The Encyclopedia of Peace Psychology

Dedicated to Milton Schwebel
with gratitude and admiration

The Encyclopedia of Peace Psychology

Edited by

Daniel J. Christie

Volume II
Eq–Po

A John Wiley & Sons, Ltd., Publication

This edition first published 2012
© 2012 Blackwell Publishing Ltd.

Blackwell Publishing was acquired by John Wiley & Sons in February 2007. Blackwell's publishing program has been merged with Wiley's global Scientific, Technical, and Medical business to form Wiley-Blackwell.

Registered Office
John Wiley & Sons Ltd, The Atrium, Southern Gate, Chichester, West Sussex, PO19 8SQ, UK

Editorial Offices
350 Main Street, Malden, MA 02148-5020, USA
9600 Garsington Road, Oxford, OX4 2DQ, UK
The Atrium, Southern Gate, Chichester, West Sussex, PO19 8SQ, UK

For details of our global editorial offices, for customer services, and for information about how to apply for permission to reuse the copyright material in this book please see our website at www.wiley.com/wiley-blackwell.

The right of Daniel J. Christie to be identified as the author of the editorial material in this work has been asserted in accordance with the UK Copyright, Designs and Patents Act 1988.

Library of Congress Cataloging-in-Publication Data

The encyclopedia of peace psychology / edited by Daniel J. Christie.
    p. cm.
  Includes bibliographical references and index.
  ISBN 978-1-4051-9644-4 (hardcover: alk. paper)
  1. Peace—Psychological aspects—Encyclopedias.   2. Peace—Encyclopedias.   I. Christie, Daniel J.
  JZ5533.E65 2011
  303.6′6—dc22

                                        2011009305

A catalogue record for this book is available from the British Library.

This book is published in the following electronic formats: Wiley Online Library 9780470672532

Set in 10.5/12pt Dante by Toppan Best-set Premedia Limited

Printed and bound in Singapore by Markono Print Media Pte Ltd

1   2012

Managing Editors and International Advisory Board Members

Brief Contents

Volume I

List of Entries by Topic   ix
Notes on Contributors   xv
Preface   liii
Acknowledgments   lvii

Encyclopedia of Peace Psychology A–Em   1–416

Volume II

List of Entries by Topic   ix

Encyclopedia of Peace Psychology Eq–Po   417–844

Volume III

List of Entries by Topic   ix

Encyclopedia of Peace Psychology Po–Z   845–1193

Name Index   1194
Subject Index   1221

List of Entries by Topic

Activism
Activism, Antiwar
Activism, Psychology of Social
Emotional Appeals, Mobilizing through
Mobilization: Peaceful and Violent
Nonviolent Democratic Transitions
People Power
Psychologists for Social Responsibility
Self-Efficacy

Aggression
Aggression
Cyberbullying
Sexual Harassment

Biological perspective
Aggression and Competition
Evolutionary Psychology

Children
Bullying
Child Soldiers
Child Soldiers and Mental Health
Children, Peace and Aggression in
Children and Armed Conflict: Strategic
    Review of Machel Study
Children's Conceptions of Peace
Gangs and Political Violence, Children and
    Youth Involvement in
Socialization
Violence, Youth
Violent Video Games and Aggression

Civil society
Civil Society Cooperative Projects for
    Peace

Cognition
Cognition: Creative versus Dogmatic
Cognitive Complexity

Conflict
Attribution Theory, Intergroup Conflict
    and
Conflict, Asymmetric
Conflict, Culture of
Conflict, Escalation and De-escalation of
Conflict Resolution, Sociopsychological
    Barriers to
Conflict, Ethos of
Conflict, Intractable
Conflict Escalation, Psychological Factors
    in
Game Theory: Conflict and Cooperation
Human Needs Theory, Conflict, and Peace

Conflict management
Alternative Dispute Resolution
Communication, Listening, and Conflict
    Resolution Skills
Conflict Management, Proactive
Conflict Management, Resolution, and
    Transformation
Conflict Management Styles
Conflict Resolution, Interactive

Conflict Resolution in Nonhuman Primates
Conflict Resolution in Schools
Conflict, Reduction of Intergroup
Conflicts, Constructive
Constructive Controversy
Dispute Resolution, Online
Identity-Based Conflicts, The ARIA
    Contingency Approach to
Identity Conflicts, Managing Intractable
Markov Chain Models of Negotiators'
    Communication
Mediation
Negotiating Strategies and Processes,
    Psychological Aspects of
Negotiation, Principled
Negotiations and Trust
Peace, Overcoming Psychological–
    Cognitive Barriers to
Peace Zones
Peacekeeping, Psychology of
Ripeness Theory

Contact theory
Common Ingroup Identity Model
Contact Theory: Extended and Parasocial
Contact Theory, Intergroup
Corporate Social Responsibility: Applying
    Contact Theory and Mediation
Deprovincialization

Coping
Coping: Emotion and Problem-Focused
Terror Management Theory: Why War?
Humanitarian Workers, Managing Stress in

Critical perspective
Critical and Radical Psychology
Critical Security Studies
Discourse Theory and Peace

Culture
Cultural Carriers
Culture and Conflict
Culture of Peace
National Political Cultures
Tribal Culture and Violence

Decision-making
Decision-Making, Psychological
    Dimensions of Foreign Policy
Decision-Making, the Role of Emotions in
    Foreign Policy

Drama theory
Drama Theory

Dynamical systems theory
Dynamical Systems Theory: Applications
    to Peace and Conflict

Education
Action Teaching
Anti-Bias Education
Coexistence Education
Peace and Conflict Studies versus Peace
    Science
Peace Education
Peace Education: Lessons Learned in
    Israel/Palestine, Research on
Simulation: Learning through Role Playing
    and Design
Social and Emotional Learning

Emotion
Affect: Origins and Targets of Hate
Emotion
Emotional Climate for Peace
Emotional Orientation, Collective
Emotions in Violence and Peace,
    Intergroup
Fear, Politics of
Guilt: Personal and Collective
Negotiation, Role of Emotions in

Empathy
Empathy
Empathy, Ethnocultural
Empathy, Intergroup: Regarding the
    Suffering of Others
Empathy in the Process of Forgiveness
Empathy Training and Listening Skills
Prosocial Behavior

Ethics
Do No Harm
Ethical Considerations in Peace Psychology
Interrogation, Psychology and

Forgiveness
Apologies and Forgiveness
Forgiveness, Intergroup
Forgiveness, Interpersonal
Restorative Conferencing, Method of
Restorative Justice

Gender
Gender and International Relations
Gender and Terrorism
Gender-Based Violence
Gender Inequality
Gendering Peace Psychology
Girls in Armed Groups
Women and Peace Hypothesis

Global issues
Climate Change and Violence
Globalization and Conflict

Group processes
Bystander Intervention
Diffusion of Responsibility
Groupthink

Human rights
Children and Human Rights
Human Rights and Human Rights
   Violations, Psychological Aspects of
Humiliation and Dignity
Monitoring Human Rights in Educational
   Settings

Ideology
Conservative Ideology
Ideology
Protestant Work Ethic
System Justification Theory

Indigenous peacemaking
Child Soldiers, Traditional Healing and
Native Peacemaking

Influence processes
Normative Influence, Theories of
Social Influence

Intergroup relations
Collective Narcissism
Colonialism and Postcolonialism:
   Psychological Dimensions
Cooperation and Competition
Cooperative Learning
Dehumanization, Infrahumanization, and
   Naturalization
Delegitimization
Desegregation
Hetero-Referentiality and Divided Societies
Intergroup Conflict, Theories of
Intergroup Hatred: Psychological
   Dimensions
Occupation
Othering of People and Phenomena
Police–Community Relations
Security
Social Dilemmas
Social Interdependence Theory
Tolerance for Diverse Groups
Transitional Context
Trust and Distrust
Victimhood, Collective

International relations
Diplomacy, Preventive
Image Theory
International Relations, Psychological
   Perspectives on
Just War Theory
Patriotism and Nationalism
Power: Hard, Soft, and Smart
Security Dilemma in Structural
   International Relations Theory

Intervention methods
Appreciative Inquiry
Children, Psychosocial Interventions with
Dialogue Methods
Interfaith Dialogue
Intergroup Violence and Psychosocial
   Interventions, Cycles of

Peace and Coexistence Programs in the
    Israeli–Palestinian and Middle East
    Context
Post-Conflict Psychosocial Intervention
Post-Violence Reconstruction
Psychosocial Accompaniment of Victims
    of Political Violence
Storytelling as a Peacebuilding Method
TRANSCEND Method
Us and Them: Moderating Dichotomous
    Ingroup/Outgroup Thinking

Levels of analysis
Conflict: Levels of Analysis
Ecological Model
Levels of Analysis Problem

Liberation psychology
Conscientization
Liberation Psychology
Praxis
Problematization

Media
Media and Peace: Emerging Technologies
Media and Peace: Traditional Outlets
Media Violence, Effects of
Peace Journalism

Military
Humanitarian Military Interventions,
    Support for
Militarism and Who Benefits
Militaristic Attitude
Military Psychology
Psychological Warfare
Suicide among War Veterans
War: US Children and Parental
    Deployment
War Veterans and Family Violence

Moral
Moral Conviction
Moral Development
Moral Disengagement
Moral Exclusion

Nonviolence
Alternatives to Violence
Nonviolence, Psychology of
Pacifism, Psychology of
Values, Nonviolence, and Peace
    Psychology

Obedience
Lucifer Effect
Obedience
Obedience to Authority

Peace psychology
Peace Psychology: Contributions from
    Africa
Peace Psychology: Contributions from Asia
Peace Psychology: Contributions from
    Europe
Peace Psychology: Contributions from
    North America
Peace Psychology: Definitions, Scope, and
    Impact
Peace Psychology, Philosophical
    Foundations of
Peace Psychology in Australia
Positive Psychology and Peace Psychology
Sport and Peace Psychology

Peace studies
Peace, Positive and Negative
Peace Studies, Psychological Contributions
    to

Personality
Authoritarian Personality
Nonviolent Dispositions
Peaceful Personality

Political psychology
Political Psychology and Peace

Positioning theory
Positioning Theory

Prejudice
Anti-Semitism, Psychology of
Discrimination

Ethnocentrism
Prejudice, Types and Origins of
Prejudice Reduction, Approaches to
Racism
Xenophobia

Reconciliation
Collective Remembering
Reconciliation, Collective Memory and
Reconciliation: Instrumental and
    Socioemotional Aspects
Transitional Justice Systems, Psychology
    and
Truth and Reconciliation Commissions,
    Psychological Impact of

Refugees
Asylum Seekers and Refugees, Attitudes
    toward
Refugee Mental Health
Refugee Mental Health Interventions
Refugees and Asylum Seekers: Stereotyping
    and Prejudice

Research methods
Archival Research
Comparative Case Studies
Disaster Research
Experimentation, Design, and Analysis
Grounded Theory
Internet Data Collection
Laboratory Experiments
Meta-Analysis
Minimal Group Paradigm
Multidimensional Scaling Methods in Peace
    Psychology
Narrative Analysis
Narrative Psychology
Participatory Action Research,
    Community-Based
Personality Processes in Interpersonal
    Conflict, Assessing
Political Personality Profiling
Qualitative Methods and Coding
Quantitative Methods and Coding
Questionnaires in Conflict Research, Use
    of

Role Playing as a Training and Assessment
    Tool
Survey Research in Peace Psychology

Resilience
Children and Political Violence
Children and Resilience
Children's Exposure to Violence

Social identity theory
Collective Efficacy
Social Identity Theory

Social justice
Counseling and Social Justice
Equity Theory
Relative Deprivation Theory
Restorative Justice: Some Archetypal Roots
Social Dominance Theory
Social Injustice
Social Justice Education

Social psychology
Social Psychological Peace Research

Social representations
Collective Memories of Intergroup
    Conflict
Siege Mentality
Social Representation Theory
Social Representations of History
Social Representations of Reconciliation
Social Representations of War and Peace
Symbols, Symbolism, and Mass Action

Spirituality
Buddhism and Peace Psychology
Mindfulness
Psychospiritual Harmony

Stereotype
Stereotype Threat and Intergroup Relations
Stereotypes

Terrorism
Counterterrorism, Psychological Aspects
    of

Suicide Terrorism
Terrorism, Psychology of
Terrorists, Psychology of

Threat
Intergroup Threat Theory
Mortality Salience in Peace and Conflict
Threat, Kinds and Effects of
Threats, Inflation of National Security

Trauma
Post-Traumatic Stress Disorder and Peace
Trauma – from an Individual and a Group
   Perspective

Trauma, Intergenerational Transmission of
Traumatic Stress, Perpetration-Induced

Violence
Domestic Violence: Feminist Perspective
Family Violence and Abuse
Genocide and Mass Killing: Origins and
   Prevention
Language, Violent and Peaceful Uses of
Psychosocial Impact of Political Violence
Seville Statement on Violence

Equity Theory

ELAINE HATFIELD, RICHARD L. RAPSON,
AND LISAMARIE BENSMAN

On June 4, 2009, President Barack Obama delivered his now well-known Cairo speech, in which he proposed "a new beginning." He pointed out that Israelis and Palestinians had suffered terribly from religious wars and conflict. The Israelis, subjected to centuries of persecution, faced annihilation as a people in the Holocaust. The Palestinians, victims of colonialism and Cold War policies, had faced the daily humiliations of occupation for more than a half-century. Although these grievances, social injustices, horrors, and deaths could never be forgotten or forgiven, it was, he argued, time to start anew. In the end – whether the peace process took 1 year, 10 years, or 1,000 years – Palestinians and Israelis must find some way to share the Holy Land.

Critical reactions were fierce and immediate. Zealots on both sides insisted that God and social justice were on their side. A few Israelis stood outside the US consulate, waving portraits of Obama wearing a Palestinian headscarf, with "Jew Hater" scrawled beneath his portrait. One protester declared, "We will never sacrifice the cherished conviction that we (and only we) are the rightful inheritors of the lands of the Ken'ites and the Ken'izites, the Kad'mon-ites and the Hittites, the Per'izzites and the Reph'aims, the Am'or-ites and the Canaanites, the Girgashites and the Jeb'u-sites . . . " On the Palestinian side, social commentators such as Mirza Beg, fired back:

While talking of violence by Palestinians, I wish he [Obama] would have also commented on much worse violence inflicted on the Palestinians by Israelis, as is obvious by the death toll in many of the Israeli military operations. The toll of violence in Gaza last January was approximately 1,300 Palestinians killed, mostly civilians, to about six Israeli soldiers . . .

The *cri de coeur* that comes through these passionate outcries is: "It's not fair" and "Your suffering is nothing compared to our own. Restitution must be paid."

The Palestinians and the Israelis are not the only peoples who find themselves swept up in arguments about the nature of social justice in the midst of political, religious, and ethnic conflicts. In the past decade, the world has witnessed a plethora of the horrific: suicide bombers, mass murder, genocide, crimes against humanity, and global terrorism. We have only to speak the names Serbia and Bosnia, Northern Ireland, Cambodia, Rwanda, Darfur, Palestine and Israel, the World Trade Center, and a host of others to despair.

Social psychologists have devoted a great deal of thought to trying to unravel the mysteries of good people's willingness to commit staggering wrongs – to engage in orgies of killing and torture in the name of God and social justice. Some political policymakers and psychologists have argued that one can best understand the white heat of people caught up in such holy crusades (such as the Arab–Israeli clash) by considering: (1) the cultural, historical, and economic factors sparking such conflicts; (2) the cognitive and rational calculations of combatants; and (3) the turbulent cognitions and emotions – the shame, fear, rage, sorrow, hatred, and despair – of people caught up in such holy crusades.

In this essay, we will discuss one additional factor that has been found to be important in shaping people's cognitive and emotional reactions to others: their perceptions as to what is fair or unfair. It is our hope to provide a few insights into the powerful forces that unite people or divide them from their fellows, and to aid a better understanding of the factors that provide a shared vision, push emotions to a fever pitch, and contribute to people's perplexing and unrelenting willingness to engage in Holy Wars – no matter how wasted the effort, how horrendous the costs, and how devastated a suffering humanity. Let us begin by discussing equity theory. (See RELATIVE DEPRIVATION THEORY; SOCIAL INJUSTICE; MORAL EXCLUSION; MORAL DISENGAGEMENT.)

AN OVERVIEW OF EQUITY THEORY

In the eleventh century, St. Anselm of Canterbury argued that the will possesses two competing inclinations: an affection for what is to one's own advantage and an affection for justice. The first inclination is stronger, but the second matters, too. Equity theory, too, posits that in social relationships, two concerns stand out: First, how rewarding are people's societal, familial, and work relationships? Second, how fair and equitable are those relationships? According to the theory, people feel most comfortable when they are getting exactly what they deserve from their relationships – no more and certainly no less.

The Theoretical Formulation

Equity theory consists of four propositions designed to predict when individuals will perceive that they are justly (or unjustly) treated and how they will react when they find themselves enmeshed in unjust relationships:

Proposition 1. Men and women are "hardwired" to try to maximize pleasure and minimize pain.

Proposition 2. Society, however, has a vested interest in persuading people to behave fairly and equitably. Groups will generally reward members who treat others equitably and punish those who treat others inequitably.

Proposition 3. Given societal pressures, people are most comfortable when

they perceive that they are getting roughly what they deserve from life and their relationships. If people feel overbenefited, they may experience pity, guilt, and shame; if underbenefited, they may experience anger, sadness, and resentment.

Proposition 4. People in inequitable relationships will attempt to reduce their distress through a variety of techniques – by restoring psychological equity (convincing themselves that an inequitable relationship is indeed fair), by restoring actual equity (setting things right), or by abandoning the relationship.

During America's civil war, for example, many slave owners, when challenged about the morality of slavery, defended themselves, restored *psychological equity* (and reduced their guilt) by arguing that Africans were an inferior race that was better off under slavery than free. (In fact, most slave owners refused to use the word "slavery"; instead they opted for the bland euphemism "the peculiar institution.") A few slave holders worked to set things right by freeing their slaves and making recompense – thus restoring *actual equity.* Finally, most Southerners elected to deal with their conflicting ideals by voting to leave the Union, risking what would turn out to be a hideous war and unfathomable death and destruction.

What Constitutes an Equitable Relationship?

Technically, equity is defined by a complex formula (Walster, 1975). In practice, however, a person's perception of social equity in a given relationship can be reliably and validly assessed via a simple measure. Specifically, people are asked: "Considering what you put into your relationship, compared to what you get out of it . . . and what your partner puts in compared to what (s)he gets out of it, how does your relationship 'stack up'?" Respondents are given the following response options:

+3 I am getting a much better deal than my partner.
+2 I am getting a somewhat better deal.
+1 I am getting a slightly better deal.
 0 We are both getting an equally good, or bad, deal.
−1 My partner is getting a slightly better deal.
−2 My partner is getting a somewhat better deal.
−3 My partner is getting a much better deal than I am.

On the basis of their answers, persons can be classified as overbenefited (receiving more than they deserve), equitably treated, or underbenefited (receiving less than they deserve).

SOCIAL JUSTICE AND EQUITY: A FEW QUESTIONS

Social commentators interested in fostering peace and social justice have often posed some difficult questions: First, is the desire for social justice and equity a cultural universal? Second, do societies differ in who is included in the "family of man," and thus deserve to be treated with respect and fairness? Third, do they differ in who is banished from the elect? Or, who can be dismissed as "Godless infidels," "heathens," "strangers," "less than human – animals," to be despised and abused at will? Finally, do societies differ in what is considered profitable, fair, and equitable?

The Universality of a Desire for Equity

Most scholars generally agree that a concern with fairness and equity is a cultural universal. In the past 25 years or so, many have

proposed that such desires are written in the mind's architecture. As evolutionary psychologists Leda Cosmides and John Tooby (1992) observed:

> It is likely that our ancestors have engaged in social exchange for at least several million years . . . Social exchange behavior is both universal and highly elaborated across all human cultures – including hunter-gatherer cultures . . . as would be expected if it were an ancient and central part of human life.

They contend that notions of social justice came to be writ in the mind's "architecture" because such concerns possessed survival value. A concern with social justice, in all its forms, they contend, is alive and well today (in all cultures and all social structures) because, in most instances, fairness remains a wise and profitable strategy. This begs the questions as to what is meant by "fairness" and "fairness to whom?" The history of humans, after all, has not been characterized by peace.

Paleoanthropological evidence supports the view that notions of social justice and equity are extremely ancient, albeit often with violent consequences. Ravens, for example, have been observed to attack those who violate social norms. Dogs get fiercely jealous if their playmates receive treats and they do not. Wolves that don't "play fair" are often ostracized – a penalty that may well to lead to the wolves' death.

Primatologists have amassed considerable evidence that primates and other animals do care about fairness. In one study, Sarah Brosnan and Frans de Waal (2003) found that female monkeys who were denied the rewards they deserved became furious. They refused to "play the game" (refused to exchange tokens for a cucumber) and disdained to eat their "prize" – holding out for the grapes they thought they deserved. If severely provoked (the other monkey did nothing and still got the highly prized grapes instead of the cucumber) capuchins grew so angry that they began to scream, beat their breasts, and hurl food at the experimenter.

Do Societies Differ in Who is Included in the "Family of Man"?

Almost all religions endorse some variant of the golden rule: "Love thy neighbor as thyself" and "Do unto others . . . " Historically, however, societies have been found to possess very different ideas as to who those privileged "neighbors" are. In some cultures, one's "neighbors" mean close kin, members of their tribe, adherents to their religion, or fellow nationals. In others, there is a belief that there ought to be "justice for all," and a sense of universal brotherhood.

In attempting to predict whether people will possess a parochial or broad and inclusive view of who merits fair and equitable treatment, cultural researchers have attempted to classify various societies on a variety of dimensions. They point out that the world's cultures differ profoundly in the extent to which they are family centered or universalistic, value collectivism or individualism, traditionalism or modernism, whether they are rural or urban, religious or secular, poor or affluent. They have found that societal values have a profound impact on whether people assume that principles of fairness and justice are applicable only to family and clan or whether they accept the notion that principles of fairness and equity apply to all. Thus, cultural norms may trump biology in these matters, although globalization could conceivably lead to the dominance of "fairness" hardwiring.

Do Societies Differ in What is Considered Fair and Equitable?

Even if societies agree that equity is important in a given relationship, citizens may differ as to the inputs and outcomes that they think ought to "count" in those relationships. Here are some dominant views:

- "All men are created equal." (US idealism)
- "The more you invest in a project, the more profit you deserve to reap." (US capitalism)
- "To each according to his need." (Communism)
- "Winner take all." (Dog-eat-dog capitalism)
- "It's a man's world. (Traditional societies)

Given the fact that people of good will can differ so markedly as to the meaning of fairness and equity, as to how broadly the imperative for equity must be applied, and as to how equity ought to be calculated, it is not surprising that so many opportunities for cultural misunderstanding and conflict exist. Let us hope that, in dialogue and in the development of a global culture, commonalities between peoples can overcome the narrow definitions of "the other" that have so defaced human history.

SEE ALSO: Moral Disengagement; Moral Exclusion; Relative Deprivation Theory; Social Injustice.

REFERENCES

Brosnan, S. F., & de Waal, F. B. M. (2003). Monkeys reject unequal pay. *Nature, 425,* 297–299.

Cosmides, L., & Tooby, J. (1992). Cognitive adaptations for social exchange. In J. H. Barkow, L. Cosmides, & J. Tooby (Eds.), *The adapted mind.* (pp. 161–228). New York, NY: Oxford University Press.

Walster, G. W. (1975). The Walster et al. (1973) equity formula: A correction. *Representative Research in Social Psychology, 6,* 65–67.

ADDITIONAL RESOURCES

Hatfield, E., Rapson, R. L., & Aumer-Ryan, K. (2008). Social justice in love relationships: Recent developments. *Social Justice Research*, 21, 413–431. New York, NY: Springer.

Hatfield, E., Walster, G. W., & Berscheid, E. (1978). *Equity: Theory and research*. Boston, MA: Allyn & Bacon.

Sernau, S. R. (2009). *Global problems: The search for equity, peace, and sustainability* (2nd ed.). Boston, MA: Allyn & Bacon.

Ethical Considerations in Peace Psychology

MARK M. LEACH

The marriage of ethics and peace psychology is a natural one as they are both concerned with human rights, which are predicated on the promotion of positive, empathic, and egalitarian motivations. Peace psychology has a clear moral component and has been committed to advancing the decrease of violence and the promotion of nonviolence as well as pursuing social justice. It has transitioned from a post-Cold War mentality to include a greater geohistorical context, inclusion of multiple levels of analysis, and increased understanding of multiple worldviews (Christie, Tint, Wagner, & Winter, 2008). Similar motivations emerge within professional ethics, regardless of discipline. The field of ethics has always been intimately connected with morality, and has promoted positive behaviors and attempted to avoid potentially damaging behaviors. It has recently become more globally aware of context, includes multiple levels of analyses, and has also begun to increase sensitivity to multiple cultures and worldviews. Global consciousness within psychological ethics has become increasingly prominent in recent years with the development of ethics codes for the international community. Psychology itself may be working toward an underlying morality on an international level.

EXAMPLES OF INTERSECTIONS OF PEACE PSYCHOLOGY AND ETHICS

There are multiple examples of the intersection of sociopolitical events and sound ethical practice, though only a few will be mentioned. During and post-World War II, German psychology changed based on government intervention. For example, East and West German psychologies differed (Rösler, 2009), with issues such as social justice and free speech taking center stage. Ferrero (2009) described how military coups in Argentina changed the acceptance of psychology, with the discipline itself perceived as a national threat. Leach, Akurst, and Basson (2003) discussed the influence of the South African apartheid system that created two psychologies in that country, including psychology's roles in violating human rights and maintaining the governmental status quo. More recently, it was noted that a very small number of US psychologists were involved with interrogations in military prisons. It is through a discussion of ethics and ethics codes that the overlap with peace psychology becomes even more focused.

HISTORY

Ethics and ethics codes have multiple functions, two of which are to protect the public and offer guidance for appropriate professional behavior. One of the first known codes of laws, based on ethics and morals, is the Code of Hammurabi (1795–1750 BCE), a code that highlighted a broad range of professional and personal behaviors. It was developed to assist individuals with socially appropriate behaviors and guide good citizenry. The Hippocratic Oath (500–400 BCE) established the tradition that good professional behaviors should be guided by sound ethical principles and still serves as the foundation for ethical medical practice.

More modern ethics documents were developed after World War II when it became public that many of the atrocities during the war were committed by professionals. Three notable attempts to develop ethics codes by a range of professions, including psychology, were partially derived from the Nuremberg Code of Ethics in Medical Research (www.hhs.gov/ohrp/irb/irb_appendices.htm), a code with ten principles designed to regulate medical research experiments with humans. Many of the principles outlined (e.g., informed consent) are found within many national psychology ethics codes today and are considered foundations for ethical research and applied practices. In 1948 the Declaration of Geneva of the World Medical Association (WMA) emphasized broad medical humanitarian values. In the same year, the Universal Declaration of Human Rights (www.un.org/Overview/rights.html) was also developed and was the first international document that detailed universal human rights. It is a morally grounded code that has become entrenched in ethical and legal codes in many countries. Years later, the WMA constructed the 1964 Declaration of Helsinki (www.wma.net/e/ethicsunit/helsinki.htm), also focused on human ethical research, and though the Nuremberg Code and Declaration of Helsinki are not decreed by international law their ramifications can be seen in institutional review boards internationally. Ethics codes have been developed by national, regional, and international psychological organizations, topics to which we now turn.

NATIONAL CODES

Codes of ethics are now found within diverse professional organizations, including real estate, journalism, sociology, and anthropology. The American Psychological Association (APA) developed the first code of ethics for the psychology profession in 1953, though there was initial resistance to creating such a code for a number of reasons, including the belief that a profession cannot codify individual ethical and perhaps moral behaviors. The latest version developed in 2002 is considered one of the most comprehensive codes of ethics in psychology. At least 50 other national psychological organizations now have codes of ethics.

Though codes themselves differ in structure and format, regardless of the profession, they generally emphasize principles and standards. Principles are aspirational, overarching guidelines that provide the foundation for solid ethical reasoning. Strictly, however, they are non-enforceable. For example, beneficence (benefit others), nonmaleficence (do no harm), respect for individual rights and dignity (autonomy), integrity (honesty), fidelity and responsibility (creating loyalty and trust), and justice (fairness) are principles that have been found in a variety of codes across a variety of professions, though determining whether an individual psychologist does not abide by a principle is difficult to determine. Some professional organizations are increasingly focusing on principle-based social justice issues in their codes. An ongoing issue is the primacy of principles when they conflict. In essence, which principle should take precedence when situations arise that call for principled guidance? The successful resolution of the ethical dilemma on an individual level is often dependent upon the interpretation of the situation and the principle itself.

Standards are specific guidelines that are often consulted when an ethical dilemma arises. They are enforceable rules that direct ethical practices and are "legalistic," though no series of standards can account for the multitude of possible ethical issues that can arise. Though similar standards may appear across national ethics codes, they can be interpreted differently based on culturally accepted legal practices.

Ethical principles can be observed within the oft-cited distinction between positive and negative peace. Positive peace promotes conditions that lead to social justice, consistent with many of the ethical principles noted above (e.g., beneficence, justice). Negative peace refers to the prevention and mitigation of harmful events, consistent with the principle of nonmaleficence. Western psychology may emphasize negative peace in part because the APA code emphasizes "legalistic" guidelines rather than including aspirational language (Leach & Harbin, 1997).

However, there are movements within psychology that are aspirational and emphasize a shift toward egalitarianism and social justice. Liberation psychology, for example, was initiated in the 1980s by an El Salvadorian Jesuit priest and psychologist, Ignacio Martín-Barí, and furthered by Maritza Montero. The movement has become an influential force not only across Latin America but other countries across the world. (See LIBERATION PSYCHOLOGY.) It criticizes the domination of Western individualistic, decontextualized, and dispassionate psychological thought, and emphasizes social transformation to decrease structural and institutional inequities among peoples. Other movements in psychology, including radical psychology and peace psychology, also have emancipatory agendas. (See CRITICAL AND RADICAL PSYCHOLOGY; PEACE PSYCHOLOGY: DEFINITIONS, SCOPE, AND IMPACT.)

In a number of countries, professional ethics codes have been revised with the aspirational language of human rights. Canada and New Zealand have been in the forefront of efforts to integrate ethical principles and standards. By doing so, psychologists can better understand how both principles and standards can assist them in good ethical decision-making. Research into comparisons among principles and standards

multinationally has yielded interesting results, which are closely aligned with values found within peace psychology. For example, Leach and Harbin (1997) compared ethics codes among 24 countries and found significant overlap of principles. There seemed to be some agreement regarding the principles outlined in the APA code (e.g., Respect for People's Rights and Dignity, Concern for Other's Welfare, Social Responsibility), and among 10 standards that approached almost unanimous agreement, including Avoiding Harm, (Avoiding) Exploitative Relationships, and Informed Consent (which is closely connected to allowing others to make informed choices). (See DO NO HARM.)

REGIONAL CODES

While national organizations with similar cultures have created a code of ethics by which they abide, on a larger scale, in 1995 the European Federation of Psychological Associations (EFPA) initially developed a Meta-code on Ethics that is largely principled (revised in 2005). This organization is composed of 34 national psychological associations in Europe and provides a forum for European cooperation. Each country's ethical code should be in accord with the EFPA code of ethics, which highlights four principles: Respect for Person's Rights and Dignity, Competence, Responsibility, and Integrity. Other organizations on other continents (i.e., Asian Regional Union of Psychological Societies; Interamerican Society of Psychology; Middle East/North Africa) have begun considering similar efforts in their geographic regions.

INTERNATIONAL DOCUMENTS

A recently developed document has made a significant impact on psychological ethics, and will continue to do so. The International Union of Psychological Science (IUPsyS), an international psychological organization composed of national psychological organizations and not individuals, along with the International Association of Applied Psychology (IAAP) and the International Association for Cross-Cultural Psychology (IACCP), joined efforts to develop the Universal Declaration of Ethical Principles for Psychologists (Gauthier, 2008). This Declaration, based on human values, is the first internationally approved set of moral principles for the profession of psychology. It is not an ethics document and is nonenforceable; however, the document attests to a global, focused movement in psychology emphasizing human rights. It sets a high moral tone for psychological practice and can assist national organizations with their own codes of ethics.

There are many international organizations that have developed their own ethics documents or follow existing documents. For example, the International Test Commission has developed a document that outlines common test practices to assist psychologists with their test procedures, regardless of country of origin. Psychologists for Social Responsibility, a group comprised of psychologists from around the world, promote peace, social justice, and human rights. Finally, the Committee on the Psychological Study of Peace is a multinational group formed through the IUPsyS and is committed to advancing peace initiatives. There are many other international organizations that adhere to ethics documents. When considering international ethics, as with other areas, cultural variations become more prominent.

SUMMARY

Just as peace psychology is an international movement with individuals from a range of professional and personal backgrounds striving to understand the factors associated with optimal human functioning, so too are those who promote sound ethical judgment. Professional ethics has become a global enterprise in psychology and many other disciplines. Increasingly, the Universal Declaration of Human Rights is considered when national psychological organizations develop or revise their codes of ethics. International documents, including the Universal Declaration, help bring communities of psychologists together to speak with a consistent ethical voice, though we must always be reminded of the cultural interpretations that influence good practices. The greater the number of people with similar motivations to promote human rights and social justice, the greater the likelihood that peace will become more sustainable.

SEE ALSO: Critical and Radical Psychology; Do No Harm; Liberation Psychology; Peace Psychology: Definitions, Scope, and Impact.

REFERENCES

Christie, D. J., Tint, B. S., Wagner, R. V., & Winter, D. D. (2008). Peace psychology for a peaceful world. *American Psychologist, 63,* 540–552.
Ferrero, A. (2009). A South American experience of the transition from dictatorship to democracy. In D. Wedding & M. J. Stevens (Eds.), *Psychology: IUPsyS global resource* [CD-ROM] (10th ed.). Hove, UK: Psychology Press.
Gauthier, J. (2008). Universal Declaration of Ethical Principles for Psychologists. In J. E. Hall & E. M. Altmaier (Eds.), *Global promise: Quality assurance and accountability in professional psychology* (pp. 98–105). New York, NY: Oxford University Press.
Leach, M. M., Akurst, J., & Basson, C. (2003). Counseling psychology in South Africa: Current political and professional challenges and future promise. *Counseling Psychologist, 31,* 619–640.
Leach, M. M., & Harbin, J. J. (1997). Psychological ethics codes: A comparison of

twenty-four countries. *International Journal of Psychology*, 32, 181–192.

Rösler, H.-D. (2009). Professional change and professional ethics of psychology in East Germany. In D. Wedding & M. J. Stevens (Eds.), *Psychology: IUPsyS global resource* [CD-ROM] (10th ed.). Hove, UK: Psychology Press.

ADDITIONAL RESOURCES

http://www.am.org/iupsys/resources/ethics/ index.html (International Union of Psychological Science)

http://www.psypress.com/iupsys/ (Psychology: IUPsyS International Resource CD)

Lindsay, G., Koene, C., Ovreeide, H., & Lang, F. (Eds.). (2008). *Ethics for European Psychologists*. Cambridge, MA: Hogrefe and Huber.

Ethnocentrism

THOMAS KESSLER AND IMMO FRITSCHE

William Graham Sumner (1840–1910) was the first to describe and conceptualize ethnocentrism in his 1906 book, *Folkways: A Study of the Sociological Importance of Usages, Manners, Customs, Mores, and Morals*. Ethnocentrism has been frequently used as a concept to explain ingroup favoritism, prejudice, and intergroup conflict in various disciplines including psychology, sociology, anthropology, political science, and evolutionary biology.

Although ethnocentrism often refers to one's own culture and ethnic heritage, it extends to all social groups to which one belongs, is attached, and identifies. Moreover, ethnocentrism is often conceived of as a socially problematic syndrome that fosters a sense of ingroup superiority and negativity towards outgroups. Such a perspective neglects potential positive aspects of ethnocentrism such as loyalty to the ingroup, support of ingroup members, coordination of collective actions, and the high levels of cooperation within the ingroup.

Ethnocentrism comprises a variety of interrelated attributes. Sumner characterized the concept in 18 sentences, while LeVine and Campbell (1972) list 23 distinct facets. These lists have been summarized into three basic components. First, epistemic ethnocentrism involves the distinction between an ingroup (the "insiders"/ "us") and an outgroup ("outsiders"/"them"). An ingroup has epistemic primacy inasmuch as other people and outgroups are scaled with reference to the ingroup. Second, ingroup superiority denotes that ingroups are perceived positively and usually more positively than outgroups. Third, outgroup evaluation traditionally has been conceived of as negative. However, more recent research demonstrates that appreciation of the ingroup can be accompanied by a variety of different attitudes towards outgroups ranging from positive appreciation, tolerance, and ignorance of differences, to active competition, derogation, and hostility.

FACETS OF ETHNOCENTRISM

Epistemic Ethnocentrism

At a very basic level, ethnocentrism refers to the distinction between ingroup and outgroup. According to Sumner (1906, p. 12) "a differentiation arises between ourselves, the we-group, or ingroup, and everybody else, or the others-groups, outgroups." This characterization is ambiguous, as "outgroup" may either refer to all non-ingroups or to a specific outgroup. This distinction is important because differentiating the ingroup from all non-ingroups may lead to generalized prejudice, whereas the reference to specific outgroups implies the development of specific intergroup relations with unique evaluations of outgroups (e.g., "we do like/ dislike members of group X").

The ingroup–outgroup differentiation also refers to the epistemic primacy of the ingroup; "one's own group is the center of everything, and all others are scaled and rated with reference to it" (Sumner, 1906, p.13). Ingroup culture, tradition, norms, and values are taken as givens and the cultural practices of other groups or outgroups are perceived and evaluated relative to the ingroup culture. This facet of ethnocentrism develops basically because people are socialized within ingroups. Children, for instance, are all born into a particular society or culture and learn its conventions, values, and norms (e.g., language, local dialect, food taboos, clothing, conventions such as greeting, forming contracts, exchanging items, etc.) before they encounter outgroup members. In their development, children acquire the culture and its rules without reflecting, criticizing, and reasoning about it. Ingroup conventions, rules, values, and norms are the basic knowledge about how life, social interactions, and social reality work. Thus, people tend to conceive of ingroup norms as a matter of fact, rather than as arbitrary conventions and a matter of chance or taste. Moreover, the ingroup provides the point of departure when people start to think about themselves and various alternative ways to live. Thus, whenever some new ways of life are encountered (e.g., by intergroup contact) the actions of others are evaluated against the background of cultural knowledge about the ingroup. This primacy of the ingroup is also echoed by Allport when he writes: "Although we could not perceive our own ingroups excepting as they contrast with outgroups, still the ingroups are psychologically primary. We live in them, by them, and, sometimes, for them. Hostility towards outgroups helps strengthen our sense of belonging, but it is not required" (Allport, 1954, p. 42). Groups are formed and maintained by the acquisition and repeated mutual confirmation of ingroup attributes, which lead to shared identity. The adherence to ingroup norms fosters certainty, coordination, and cooperation within groups. However, between-group interactions have the strong potential for misunderstandings that lead to feelings of embarrassment and intergroup anxiety that fosters distrust, avoidance, and a lack of cooperation.

Ingroup Superiority

As a consequence of this ingroup centrism, a favorable ingroup evaluation and preferential ingroup treatment develops. Ingroup norms and values are positive because they regulate social interactions within the group in a mutually beneficial way. They also define who "we" are, what can be expected from fellow group members, and what counts as correct and appropriate behavior. Ingroup knowledge is not only restricted to factual knowledge, but extends also to evaluative and moral issues. Thus, the ingroup is seen as positive and moral and outgroups, as they are different, tend to be seen as less positive and less moral. For instance, research has demonstrated that ingroup members develop universal ingroup stereotypes including attributes like being trustworthy, peaceful, moral, loyal, and reliable (Brewer, 2007). Given this general and mutual expectation of ingroup members, their interactions lead to successful coordination and cooperation that will be interpreted as positive, whereas similar behaviors performed by an outgroup member can be seen as potentially treacherous and dangerous.

This positivity of the ingroup seems to be equated with a superiority of the ingroup relative to outgroups when Sumner suggests: "The insiders in a we-group are in a relation of peace, order, law, government, and industry, to each other. Their relation to all outsiders, or others-groups, is one of war and plunder, except so far as agreements have modified it" (Sumner, 1906, p.12).

Outgroup Evaluation

Sumner (1906) conceived of intergroup relations as problematic and proposed that positive intragroup relations are negatively related to relations to outgroups. Positive relations within groups even seem to be based on intergroup conflict: "The relation of comradeship and peace in the we-group and that of hostility and war towards others-groups are correlative to each other. The exigencies of war with outsiders are what make peace inside, lest internal discord should weaken the we-group for war" (p. 12). Although this suggestion seems to be very intuitive, research has not confirmed this negative relation between ingroup positivity and attitudes towards the outgroup. Although ingroup members seem to prefer their ingroup (to be precise, they prefer their ingroup more than outgroup members prefer it), this does not necessarily imply a particular negativity toward outgroups. Intergroup relations vary in quality because, on the one hand, intergroup negotiations, agreements, and cooperation foster positive relations and, on the other hand, misunderstanding, explicit competition, and perceived moral duty may lead to fighting against an outgroup.

CAUSES OF ETHNOCENTRISM

One of the first attempts to explain ethnocentrism was based on the notion of an authoritarian personality. According to this approach, people high in authoritarianism have an increased tendency to adhere to ingroup conventions, to submit to local or ingroup authorities, and to punish people who are seen as deviating from ingroup norms. Authoritarian tendencies seem to become most prevalent in times of threat from outgroups, but also as a consequence of the economic situation or other threats. Although much evidence has been accumulated concerning the relation between authoritarianism and prejudice, this research is notoriously unclear about the causal relations between individual differences and prejudice. Differences in authoritarianism may determine prejudice; however, group processes may simultaneously determine both authoritarian tendencies as well as prejudice against outgroups. (See AUTHORITARIAN PERSONALITY.)

Realistic group conflict theory (LeVine & Campbell, 1972) proposes that the structural relations between social groups determine attitudes and behavior towards the ingroup and outgroups. (See INTERGROUP CONFLICT, THEORIES OF.) With negative interdependence (e.g., one group's win is the other group's loss), ingroup members tend to perceive an outgroup as a threat, they become more loyal to the ingroup and less tolerant to ingroup deviants, as well as negative towards the outgroup. Here, realistic group conflict theory stresses the positive effects of threat to an ingroup for ingroup cohesion and cooperation. Positive interdependence between social groups (e.g., all groups can only win or lose together), in contrast, leads to more favorable intergroup relations. (See SOCIAL INTERDEPENDENCE THEORY; COOPERATION AND COMPETITION.) This theory would explain ethnocentrism as a result of the structural preconditions between the groups instead of individual differences (although individual differences could be the outcome of a certain intergroup structure).

However, several empirical findings seem to indicate that intergroup competition (i.e., negative interdependence) is not necessary for the development of ethnocentric attitudes (Brewer, 2007). The simple categorization of people into ingroup and outgroup seems to foster ethnocentric attitudes as the ingroup is favored over the outgroup, even in minimal situations. (See SOCIAL IDENTITY THEORY.) Self-categorization as a group member can be sufficient to motivate people to favor their ingroup and try to demonstrate that their ingroup is positively distinct from an outgroup on valued dimensions.

PSYCHOLOGICAL PROCESSES UNDERLYING ETHNOCENTRISM

Current research indicates that one basic psychological process underlying ethnocentrism is the categorization of people into ingroup and outgroup. When people define themselves as members of a particular group, they are likely to adopt self-views and attitudes that are in line with the ingroup stereotype (self-stereotyping). This makes group members more similar to each other and may differentiate them from members of other groups. This process may also lead to the perception of a shared identity.

The positivity of the ingroup may be acquired by several basic psychological processes. Mere exposure to ingroup features (e.g., the familiarity with them) can lead to a more positive evaluation. Moreover, people learn first about their ingroup. As interactions within groups tend to be positive, people learn predominantly positive features of the ingroup. When they encounter outgroups, they learn what differentiates outgroups from their ingroup, which tend to be negative features. This tendency is also supported by the potential for misunderstandings to occur in attempts at intergroup cooperation, which leads to actual nonpositive experiences. These basic psychological processes are supplemented by motivational tendencies to protect the ingroup and to see it as positively distinct from outgroups. One prominent process may be the evaluation of all groups according to a common frame of reference that is based on the projection of ingroup attributes. Motivational processes are likely to be triggered whenever a valued ingroup is perceived to be threatened by an outgroup, either in material or symbolic terms. Thus, studies show consistently that a perceived threat to the ingroup (and sometimes threat to the individual) leads to negative attitudes toward outgroups, an enhanced endorsement of ingroup attributes and also to enhanced ingroup identification. (See INTERGROUP THREAT THEORY; THREAT, KINDS AND EFFECTS OF; TERROR MANAGEMENT THEORY: WHY WAR?)

MEASUREMENT OF ETHNOCENTRISM

There are several measures of ethnocentrism in the literature. Such measures often focus on one aspect of ethnocentrism, such as scaling other groups against ingroup standards, ingroup superiority, or generalized prejudice against outgroups. In the area of consumer behavior, measures of consumer ethnocentrism assess the tendency for consumers to buy local or ingroup products. In a recent attempt to measure ethnocentrism comprehensively, Bizumic, Duckitt, Popadic, Dru, and Krauss (2009) developed a scale of ethnocentrism that assesses intragroup ethnocentrism (representing ingroup cohesion and devotion to ingroup norms) and intergroup ethnocentrism (based on four facets including ingroup preference, ingroup superiority, purity, and exploitativeness). Intergroup ethnocentrism seems to be related to more negative attitudes toward outgroups, whereas intragroup ethnocentrism is related to ethnic identification and religiosity. This scale captures the notion that the basis of ethnocentrism is a strong ingroup focus. Relations to outgroups, however, are more complex and are not always just the flip side of ingroup love.

OVERCOMING ETHNOCENTRISM

Although the relation between ethnocentrism and outgroup devaluation is not as straightforward as Sumner assumed, ethnocentrism has the potential to produce negative intergroup relations. (See CONTACT THEORY: EXTENDED AND PARASOCIAL; CONTACT THEORY, INTERGROUP.) How could ethnocentric tendencies be reduced? According to Allport (1954), contact between members of different groups has the potential to reduce prejudice and intergroup conflict. Through intergroup contact people learn new things about the outgroup in order to change stereotypes, they develop affective ties to outgroup members by establishing outgroup friends, and they may also reappraise their ingroup. This ingroup reappraisal may be one crucial factor in changing ethnocentric tendencies because it involves a reassessment of the notion that the ingroup represents the one possible way of living. Reappraising the ingroup may not necessarily reduce the value of the ingroup but it may lead to a "deprovincialization" of the ingroup. (See DEPROVINCIALIZATION.) This is the recognition that although other groups live a different life and conform to different norms and values they nonetheless live a valid life and conform to valid norms and values. People may prefer living according to ingroup norms and values, but also recognize that other ways of living can be equally respectable.

SEE ALSO: Authoritarian Personality; Contact Theory: Extended and Parasocial; Contact Theory, Intergroup; Cooperation and Competition; Deprovincialization; Intergroup Conflict, Theories of; Intergroup Threat Theory; Social Identity Theory; Social Interdependence Theory; Terror Management Theory: Why War?; Threat, Kinds and Effects of.

REFERENCES

Allport, G. (1954). *Nature of prejudice.* Cambridge, MA: Perseus Books.

Bizumic, B., Duckitt, J., Popadic, D., Dru, V., & Krauss, S. (2009). A cross-cultural investigation into a reconceptualization of ethnocentrism. *European Journal of Social Psychology, 39*, 871–899.

Brewer, M. B. (2007). The importance of being we: Human nature and intergroup relations. *American Psychologist, 62*, 728–738.

LeVine, R. A., & Campbell, D. T. (1972). *Ethnocentrism: Theories of conflict, ethnic attitudes, and group behavior.* New York, NY: Wiley and Sons.

Sumner, W. G. (1906). *Folkways: A study of the sociological importance of usages, manners, customs, mores, and morals.* New York, NY: Dover Publications.

Evolutionary Psychology

DANIEL PAQUETTE

Evolutionary psychology focuses specifically on the evolution of the human mind. It has adopted as its own the basic theories of sociobiology, which itself is the product of the integration of ethology, ecology (population dynamics), and neo-Darwinism. Ethology is the descriptive, causal, and comparative study of the behavior of animals (including humans) in their natural environment. Like psychology, ethology focuses as much on the external causes (trigger stimuli) as on the internal causes (nervous and endocrine mechanisms) of behavior, as well as on postconception development (ontogenesis). However, it analyzes animal and human behavior essentially from an evolutionary perspective. Ethology is thus also and primarily interested in so-called distal or ultimate causes – that is to say, the evolution of behaviors in species over generations (phylogeny), and the biological functions of behaviors (i.e., their adaptive or survival value to individuals). Like organs, behavior is a means of adaptation to the environment and evolves primarily through the mechanism of natural selection (Darwin, 1859). Natural selection is the mechanism by which those individuals who have adapted least to the conditions of their environment (due to hereditary characteristics they may in turn pass on to their descendents) reproduce less than better adapted individuals. Over generations (i.e., thousands of years), differential reproduction and mortality ensure that certain characteristics become more widespread than others in a population. The discovery of the laws of heredity (Mendel) and molecular biology in the 20th century clarified the role of natural selection without fundamentally questioning it. Similarly, the work of certain anthropologists, psychologists, and biologists concerning the concept of cultural selection (culturally transmissible traits also offering reproductive advantages) has also contributed to our thinking about the mechanisms of human evolution.

Sociobiology is the systematic study of the biological basis of all social behaviors (Wilson, 1975). Its aim is to understand how social behaviors ensure the reproductive success of the individuals. Adaptations are often interpreted in terms of the survival of the species although, according to Darwin and his successors, it is the individual who is the unit of selection. Stressing the temporary nature of the individual, Dawkins (1976) instead considers the gene to be the fundamental unit of selection. To him, living beings are survival machines built by genes to ensure their own preservation over time. The individuals who survive best are those who possess the most effective combinations of genes. According to this theory, the selfishness of the individual results from the gene's selfishness and any altruistic behavior camouflages the selfish objective of increasing the transmission of the altruist's genes.

The fundamental principle of sociobiology is that individuals tend to behave in such a way as to maximize their reproductive success – in other words, to increase the transmission of copies of their genes over generations. The main basic concepts and theories of sociobiology adopted by evolutionary psychology are kin selection theory,

parental investment theory, sexual dimorphism, sexual selection, and reciprocal altruism theory. According to kin selection theory, an individual may obtain a genetic advantage by helping other related individuals. In fact, the probability of an altruistic or a selfish act is proportional to the relationship coefficient for two individuals. The more genes two individuals share, the more altruistic gestures there will be between them and the less aggression there will be. Thus, in adulthood we would expect to find less aggression between two brothers than between two cousins, and less between two cousins than between two strangers. When carried to its limit, altruism benefits the progeny of related individuals to the detriment of the altruist's own progeny. This theory also offers a biological explanation for such things as nepotism, the pronounced altruism of parents towards their children, and fraternal jealousy. Parent–child conflict and sibling conflict result from the fact that genetic advantages for parent and child are not the same. Sharing 50% of their genes with each of their children, parents are better off investing equally in each of their offspring while each child (who shares 100% of his genes with himself and only 50% with his brothers and sisters, and for whom it is therefore more advantageous to have direct progeny than to foster the progeny of a relative) tries to receive more than his/her share, resulting in sibling competition or aggression. One would therefore expect even more sibling aggression if parents display a preference for one child. (See AGGRESSION AND COMPETITION.)

Parental investment theory predicts that the sexual partner is chosen by the parent who makes the greatest parental investment. In mammals, due to the enormous investment involved in pregnancy, females are unable to have a quantitative reproductive strategy (maximization of the number of descendants) and must instead adopt a qualitative strategy centered on gene quality, hence the importance of choosing the father of their children. Sexual selection is a particular form of natural selection that favors the development of differences between sexes both in morphology and behavior (Darwin, 1871). The sexual dimorphism observed in a certain number of mammal species in which, for example, the male is bigger and more aggressive than the female, is explained by the selective pressure of two factors: intermale competition for access to females, and the female tendency to choose dominant males. Different mating systems (monogamy, polygyny, polyandry) found in nature result in conflict between males and females in a given environment, due to the fact that males and females have different reproductive strategies. The genetic ideal for males is to have the most sexual partners possible (maximization of reproductive success) while leaving parental investment to the other parent. Depending on the species, females will adopt one of the following two strategies: They either choose a male based on the quality of the genes to be transmitted to the children, or they choose a "faithful" male who will share the enormous cost of raising the young. According to Paquette (2004), the reduction in sexual dimorphism over the course of human evolution supports the idea that the human species has an ancient tendency to polygyny (shared with its primate cousins) and a recent tendency to monogamy (due to the growth of the brain and neoteny). This would mean that both female strategies may be found in our species, depending on the environment (access to resources). In certain cases, the female chooses a dominant male who will provide the children with genes that will eventually allow them to achieve a high rank of dominance, and in others she chooses a male who will share with her the enormous cost of raising the offspring, a male who will participate either as a provider of care or as a provider of financial resources. Thus one would expect the majority of interparental conflicts to concern parental investment (direct or indirect) or sexual jealousy.

The theory of reciprocal altruism (Trivers, 1971) offers an explanation for helping behaviors between unrelated individuals of a same species. Reciprocal altruism is the nonsimultaneous exchange of services between two unrelated individuals. It evolves in species capable of individual recognition and of remembering past events. Such behavior is selected over the course of evolution if both partners receive more than they contribute: For example, the cost of supporting an ally against an adversary is low compared to the benefits of a high dominance status. Game theory specialists from various disciplines have demonstrated that the strategy that procures the most resources for the individual over the long term is cooperation. (See GAME THEORY: CONFLICT AND COOPERATION.) Trivers considers that reciprocal altruism has likely played an important role over the course of hominid evolution. All cultures have established rules of reciprocity, which ensure social cohesion and thus permit each individual to survive in hostile environments (predation, disease, famine, natural catastrophes, intraspecific aggression, etc.).

In effect, evolutionary psychology studies everything that is in anyway related to the human brain: sex differences, individual survival activities (such as locating and acquiring resources, defending oneself against danger), the choice of sexual partners, social behavior, moral development, kin relationship, cognition, language, emotions, psychopathology, etc. Through its examination of the adaptive value of human characteristics, evolutionary psychology provides an integrating framework that affords a better understanding of the different proximal mechanisms highlighted by researchers in the humanities and the social sciences. Thus, the past two decades have seen the development of subdisciplines such as evolutionary cognitive psychology, evolutionary social psychology, evolutionary developmental psychology, and evolutionary personality psychology (Buss, 2005).

Evolutionary psychology is essentially based on three heuristic postulates (Tooby & Cosmides, 1990). First, the psychological traits that are characteristic of the human species are essentially the result of adaptations that occurred during the Pleistocene, a period that began 1.8 million years ago and ended 10,000 years ago. In short, our brain is adapted to life in groups of a few dozen to 300 hunter-gatherers. Second, our mind is not a general-purpose problem-solving system, but a modular structure composed of between a few hundred and 3,000 mental modules (neural circuits), each linked to an innate pattern of behavior. Third, the modules that evolved in the ecological and social environment of the Pleistocene represent completed evolution and form the psychological universals that make up human nature. Without denying the importance of cultural diversity, evolutionary psychologists believe that the latter actually masks underlying psychological uniformity. Of course, there are a number of objections to each of these postulates – for example, that we have little information on this ancestral environment, that human evolution during the historical era is perhaps not as negligible as claimed, and that this modular decomposition bears little relation to the functional decomposition of the brain in the neurosciences. However, there are two points that should be mentioned about evolutionary psychology. The first is that evolutionary psychologists do not consider all psychological characteristics or all behaviors to be necessarily adaptive. The second is that evolutionary psychology, like ethology or sociobiology, is not deterministic: The effect of genes is envisaged in terms of predispositions rather than causes. (See SEVILLE STATEMENT ON VIOLENCE.) Thus it is always important to remain wary of people who try to justify human behaviors or social inequalities based on evolutionary theories, for the latter address biological predispositions which are dependent on the environment for their actualization. Furthermore, as Dawkins (1976) has said, evolution has given us a conscience that allows us to make choices that may run counter to our predispositions if we so desire.

SEE ALSO: Aggression and Competition; Game Theory: Conflict and Cooperation; Seville Statement on Violence.

REFERENCES

Buss, D. M. (2005). *The handbook of evolutionary psychology*. Hoboken, NJ: John Wiley & Sons.

Darwin, C. (1859). *On the origin of species by natural selection*. London, UK: John Murray.

Darwin, C. (1871). *The descent of man and selection in relation to sex*. London, UK: John Murray.

Dawkins, R. (1976). *The selfish gene*. Oxford, UK: Oxford University Press.

Paquette, D. (2004). Theorizing the father–child relationship: Mechanisms and developmental outcomes. *Human Development, 47*(4), 193–219.

Tooby, J., & Cosmides, L. (1990). On the universality of human nature and the uniqueness of the individual: The role of genetics and adaptation. *Journal of Personality, 58*, 17–67.

Trivers, R. L. (1971). The evolution of reciprocal altruism. *Quarterly Review of Biology, 46*, 35–57.

Wilson, E. O. (1975). *Sociobiology: The new synthesis*. Cambridge, MA: Harvard University Press.

Experimentation, Design, and Analysis

MICHAEL R. HULSIZER AND
LINDA M. WOOLF

Peace psychology researchers have a multitude of methodologies available to explore the diverse areas of inquiry which compose the field of peace psychology. For example, researchers may choose a qualitative approach through the use of field studies, ethnographies, oral histories, or case studies. Although many of these approaches are more commonplace in disciplines such as women's studies and anthropology, there are an increasing number of psychologists utilizing these methodologies given the richness of the resultant data and the challenges of international research. (See QUALITATIVE METHODS AND CODING.) However, the most prevalent research approach in psychology involves the investigation of quantitative data – often collected through archival data, interviews, surveys, quasi-experiments, and/or experiments. (See ARCHIVAL RESEARCH; SURVEY RESEARCH IN PEACE PSYCHOLOGY.) The focus of this essay is on experimentation using quantitative data.

The goal in quantitative research is to represent abstract concepts numerically to statistically demonstrate associations between variables, identify differences between groups, or infer a causal relationship. However, the path from data collection to statistical analysis is fraught with risk. First, researchers need to take care when developing quantitative measures to ensure that they are reliable, have high construct validity, and are culturally appropriate. Second, researchers need to develop a research design that has high internal validity, sufficient power, and can lend itself to statistical analysis. Third, researchers need to select statistical analyses that will enable the researcher to address the experimental hypothesis. Finally, it is imperative that researchers conduct all studies ethically with an eye towards protection of participants.

DEVELOPING APPROPRIATE MEASURES

The process by which an abstract concept is translated into a quantitative measure appears, at first glance, to be a simple endeavor – simply pose the question and measure the response. However, the researcher needs to consider two important issues when developing and/or selecting quantitative measures. The first issue that needs to be taken into consideration is construct validity – the degree to which the operational definition of the variable (i.e., how it is being measured) accurately reflects the underlying abstract concept. There are a number of indicators of construct validity available to researchers including face validity (measure appears to assess what it purports to measure), predictive validity (scores can predict future behavior), concurrent validity (participants with differing characteristics score in predicable fashion), convergent validity (scores on the measure are strongly associated with participant scores on a similar measure), and discriminant validity (scores on the measure are not related to dissimilar measures).

Most researchers in psychology rely on face validity when developing their own measures. However, greater confidence in a measure can be gained by establishing the construct validity of the measure through a number of indicators.

According to Woolf and Hulsizer (2011), there are unique threats to construct validity which occur within the realm of international research – an area in which peace psychologists are prolific. Specifically, it is essential that investigators monitor the degree to which the measures used are equivalent across cultures and groups. In assessing the construct validity of international measures, investigators need to develop an awareness of three sources of nonequivalence – translation, conceptual, and metric. Translation equivalence is necessary when conducting research on one population while using experimental measures developed and standardized with another population. According to the *Guidelines for Research in Ethnic Minority Communities* (Council of National

Psychological Associations for the Advancement of Ethnic Minority Interests, 2000), the proper translation of experimental measures involves the use of the back-translation method – using multiple translators to convert the measure to the target language and back to the original language until equivalence is achieved. Conceptual equivalence is the degree to which theoretical concepts or constructs are the same between two cultures. Metric equivalence represents the ability to compare the specific scores on a scale of interest across cultures. To address these equivalence concerns, the guidelines recommend that researchers work collaboratively with indigenous investigators.

Second, researchers need to examine the reliability of the measure. Test–retest reliability is the most commonly used technique to assess reliability. For this approach, participants complete the measure twice. The greater the similarity between scores and the greater the time gap, the more reliable the measure is rated. Similarly, when two or more individuals are coding data (e.g., interviews or observational data) the researcher will often use interrater reliability to evaluate the credibility of the measure. For research involving a multi-item questionnaire, researchers should assess the internal consistency reliability of the measure. This analysis examines the extent to which a participant responds consistently to similar items throughout the questionnaire and is typically examined using Chronbach's alpha.

EXPERIMENTAL DESIGN

A challenge in experimental research is developing a design which can establish a cause and effect relationship. At the most basic level, establishing a cause and effect relationship through experimental design involves measuring the effect of an independent variable on a dependent variable.

For example, a researcher could study the effects of several levels of television violence (independent variable) on aggressive behavior (dependent variable) in children. The independent variable is manipulated by the researcher. Categorical variables, such as gender, may also be used as an independent variable. The dependent variable, or outcome variable, is designed to measure the effect of the independent variable.

A between groups design involves the random assignment of participants to one of the levels of the independent variable (e.g., one participant may be randomly assigned to view a television program that is high in violence while the next participant may be randomly assigned to a program that is moderately high in violence).

In contrast to a between groups design, a repeated measures design enables each participant to take part in all levels of the independent variable. Therefore, in a repeated measures design, each participant is her/his own control group, given that they would eventually participate in all levels of the independent variable (Keppel & Wickens, 2004). The aforementioned designs are relatively simple. More complex designs may involve two or more independent variables (each with two or more levels) and multiple dependent variables (i.e., factorial and multivariate designs, respectively), or a combination of between and repeated measures (i.e., a mixed design), and numerous additional design elements engineered to clarify the effects of independent variables on dependent variables.

A study has high internal validity when the researcher has a high degree of confidence that changes in one variable caused the changes in the outcome variable. To achieve high internal validity, the researcher needs to utilize a design that eliminates or minimizes all threats to internal validity (see Shadish, Cook, & Campbell, 2002). In addition, researchers need to pay particular attention to external validity, especially in relation to participant selection procedures. According to Keppel and Wickens (2004), random, representative sampling can greatly assist the external validity, or generalizability, of the research results. Haphazard sampling, or samples of convenience, may be easier to gather but potentially introduce a host of problems in interpreting precisely what the results of a study mean. It is vital that researchers collect as many participants as possible as a means to increase statistical power – that is, the likelihood of being able to detect a statistically significant impact of the independent variable on the dependent variable.

STATISTICAL ANALYSES

Knowing which statistical technique to use can be challenging. Fortunately, there are a number of resources available to assist researchers (e.g., Howell, 2011). Generally, traditional statistical textbooks cover three primary areas. The first category of statistical analyses is descriptive statistics. As the name suggests, these statistics (e.g., mean, standard deviation) describe the research sample. The second category involves measures of association such as correlation, which refers to the strength and direction of the association between two or more variables. The Pearson product–moment correlation coefficient is appropriate for most correlation analyses that are examining the relationship or association between two variables. Regression analyses typically involve a predictor variable and outcome variable. The stronger the association between the predictor and outcome variable, the more accurate one can make predictions of outcomes based on knowledge of the value of the predictor variable. There are several regression analyses available for researchers ranging from ordinary least squares analyses to multiple regression using a variety of approaches (e.g., hierarchical, stepwise);

however, these topics are beyond the scope of the current article. Regardless of the analysis, care needs to be taken when interpreting correlation and regression analyses given that they cannot be used to determine causality. Inferential statistics, such as *t* tests and analysis of variance (ANOVA) are appropriate for the analysis of experiments and are the third major category of statistical analyses. These analyses allow the researcher to make inferences about a specific population based on sample data. Finally, advanced level statistical analyses such as meta-analysis are also becoming more popular in the literature. (See META-ANALYSIS.)

Currently available statistical software programs (e.g., PASW, SAS) ensure that sophisticated statistical analyses are a mere point and click away. In addition, there are a number of step-by-step guide books available (e.g., George & Mallery, 2010). Upon first glance at these programs, researchers may be overwhelmed by the sheer number of statistical analyses available. Care should be taken to select the right analysis given the constraints of the data. Researchers also need to be cognizant of any threats to statistical conclusion validity – the extent to which the study can be properly analyzed (Shadish et al., 2002). Some threats to statistical conclusion validity include violating statistical assumptions, "fishing" for statistical results by continuing to analyze data in various ways after statistical analyses of the initial hypothesis have been completed, using unreliable measures, and having low statistical power. Most of the potential threats can be addressed with good research design, a sufficient number of participants, and appropriate statistical analyses.

RESEARCH ETHICS

The American Psychological Association's *Ethical Principles of Psychologists and Code of*

Conduct (2002) highlights a range of research ethics topics. According to the *Ethical Principles*, researchers conducting any study must inform participants about a variety of features such as purpose, procedures, risks and benefits, the limits of confidentiality, and the right to withdraw from participation. Although all of these concerns are fundamental to psychological research, issues of informed consent and confidentiality are especially important in cross-cultural peace psychology research, particularly in relation to protection from harm. (See DO NO HARM.) For researchers working cross-culturally, consent forms must be developed with an understanding of the local culture. Specifically, consent forms need to be inclusive of special needs related to language, reading ability, nation-specific legal standards, and cultural norms. Moreover, it is important to note that in some cultures, women may not be culturally free to give informed consent but must first receive the consent of a male guardian. It is imperative in all research that investigators carefully protect the confidentiality of all participants (e.g., including no easily identifiable information about the participants on forms, questionnaires, etc.). Researchers must be particularly cautious in cultures where data may be legally taken by family members, religious officials, or governmental agents for use against the well-being of the participant or where small group, aggregate data may be used against an entire minority population.

CONCLUSION

Significant advances in the field of peace psychology have been made over the past several decades. Some of this growth can be attributed to the increased use of appropriate experimental methods. Researchers need to utilize the most effective research design

to neutralize specific threats to construct, internal, external, and statistical conclusion validity. In addition, appropriate analyses are critical for establishing associations or inferring a causal relationship between variables of interest. The continued use of effective research design and analyses will further deepen our understanding of the field of peace psychology.

SEE ALSO: Archival Research; Do No Harm; Meta-Analysis; Qualitative Methods and Coding; Survey Research in Peace Psychology.

REFERENCES

American Psychological Association. (2002). *Ethical principles of psychologists and code of conduct*. Retrieved from http://apa.org/ethics/code2002.html

Council of National Psychological Associations for the Advancement of Ethnic Minority Interests. (2000). *Guidelines for research in ethnic minority communities*. Washington, DC: American Psychological Association.

George, D., & Mallery, P. (2010). *SPSS for Windows step by step: A simple study guide and reference, 17.0 update* (10th ed.). Boston, MA: Pearson Education.

Howell, D. C. (2011). *Fundamental statistics for the behavioral sciences* (7th ed.). Belmont, CA: Wadsworth.

Keppel, G., & Wickens, T. D. (2004). *Design and analysis: A researcher's handbook* (4th ed.). Englewood Cliffs, NJ: Prentice Hall.

Shadish, W. R., Cook, T. D., & Campbell, D. T. (2002). *Experimental and quasi-experimental designs for generalized causal inference*. Boston, MA: Houghton Mifflin.

Woolf, L. M., & Hulsizer, M. R. (2011). Why diversity matters: The power of inclusion in research methods. In K. D. Keith (Ed.), *Cross-cultural psychology: Contemporary themes and perspectives* (pp. 56–72). Oxford, UK: Wiley-Blackwell.

ADDITIONAL RESOURCES

Cook, T. D., & Campbell, D. T. (1979). *Quasi-experimentation: Design and analysis issues for field settings*. Boston, MA: Houghton Mifflin.

Grimm, L. G., & Yarnold, P. R. (Eds.). (1995). *Reading and understanding multivariate statistics*. Washington, DC: American Psychological Association.

Kirk, R. E. (1995). *Experimental design: Procedures for the behavioral sciences* (3rd ed.). Pacific Grove, CA: Brooks/Cole.

F

Family Violence and Abuse

ANDREA E. MERCURIO

The field of family violence and abuse is multifaceted, complex, and still in its infancy. The notion of family violence has traditionally been understood as violence between and among members of an immediate family (e.g., a parent who strikes a child or a husband who hits his wife). The subfields of intimate partner violence (the preferred term for marital/spousal abuse) and child physical and sexual abuse have probably garnered the most scholarly attention. However, family violence and abuse takes diverse forms and researchers have begun to direct greater empirical efforts towards understanding the areas of child neglect, elder abuse, and sibling abuse; moreover, particularly in the United States, there is an increased focus on interpersonal violence that occurs outside the boundaries of conventional definitions of the family (e.g., violence between partners in same-sex relationships).

The area of family violence and abuse is beset with controversy. At the most basic level, scholars at times disagree about what constitutes a family, which invariably leads to inconsistencies in how family violence is defined, measured, and understood. Some have argued that the term intimate might be more suitable than family given the changing cultural and legal landscape of what is meant by family, as well as the fact that interpersonal violence does not always fall neatly within the scope of popular descriptions of the typical family. However, others have adopted a more flexible understanding of family, allowing for the consideration of abusive relations that occur outside the traditional family unit. A related issue concerns our understanding of what should be considered abusive. As many researchers have noted, definitions of abuse differ considerably in the extent to which they focus on such things as causes, effects, motivations, frequency, and intensity. There have been some attempts to differentiate among interrelated terms like violence, abuse, and maltreatment, but examination of the literature suggests that within the United States and internationally there is no universal agreement among scholars and professionals (Malley-Morrison, 2004). Differences in how family violence is conceptualized and discrepancies in what behaviors (or lack thereof) are or are not considered abuse

The Encyclopedia of Peace Psychology, First Edition. Edited by Daniel J. Christie.
© 2012 Blackwell Publishing Ltd. Published 2012 by Blackwell Publishing Ltd.

clearly have important implications for the likelihood that victims will receive assistance from the legal, medical, or social service communities.

One of the most contentious debates in the field of family violence concerns the extent to which corporal punishment, a physical disciplinary technique, should be viewed as a form of abuse or as an acceptable alternative for socializing children who misbehave. Some social scientists and child advocates have taken the staunch position that corporal punishment is abusive, harmful, and should be legally banned, as it has already been in a number of European countries such as Sweden, Finland, Norway, Germany, Greece, Hungary, and Portugal, among others. Opponents of corporal punishment cite empirical evidence suggesting that its use is linked to aggression, delinquency, and other adverse health outcomes such as suicide and problem drinking (e.g., Straus, 1994). Not surprisingly, proponents of corporal punishment often reject these findings and refer to research demonstrating that physical discipline may be an effective back-up strategy to nonphysical tactics or successful when used in combination with other techniques (e.g., Larzelere, 1994). (See CHILDREN, PEACE AND AGGRESSION IN.)

Finally, controversy continues over research suggesting that women commit physical acts of violence against their partners in equal proportion to men. Data collected in the United States from crime reports such as the National Crime Victimization Survey (NCVS) suggest that men commit violent acts towards their partner more often, while data gathered in the United States and Canada from nationally representative self-report surveys indicate women and men are equally likely to carry out assaults on their partner. Females, however, still constitute a highly vulnerable group, as statistics indicate that they reportedly sustain greater injury from domestic violence disputes than males.

Global prevalence rates of different forms of family violence and abuse are difficult to estimate due to the many challenges associated with conducting large-scale epidemiological studies across varied cultural and social settings. Estimates of various types of abuse vary widely by country due, in part, to differences in methodology. However, cross-cultural research on the scope of family violence is accumulating. Internationally, population studies in 50 different countries reveal that (a) women are more likely to be physically and/or sexually attacked or killed by a former or current partner than by anyone else; and (b) women around the world experience a lifetime prevalence of physical partner abuse ranging from around 10% (e.g., in Japan) to 62% (e.g., in Peru) (Kar & Carcia-Moreno, 2009). Moreover, according to the World Health Organization (WHO), a number of international studies have indicated that 25–50% of all children report severe and frequent physical abuse, depending on the particular country under study (World Health Organization, 2006). Many other children also endure emotional abuse and neglect, although the magnitude of these problems worldwide is not yet fully known.

Just as there is no single definition or understanding of family violence and abuse, there is no single theory that adequately accounts for all instances of family violence. The various models and theories frequently emphasize different causal factors and approach the issue from different theoretical levels of analysis. Existing theories of family violence are often organized into a macrosystem, exosystem, and microsystem framework, depending on how broad or narrow is the scope of the particular theory. (See ECOLOGICAL MODEL.) Similarly, other scholars categorize the theories into psychological/individual-level approaches, social psychological approaches, and sociocultural approaches. Theories that fall under the rubric of an individual-level approach often link personality characteristics, mental illness, alcohol and substance use, and other intra-individual processes to acts of aggression within the family. Although there is evidence that links psychopathology, and particularly substance abuse, to violence, there is also recognition that there are many people with these problems who do not engage in violence toward family members. Thus, these theories fail to explain why many people with mental illness and personality disorders, for example, do not engage in violent acts toward family members. Social psychological approaches examine external environmental factors that impact on the family unit. Theories that consider factors like stress, family structure, family interactions, learning, and the transmission of violence all fit within a social psychological analysis. Finally, sociocultural approaches offer a macrolevel of analysis that focuses on broad cultural, social, and structural factors that may lend themselves to promoting violence within families (e.g., patriarchy or poverty). For example, feminist theorists view violence as a function of male privilege and power and as a means by which men, the dominant members of society, uphold their status in the family setting and in a patriarchal society. However, these perspectives are unable to account for women's violence against their partners, which may be similar in prevalence to men's violence against their partners, at least in the United States (Straus, 2005). Moreover, feminist-inspired theories offer less insight into our understanding of other forms of violence, such as sibling abuse and elder abuse. (See DOMESTIC VIOLENCE: FEMINIST PERSPECTIVE.)

Research efforts have identified a multitude of factors that make an individual more susceptible to family violence and abuse. Many researchers suggest that family violence is best understood by considering the complex interplay of factors that occur at different levels (e.g., the individual level, the relationship level, the community level, and the society level). Risk factors at each level have been associated with the occurrence of family violence but not much is known about the relative importance of these risk factors in causing family violence, and the most significant factors are likely to vary by country and by the particular type of family violence. Common risk factors for family violence across nations include younger age, gender inequality, social and cultural norms which foster traditional gender roles, marital conflict, poverty, economic stress, alcohol and substance abuse, social isolation, and unemployment.

The physical and psychological effects of violence on family members are both immediate and long-lasting. Physical injury, one of the most obvious, visible, and immediate consequences of violence within families, is only one of countless effects that abuse can have on an individual. Victims of child physical abuse may experience impaired social and emotional development, suffer from substance abuse problems and psychiatric illnesses, and engage in aggressive and antisocial behavior and criminal activity. There is evidence that children subjected to emotional abuse and neglect experience similar types of problems. International research on physical and sexual violence against women by intimate partners paints a similarly unpleasant picture concerning the negative impact of abuse. The WHO's *Multi-country Study on Women's Health and Domestic Violence against Women*, which included interviews of over 24,000 women in 15 different settings and 10 different countries, found that women who experienced physical or sexual violence by an intimate partner were more likely to report poorer health, higher levels of emotional distress, thoughts of suicide, and more problems carrying out daily activities (World Health Organization, 2005).

The last four decades of research have produced considerable knowledge about family violence in many nations around the world and improved our understanding of the individual, social, and cultural factors that contribute to its development and sustain it over time. The evidence clearly suggests that violence in families is a significant international public health problem that deserves increased attention. However, more extensive, systematic, and comprehensive research efforts are needed to advance our knowledge of the causal factors involved in family violence so that effective intervention and prevention programs can be developed and implemented, especially in countries were data are currently limited. The problem of family violence is not new and clearly there is still much work to be done so that all individuals can lead full and productive lives, free from abuse and its devastating impact on health and well-being.

SEE ALSO: Children, Peace and Aggression in; Domestic Violence: Feminist Perspective; Ecological Model.

REFERENCES

Kar, H. L., & Garcia-Moreno, C. (2009). Partner aggression across countries. In K. D. O'Leary & E. M. Woodin (Eds.), *Psychological and physical aggression in couples: Causes and interventions*. Washington, DC: American Psychological Association.

Larzelere, R. E. (1994). Should the use of corporal punishment by parents be considered child abuse? No. In M. A. Mason & E. Gambrill (Eds.), *Debating children's lives: Current controversies on children and adolescents* (pp. 204–209, 217–218). Thousand Oaks, CA: Sage.

Malley-Morrison, K. (Ed.). (2004). *International perspectives on family violence and abuse: A cognitive ecological approach*. Mahwah, NJ: Erlbaum.

Straus, M. A. (1994). Should the use of corporal punishment by parents be considered child abuse? In M. A. Mason & E. Gambrill (Eds.), *Debating children's lives: Current controversies on children and adolescents* (pp. 196–222). Newbury Park, CA: Sage.

Straus, M. A. (2005). Women's violence towards men is a serious social problem. In D. R. Loseke, R. J. Gelles, & M. M. Cavenaugh (Eds.), *Current controversies on family violence* (pp. 55–77). Newbury Park, CA: Sage.

World Health Organization. (2005). *WHO multi-country study on women's health and domestic violence against women*. Retrieved September 3, 2009, from http://www.who.int/gender/violence/who_multicountry_study/summary_report/summary_report_English2.pdf.

World Health Organization. (2006). *Preventing child maltreatment: A guide to taking action and generating evidence*. Retrieved September 3, 2009, from http://whqlibdoc.who.int/publications/2006/9241594365_eng.pdf.

Fear, Politics of

DANIEL BAR-TAL AND NIMROD ROSLER

Research about the role and effects of fear in politics and conflicts has received contributions from scholars in different domains, such as psychology, political science, international relations, and history.

Psychologists tend to define fear as a primary emotion which includes aversive feelings, physiological changes such as increased sweating and accelerated heart rate, and behavioral intentions of fight, flight, or avoidance in relation to the threatening stimulus. On the level of primary affect, fear is related to homeostasis. It arises in situations of perceived threat and danger to the organism (the person) and/or his/her environment (the society), and enables them to respond adaptively. Threats and dangers, which can be detected in present situations or generalized from past experiences, can be related specifically to a particular individual (e.g., as stimulated by noise, darkness, a dog, or social rejection) or be evoked in collective situations (e.g., political persecution, terror attack, or war). On the personal level, fear is a component of more complex reactions and feelings, such as panic, dread, anxiety, despair, caution, submission, guilt, shame, prudery, or cowardliness. On the collective level, fear can also serve as a social construction aimed at securing the conformity of members of society to current attitudes, values, and social hierarchies. (See EMOTION.)

Fear can be acquired by exposure to situations that are perceived as threatening the person or their society, or by information received about certain objects, events, or people. Once the information about threatening – or potentially threatening – stimuli is acquired through different modes of learning, it is stored as either implicit or explicit memory about emotional situations. Subsequently, both types of memory influence appraisal of a particular situation as threatening. Implicit affective memory unconsciously arouses reactions of fear in view of a particular cue, and is particularly resilient, exhibiting little fading with the passage of time. Furthermore, LeDoux (1996) points out how implicit affective memory unconsciously arouses reactions of fear in view of a particular cue. Fear is especially powerful when it is based on implicit memory. Its effect is stronger than that of explicit memory because it arouses fear spontaneously and automatically, overcoming cognitive control, rationality, and logic.

PSYCHOLOGICAL AND POLITICAL EFFECTS

Fear dominates and controls thinking because the connections from the limbic (affective system) to the cortical structures (cognitive system) are more numerous than those in the opposite direction, from the cognitive system to the emotional system (LeDoux, 1996). As a result, fear floods consciousness and leads to automatic behavior, preparing the individual to cope with the threatening situation.

Once fear is evoked, it limits activation of mechanisms of regulation and stalls consideration of various alternatives because of its egocentric and maladaptive patterns of reactions to situations that require creative and novel solutions for coping. The empirical evidence provided by LeDoux (1996) shows that fear has limiting effects on cognitive processing. It tends to cause adherence to known situations and avoidance of risky, uncertain, and novel ones; it tends to cause cognitive freezing, which reduces openness to new ideas, and resistance to change.

Finally, fear motivates defense and protection from events that are perceived as threatening. When defense and protection are not efficient, fear may lead to aggressive acts against the perceived source of threat. That is, when in fear, human beings sometimes tend to cope by initiating fight, even when there is little or nothing to be achieved by doing so. Thus, Thucydides, writing in the fifth century BCE about the Peloponnesian War, Thomas Hobbes, and scholar of international relations Kenneth Waltz all consider fear as an important factor for wars and mistrust, as well as for the creation of political institutions that regulate aggression, such as a state.

However, from another perspective, the dominant influence of fear on human cognition makes it an effective instrument for attitude and behavior change generally, and political persuasion specifically. Messages triggering moderate fear levels were observed as early as the 1950s by Janis and Feshbach (1953) to be effective for persuasion generally. Correspondingly, political scientists Michael MacKuen and George Marcus (see Neuman, Marcus, Crigler, & MacKuen, 2007) point out that fear facilitates reconsideration of current attitudes and ways of action, and intense collection of relevant information and engagement in its processing. These processes may potentially lead to change in attitudes and political actions, thus providing opportunities for political persuasion.

FEAR AS A COLLECTIVE PHENOMENON

Fear is not merely an individual emotional phenomenon, but can evolve as a context or political and social atmosphere, thus becoming a collective emotion. Furthermore, since individual emotions are created under the influence of common social norms, it is natural that under certain circumstances, fear becomes pervasive in society either spontaneously or through deliberate social processes. Such social circumstances are inclined to include state terror or intense intergroup conflicts.

Corradi, Fagen, and Garretón (1992), for example, analyzed the formation of the collective emotional orientation of fear in four South American societies: Argentina, Brazil, Chile, and Uruguay. In these cases, fear developed in reaction to certain threatening societal conditions: Members of these four societies were subjected to systematic and consistent terror, and as a result, they perceived the political system as the source of life-threatening dangers. This perception was shared by a substantial segment in each society, resulting in a "fear culture."

Recently, the terror attacks in the United States on September 11, 2001 demonstrated the emergence of a collective fear orientation. The unexpected loss of life and destruction, together with uncertainty and potential additional attacks, brought about the development of large-scale fear that can characterize collectives. (See TERROR MANAGEMENT THEORY: WHY WAR?.)

FEAR IN INTRACTABLE CONFLICTS

The prolonged experience of violence inherent to vicious and harsh intractable conflicts affects the personal life of society members and marks their behavior. In these stressful situations, society members tend to process information selectively, focusing on the evil acts of the adversary, which are threatening and full of dangers. These experiences become embedded in the collective memory, get incorporated into cultural products, and are then disseminated via society's channels of communication. Eventually, they serve as a fertile ground for the formation of the collective fear orientation (Jarymowicz & Bar-Tal, 2006).

Political scientist Jennifer Mitzen suggested that states and societies engulfed by prolonged conflicts may give precedence to continuing the routine of the conflict since it becomes a major part of their national identity. The conflict and the consequent collective fear orientation can paradoxically provide them with a stable cognitive environment and ontological security. If absent, societies in conflict may construct an ongoing discourse of danger and fear in order to prevent existential threat to their common identity (Mitzen, 2006).

Of course, the formation of a collective fear orientation in cases of intractable conflict is inevitable due to the impact of real threats, dangers, and other negative emotional information on the human mind. Accumulated evidence in psychology shows that negative events and information are well attended to and remembered and that they have determinative influence on evaluation, judgment, and action tendencies. This negativity bias is an inherent characteristic of the negative motivational system, which operates automatically at the evaluative–categorization stage. The negative motivational system is structured to respond more intensely than the positive motivational system to comparable levels of motivational activation. This tendency reflects adaptive behavior, since negative information, especially related to threats, may require an immediate defensive reaction. (See

INTERGROUP THREAT THEORY; THREAT, KINDS
AND EFFECTS OF.)

A collective fear orientation cuts deeply
into the psychic fabric of society members
and becomes linked with a social ethos of
conflict. The collective fear orientation
becomes embedded in the societal ethos
simply because fear is functional and adaptive. Fear prepares society members for
better coping with the stressful situation on
a very primary level. This preparation is
achieved in a number of ways: (a) it mobilizes constant readiness for potential dangers
against unwished-for surprises; (b) it directs
attention and sensitizes society to cues that
signal danger and to information that implies
threat; (c) it increases affiliation, solidarity,
and cohesiveness among society members in
view of the threat to individuals and to
society at large; and (d) it mobilizes society
members to act on behalf of the society, to
cope with the threat, to act against the
enemy and defend the country and society.

In addition to the above-noted functions
of the collective fear orientation, there are
also other consequences. It may lead to a
collective freezing of beliefs. A society in
intractable conflict tends to adhere to certain
beliefs about the causes of threat, about the
conflict, about the adversary, and about
ways of coping with the dangers. It has difficulty in entertaining alternative ideas, solutions, or courses of action. As Abraham
Maslow noted, all those psychological and
social factors that increase fear cut impulses
to know.

Furthermore, the collective fear orientation tends to limit society members' perspective by binding the present to past
experiences related to the conflict, and by
building expectations for the future exclusively on the basis of the past. This seriously
hinders the disassociation from the past
needed to allow creative thinking about new
alternatives that may resolve the conflict
peacefully (Jarymowicz & Bar-Tal, 2006). A
society oversensitized by fear tends to

misinterpret cues and information as signs
of threat and danger, searching for the smallest indication in this direction, even in situations that signal good intentions. The fear
also causes great mistrust and delegitimization of the adversary. In addition, lines of
political research show that fear leads people
to increased ethnocentrism and intolerance
towards outgroups (e.g., Duckitt & Fisher,
2003). Finally, the collective fear orientation
is a major cause of violence. A society in fear
tends to fight when it copes with threatening
conditions. Fight is a habituated course of
action, based on past experience, and thus,
again, a society fixates on coping with threat
in a conflictive way, without exploring new
avenues of behavior that can break the cycle
of violence (Lake & Rothchild, 1998).

SUMMARY

Fear as a primary and dominant emotion has
major influences over cognition and behavior both in the individual and at the collective level. It enables rapid responses to cope
with the threatening situation, but usually
creates constraining consequences for cognitive processing. Fear characterizes individuals and societies living in intractable conflicts
as a result of threatening experiences of violence. It is functional to cope with the situation, but at the same time the collective fear
orientation feeds the continuation of the
intractable conflict, creating a vicious cycle
of fear, freezing, and violence.

SEE ALSO: Emotion; Intergroup Threat
Theory; Terror Management Theory: Why
War?; Threat, Kinds and Effects of.

REFERENCES

Corradi, J. E., Fagen, P. W., & Garretón, M. A.
(Eds.). (1992). *Fear at the edge: State terror and
resistance in Latin America.* Berkeley, CA:
University of California Press.

Duckitt, J., & Fisher, K. (2003). The impact of social threat on worldview and ideological attitudes. *Political Psychology, 24*, 199–222.

Janis, I. L., & Feshbach, S. (1953). Effects of fear-arousing communication. *Journal of Abnormal and Social Psychology, 48*, 78–92.

Jarymowicz, M., & Bar-Tal, D. (2006). The dominance of fear over hope in the lives of individuals and collectives. *European Journal of Social Psychology, 36*, 367–392.

Lake, D. A., & Rothchild, D. (Eds.). (1998). *The international spread of ethnic conflict: Fear, diffusion, and escalation.* Princeton, NJ: Princeton University Press.

LeDoux, J. E. (1996). *The emotional brain: The mysterious underpinnings of emotional life.* New York, NY: Simon and Schuster.

Mitzen, J. (2006). Ontological security in world politics: State identity and the security dilemma. *European Journal of International Relations, 12*, 341–370.

Neuman, W. R., Marcus, G. E., Crigler, A. N., & MacKuen, M. (Eds.). (2007). *The affect effect: Dynamics of emotion in political thinking and behavior.* Chicago, IL: University of Chicago Press.

Forgiveness, Intergroup

HERMANN SWART AND MILES HEWSTONE

Memories of past events and conflicts often remain inextricably woven into the fabric of the present in the lives of both victims and perpetrators living in post-conflict societies. Interpersonal forgiveness is important in the process of repairing the relationship between individuals previously in conflict. An act of interpersonal forgiveness allows the victim to let go of their feelings of anger and hurt felt towards the perpetrator and, in essence, cancels the "debt" owed on the part of the perpetrator. The victim thereby gives up their right to revenge, which allows the victim and the perpetrator to work towards repairing their relationship. (See FORGIVE-NESS, INTERPERSONAL.)

This understanding of interpersonal forgiveness can, in many ways, be extended to the realm of post-conflict intergroup relations. The concept of forgiveness between groups, or intergroup forgiveness, where "I as a member of my group" forgive "them as a group" for the harm that "their group" have caused "me and/or my group" has begun to gain momentum within the social psychological literature as an important psychological mechanism in the development of peace and reconciliation in post-conflict societies (Cairns, Tam, Hewstone, & Niens, 2005; Hewstone et al., 2004; Wohl & Branscombe, 2005).

In this article we briefly explore the concept of intergroup forgiveness and consider how it compares to interpersonal forgiveness. We also discuss how intergroup forgiveness may be achieved and what variables play an important role in either promoting or inhibiting intergroup forgiveness. Finally, we briefly consider ideas for future research on intergroup forgiveness.

THE CONCEPT OF INTERGROUP FORGIVENESS

Social psychologists have for a number of decades understood the importance of differentiating between interpersonal-level behavior and intergroup-level behavior. There is an overwhelming body of research that supports the idea that individuals behave differently towards one another when group categories are made salient as compared to when group membership is not salient. Given this understanding, it is all the more surprising that, while there is an ever-growing body of literature on interpersonal forgiveness, the social psychological inquiry into intergroup forgiveness has only just recently begun to emerge.

Forgiveness may be regarded as an unfolding prosocial process of volitional change of affective, cognitive, and behavioral attitudes that serve to motivate the victim to modify or repair their relationship with the offender by pursuing relationship-constructive, as opposed to relationship-destructive, actions. It is worth emphasizing the *volitional* nature of forgiveness. As a complex prosocial transformation that can be powerfully healing, reconciling, and future-oriented, it cannot be prescribed or coerced. To do so could add to the cycle of violence rather than diminish it.

At first glance intergroup forgiveness and interpersonal forgiveness seem very similar to one another insofar as they both involve the giving up of the right to revenge against the perceived perpetrator(s). From an interpersonal perspective the perpetrator(s) would be one or more specific individuals, whereas from an intergroup perspective the perpetrator(s) may comprise a collection of (often anonymous) individuals from a specific social group. However, upon closer inspection intergroup forgiveness appears to differ from interpersonal forgiveness in a number of important ways (Hewstone et al., 2004).

First, interpersonal forgiveness is generally a private affair between individuals. Intergroup forgiveness, on the other hand, is often the subject of intense public scrutiny, and calls for intergroup forgiveness are frequently made with strong political undertones. Second, interpersonal forgiveness is more likely to follow subsequent to some form of apology or acknowledgment of guilt on the part of the perpetrator. Despite the groundswell of public apologies by perpetrator groups in post-conflict societies around the world, such apologies made by one group towards another are often received with skepticism. (See APOLOGIES AND FORGIVENESS.) Third, while interpersonal forgiveness is generally more likely to occur when there exists a fair chance that the consequences of the wrongdoing will disappear with time, the consequences of intergroup conflict are often of such a nature that

they are very difficult to erase. A fourth distinction between interpersonal and intergroup forgiveness is that while it is often possible to distinguish between a distinct victim and perpetrator in an interpersonal dispute, such distinctions become more difficult to make when dealing with intergroup conflicts characterized by cycles of violence and revenge. In such cases it becomes more challenging to identify who it is that should be asking for forgiveness and who should be doing the forgiving.

Given these differences, interpersonal forgiveness might not be sufficient for improving intergroup relations in the aftermath of conflicts characterized not only by group-based violence but also by atrocities. As such, these differences highlight the importance of further research into how best to achieve intergroup forgiveness in post-conflict societies. Importantly, given the differences between interpersonal and intergroup forgiveness pointed out above, such research should measure intergroup forgiveness at the community or group level rather than at the individual level of personalized trauma (Cairns et al., 2005).

The idea of forgiveness is often synonymous with forgetting about the wrongdoings one has suffered, and with reconciliation. As far as forgiving and forgetting is concerned, this is not always possible within societies characterized by a history of intractable conflict, nor is it necessarily desirable. In fact, a minimum degree of remembering the past is necessary in order for any forgiveness to occur. (See RECONCILIATION, COLLECTIVE MEMORY AND.) Calls for forgiveness in societies attempting to achieve post-conflict reconciliation are common. However, the precise nature of the relationship between forgiveness and reconciliation remains as yet unresolved. It is unclear whether intergroup forgiveness is required in order to promote reconciliation, or whether reconciliation is necessary before intergroup forgiveness is possible. It may well be that intergroup forgiveness is likely to encourage greater reconciliation that, in turn, will further strengthen the desire towards intergroup forgiveness. Exploratory research suggests that there are subtle, yet meaningful differences between forgiveness, forgetting, and reconciliation (Hewstone et al., 2004). (See RECONCILIATION: INSTRUMENTAL AND SOCIOEMOTIONAL ASPECTS.) We turn now to a brief discussion on how intergroup forgiveness might be achieved.

ACHIEVING INTERGROUP FORGIVENESS

Achieving peace and reconciliation in post-conflict societies has featured strongly on the international agenda over the past two to three decades. More often than not, the most persistent calls for forgiveness and reconciliation are made by foreign politicians who are removed from the conflict itself. Historical perpetrator groups are asked to apologize, and truth commissions are established to create a collective memory of the past by bringing erstwhile victims and perpetrators together in mediated, public dialogue. As alluded to earlier, while apologies by historical perpetrator groups are welcomed by some they are also received with cynical skepticism by others, often because they do not go as far so as to include an explicit acknowledgment of guilt or any commitments towards making concrete reparations. (See TRANSITIONAL JUSTICE SYSTEMS, PSYCHOLOGY AND.)

Empirical research on intergroup forgiveness in post-conflict societies faces a number of challenges, not the least of which is the potential to heighten intergroup anxiety and distrust. These challenges notwithstanding, the newly emerging body of research on intergroup forgiveness, within the context of Northern Ireland in particular, has begun to explore the group-level correlates of intergroup forgiveness (for reviews, see Cairns et al., 2005; Hewstone et al., 2004, 2006).

Positive intergroup contact experiences, particularly those that have acquaintance potential and encourage the development of cross-group friendships, have emerged as among the strongest predictors of a greater willingness to forgive the outgroup (even among segments of the population which have suffered the most during the conflict; see Hewstone et al., 2006). Our research suggests that this relationship between intergroup contact and forgiving the outgroup is mediated by reduced anger-related emotions, increased outgroup trust, increased perspective taking, and increased affective empathy towards the outgroup. Being able to put yourself "in the shoes" of the outgroup and recognizing the humanity in the outgroup by empathizing with them appears to be an important step towards being willing to forgive them. Conversely, dehumanizing the outgroup discourages outgroup forgiveness. Thus, positive intergroup contact experiences through cross-group friendships not only mitigate those potential factors that may inhibit the willingness to forgive, such as anger, hatred, and the dehumanizing of the outgroup, but also augment those factors that promote a willingness to forgive the outgroup, such as trust and empathy (Tam et al., 2007). (See EMPATHY IN THE PROCESS OF FORGIVENESS; CONTACT THEORY: EXTENDED AND PARASOCIAL; CONTACT THEORY, INTERGROUP.)

Moreover, the degree of direct and indirect exposure to the conflict is a further important predictor of forgiveness. In Northern Ireland, for example, a greater degree of direct and indirect experience of victimization and violence during "the Troubles" is associated with a greater reluctance to acknowledge the wrongs committed by the ingroup in the course of the intergroup conflict, and with a reduced willingness to forgive the outgroup for the wrongs they have committed (Cairns et al., 2005; Hewstone et al., 2004, 2006).

Recent survey and experimental evidence suggests that group identity and categorization also play an important role in outgroup forgiveness. It seems reasonable to expect that a greater degree of identification with the ingroup would be associated with greater ingroup bias and a reduced willingness to forgive the outgroup. Survey and experimental data from Northern Ireland support this prediction; not only are higher levels of ingroup identification negatively associated with outgroup forgiveness, but they are also associated with ingroup bias. High ingroup identifiers are more willing to forgive ingroup perpetrators of group-based violence than they are outgroup perpetrators. This may be because the ingroup views the violence perpetrated by them during the conflict as justified. Similarly, those individuals who fought in the liberation struggle against the apartheid regime in South Africa were unhappy with the Truth and Reconciliation Commission's report that was released after the hearings were concluded, which condemned the violence perpetrated on both sides of the apartheid struggle. Those fighting for the liberation forces felt that their acts of violence were justifiable in the face of apartheid oppression (Thompson, 2001; see also Gibson, 2004). (See TRUTH AND RECONCILIATION COMMISSIONS, PSYCHOLOGICAL IMPACT OF.)

A possible solution to this problem of strong ingroup identification is to encourage broader category inclusiveness within post-conflict societies. Wohl and Branscombe (2005) ran a series of experiments testing whether increasing category inclusiveness would lead to greater forgiveness of a historical perpetrator group (Germans and White Canadians) and reduced collective guilt assignment for their wrongdoing by historical victim groups (Jewish North Americans and Native Canadians, respectively). Category inclusiveness was manipulated by varying the degree of the uniqueness of the historical perpetrator group's harmful actions towards the ingroup. As predicted, varying levels of increased category inclusiveness (ranging from the intergroup level to the maximally inclusive human level) were associated with a greater willingness to forgive the outgroup and reduced expectations that the outgroup should experience collective guilt for their actions.

CONCLUSIONS

While forgiveness will not solve intergroup conflict in and of itself, it provides an opportunity for post-conflict reconciliation. It offers post-conflict societies hope for the future as it orients groups towards a shared future, as opposed to continuously recycling the past in the form of reprisals and counter-reprisals. Policymakers are encouraged to give serious consideration to the role of positive intergroup contact as a means of achieving a greater willingness to forgive the outgroup, while also encouraging greater category inclusiveness that extends beyond the intergroup level. (See COMMON INGROUP IDENTITY MODEL.)

Our understanding of intergroup forgiveness would be benefited by a deeper understanding of how intergroup forgiveness relates to interpersonal forgiveness. Furthermore, it is as yet unclear precisely *when* intergroup forgiveness should be encouraged within the cycle of conflict. Most of the research on intergroup forgiveness to date has been correlational in nature, and has been undertaken at the post-conflict phase of intergroup relations. Although ambitious, it would be of great value if further research were able to explore the nature of intergroup forgiveness and its correlates over the course of intergroup relations that spans the transition from conflict to post-conflict relations.

SEE ALSO: Apologies and Forgiveness; Common Ingroup Identity Model; Contact Theory: Extended and Parasocial; Contact Theory, Intergroup; Empathy in the Process of Forgiveness; Forgiveness, Interpersonal; Reconciliation, Collective Memory and; Reconciliation: Instrumental and Socioemotional Aspects; Transitional Justice Systems, Psychology and; Truth and Reconciliation Commissions, Psychological Impact of.

REFERENCES

Cairns, E., Tam, T., Hewstone, M., & Niens, U. (2005). Intergroup forgiveness and intergroup conflict: Northern Ireland, a case study. In E. L. Worthington, Jr. (Ed.), *Handbook of forgiveness* (pp. 461–475). New York, NY: Routledge.

Gibson, J. L. (2004). *Overcoming apartheid: Can truth reconcile a divided nation?* New York, NY: Russell Sage Foundation.

Hewstone, M., Cairns, E., Voci, A., Hamberger, J., & Niens, U. (2006). Intergroup contact, forgiveness and experience of "the Troubles" in Northern Ireland. *Journal of Social Issues, 62,* 99–120.

Hewstone, M., Cairns, E., Voci, A., McLernon, F., Niens, U., & Noor, M. (2004). Intergroup forgiveness and guilt in Northern Ireland: Social psychological dimensions of "the Troubles." In N. R. Branscombe & B. Doosje (Eds.), *Collective guilt: International perspectives* (pp. 193–215). New York, NY: Cambridge University Press.

Tam, T., Hewstone, M., Cairns, E., Tausch, N., Maio, G., & Kenworthy, J. (2007). The impact of intergroup forgiveness in Northern Ireland. *Group Processes and Intergroup Relations, 10,* 119–135.

Thompson, L. (2001). *A history of South Africa* (3rd ed.). New Haven, CT: Yale University Press.

Wohl, M. J. A., & Branscombe, N. R. (2005). Forgiveness and collective guilt assignment to historical perpetrator groups depend on level of social category inclusiveness. *Journal of Personality and Social Psychology, 88,* 288–303.

Forgiveness, Interpersonal

RAYMOND F. PALOUTZIAN AND
ANI KALAYJIAN

The twentieth century saw no fewer than 80 million people killed due to war, genocide, massacre, and other acts of violence. The twenty-first century began with global jihad and more of the same destructive behaviors. When will it end? Forgiveness and reconciliation may be among the most difficult behaviors required of people, but an increasing number of scholars, practitioners, and leaders are beginning to think that without forgiveness and reconciliation the future of humans looks bleak. (See FORGIVENESS, INTERGROUP; APOLOGIES AND FORGIVENESS; EMPATHY IN THE PROCESS OF FORGIVENESS; RECONCILIATION: INSTRUMENTAL AND SOCIOEMOTIONAL ASPECTS; RECONCILIATION, COLLECTIVE MEMORY AND; SOCIAL REPRESENTATIONS OF RECONCILIATION.) The complexities involved in bringing vast numbers of people and governments to adopt and practice forgiveness and reconciliation as priorities over grudge-holding and reprisal are daunting. The challenge is to demonstrate to people and governments that forgiveness, reconciliation, and peace are of value and in their self-interest. The vision of peace is big; steps small and large must be taken. Tutu (1999) bluntly stated in the title to one of his books: *No future without forgiveness.*

Forgiveness in the real world is not the simple idea that is sometimes conveyed in moral lessons to children. To the contrary, it is complicated and very challenging. It is not an end state to arrive at but is instead a process that takes time, work, and risk, perhaps requiring a lifetime of persistence and hope combined with the stamina and clear-sightedness to live with an uncertain outcome. Below we briefly sketch the basic issues and offer key resources for further study.

THE NEED OF FORGIVENESS

The need for humans to forgive may be a consequence of more basic, wired-in tendencies (McCullough, 2008). A phylogenetically primitive response to attack is to counterattack, because doing so increases the probability of survival and reproduction of oneself and one's group. The inculcation of more lofty ideals such as loving one's enemy or forgiving those who have hurt you no doubt developed later. Thus it became possible for humans to live in groups and form societies. Since then, humans have continually lived with the opposing forces of the tendency to attack or at least be cautious of or avoid the harm-doer, and the ideals of forgiveness, reconciliation, and loving one's enemy, which are prescribed by high ethics and religions. This latter approach – forgiving – requires one to forego the gratification that would come from counterattack and to learn to perform positive, reparative reactions instead; this, for the "higher" good of oneself and the group. For us to understand the potentials and limits of forgiveness, we need to understand what it means.

WHAT FORGIVENESS MEANS

Various writers have said what forgiveness is not. It is not saying that the transgression is OK, that the perpetrator should go unpunished, that you have to forget what happened, or that you have to pretend or feel that the transgression never occurred. But it is far more difficult to say what it is.

One conceptualization of forgiveness, applicable to courts of law and reflected in some theologies, says that only God (or the proper entity of authority) can forgive; ordinary humans cannot. Thus, in a courtroom, the judge can declare a wrongdoer guilty of a crime and then free that person from punishment, i.e., legally forgive the person for the crime. This notion of forgiveness is of little use in complex human interactions. In fact, it may be a barrier to forgiveness between people because an offender may think that he or she does not have to confess or ask the victim to forgive, because doing so is up to God. Similarly, the victim may think that he or she does not need to forgive the offender because that is God's prerogative; it is not even our responsibility to do so. The problem with this view is that it places genuine interpersonal forgiveness off the table as a viable human option. But it is precisely at this on-the-ground human level that the most important forgiveness processes are needed and can happen. A blend of scholarly opinion suggests that interpersonal forgiveness is a process in which a person shifts from a tendency to react to harm by retaliating, to a more peaceful response of not hurting, and in the ideal case, of feeling and behaving prosocially toward the perpetrator. This does not preclude protecting oneself from the perpetrator, but does signal a change in one's orientation, and perhaps motivations, toward the perpetrator. Psychological factors, both intrapersonal and interpersonal, affect this.

Intrapersonal and Interpersonal

Intrapersonal factors can foster a sense of personal peace and comfort following victimization. This would include giving up feelings of hatred or revulsion toward the perpetrator, or the desire for revenge. One comes to "rest" or at least feels nonhostile, no longer angry, internally. This process does not require active involvement of or contact with the offender; the benefit is to oneself (Worthington, 2005). Forgiving in this way is desirable especially in cases where the offender is not available. In contrast, interpersonal forgiveness involves reciprocal contact, active participation of both victim and perpetrator. This is a bilateral interpersonal transaction of mutual exchange of perceptions of past events, feelings, attitudes, and (ideally) commitments for future behavior. An ultimate aim is to extend forgiveness from an internal process for oneself to a social process for the common good. With reconciliatory behavior as an ideal goal, this seems necessary for fully peaceful social relationships to be established.

Attitudes, Feelings, and Behavior

The distinction between intrapersonal and interpersonal forgiveness is related to basic distinctions between forgiving attitudes, feelings, and behaviors. It is possible to hold forgiving attitudes and feelings toward a perpetrator and harm them nevertheless. It is likewise possible to hold hostile attitudes and feelings and nevertheless behave in kind and compassionate ways toward the offender. Attitudes, feelings, and actions – and therefore intrapersonal and interpersonal forgiveness – can, but do not necessarily, correspond. In combination, the probability of genuine reconciliation would be enhanced.

DIMENSIONS OF FORGIVENESS

Forgiveness is not a state but a multidimensional process (Worthington, 2005). People can be at high, medium, or low levels on its many dimensions. One result of this is that all cases are unique (yet have common theoretical aspects), so that the application of knowledge to facilitating forgiveness requires the skill to fine-tune the process for a particular person. There is no simple textbook formula. The dimensions on which the forgiveness process can vary include but are not limited to: variations in forgiveness attitudes and behaviors, intrapersonal and interpersonal emphases, dealing with the full versus partial scope of the offense, the time lag since the offense, degree of closure attained, a positive versus negative outcome, a public versus private process, and whether

the victim receives acknowledgment and reparation. The position of one's forgiveness process on the above and related dimensions, combined with personal, social contextual, and life history factors, provides a complex mix of factors that determine the outcome of forgiveness efforts (Kalayjian & Paloutzian, 2009).

CULTURAL FACTORS

Forgiveness processes can vary greatly by culture and religion. In the case of cultures, for example, a common Western approach to dealing with a youth offender might be to involve the person in professional counseling. A process of helping the youngster develop his or her self-esteem may be used, and there may be little emphasis on public displays of confession, remorse, or facing the victims. In some Western countries there seems to be some current expectation that youth give community service as compensation to the community at large, instead of giving to the person whom they have harmed. Other cultures, such as some in Africa (Kalayjian & Paloutzian, 2009), may highlight seemingly opposite factors, such as public confession, facing the victim, and deliberately (but restoratively) shaming the perpetrator. The experiences of African Gacaca Community Courts (whose motto is "Justice for Reconciliation") suggests that reconciliation at the interpersonal level is possible only when, on the one hand, the perpetrator has come to terms with his or her offense, repented from it, and confessed and asked for forgiveness; and on the other hand, the victim has healed from the wounds and is ready to forgive. Thus, forgiveness alone will not necessarily lead to reconciliation, although may facilitate it. Forgiveness alone can help heal emotional wounds of the individual victim even if the offender refuses to acknowledge the offense, but it will not by itself restore group harmony or bring about peace on a large scale. Reconciliation is the restoration of a broken relationship, where both parties are actively involved. (See RESTORATIVE JUSTICE; GENOCIDE AND MASS KILLING: ORIGINS AND PREVENTION.)

Additional cultural differences may profoundly influence forgiveness and reconciliation. For example, cultures differ greatly in whether it is OK for a person to publicly lose face. Fessing up to one's failures or giving in to the opposite side may be acceptable flaws in one culture and be psychologically forbidden, unforgivable sins, in another. Such differences can greatly affect the possibility that a forgiveness process can take hold.

Religions can likewise encourage or discourage interpersonal forgiveness. The texts of some world religions, such as Christianity, teach unconditional forgiveness; while others, such as Islam or Judaism, may focus on justice, reparation, and acknowledgment as necessary before forgiveness takes place. At the more human level of religion on the ground, religious organizations can sometimes make forgiveness and loving one's enemy a top priority; while at other times they might foster prejudice and suspicion of other religious groups.

ETHICS

Ethical issues are inherent in any consideration of forgiveness. To illustrate, what if anything is the victim of a crime entitled to? Should his or her government pay the medical or legal expenses due because of the perpetrator's offense? Should the victim be entitled to harm the perpetrator? If so, where does the cycle of violence end? If not, can we assure the victim of proper justice? To what, if anything, is the perpetrator entitled? In most modern countries the person is at a minimum entitled to being considered innocent instead of guilty before the law,

until proven contrary based on evidence in some fair procedure. What about being entitled to receive, or required to give, at an interpersonal level? Extrapolating to larger units of analysis, how do these same issues apply when taken from the simple illustration of one perpetrator and one victim to the international level of nation-against-nation hostilities? Add to this the notion of entitlements to the generations-later offspring of those against whom a great crime was committed by a bygone empire, such as the offspring of Armenians who survived the 1914–1923 genocide or the descendents of Jewish Holocaust survivors, or the descendents of American slaves. They inherit the consequences of the entrapment, poverty, and harm done to their ancestors just as others inherit the wealth and other benefits of their better-off ancestors. Who is entitled to what? In general, how do we approach even talking about, let alone solving, dilemmas such as these passed on from generations?

DIALOGUE

Are there concrete procedures that can be implemented to facilitate intrapersonal and interpersonal forgiveness on the path toward reconciliation and peace? In addition to directing you to the references listed below, we highlight the following two procedures.

First, a seven-step biopsychosocial and ecospiritual model has been used successfully in over 25 countries post-calamities (Kalayjian & Eugene, 2009). The steps are to assess levels of stress and trauma due to victimization; encourage expression of feelings; provide empathy and validation; encourage discovery and expression of meaning; provide didactic information; eco-centered connecting with nature; and teach breathing and movement exercises. Through these steps, various aspects of traumatic victimization are identified, explored, processed, and integrated within the self, and intrapersonal forgiveness can be facilitated.

Second, systematic dialogue processes are a valuable tool to facilitate interpersonal forgiveness. Various models of dialogue procedures exist (Lederach, 1997; Kalayjian & Paloutzian, 2009), but each one involves direct contact between opposing parties to allow open discussion and honest hearing of the views of those on opposite sides. Besides setting a safe, open, and affirming atmosphere for opposing parties to speak to each other in a plain and clear way, genuine dialogue sets the stage for collaboration among parties so that they can become co-workers taking concrete steps toward their joint goal – peace.

SEE ALSO: Apologies and Forgiveness; Empathy in the Process of Forgiveness; Forgiveness, Intergroup; Genocide and Mass Killing: Origins and Prevention; Reconciliation, Collective Memory and; Reconciliation: Instrumental and Socioemotional Aspects; Restorative Justice; Social Representations of Reconciliation.

REFERENCES

Kalayjian, A., & Eugene, D. (2009). *Emotional healing around the world: Rituals and practices for resilience and meaning-making.* New York, NY: ABC-CLIO.
Kalayjian, A., & Paloutzian, R. F. (Eds.). (2009). *Forgiveness and reconciliation: Psychological pathways to conflict transformation and peace building.* New York, NY: Springer.
Lederach, J. P. (1997). *Building peace: Sustainable reconciliation in divided societies.* Washington, DC: United States Institute for Peace Press.
McCullough, M. E. (2008). *Beyond revenge: The evolution of the forgiveness instinct.* San Francisco, CA: Jossey-Bass.
Tutu, D. (1999). *No future without forgiveness.* New York, NY: Doubleday.
Worthington, E. L. (Ed.). (2005). *Handbook of forgiveness.* New York, NY: Routledge.

ADDITIONAL RESOURCES

American Psychological Association. (2007). *Resolution on religious, religion-based and/or religion-derived prejudice.* Retrieved from http://search.apa.org/search?query=APA%20Policy%20on%20Religious%20Discrimination.

G

Game Theory: Conflict and Cooperation

EDUARD BRANDSTÄTTER

Philosopher Jeremy Bentham envisioned a society in which people strive for "the greatest good for the greatest number of people." All too often, however, striving for one's own good opposes that of others – leading to conflict rather than greatest happiness. Such conflicts are common and range from two children craving the same cake to nations negotiating thorny peace treaties. In this article I focus on conflicts and cooperation. (See COOPERATION AND COMPETITION.) To this end I describe a scientific school of thought, known as *game theory*, which offers a fruitful framework for classifying conflicts and for overcoming them by promoting cooperation.

When do conflicts occur? Consider the example of two children craving the same cake. On the one hand the conflict arises from the children's *identical* interests, because both want the *same* cake (i.e., not different ones). On the other hand the conflict arises from the children's *opposing* interests, because each child wants the whole

cake for herself and nothing for the other. Thus, whether a conflict results from identical or opposing interests merely depends on the frame one takes. Anyway, few doubts exist that the cake situation (i.e., one cake and two children) is likely to promote a *social dilemma*. In a social dilemma each party can benefit by pursuing personal interests at the expense of others. If everybody, however, pursues personal interests, an inferior collective outcome ensues and everyone would be better off by cooperating. (See SOCIAL DILEMMAS.) In the cake example, insisting on personal interests only (e.g., each child wanting the whole cake) triggers endless conflicts but no solution, and each child will be worse off by getting nothing. Research has identified different kinds of social dilemmas, and the most important ones are the *prisoner's dilemma*, the *commons dilemma*, and the *public goods dilemma* (see Luce & Raiffa, 1957).

Consider the *prisoner's dilemma* first. Suppose you and your partner have been arrested by the police for killing a friend. You are imprisoned in separate cells and cannot communicate. Each of you receives a separate visit from the police officer, who offers each of you the opportunity to reduce

The Encyclopedia of Peace Psychology, First Edition. Edited by Daniel J. Christie.
© 2012 Blackwell Publishing Ltd. Published 2012 by Blackwell Publishing Ltd.

Table 1   Prisoner's dilemma: 2 × 2 game

		Other	
		Cooperate	Defect
Self	Cooperate	1, 1 (C_S, C_O)	10, 0 (A_S, D_O)
	Defect	0, 10 (D_S, A_O)	5, 5 (B_S, B_O)

Note: Left and right numbers in each cell correspond to years in prison for *Self* and *Other*, respectively.
"Cooperate" represents staying silent and "Defect" represents charging the partner. Brackets signify the game in general form; for example, B_S = outcome for *Self* when both parties defect.

personal imprisonment by charging your partner with the crime (without confessing yourself). Thus, each of you is faced with two options: staying silent or charging your partner. When you stay silent you *cooperate* with your partner (but not with the police); when you charge your partner you *defect* – resulting in four different combinations (Table 1): First, if you and your partner cooperate by staying silent, you will both be imprisoned for 1 year (upper left cell). Second, you can reduce your imprisonment by defection: If you defect but he cooperates – that is, you charge your partner but he stays silent – you will be released and your partner will be imprisoned for 10 years (lower left cell). Third, the same holds for your partner (upper right cell). Fourth, if you both defect by charging each other, you will both be imprisoned for 5 years (lower right cell).

Game theory makes a specific prediction about people's behavior, assuming that they are (a) rational and (b) pursuing their own interests. For the dilemma shown in Table 1, staying silent may result in a 1-year sentence. This sentence can be removed by charging the partner. A rational and self-interested person will recognize that the partner will also think so and act accordingly. Consequently, game theory predicts that each person will charge the partner to avoid a

10-year sentence – resulting in a stable *equilibrium*.

It is intuitively clear that people's behavior in the prisoner's dilemma strongly depends on the numbers (i.e., years of imprisonment) chosen. Different combinations of numbers result in 78 different games, each having its own strategic properties (Rapoport & Guyer, 1966). In the prisoner's dilemma, for instance, $A > B > C > D$, while in another famous game, the chicken game, $B > A > C > D$. Table 1 presents a 2 × 2 prisoner's dilemma involving two people. Prisoner's dilemmas can, however, easily be extended to more than two parties, resulting in an *n*-party prisoner's dilemma. The dilemma underlies some of the most important decisions people make, including choices between helping and not helping, working or loafing, and arming or disarming (Pruitt, 1998).

The commons dilemma and the public goods dilemma represent two other major social dilemmas. In the *commons dilemma* a self-interested person tries to *take* as much as possible from a common good. This happens, for example, when each of several fishers aims at fishing as much as possible from a lake. If the lake is overfished and depleted, however, all fishers lose. In the *public goods dilemma*, in contrast, a self-interested person tries to *contribute* as little as possible to a common good (rather than taking out as much as possible). Tax-paying is a prime example of a public goods dilemma, because personal self-interest prescribes withholding taxes. If nobody pays taxes, however, everybody is worse off.

WHEN DO PEOPLE COOPERATE?

The degree of people's cooperation in social dilemmas depends on many different factors. The most important one, probably, is the *structure of the game*. In the prisoner's dilemma (Table 1), for example, low levels of C and A decrease imprisonment from cooperation, whereas high levels of D and B increase imprisonment from defection. Consequently, cooperation rises when C and A are low and when D and B are high. This pattern holds for losses, as in Table 1, in which cell entries represent years of imprisonment. If a different context implies that cell entries represent gains (e.g., amounts of money), the reverse pattern holds.

Another prominent factor influencing how much people defect or cooperate is *social norms*, such as the peacekeeping Golden Rule, which prescribes treating others in the way one wants to be treated by them. If this is the case, defection (and retaliation) is not allowed. Surprisingly, game theory predicts the opposite. In a prisoner's dilemma game, Axelrod (1984) tested different strategies against each other and found that one simple strategy, tit-for-tat, outperformed all other strategies. Tit-for-tat is cooperative at the first move and then always mirrors the last move of the partner. That is, tit-for-tat leads to cooperation if the partner has just cooperated and to defection if the partner has just defected. Unlike the prescription from the Golden Rule and unlike Christian ethics, tit-for-tat recommends retaliation and defection. Might scientific knowledge contradict religious rules? Unlikely – because tit-for-tat has shortcomings, too. Imagine that tit-for-tat plays against itself and an error occurs. That is, one party switches from cooperation to defection. By mirroring the partner, the other party retaliates and permanent defection ensues. This problem, however, can be solved if tit-for-tat slowly retaliates and slowly forgives. In these cases, tit-for-tat does not mirror the partner's move immediately but waits for one more move of the partner (i.e., tit-for-tat + 1). More importantly, experiments with participants have found that tit-for-tat rarely extends beyond the period in which it was used. If one person stops playing tit-for-tat, cooperation declines. This is not the case if the other party had been cooperating consistently.

People also cooperate when they endorse large *time horizons*, while short time horizons promote defection. That is, social dilemmas can be played once or repeatedly. If played repeatedly, people realize that they lose in the long run by mutual defection. Many people, however, only learn this lesson through long and exhausting periods of mutual defection. This is not unlike peace treaties, which become more likely when people feel strained after long periods of war time.

Communication constitutes another major factor that increases people's degree of cooperation. In the standard social dilemma, as in Axelrod's (1984) computer simulations, communication was not allowed. Communication, however, is beneficial in many different ways. Through communication, people can agree upon social norms for cooperation and impose sanctions on partners who do not adhere to these norms. A third benefit of communication is that it often fosters group identity, which in turn triggers cooperation. Through communication, people may publicly commit themselves to cooperate. Research from dissonance theory has shown that public commitment helps in implementing personal intentions. When people communicate, they often establish a long-term perspective, which also promotes cooperation. Finally, communication has been shown to trigger expectations that the other party will cooperate. Overall, communication constitutes a major force in fostering cooperation. The neglect of communication in Axelrod's computer simulations, therefore, offers another reason for adopting caution in substituting ethical universals with findings from computer simulations.

People also cooperate more when they like each other, and when they endorse certain *values* (Deutsch, 1973). Values of cooperation [max *(Self + Other)*] produce more cooperation than values of self-interest (max *Self*), which produce more cooperation than values of competition [max *(Self − Other)*]. A purely competitive person, note, prefers 100 for herself and 80 for the partner to a situation where both get 120.

Cooperation further increases if the *number of parties* is small. That is, the more parties that participate in a social dilemma, the more often they will defect. This effect, however, only holds for up to eight parties. If there are more than eight parties, little or no further defection occurs. Taken together, people's cooperation is and can be influenced by many different factors.

GREATEST GOOD FOR
THE GREATEST NUMBER OF PEOPLE?

Bentham envisioned a society that strives for "the greatest good for the greatest number of people." While human conflict seems inevitable, striving for the greatest good remains an enticing goal. Game theory shows that utility maximization is possible despite people's opposing interests; through mutual cooperation rather than defection, joint utility can be maximized. Maximizing utility despite opposing interests is relevant in many real-life situations such as sharing or not sharing goods, paying or not paying dues, and pursuing or avoiding peace. The theory's findings can thus help to promote peace among people, groups, institutions, and nations in the future.

SEE ALSO: Cooperation and Competition; Social Dilemmas.

REFERENCES

Axelrod, R. (1984). *The evolution of cooperation*. New York, NY: Basic Books.

Deutsch, M. (1973). *The resolution of conflict*. New Haven, CT: Yale University Press.

Luce, G. D., & Raiffa, H. F. (1957). *Games and decisions*. New York, NY: Wiley.

Pruitt, D. G. (1998). Social conflict. In D. T. Gilbert, S. T. Fiske, & G. Lindzey (Eds.), *Handbook of social psychology* (4th ed., pp. 470–503). New York, NY: Oxford University Press.

Rapoport, A., & Guyer, M. (1966). A taxonomy of 2 × 2 games. *General Systems, 11*, 203–214.

ADDITIONAL RESOURCES

Dixit, A. K., & Nalebuff, B. J. (1993). *Thinking strategically: The competitive edge in business, politics, and everyday life*. New York, NY: W. W. Norton.

Excellent website on philosophy that contains a concise summary of game theory: http://plato.stanford.edu

Gangs and Political Violence, Children and Youth Involvement in

KATHLEEN KOSTELNY

Worldwide, young people are impacted by both gang and political violence. Although gang violence and political violence have different origins and are typically analyzed separately, this article focuses on their similarities and areas of overlap in order to emphasize the similarity of impact on young people's lives and the forces which build cultures of violence. Whether in zones affected by gang violence or political violence, children and youth are witnesses and victims. They are also prominent actors. In order to build cultures of peace, children and youth must be given alternative nonviolent options and socialized for peace. (See CHILDREN, PEACE AND AGGRESSION IN; SOCIALIZATION.)

CONTEXT OF GANGS AND POLITICAL VIOLENCE

Political violence and gang violence partially overlap, with some young people being involved in both. For the most part, however, they are separate entities having many similarities. Political conflicts are currently ongoing in more than 30 countries. Unlike conflicts decades earlier, contemporary conflicts occur increasingly within state borders. Children and youth are affected as communities are deliberately targeted. Moreover, it is estimated that there are approximately 300,000 children (defined by international law as persons under 18 years of age) actively involved in armed forces or groups in a variety of roles. The availability of light, high-powered weapons where political conflicts are waged enables children and youth to operate them. Armed forces and groups often prefer teenagers as fighters because of their strength, fearlessness, and willingness to take risks. They are also easily manipulated and have a limited sense of their own mortality. (See CHILD SOLDIERS.)

Gangs are even more widespread, present in zones of political conflict as well as areas with no political conflict. Gangs exist in most countries and are found in many urban and an increasing number of rural communities. It is estimated there are tens of millions of gang members worldwide, the majority of whom are young people. In the United States the number of gangs and gang members has increased significantly over the past three decades – to at least 26,000 gangs and 775,000 gang members. The typical age range for gang members in the United States is 12–24 years, and the average age is 17 years, although younger members are becoming more common. Males are predominantly involved in gangs, though there is increasing female involvement, as well as all-female gangs. Gangs have become more prevalent and more violent than in previous decades, attributable also to the increasing availability of semiautomatic and high-powered weapons.

REASONS YOUTH ENTER ARMED FORCES OR GROUPS AND GANGS

A number of factors influence how children and youth become members of gangs or armed groups. Young people enter gangs and armed groups, either by force or voluntarily.

Forced Entry

In some political conflicts, children and youth are forcibly recruited. For example, in Sierra Leone they were abducted at gunpoint by the Revolutionary United Front (RUF) and forced to join or else be killed. Though the United Nations' Optional Protocol on Children's Involvement in Armed Conflict prohibits children younger than 18 from fighting in armed forces and groups, some groups, such as the Lord's Resistance Army (LRA) in northern Uganda, have abducted children less than 10 years of age to become part of their fighting force.

Gangs also use intimidation and coercion to compel young people to join. Gang members in the United States have followed young boys on their way to and from school, threatening them with violence if they do not align themselves with their gang. Children and youth who resist have been harassed, beaten, and shot.

Nonforced Entry

Young people also decide to join gangs and armed groups. During political violence, children, and especially youth, join voluntarily out of ideological commitment and view themselves as freedom fighters committed to a higher cause (Garbarino, Kostelny, & Dubrow, 1991). Many youth find meaning through participation in a liberation struggle and use violence as a way of helping to liberate their people, as was the case in South Africa, Occupied Palestinian Territories (oPt), Nicaragua, and Sri Lanka.

Some gangs also provide a sense of identity and meaning. During the 1960s in Chicago, some youth joined the Blackstone Rangers, which promoted itself as a civil rights organization. Though it later evolved into one of the most dangerous and powerful gangs in the United States, involved in crime and drug trafficking, many youth, frustrated with discrimination and poverty, were drawn to the gang's espousal of equal rights for African Americans.

Often, decisions to join armed groups or gangs are not "voluntary," but a result of difficult or extreme circumstances and a combination of "push" and "pull" factors. Fleeing emotional, physical, or sexual abuse in their family is a "push" factor for young people. In Sri Lanka and Columbia, girls joined armed groups to escape sexual abuse at home, or forced marriage. Both armed groups and gangs may also act as a surrogate family, providing physical and social support, and a sense of belonging – a strong "pull" factor. In the United States, young children who have a difficult family life are drawn to gangs who provide recreational opportunities and act as mentors and surrogate parents when parents are not emotionally available.

Poverty is another "pull" factor for joining. In armed forces and groups, young people join as a means of obtaining food, shelter, and medical care. Though they may join voluntarily, because of hardships, they may have no other options of survival. With regard to gangs, young people may join for material gain. Gangs are more prevalent in economically distressed areas with high levels of unemployment, low education levels, overcrowding, and few social supports. Some gangs provide food and clothes, and young people have been enticed into gangs because they have been given expensive athletic shoes and clothes, or attracted by money from the drug economy.

Children and youth also join to achieve prestige or power. Many feel that because they have a gun, wear a uniform, or dress in a certain manner, they are treated with respect that they never had outside the group. Joining a gang also brings protection from other gangs or dangerous people.

Still other children and youth join armed groups because of family ties. In northern Afghanistan, young people frequently joined the Northern Alliance to fight the Taliban because their fathers, brothers, or uncles were part of the armed group. In the LRA, children are born into the armed group. Similarly, in US communities where there is a prevalent gang influence, children grow up with family members who are in gangs and who identify from an early age with a particular gang, even before they are formally inducted. Children learn from an early age the symbols and language of gangs, and to identify who is part of the gang and who is the opposition.

ROLES AND EXPERIENCES

Children and youth are engaged in diverse roles and have a variety of experiences in armed groups and gangs that vary according to context and gender. Not all youth involved in political conflict or gangs are combatants or engaged in violence.

Political Violence

In contexts of political violence, many children and youth serve as combatants. Some are forced into this role, while others eagerly take on a role as assassin or torturer. Initiation into some armed groups such as the RUF requires a new recruit to brutally kill someone, often from their own community or even family. However, in addition to combatants, many others serve a variety of roles, including porters, cooks, bodyguards, and spies (Wessells, 2006). Girls, in particular, are recruited to serve as sex slaves and to carry heavy loads. Many youth have multiple roles with an armed force or group.

Within these diverse roles young people are exposed to an array of violence, including witnessing killings, severe beatings, maiming, and other acts of extreme violence. Many also experience sexual exploitation, which varies according to context. In northern Uganda and Sierra Leone many girls were abducted by armed groups and sexually exploited as "soldiers' wives." (See GIRLS IN ARMED GROUPS.) However, in other contexts, such as the Liberation Tamil Tigers Eelam in Sri Lanka, girls are not sexually exploited, and some groups expressly prohibit sexual exploitation. In Afghanistan, where young recruits were male, it was not uncommon for older soldiers to sexually abuse young boys. However, because of strong taboos, little is known about the prevalence of the exploitation of boys in armed groups.

There is also a variety of experiences with regard to drug use. In Sierra Leone, young people were given amphetamines and other drugs to make them fearless when they fought. In Afghanistan, though massive opium stocks exists, drug use was not evident as it was in violation of their Islamic beliefs.

Gangs

Young people in gangs have a variety of roles as well: as lookouts, drug carriers, enforcers, and fighters. Some of the activities gangs are involved with are robberies, prostitution, street crime, drug trafficking, and murder. Adolescent gang members commit a majority of violent offenses. In some gangs, new recruits are also required to kill someone as part of their initiation. In the United States initiations have included drive-by shootings and shooting into a crowd of people. Young

people in gangs may also be involved in multiple roles – for example, as a lookout as well as a drug carrier.

Similar to armed forces and groups, sexual exploitation occurs. Female members of gangs, including in the United States and Mexico, have been reported to experience sexual abuse by male gang members. Drug use is also common in gangs. A major difference between armed forces and gangs, however, is that drug selling and distribution is a major activity for gangs.

IMPACT

Death and physical injuries are the most visible impacts of the violence that occurs in gangs and armed groups. Additionally, young people witness violence to parents, family, friends, and community members. Emotional impacts include depression, anxiety, fearfulness, psychosomatic distress, sleep disturbances, depression, and post-traumatic stress disorder. Other negative impacts include identification with the aggressor, hopelessness about the future, and socialization into a model of aggression and revenge. However, the particular response depends on an array of factors including the young person's temperament, pre-existing problems, available social support in the family, community, and culture, and the meaning that is attributed to their experiences. Those who believe they are fighting for a cause and see the violence as meaningful suffer less negative impacts than do youth who believe the violence is random and meaningless (Punamaki, 1989).

Interventions

When large numbers of young people involved in gangs and armed conflict lack livelihoods and alternatives to being combatants, the cycle of violence will continue. Alternative options that are holistic and culturally appropriate must be provided in order to promote peace. In Sierra Leone, young people from an armed group were brought together with other young people in the community using a superordinate goals approach. They cooperated on achieving a common goal of improving the well-being of young children, while engaged in a civic works project and earning an income. The young people who had been in an armed group were able to cast off their combatant identities and reintegrate into their communities as productive members in civilian life.

Likewise, gang interventions must be holistic, providing opportunities such as life skills, recreational opportunities, job training, and livelihoods. Linking young people with mentors who can be successful role models and provide emotional support is also key. Many of the interventions useful in supporting children and youth associated with armed forces and groups may also be useful in reintegrating former gang members. In either case, socializing for peace is crucial in stemming cycles of violence.

SEE ALSO: Child Soldiers; Children, Peace and Aggression in; Girls in Armed Groups; Socialization.

REFERENCES

Garbarino, J., Kostelny, K., & Dubrow, N. (1991). *No place to be a child: Growing up in a war zone*. Lexington, MA: Lexington Books.
Punamaki, R. (1989). Political violence and mental health. *International Journal of Mental Health, 17*, 3–15.
Wessells, M. (2006). *Child soldiers: From violence to protection*. Cambridge, MA: Harvard University Press.

ADDITIONAL RESOURCES

Cairns, E. (1996). *Children and political violence*. Oxford, UK: Blackwell.

http://www.ncjrs.gov (Office of Juvenile Justice and Delinquency Prevention)

Gender and International Relations

CAROLYN M. STEPHENSON

The conceptualization of gender in international relations is relatively new. International relations as a field of study was one of the most reluctant to acknowledge the relevance of gender, with articles in major journals not appearing until the late 1980s and early 1990s. The majority of scholars in international relations, and especially international security studies, are male, reflecting the gender balance in the practice of international relations. While women were always a part of international relations, as Cynthia Enloe showed with her landmark book *Bananas, Beaches and Bases* (1989) they had largely been invisible. Initial feminist concerns focused on discrimination against women and on increasing the inclusion of women in political, economic, and social structures.

Gender, however, is not only about biological males and females, but also about the social construction of men and women and how their identities are mobilized under particular historical conditions. It examines and attempts to understand how the discourses, institutions, and practices that underlie gender inequalities are constructed, maintained, legitimized, and changed. (See GENDER INEQUALITY.) In international relations, it is argued that the very construction of the international, of the state, politics, power, war, and peace, is gendered. (See GENDERING PEACE PSYCHOLOGY.) While liberal feminists began with an approach often described as "add women and stir," radical feminists attempted to change conceptualizations of politics itself, contending that "the personal is political" and, along with other critics of traditional international relations theory, that security issues should not be considered "high politics" while other issues were relegated to lower status. Gender theorists generally reject essentialist arguments that gender differences are biologically determined (reproduction, size, etc.), and argue that culture and structure, and the socialization of women and men into different roles, determine the differential representation of women and men in international relations (Tickner, 1992). Most gender theorists today argue that there is no such thing as a women's standpoint, because women stand in different places dependent on their race, class, geography, culture, and other factors.

Mainstreaming a gender perspective, rather than simply adding women, became a guideline for the United Nations and many other international organizations. In 1997 the United Nations Economic and Social Council (ECOSOC) defined the concept of mainstreaming:

> Mainstreaming a gender perspective is the process of assessing the implications for women and men of any planned action, including legislation, policies, or programs, in any area. It is a tool for making women's as well as men's concerns and experiences an integral dimension in the design, implementation, monitoring, and evaluation of policies and programs in all political, economic, and societal spheres so that women and men benefit equally and inequality is not perpetuated. The ultimate goal is to achieve gender equality.

While women have been underrepresented in formal international politics, women have long been involved in peace movements and attempts to change international relations. In the first wave of the women's movement, when Lucretia Mott and Elizabeth Cady Stanton returned to the United States from the 1840 London Anti-Slavery Conference, where women were unable to gain access,

and initiated the 1848 Seneca Falls Conference, women banded together to gain the vote and the ability to have an influence on the abolition of slavery, prohibition of alcohol, and other peace and social justice issues. New Zealand was the first in 1893 to grant full voting rights to women. Aletta Jacobs, the first woman physician in Holland and founder of the Dutch suffrage movement, called the First International Women's Peace Congress at the Hague, with 1,136 voting members, and resolutions from which Jane Addams (second woman Nobel Peace Prize winner) carried to seven governments. Jeannette Rankin, the first woman elected to the US Congress in 1916, voted against both world wars, being the only member of the House to vote against World War II. April 1919 saw the Second International Congress of Women in Zurich form itself into the Women's International League for Peace and Freedom (WILPF). Emily Greene Balch (third woman Nobel Peace Prize winner), an economist/ sociologist who had been removed from the Wellesley faculty for her outspoken pacifism, served as director of the main office of WILPF in Geneva, working at international relief and reconstruction, and cooperating with League of Nations commissions on white slavery, narcotics, and labor rights.

In the second wave of the women's movement, from the 1970s, President Carter's February 1980 proposal to register women and men for the draft reopened the debate over whether women have, or should have, a particular relationship to peace. (See WOMEN AND PEACE HYPOTHESIS.) Polls and research have shown that the deepest divisions between men's and women's attitudes are on issues of war and peace (Goldstein, 2001), and that states with higher gender equality tend to initiate wars less often, to be less involved in internal armed conflict or human rights abuses, to be more democratic, and less corrupt. However, it appears that the primary factor is liberal democracy (freedom of the press, rule of law) and participation, rather than gender equality, although these are highly correlated.

The United Nations has been important in the development of gender equality. The UN Charter included references to the equality of men and women. The Economic and Social Council created the Commission on the Status of Women (CSW) in 1946. The United Nations General Assembly declared 1975 as International Women's Year, holding the first of four major conferences on women in Mexico City, with the theme Equality, Development and Peace. Out of this came the UN Decade for Women 1976–1985 and in 1979 the Convention on the Elimination of All Forms of Discrimination Against Women (CEDAW). American feminist leaders Betty Friedan and Congresswoman Bella Abzug came to the UN Conferences with American feminist views of the primacy of individual women's rights and discovered other feminisms that involved more communal views, in turn influencing third world feminists toward stronger views on women's rights. As a founder of the Women's Environment and Development Organization in 1991, Abzug began to incorporate environmental concerns as well as peace concerns into the women's movement and, along with other environmental organizations, into the UN Conferences on Women (Winslow, 1995). At the 1985 Decade Review Conference in Nairobi, Wangari Maathai, Kenyan activist for women's rights and democracy, and founder of the Green Belt movement in 1977, was a substantial influence, also linking these issues. Maathai won the 2004 Nobel Peace Prize for her work.

Gradually, there had come to be a realization that working for the rights of women could not succeed without examining the gender implications of all policies. Development aid did not lift all boats equally, often resulting in a decline, rather that an improvement, in the status of women (Boserup, 1970). Thus there came to be a specific focus on women in development (WID), to ensure that development improved the equality of women with men. Over the course of time, the UN and others shifted to focus on the linkage of gender and development (GAD), looking at underlying structures rather than trying to improve the status of women in isolation.

In the 1994 edition of the *Human Development Report* there was discussion of the need to pay attention to gender issues, and a gender-disparity-adjusted version of the Human Development Index (HDI) was introduced for 43 countries. The Human Development Index itself was an attempt to get away from the purely economic indicators of development and included, in addition to GNP per capita, measures of education and health. In the 1995 edition, two significant new indicators allowed measurement of overall gender impacts on human development. While the HDI measures the average achievement of a country in basic human capabilities, the Gender-related Development Index (GDI) imposes a penalty for inequality on the HDI, thus adjusting the HDI downwards for gender inequality. The Gender Empowerment Measure (GEM) examines whether women and men are able to participate in economic and political life and take part in decision-making. While other gender-related indices (such as female vs. male school enrollment and literacy, female as a percentage of male participation rates in professions and government, death rates by sex, etc.) continue to be available and important, this was first time one could look at women's access to resources and their status and power in the society overall. Thus gender increasingly became a variable one could measure in connection with other variables.

Overcoming cultural factors that allow gender discrimination and violence against women is also important. Changing structural economic and political conditions that allow or encourage gender inequality can be facilitated by changing stereotypes of men and women. Among those that most relate to cultures of peace are the stereotypes of masculinity as warlike and strong and femininity as peaceful and weak. Feminist conceptualizations of men and women have begun to separate conceptualizations of strength from those of violence (Reardon, 1985; Stiehm, 1983).

While women have continued to be active in peace movements, they have also entered the regular sphere of international relations practice in greater numbers, in the process sometimes beginning to change gendered conceptualizations of security as based in coercive force. Women have continued to work both on women's rights and on broader social justice and peace issues. Jody Williams and the International Campaign to Ban Landmines (ICBL), in coordination with the Canadian government in the Ottawa Process, produced the Land Mines Convention, which was signed in December 1997 and came into force in record time in March 1999. The achievement of the signing of the treaty won Jody Williams and the ICBL the 1997 Nobel Peace Prize. In October 2000, women leaders in WILPF and the NGO Working Group on Women and International Peace and Security worked with Ambassador Anwarul Chowdhury of Bangladesh to pass Security Council Resolution 1325 on Women, Peace, and Security, which urged both the protection of women in armed conflict and their participation in peace negotiations.

Women appear to have different attitudes toward war and peace and international security than men, and even to define peace and security differently. Participants in the 1996 Expert Group Meeting on Political Decision-Making and Conflict Resolution: The Impact of Gender Difference argued that

a broad range of research and experience over several decades indicates that most women appear to have somewhat different definitions of peace, security, and sovereignty than most men. In general, women's approaches to violence, conflict, and the resolution of conflict appear to be somewhat different than those of men in positions of decision-making in peace and security matters. (para. 29)

In 2006 the Women's Peace Initiative, established by six of the 12 women winners of the Nobel Peace Prize, argued for a different definition of peace:

We believe peace is much more than the absence of armed conflict. Peace is the commitment to equality and justice; a democratic world free of physical, economic, cultural, political, religious, sexual, and environmental violence and the constant threat of these forms of violence against women – indeed against all of humanity.

While this definition is not unique to women, it is one that appears to be more widely shared among women than among men.

CONCLUSION

By the time of the UN's Beijing Fourth World Conference on Women in 1995, the international system had come to recognize that gender is a significant factor in development, in education, in health, in democracy, and in peace and conflict matters. In the Beijing Declaration, governments committed themselves to implementing the Platform for Action and ensuring that a gender perspective was reflected in all their policies and programs. While equality between men and women is also specifically delineated as one of the eight domains of the UN's Culture of Peace, in actuality gender equality is highly correlated with success in the other domains (Stephenson, 2008). One sees considerable linkage between the 12 critical areas of concern for women identified in the 1995 Beijing Platform for Action and the eight domains of the Culture of Peace. Among the Beijing Platform's critical areas of concern are: the burden of poverty on women, unequal access to education and healthcare, violence against women, the effects of armed conflict on women, inequality between men and women in power and decision-making, the human rights of women, stereotyping of women, and inequality in access to resources and the management of natural resources (para. 44).

Gender gaps continue in all of these areas, but they are narrowing in some. The Global Gender Gap Report 2006 shows that Sweden, Norway, Finland, and Iceland rank highest in gender equality. Its Gender Gap Index, based on four critical areas of inequality – (1) economic participation and opportunity, (2) educational attainment, (3) political empowerment, and (4) health and survival – shows improvement in the scores of all top 20 countries. Gender analysis is making a difference in international relations.

SEE ALSO: Gender Inequality; Gendering Peace Psychology; Women and Peace Hypothesis.

REFERENCES

Boserup, E. (1970). *Women's role in economic develoopment*. New York, NY: St. Martin's Press.
Enloe, C. (1989). *Bananas, beaches, and bases*. London, UK: Pandora Press.
Goldstein, J. S. (2001). *War and gender: How gender shapes the war system and vice versa*. Cambridge, UK: Cambridge University Press.
Reardon, B. (1985). *Sexism and the war system*. New York, NY: Teachers College Press.
Stephenson, C. M. (2008). Gender equality and a culture of peace. In J. de Rivera (Ed.), *Handbook for building cultures of peace*. New York, NY: Springer.
Stiehm, J. H. (Ed.). (1983). *Women and men's wars*. New York, NY: Pergamon. (Previously published in 1982 as a special issue of *Women's Studies International Forum, 5*(3)).
Tickner, J. A. (1992). *Gender in international relations: Feminist perspectives on achieving global security*. New York, NY: Columbia University Press.
Winslow, A. (Ed.). (1995). *Women, politics, and the United Nations*. Westport, CT: Greenwood Press.

ADDITIONAL RESOURCES

"Nobel women's initiative – about us." Retrieved March 24, 2010, from www.nobelwomensinitiative.org
http://www.unifem.org/progress/2008/fs_topicindex.html (UNIFEM: Progress of the World's Women 2008/2009)
http://www.weforum.org/en/initiatives/gcp/Gender%20Gap/index.htm (World Economic Forum: The Global Gender Gap Report 2007)

Gender and Terrorism

NAJMA NAJAM

It is well documented that the world's active combat forces have been almost all male. With the exception of the legends of Amazons, there have been no known formal female fighting forces. History does record women such as Joan of Arc (France), Jhansi ki Rani, Razia Sultana (Indian subcontinent), and more recently Phoolan Devi (India) who led fighting forces comprised of men, but these are a rare occurrence. Similarly, in the last few decades, more men than women have been involved and are visible in acts of terrorism, including suicide attacks across Afghanistan, Kashmir, Sri Lanka, Bosnia, Palestine, Turkey, Chechnya, and elsewhere (barring Russia, where women have been active and quite visible).

The low level of involvement (and lower visibility) of females in terrorism and suicide attacks has been explained through two distinct but sequentially related frameworks. One deals with antecedent conditions of terrorist acts; the other explains women's involvement in terrorism as a consequence of the conditions experienced. The former models draw on biological, sociobiological, social, learning, and cultural/political frameworks. The latter explains women's involvement in terrorism as a consequence of the conditions women have undergone, such as social change (i.e., modernization), identification, revenge, and alienation. The two frames are sequentially related because consequent conditions can, in turn, become antecedent conditions for terrorism and suicide attacks. (See TERRORISM, PSYCHOLOGY OF; TRIBAL CULTURE AND VIOLENCE; WOMEN AND PEACE HYPOTHESIS.)

ANTECEDENT INTERPRETATIONS

These fall into two main categories, the biological/sociobiological and the social psychological.

Biological/Sociobiological

Biological differences   In animals, males are biologically equipped and ready for combat, being physically stronger, whereas females physically and biologically are equipped for giving birth and nurturing. Further, male animals have bigger and more ferocious tools, such as larger canines in male baboons. The same biological differences continue on the higher phylogenetic scale. However, in humans the extensions of tools for fighting are weapons and guns, which are highly visible and give the appearance of being powerful. This is illustrated by pictures of young boy soldiers in Africa and Afghanistan carrying big guns, and of Afghani fighters standing on tanks to show off their conquest. Interestingly, in Afghani fighters, male masculinity ideals are strong, and the torture of male enemies frequently focuses on the

male sexual organs (pictures serve as documentary evidence of the grotesque and brutal nature of such torture).

Territoriality   In animals, territoriality has been well documented, from the observations on the male stickleback fish to horses, cats, canines, etc. In humans, demarcation of property, village, and country boundaries also reflects territoriality. This can be extended to understand and explain terrorism as "territoriality" (males fight for their territory).

Social Psychological

Social learning perspective   Bandura's social learning perspective suggests that in cultures that value aggression, aggression is transmitted through childrearing practices. Where the culture transmits aggression in males, aggression is rewarded and reinforced. Boys are encouraged to respond with aggression in a fight and not to return home defeated. The elder females, including the mother, encourage aggressive behavior and language in young males. For example, in the Pakhtoon culture this begins at birth, when more guns are fired to announce the birth of a son than a daughter.

Role modeling   Human behavior is learned through observations (i.e., through modeling). From observing older members, a child forms an idea of how behaviors are to be performed, and this becomes a template for later action and behavior. In the famous BO-BO doll experiment it was demonstrated that aggression is learnt through watching adult behaviors. Thus, a society encourages aggressive behavior to the extent that it furnishes successful aggressive male role models and rewards aggressive actions. Further, the imitation of adult roles and reinforcement of imitated behaviors also ensures that females have a more nurturant role; girls spend more time playing with dolls, boys with guns (Bandura, 1977).

Gender role differentiation   In cultures and societies where there is greater gender role differentiation there is also greater segregation between the genders, and greater inequality that is visible in many activities. In such societies, males are traditionally associated with aggression, learning and knowing how to fight from early childhood, while females are associated with nurturing, caring, and life-giving. Further, such gender-split cultures tend to be more violent – the Taliban being a recent example (Stout, 2002). In such societies, women are affected by conflict and war – the more violent the conflict, the more serious are the consequences for women (75% of refugees of the Afghan War were women and children).

Differences in goals   Men typically strive to build societies based on political and religious ideals rather than on protecting and bettering the lives of their children and families. This can also be interpreted as pressured manhood, an insecurity which needs dramatic proof of manhood through violence and aggression (namely, acts of terrorism). Similarly, the fighting force/terrorist organization is seen as a hypermasculine force that involves expression of masculinity through violence, organizational obedience, and dominance. Women strive to protect and support their families. The Afghan War is a case in point, where a whole generation of women is widowed and children are without fathers, where the grandmother becomes the head of the household – being the only surviving elder.

CONSEQUENT INTERPRETATIONS

An act of terrorism can be a consequence of the conditions that a person has experienced. Rapid changes in – or rigidity of – social norms or even painful experiences (e.g., rape, loss of male relatives through aggression) have led to females' involvement in acts of terrorism. Thus, female suicide terrorism is possible even in societies where cultural or religious norms restrict women's movements and access to public spheres or where the traditional systems are breaking down and/or undergoing rapid change and where women are undergoing traumatic experiences.

Changing Societies: Greater Equality

In societies undergoing rapid change, modernization and a rise in the general level of education created equity for jobs and education for females; also created was equity for acts of aggression (e.g., Chechnya, Turkey, Palestine, Sri Lanka). The first terrorist organizations to recruit women were more secular, while the more right-wing/conservative organizations did not include women at any level. As a case in point, in 2004 violent suicide attacks and explosions were set off by female suicide bombers in Tashkent (Uzbekistan), a former Soviet state with equitable education and other opportunities. In Turkey (a secular Muslim state), 14 of 21 suicide attacks were reported to be carried out by females. Similarly, the LTTE (Tamil Tigers) in Sri Lanka (a state that had the world's first female prime minister and is known for the highest education rates for women in the Indian subcontinent) had women fighters and suicide bombers: of 200 recorded suicide attacks, 30–40% were by women. One female suicide bomber even blew herself up along with an eminent scion of the Gandhi family. Further, 46 incidents in which women were involved were reported between 1969 and 2005, about 1.3 attacks per year. Thus, it appears that the greater the opportunities for women's education and the greater the equity for employment, the greater is the acceptance of women as fighters and terrorists within that culture. This is supported by the fact that there is greater visibility of women in Iraq, Jordan, Lebanon, Israel, and Chechnya and less visibility in Palestine and Afghanistan. There is also a change over generations, with younger Chechnyan women, for example, more accepting of their roles in violent activity and more involved in terrorism as compared to their mothers' generation. Thus, increased participation of women in society, and equitable opportunities associated with women's liberation, appear to be important factors in women joining terrorist organizations as equals.

Women's Identity and the Availability of New Roles

Some women identify with the goals and roles prescribed by men and support men's acts of aggression by nurturing aggression in their male counterparts; they also support children who commit acts of aggression (as in Afghani society). In addition, women can play an indirect role by acting as recruiters, supporters, planners, and patrons of violence. Examples of highly qualified women include Ume-Usama, who actively recruited volunteers for suicide missions via the Internet, and Dr. Afia, a neuroscientist trained at the Massachusetts Institute of Technology who was involved with fundraising to support terrorist activities. These women took on roles allowed within the boundaries defined by the ultraconservative nature of the organizations of their affiliation. Thus, through strong identification with the goals and roles identified by men, they chose a different path to terrorism – a supportive but not actively visible role.

Revenge

Female suicide terrorism has also been reported to take place when close male relatives have been adversely affected by violence – physically tortured, raped, or killed. These women opt to revenge their personal losses. Their grief, loss, and stigma are channeled into acts of terrorism.

WOMEN'S PARTICIPATION: OTHER PERSPECTIVES

In strongly gender-divided traditional societies, the involvement of females in terrorism/ suicide attacks becomes a symbol of commitment to the cause and brings great visibility to the cause. For instance, Leila Khaled, a Palestinian woman involved in a 1970 hijacking, brought the Palestinian issue to the forefront. In addition, in highly gender-divided societies, an act of terrorism by women may also be motivated by a rebellious attitude, in order to break away from norms and achieve recognition and equality.

At the same time, women in a traditional society with a strong male–female divide would be ostracized for breaking social norms and mores by getting involved in organizations that are active fighting forces. Further, since suicide bombing would expose their body parts, this act would certainly not be acceptable in some societies (such as Afghanistan). Any woman who chooses to do so in such societies enters a one-way street, as her family or the society would not accept her if she survived. No one would accept her as a bride in a house.

In summary, in the present turbulent times, this is an area for further investigation by gender specialists, social psychologists, and especially researchers focusing on the causes and consequences of terrorism.

SEE ALSO: Terrorism, Psychology of; Tribal Culture and Violence; Women and Peace Hypothesis.

REFERENCES

Bandura, A. (1977). *Social learning theory*. New York, NY: General Learning Press.

Stout, C. E. (Ed.). (2002). *The psychology of terrorism: A public understanding*. Westport, CT: Praeger.

ADDITIONAL RESOURCES

Authors unknown. (2005). OSCE ODIHR: Background paper on female suicide terrorism: Consequences for counter-terrorism. OSCE Technical Expert Workshop on Suicide Terrorism, Warsaw, Poland.

Berko, A., & Perez, E. (2006). Women in terrorism: A Palestinian feminist revolution or gender oppression. Retrieved July 6, 2009, from www.terrorism-info.org.il/malam_multimedia/English/eng_n/html/women_terror_e.htm.

Davis, J. (2006). Women and terrorism in radical Islam: Planners, perpetuators, patrons? Revolution or evolution? Emerging threats to security in the 21st century. Presented at the 1st Annual Graduate Symposium at Dalhousie University, Halifax, Canada.

Gender-Based Violence

OLIVERA SIMIC

For a long time, gender-based violence (GBV) has been viewed as a private or family matter. Over the last two decades there has been a shift in thinking about GBV, and it is now viewed as a societal problem, primarily as a human rights violation and public health problem. Although GBV is often interchangeably used with "sexual violence" and "violence against women," it is useful to distinguish GBV from other forms of violence. GBV is a deliberately broad term in order to recognize the gendered elements in nearly all forms of violence against women and girls, whether it is perpetrated through sexual violence or through other means.

The term GBV refers to violence that targets individuals or groups on the basis of their gender, which is the primary motive or risk factor. Although GBV affects both women and men, women and girls are by far the most affected. Women and men are also affected by GBV in different ways. Globally, "men experience a higher level of physical violence than women as a result of war, gang-related activity, street violence, and suicide, while women and girls are more likely to be assaulted or killed by someone they know, such as an intimate partner" (Bott, Morisson, & Ellsberg, 2005). However, while GBV affects both sexes, leading feminist scholars like Cynthia Enloe argue that "violence is fundamentally masculinist, but I am not prepared to say that only men act violently" (Enloe, 2004, p. 133).

In 1993 the United Nations Declaration on the Elimination of Violence against Women promulgated in its Article 1 the first official definition of GBV as "any act of gender-based violence that results in, or is likely to result in, physical, sexual or psychological harm or suffering to women, including threats of such acts, coercion or arbitrary deprivations of liberty, whether occurring in public or in private life." This definition encompasses acts of physical, sexual, and psychological violence in the family, community, or condoned by the state. The 1995 Beijing Platform for Action expanded on this definition and included violations of the rights of women in situations of armed conflict. Any of these abuses can have serious impact on women and girls' health, and in some instances can result in death.

Although violence is a traumatic experience for both women and men, GBV is predominantly inflicted by men on women and girls. It is estimated that, worldwide, one in five women will be victims of rape or attempted rape in their lifetimes. At least one in three women have been beaten, coerced into sex, or otherwise abused in their families (Heise, Ellsberg, & Gottemoeller, 1999). Each year, hundreds of thousands of women and girls are trafficked and enslaved for the purpose of sexual and labor exploitation. Although GBV persists in every country in the world, high rates of GBV occur in patriarchal societies.

Widespread and pervasive, GBV is the most socially tolerated and recognized human rights violation in the world. It is a universal problem that occurs across cultures and cultural groups. In many cultures, GBV is viewed as legitimate, goes unrecognized, or remains culturally accepted. Such cultures may have norms, beliefs, and social institutions that legitimize, and therefore perpetuate, GBV. Although it occurs in both the public and private spheres, it is harder to detect and recognize GBV in the home than in public. For example, the same acts of GBV that would be punished if directed at a neighbor or an employee often go unchallenged when men direct them towards a woman or a girl, especially within the family.

Varying aspects of GBV are perceived differently across cultures, yet women are increasingly exposed to all its forms. Across cultures, GBV serves to perpetuate male power and control, which are often expressed as violence or coercion and are sustained by a culture of silence and denial. It aims to reinforce gender hierarchies and perpetuate gender inequalities. (See GENDER INEQUALITY.) According to Watts and Zimmerman (2002) GBV includes:

• Rape or sexual assault
• Intimate partner violence
• Sexual harassment
• Stalking
• Trafficking
• Forced prostitution
• Exploitation of labor
• Debt bondage of women and girls
• Sex-selective abortion
• Physical and sexual violence against prostitutes
• Female infanticide
• Deliberate neglect of girls
• Rape in war

GBV can also occur in different forms throughout the life cycle of a woman, as illustrated in Figure 1 (adapted from Heise, 1994).

Feminist researchers emphasize that GBV is inextricably linked to gender-based inequalities and the violent expression of masculinity (Welsh, 2001). Such researchers challenge the behavior of men and the power relations between the sexes that underpins it. The research evidence indicates that the majority of crimes are committed by men towards women and that they are particularly responsible for physical and sexual violence. These two types of violence are intertwined, since sexual violence is largely carried out with physical force. For men, formative influences include socialization and culturally dominant beliefs regarding acceptable masculine behavior (Galtung, 1996). Masculinity is often associated with characteristics such as aggressiveness, dominance, strength, competitiveness, and control. These characteristics result from a combination of biological, cultural, and social influences in a given society. However, neither violent attitudes nor behaviors are uniform for all men within a given society (Madrigal, 2006).

GBV has long-term health, social, and economic consequences. A number of studies have analyzed the costs of GBV, although these studies have been limited largely to developed countries. Those studies that focus on developing countries mainly concentrate on the macrolevel, analyzing costs to national governments rather then costs to individuals – in particular, women, households, and communities. Despite these limitations, such studies brought the issue of GBV to the forefront of development studies, recognizing it as a development concern as well as a serious impediment to economic growth. Thus, it is crucial that GBV is reframed as a public health and development issue, rather than solely a women's human rights issue, in order to mobilize attention and cooperation across sectors when developing prevention and response programs.

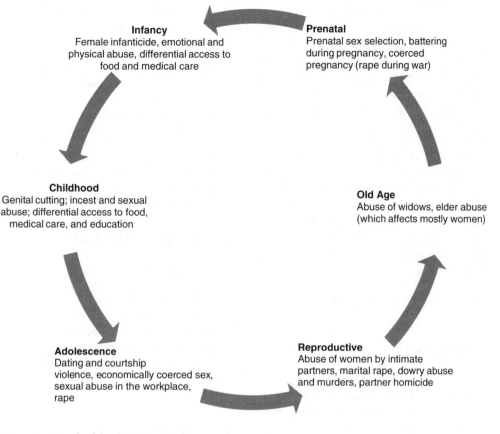

Figure 1   Gender-based violence.

Serious sexual and reproductive health injuries can result from GBV, including sexually transmitted infections such as HIV/AIDS, induced abortions, unintended pregnancies, adverse pregnancy outcomes, and miscarriages. Mental health consequences can include risk of depression, sleep difficulties, post-traumatic stress disorder, emotional distress, and eating disorders. Deaths from GBV include honor killings, female infanticide, suicide, and maternal death resulting from unsafe abortions. In terms of social and economic costs, GBV has enormous consequences, affecting not only women who may suffer from isolation and inability to work, but also affecting the whole family and community (World Health Organization, 2008). Women who are affected by GBV have limited ability to take care of themselves, their children, and other family members. The health costs of GBV are significant for health service providers as well. The high costs highlight the scope and seriousness of a problem that drains resources and ripples through households to the community and society at large.

GBV is a major impediment to achieving gender equality and also a serious obstacle to making real progress towards development and peace. It reflects and reinforces inequality between women and men and can leave deep psychological scars, damaging the health of women and girls in general and even resulting in death. Any strategy to confront GBV must address the root causes of abuse which are deeply rooted in structural relationships of inequality. This means challenging the social attitudes and beliefs that support men's violence and renegotiating the balance of power between women and men at all levels of society. GBV prevention programs should increase community based education and awareness of violence and its consequences, as well as expand resources for women survivors. They should target the whole community, and engage with men and women, boys and girls in order to change attitudes about gender inequalities and the acceptability of violence.

SEE ALSO: Gender Inequality.

REFERENCES

Bott, S., Morisson, A., & Ellsberg, M. (2005). Preventing and responding to gender-based violence in middle and low income countries: A global review and analysis. World Bank Policy Research Working Paper No. 3618. Washington, DC: World Bank.

Enloe, C. (2004). *The curious feminist: Searching for women in the new age of empire*. Berkeley, CA: University of California Press.

Galtung, J. (1996). *Peace by peaceful means: Peace and conflict, development and civilization*. Oslo, Norway: International Peace Research Institute.

Heise, L. (1994). Violence against women: The hidden health burden. World Bank Discussion Paper. Washington, DC: World Bank.

Heise, L., Ellsberg, M., & Gottemoeller, M. (1999). *Ending violence against women: Population reports*. Series No. 11. Baltimore, MD: Johns Hopkins University School of Public Health, Population Information Program.

Madrigal, L. J. (2006). Masculinities: Hopes to change. In M. Baltodano, M. Blyth,
L. Madrigal, S. Mabetembe, & W. Robins (Eds.), *Celebrating changes: Exploring equality and equity of diakonia in the church* (pp. 51–59). Geneva, Switzerland: World Council of Churches.

Watts, C., & Zimmerman, C. (2002). Violence against women: Global scope and magnitude. *Lancet, 359*, 1232–1237.

Welsh, P. (2001). *Men aren't from Mars: Unlearning machismo in Nicaragua*. London, UK: Catholic Institute for International Relations.

World Heatlh Organization (2008). *Violence against women*. From http://www.who.int/mediacentre/factsheets/fs239/en/index.html.

ADDITIONAL RESOURCES

www.undp.org/unifem (United Nations Development Fund for Women)

www.whiteribbon.ca/eindex.html (White Ribbon Campaign: a group of "men working to end men's violence against women"; offers a newsletter, educational material for adolescent and adult men about violence against women, and counseling resources for abusers)

Gender Inequality

BERNICE LOTT

This article is about gender, and the significant national and international social, economic, and political problems associated with inequality in status and resources between women and men. Sexual identification at birth appears to be universal across the globe, and this recognition of a baby's sexual category is followed everywhere by the development of gender – a socially constructed category of relationship to other human beings that characterizes all of us throughout our lives. Because the behaviors expected of girls and boys, women and men, are, for the most part, unrelated to the few biological imperatives or biological distinctions between the sexes, we use the word gender to refer to these human groups. Gender serves to organize social relations and interactions at the structural or institutional level as well as at the individual level, each of which reinforces the other. Gender incorporates culturally normative prescriptions and proscriptions with respect to behavior, expectations, and the designation of gender-appropriate environments. Especially implicated in gender relationships is relative power, or access to resources. Almost universally, beliefs about gender reinforce men's privilege, as do the realities of daily life. (See WOMEN AND PEACE HYPOTHESIS; DOMESTIC VIOLENCE: FEMINIST PERSPECTIVE; GENDER AND INTERNATIONAL RELATIONS; GENDER-BASED VIOLENCE; GENDERING PEACE PSYCHOLOGY.)

Historical and contemporary data support the conclusion that women's lesser social status relative to men's is a ubiquitous feature of human societies. It is a stark reality that women have been, and continue to be, denied full social equality with men. Men have treated women as property, objectified them, and erected barriers to their access to full societal participation and equitable rewards. These realities vary with regions of the world, nations, institutions, cultures, and historical period. There are variations, as well, in the agents and processes that maintain inequality and in the significance of such categories as social class, ethnicity, age, and sexual preference as they interact with gender.

Women and men are still, more often than not, excluded from what is considered to be the domain of the other. For women, across ethnicities and social classes, this results in more limited access than comparable men to human welfare resources, fewer positions of high status, and narrower opportunities for personal growth and development. For example, in the United States at the end of the first decade of the twenty-first century, "elite" women constituted 16% of the membership of the House of Representatives, about 22% of all state legislators, 15% of corporate officers, 25% of physicians, and a third woman had been added to the nine-member Supreme Court.

There is agreement among social scientists that the major manifestations or dimensions of gender inequality are found in the realms of income or economic activity, and political power. With respect to the former, it is instructive to examine the East Asian countries that have achieved outstanding economic growth in the past several decades. This growth has followed the hard work and sacrifice promoted by the governments but has not been accompanied by workforce gender equality. Instead, the patriarchal relations of households have been largely reproduced and women in these countries are found in the most poorly paid global production industries where they serve as a supply of compliant workers (Steel & Kabashima, 2008).

Another enlightening and important comparison can be made with Scandinavian countries in which there are a variety of policies designed to increase gender equity, such as paid work leave, flexible employment hours for parents, and subsidized child and after-school care. These and other policies have "achieved the lowest level of material inequality between men and women" in the world, yet these countries "have some of the most sex-segregated occupational structures of advanced industrial societies" (Ridgeway, 2009, p. 156). Family friendly policies in these countries have enabled married women to stay in the workforce, but not at the highest levels of responsibility or compensation. Thus, there appears to be no automatic carry-over from a nation's economic health and material circumstances to women's workforce status.

Strongly correlated with women's position in the workforce are women's economic circumstances and women's access to resources that provide for material well-being. Among those living in poverty in today's world, 70% are women and children. In low-income nations as well as in moderate and high-income nations, women, as a group, have jobs of lesser status and earn less income than men, and are far more likely to be poor. In the United States, for example, women who are employed full-time outside the home earn 77 cents for every dollar earned by a man. For African-American women, it is 66 cents and, for Latinas, it is 55 cents. In 2006, men with high school diplomas made more than $13,000 more a year than comparable women, and men with bachelor's degrees made $23,000 more than women with similar degrees. As women and men grow older, the difference in their earnings increases.

A study of 18 affluent democracies in the Western hemisphere found nearly universal overrepresentation of women among the poor across the years from 1969 to 2000. This overrepresentation of women, across a wide age span, was only weakly related to a country's overall level of economic inequality. In other words, concluded the researchers, "one cannot . . . reduce the gender inequality in poverty to overall poverty" (Brady & Kall, 2008, p. 996).

Matching the universality of gender inequality in the economic sphere is the sharp and pronounced lack of equity in the realm of politics and government. Despite the leadership position of a woman in the United States as Speaker of the House of Representatives (following the 2008 election), the membership of that body is only 16% female. This figure is strikingly similar to that for the world at large in which 17% of the seats in national parliaments are occupied by women. Not surprisingly, the five countries in which the parliamentary representation of women was greater than 30% in 2000 are the Scandinavian nations. What is surprising, however, is the growing political power of women in developing countries.

In Rwanda, for example, women have been elected to 55% of seats in the lower house of parliament. Some attribute this phenomenon to the civil conflicts that have served as catalysts for change. Civil wars have highlighted women's disproportionate suffering as victims of sexual crime, increased women's participation in human rights and peace movements, increased the pool of women candidates, and contributed to change in traditional gender beliefs. Wars that have been fought against governments rather than to gain territory appear to be more likely to enhance women's political position.

A study by Hughes (2009) of the parliamentary representation of women in 36 high-income, 86 mid-income, and 63 low-income countries (as of the end of 2000) found some striking significant variables associated with higher representation. These are: a Marxist-Leninist ideology, a proportional representation voting system, a left-of-center political party, and less national religious orthodoxy. Taken together with the influence of civil conflict on women's political position, these findings appear to challenge the assumption that political equality requires, as precursors, women's economic and social equality. Women's important participation and representation in the political sphere seems to have occurred in some countries despite persistent gender inequality in other spheres.

Some scholars attribute the persistence of gender inequality to the universal division of household labor relating to the care of children. Shared among all countries, with some but few variations, is the assumption and prescription that mothers (or other women) will bear the greater responsibility for the welfare and development of children. Thus, it is almost always the case that women's time and energy are devoted to a far greater extent than men's to tasks and behaviors centering on the care of children.

It has been concluded by some that this "unequal gender division of labor constitutes a barrier – perhaps the most important barrier – to further progress in realizing the goals of opportunity between men and women" (Brighouse & Wright, 2008, p. 362). It may well be that this single difference in what is expected of women and men in family households is of enormous significance in contributing to gender inequality in the more public spheres of economics and politics. The circularity of inequality is maintained as the public forms reinforce and contribute to those within the family and vice versa.

Except for a very small minority of persons, the ideal of having mothers and fathers contribute equally to the care of their children is not realized currently in any society. Even countries like those in Scandinavia, and some in Europe, that have family–work policies that assist parents in better gender-balanced child-rearing practices have not achieved the ideal. In higher-income countries, despite women's greater opportunities for education and training and greater participation in politics, civic affairs, and high status employment, motherhood inevitably brings a set of expectations that are different and more complex and demanding than those of fatherhood. These expectations do not simply suddenly appear when adults become parents. Girls/women and boys/men are prepared within their societies for their roles as parents from early childhood and throughout life by their families, schools, language, religions, media, and social institutions. Thus, the proposition that unequal parenting responsibilities constitute a primary factor in maintenance of gender inequality has a high probability of being empirically accurate. There are, of course, variations among and within countries in the extent to which parenting is gender-unequal, with social class and

sexual minority status contributing most to the variation.

Even when running for high elected office in the United States, the image of a woman as mother is an inevitable accompaniment of any description, as was true in 2008 for both Hillary Clinton and Sarah Palin. The assumption remains strong that, when children are born, it is the mother (or a mother substitute) who assumes primary responsibility for their rearing and for their health and welfare, particularly when they are young. A continuing debate in the US media is whether motherhood responsibilities take precedence over a career for educated middle-class (and White) women. Some argue that "career women" are more likely to have problematic marriages and be less likely to be happy wives and mothers. Generally missing from discussions of conflicts between work and parenting is attention to social class and ethnicity. Black women, in general, in the United States see employment as compatible with motherhood, due to a mixture of historical and current special circumstances. Also typically absent from media discussions of parenting is the role of fathers, husbands, and male partners.

When current levels of gender inequality are compared with levels that have existed in the past, in both low-income and high-income countries, it is possible to see progress and anticipate even more positive change. However, the relatively small number of women found today in powerful and high status political or economic positions are invariably "tokens," or "exceptions," their positions neither reflecting nor seriously affecting the status of the women in their countries. But it is likely that they do have a positive influence on changing gender stereotypes and expectations by challenging them. As women's public participation in the economic life of their countries has increased, there has been a corresponding change in many parts of the world in the traditional content of gender stereotypes.

The 2000 Gallop International Millennium Survey obtained answers to questions from close to 55,000 persons in 60 nations. Included were six items on gender equality, such as: education is more important for boys than girls; men make better political leaders than women; and a woman needs children to be fulfilled. The data indicate that egalitarian gender beliefs are largely supported, with those in wealthier nations subscribing to them more than those in low-income countries. But gender equality was found to sometimes have ambiguous meanings and to have different meanings in different countries, particularly where the focus was on specific issues related to "women's rights."

Gender inequality in a society is present in all spheres and institutions – family, education, economic, and political. Because women and men are exposed to different circumstances, constraints, and stressors, there are significant and far-reaching consequences for health and for physical and psychological well-being. A relationship has been found between gender inequality and differences between women and men in subjective experiences of well-being. Data from a study of 57 countries indicated that gender differences in subjective well-being "are influenced by unequal access to individual resources and . . . the degree to which women are disadvantaged or excluded from societal resources and opportunity structures" (Tesch-Romer, Motel-Klingebiel, & Tomasik, 2008, p. 342).

What is clear from all available data is that gender inequality has widespread consequences of enormous importance for personal opportunities and interactions, development, experience, and satisfaction with life, corresponding to societal effects on institutions, and cultural effects on beliefs and practices. Some see the oppression of women as the major human rights issue and moral challenge in today's world. Kristof and WuDunn (2009), for example, argue convincingly that putting an end to the routine raping, selling, and beating of women will not only lead to increased access to sources of power for women but will also constitute the most effective solution to global poverty and political extremism.

A related argument is that since poverty is a major index of women's inequality, any program to eradicate poverty must begin with attention to women's lives. Women, who constitute 50% of the adult population of the world, one-third of its official workforce, and 50% of its food producers, own only 1% of the world's property, earn only 10% of its income, and are two-thirds of all those who are illiterate. Emerging policy for developing nations has begun to emphasize education for women as vital not only to their empowerment but also to the advancement of their societies. Education enables women to play a larger role in social and political decision-making in families, communities, and nations, thus expanding the range of responsible voices committed to social change.

SEE ALSO: Domestic Violence: Feminist Perspective; Gender and International Relations; Gender-Based Violence; Gendering Peace Psychology; Women and Peace Hypothesis.

REFERENCES

Brady, D., & Kall, D. (2008). Nearly universal, but somewhat distinct: The feminization of poverty in affluent Western democracies, 1969–2000. *Social Science Research, 37*, 976–1007.

Brighouse, H., & Wright, E. O. (2008). Strong gender egalitarianism. *Politics and Society, 36*, 360–372.

Hughes, M. M. (2009). Armed conflict, international linkages, and women's parliamentary representation in developing nations. *Social Problems, 56*, 174–204.

Kristof, N. D., & WuDunn, S. (2009, August 23). The women's crusade. *New York Times Magazine*, 28–39.

Ridgeway, C. L. (2009). Framed before we know it: How gender shapes social relations. *Gender and Society, 23*, 145–160.

Steel, G., & Kabashima, I. (2008). Cross-regional support for gender equality. *International Political Science Review, 29*, 133–156.

Tesch-Romer, C., Motel-Klingebiel, A., & Tomasik, M. J. (2008). Gender differences in subjective well-being: Comparing societies with respect to gender equality. *Social Indicators Research, 85*, 329–349.

ADDITIONAL RESOURCES

Lott, B. (2010). *Multiculturalism and diversity: A social psychological perspective*. Oxford, UK: Wiley-Blackwell.

UN Commission on the Status of Women (2006). *Fiftieth session 27 February–10 March 2006*. Retrieved from http://www.un.org/womenwatch/daw/csw/50sess.htm.

UNFPA *Gender Equality Fact Sheet*. (2005). Retrieved from http://www,unfpa.org/swp/2005/presskit/factsheets/facts_gender.htm.

Gendering Peace Psychology

MIRIAM SCHROER-HIPPEL

Gender perspectives are central to peace psychology. This may be argued from the point of view of gender and conflict studies, a growing interdisciplinary field of research. Thorough analyses of gender relations and their intersections with other categories, such as ethnicity, sexuality, and class, have contributed substantially to understanding the dynamics of violent conflict. From this point of view, any discipline concerned with the study of peace and conflict cannot do without a gender analysis. Besides this, the relevance of gender perspectives to peace psychology may be argued from a normative stance. Most definitions of peace psychology emphasize a normative commitment towards negative and positive peace, towards ending direct violence and achieving social justice. It was mainly feminist scholars and activists who pointed out that this should apply to both men *and* women. In a broad debate, feminist definitions of peace, conflict, and security have been developed. They account for diverse forms of violence against women and men, including violence in the so-called private sphere of the home, and define gender equality as an inseparable part of peace. Three threads of gendering peace psychology will be discussed in this article: (1) gendered experiences in peace and conflict, (2) gendering methods of conflict management, and (3) gender theoretical analysis of the formation of war and peace.

In the first thread, gender is deployed as an analytic research tool to differentiate between men and women, studying experiences of men and women in their gendered positions. Many scholars in this field account for diverse positions among women and men. This research has been influential to the second thread on gendering methods of conflict management. Their main argument is that conflict management should contribute to an inclusive, gender-just peace. Gender is defined as socially constructed by most scholars within the previous threads: they reject notions of inherent female competencies for nonviolence or natural male tendencies towards violence. (See WOMEN AND PEACE HYPOTHESIS.) But in the third thread, gender itself comes in as a research subject. Processes of the social construction of gender are studied in order to understand the dynamics of violent conflict.

Within peace psychology, gendered perspectives have had an ambivalent and at times marginalized position, but they increasingly become part of the discipline's definitions and debates. The third thread, gender theoretical analysis of the formation of war and peace, developed mainly outside of peace psychology, but rather within feminist psychology as well as gender and conflict studies. It is argued here that this perspective provides considerable potential for future research and practice in peace psychology.

STUDYING GENDERED EXPERIENCES IN WAR AND PEACE

A first thread of gendering peace psychology started from the critique that peace psychology had in many cases taken men's positions as a norm and neglected specific experiences of women and girls in armed conflict as well as their contributions to peacebuilding. An extensive body of studies, covering a wide range of conflict settings, is dedicated to the aim of "bringing women in" and contributing towards more gender-just peacebuilding processes. The research was initially grouped around roles of women in war and peace: victims, activists, and perpetrators. Later, also, men's roles and experiences were researched from a critical gender perspective. Further references on the first two threads can be found in Costin's (2006) overview.

This research relates to feminist activists' critique of political policy ignoring the enormous extent of sexualized violence against women in wars. It is, at the same time, part of a research perspective within gender and conflict research. Feminist political scientists criticized international relations theory for excluding experiences of women from the research agenda on conflict. In sociological and anthropological studies, the symbolic meaning of systematic rape was analyzed as a means to humiliate the enemy men for failing to protect "their" women. Feminist

psychologists added their perspective by studying coping and empowerment strategies of war-affected women. They discussed which reactions of the family and the local and international community helped or hindered healing processes. Controversial discussions on approaches to healing the traumas of gender-based violence questioned Western individualistic therapy models in favor of more community based approaches. In a second step, feminist scholars criticized media discourses for reducing women to victimhood and women being excluded from peace negotiations and peacebuilding.

Feminist psychologists documented women activists' perspectives and contributions to reconciliation and peacebuilding, as well as the contribution of "ordinary" women to post-conflict reconstruction. A small, but increasing number of feminist studies focused on women as part of nationalist and militant movements, on men's socialization into the military, and on men's experiences of violence, including sexualized violence.

Studying gendered experiences in war and peace provides a more systematic and more complete picture. Using gender as a differentiating tool is necessary to assess gender inequality and gendered division of labor in war and peacebuilding, as well as the specific needs of men and women in their gendered positions. These studies provided the empirical background for developing more inclusive, gender-sensitive peacebuilding measures. The perspective has, at the same time, been criticized for simplification and re-establishing gender stereotypes by subsuming women's experiences to roles of victims and peacemakers. This is seen as problematic, as it echoes dominant war discourses, which might be flexible enough to subsume the figure of the female peacemaker under the dominant dichotomy of weak, peaceful, female victims to be protected by hypermasculine warriors.

Evaluated from a research perspective, this thread is at its strongest when it accounts for diverse experiences of men and women and strongly links the study of gendered experiences to gender theoretical analysis of conflict.

GENDERING METHODS OF CONFLICT MANAGEMENT

Peace psychology contributes to peace and conflict studies by improving methods of conflict management. They range from face-to-face methods such as mediation, to larger processes such as psychological aspects of peacebuilding, as well as collective action. Feminist scholars criticized conflict management methods that did not consider barriers to equal participation, and consequently contributed to the exclusion of women from peace practice. Furthermore, methods were not directed towards achieving an inclusive, gender-just peace. This led, they argued, to neglecting women's peacebuilding and security needs, to ignoring the long-term contributions of women peace activists, and to re-establishing women's exclusion from the public arena. The process of engendering methods of conflict management has only started. One example is the engendering of Burton's human needs theory (Reimann 2002). Others include problem-solving workshops, mediation, civil political discourse, or psychological aspects of societal reconstruction. This thread is related to broader practice-oriented debates on gendering peacebuilding, reconstruction, and peace-support operations. Gender-sensitive evaluations as well as activists' accounts suggest that, even if gendered methods are provided, their implementation cannot be taken for granted.

Gendering methods of conflict management contributes to the theoretical underpinning of practical tools and implies immense potential for improving peace work. This line of discussion has provoked reflection on more inclusive accounts of peace and peacebuilding. At the same time, gender is almost exclusively discussed in terms of gender equality, which is then mainly translated into empowering women. Some approaches of gendering peacebuilding include perspectives on men and masculinities, aiming at challenging the primacy of militarized, hegemonic masculinity (e.g., Breines, Connell, & Eide, 2000). Future perspectives in gendering conflict management may benefit from the gender theoretical perspectives described below.

GENDER THEORETICAL ANALYSIS OF THE FORMATION OF WAR AND PEACE

Gendering peace psychology, here, relates to applying elements of gender theoretical frameworks, developed within gender and conflict studies, to the psychological study of peace and conflict. A small number of scholars made use of these perspectives, mainly within feminist psychology and other debates outside of peace psychology. In the following, central elements of these theoretical frameworks will be outlined, followed by examples of several discussions drawing on them.

According to Reimann (2002, p. 3), three dimensions of gender have been suggested as relevant to the study of peace and conflict: (1) the individual gender identity (social norms and socially constructed individual identity), (2) the symbolism of gender (classification of stereotypical gender dualisms), and (3) the structure of gender (the organization and institutionalization of social action in the public and private sphere). Gender is taken into account with its multiple intersections with other categories of power, such as ethnicity, race, sexuality, and class. Masculinity studies, especially the paradigm of hegemonic masculinity (applied, for example, in Breines, Connell, & Eide, 2000), suggests that in addition to inequalities between men and women, hierarchies between men must be studied. Hegemonic masculinity is defined as the dominant form of masculinity, a cultural ideal linked to material advantages. The subordination of gay men and the exclusion of non-White and working-class men are seen as important aspects of the formation of hierarchy. Using these and other concepts, gender and conflict studies have contributed to the understanding of the formation of violent conflict. Empirical studies showed for different conflict regions how the ethnicized Other was constructed through notions of gender and sexuality in a way that justified and enabled extreme forms of violence. Discourse analyses showed how notions of masculinity were militarized, based on the subordination of women, gay men, and men with disabilities. The nation-state and modern armies were analyzed as gendered institutions with highly gendered practices. It was studied how individual men and women were mobilized into ethnicized, violent conflict.

Feminist psychologists from different geographical locations have drawn on some of these perspectives. In the research field on aggression and violence, feminist psychologists contributed to the deconstruction of essentialist notions of gender, pointing to underlying dimensions of power. Their critique was applied to psychological theories of individual aggression as well as to essentialist accounts of soldiering, war, and racism within multiple disciplines (cf. Hunter, Flamenbaum, Sunday, & Genes and Gender Conference, 1991). This debate did not go into detail concerning the power relations of race and ethnicity.

A substantial bridge between the gender theoretical frameworks and psychological inquiry was provided by feminist psychologists studying identities of minority and majority groups. Critical to social psychological approaches, they introduced feminist analyses of "gender and nation" and the

concept of intersectionality to psychological debates (Bhavnani & Phoenix, 1994; Marshall 1999). Neither gender nor ethnicity should be used as separate, fixed variables in the psychological inquiry of ethnic identities, suggested Marshall (1999). Identities should rather be studied as processes in the context of shifting national and global constellations of power (Bhavnani & Phoenix, 1994). Research on minorities should, according to these arguments, connect individual agency with an analysis of the position of a studied group within a society.

Even though they provide insight into central topics of peace and conflict, these approaches have been drawn upon only by a few psychological studies on peace and conflict. For the Kashmir conflict, for example, it was shown how men's ways of joining militant groups were related to culturally available images of the male freedom fighter and to developing a group identity as victims (Sonpar, 2006). Other researchers traced how gender may become a site of enforcing national purity, for example by obliging a refugee woman in Congo to accept a last name that suggests ethnic homogeneity. Scandinavian studies used intersectional perspectives to analyze, for example, the position of children from minority communities in schools.

This thread of psychological scholarship might be a fruitful contribution to gender and conflict studies. While most gender study scholars focus on symbolic and structural aspects of gender, a future contribution of peace psychologists might be to analyze how individual identity and agency are formed in conflict and peacebuilding vis-à-vis dominant gendered and ethnicized structures and symbolisms.

The gender theoretical perspective has implications for peace psychology and psychology in general. It urges psychologists to reflect on the use of identity categories in psychological theorizing and research. From this perspective, it is crucial to study relations of power and inequality within the study of identity. It implies understanding identity not only as the result of a construction, but analyzing the processes of the construction of Otherness. Excluding these critical perspectives can promote the reconstruction and naturalization of categories of difference such as culture, ethnicity, and religion. These are the very categories used to construct irreconcilable polarizations needed for war.

SEE ALSO: Women and Peace Hypothesis.

REFERENCES

Bhavnani, K.-K., & Phoenix, A. (Eds.). (1994). *Shifting identities, shifting racisms: A feminism and psychology reader.* London, UK: Sage.
Breines, I., Connell, R., & Eide, I. (Eds.). (2000). *Male roles, masculinities and violence: A culture of peace perspective.* Paris, France: UNESCO.
Costin, A. (2006). The feminist approach. In H. Blumberg, A. P. Hare, & A. Costin (Eds.), *Peace psychology: A comprehensive introduction* (pp. 37–45). Cambridge, UK: Cambridge University Press.
Hunter, A. E., Flamenbaum, C. M., Sunday, S. R., & Genes and Gender Conference. (Eds.). (1991). *On peace, war, and gender: A challenge to genetic explanations.* New York, NY: Feminist Press at the City University of New York.
Marshall, H. (1999). Intersections of gender, "race" and nation. *Feminism and Psychology,* 9(4), 479–486.
Reimann, C. (2002). *"All you need is love." . . . and what about gender? Engendering Burton's human needs theory* (vol. 10). Bradford, UK: Department of Peace Studies, University of Bradford.
Sonpar, S. (2006). *Violent activism: A psychosocial study of ex-militants in Jammu and Kashmir.* New Delhi, India: AMAN Charitable Trust, Initiative for a Just and Compassionate Society.

ADDITIONAL RESOURCES

http://www.international-alert.org/gender/index.php (International Alert)
http://www.jmm.sagepub.com/ (*Men and Masculinities* journal)
http://www.peacenews.info/issues/2443/ (Peace News)

Genocide and Mass Killing: Origins and Prevention

ERVIN STAUB

Similar influences lead to genocide and mass killing, and mass killing can be a way station in the evolution of genocide. Early, genuine prevention requires a response to predictive conditions before it is clear what type of group violence will develop. The United Nations Genocide Convention defines genocide as "acts committed with intent to destroy in whole or in part, a national, ethnic, racial, or religious group." The genocide convention does not appropriately clarify what is the meaning of "in part," that is, when killing *some* members of a group is genocide and when it is not. The definition is also incomplete in not including the killing of political groups as genocide – which has been named politicide (Harff, 2003).

The definitions of genocide offered since the Convention are similar, but differ in some important details. In my definition, violence against a group is genocide when a government or some group acts to eliminate a whole group of people, whether by directly killing them or creating conditions that lead to their deaths or inability to reproduce (Staub, 2011). In contrast, mass killing is "killing (or in other ways destroying) members of a group without the intention to eliminate the whole group, or killing large numbers of people" without a focus on group membership (Staub, 1989, p. 8).

Essential questions in understanding the origins of extreme group violence include: What are the motivations of perpetrators, how do they evolve, how did inhibitions decline? What are the instigating conditions? What do characteristics of cultures and societies contribute? What is the psychology of perpetrators and passive bystanders? While many influences contribute to genocide and mass killing, an essential source of groups turning against other groups is the human proclivity to differentiate between "us" and "them" and the tendency to devalue them. If we understand origins, what might be the avenues to prevention? (See US AND THEM: MODERATING DICHOTOMOUS INGROUP/OUTGROUP THINKING.)

INSTIGATORS OF GENOCIDE AND MASS KILLING

The following are conditions in a society or in a group's relationship to another group that have great impact on people. They give rise to psychological reactions in individuals and whole groups, and actions and events in a society or social group that lead the group to turn against another group, often a subgroup of the society (Staub 1989, 2011; see also Hamburg, 2007).

Difficult Life Conditions

These include severe economic problems, great political conflicts within a society, or extensive, rapid social changes, and any combination thereof. They have intense psychological impact. They frustrate universal, basic psychological needs for security, positive identity, feelings of effectiveness and control, positive connection to people, and comprehension of reality. (See HUMAN NEEDS THEORY, CONFLICT, AND PEACE.)

Group Conflict

This takes two forms: (a) Conflict involving "vital" interests, such as need for territory as living space. Even though these conflicts have "objective" elements, such as the

territory both sides need, the psychological elements (devaluation of another, fear and distrust, unfulfilled basic needs) make the conflict especially difficult to resolve. (b) Conflict between a dominant and a subordinate group in a society. Frequently, demands by the subordinate group for greater rights or more participation in society start active violence between the groups that may end in genocide or mass killing.

Conflicts between groups also tend to frustrate basic needs – certainly the need for security, but also others. Dominant groups, faced by demands from a subordinate group, often protect not only their rights and privileges, but also their worldview (their comprehension of reality and of their own place in the world). Group conflicts and difficult life conditions often combine as instigators.

Self-Interest

At times, when a group and its members are devalued and powerless, a powerful group may engage in actions that advance its interests but directly or indirectly destroy that group. Taking territory from or developing their land has been one form of destruction of indigenous groups (Totten, Parsons, & Charny, 1997).

NEED FULFILLMENT IN DIFFICULT TIMES OR IN CASE OF CONFLICT

Cooperative efforts between subgroups of society addressing life problems, or groups resolving conflict through negotiation and mutual concessions, could fulfill psychological and (over time) material needs. This constructive mode of need fulfillment often does not happen. Instead, psychological and social "processes" arise that often become the starting point for violence. Individuals turn to some group for security, identity, connection, and feelings of effectiveness. They elevate this group by devaluing others.

The group scapegoats another group for life problems or blames the other group for their conflict. People turn to ideologies that offer a vision of a better life (nationalism, communism, Nazism, Hutu power in Rwanda), but also identify enemies who must be "dealt with" (which often means in the end that they must be destroyed) in order to fulfill the ideology. (See IDEOLOGY.)

THE EVOLUTION OF DESTRUCTIVENESS

As a group turns against a scapegoat or ideological enemy, as it blames another group for conflict, often it begins to take actions that harm the other group and its members. Individuals and whole groups "learn by doing." As they harm others, perpetrators, bystanders, and the society begin to change. They engage in just-world thinking; based on the belief that the world is a just place, they see those who suffer as deserving their suffering. They adapt or habituate to each new level of violence. They justify their actions by increasing devaluation of victims, and progressively exclude them from the moral realm, the realm of people to whom moral values and standards apply. They may engage in a reversal of morality: killing "these people" becomes the right thing to do. They may also replace moral values that protect other people's welfare with other values, such as obedience to authority or loyalty to the group. Individuals change, the norms of social behavior change, new institutions are created to serve violence (e.g., paramilitary groups). (See MORAL EXCLUSION; MORAL DISENGAGEMENT.)

CULTURAL CHARACTERISTICS THAT CONTRIBUTE TO VIOLENCE

Certain characteristics of a culture make it more likely that in difficult times or in the face of group conflict the psychological reactions and social processes described above take place.

One of them is cultural devaluation, a history of devaluation of a subgroup of society. Certain forms of it, like seeing the other as lazy or less intelligent, are not as dangerous as other forms, like seeing the other as manipulative, morally bad, or dangerous, an enemy that intends to harm one's own group. When another group is greatly devalued, but still does relatively well in society – its members have good jobs, are fairly well off, and so on – the potential for them to be victimized is particularly great. This was the case with the Jews in Germany, the Armenians in Turkey, and the Tutsis in Rwanda. An ideology of antagonism is another cultural characteristic: groups develop intense, mutual hostility, seeing the other as their enemy, and themselves as the enemy of the other. Being an enemy of the other can become a part of group identity.

Overly strong respect for authority is another cultural contributor to violence. Accustomed to being led, in difficult times people are more likely to turn to leaders and ideological groups. They are unlikely to oppose leaders who move the group toward violence. They are also more likely to follow direct orders to engage in violence. Related to this is a monolithic (versus pluralistic) culture. The less varied are the values in a society, the less freedom to express them, the less likely that people will oppose the evolution of hostility and violence. These tendencies are intensified in an authoritarian political system. When members of all groups in a society have the right to express themselves and participate, an evolution towards genocide becomes less likely. Democracies, especially mature ones that have well-developed civic institutions, are unlikely to engage in genocide. (See OBEDIENCE.)

Unhealed wounds of a group due to past victimization or suffering can also contribute to group violence. When a group has been victimized in the past, its members will feel diminished and vulnerable. They will see the world as a dangerous place. In the face of new threat or conflict they will be inclined to believe that they need to protect themselves. They may become perpetrators as they engage in unnecessary violent self-defense. A history of violence in a society as a means of resolving conflict also makes new violence more likely (Harff, 2003). (See VICTIMHOOD, COLLECTIVE.)

THE ROLE OF BYSTANDERS

Passivity by bystanders greatly encourages perpetrators. It helps them believe that what they are doing is right. Unfortunately, bystanders are often passive, continuing with business as usual, which represents a form of complicity. Sometimes they support and help perpetrators. Internal bystanders (members of the population) often show no opposition to increasing hostility and participate in discrimination against a victim group. As a result, just like perpetrators, they change. It is difficult to oppose one's group, especially in difficult times, and as members of the same society as the perpetrators, bystanders have also learned to devalue the victim group. To reduce their empathic distress and feelings of guilt, they tend to distance themselves from victims. As they change, at least some bystanders become perpetrators (Lifton, 1986).

External bystanders, outside groups and other nations, also usually remain passive, continue with business as usual, or even support perpetrators. Nations historically have not seen themselves as moral agents and instead used national interest, defined as wealth, power, and influence, as their guiding value. Sometimes historical ties to a country and a particular group in it lead nations to support the perpetrator group.

THE ROLE OF LEADERS

To an important extent, it is the inclinations of populations, created by the conditions in society and culture, that create the possibility and likelihood of mass killing or genocide. To some degree, people select leaders who respond to their inclinations and fulfill their needs at the time. Still, leaders and the elite of a society have an important role in shaping and influencing events. They can attempt to deal with problems in a society and conflicts between groups by peaceful means. Or they can scapegoat and offer destructive ideologies. They can use propaganda to intensify devaluation and instigate violence against a group. They can create institutions, such as propaganda tools (media), and state offices that serve persecution and paramilitary groups that perpetrate violence. Often, leaders who do this are said to have as their motives gaining support and enhancing their power. But leaders and elites are also members of their society, as impacted by life conditions, group conflict, and culture as are members of their group.

WHAT MIGHT BE DONE TO REDUCE MASS KILLING AND GENOCIDE?

Halting Persecution and Violence

There are increasing numbers of United Nations and international conventions which function as international laws prohibiting mass violence. However, there are few effective institutions to enforce them, and even fewer to engage in early, effective prevention. The International Criminal Court, not yet ratified by the United States in 2011, can at least in principle punish perpetrators.

To create an effective mechanism of prevention requires a change in values, a long-term goal to which each person can contribute. Early warning is important, but repeatedly when information about impending violence is available, as in the case of Rwanda, the international community has not responded. Institutions are needed, both within the UN and national governments, that can activate actions by the community of nations.

Late prevention includes diplomatic efforts to communicate disapproval of violence and of consequences if violence continues, and offers of mediation and incentives to halt violence. These actions must be taken with awareness of the history of groups, their woundedness when that exists, and their culture. They must be accompanied or followed, as needed, by withholding aid, sanctions, boycotts – especially designed to affect leaders – and the use of force, if necessary.

Prevention and Reconciliation

Helping groups overcome devaluation and develop more positive attitudes toward each other is an important aspect of prevention. One avenue for this is humanizing the other through positive words (by leaders, in the media, in literature, etc.) and positive actions. Another is significant, positive contact, especially through shared effort for joint goals. Helping former victims heal is also important for prevention. Understanding the influences that lead to mass violence, and their impact on people, can contribute to healing and generate active bystandership (Staub, Pearlman, Gubin, & Hagengimana, 2005). (See BYSTANDER INTERVENTION.)

While reconciliation usually refers to promoting mutual acceptance after great violence, it is also a means of prevention. Assumptions of responsibility and expressions of regret by perpetrators (or mutually, when violence was two-sided) contribute to reconciliation. Establishing the truth about past actions, and the punishment of especially responsible perpetrators (but not revenge on a whole group), contribute to

reconciliation. (See TRANSITIONAL JUSTICE SYSTEMS, PSYCHOLOGY AND.)

Socialization of children at home and in school can make participation in violence and passive bystandership less likely. Such socialization helps children fulfill basic needs, and develops inclusive caring that expands beyond the boundaries of the group, ideally to all human beings. It develops critical consciousness and critical loyalty so that people will use their judgment and be less likely to follow destructive leaders. (See SOCIALIZATION.)

Equitable economic development of a country, which reduces inequality and the experience of injustice, makes group conflict less likely. Developing democratic institutions and pluralism makes resistance to influences leading to violence more likely.

SEE ALSO: Bystander Intervention; Human Needs Theory, Conflict, and Peace; Ideology; Moral Disengagement; Moral Exclusion; Obedience; Socialization; Transitional Justice Systems, Psychology and; Us and Them: Moderating Dichotomous Ingroup/Outgroup Thinking; Victimhood, Collective.

REFERENCES

Hamburg, D. (2007). *Preventing genocide: Practical steps toward early detection and effective action*. Boulder, CO: Paradigm Publishers.
Harff, B. (2003). No lessons learned from the Holocaust? Assessing risks of genocide and political mass murder since 1955. *American Political Science Review*, 97(1), 57–73.
Lifton, R. J. (1986). *The Nazi doctors: Medical killing and the psychology of genocide*. New York, NY: Basic Books.
Staub, E. (1989). *The roots of evil: The origins of genocide and other group violence*. New York, NY: Cambridge University Press.
Staub, E. (2011). *Overcoming evil: Genocide, violent conflict and terrorism*. New York, NY: Oxford University Press.
Staub, E., Pearlman, L. A., Gubin, A., & Hagengimana, A. (2005). Healing,

reconciliation, forgiving and the prevention of violence after genocide or mass killing: An intervention and its experimental evaluation in Rwanda. *Journal of Social and Clinical Psychology, 24*(3), 297–334.

Totten, S., Parsons, W. S., & Charny, I. W. (Eds.). (1997). *Century of genocide: Eyewitness accounts and critical views.* New York, NY: Garland.

Girls in Armed Groups

SUSAN MCKAY

Throughout the world, girls – internationally defined as females up to 18 years of age – participate in armed opposition groups. Their presence in these groups, usually covert, has become widely recognized during the past decade and investigated by scholars and nongovernmental groups such as Save the Children, World Vision, and ChildFund (Denov, 2008, 2010; McKay 2005, 2006; McKay & Mazurana, 2004; Wessells, 2006). Although we have had reports since 1990 of girls' participation in armed forces (government militaries) and armed opposition groups in more than 55 countries (McKay & Mazurana, 2004), they remain overlooked. Because so many armed opposition groups in sub-Saharan African conflicts depend upon girls to build and maintain the infrastructure of military groups through their productive and reproductive work, this discussion focuses upon this geographic region. However, throughout the world, girls carry out similar support functions.

Interest has grown recently in accounting more accurately for girls' presence in armed groups. Although difficult to estimate, in many armed opposition groups – particularly in Africa – girls are thought to constitute 10–30% of child soldiers. Higher percentages have been suggested in some armed conflicts and, in others, girls are thought not to be present. Solid data are lacking, however, to support these "guesstimates," and citing high percentages may be inaccurately used as "hype" to draw greater attention to their plight. A significant reason that more precise numbers are not available is because most do not go through formal disarmament, demobilization, and reintegration programs (DDR), whereas large numbers of boys do. Instead, girls typically find their own way back to their communities or to that of friends or other family members. Because their presence in armed groups is denied or greatly underestimated, and because DDR processes are designed primarily to remove boys and men with guns from militarized groups, girls avoid these programs. They may also be unaware that DDR exists or think they are not eligible – especially if they don't have a gun. Consequently, they experience gender discrimination because they do not receive the benefits that males do. (See CHILD SOLDIERS; CHILD SOLDIERS AND MENTAL HEALTH.)

This lack of recognition and marginalization about the essential roles that girls and older females carry out within these groups is evidence of gender discrimination and disregard for girls' and women's human rights. Fortunately, this neglect is now changing because advocacy groups and the United Nations Security Council have called attention to the issues through UN Resolution 1325 (adopted October 31, 2000) and UN Resolution 1820 (2008), which demand greater attention to the human rights of girls and women who are affected by violence and armed conflict (United Nations, 2002; Mazurana & Carlson, 2006).

Girls become members of armed opposition groups in diverse ways. In many sub-Saharan African wars, common entry modes are abduction from their homes, schools, and marketplaces and even as they are walking along roads. Girls may join of their own volition – perhaps escaping abusive conditions at home or because they are seeking improved access to food and security. They also may join with family members and friends and/or be enticed by political promises during wars of liberation. Some girls are born into armed groups whereas others are orphans or street children who are recruited. They also may be press-ganged in schools or lured by promises of scholarships or other benefits.

Girls' ages vary upon entry, with some as young as 5 or 6 years of age. Young girls fetch water, help with childcare, do errands, and act as porters. Prepubescent and pubescent girls provide increasingly significant contributions to the work of the armed group. They farm and cook, and serve as armed combatants and spies. Concerning the latter roles, girls are less likely than boys to raise suspicion when they mingle in marketplaces and other village meeting places where they may obtain valuable information. Another role is providing first aid and healthcare.

When they are pubescent or before, many become "bush wives" of commanders. Girls who do not have a bush husband who can provide protection may be repeatedly used for sexual purposes by many men. Thus, being a bush wife conveys some advantages, although abuse and rape are characteristic of these liaisons. Whereas rape, sexual violence, and forced "marriage" and "motherhood" are common in sub-Saharan Africa, other armed groups (e.g., the Liberation Tigers of Tamil Eelam in Sri Lanka) eschew these practices.

Their initiation upon entry into armed groups typically involves witnessing and being forced to participate in atrocities. In African civil wars, these are often directed at civilians – including family members and friends. When girls remain with an armed group for an extensive time, military life in the armed group may come to seem normal. The transition, however, is brutal, as they are torn from families, face incredibly harsh conditions, and suffer profound physical and psychological effects such as exhaustion, malnutrition, headaches (from

beatings), scabies and other skin disorders, chest pain, genital and other injuries from sexual violence, and sexually transmitted diseases.

Due to misogyny and sexism, girls face distinct gender-specific abuses and remain subservient to boys and men, although some girls and women who become commanders' "wives" gain a modicum of power over others. Most girls are raped immediately and repeatedly, although small girls may be terrorized in other ways. Besides rape, girls are subjected to continual sexual violence, including gang rape and having their genitals, breasts, or other body parts mutilated. Death may be the result. Given this brutal treatment, transmission of sexual infections is common, and many girls become pregnant and give birth in the bush. Lack of medical care means that complications during pregnancy and childbirth are seldom treated. Many girls and their infants are thought to die, although gathering accurate data about incidence and prevalence has not been possible, and this information is derived from testimonials from girls themselves (McKay & Mazurana, 2004; Denov, 2008, 2010).

Girls' lives within armed groups becomes progressively militarized. They typically undergo military training, although they may only learn how to cock and load guns. With greater age and experience, girls may become intermittent and regular fighters, with some attaining the rank of commander. They risk their lives in combat activities, and some have reported their own participation in atrocities (McKay, 2005). They may attempt to escape from the armed group, but they do so at their peril – if found, they are often killed.

Regardless of whether they escape or the armed conflict ends, returning and reintegrating into normal life is difficult. Most girls go straight home (if their homes still exist) – called self- or spontaneous reintegration – and they bypass formal programs.

Therefore, they do not receive focused organizational assistance. This is worsened by a strategy of secrecy whereby they slip back and don't want anyone to know what happened to them. Thus if NGOs or other groups institute programs in the community, they may avoid participation. When returning to their own families doesn't work out, they may live with families of friends or with other former girl soldiers. This has been especially noted among some girl mothers who find that the best arrangement is to share a household with others in the same situation so that they share childcare and income. Some bush wives stay with their "husbands" as another alternative. Bush husbands are sometimes accepted as marriage partners by the families of returning girls. More often, both the girls and their families do not want the relationship to continue.

Girls who remain in an armed group for a long time and later escape or are let go because the conflict ends are likely to be regarded with suspicion and fear when they return to their communities. Although initially most will be welcomed back by their families, community members may be less welcoming – especially if they bring with them children born of bush marriages. These girls may be taunted with names such as "rebel wife" and their children similarly labeled and stigmatized. In addition to stigma, girls may face threats, physical abuse in their homes, and sexual violence by boys and men in the community. Whereas boys often receive some training and financial support from DDR programs, girls are faced with few options in securing livelihoods. Without adequate resources to feed and care for themselves and their children, they strain family reserves, since family members are usually struggling with poverty and the effects of armed conflict. Consequently, many girls engage in sex work to survive – often with "boyfriends" with whom they exchange sex for food and small amounts of money.

After months or years in armed groups, girls may find it difficult to resume traditional gender roles valued by the community. Often, they engage in behaviors that cause them difficulty in being accepted. They may be aggressive, quarrelsome, and verbally abusive and also lie, steal, and use drugs. Psychologically, girls feel worry, nervousness, and anxiety and are isolated, with no hope for a more positive future (McKay & Mazurana, 2004). Interestingly, although intuitively it might seem that girls would fare better when they are no longer in an armed group, this is not necessarily true. As commanders' wives, some girls enjoyed privileged status, and the looting of goods, food, and medicine gave them better access to resources within an armed group than when they return. Also, some of these girls enjoyed a sense of power and increased agency because of their roles in the armed group.

When they return, shame is a particularly significant emotion because of experiences such as rape, forced motherhood, participating in combat, and committing atrocities, all of which violate gender and community norms. When they have identifiable tattoos or scars they may feel shame because they have been "branded" as part of the armed group (McKay & Mazurana, 2004). "Undoing shame" and reintegrating so they become accepted and contributing members of the community are facilitated when girls can contribute to household resources. Support programs can offer psychosocial support in dealing with difficult experiences via such expressive modalities as drama, music, and art that are culturally appropriate and bring together girls with the community. For example, performing a drama can convey to the community their experiences and enable dialogue about their present situations. Also, in some cultures, rituals (sometimes gender specific) may be significant in reconnecting the child to the community, and facilitating social reintegration. These rituals can support healing for girls and also their communities (McKay & Mazurana, 2004).

Because most girls have not gone through DDR and received skills training or further education, they have few livelihood options unless NGOs or grassroots groups sponsor programs to improve their opportunities. If they are fortunate enough to enroll in training, markets for goods they produce (e.g., soap and tailoring) are often limited. Also, the training may be too short for them to achieve marketable skills. Some girls return to school; however, those who were in an armed group for a long time may be far behind their age peers and uncomfortable in school with younger children. Also, if they have children, they may not have childcare, so they are unable to attend school. Some training programs have accelerated school programs to make it easier for girls to participate in school with childcare provided.

The situation of girls who return from armed groups is difficult – their girlhoods have been stolen, and they have suffered human rights violations in the extreme. Yet, with psychosocial support from families and community members, healthcare for themselves and their children, and livelihood opportunities, most are able to move forward with their lives, care for their children, and become respected members of their community. There is a tendency on the part of the international community to focus upon the trauma experienced by these girls (and all child soldiers), but as a group they show great resilience if given support that enables them to reintegrate. (See CHILDREN AND RESILIENCE.)

SEE ALSO: Child Soldiers; Child Soldiers and Mental Health; Children and Resilience.

REFERENCES

Denov, M. (2008). Girl soldiers and human rights: Lessons from Angola, Mozambique, Sierra Leone, and northern Uganda. *International Journal of Human Rights*, 12(5), 813–836.

Denov, M. (2010). *Child soldiers: Sierra Leone's Revolutionary United Front*. Cambridge, UK: Cambridge University Press.

McKay, S. (2005). Girls as "weapons of terror." In C. Ness (Ed.), Special issue on gender and terrorism. *Studies in Conflict and Terrorism*, 28(5), 385–397.

McKay, S. (2006). The inversion of girlhood: Girl combatants during and after armed conflict. In N. Boothby, M. Wessells, & A. Strang (Eds.), *A world turned upside down: The social ecologies of children in armed conflict* (pp. 89–109). Bloomfield, CT: Kumarian Press.

McKay, S., & Mazurana, D. (2004). *Where are the girls? Girls in fighting forces in northern Uganda, Sierra Leone and Mozambique: Their lives during and after war*. Montreal, Canada: Rights and Democracy.

Mazurana, D., & Carlson, C. (2006, September). *The girl child and armed conflict: Recognizing and addressing grave violations of girls' human rights*. United Nations Division for the Advancement of Women (DAW) Expert Group Meeting on the Elimination of all Forms of Discrimination and Violence Against the Girl Child. Florence, Italy.

United Nations. (2002). *Women, peace and security: Study submitted by the Secretary-General pursuant to Security Council resolution 1325 (2000)*. New York, NY: United Nations.

Wessells, M. (2006). *Child soldiers: From violence to protection*. Cambridge, MA: Harvard University Press.

ADDITIONAL RESOURCES

http://www.child-soldiers.org/home
http://www.un.org/children/conflict/_documents/parisprinciples/ParisPrinciples_EN.pdf
http://www.un.org/children/conflict/english/index.html

http://www.uwyo.edu/girlmothersparsupport/
    docs/PAR%20Final%20Report%20June%20
    30%202010%20doc.pdf

Globalization and Conflict

MARC PILISUK AND GIANINA PELLEGRINI

Globalization refers to a complex set of cultural, economic, political, and environmental changes. They reflect a transfer from diverse, separate, and local options to standardized, interconnected, centralized, and global ones. At the onset of the twenty-first century globalization is perhaps the most potent force affecting human behavior and experience. Many symbols are recognized globally, goods and information cross borders instantaneously, and we have exciting opportunities to know about others. Globalization affects what we wear, what we eat, who shall have enough to eat, the safety of our air and water, where we reside, our options for employment, the availability of human services, the shaping of values by which we assign meaning to life, how we shape and are shaped by technologies, the potential for financial stability and equity in the world, the possibilities for survival of an endangered planet, and the arena in which individuals and communities retain a measure of control over their lives. Globalization also affects the physical composition of the planet and the selection of which forms of life are to survive and which to be eliminated. Globalization includes vast changes in the power to make economic decisions at every level. It is the economic side of globalization that is strongly linked to conflict and which assumes relevance to each individual's own work, home and community life, and political participation. The purpose here is to examine the pathways that constitute the increased global interconnectedness, the forces that are creating and using these pathways, and the consequences to quality of life and distribution of wealth and of power. (See MILITARISM AND WHO BENEFITS.)

From their onset, humans lived in small bands who hunted or foraged within small environmental locales. Value placed upon others in their band and upon their local ecology was essential to survival. About 5,000 years ago, our species began to move away from community based forms of organization and we began to organize ourselves by a dominator hierarchy. (See HUMILIATION AND DIGNITY.) It was the beginning of a move toward larger collectivities and eventually the move to empire. Even with the evolution of nation-states and well into the era of the industrial revolution most people lived in small communities relating to their peers and to their habitat in a direct and personal way. But the dominator hierarchy spread at all levels of society, from the relationships among nations to relationships within families, relationships between genders and between races (Korten, 2009). At the global corporate level, multinational corporations express Western masculine values of domination, power, and control and devalue feminine perspectives that tend to be holistic, collaborative, spiritual, and friendlier to the environment (Seager, 1993).

Where rulers once were kings and emperors, they are now corporate CEOs and hedge fund managers. The system has evolved. Actual rule of the economy has been by Wall Street institutions through the system of money, which translates into a system of power. Some indigenous communities and many nations have employed democratizing processes, but globalization has provided a fertile context for preserving the dominator hierarchy. Democracy, media, and elections, which could require accountability, have evolved into tools by which this powerful elite can manage a consensus and thereby not need to rely entirely upon police force to justify their special privilege (Pilisuk, 2008).

The way we are supposed to think about the economy is that a rising stock market indicates economic growth or generation of resources for productive activity. However, most of the Wall Street funding is in speculation. At least 90% of the trading that goes on in Wall Street has nothing to do with assisting real businesses (Prins, 2009). Financiers are just gambling by exchanging pieces of paper in expectation of either a bubble or a fall. This has absolutely nothing to do with real wealth. When we are told that the economy is expanding, it actually means that rich people are getting richer or getting richer faster than the rest of us.

Money managers are now running the global economic system. With funds larger than the budgets of many governments they have the ability to direct development, or to undermine it, in countries desperate for credit. Any understanding of how a corporate elite dominates global development owes much to the personal history of John Perkins (2006). His clandestine position, first with the National Security Agency and then transferred to a private company, was predicated upon an ability to make inflated economic forecasts and sell large loans to heads of state in undeveloped countries. The loans were always for the development of infrastructure, oil drilling and pipelines, dams, electric power grids, and building complexes. The contracts would be awarded to giant corporation giants like Bechtel or Halliburton. The inducements to foreign leaders included military and police aid, lucrative financial benefits, recognition in US diplomatic circles, and even the procurement of personal mistresses (Perkins, 2006). The contracts would make a small group within the accepting country very wealthy. They would make the particular nation a client state, dependent upon further loans and adjustments to repay the debts and unable, therefore, to use the country's resources for sustainable productivity for its farmers, education and healthcare for its children, and protections for its environment.

Some populist leaders found the terms unacceptable. Many of those who refused the loan terms were removed in coups, assassinations, or plane or helicopter "accidents." If that did not produce a compliant government, the next steps were to foment a violent revolt and finally to send in the bombs and the marines. Variations of this happened in the Dominican Republic, Zaire, Iran, Guatemala, Chile, and Panama. Now in the global empire, military conflicts have become asymmetric, pitting groups of resisters adept at car bombing or kidnapping and able to melt back into the villages of their families, against highly trained, high-tech military occupiers with massive firepower often sent as an armed drone from a computer continents away (Pilisuk, 2008).

The major ongoing interventions, occurring without the fanfare of war, have been economic. The manipulation of local economies has been part of a worldwide effort to impose what has been labeled the Washington Consensus. This has been forced on developing countries via procedures of the US government, the World Bank, the International Monetary Fund, and the World Trade Organization. The basic tenets are reforms calling for economic deregulation, privatization, encouragement of foreign investment, unrestricted movement of capital, liberalization of trade policies, and reduction in public expenditures. This program of "neoliberalism" has been aggressively pushed as primary US foreign policy. The strategy is focused upon pressuring developing countries that are dependent on aid from major international lending agencies and the United States to implement structural adjustment programs that prescribe the required changes that a specific country must make in order to be considered credit worthy. Meanwhile, the arable land and the oil and mineral reserves are usurped from local communities (Korten, 2009). Patents on their seeds remove this natural resource from their local economies and water rights are ceded to corporate investors. Some residents are forced to migrate, others are lured by false promises into indentured labor or trafficked, and 27 million are slaves (Bales, 2005).

Increasingly, US strategy has been to support governments subservient to US corporate interests and to provide the military aid that keeps them in power. Such governments are associated with financial indebtedness and military control over their dissenters. US officials have come to regard the facade of a highly fortified Green zone, with lush accommodations for visiting officials, as the US ally, rather than the people of the country. This makes sense if one recalls that it is an elite network of diplomatic, financial, and military ties that determines the paths of information and influence (Pilisuk, 2008).

Globalization fuels a conflict for jobs. One of the great economic trends of the past 50 years has been the movement of the industrial heartland of America from the Midwest to China, to India, and to the developing world. Much of the production of the West is now in countries where the labor standard under which products are made is far inferior to where it had been made in Western Europe or in the United States. Factory sweatshops and dangerous mining and corporate farming reduce people to destitution. Labor organizers in every continent are harassed and in fact killed while profits, drained from local communities by transnational corporations, go to enlarge remote financial empires.

The top officials and board members of international corporations reap the benefits of environmental degradation. With environments destroyed, no new frontiers to exploit, and middle-class consumers lacking credit to fulfill heavily marketed needs, the global elite have created fictitious transactions as a justification for collecting fees from the system. They have been raiding and repackaging the equity of financial investments that were intended to be a cushion against risk (Prins, 2009).

Many of their derivatives were ultimately sold off to local municipal trust funds, to pension funds, or university endowments. The total financial claims built up through the bubble greatly exceed the real wealth of the planet, which means that they are fictitious and can never be realized. Money in the global economy has been changed from a medium of value to a storehouse of expectations. It is drained from the environment and from communities and it accumulates at the top.

The names of the beneficiaries are known and reports of their annual salaries, sign-on bonuses, and severance pay are available but not publicized. The excessive wealth of a small few is astounding: "793 billionaires possess $2.6 trillion dollars, which according to the Committee for the Cancellation of Third World Debt (CADTM) is the sum equal to 'the entirety of developing countries' foreign debt" (Kempf, 2008, p. 47). What do the molders of the global economy do with this money?

A relatively small part of the concentrated wealth goes into lavish consumption on expensive clothing, multiple homes, vacations, art collections, and "yacht wars" to establish prestige. The hyper-rich live in secluded mansions, gated communities, and restricted penthouses apart from the common space shared by others (Kempf, 2008). But much wealth is invested into campaign contributions, consolidation of media, lobbying with well-paid government and military retirees, and funding think tanks and endowed programs with experts who share their views. Some goes to provide corporate messages into media news and some to underwriting and public image advertising (Pilisuk, 2008).

The answer to exploitative economic globalization is to dismantle and decentralize corporate entities that have grown too large to fail. In finance this may not require the government to run a nationalized banking system, but it will need a transition toward community banks, restoring the local financial institutions where people could deposit their savings, and the banks could make loans to people who were buying a house or running a business. International standards upholding human dignity can permit some shifts to local commerce. The data show that people who shop in a farmers' market have ten times the number of conversations of people who shop in a supermarket. You meet people and get acquainted with the farmer who grows your produce. This is all about building relationships. We have monetized the economy and a part of that process is monetizing relationships (Korten, 2009). This diminishes our humanity. When everything has a price then nothing, neither the purity of water nor the sound of songbirds, is sacred.

In a world that has become so intricately interconnected it is no longer satisfactory to solve one problem at a time without regard for the impact of the solution on other people and places. So this account of globalization ends with questions worth further study. How is our collective history constructed so that we have come to see exploitation and destruction of people and planet as natural costs of an inevitable path to progress? Who has sanctioned the arrogance of detachment from nature and permitted excluding the indigenous wisdom of cultures that knew better? How have values of individualism and freedom been molded and tapped to permit a construction of reality in which the consequences of corporate greed are seen as isolated problems and not cause for a change in power?

SEE ALSO: Humiliation and Dignity; Militarism and Who Benefits.

REFERENCES

Bales, K. (2005). *Understanding global slavery: A reader*. Berkeley, CA: University of California Press.
Kempf, H. (2008). *How the rich are destroying the earth*. White River Jct., VT: Chelsea Green.
Korten, D. C. (2009). *Agenda for a new economy: From phantom wealth to real wealth*. San Francisco, CA: Berrett-Koehler.
Perkins, J. (2006). *Confessions of an economic hitman*. New York, NY: Plume.
Pilisuk, M. (2008). *Who benefits from global violence and war: Uncovering a destructive system* (with J. A. Rountree). Westport, CT: Greenwood/Praeger.
Prins, N. (2009). *It takes a pillage: Behind the bailouts, bonuses, and backroom deals from Washington to Wall Street*. Hoboken, NJ: John Wiley & Sons, Inc.
Seager, J. (1993). *Earth follies: Coming to feminist terms with the global environmental crisis*. New York, NY: Routledge.

ADDITIONAL RESOURCES

http://www.davidkorten.org and its companion website http://thegreatturning.net
http://www.ifg.org (International Forum on Globalization)
http://www.stopcorporateabuse.org/ (Corporate Accountability International)

Grounded Theory

ANNA MADILL

Grounded theory methodology evolved during Barney Glaser and Anselm Strauss's (1965) seminal study on the awareness of dying. Grounded theory represented a radical, qualitative alternative to the quantitative sociology of the time and sought to provide a way of capturing lived experience. It was also developed as a method for bridging the gap between theory and empirical research in the social sciences. Glaser and Strauss (1967) outline the *constant comparative method* as a procedure for generating theory from qualitative data (texts such as observations, interviews, and documents) in terms of four iterative stages. (See QUALITATIVE METHODS AND CODING.)

First, the data are inspected for differences and similarities between groups and cases, incident to incident. Categories are generated from this comparison that capture patterns in the data at an abstract level – for example, nurses' perception of the *social loss* entailed by the death of a patient. Properties and dimensions of categories are also identified which elaborate theoretically important aspects of a category and its range – for example, the *degree* of social loss as estimated by the nurses' perception of the patient's *age, occupational worth*, and *education*. Notes about the development of categories, their properties, and dimensions should be documented during analysis in the form of memos. As comparative analysis continues, new categories and properties emerge while those already identified are substantiated or amended. The researcher may start data collection anywhere relevant to the topic of interest. However, as categories are developed, selection of further material is conducted on the basis of theoretical sampling guided by the requirements of the developing theory. Hence, additional material is gathered which potentially offers interesting contrasts to the earlier data and fills gaps in the analysis.

The constant comparison of material generates categories but also suggests hypotheses about the relationships between categories which may be verified through the analysis of further data. Hence, stage two involves the integration of categories into a model. This is guided by the identification of a core theme representing the emerging theory in its most abstract form.

Stage three, delimiting the theory, is the point at which the researcher begins to wind down data collection and analysis. This occurs when theoretical saturation is reached: that is, when further data brings little elaboration of the theory, and the researcher can identify and focus on a few high-level concepts of greatest relevance. Finally, in stage four, the researcher writes up the theory drawing from the coded data and collating the memos on each relevant category. The theory should be systematic and "couched in a form that others going into the same field could use" (Glaser & Strauss, 1967, p. 113).

Strauss and Juliet Corbin (1990, 1998) offer a revised and elaborated exposition of grounded theory, specifying three major stages through which the researcher will cycle: open coding, axial coding, and selective coding.

Open coding entails close scrutiny of the data for recurring themes, ideas, or phenomena which can be clustered together at a more abstract level to form categories. This is conducted through a constant comparative analysis of the data which, during an early stage, proceeds on a detailed line-by-line basis and may develop to incident-to-incident and category-to-category comparisons. The properties, or characteristics, of each category are identified, as are the dimensions along which properties range.

Axial coding is the process in which the researcher uncovers relationships between categories through which they are linked at a conceptual level. These relationships may be explicit or, more likely, implicit in the data and require a level of inference to determine. To aid this process, Strauss and Corbin provide two organizing schemes which can be used in tandem as guides: the paradigm model and the conditional/consequential matrix. Although aspects of these schemes are mentioned by Glaser and Strauss (1967), Strauss and Corbin present a highly developed and systematized account of these features of the method.

The paradigm model consists of four interlinking components: phenomenon, conditions, action/interaction strategies, and consequences. Some of the categories developed in open coding will be central to the developing theory: phenomena. Categories standing for important phenomena can be identified as they are ideas, events, or happenings which require management by participants. Other categories identified during open coding will be subcategories of a phenomenon as they can be linked to it within a specific framework such as that offered by the paradigm model as follows. Conditions are events or situations that impact on phenomena. They can be divided into causal (leading to the occurrence of a phenomenon), intervening (mitigating the impact of causal conditions), or contextual (circumstances requiring a response). Action/interaction strategies are the tactics by which a phenomenon is managed. Strategies can be routine (e.g., ward protocols) or strategic (e.g., when a problem requires a purposeful solution). Consequences represent the range of outcomes in response to action/interaction strategies, or to the lack of them.

Strauss and Corbin (1990, p. 110) suggest that about five or six categories are developed by way of the paradigm model in a typical analysis. Not all subcategories of the paradigm are necessarily identified in initial open coding, and completing the paradigm may indicate gaps in the analysis which may be filled through reanalysis of material or theoretical sampling of further data.

The second scheme which can be used in combination with the paradigm model to guide the conceptual integration of categories during axial coding is the conditional/consequential matrix. The matrix draws the researcher's attention to the different types of context impinging on, and impacted by, the topic of investigation. Contexts range from the micro (e.g., the individual or immediate family) to the macro (e.g., the national or global).

The third stage in a grounded theory analysis as outlined by Strauss and Corbin is selective coding during which the evolving theory is refined. Selective coding involves deciding upon, and committing to, a central organizing concept or core category. Further strategic data collection can also be conducted where the initial material failed to provide sufficient detail about aspects of the developing theory. This can be done on the basis of discriminate sampling where participants are selected and/or data eliciting methods, such as interview questions, amended with the purpose of focusing on the phenomena of particular interest. A further technique is to revisit original data.

A final aspect of Strauss and Corbin's approach is that throughout the stages of open, axial, and selective coding the researcher should be writing memos. These are notes on ideas raised by the analysis and focus on the conceptual, rather than descriptive, level. The content of memos depends on the phase of analysis. For example, during open coding, codes notes might document ideas around potential category labels and the possible category properties and dimensions. Theoretical notes written in the axial coding stage would likely contain observations on potential links between categories and comments on further theoretical sampling required to check these links. Sorting is the final step, where memos are organized in a way that shows how categories related to the core category. Hence, memos provide an audit trail through the analysis and form the basis for reintegrating the fractured data at a conceptual yet grounded level.

Although Glaser (1978) published his procedural elaboration of grounded theory before Strauss and Corbin (1990, 1998), his writings have had less impact, at least according to the number of citations in the literature, and "[t]he appeal of the Strauss and Corbin version probably comes from its promise of simplicity, procedural structure and verifiability" (Rennie, 1998, p. 115).

However, Glaser's (1978) elaboration of method contains some interesting differences in emphasis to Strauss and Corbin.

For Glaser, the initial open coding of material produces substantive codes which, he emphasizes, must fit, work, and be relevant. Fit requires that codes describe important aspects of the data at the conceptual level without artificially forcing material into a preconceived pattern. Codes work if, when integrated into a theory, they explain and predict phenomena central to that theory. Finally, codes are relevant if they allow core problems and processes to emerge. Codes are modified through the analysis of subsequent data collected through theoretical sampling in order to hone their fit, work, and relevance.

Throughout this process Glaser stresses the use of memos and, although Strauss and Corbin incorporate this into their procedure, memos appear central to Glaser's approach. Memoing requires that the researcher notes systematically his/her ideas about the codes as they develop in order to articulate and speculate on their interrelationships whilst the researcher is immersed in the data. Memos help the researcher discover the core category around which the theory is emerging. This then forms the basis of further selective theoretical sampling, selective coding, and memoing.

Selective coding involves theory integration as the researcher begins to focus coding on material relevant to the core category. In all, Glaser (1978, p. 71) recommends that 10–15 codes are sufficient for a substantive theory. To aid theory integration, Glaser identifies 18 families of theoretical codes (not an exhaustive list), the first of which is the paradigm model favored by Strauss and Corbin. Theoretical codes are at a higher level of abstraction than substantive codes and conceptualize how categories may relate together in a theory. As coding and memoing reaches saturation, analysis can move towards the sorting of the memos

themselves. Sortibility is a feature of the rigor and organization with which the researcher has written his/her memos. That is, the format of the memos should allow for easy identification of content so that relevant memos can be pulled together. The writing of theory then evolves from the sorted memos guided by the theoretical codes and can be evaluated on the criterion of credibility – that is, the theory should be integrated and relevant, and should work.

The difference between Glaser's approach and that of Strauss and Corbin is articulated vehemently in Glaser's (1992) response to the first edition of the *Basics of Qualitative Research* (1990). The main difference is presented as that of allowing theory to *emerge* from the data (bottom-up induction) versus *forcing* of material into a preconceived structure. Glaser argues that increasing the detail of the procedures, such as with axial coding, risks imposing an artificial framework and encourages sticking too rigidly to a set of procedures, and that both may take researchers away from patterns inherent in the data themselves. In particular, Glaser expresses bewilderment with Strauss and Corbin's dedication to the one paradigm model when many different kinds of organizing structures can be identified. In essence, Glaser (1992) argues that Strauss's revised method mitigates the main strength of the approach as originally formulated – development of theory grounded in the data – and suggests that Strauss and Corbin's variant would be more correctly termed "full conceptual description" than grounded theory.

Glaser also disputes Strauss and Corbin's claim that grounded theory is inherently verificational, arguing that the method produces only theory that must be subjected to the logico-deductive procedures of natural science in order to be verified. However, contemporary grounded theory methodologist Kathy Charmaz (2006) takes issue with the idea that grounded theory is, or should be, verificational at all. She argues that confirming ideas through the constant scrutiny of additional data is not the same as verification as understood in the philosophy of science and that grounded theory should be considered, instead, to offer *plausible explanations*. In doing so, Charmaz offers an *interpretative* as opposed to an *objectivist* version of grounded theory. She challenges the situating of grounded theory within a positivist tradition through utilizing critique of the notion that rigorous operationalization of method will reveal the meaning of qualitative data – for example, in terms of a core category. Instead, she argues that data, such as interviews, are already co-constructed by researcher and participant. Moreover, she draws on a constructionist position in her understanding that the researcher's analysis of the data is necessarily interpretative: that is, that the *meaning* of the data is created during the process of the researcher's engagement with the data and is not already there, waiting to be discovered. Charmaz's interpretativist variant of grounded theory has been well-received and resonates with current directions in qualitative research.

SEE ALSO: Qualitative Methods and Coding.

REFERENCES

Charmaz, K. (2006). *Constructing grounded theory: A practical guide through qualitative analysis*. London, UK: Sage.

Corbin, J., & Strauss, A. (1998). *Basics of qualitative research: Techniques and procedures for developing grounded theory* (3rd ed.). London, UK: Sage.

Glaser, B. G. (1978). *Theoretical sensitivity*. Mill Valley, CA: Sociology Press.

Glaser, B. G. (1992). *Basics of grounded theory analysis: Emergence vs. forcing*. Mill Valley, CA: Sociology Press.

Glaser, B. G., & Strauss, A. (1965). *Awareness of dying*. Chicago, IL: Aldine.

Glaser, B. G., & Strauss, A. (1967). *The discovery of grounded theory: Strategies for qualitative research*. Chicago, IL: Aldine.

Rennie, D. L. (1998). Grounded theory methodology: The pressing need for a coherent logic of justification. *Theory & Psychology, 8*, 101–119.

Strauss, A., & Corbin, J. (1990). *Basics of qualitative research: Grounded theory procedures and techniques*. London, UK: Sage.

ADDITIONAL RESOURCE

Teaching Qualitative Research Methods at Undergraduate Level (TQRMUL) Dataset Teaching Resources: http://www.psychology.heacademy.ac.uk/Webdocs_not_nof/tqrmul/dataset/

Groupthink

DANIEL M. MAYTON II AND
M. ZACHARY BRINK

Sometimes groups make good decisions. Sometimes their decisions are disastrous. (See DECISION-MAKING, PSYCHOLOGICAL DIMENSIONS OF FOREIGN POLICY; DECISION-MAKING, THE ROLE OF EMOTIONS IN FOREIGN POLICY.) While reading about the poor decision-making that led to the Bay of Pigs invasion in 1961, Irving Janis (1982) began to develop the concept of groupthink. Asking how could so many smart people make stupid decisions when placed in groups, Janis analyzed policymakers and their processes of decision-making in many different instances. He proposed the Orwellian-like term groupthink in 1972 to describe a particular ailment of policymaking groups. Janis defined groupthink as "a mode of thinking that people engage in when they are deeply involved in a cohesive ingroup, when the members' strivings for unanimity override their motivation to realistically appraise alternative courses of action" (p. 9). Groupthink is further characterized by "a deterioration of mental efficiency, reality testing, and moral judgment that results from ingroup pressures" (p. 9).

SYMPTOMS OF GROUPTHINK

Janis (1982) scrutinized many policy fiascos to identify the symptoms of groupthink. While not every fiasco is the result of groupthink, understanding groupthink can help us understand many fiascos and learn how to avoid them. In addition to the Bay of Pigs invasion, Janis considered other examples of groupthink: the failure to recognize the warning signs for the attack on Pearl Harbor, the escalation of the wars in Korea and Vietnam, the Watergate cover-up, the rescue of hostages in the US embassy in Iran. Based on these analyses, Janis proposed eight symptoms of groupthink: (1) an illusion of invulnerability, (2) collective rationalization, (3) a belief in an inherent morality, (4) stereotyped views of outgroups, (5) direct pressure on dissenters, (6) self-censorship, (7) an illusion of unanimity, and (8) self-appointed mindguards.

Much has been written in the press and in academic journals about the US decision to invade Iraq in 2003 as an example of groupthink. While there are some differing viewpoints, the Bush administration's decision-making is generally recognized as possessing many symptoms of groupthink in the lead-up to the war (Cairo, 2009) and the strategy used after the invasion (Fitzsimmons, 2008). Therefore, the decision to launch an attack on Saddam Hussein's Iraq in 2003 will be used to help illustrate each of these eight symptoms.

When groups possess an illusion of invulnerability, they are extremely optimistic about their plan of action and this optimism encourages them to take risks without properly assessing the consequences of their actions. This can be dangerous when the decisions to be made include either potential

loss of human life or factors that may affect the quality of living for any number of people. The United States was the lone military superpower as the twenty-first century began. Many in the Bush administration's inner circle (Vice-President Dick Cheney, Secretary of Defense Donald Rumsfeld, and Assistant Secretary of Defense Paul Wolfowitz, along with advisors Elliott Abrams, Richard Armitage, John Bolton, Eliot Cohen, and Lewis Libby, among others) had been active in the late 1990s in the think tank Project for the New American Century (PNAC) that adopted principles designed to ensure continued US military greatness and outlined a strategy to assure US military and economic hegemony well into the future. Following 9/11, these members, now in the Bush administration, dusted off their Iraqi regime-change ideas to push for an Iraqi invasion with a sense of invulnerability.

Collective rationalization exists when group members know they are correct, or rational, in their way of thinking, so they believe there is no point in questioning their assumptions or giving any credit to warnings about them. Prior to the invasion of Iraq, Germany and France expressed serious concerns, but were dismissed as being "old Europe" by Defense Secretary Rumsfeld. The International Atomic Energy Agency (IAEA) was also dismissed as ineffectual when it found no evidence of weapons of mass destruction (WMD) in its inspections of Iraq. Faulty US intelligence was presumed to be correct, not the IAEA.

A belief in an inherent morality may be one of the most dangerous symptoms of groupthink. Because the group believes in its own morality, any strategy that is decided upon must be moral. Unfortunately, the belief in the correctness of the plan often leads people to assume that not only is their plan correct, but it's also ethically and morally correct. President Bush's strong religious beliefs provided some support for this symptom, as did the "we are the good guys" mentality presented by many in the administration during speeches and press conferences.

Groupthink is also characterized by stereotyped views of outgroups and their leaders as too evil, stupid, or inept to be concerned about. Certitude about the righteousness of the ingroup's views and the ineptitude of the outgroup can diminish concerns about conflict. Following 9/11, President Bush referred to the fight against the perpetrators as a Crusade and during his 2002 State of the Union Address to the country he dubbed Iraq one of the "Axis of Evil" countries. In the lead-up to the invasion of Iraq, additional time to allow IAEA inspectors to find WMD was not regarded as necessary because negotiation and diplomacy were not expected to work with a leader like Saddam Hussein. Moreover, stereotypes of Iraqi soldiers and civilians may have played a role in making a plan for post-invasion activities unimportant, as US soldiers were expected to be greeted as liberators. (See STEREOTYPES.)

Direct pressure on dissenters within a group, self-censorship, and mindguards can increase the chance of groupthink. Some members of a group may wish to express their concerns about the plan, but realize they may receive hostile reactions from others if they do. This pressure builds an understanding within the group that nobody is to express any doubts or deviations from the given consensus of the plan. The stronger the cohesiveness within the group, the stronger this pressure is likely to be. Self-censorship occurs when the members of the group do not express their concerns because of strong commitment to the goals of the group and/or because they feel strong pressures to toe the line within the group. The external pressure becomes internalized and dissent is not voiced. Mindguards within the group are self-appointed members who work individually to quell dissent with the goal of protecting and preserving the current plan of action. These mindguards discount or disregard information that could cause a problem for the plan, and keep it from ever reaching the leader of the group.

The Bush administration was a cohesive group to begin with and had few potential dissenting voices. Secretary of State Colin Powell was one dissenting voice, but even this retired four-star general succumbed to the pressure epitomized by President Bush's admonition that "You're either with us or against us." At other times Powell was left out of some deliberations altogether (Cairo, 2009). Harsh administrative public reaction to military leaders who questioned war plans also pressured others to be silent with their concerns. Woodward (2004) suggests that just before the invasion of Iraq, Powell acquiesced to the plan to attack Iraq out of a sense of duty; however, this shift may have had an element of self-censorship too. Self-censorship also existed in the American news media as reporters and news anchors generally did not bring up opposition views to invasion for fear of being labeled unpatriotic. In the lead-up to the Iraq invasion many media outlets served as mindguards for the administration by calling out dissenters on their programs or failing to cover dissenting viewpoints altogether in order to support the publically stated plan. However, Fitzsimmons (2008) concludes that if groupthink is already present, the impact of the media is negligible.

Unfortunately, with pressures against dissent and with self-censorship the group may develop an illusion of unanimity. Since no doubts or opposing opinions are being expressed, then the group may assume everybody is in agreement. The spate of books that have been written by and about former members of the Bush administrations (e.g., Tenet, 2007) speaks to the feelings that some experienced the administration's unanimity behind its plan to go to war.

Groupthink can often be expected when the previously mentioned symptoms are seen within a decision-making group's behavior, but not always. Groupthink tends to occur under specific conditions, which include a highly cohesive group and considerable pressure to expeditiously turn out a decision. A group can take steps to reduce the chance that they make the mistake of falling into groupthink.

PREVENTING GROUPTHINK

Groupthink is not the inevitable outcome of policymaking groups. Janis (1982) has suggested nine measures that can be taken to prevent the syndrome from taking hold:

1. The leader should assign every member of the decision-making group to the position of critical evaluator and therefore allow for their own decisions to be questioned. This will increase the likelihood of members airing doubts and speculations about preferred plans of action.
2. The leader must present the group with the conflict without stating his or her preferred plan of action so the group atmosphere is likely to be more open and accepting of alternative plans of action. It is necessary that the group be briefed on limitations, but if the leader does not express his/her desired outcome, the group will feel less pressure for any specific outcome.
3. The initial group should regularly assign different groups and committees the same problem in order to open up the policymaking team to outside opinions from those that may not be within the immediate group.

The following solutions have the specific goal of offsetting insulation of the policymaking group:

4. The initial group should regularly break up into smaller subgroups for a more focused discussion of plans that may not have had a chance to be heard in the larger group. After breaking apart, the groups should then converge and discuss any ideas or concerns considered while separated.
5. Every member should regularly meet with trusted colleagues to discuss the group's deliberations. It is very important to consider the reactions of those outside of the group who have different perspectives. After hearing these new reactions, each member should report back to the group and scrutinize any plan they may be considering.
6. The group should regularly invite experts to share their knowledge, to analyze, and to express their concerns about the group's plans. The experts should play the role of evaluator and challenger in order to strengthen the idea that any one specific course could potentially be flawed.

The final solutions are aimed at thwarting any form of leadership bias:

7. One capable and calculating member of the group should be assigned as the devil's advocate for every meeting of the group. The goal of this person should be to question and pierce as many holes through that plan as possible, plus to seek alternatives, even if the current plan appears foolproof.
8. If any issue or decision specifically involves a rival, it's important not to underestimate their abilities. Much time should be spent assessing the rival's strategies, strengths, weaknesses, capabilities, resources, history, culture, warning signals, threats, and intentions without stereotyping.
9. Once the group has reached a decision, they should hold a "second chance" meeting with the explicit goal of expressing doubts and approaching the issue

from different viewpoints before finally going forward with the plan.

The end goal of these different measures is to allow as many different points of view as possible to speak freely in order to analyze and understand every single possible option, and the potential positive and negative outcomes of every plan. Only after viewing every possibility can the policy-making group find the single best course of action.

CONCLUSION

While it is unclear whether the symptoms cause groupthink or if they are the residual effects of groupthink, they do seem to be found within groups that have made decisions that have resulted in fiascoes. Groupthink has been criticized for its lack of strong research backing, but case studies have been compelling. The prescriptions for open-minded leaders to avoid groupthink have been shown to prevent poor decision-making in some instances, while the prognosis for closed-minded leaders to successfully avert groupthink is less positive (Kowert, 2002).

SEE ALSO: Decision-Making, Psychological Dimensions of Foreign Policy; Decision-Making, the Role of Emotions in Foreign Policy; Stereotypes.

REFERENCES

Cairo, M. (2009, February). From multiple advocacy to groupthink: George W. Bush and the decision to invade Iraq. A paper presented at the meeting of the International Studies Association, New York, NY.
Fitzsimmons, D. (2008). Coherence in crisis: Groupthink, the news media, and the Iraq war. *Journal of Military and Strategic Studies*, 10(4), 1–52.
Janis, I. L. (1982). *Groupthink: Psychological studies of policy decisions and fiascoes* (2nd ed.). Boston, MA: Houghton Mifflin.
Kowert, P. A. (2002). *Groupthink or deadlock: When do leaders learn from their advisors*. Albany, NY: State University of New York Press.
Tenet, G., with Harlow, B. (2007). *At the center of the storm: My years at the CIA*. New York, NY: HarperCollins.
Woodward, B. (2004). *Plan of attack*. London, UK: Simon and Schuster.

Guilt: Personal and Collective

MICHAEL J. A. WOHL & NYLA R. BRANSCOMBE

PERSONAL GUILT

Guilt is an unpleasant emotion that is evoked when people's behavior deviates from salient moral standards concerning how other people should be treated. Simply deviating from these standards, however, is insufficient to experience guilt. For guilt to occur, the individual must recognize that his or her behavior is inconsistent with what is normative with regard to the treatment of others and accept personal responsibility for the harm inflicted. For example, John might feel guilt if he knowingly and unjustifiably failed to hire a person because of his/her race or ethnicity rather than the merit of that particular applicant.

Importantly, guilt can be distinguished from simple fear of punishment by external sources. People could be afraid that their actions will lead to reprisal, but feel no guilt for committing the act. Likewise, potential judiciary decisions of guilt can be quite removed from the emotional experience of guilt. People do not necessarily feel guilt just because others judge their actions to have violated a moral standard. Guilt is predominantly experienced when responsibility is accepted for action that is perceived to be illegitimate, harmful to others, and deemed to be within the person's own control. By contrast, shame (an emotion term that is often used interchangeably with guilt) is typically experienced for outcomes deemed outside personal control and when made public portrays the perpetrator as weak or inferior. Distinguishing the two emotions further, guilt is experienced when harm is directed toward another person or persons, whereas this is not a precondition for the experience of shame. In shame, potential loss of reputation and stature are paramount, whereas with guilt the harm inflicted on another is focal. John might feel guilt for illegitimately failing to hire a minority group applicant when it was within his power to do so, but shame if he believes others perceive him to be a racist because of this choice.

More generally, guilt has been conceptualized as a self-conscious emotional state that results when an actor causes, foresees causing, or is linked with illegitimate harm. As such, guilt is not restricted to events that have already occurred, but may also include anticipated negative events as well as past negative events with which people believe themselves to be associated. Thus, guilt is relevant to a variety of daily experiences, and is important for understanding moral behavior and social cohesion.

Indeed, because moral standards are culturally anchored, to feel guilt an individual must internalize the morals of the society to which they identify (Devine & Monteith, 1993). In this way, guilt is functional. It serves as the social glue that binds members of a society together by forcing people to pay attention to how their behavior can negatively affect others and subsequently feel badly about their wrongful behavior. If guilt was not experienced, people would care little about the harm they inflict on other people or their property. The anticipation of feeling guilt is consequentially a motivating factor to abstain from engaging in behavior that violates normative standards. In effect, guilt serves to effectively regulate social behavior and facilitate peaceful coexistence between individuals.

As a result of its role in social regulation, guilt is often considered a higher-order, social emotion. Whereas emotions such as fear serve to initiate the fight or flight response, guilt involves complex cognitive processing that can motivate behavior beyond the initial felt experience. Specifically, after the initial harmful behavior occurs and guilt is experienced, the person who committed the harm may begin to look for ways that the harm can be repaired. The means by which this repair is undertaken can take many forms. People may apologize for the wrong committed, pledge to change their behavior, provide financial reparations for damages, or otherwise make up for the harm done (Baumeister, Stillwell, & Heatherton, 1994). (See APOLOGIES AND FORGIVENESS.) There are times, however, when there are no obvious means by which reparation can be made. In the case of a person who has discriminated against someone based on group membership, there may be no means to repair the harm done to that particular harmed individual. Even with no obvious route of repair for that specific individual, guilt can still facilitate positive social behavior because a person can always decide to refrain from such harm-doing and behave differently in the future when faced with a similar situation. To this end, guilt can be beneficial for the facilitation and maintenance of positive interpersonal relations.

COLLECTIVE GUILT

As anyone who is aware of world politics knows, intense emotions can be elicited in response to adversarial relations between social groups (Branscombe & Doosje, 2004).

Importantly, emotions such as guilt elicited by salient intergroup inequality depend primarily on belonging to the social group that has perpetrated harm on another group, and not necessarily on individual actions. Therefore, feelings of guilt can arise not only due to personal behavior that violates social norms, but may also result from the behavior of other members of one's group. For example, European Americans may feel guilt for the historical enslavement of African Americans. European Americans who feel guilty for the harm done to African Americans do not necessarily experience guilt for harm that they have committed *personally*, but rather they feel *collective* guilt because they perceive members of their own group as having committed illegitimate harm against members of another group. Thus, negative events that elicit collective guilt are ones in which the victim and perpetrator are perceived as members of social groups, rather than individuals (Branscombe, 2004).

Although some have argued that in the absence of personal responsibility a person should not feel guilt for harmful behaviors committed by others, the reality is that people can and do feel collective guilt. This is because part of people's sense of self is derived from the groups to which they perceive themselves as belonging. Just as events for which the personal self is responsible can elicit emotions such as guilt, appraisal of events that involve a person's group can likewise trigger such emotions based on the collective self. In order to experience collective guilt, people must perceive themselves as members of a social group that has illegitimately harmed another social group (Branscombe, 2004). The potential for collective guilt is not restricted to instances of historical injustices. It can also be experienced for harmful behavior one's own group is currently committing. Indeed, awareness of a wide range of contemporary intergroup inequalities may elicit collective guilt.

Although John might not hold prejudicial attitudes toward minority groups and has not personally discriminated against them, collective guilt might still be experienced if he perceives his group as routinely engaging in discriminatory hiring practices against minority group members.

The factors that lead group members to feel collective guilt for historical or contemporary harm toward members of other groups are not unlike those required for the experience of personal guilt. In addition to acknowledging the self to be a member of a group that has illegitimately harmed another group, group members must hold their group responsible for the harm done. In the absence of perceived ingroup responsibility, little collective guilt will be experienced. Because it is unpleasant to believe one's group has illegitimately harmed another social group, various strategies can be employed to deflect ingroup responsibility for the harm inflicted (Wohl, Branscombe, & Klar, 2006). One strategy group members use to reduce ingroup responsibility is to shift the focus of attention from the ingroup to the outgroup. For example, inequality and discrimination can be framed in terms of the advantages experienced by the ingroup (e.g., occupying well-paying jobs) or the disadvantages experienced by the outgroup (e.g., occupying poor-paying jobs). By shifting focus, the harm committed becomes more about "them" and less about what "we" did, which reduces the likelihood that collective guilt will be experienced (Powell, Branscombe, & Schmitt, 2005). Group members can also blame the outgroup for the harm its members experience in order to reduce feelings of collective guilt. The Nazis, for instance, blamed much of Germany's ills on the Jews. By doing so, Germans could feel less responsible for the harm they inflicted. Ingroup responsibility can be also undermined to the extent that the harm committed is seen as isolated in a few deviant ingroup members and not a reflection on the ingroup as a whole. By psychologically isolating the wrongdoers from the group, the ingroup as a whole can be shielded from responsibility.

Importantly, even when responsibility is accepted, this does not guarantee that group members will feel collective guilt. In addition to acceptance of responsibility, group members must also perceive that the ingroup's harmful actions toward the outgroup were illegitimate. In particular, collective guilt requires that people perceive that their group violated a moral standard coupled with a belief that there is no justification for having done so. Because people are motivated to see their ingroup in a positive light, collective guilt is often undermined by legitimization processes. One means by which members can legitimize their group's actions is by arguing that the ingroup was simply responding to the harmful behavior perpetrated by the outgroup. That is, the ingroup was forced to commit harm in response to the aggressive actions initiated by the outgroup. Although responsibility is accepted for the harm the ingroup inflicted, that harm is justified as a means of protecting the ingroup from an aggressive outgroup. Accordingly, derogation and harm to an outgroup can be seen as a legitimate response to the threat posed by the outgroup (Wohl et al., 2006).

Because of the many strategies people have for preventing and undermining feelings of collective guilt, it may be an emotion that is experienced relatively infrequently. When it is experienced though, group members must come to grips with the fact that their group has violated agreed-upon moral standards. People want to believe that the groups to which they belong are good, especially those who feel a strong sense of connection to their ingroup. Collective guilt undermines these perceptions, thus leaving group members to question the positivity of their ingroup. However, it is precisely the motivation to see the ingroup in a positive

light and alleviate feelings of collective guilt that can lead group members to repair the wrongs their group has inflicted on another group.

By correcting wrongs committed by the ingroup, group members can once again perceive their group to be moral. Just as personal guilt is associated with the desire to take corrective action, so too does collective guilt motivate group members to restore justice and make amends for their group's harmful behavior. Indeed, collective guilt has been found to predict support for affirmative action policies, financial reparations, and the desire for group leaders to offer a public apology to groups that have been victimized by the ingroup (e.g., Canadian and Australian governmental apologies to their respective Native populations for the forced displacement and years of discrimination endured).

It should be noted, however, that simply feeling collective guilt might not be sufficient to elicit support for reparative action. Group members must feel they are efficacious with regard to bringing about change. If repair is seen to be especially difficult to achieve, then the need to restore justice might be outweighed by the perceived difficulty of doing so. Perhaps counterintuitively, if correcting the harm done is seen as relatively easy to accomplish, then the intensity of collective guilt may be also low and thereby undermine any motivation to repair the wrongs that have been committed by the ingroup. Compensatory action is most likely to occur when the importance of restoring justice is high, and the effort needed to restore justice is feasible, but not so difficult that it outweighs the value of repairing the wrongs committed (Schmitt, Miller, Branscombe, & Brehm, 2008).

The collective guilt that national and ethnic groups experience for the harm committed against other groups may be critical for changing the nature of intergroup relations and the quest for peace and justice. It is when immoral and unjust behavior is confronted that guilt is experienced, be it personal or group-based. By experiencing guilt, moral standards and the desire to adhere to those standards are reinforced.

SEE ALSO: Apologies and Forgiveness.

REFERENCES

Baumeister, R. F., Stillwell, A. M., & Heatherton, T. F. (1994). Guilt: An interpersonal approach. *Psychological Bulletin, 115*, 243–267.

Branscombe, N. R. (2004). A social psychological process perspective on collective guilt. In N. R. Branscombe & B. Doosje (Eds.), *Collective guilt: International perspectives* (pp. 320–334). New York, NY: Cambridge University Press.

Branscombe, N. R., & Doosje, B. (Eds). (2004). *Collective guilt: International perspectives*. New York, NY: Cambridge University Press.

Devine, P. G., & Monteith, M. J. (1993). The role of discrepancy-associated affect in prejudice reduction. In D. M. Mackie & D. L. Hamilton (Eds.), *Affect, cognition, and stereotyping: Interactive processes in group perception* (pp. 317–344). San Diego, CA: Academic Press.

Powell, A. A., Branscombe, N. R., & Schmitt, M. T. (2005). Inequality as ingroup privilege or outgroup disadvantage: The impact of group focus on collective guilt and interracial attitudes. *Personality and Social Psychology Bulletin, 31*, 508–521.

Schmitt, M. T., Miller, D. A., Branscombe, N. R., & Brehm, J. W. (2008). The difficulty of making reparations affects the intensity of collective guilt. *Group Processes and Intergroup Relations, 11*, 267–279.

Wohl, M. J. A., Branscombe, N. R., & Klar, Y. (2006). Collective guilt: Emotional reactions when one's group has done wrong or been wronged. *European Review of Social Psychology, 17*, 1–37.

H

Hetero-Referentiality and Divided Societies

RAGINI SEN

It has been observed that events, as represented in groups, form a narrative network that informs the actions, cognitions, and affects of their holders. Antagonistic groups, politically inspired events, and the derivative interpretations following from their narratives, generally help create hetero-referential situations. Each group's representation is validated by, and indeed depends on, the respective antagonistic representation of the other group. (See NARRATIVE ANALYSIS; NARRATIVE PSYCHOLOGY; SOCIAL REPRESENTATION THEORY; SOCIAL REPRESENTATIONS OF HISTORY.)

We wish to call two systems of representations "hetero-referential" if both groups refer to the same series of events, if the shared events are represented in a "180 degree" antagonistic fashion and in the manner of a zero sum game by each group. Each group's enjoyable experience entails the other group's loss and each group's painful experience entails the other's joy.

This situation is a characteristic of historically related ethnic groups, states, or nations, whose proximity and antagonistic interests inextricably link their fate inversely to the other's fare. Without a certain degree of mutual – or, if you want, empathic – background knowledge of the others' way of storytelling and symbolic resources hetero-referential representations tend to reconstruct and perpetuate the conflict over time.

REPRESENTATIONAL SYSTEMS

Social representation theory delineates three kinds of representations whose objective is to enable members of a group to function in a familiar and self-evident world. These representations are not fixed entities but can shift across time, and it can be argued that this tripartite classification is sometimes indicative of different phases in the overall life span of groups and societies.

Hegemonic representations are shared by almost all members of a society and by default are uniform and coercive. They signify social identity and the individual in this situation has a curtailment of degrees of

The Encyclopedia of Peace Psychology, First Edition. Edited by Daniel J. Christie.
© 2012 Blackwell Publishing Ltd. Published 2012 by Blackwell Publishing Ltd.

freedom. Consensual or hegemonic social representations facilitate conflict resolution and subgroup reconciliation. Liu, Lawrence, Ward, and Abraham (2002), for instance, investigated social representations of history in Malaysia and Singapore and found predominantly hegemonic social representations of history across ethnic groups. They showed that such hegemonic representations were associated with positive correlations between ethnic and national identity. (See SOCIAL REPRESENTATIONS OF HISTORY.)

Emancipated representations are created when members of a society are differentially exposed to new information. They are an outgrowth of circulation of knowledge belonging to subgroups that are generally closely linked and in this case each group creates and shares its own version of a common story. The significant fact being that they claim subgroup variations that complement one another.

However, polemic representations are constructed when a society is in a state of turmoil and reflect contradictory or mutually exclusive interpretations usually arising in the context of a social controversy. The society as a whole does not share them and they are a result of antagonistic relations between its members. This characteristic is clearly visible in debates on policy issues which lead to social change. A pointer is the healthcare reform issue debated in the United States. Such debates are based on a discourse, which is structured by two different representations, which are to a large extent dependent on the political view preferred by the group and its position in a social class hierarchy. Because of the power of polemic representations to bring controversies in a society upfront, they can be considered as good tools for creating political opinions and help mobilize collective actions, especially in divided societies. Polemical representations are one of the major mainstays of hetero-referentiality. (See NATIONAL POLITICAL CULTURES.)

HETERO-REFERENTIAL REPRESENTATIONS

Hetero-referential representations are a borderline case of polemic representations and of holomorphic representations. They are polemic because they imply antagonism in interaction and access to resources. They are holomorphic because each of the two groups is not only aware of its own course of action and justification, but also has some general knowledge of patterns of perception, feelings, and judgment, and the course of action of the other group.

Montiel's (in press) and Sen and Wagner's (2005) research clearly illustrate the existence of hetero-referential situations, which exist in a divided society. Montiel's research findings show two stories of "People Power" (or EDSA I): one in the collective mind of civilians, the other in the group mind of military leaders. In the Philippines in 1986 People Power toppled the 14-year Marcos dictatorship (1972–1986) and ushered in a more democratic government under President Aquino. People Power or EDSA I was a political event which was not just an episodic moment in 1986 but was a collective experience shared nationwide. This dramatic political event was not only recognized domestically but was also globally showcased as a model for nonviolent democratic transitions. Civilians viewed People Power as potent and good. Conversely, the military believed that the 1986 People Power was an aborted coup that succeeded because of the military's withdrawal of support from President Marcos. In the social representations of the military, People Power was weak and bad. (See PEOPLE POWER.)

Montiel argues that the two stories are not only antagonistic; they are also hetero-referential. They are hetero-referential because both narratives of the conflicting groups are about the same episode, include the same story elements, but carry different plots where the narrative claimed by each group elevates the ingroup at the expense of the outgroup. Each narrative likewise arouses strong group emotions, generating intense positive emotions toward one's ingroup and hostility toward the outgroup. Her surmise was that the stories of People Power are polemical because each group, civilian or military, constructs its own account of recent history to vitalize their respective social identities in the Philippines' political arena. The protagonist or central hero varies according to the storyline that is accepted.

Research conducted by Sen and Wagner (2005; Wagner, Holtz, & Kashima, 2009) on Muslim–Hindu conflicts in India revealed that, based on the creation of polemical and holomorphic representations, Hindu revivalists created a vitiated atmosphere which led to the formation of outgroups and ingroups during the 1990s–2004. In India in the 1990s, in order to consolidate their position, members of the Hindu right-wing political spectrum sparked the controversy surrounding Babri Masjid (mosque) which became the core symbol at the center of divisive politics being practiced all through the decade. Hindu ideologues claimed that the place on which the Babri Masjid was located was the birthplace of Lord Ram, who is a central Hindu deity. Based on this claim they demolished the mosque in 1992. This created an emotional charge and permitted the organization of riots and communal hatred.

The Babri Masjid had created a hetero-referential situation *par excellence* – a symbol of collective grief amid the Muslims and collective triumph amid the Hindus. It retained the power to stoke divisive politics. In political discourse Babri Masjid dictated terms and controlled the emotional reins. It was a "canonic thema," shrouded by suppressed fury felt with equal intensity by both Muslims and Hindus who interpreted the situation along entirely different storylines. In this hetero-referential situation, Ram and Allah both became hostages of communal forces and helped heighten hetero-referentiality.

The examples of discourse given above are indicative of a change in social dynamics wherein the boundaries of a focused outgroup along with consolidation of the ingroup were becoming pronounced and the Other was assuming a clear and negative character. The escalation of passion and emotion associated with such collective uprisings was a result of a tale read differently by two antagonistic groups.

HETERO-REFERENTIALITY AND STRUCTURAL FACILITATION

Story structures involving two groups define and foster one's own identity and in doing so also set up boundaries within which the other group is symbolically located. Such structures also decide the role that is to be assigned to the group in the plot of the story (Pratkanis, 2000). This simultaneous locating and role casting, i.e., altercating, of the collective Other is the final keystone in the architecture of hetero-referential representational systems.

In hetero-referential situations, usually, antagonism is fueled by simultaneous claims for a geographic area, for resources, or for ideological and religious claims of supremacy. The representational and ideological system that emerges in the long historical development of such conflicts provides the collective mental harness of justification that is further elaborated by ideologues' attempts at estranging and dehumanizing the Other. For instance, Sen and Wagner (2005) argue that Hindu ideologues had begun to impose the idea of jihad (holy war) in the branding of the Muslim community, and Montiel (in press) shows that People Power was given the label of weak and bad by the military, which are clear cases of altercating. Such a collective representational harness is the structural precondition for atrocities to be taken as normal and for their perpetrators to be praised as heroes.

The structural and behavioral logic investigated in the Stanford Prison Experiment (Haney, Banks, & Zimbardo, 1973) illustrated similar opposed systems of widely shared justificatory representations. It is not the personality or some ingrained evilness that makes people perpetrate against the Other, but the ideological and/or physical structure of the situation. It does not take a prison structure with well-defined participants being prisoners or guards, but only the outspoken or silent encouragement of an authority or the actual or projected consensus of other ingroup members to prepare the perpetrators.

In the case of groups confronting each other, the representational systems of each not only comprises cognitive and affective components, but also have behavioral implications. In other words it can be said that representations, once created, are enacted in discourse as well as in overt behavior. As much as shared systems of representations unite the members of the ingroup and create their unique identity, to the same extent shared hetero-referential representations exclude members of the outgroup from being seen as human beings with a right to their own way of life.

When this happens essentialist ascriptions transform the target group's attributed negative characteristics into a natural trait. Once ascriptions such as "all Muslims are terrorists" or "ethnic hybrids are inferior" are entrenched in discourse, they are not easily shed. On the basis of naturalization and dehumanizing/infrahumanizing rhetorics, apparent differences between social groups are sharpened and this increases the rifts in the social fabric of societies (Wagner, Holtz, & Kashima, 2009). The storylines and perceptions do not match and mutual antagonism is the result, which paves the way for

sustaining conflict. (See DEHUMANIZATION, INFRAHUMANIZATION, AND NATURALIZATION.)

There is a host of politicians around the world whose politics also rests on the creation of antagonistic situations, which serve a divisive purpose and help engender conflict. Given this, hetero-referentiality can perhaps be utilized as a tool for analyzing social controversies, which are often enough part of public discourse in almost all societies.

SEE ALSO: Dehumanization, Infrahumanization, and Naturalization; Narrative Analysis; Narrative Psychology; National Political Cultures; People Power; Social Representation Theory; Social Representations of History.

REFERENCES

Haney, C., Banks, C., & Zimbardo, P. (1973). A study of prisoners and guards in a simulated prison. Washington, DC: Office of Naval Research, Department of the Navy.

Liu, J., Lawrence, B., Ward, C., & Abraham, S. (2002). Social representations of history in Malaysia and Singapore: On the relationship between national and ethnic identity. Asian Journal of Social Psychology, 5, 3–20.

Montiel, C. J. (in press). Social representations of democratic transition: Was the Philippine People Power One a nonviolent power shift or a military coup? Asian Journal of Social Psychology.

Pratkanis, A. (2000). Altercating as an influence tactic. In M. A. Hogg & D. J. Terry (Eds.), Attitudes, behavior, and social context: The role of norms and group membership. Mahwah, NJ: Erlbaum.

Sen, R., & Wagner, W. (2005). History, emotions and hetero-referential representations in intergroup conflict: The example of Hindu–Muslim relations in India. Papers on Social Representations, 16, 2.1–2.23.

Wagner, W., Holtz, P., & Kashima, Y. (2009). Constructing and deconstructing essence in representing social groups: Identity projects, stereotyping, and racism. *Journal for the Theory of Social Behaviour, 39*(3), 363–383.

Human Needs Theory, Conflict, and Peace

H. B. DANESH

Although the concepts of human needs, conflict, and peace are interrelated and affect all aspects of human life, academics and practitioners have usually addressed them in a rather fragmented manner. Human needs theories propose that all humans have certain basic universal needs and that when these are not met conflict is likely to occur. Abraham Maslow proposed a hierarchy of needs beginning with the need for food, water, and shelter followed by the need for safety and security, then belonging or love, self-esteem and, finally, personal fulfillment and self-actualization. Later in his life Maslow (1973) proposed self-transcendence as a need above self-actualization in the hierarchy of needs.

John Burton (1990) also identifies a set of needs, which he considers to be universal in their occurrence but with no hierarchical significance. His list of needs includes distributive justice, safety and security, belongingness, self-esteem, personal fulfillment, identity, cultural security, and freedom. While Maslow and Burton emphasize human biological, psychological, and social needs, Marshall Rosenberg introduces a new set of needs that could best be categorized as psycho-spiritual in nature, among them the need for love integrity, celebration and mourning, and spiritual communion. Likewise, Max-Neef and his colleagues added their own uniquely understood human needs, including the need for creation, and leisure and idleness (for a comparative review of these theories see Kok, 2007). Simon Hertnon (2005) proposes the theory of universal human needs based on just two

needs: survival and betterment. Under survival needs he identifies physical and mental well-being, respect from others, and self-esteem (all required for happiness), and a safe and healthy environment, logical reproductive practices, appreciation of life, and doing good things (all required for contentment). There are still many other formulations of human needs. As is clear from this brief review, the concept of human needs is an evolving concept in the search for a more universal, integrated framework. Such a framework will be addressed later in this article. (See CONFLICT RESOLUTION, INTERACTIVE; INTERGROUP CONFLICT, THEORIES OF.)

Human needs theorists distinguish between human needs and interests, and argue that human conflicts emerge when people's efforts to meet their fundamental needs are frustrated. It is further argued that conflict and even violence are inevitable because human needs are nonnegotiable, while human interests are open to negotiation and compromise. The line of demarcation between needs and interests, however, is not very clear and is itself subject to dispute.

While human needs theory is accepted as a valid and useful model for understanding some of the fundamental aspects of human behavior, there are nevertheless significant questions that remain to be answered. How can we define human needs? Are human needs universal or cultural in nature? Is there indeed a hierarchy of needs, making some needs more important than others? How can we distinguish between human needs and human interests? Is the nature of conflicts emerging from unmet needs essentially different from those caused by differing sets of interests? These questions concerning needs, interests, and conflict require a better understanding of the nature of human conflicts and their genesis. In this regard it should be noted that there is general agreement among most scholars and practitioners that issues of security, identity, and recognition play fundamental roles in the creation of severe and intractable conflicts.

Early elements of conflict theory can be found in the writings of Machiavelli and Thomas Hobbes. Current generally held views on the nature and role of conflict in human life, although varied, are fundamentally based on the notion that conflict is an inherent aspect of human nature and, as such, is not only inevitable but even necessary. For example, Galtung, Jacobsen, Brand-Jacobsen, and Tschudi (2000) comment that conflict and incompatible goals are as human as life itself; dead humans are the only humans free of conflict. In contrast, war and violence come and go, like slavery, colonialism, and patriarchy. Others consider conflict useful for identity development, social change, creativity, and enlivening human relationships.

The four basic assumptions of modern conflict theory are competition, structural inequality, revolution, and war. Competition takes place in the context of the scarce resources required for satisfaction of both needs and interests. Structural inequality refers to the inevitable unequal distribution of power, which often results in conflict between social classes, giving birth to revolutions. War likewise has its genesis in the same dynamics of competition, limited resources, and unequal distribution of power. These notions, along with the idea that conflict is an inherent aspect of human nature, are problematic. They justify human conflict and violence as natural expressions of the concept of the *survival of the fittest* that informs the biological theory of evolution. Likewise, the idea of social Darwinism (as applied to economic, political, and social practices) is invoked to justify extremes of wealth and poverty, cut-throat political competition, and competitive, aloof social relationships. These are fertile grounds for ongoing, intractable conflicts, which by their very presence make satisfaction of the basic human needs of all involved extremely

difficult or impossible and render the human eternal quest for peace utopian and unrealistic.

Although peace has always been the central objective of many religions, poets, mystics, philosophers, writers, and ordinary people, there is neither an agreed upon definition of peace nor consensus on how to achieve it. In fact, there is not even a definitive agreement that peace is necessarily always desirable. Views on the nature and types of peace include Immanuel Kant's notion of perpetual peace; Johan Galtung's concept of negative peace (absence of war) and positive peace (presence of harmony); Salomon and Nero's classification of microlevel peace (harmony between individuals) and macrolevel peace (absence of war, armed conflict, and violence at the level of the collective); Ben-Porath's holistic and narrow (conflict resolution-based) categories of peace; and the democratic peace theory based on the notion that democracies do not go to war with one another. Some current scholars hold the view that the democratic peace theory is a new version of Kant's concept of peace put forward in his 1795 essay *Perpetual Peace* (see Barash & Webel, 2008).

This range of views about peace clearly indicates the need for a more systematic, comprehensive, integrated approach to the concept of peace, its definition, forms of expression, prerequisites for its creation, and its relationship with conflict and human needs. The remainder of this article outlines the main elements of an integrated formulation of issues of conflict, peace, and human needs. This formulation is based on currently accepted views on human needs, conflict, and peace and on my own observations and research in the decade-long course of the implementation of the Education for Peace Program involving some 100,000 children and youth along with their teachers and parents, as well as community leaders, in several countries in Europe, North

America, and Africa. These populations included individuals from war-ravaged, poverty-stricken, authoritarian societies as well as from prosperous, democratic countries.

In 2002, Danesh and Danesh put forward the notion that unity, not conflict, is the primary law operating in all human conditions and that conflict is simply absence of unity. They further argued that both conflict resolution and peace creation are specific processes of unity building. They defined unity as a conscious and purposeful condition of convergence of two or more unique entities in a state of harmony, integration, and cooperation to create a new evolving entity or entities, usually of a same or higher nature.

Later, I formulated the integrative theory of peace (ITP), which holds that our understanding of human needs, as well as conflict and peace, is shaped by our respective worldviews – our view of reality, human nature, purpose of life, and human relationships (Danesh, 2006).

The ITP asserts:

- Peace is a psychosocial and political as well as moral and spiritual condition requiring a conscious approach, a universal outlook, and an integrated, unifying strategy.
- Peace is the expression of a unity-based worldview.
- The unity-based worldview is the prerequisite for creating both a culture of peace and a peace-based approach to conflict resolution.
- Only a dynamic, progressive, conscious, and all-inclusive state of peace resulting from a unity-based worldview is capable of meeting the fundamental tripartite human needs – survival, association, and transcendence – which shape all human endeavors and life processes at both individual and collective levels.

Of these needs, survival is the most immediate, association the most compelling, and transcendence the most consequential. Not surprisingly, much of human knowledge, effort, and attention has always been, and still is, focused primarily on our survival needs. Most scientific theories give primacy to survival in their explanation of various human activities and behavior. They explain that much of the biological tendencies and psychosocial preoccupation of individuals and groups is limited to concerns for their personal and/or group survival. Within the developmental paradigm of ITP, a reasonable level of preoccupation with survival needs is both understandable and necessary. However, the fact that this focus in the modern world has now reached unhealthy proportions – expressed in the extreme self-centered individualism and/or collective coercion in many societies – merits serious attention and modification.

Association needs refer to issues of human relationships such as equality, freedom, and justice. Different societies address these needs with varying degrees of success, and much remains to be done with respect to these needs in every society. In fact, the major contemporary schools of thought view most, if not all, human needs within the context of both survival and association needs. They concentrate on the twin issues of economic conditions and modes of governance with a focus on safety, security, and economic development, on the one hand, and democracy, freedom, human rights, and personal success and happiness, on the other. These programs, although valuable, basically either ignore the third category of human needs – the need for transcendent purpose and meaning – or relegate such needs to a subsection of the second category. Even with respect to human association needs, little, if any, effort is made to understand and develop the main sources of all human relationships and associations

Table 1 Correlation of concepts of worldview, human needs, human rights, conflict, and peace

Worldview	Human needs	Human rights	State of conflict	State of peace
Survival-based worldview	Survival needs (food, shelter, healthcare . . .) *First-order needs*	Right to security and sustenance	Fear-based and power-based conflict *Suppressed conflict*	Force-based peace *Authoritarian oppression*
Identity-based worldview	Association needs (justice, equality, freedom . . .) *Second-order needs*	Right to equality, personal freedom, and happiness	Competition-based conflict *Survival of the fittest*	Conflict-based peace *Adversarial democracy*
Unity-based worldview	Spiritual needs (transcendent meaning/ purpose) *Third-order needs*	Right to truth, justice, and freedom of spiritual conviction	Unity in diversity *All-centered relationships*	Unity-based peace *Consultative democracy*

– unity, with its animating force: love. Such programs neither consider the dynamics of human love in all its grandeur, depth, and creativity, nor consider the powerful and creative force of unity as a worthy subject of scientific inquiry and experimentation. Even in their emphasis on such lofty issues as equality, justice, and freedom, they underline the existing divisions, dichotomies, and conflicts and do not approach them from a truly universal perspective in the context of the principle of unity in diversity. Consequently, the supraordinate human need for transcendence and spirituality receives little, if any, attention from parents, teachers, and the community at large. Even when issues of religion and morality are included in the education of each new generation, unfortunately in most cases these concepts are taught within the parameters of survival- and identity-based worldviews revolving around concepts of otherness, conflict, and the superiority of one group over others (Danesh, 2006).

This brief review of the integrative formulation of human needs, conflict, and peace, outlined above becomes clearer when

the role of worldview regarding these issues is further delineated. Table 1 depicts the link between worldview, human needs, human rights, conflict, and peace.

From this review it is evident that our understanding of the relationship between human needs, conflict, and peace is evolving and calls for further research and deliberation.

SEE ALSO: Conflict Resolution, Interactive; Intergroup Conflict, Theories of.

REFERENCES

Barash, D., & Webel, C. (2008). *Peace and conflict studies*. Thousand Oaks, CA: Sage.

Burton, J. (1990). *Conflict: Resolution and provention*. New York, NY: St. Martin's Press.

Danesh, H. B. (2006). Towards an integrative theory of peace education. *Journal of Peace Education*, 3(1), 55–78.

Danesh, H. B., & Danesh, R. (2002). Has conflict resolution grown up? Toward a new model of decision making and conflict resolution. *International Journal of Peace Studies*, 7(1), 59–76.

Galtung, J., Jacobsen, C. G., Brand-Jacobsen,
    K. F., & Tschudi, F. (2000). *Searching for peace:
    The road to TRANSCEND*. London, UK: Pluto
    Press in association with TRANSCEND.
Hertnon, S. (2005). Theory of universal human
    needs. Retrieved April 5, 2011, from http://
    www.nakedize.com/universal-human-needs.
    cfm#human-needs
Kok, H. (2007). Reducing violence: Applying
    the human needs theory to the conflict in
    Chechnya. *Review of International Law and
    Politics*, 3(11), 89–108.
Maslow, A. H. (1973). *The farther reaches
    of human nature*. Harmondsworth, UK:
    Penguin.

ADDITIONAL RESOURCES

Christie, D. J. (1997). Reducing direct and
    structural violence: The human needs theory.
    Peace and Conflict: Journal of Peace Psychology,
    3, 315–332.
Doyal, L., & Gough, I. (1991). *A theory of human
    needs*. London, UK: Macmillan.

Human Rights and Human Rights Violations, Psychological Aspects of

JOST STELLMACHER AND GERT SOMMER

The Universal Declaration of Human Rights
(UDHR) adopted on December 10, 1948 by
the General Assembly of the United Nations
is the major reference document for international human rights. The UDHR and
the subsequent International Covenants
on Human Rights of 1966 (on Economic,
Social, and Cultural Rights and on Civil and
Political Rights) represent the International
Bill of Human Rights. In these documents,
two generations or dimensions of human
rights have been distinguished. The first
dimension consists of civil and political
human rights, for example the prohibition
of discrimination, the right to life, the

prohibition of torture or inhuman treatment, the right to freedom of thought, of
opinion and expression, the right to seek
asylum. The second dimension is made up
of economic, social, and cultural human
rights, for example the right to work, protection against unemployment, the right to
equal pay for equal work, the right to remu-
neration ensuring an existence worthy of
human dignity, the right to a standard of
living adequate for one's health and well-
being, including food, housing, and medical
care, and the right to education. In addition,
a third generation of human rights has been
discussed in the United Nations but not yet
adopted. It includes mainly the right of
peoples to peace, the right to development,
and the right to a healthy environment.
(See ETHICAL CONSIDERATIONS IN PEACE
PSYCHOLOGY.)

Three principles characterize the UDHR:
(1) human rights are *inalienable* and a
"common standard of achievement for all
peoples and all nations" (preamble of the
UDHR); (2) human rights are *indivisible*, i.e.,
every right of the UDHR must be acknowledged and realized; (3) human rights are *universal*, i.e., they apply to every person and in
every situation.

During the Cold War, a bisection of
human rights was common: Western countries stressed civil rights, whereas Eastern
countries stressed economic rights. This
bisection seems to hold true even now.
However, the UDHR emphasizes the indi-
visibility of human rights. Likewise, the
former president of the United States,
Franklin D. Roosevelt, required four
freedoms in his presidential address of
January 6, 1941: freedom of speech and
expression, freedom to worship God,
freedom from want, which means "economic understandings, which will secure to
every nation a healthy peacetime life for its
inhabitants," and freedom from fear, which
is a reduction of armaments to avoid physical aggression among nations.

IMPORTANCE AND KNOWLEDGE

The UDHR can be regarded as one of the most important documents of the twentieth century because it defines a catalogue of inalienable rights, which should be valid for all people of the world. Indeed, empirical studies show that the realization of human rights is evaluated as very important. For example, a representative survey in Germany (Stellmacher, Sommer, & Brähler, 2005) showed that 76% of respondents rated the worldwide realization of human rights as "extremely important." Similar results have been found in several studies across different nations (Sommer & Stellmacher, 2009) – from North America (McFarland & Mathews, 2005) and Western Europe (e.g., Finland, Germany, Netherlands, and Norway) to Bulgaria and Russia (Puncheva-Michelotti, Michelotti, & Gahan, 2008), Serbia and Guatemala. However, this seemingly strong support for human rights must be considered critically, because actual knowledge of human rights remains poor. When people are asked to recall all the human rights they know, on average only two to four human rights can be recalled. The UDHR, however, contains 30 articles with more than 100 single rights. Poor knowledge of human rights has been confirmed in several samples (students, nonstudents, and representative samples) and in different nations (the United States, Western and Eastern Europe, Guatemala) (Sommer & Stellmacher, 2009).

Moreover, there is a sharp distinction between civil and economic human rights. In spontaneous listings of human rights, respondents recall primarily civil human rights, whereas economic human rights are hardly known. This result was confirmed when people were asked to identify human rights from a list of different rights, including also nonhuman rights (Stellmacher et al., 2005). Thus, the cognitive representation of human rights seems to consist of only a few civil human rights and is in line with the bisection of human rights made by politicians and media. This implies that more extensive human rights education is needed.

PSYCHOLOGICAL DIMENSIONS OF HUMAN RIGHTS ORIENTATIONS

Different attitudes toward human rights can be distinguished. In an international study with students from 35 countries, Doise, Spini, and Clémence (1999) distinguished four types of respondents according to their attitude patterns about human rights: the advocates, having a positive attitude towards human rights; the skeptics with a less positive attitude; the personalists, showing strong personal involvement while being skeptical of the government's effectiveness in enforcing human rights; and the governmentalists, showing little personal involvement while being convinced of the government's effectiveness in enforcing human rights. Similarly, McFarland and Mathews (2005) identified three major dimensions of human rights orientations: endorsement (i.e., general support for human rights principles), restriction (i.e., support for human rights restrictions under conditions of crisis), and commitment (i.e., preference for human rights policies vs. nationally focused goals). Cohrs, Maes, Moschner, and Kielmann (2007) showed that the endorsement of human rights has an impact on the amount of behaviors aimed at promotion of human rights. In Germany, about 1% of the population could be identified as the core of activists in human rights protection.

PSYCHOLOGICAL CONCEPTS AND HUMAN RIGHTS VIOLATIONS

The UDHR incorporates more than 100 single rights and represents a very high standard of achievement. This means that every country violates human rights in a more or less extensive way. Even Western democracies, which do quite well in realizing civil rights within their boundaries, may contribute to human rights violations when, for instance, they support authoritarian governments or fight other democracies because they do not fit with their ideology or political and economic interests. Since the terror attacks in the United States in 2001, civil and political rights have been constricted in many Western countries. The armed forces of Western countries have been involved in torture and other inhuman treatment. Also, it might well be argued that the economic system of neoliberalism pushed by the leading industrialized Western countries is at least partly accountable for economic human rights violations in developing countries. Major reasons for the acceptance of human rights violations under specific circumstances might be political and economic interests. However, psychological processes also play an important role. (See INTERROGATION, PSYCHOLOGY AND.)

Psychological studies have shown that human rights violations are perceived and evaluated in different ways depending on the situation and predisposing characteristics of the personality of the observer. Staerklé and Clémence (2004) found a principle–application gap in the evaluation of human rights violations. Their participants revealed a large gap between the support for general principals of human rights and the evaluation of concrete violations of those principles. This result indicates that human rights violations tend to be more acceptable in situations where the attributes and actions of the victim are available to be used to justify the violations. Other studies show that persons are more willing to accept human rights violations conducted by institutions of the home country than conducted by institutions of foreign countries. In the same way, human rights violations in the home country conducted by established authorities are more acceptable than human rights

violations in foreign countries conducted by foreign governments (Stellmacher & Sommer, 2008). These results reflect a double standard in the evaluation of human rights violations.

Besides these context effects, individuals differ systematically in the way they think and behave regarding human rights and human rights violations. The most prominent individual differences in this context are the right-wing authoritarian and social dominance orientations. Persons with high authoritarian or high social dominance orientations are more willing to accept human rights violations conducted by their own country. Furthermore, such persons have a more negative orientation toward human rights in general. Persons with high authoritarian or social dominance orientations show less general support for human rights, are more willing to accept restrictions of human rights in times of crisis, and prefer nationally focused goals in comparison to human rights policies (McFarland & Mathews, 2005; Cohrs et al., 2007). Reasons for this might be that persons high on right-wing authoritarianism believe in the superiority of their own group and will follow the values and norms of the authorities of their ingroup more than universal values and norms, as represented by human rights. Also, persons with high social dominance orientations will oppose human rights because they are in contradiction to the hierarchy-enhancing ideologies of social dominators, which function as legitimization of inequality and discrimination.

Other research examining the relationship between human rights and personal values found that universalism and benevolence values showed positive correlations to human rights attitudes, while power and security values showed negative correlations (e.g., Cohrs et al., 2007). These results demonstrate that values can support or impede a positive orientation toward human rights.

(See VALUES, NONVIOLENCE, AND PEACE PSYCHOLOGY.)

Further individual differences which show an impact on human rights attitudes and behaviours are: (1) dispositional empathy, with a positive correlation to human rights commitment and endorsement; (2) nationalism, with negative correlations to human rights attitudes and the tolerance of human rights violations of the home country; and (3) ethnocentrism, with negative correlations to human rights commitment and positive correlations to the support for human rights restrictions under conditions of crisis (McFarland & Mathews, 2005; Sommer & Stellmacher, 2009). (See EMPATHY; PATRIOTISM AND NATIONALISM; ETHNOCENTRISM.)

Additionally, some recent studies show that individual differences interact with context effects regarding the evaluation of human rights violations. Compared to human rights violations by a foreign government, violations by one's own government are more tolerated when authoritarianism or social dominance orientations are elevated (Sommer & Stellmacher, 2009). (See SOCIAL DOMINANCE THEORY; AUTHORITARIAN PERSONALITY.)

The above results send an important message about human rights education programs: It is not only important to enhance the knowledge and the importance of human rights; it is also important to reduce personality characteristics which are at odds with the idea of human rights.

HUMAN RIGHTS EDUCATION

The empirical results demonstrate the necessity of more extensive human rights education. If people are unaware of feasible regulations for human rights, the threat rises that wars can be legitimated with the argument that another government is violating human rights. However, human rights violations are a self-evident and essential part of every violent conflict and every war. Thus, conducting wars in order to enforce human rights will in itself increase the danger of human rights violations.

Several important declarations of the United Nations Education, Science, and Culture Organization (UNESCO) have stressed the close relationship and interdependence between human rights, peace, and democracy. While peace is often defined negatively as the absence of war, peace can also be defined positively, using the UDHR as reference. In a culture of peace, as declared by the UN General Assembly, human rights are one of seven core elements. These elements are perceived as being major targets for general education, which is why UNESCO calls for a transformation of traditional education. Additionally, human rights education is defined by the UDHR as a human right in itself (preamble and Article 26). The UN General Assembly stressed the necessity of human rights education by announcing the Decade for Human Rights Education for 1995–2004, followed by the World Program for Human Rights Education, 2005–2015. (See CULTURE OF PEACE.)

Although a lot of suggestions for human rights education programs have been developed (e.g., Benedek, 2006), scientific evaluations of those programs are rare. This is another major field for psychology research. For instance, evaluation studies by Stellmacher and Sommer (2008) showed that human rights education can be effective. They demonstrated that just five human rights sessions during a university seminar on peace psychology not only enhanced knowledge of human rights, but also influenced the attitudes towards human rights positively and decreased ethnic prejudice. Altogether, if people are unaware of their rights, then those rights are of little relevance. Thus, human rights education in schools, universities, and other public educational institutions is of great importance. And the realization of human rights is of high priority for a culture of peace.

SEE ALSO: Authoritarian Personality; Culture of Peace; Empathy; Ethical Considerations in Peace Psychology; Ethnocentrism; Interrogation, Psychology and; Patriotism and Nationalism; Social Dominance Theory; Values, Nonviolence, and Peace Psychology.

REFERENCES

Benedek, W. (2006). *Understanding human rights: Manual on Human Rights Education.* Retrieved August 28, 2009, from http://www.etc-graz.at/typo3/index.php?id=818.

Cohrs, J. C., Maes, J., Moschner, B., & Kielmann, S. (2007). Determinants of human rights attitudes and behavior: A comparison and integration of psychological perspectives. *Political Psychology, 28,* 441–469.

Doise, W., Spini, D., & Clémence, A. (1999). Human rights studied as social representations in a cross-national context. *European Journal of Social Psychology, 29,* 1–29.

McFarland, S., & Mathews, M. (2005). Who cares about human rights? *Political Psychology, 26,* 365–385.

Puncheva-Michelotti, P. Y., Michelotti, M., & Gahan, P. G. (2008). *Comparison of the determinants of human rights perceptions and their relationship with corporate social responsibility in Russia and Bulgaria.* Social Science Research Network. Retrieved October 13, 2008, from http://ssrn.com/abstract=1283988.

Sommer, G., & Stellmacher, J. (2009). *Menschenrechte und Menschenrechtsbildung. Eine psychologische Bestandsaufnahme* [Human rights and human rights education: A psychological review]. Wiesbaden, Germany: Verlag für Sozialwissenschaften.

Staerklé, C., & Clémence, A. (2004). Why people are committed to human rights and still tolerate their violation: A contextual analysis of the principal–application gap. *Social Justice Research, 17,* 389–406.

Stellmacher, J., & Sommer, G. (2008). Human rights education. *Social Psychology, 39,* 70–80.

Stellmacher, J., Sommer, G., & Brähler, E. (2005). Human rights: Knowledge, importance and support – Results of two representative studies in Germany. *Peace and Conflict: Journal of Peace Psychology, 11,* 267–292.

ADDITIONAL RESOURCES

Moghaddam, F. M., & Vuksanovic, V. (1990). Attitudes and behavior toward human rights across different contexts: The role of right-wing authoritarianism, political ideology and religiosity. *International Journal of Psychology, 25,* 455–474.

Universal Declaration of Human Rights. Retrieved August 28, 2009, from http://www.un.org/en/documents/udhr/

Humanitarian Military Intervention, Support for

SAM G. MCFARLAND

When world leaders gathered for the United Nations World Summit in September 2005 they adopted a new policy called "responsibility to protect." This policy committed the UN to protecting populations that are threatened with genocide, crimes against humanity, and ethnic cleansing when their national government cannot or will not do so. In dire situations, and when lesser methods cannot succeed, the responsibility to protect obligates the UN or a designated regional group (e.g., NATO, the African Union) to enter a country with military force to protect people from these horrible crimes. (See GENOCIDE AND MASS KILLING: ORIGINS AND PREVENTION; HUMAN RIGHTS AND HUMAN RIGHTS VIOLATIONS, PSYCHOLOGICAL ASPECTS OF.)

This policy was initiated following tragic failures during the 1990s. The most significant was the failure of the UN to intervene to stop the 1994 genocide in Rwanda, which took between 800,000 and 1 million lives in just 100 days. Many world leaders felt great guilt over that failure. Also, the "ethnic cleansing" in Bosnia in the mid-1990s took 200,000 lives, but neither the UN nor NATO intervened for three years. The slaughter of virtually all the male population of the city of Srebrenica in July 1995 took more than 8,000 lives. Despite a UN promise of protection, neither the UN nor NATO tried to stop this slaughter. In 1999 Serbian President Slobodan Milosevic tried to expel at gunpoint all ethnic Albanians from Kosovo province.

Because the governments of these countries were complicit in these killings and abuses, civilians within them needed protection from outside. The UN and other international bodies had to decide whether and how to provide it. The day before the World Summit, General Romeo Dallaire, the powerless commander of UN forces in Rwanda during that genocide, wrote an impassioned plea in the *New York Times* to adopt the responsibility to protect:

> Because the United Nations Security Council members demonstrated inexcusable apathy, I and my small United Nations peacekeeping contingent were forced to watch the slaughter up close with no mandate to intervene. Governments of the world have the chance at the United Nations world summit meeting in New York to make "never again" a reality by agreeing to accept their responsibility to protect civilians in the face of mass murder.

The decision to intervene is never easy, and the issues are complex. Under the responsibility to protect policy, military intervention is limited to genocide and other situations that threaten major loss of life. Further, intervention must follow a careful analysis that all other means for ending the bloodshed have failed or would fail. (For a thorough discussion, see Evans, 2008.)

Humanitarian military intervention poses a difficult issue for peace psychologists and for all who yearn for peace and abhor violent conflict. On the one hand, we are interested, above all else, in creating and preserving peace. For example, the central aim of the Society for the Study of Peace, Conflict, and Violence (Division 48 of the American Psychological Association) is "applying the knowledge and methods of psychology in the advancement of peace and prevention of violence and destructive conflict." (See PEACE PSYCHOLOGY: DEFINITIONS, SCOPE, AND IMPACT.) Military action, even for the purpose of ending a mass killing, appears to contradict that goal. On the other hand, we deeply value all human life. In short, should those who value human life so dearly support or oppose military intervention when its purpose is to prevent a genocide or mass killing?

International policies and moral quandaries aside, there is a limited but growing research literature on individual differences that affect support for humanitarian military intervention. This article reviews that research and offers new data to resolve a difference between findings in America and Germany.

In perhaps the first relevant study, Pratto, Sidanius, Stallworth, and Malle (1994) introduced social dominance orientation (SDO), defined as "the extent that one desires that one's ingroup dominate and be superior to outgroups" (p. 742). They found that the SDO correlated positively, $r = .31$, with support for wars of national self-interest (e.g., "to protect our economic interests"), but negatively, $r = -.41$, with support for wars for humanitarian ends (e.g., "to protect unarmed civilians"). Those low in social dominance were more willing than others to use military force for humanitarian ends, but less willing for nationalistic reasons. (See SOCIAL DOMINANCE THEORY.)

A decade later, McFarland and Mathews (2005) developed a scale of "human rights scenarios" (HRScene) that described historical and current events and offered respondents choices that range from acting on national self-interest to investing national resources, including military forces, to defending citizens against severe human rights violations, particularly against genocide. A sample item reads as follows:

In the central African country of Rwanda, rival tribal groups, Hutu and Tutsi, had a growing hatred. In 1994 the Hutu extremists began killing all Tutsi, including women, children, and babies. It quickly became evident that a deliberate genocide was beginning. United Nations personnel in the country urged the UN to send troops to stop the genocide and said that such a mission could succeed. However, the mission would be dangerous and costly. Do you think the President of the United States should have

(a) sent American troops along with other nations to stop the genocide?
(b) offered supplies and transportation to troops from other nations, but not sent American troops?
(c) not become involved if no vital American interests were at stake?

Other items asked whether the United States should send forces to Sudan along with other nations to stop that ethnic cleansing, and the like. One item, borrowed from the Gallup Organization, asked whether the US military should be used "to stop mass killings and ethnic cleansing," with responses ranging from "much less often" to "much more often" than now. Replicating Pratto et al. (1994), McFarland and Mathews found, for an American sample of mostly adults, that the HRScene correlated −.52 with the SDO. Further, support for military intervention was positively correlated .56 with "globalism" (i.e., a concern for humanitarian and other global needs such as "combating world hunger" and "protecting the natural environment"), .34 with

dispositional empathy (e.g., "I am often quite touched by things that I see happen"), .29 with principled moral reasoning, and .22 with self-rated political liberalism. Negatively, it correlated −.57 with ethnocentrism, −.33 with right-wing authoritarianism (RWA), and −.30 with an attitude of fatalism (e.g., "Our world has its basic and ingrained dispositions, and you really can't do much to change it"). McFarland and Mathews provide information on these various measures. (See EMPATHY; MORAL DEVELOPMENT; IDEOLOGY; ETHNOCENTRISM; AUTHORITARIAN PERSONALITY.)

Data collected by this author in 2009 reconfirmed all of these relationships with support for military intervention on the HRScene except for globalism, which was not assessed. In both McFarland and Mathews and the 2009 sample, support for military intervention was not related to age, sex, education level, or self-reported religiousness. Interestingly, many studies have found authoritarianism and social dominance *positively* predict support for military action for national self-interest (e.g., McFarland, 2005), but they *negatively* predict support for military intervention to end mass killings of non-Americans.

However, studies conducted in Germany appear directly to contradict the American findings for authoritarianism and the social dominance orientation on humanitarian intervention. Fetchenhauer and Bierhoff (2004) developed a ten-item Attitude Toward Military Enforcement of Human Rights scale (ATMEHR) (e.g., "It is still better to go to war for a few months than to sit back and accept long-term violations of human rights."). For a sample of German students, three factors predicted scores on the ATMEHR. In contrast to McFarland and Mathews (2005) and this author's (2009) data, authoritarianism correlated *positively*, $r = .25$, with support for military intervention. Second, "aggressive sanctioning," a willingness to use force against those who engage in antisocial behavior (e.g., parking in a handicapped slot, driving while drunk) correlated .27 with the ATMEHR. The ATMEHR was predicted by civil engagement with human rights (e.g., "I take part in campaigns that are aimed at the enforcement of human rights") only for those who were high in aggressive sanctioning. Finally, being male rather than female correlated .18 with the scale. The ATMEHR was unrelated to a measure of social responsibility, or to "constructive sanctioning" of antisocial behaviors (e.g., kindly asking the offender to stop).

For a later sample of German students and nonstudent adults, Cohrs, Maes, Moschner, & Kielmann (2007) found that authoritarianism correlated .43 with the ATMEHR, replicating Fetchenhauer and Bierhoff (2004), and .45 with the SDO. These correlations contrast with the American studies cited above, where the SDO and RWA correlate *negatively* with support for military intervention. Cohrs et al. (2007) also found that support for military intervention on the ATMEHR correlated strongly with the values of universalism (negatively) and power (positively).

Are these American–German differences due to cultural differences? Or are they due to differences between the ATMEHR and HRScene, both of which claim to measure support for military intervention? The scales appear quite different: The items on the ATMEHR emphasize the use of military force, albeit for human rights, and do not mention particular genocides or other abuses. In contrast, items on the HRScene focus first on specific crimes against humanity in other countries, and it then asks if military force should be used to stop these crimes.

For this article, I tested this issue by administering both the ATMEHR and HRScene to 75 American students along with the RWA, SDO, and the Schwartz measures of universalism and power. The

ATMEHR and HRScene correlated just .15, *ns*. Their patterns of correlations largely replicated the differences cited above. The RWA correlated .25, $p < .05$ with the ATMEHR, replicating the German results, but −.36, $p < .01$, with HRScene, replicating the American results. The SDO correlated .06, *ns*, with the ATMEHR, but −.39, $p < .01$, with HRScene. Similarly, the values of universalism and power correlated respectively .04, *ns*, and .29, $p < .01$ with the ATMEHR, but .36, $p < .01$, and −.02, *ns*, with the HRScene. Further, the ATMEHR correlated .10, *ns*, with ethnocentrism, while the HRScene correlated with ethnocentrism −.36, $p < .01$. (See VALUES, NONVIOLENCE, AND PEACE PSYCHOLOGY.)

In summary, the differences between the German and American results appear due, at least in large part, to the different measures of support for humanitarian intervention. When items focus on the use of military force, even if for generic "human rights," authoritarianism, social dominance, and the value of power tend to positively predict the desire to use force. However, when questions focus on a specific genocide or mass killing of other people, authoritarianism, social dominance, universalism, and ethnocentrism negatively predict a desire to use military force to save them.

McFarland (in press) recently developed a measure of "identification with all humanity" (IWAH), a scale designed to assess a deep positive caring for all human beings. This identification expresses the sense, as Gandhi said, that "All humanity is one undivided and indivisible family." The IWAH consists of nine three-part items in the form of the following two items:

1. How much do you identify with (that is, feel a part of, feel love toward, have concern for) each of the following?
   (a) People in my community
   (b) Americans
   (c) All humans everywhere

2. When they are in need, how much do you want to help:
   (a) People in my community.
   (b) Americans.
   (c) People all over the world.

Because the three identifications are presented together, a comparison is implicitly suggested. Both raw scores for IWAH (the sum of the c. items) and residual scores (the unique variance of the c. items controlling for the other two identifications) are calculated.

McFarland (in press) found that both the raw and residual scores on the IWAH strongly predicted support for human rights (as expressed by support for the International Criminal Court, a desire to prosecute human rights abusers, and believing that governments with poor human rights records should not be supported). However, the IWAH raw and residual scores correlated .00 and .02, *ns*, in both cases, with support for military intervention on the HRScene. A plausible interpretation is that individuals high in identification with all humanity are torn between the desire not to take human life and the desire to save those who are likely to be the victims of genocide. If so, those high in identification with all humanity experience the dilemma that confronts peace psychologists and all who work for peace.

SEE ALSO: Authoritarian Personality; Empathy; Ethnocentrism; Genocide and Mass Killing: Origins and Prevention; Human Rights and Human Rights Violations, Psychological Aspects of; Ideology; Moral Development; Peace Psychology: Definitions, Scope, and Impact; Social Dominance Theory; Values, Nonviolence, and Peace Psychology.

REFERENCES

Cohrs, J. C., Maes, J., Moschner, B., & Kielmann, S. (2007). Determinants of human rights attitudes and behavior: A comparison and integration of psychological perspectives. *Political Psychology, 28,* 441–469.

Evans, G. (2008). *The responsibility to protect: Ending mass atrocity crimes once and for all.* New York, NY: Brookings Institution Press.

Fetchenhauer, D., & Bierhoff, H. W. (2004). Attitudes toward a military enforcement of human rights. *Social Justice Research, 17,* 75–92.

McFarland, S. G. (2005). On the eve of war: Authoritarianism, social dominance, and American students' attitudes toward attacking Iraq. *Personality and Social Psychology Bulletin, 31,* 360–367.

McFarland, S. G. (in press). "Identification with all humanity" as a moral concept and psychological construct. In Y. Araki & M. Karasawa (Eds.), *Intergroup behavior and political psychology.* Tokyo, Japan: Ohfu Politics Library.

McFarland, S. G., & Mathews, M. (2005). Who cares about human rights? *Political Psychology, 26,* 365–385.

Pratto, F., Sidanius, J., Stallworth, L. M., & Malle, B. F. (1994). Social dominance orientation: A personality variable predicting social and political attitudes. *Journal of Personality and Social Psychology, 67,* 741–763.

Humanitarian Workers, Managing Stress in

AMANDA ALLAN AND NICK HASLAM

Humanitarian workers are people who work in theaters of humanitarian crisis that may have been instigated by natural environmental disasters, famine, conflict, or epidemics. These events invariably threaten the homes, livelihoods, safety, security, health, wellbeing, and fabric of the community of large groups of people. The role of a humanitarian worker is to alleviate suffering and to save lives. (See DISASTER RESEARCH.)

RISK FACTORS

Humanitarian workers are repeatedly exposed to situations and phenomena more extreme than most people experience. In the course of their work, they may witness the traumas, helplessness, losses, grief, severe injuries, deaths, and destruction of the livelihood of people *en masse*. Humanitarian workers may be exposed to extreme temperatures and be required to function with basic and inadequate equipment. They often endure lengthy separations from loved ones and live intimately with other aid workers in makeshift and often uncomfortable conditions.

Stress experienced by humanitarian workers can be precipitated by a wide range of risk factors inherent in the humanitarian system itself; factors that are embedded in the interacting environmental, organizational, management, workplace, team, and living contexts of humanitarian work. Humanitarian workers usually operate under the coordination of an organization or organizing body and in teams, which can impose further challenges. Variability in organizational factors such as size of the organization; organizational ethos, goals, budget, governance, and management capacity; as well as diversity of motivation, professionalism, standards, and training within the workforce can pose an additional array of challenges for the humanitarian worker.

Given the variability of conditions and the multiplicity of demands, it is not surprising that stress is an inevitable outcome of humanitarian work. The cost of caring can be high and the contexts and the conditions under which humanitarian workers operate laden with a multitude of strains and stressors. Table 1 summarizes a sample of field- and work-related factors that can substantially increase the potential for strain and accumulative stress in the course of work.

Current research and anecdotal evidence indicates that stress in humanitarian workers is most likely when:

- too much is demanded of the humanitarian worker with insufficient resources to meet the demand;
- the humanitarian worker has unreasonable expectations and a lack of control and influence to adequately mitigate the impact of the demands of the humanitarian context and their own workload;
- there is a lack of clarity of the humanitarian worker's role;
- there is inadequate support both to accomplish the humanitarian goals and to remain resilient under harsh conditions;
- there are difficult relationships or obstacles to constructing effective relationships in the field (e.g., not speaking the language or understanding the culture);
- there are changing circumstances or factors (timelines, staffing capacity, role definitions, available resources, weather) that impact the capacity of the humanitarian worker to do his/her job; and
- there is insufficient appreciation of the effort required to undertake the role.

Unique psychological risk and resiliency factors of individual humanitarian workers interact with contextual risk factors to determine the nature and impact of stress that will be experienced. A sample of personal risk factors of individual humanitarian workers is presented in Table 2.

The cumulative impact of these personal risk factors contributes to a degenerative stress response and reduced levels of resiliency.

BIOPSYCHOSOCIAL MODEL OF STRESS

A biopsychosocial approach is proposed as a helpful and practical theoretical perspective

Table 1 Contextual risk factors

Environmental	Organizational	Management
• Physical demands (of climate, topography, and public health issues) • Insecurity and instability • Human suffering, displacement, and mortality • Inadequate public health and sanitation • Poverty or inequitable affluence • Time frames and tempo of both the emergency response and community momentum • Availability of resources in the community to do the job • Lack of civil law and order • Breaches of humanitarian rights and civil liberties • Incongruent religious and spiritual practices • Language and cultural barriers	• Incompatible organizational ideology • Difficult organizational politics and bureaucracy • Absent or burdensome organizational structure, processes, and governance • Ineffective occupational health and safety, and human resources, policies and practices • Inactive grievance, gender equity, structural violence, sexual harassment, and disability policies • Job insecurity • Inadequate or inequitable salary and conditions • Lack of career development opportunities • Inadequate staff resources • Lack of professional development and training	• Absence of supportive leadership • Unnecessary or destructive autocratic and authoritarian styles • Unclear authority • Inexperienced managers • Burnt-out managers • Poor information or communication flow • Local expertise insufficiently recognized • Lack of recognition of staff team efforts • Poor management of protocols and systems

Workplace	Team	Living
• Inhospitable or uncomfortable working conditions • Large or overwhelming workload • Long hours • Dangerous or difficult tasks • Mentally and emotionally draining work • Overwhelming responsibility • Lack of sense of accomplishment • Mismatch of skills and competency and job requirements • Lack of resources to do the job • Limited opportunities for restorative breaks • Insufficient technology • Working remotely or in isolation	• Low morale, lack of leadership and inspiration • Team conflict • Poor coordination of the team • Language difficulties • Conflicting values and priorities • Poor communication • Competitiveness • Stressed or tired colleagues • Lack of support and compassion within the team • Personality clashes or lack of cohesion • Unhealthy coping behaviors within the team • Serious injury or death of a colleague	• Uncomfortable living quarters • Poor sanitation and hygiene • Poor dietary options • Lack of privacy • Insecure housing • Little separation between living quarters and workplace • Noisy living conditions • Lack of recreational opportunities • Limited access to prayer or meditation • Decreased contact with family and friends • Demanding travel conditions from home to work

Table 2   Personal risk factors

- Decreased levels of cognitive functioning (alertness, concentration, memory, response)
- Fatigue levels
- Lack of sense of agency or control
- Low confidence
- Lack of sense of competency
- Feelings of helplessness
- Uncertainty of role
- Feelings of worry, anxiety, irritability, anger, sadness, grief, depression
- Feeling like not coping
- Poor emotional regulation
- Inability to anticipate
- Lack of sense of achievement
- Desensitization to risks
- Loss of compassion
- Intensity and loss of humor
- Unrealistic expectations of self and others
- Sense of not belonging
- Needing to be alone
- Inability to maintain healthy routines (sleep, diet, rest, exercise, prayer, socializing)
- Not feeling well (headaches, elevated heart rate, nausea, exhausted, pains)
- Disturbed by bad memories, nightmares, recurring thoughts

for understanding the phenomenon of stress and how to manage it. Biopsychosocial models of stress (e.g., Bernard & Krupat, 1994) are usually based on three components of stress: internal, external, and an interaction between the external and internal components.

The *internal component* involves a set of neurological and physiological reactions to stress. Hans Selye (1956), the pioneer of the term "stress," conceived in the 1930s that stress was the response of the body to a demand (a "stressor"). He also suggested that stress could both enhance functioning and capacity ("eustress") or overload functioning and capacity ("distress"). Although an individual may be able to resist the impact of a stressor at first, if the stressor is

persistent and coping resources become depleted, cumulative biological exhaustion is likely to be an outcome over time.

More recently, the fields of neurochemistry and physiology are playing a major role in furthering our understanding of the bioscience of internal stress. "Allostatic load" is a term suggested by McEwen (2000) to describe the physiological costs to the body resulting from chronic exposure to the neural or neuroendocrine stress response and the ongoing adaptive efforts to maintain stability (homeostasis) in response to stressors. There are four main conditions that contribute to allostatic load: (1) repeated stress responses to new stressors; (2) failure to adjust the stress response to similar stressors; (3) failure to moderate or turn off a stress response; and (4) an inadequate stress response that results in the activation of other stress responses.

External components of stress are concerned with the factors that are responsible for precipitating a stress response such as the environmental risk factors outlined above.

The *interactional components* are concerned with the unique and subjectively variable appraisals and reactions to potential stressors which will be influenced by prior experience, expectations, current stress and fatigue levels, life experience, social and cultural backgrounds, coping styles, and motivation.

It is essential that the modern humanitarian worker is sufficiently educated in a biopsychosocial model of stress management before embarking on field assignments to help maintain an informed, responsible, and resilient response to the work.

Wider reading on the topic of stress and resilience will assist in gaining a comprehensive understanding of the diversity of stress outcomes experienced by humanitarian workers as manifested in conditions or behaviors such as hypervigilance (constant alertness and responding as if to unsafe, insecure, or unstable contexts); burnout (accumulative emotional, cognitive, and physical exhaustion); compassion fatigue (exhaustion from giving and empathizing with beneficiaries); primary, secondary, and vicarious trauma responses (psychological disturbance and experiencing of or witnessing the traumatic stories of others) as well as ways of best treating these manifestations with professional support.

MANAGING STRESS

An implication of the biopsychosocial model of stress management is that systematic consideration be given to the biological, psychological, and social factors of preparing and sustaining assignment capability.

Prior to assignment and regardless of previous aid experience, humanitarian workers should undertake a stress fitness analysis, physical and mental health screening, stress management and resilience training and assistance to design an assignment self-care plan that includes strategies for accessing support from peers, managers, family, friends, and professionals. Rest and recreation plans and well-being routines should be thought through at a pragmatic level.

In addition to being well educated in personal stress management, humanitarian workers should also be well versed in the range of environmental stressors and strains (external components) they are likely to encounter in the course of their work. They should make themselves aware of policies and protocols that an organization has in place to support staff and to mitigate the impact of stress, for example, in relation to critical incidents, security, and medical evacuations. Humanitarian workers should ensure they receive an accurate briefing about their assignment and the broader operational context. Essentially, they should seek out stress and security management training. A system for regularly monitoring stress levels and effectiveness of support should be identified and negotiated with the employing agency. Exit from the assignment and field environments, homecoming, and reintegration experiences should be anticipated and support plans put in place such as assignment debriefings and family education. (See COPING: EMOTION AND PROBLEM-FOCUSED.)

The management of stress in humanitarian workers is the joint responsibility of employing organizations and the aid worker. Systematic and consultative organizational processes will more effectively mitigate the impact of contextual risk factors that contribute to undermining resilience.

In summary, four key screening processes are recommended for organizations to proactively reduce the impact of stress and to enhance resilience:

1. screening of the field contexts, security issues, conditions, and resources that a humanitarian worker is likely to encounter in the field;
2. screening of personal expectations, field readiness, stress fitness, monitoring and coping capacity of the individual humanitarian worker prior to entering the field;
3. screening of the capacity of the organization and project managers to mitigate, manage, and monitor the impact of the strains on their team of humanitarian workers; and
4. evaluation of the capacity of the employing agency to facilitate additional support such as critical-incident medical and mental health support for the humanitarian worker if and when needed.

A baseline of screening assists organizations to subsequently design systematic staff support strategies for the mitigation of stress.

Although this essay has focused on stress and resilience, it is worth acknowledging that most aid workers feel they gain more by what they have received because of the experience than what they may have endured. However, to be a sustainable and effective humanitarian worker, it is imperative that the cost of the stress of undertaking humanitarian work and knowledge of how to mitigate its effects are understood and addressed.

SEE ALSO: Coping: Emotion and Problem-Focused; Disaster Research.

REFERENCES

Bernard, L. C., & Krupat, E. (1994). *Health psychology: Biopsychosocial factors in health and illness*. New York, NY: Harcourt Brace.
McEwen, B. S. (2000). Allostasis and allostatic load: Implications for neuropsychopharmacology. *Neuropsychopharmacology, 22*,108–124.
Selye H. (1956). *The stress of life*. New York, NY: McGraw-Hill.

ADDITIONAL RESOURCES

Antares Foundation. (2006). *Managing stress in humanitarian workers: Guidelines for good practice* (2nd ed.). Amsterdam, The Netherlands: Antares Foundation. Retrieved from http://www.antaresfoundation.org/download/managing_stress_in_humanitarian_aid_workers_guidelines_for_good_practice.pdf
Salama, P. (1999). The psychological health of relief workers: Some practical suggestions. *Humanitarian Exchange Magazine, 15*. Retrieved from http://www.odihpn.org/report.asp?id=1043
Schabracq, M. J., Winnubst, J. A. M., & Cooper, C. L. (Eds.). (2003). *The handbook of work and health psychology* (2nd ed.). Chichester, UK: John Wiley & Sons, Ltd.

Humiliation and Dignity

EVELIN G. LINDNER

Humiliation and dignity are of crucial significance for peace, and for the field of peace psychology. Already the very definition of

peace is deeply interwoven with humiliation and dignity. In a normative frame defined by human rights, peace is conceptualized as successful dialogue embedded in mutual respect for every participant's equality in dignity. In contrast, throughout history, peace often meant calm and quiet achieved through success in inflicting humiliation on one's population. Still today, the latter definition of peace reigns in large parts of the world. Both definitions are mutually exclusive, and both camps tend to feel insulted and humiliated when criticized by the other, something that, in turn, can be disruptive of peace.

The definition of humiliation that Evelin Lindner developed is as follows: Humiliation is a complex phenomenon that entails acts of humiliation responded to with feelings of humiliation. Humiliation as an act means the enforced lowering of a person or group, a process of subjugation that damages or strips away their pride, honor, or dignity. To be humiliated is to be placed, against one's will (very occasionally with one's consent as in cases of religious self-humiliation or in sadomasochism) and often in deeply hurtful ways, in a situation that is greatly inferior to what one feels one should expect. Humiliation entails demeaning treatment that transgresses established expectations. It may involve acts of force, including violent force. At its heart is the idea of pinning down, putting down, or holding to the ground. Indeed, one of the defining characteristics of humiliation as a process is that the victim is forced into passivity, acted on, and made helpless. People react in different ways when they feel humiliated. Some people may experience rage. When this rage is turned inward, it can cause depression and apathy. Rage turned outward can express itself in violence, even in mass violence when leaders are available to forge narratives of group humiliation. Leaders such as Nelson Mandela, in contrast, translate humiliation into constructive social change (adapted from Desmond Tutu in

528   HUMILIATION AND DIGNITY

Lindner, 2010, p. 1; 2006, p. 172; see also www.humiliationstudies.org/whoweare/evelin.php).

The significance of humiliation and dignity at the present juncture in human history can only be understood by using a larger geohistorical lens. In 1757, in the English language, the connotations of the verbs to humiliate and to humble parted in opposite directions. Until that time, the verb to humiliate did not signify the violation of dignity. To humiliate meant merely to lower, to humble, or to remind underlings of their "due lowly place." Peace was defined as successful subjugation of inferiors by way of routine humiliation that was regarded as prosocial.

Medieval Christianity stressed the misery and worthlessness of *homo viator*, earthly man. Life on Earth meant suffering, which had to be accepted with dutiful and obedient humility and submissiveness. At best, happiness could be expected in afterlife. This frame of mind characterized not only medieval Christianity. History attests that in the wake of the crucial turning point around 10,000 years ago, when agriculture-based civilizations began to emerge from Mesopotamia to the Nile, otherwise widely divergent societies followed the "dominator model" rather than a "partnership model" (Riane, 1987). Hierarchies of domination, with a rigidly male-dominant "strongman" rule, both in the family and state, characterized the Samurai of Japan as much as the Aztecs of Meso-America.

In other words, the "civilized habitus" that sociologist Norbert Elias (1994) describes could also be called the "successfully humiliated habitus." The French court, the Indian caste system, the Chinese system of kowtowing, and the Japanese bow all express and reinforce strong hierarchies, all constructed around practices of successfully humiliated habitus of ritual humbling. This form of humiliation could be labeled "honor humiliation," the form that was seen as legitimate during the past millennia (and is still regarded as legitimate in contemporary honor cultures).

Honor was inescapable, and it was ranked. Honorable gentlemen had the duty to defend their honor against humiliation from peers in duels or duel-like wars. In contrast, duels were not permitted to underlings. A lord and his warriors in feudal Japan, for instance, had the legal right to use their swords to kill lower persons, such as farmers, traders, or outcasts, when they deemed it necessary, without having to expect any duel-like responses. Superiors instilled dread and apprehension in underlings and threatened them with violence and terror, from torture to killing. It was regarded as a duty for superiors to routinely humiliate their subjects to show them down to their due lowly place and thus keep stability and order, peace and quiet. Over time, continuous humbling, shaming, and humiliating became sufficient to keep subalterns in subjugation, particularly when underlings had learned to feel ashamed at even contemplating failing their master's expectations.

Inferiors (and the majority were inferiors) had to be cautious and preserve submissiveness *vis-à-vis* their superiors, at least overtly, unless they were prepared for death. It was potentially lethal to displease one's masters, and fear reigned. Women were inferiors by definition and were usually not entitled to defend humiliated honor in the same way as men. There was no female honor similar to male honor, except that women were expected to accept lowliness and subjugation with deference and display chastity. Women represented a "substrate" to male honor.

The term dignity has its etymological roots in the Latin words *decus* and *decorum* (Sanskrit *dac-as*, "fame"). For Cicero, dignity was a quality of masculine beauty. Even though it was discussed, the concept of dignity was not forged into an internally consistent set of ideas in Europe until the

Renaissance. The Renaissance began in Florence, one of the first successful global players. Giannozzo Manetti (1396–1459), son of a Florentine merchant, Marsilio Ficino (1433–1499), another Florentine humanist, and Giovanni Pico della Mirandola (1463–1494) gave philosophical and theological form to the importance of this-worldly dignity.

The concept of dignity opposes both the discourses of ranked collectivism and this-worldly suffering. It embraces life on Earth as something positive and rejects collectivist hierarchy, instead emphasizing individual rights. The Age of Reason, with the Enlightenment emerging in the eighteenth century, germinated ideas such as freedom, democracy, and the establishment of a contractual basis of rights. These ideas ultimately led to the scientific method, to the ideas of religious and racial tolerance, and to the concept of states as self-governing republics through democratic means.

The linguistic shift in the meaning of humiliation in 1757 preceded the American Declaration of Independence (July 4, 1776) and the French Revolution (August 4, 1789), both rallying points for the human rights movement. The Universal Declaration of Human Rights was adopted by the United Nations General Assembly on December 10, 1948. Article 1 reads: "All human beings are born free and equal in dignity and rights. They are endowed with reason and conscience and should act towards one another in a spirit of brotherhood." In this context, humiliation is the enforced lowering of any person or group that damages their equality in dignity. To humiliate is to transgress the rightful expectation of every human being that everybody's equality in dignity will be respected as a basic human right.

Dignity humiliation is profoundly different from honor humiliation. The linguistic shift of the meaning of the word humiliation in 1757 signals that, even though humiliation was always central to the human experience, its significance increases together with the rise of the ideals that inform human rights: the experience of humiliation becomes more intense, it affects more people, and it increases the risk for violent responses but also the chances for systemic change.

When everybody is invited as equal members into the human family, being put down hurts and humiliates more. While humiliating underlings was seen as beneficial in the context of ranked honor, this turns into a violation in a human rights context. Human rights un-rank human worthiness and are therefore not simply about dignity, but about equality in dignity or non-domination (Pettit, 1997).

Honor is a more collective feeling and institution than dignity. Honor is worn like armor, and people may defend their group's honor against humiliators merely as a duty, without much personal emotion. Dignity humiliation, in contrast, affects the core of the individual. In a human rights context, being treated as a second-class citizen contradicts its very political, cultural, and ethical spirit. Practices and institutions that once were normal – *patria potestas*, coverture, slavery, bondage, serfdom, feudalism, lords and vassals, apartheid, anthrosupremacy, speciesism – turn into *rankism* (Fuller, 2003). Rankings by sex, race, class, imperialism, age, or ability all acquire the label of illegitimately discriminatory inequality.

In an honor culture, humiliation is ubiquitous, with only masters being entitled to reject attempts to humiliate them, while underlings were required to subserviently succumb to humiliation. Human rights extend the entitlement to reject humiliation to every human being and make its application illegitimate in all cases. Millions of former subalterns, those who suffered in silence and would never have dared to raise their voice, begin to feel humiliated and request a say. Human rights generate millions of equal players, equally entitled, no longer a few aristocrats overseeing the majority of meek subjects. Moreover, not only is each humiliator now a violator, every member in a social environment that fails to protect victims turns into a violator. If the international community allows atrocities to be perpetrated in their midst, the entire human family turns into a potential perpetrator of humiliation. Standing idly by is no longer an option in a context of human rights. (See BYSTANDER INTERVENTION.)

Moral judgment depends on feelings, and feelings of humiliation are the strongest emotional driving force of the human rights movement. The ability to feel humiliated on behalf of oneself and others in the face of violations of dignity represents the emotional engine for the human rights movement. Feelings of humiliation drive *conscientization*, which, in turn, provides the motivation and energy to initiate systemic change toward a more dignified and peaceful world. Conscientization is "a psychological process in which individuals and groups are politically transformed by building a common consciousness that embraces the value of active political nonviolence" (Christie, 2006, p. 13).

Since feelings of humiliation can also be translated into acts of violence – they represent the nuclear bomb of the emotions (term coined by Lindner) – and can drive violent cycles of humiliation, peace is lost when those feelings are elicited without being guided toward Mandela-like constructive systemic change. *Hutu* means "servant," which signifies that the 1994 genocide in Rwanda was perpetrated by recently risen subalterns on their former ruling elite, a path that Mandela avoided.

Human rights call for large-scale systemic change, inspired by a new human awareness of global unity. In the spirit of the concept of a decent society (Margalit, 1996), a society in which institutions do not have humiliating effects, human rights entail the demand to build a decent world society. This requires the creation of new local and global practices and institutions that include every citizen into the stewardship of their world as a joint task where dignity is proactively increased, rather than conflict merely resolved. Peace is no longer the peace of underlings being forced and manipulated into quiet submission under systemic humiliation, but the institutionalization of dignified mutuality in dialogue among equals.

SEE ALSO: Bystander Intervention.

REFERENCES

Christie, D. J. (2006). What is peace psychology the psychology of? *Journal of Social Issues, 62,* 1, 1–17.

Eisler, R. T. (1987). *The chalice and the blade: Our history, our future.* London, UK: Unwin Hyman.

Elias, N. (1994). *The civilizing process* (2 vols.). Oxford, UK: Blackwell.

Fuller, R. W. (2003). *Somebodies and nobodies: Overcoming the abuse of rank.* Gabriola Island, Canada: New Societies.

Lindner, E. G. (2006). *Making enemies: Humiliation and international conflict.* Westport, CT: Praeger Security International, Greenwood.

Lindner, E. G. (2010). *Gender, humiliation, and global security: Dignifying relationships from love, sex, and parenthood to world affairs.* Santa Barbara, CA: Praeger Security International, ABC-CLIO.

Margalit, A. (1996). *The decent society.* Cambridge, MA: Harvard University Press.

Pettit, P. (1997). *Republicanism: A theory of freedom and government.* Oxford, UK: Clarendon Press.

ADDITIONAL RESOURCES

www.humiliationstudies.org (Human Dignity and Humiliation Studies)

www.tc.columbia.edu/ICCCR/ (International Center for Cooperation and Conflict Resolution)

www.upeace.org/ (University for Peace)

I

Identity-Based Conflicts, The ARIA Contingency Approach to

JAY ROTHMAN

A major focus of the ARIA methodology of conflict engagement is its disciplined approach to *conflict as opportunity*. Using music as its primary organizing metaphor (an "aria"), this methodology views conflict as an opportunity to foster creativity and resonance within and between people and their primary group affiliations (Rothman, 1996). While its focus was originally on creatively engaging identity-based conflicts, with the idea that the deeper the conflict the greater the need and potential for creativity, ARIA has evolved into a more comprehensive approach that builds upon and synthesizes other approaches. Thus, it has become a broader contingency model with the type of intervention suggested dependent upon the analysis of the nature and depth of the conflict. (See CON-FLICT, REDUCTION OF INTERGROUP; CONFLICT MANAGEMENT, RESOLUTION, AND TRANSFORMATION; CONFLICT RESOLUTION, INTERACTIVE; CONFLICTS, CONSTRUCTIVE; IDENTITY CONFLICTS, MANAGING INTRACTABLE.)

STEP ONE: CONFLICT ANALYSIS

ARIA begins with a detailed process of conflict analysis, asking disputants to determine the following separately and interactively: What is this conflict about? Why does it matter to you? How deep does it run? What is functional about it? What is destructive about it? For whom, when, and why? What might be done to mine its creative potential and reduce its destructiveness?

Diagnosis is a form of creative conflict engagement in itself that sometimes requires nothing additional afterward, since clarity and insight can themselves heal wounds derived from misunderstanding and misperception. However, analysis often leads to concrete plans and strategies for intervention of one form or another (e.g., from mediation to dialogue and many methods in between).

The first step in effective conflict engagement is the analytical art of "going slow to go fast," where taking the time necessary to get the definition and dynamics of a conflict

The Encyclopedia of Peace Psychology, First Edition. Edited by Daniel J. Christie.
© 2012 Blackwell Publishing Ltd. Published 2012 by Blackwell Publishing Ltd.

conceptually right to begin with can propel and even expedite practical efforts to creatively address it. Given that most people tend to have a natural and conditioned aversion to conflict, interveners commonly push quickly toward a solution which they think could overcome resistance and lessen the divide. The problem arises when there is a rush to a solution before adequate understanding of the parameters and causes of the conflict is achieved. The deeper the problem, the more likely is this premature solution seeking to occur. Often this results in solving the wrong problems and therefore exacerbates the real issues. Additionally, when conflicts are about identity they may be resistant to "solutions." Instead, a host of other types of creative process and insight-oriented ways forward may be necessary. Indeed, while it may be relatively impossible to "solve" identity conflicts, it is possible to gain insights about them and to reach agreement about their dynamics (including an often difficult and blame-filled look at the past). ARIA seeks to address this problem by introducing disputants and interveners to its contingency approach to conflict analysis and intervention as one way to engage conflicts effectively instead of fleeing from them, fighting them, or seeking to solve them prematurely or in the wrong way.

What's the Problem?

Metaphorically, picture conflict as an iceberg, with identity conflicts at the murky bottom. Goal conflicts rise above identity-based conflicts and reside translucently just beneath the water's surface. Resource conflicts are above the water and are in plain sight, the most empirical and tangible of the three.

Another way of differentiating these conflict levels is by asking the simple questions: What? What for? And why? At the top of the iceberg are the tangible *whats* of a conflict, for example, "I want that house. I understand you do too." Going down one level are the slightly less tangible *what for*s of a conflict: "I want that house because it fits my family perfectly. How about you?" Finally, the deepest level of *whys* are repositories of identities such as "I want that house because it is in a neighborhood where I have close friends and family members."

This "levels of analysis" approach visually suggests an important feature of identity-based conflict that distinguishes it from the other two. (See CONFLICT: LEVELS OF ANALYSIS.) Identity-based conflict contains within it

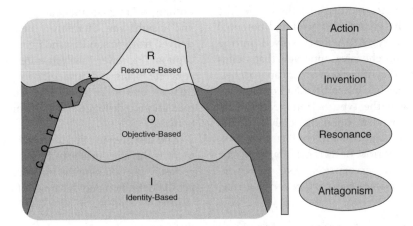

Figure 1   Conflict as iceberg.

the other two levels of conflict as well. Conceptually moving up the iceberg, a conflict, for example over *home* and one's access to and control over it (the root of many community and international identity-based conflicts), will also be about goals (e.g., goals to accomplish sovereignty and territorial integrity) and resources (e.g., economic and military strength). On the other hand, goal conflicts will be primarily about goals and resources (e.g., to establish an independent state in order to be able to gain and to control economic and military resources). And resource conflicts, while also containing the seeds of goal disputes and even identity issues, if and when they are poorly handled, are fundamentally about tangible resources and who controls them, when, and how (e.g., gaining access to and control over scarce resources).

With such a "levels of analysis" approach, the next step before focusing on solution seeking – in the form of dialogue, negotiation, or some problem-solving process that seeks to foster collaboration and coordination between conflict parties and to reduce destruction and violence – is determining the right kind of approach for which level of conflict. In their classic article, Sander and Goldberg (1994) describe the importance of "fitting the forum to the muss" making the obvious but essential point that one size cannot fit all in conflict work. Fisher and Keashly (1991) were among the first to describe the need and outlines of a contingency approach to conflict analysis and resolution.

Here are two examples, domestic and international, for applying the ARIA contingency approach. Suppose a window office becomes available in a certain department and there are two people with the same job classification who qualify for the office. How do you decide who gets it? Is this a resource, an objective, or an identity-based conflict? On the surface, this type of conflict seems like a resource-based conflict: two

employees are fighting over the office. However, the conflict could also be about deeper conflicting objectives between office personnel. Perhaps one person sees the window office as providing the necessary space for doing his or her job better. Or is it rooted even more deeply in people's sense of self-worth (e.g., "I didn't get a window office because the boss doesn't think I'm as valuable to the company as others"). ARIA suggests that interveners who seek to help parties in conflict start at the highest level that seems plausible to them, in this case viewing the problem as simply one of resource scarcity, and then inductively discover whether it is necessary to move down to deeper levels if parties are unsatisfied or if problems worsen from the intervention.

Or at the international level, imagine Israelis and Palestinians all seeking an end to the conflict and agreeing in principle about the need for a two-state solution. The next steps should be easy, right? Not at all, unless it is clear at what level they are operating. Is it about negotiating final status agreements over who gets what, when, and how (i.e., the nature of a political settlement)? Is it about the nature and purposes of that two-state solution (Is it to be demilitarized? Will Palestinian refugees be able to resettle in their old homes within Israel as part of that agreement?)? Or is it about the values and needs of each community (i.e., for identity, dignity, control over destiny, and so on, and ways in which the state will fulfill or further frustrate such existential needs and values)? (See PEACE AND COEXISTENCE PROGRAMS IN THE ISRAELI–PALESTINIAN AND MIDDLE EAST CONTEXT.)

Why is it Happening?

Having diagnosed the predominant level at which the conflict resides in the context of a certain time and place, interveners and disputants then analyze the causes of the conflict. By asking the appropriate questions (e.g., Why does this problem matter to you so much? What do you think some of its causes have been?), and utilizing the self-diagnosis of conflict participants, interveners design, or better still elicit, from the disputants themselves, an approach to address the conflict. My colleagues and I have named this process for deeply analyzing people's more profound concerns, which can be one of the gifts of engaging conflict, "The Power of Why" (Friedman, Withers, & Rothman, 2005).

STEP TWO: HOW SHOULD CONFLICTS BE ADDRESSED?

A hallmark of ARIA is the way it encourages everyone who engages in a specific conflict issue to deal with the same things, in the same way, for the same reasons. This is no small task, and unfortunately, perhaps because of the complexity of this effort, it is all too rare. Instead, in common conflict processes people often talk about different things, in different ways, for different reasons. And thus conflicts are protracted and worsen as they are surfaced and the conventional flight or fight response is further encouraged. By getting everyone to share in an analysis of what the core features or main presenting issues of a conflict and its history are, a single score is developed from which everyone can read. Next, by suggesting different types of intervention strategies and lining them up with the conflict analysis, everyone can move ahead and start off on the same footing. Paraphrasing a famous quote from philosopher Søren Kierkegaard, *conflict is to be understood backward but lived forward.*

If we look at the window conflict, we can see why each person may think they should get the window office. Viewed simply as a resource, the office assignment may be based purely on seniority or who's been there longest. In other words, the parties should be proactive and figure out the best and fairest way to divide up or allocate this resource. If it is viewed as objectives or goals based, then after probing more deeply to understand what function the office might serve, we must find ways to have that function addressed (with or without the office). For example, the desire for the window office might be based on health concerns, for example, someone may get headaches from artificial lighting, or need a larger space for holding meetings. If it is seen primarily as an identity issue, the concerns could be based on the feeling of not being valued by the company, and these deeper problems must therefore be surfaced and addressed in a more comprehensive way eventually.

In addition to being a metaphor, ARIA is also an acronym for four categories of conflict intervention that align with different conflict types: Antagonism, Resonance, Invention, and Action (Rothman, 1997).

- Surfacing of *antagonism*: mostly rooted in the past and most clearly in evidence in identity-based conflicts. Some of the conflict intervention processes used in this phase include dialogue, empowerment mediation, confrontation, and facilitation.
- Narrative excursion into the *resonance* of peoples' hopes, fears, needs, and values, often in the form of story which can be the starting point for goal-based conflicts. Some of the conflict intervention processes used in this phase include narrative mediation, storytelling, and transformative processes.
- *Invention* process of seeking creative ways to foster and promote greater resonance through concrete fulfillment of needs, values, and goals. Some of the conflict intervention processes used in this phase include interest-based bargaining, collaborative visioning, goal setting, and action research.

• *Action*-planning process of concretely designing and implementing ways to sustain and further creative inventions. Some of the conflict intervention processes used in this phase include negotiation, action planning, and techniques drawn from organizational development.

If the conflict is rooted in identity issues, then intervention processes that safely surface the hurts and indignities of the past – or antagonisms – are often necessary. If the conflict presents mainly at the goal level, then understanding and engaging each side's needs and values, their "resonance," is the suggested starting point. If the conflict is mainly about resources, then proactive processes for inventing mutual gains outcomes, or for settling differences amicably, are suggested. The intervention processes suggested by this model move up the iceberg along with the levels of analysis. For example, when starting at the identity-level, begin with antagonism and then move upwards to resonance, then invention, then action, and so forth.

Conflicts often reside at the top or bottom of the iceberg by their nature – the window office is quite concrete while the Israeli–Palestinian conflict is deeply existential. However, depending on the time and place in which the conflict is surfaced and engaged, the organizational example can be more identity based and the international example more resource based.

In the case of the window office, or territorial settlement in the Israeli–Palestinian conflict depending upon how it is analyzed at a given time and place, a concrete solution, or at least a way to concretely address the concerns, is most useful. In the ARIA approach, this is labeled *invention*. In such cases, inventive and proactive interest-based bargaining, collaborative goal setting, and negotiation strategies are often useful to begin with.

If the question about office space has to do with the goals or purposes a window office or a two-state solution will serve those seeking it, then a sustained effort to clarify the separate and overlapping objectives and values of each party is essential. We label this *resonance* to connote internal clarity about an issue, which when expressed well often forges mutual understanding of where such concerns overlap. Fostering resonance through internal and interactive goal clarification and collaborative planning is a useful way forward.

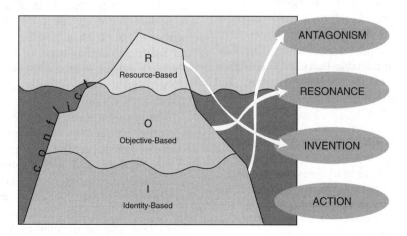

Figure 2   ARIA contingency process.

If the issue has more to do with individuals who feel that their needs and values are threatened or frustrated, then a dialogical approach may be most useful, so that the antagonisms of the past can be safely surfaced and recognized as a first step to moving towards a new future. Given that such conflicts, rooted as they are in past hurts and indignities, are often deeply antagonistic, we start this type of dialogical intervention with what we call *antagonism*.

CONCLUSION

Diagnosing a conflict's primary level and causes is not a very complex or daunting process: it simply takes dedication and the knowledge that it is important to do this before seeking a solution. A full and thoughtful diagnosis allows disputants or third parties who are assisting them to begin to develop a full intervention strategy for addressing the conflict. The ARIA process is designed to assist in this, especially in identity-based conflicts but also in more routine goal and resource conflicts, and to help transform the dissonance of conflict into the resonance of creativity and cooperation.

SEE ALSO: Conflict: Levels of Analysis; Conflict, Reduction of Intergroup; Conflict Management, Resolution, and Transformation; Conflict Resolution, Interactive; Conflicts, Constructive; Identity Conflicts, Managing Intractable; Peace and Coexistence Programs in the Israeli–Palestinian and Middle East Context.

REFERENCES

Fisher, R., & Keashly, L. (1991). The potential complementarity of mediation and consultation within a contingency model of third party consultation. *Journal of Peace Research, 28,* 29–42.

Friedman, V., Withers, B., & Rothman, J. (2006) The power of why: Engaging the goal paradox in program evaluation. *American Journal of Evaluation, 27*(2), 1–18.

Rothman, J. (1996). Reflexive dialogue as transformation. *Mediation Quarterly, 13,* 345–352.

Rothman, J. (1997). *Resolving identity-based conflict in nations, organizations and communities.* San Francisco, CA: Jossey-Bass.

Sander, F., & Goldberg, S. Fitting the forum to the fuss: A user-friendly guide to selecting an ADR procedure. *Negotiation Journal, 10,* 49–67.

ADDITIONAL RESOURCES

http://www.ariagroup.com

Rothman, J. (1992). *From confrontation to cooperation: Resolving ethnic and regional conflict.* Thousand Oaks, CA: Sage.

Identity Conflicts, Managing Intractable

C. MARLENE FIOL AND
EDWARD J. O'CONNOR

Intergroup conflicts are ubiquitous. Sometimes they stem from differences in how groups fundamentally define themselves, and from threats to their identity. When identities are implicated in a conflict, it tends to escalate to encompass an ever widening number of issues, leading parties to become trapped in an ongoing negative spiral from which it is difficult to escape. (See also INTERGROUP VIOLENCE AND PSYCHOSOCIAL INTERVENTIONS, CYCLES OF.)

Identity conflicts arise in numerous types of settings between interdependent groups. Examples include persistently negative interactions between and within professional groups and administrators, between artists and business people, between labor and management, and between and within different demographic and ethnic groups.

"When people's essential identities, as expressed and maintained by their primary group affiliations, are threatened or frustrated, intransigent conflict almost inevitably follows. For such conflicts, conventional methods of conflict management are usually inadequate and may even exacerbate the problem" (Rothman, 1997, p. 5). (See IDENTITY-BASED CONFLICTS, THE ARIA CONTINGENCY APPROACH TO.)

Although there is recognition that identity beliefs of the conflicting parties must change in order to resolve such conflicts (Kelman, 2006), we know very little about the nature of the necessary identity changes, and even less about how and why they occur. This brief essay summarizes the work we have done to address these limitations. The model we have developed entails a multiphase process by which the conflicting parties' identities shift in order to permit eventual harmonious intergroup relations.

NATURE OF INTRACTABLE
IDENTITY CONFLICTS

Intractable conflicts are *protracted* and *social* disputes that are resistant to resolution, lasting for years or even generations. For example, as of this writing, the union–management conflicts at United Airlines have been ongoing for over 20 years. Intractable conflicts are *pervasive* for those involved in the disputes. Such pervasiveness is illustrated in a recent survey of hospital CEOs in the US, which showed that problematic physician–administrator relations was one of their top concerns, second only to financial woes, given that the conflicts between these groups has often expanded to block patient and community initiatives (Fiol & O'Connor, 2009).

Many researchers view identity as being implicated in intractable conflicts. Specifically, intractable conflicts are characterized by *simplifying stereotypes* and *zero-sum conceptualizations of identity*. The identities of parties in intractable conflicts are negatively interdependent, such that a key

component of each group's identity is negation of the other. That is, for Groups A and B, a salient part of Group A's identity is *not* being like members of Group B, and vice versa. For one group to maintain its legitimacy, it must delegitimize the other. Groups bound up in intractable identity conflicts are thus in a state of *mutual disidentification*, which is strengthened by cognitive simplifications whereby parties ignore the potential plurality of outgroup members' identities.

Of all the characteristics of intractable conflicts noted above, identity is not only the most central; it also helps to explain the presence of the others. As a core construct that links the individual with larger collectives, identity explains why such conflicts are both salient and emotional. Moreover, since attacks on identity lead to information distortion, it becomes clearer why dialogue and negotiation often become emotional, persist over time, and become institutionalized.

Because of the centrality of identity in such conflicts, we refer to them as *intractable identity conflicts*. The term highlights that intractable conflicts are difficult to resolve largely because parties are trapped in ongoing mutual disidentification. Our review of the intractable conflict literature suggests that while identity is viewed as central to the formation of intractable conflicts, there has not been a systematic attempt to understand how the management of identity may help to resolve intractability and facilitate intergroup harmony. This essay summarizes how our model begins to address that gap.

MANAGING INTRACTABLE
IDENTITY CONFLICTS

Our model delineates four phases by which groups mired in intractable identity conflicts can move toward harmonious intergroup relations. (For reasons that will become clear at the end of this essay, we will describe the phases of the model in reverse order, beginning with Phase 4 and ending with Phase 1.) The *Cambridge International Dictionary* defines "harmonious" as "peaceful," which denotes agreement and accord in addition to a lack of conflict. Integrative approaches to achieving intergroup harmony (e.g., structural alignment or visioning) can sometimes achieve positive results in the absence of prolonged intractable conflict. In settings marked by intractable conflicts, however, reliance on visioning or structural alignment is usually futile. Although it is difficult to argue against bringing conflicting groups together, past attempts have demonstrated that we cannot get there by promoting integrative solutions for groups who are mired in conflicts so deep and divisive that they have become part of how the groups define themselves. Neither the structural nor visioning approach for integrating groups mired in intractable identity conflicts has generally proven successful (Fiol & O'Connor, 2009).

In fact, promoting contact between the groups and attempting to unite them around a common vision have often torn them further apart. Integrative visions and structures can be threatening because they appear to involve siding with the enemy, so they are likely to be resisted. Attempts to emphasize that "we're all in this together" when each group defines itself, in part, as unlike the other, is like a slap in the face; attempts to promote similarity when each group sees itself as fundamentally different is like pretending to be color-blind in the face of racial and ethnic differences. The most likely result of such attempts is counterforce from each group as it tries to hold onto its distinctiveness.

PHASE 4: DEVELOPING SEPARATE TOGETHERNESS

Only if the conflicting groups can maintain their autonomous identities as separate groups *and* simultaneously unite around a common purpose will traditional integrative approaches result in harmonious relations. We call this *separate togetherness*: "togetherness" because the groups collaborate around a common purpose; "separate" because they do not sacrifice their unique distinctiveness in the process.

Separate togetherness has led to harmonious relations in a number of settings. For example, conflict levels between multiple ethnic groups on the same team were lowest when both members' ethnic uniqueness *and* the success of the entire team were emphasized (Fiol, Pratt, & O'Connor, 2009). But these ethnic groups may already have been secure in their own uniqueness before they joined the team. What if this is not the case?

If a group is not secure about its own value and unique contributions to begin with, it will not be able to commit itself to the vision of a larger unit that includes the former enemy without feeling threatened. For example, neither physicians nor administrators typically seem focused on the unique value of their peer group. In fact, physicians are not usually united as a group except in their common animosity toward administrators. Fragmented administrative groups, too, find themselves coming together primarily around one of their most pressing concerns, difficult relations with their physicians (Fiol & O'Connor, 2009). In most settings plagued by such conflicts, separate togetherness will not be possible until each group feels secure about its distinctive contributions.

PHASE 3: STRENGTHENING SEPARATE GROUP SECURITY

The purpose of this phase is to build positive ties between group members who have previously felt little connection to one another except in their common dislike of the other.

It encourages the members of each group to focus on what makes them unique, distinctive, and valuable as a group and to strengthen their ties with each other based on their pride in and satisfaction with being part of such a group.

Attempts to strengthen each group's security in its unique value have sometimes led to greater satisfaction for group members, and have helped to redirect each group's attention from the negative aspects of the other to their own positive value. At other times, however, such attempts have failed to produce strong positive bonds between group members, and these groups have remained mired in their obsession with the negative other.

Efforts to develop separate group security often fail because it can be threatening to see the distrusted other strengthened. Group members may even resist strengthening the bonds between themselves and promoting their own group's value because it requires letting go of the competitive quirks that have characterized relations with their own peers. It often seems safer for members of both groups to remain on familiar ground by continuing to distrust one another and to fend for themselves individually. Group members may find it difficult to focus on their own group's positive and distinctive contributions if their main connection with their peers has been their common opposition to the other.

PHASE 2: DISENTANGLING NEGATIVE CONNECTIONS

Like fighting dragons that can no longer disengage because the battle has become their identity, such conflictive groups become so engaged in their conflict that it becomes part of how they define themselves. The negative entanglement provides a form of security – if nothing else, the security of the familiar

and the certainty that the problems each faces are primarily the fault of the other. The irony here is that groups are often more negatively entangled with the other than they are positively bonded with their own peers.

To increase the chances that group members will redirect their attention from the negative other to their own group's positive value, it is necessary to reduce the security that comes from the negative entanglements between the groups. Disentangling the negative connections is a process by which the negative ties of mutual disidentification ("We're OK because you are not") binding the groups together in a locked battle can be broken down, providing an opening for members of each group to cohere around a more positive sense of their unique contributions.

Some attempts to disentangle the negative connections between groups locked in battle have been highly successful over the long run. Other attempts have broken down before any real progress could be made. The issue is often one of readiness.

PHASE 1: DEVELOPING READINESS

Readiness to begin means individuals are committed to de-escalating the conflict. It does not necessarily mean that they *want* to engage in the processes we are describing. But readiness does mean that they are *willing* to try them, because (1) nothing else has worked; (2) the risks of trying a new path seem lower than the risks of continuing on the old; (3) they feel the negative effects of the ongoing battles; and (4) they see at least the *possibility* of a new way to relate to one another.

People's readiness to begin such a process of change does not lead directly to intergroup harmony but it facilitates the three distinct *identity shifts* (described above) which the conflicting groups must undergo in order to achieve harmony: decoupled intergroup identities, subgroup identity security, and separate togetherness. Each phase of our model provides a necessary, but insufficient, condition for intergroup harmony; and successful completion of the prior phase is necessary to carry out each subsequent phase, which is why we presented the phases in reverse order. That is, only when groups have developed readiness to begin is it possible to engage them in the process; only after the negative connections that have kept the groups enmeshed in their destructive patterns have been disentangled is it possible for each group to feel secure about its own uniqueness; and only after each group feels secure in its unique contributions is it possible for group members to focus successfully on togetherness with the other and on continued separateness as a distinctive group. Separate togetherness then becomes a foundation for harmonious relations.

SEE ALSO: Identity-Based Conflicts, The ARIA Contingency Approach to; Intergroup Violence and Psychosocial Interventions, Cycles of.

REFERENCES

Fiol, C. M. & O'Connor, E. J. (2009). *Separately together: A new path to healthy hospital–physician relations.* Chicago, IL: Health Administration Press.

Fiol, C. M., Pratt, M. G., & O'Connor, E. J. (2009). Managing intractable identity conflicts. *Academy of Management Review,* 34(1), 32–55.

Kelman, H. C. (2006). Interests, relationships, identities: Three central issues for individuals and groups in negotiating their social environment. *Annual Review of Psychology, 57,* 1–26.

Rothman, J. (1997). *Resolving identity-based conflict in nations, organizations, and communities.* San Francisco, CA: Jossey-Bass.

Ideology

JOHN T. JOST AND RICK ANDREWS

The term ideology refers to a network or system of interrelated beliefs, values, and opinions held by an individual or a group; they are typically (but by no means always) of a political nature. Generally, an ideology contains assumptions about how the social and political world *is* and how it *ought* to be. "Ideology" has come to be used in both a value-neutral sense, referring to virtually any symbolic or abstract meaning system, and also in a more critical sense to refer to a system of beliefs or ideas that are systematically distorted, so as to conceal or misrepresent certain social interests or realities.

Theorists have disagreed concerning the mental representation of ideology and whether it reflects an essentially unidimensional construct (i.e., a left–right or liberal–conservative dimension) or is inherently multidimensional. As a general rule, sociologists and political scientists have emphasized "top-down" processes associated with the communication, organization, and dissemination of ideology, that is, the activities of political parties, leaders, and the mass media. The main contribution of psychologists has been to delineate the "bottom-up" processes whereby specific ideological outcomes result from individual differences in personality as well as both situational and dispositional variability in social, cognitive, and motivational needs or tendencies that make certain belief systems more or less attractive or appealing to individuals and groups. Presumably, top-down and bottom-up processes meet "in the middle," where specific ideological messages find their natural audiences and vice versa.

TWO CONCEPTIONS OF IDEOLOGY

The origins of ideology as a philosophical concept can be traced to the late eighteenth century, in the Enlightenment writings of French philosopher Antoine Destutt de Tracy, who envisioned a "science of ideas," or what we might now term the sociology of knowledge. Marx and Engels later adapted the term, and the concept of ideology proceeded to take on two different connotations, both of which are still in circulation. According to the first, more common usage, ideology refers broadly to more or less any symbolic or abstract meaning or belief system, including scientific belief systems. This usage is typically more descriptive (in terms of its contents) and value-neutral (in terms of its politics). Social scientists conceiving of ideology in this way seek to understand the contents and the degree of stability, coherence, and consistency among specific social and/or political attitudes within the belief system of an individual or group. Under this conception, ideology is viewed essentially as an organizing cognitive structure that imposes at least some degree of attitudinal constraint across time and place. Thus, it is unlikely (but not impossible) that a given person would be classified as "leftist" on one occasion and "rightist" on another.

The concept of ideology can also refer to a system of beliefs or ideas that are systematically distorted, contrary to reality, and subject to what Marxists (and feminists) have termed "false consciousness." In these traditions, analyses of ideology often take on a critical aspect, in which hidden (sometimes unconscious) motives or interests are unmasked, and ideologies can be endorsed without much regard for logic or philosophical coherence. Use of the term in this vein also frequently connotes some stance in relation to a given social system, such as supporting or attacking the societal status quo. Tensions between these two rather different

traditions of scholarship have contributed to conceptual confusion concerning the nature and existence of ideology. According to the first conception, the holding of incoherent beliefs would seem to suggest the absence of ideology. But if there is any validity to the second conception of ideology, the inability of ordinary citizens to hold consistent, accurate beliefs about the social and political world might indicate that ideological processes are present rather than absent.

UNIDIMENSIONAL VS. MULTIDIMENSIONAL REPRESENTATIONS OF IDEOLOGY

Although ideologies can relate to cultural, economic, or religious subject matter (among other contents), the term is used most often in the political realm. Liberalism and conservatism are the two most prevalent ideologies in the contemporary United States (and in several other Western or Westernized nations), but other ideologies such as socialism, communism, fascism, and libertarianism are or have been prominent ideologies in one time and place or another. The future will likely bring new or different ideologies that have yet to take shape.

Disagreement persists over the nature and structure of even the most prevalent ideologies and how they might be represented in the human brain. It is commonly assumed that ideological space can be represented by a single (unidimensional) left–right continuum. In political philosophy, the left–right distinction can be traced back to the French Revolution, when members of the Assembly sat themselves according to whether they supported or opposed the old regime, including the church, the monarchy, and the bourgeoisie. The left–right metaphor became a powerful symbol that is now ingrained in our political vocabulary.

In addition to being heuristically useful and parsimonious, the left–right distinction seems to map onto several social psychological antinomies. Ideologies that favor traditionalism over social change and social hierarchy over egalitarianism are considered to be "right-of-center" or "conservative" ideologies. Simple self-report indicators of left–right orientation are surprisingly predictive of implicit and explicit attitudes toward social change and (in)equality, as well as many other personal characteristics. It has been suggested that the two "core" aspects of the left–right distinction (advocating vs. resisting social change and rejecting vs. accepting inequality) have coalesced into a coherent ideology because of the historical fact that traditional arrangements have tended to be rather hierarchical (i.e., less egalitarian), and most popular social change movements over the past several centuries have sought to increase the degree of social, economic, or political equality in society.

However, several proposals for a more complex (i.e., multidimensional) theory of ideological representation have been offered. Kerlinger (1984), among others, argued that liberalism and conservatism are independent dimensions that are orthogonally represented in the human mind. If this argument is correct, one could be high on both liberalism and conservatism (or low on both, which is less surprising). Others have pointed out that it is possible to be socially conservative and economically liberal, or vice versa. Social-personality psychologists have suggested that acceptance or rejection of "right-wing authoritarianism" (and accompanying perceptions of danger, threat, and the importance of conformity) underlie social values, whereas "social dominance orientation" (and perceptions of competitiveness) underlie economic values. (See AUTHORITARIAN PERSONALITY; SOCIAL DOMINANCE THEORY.)

Multidimensional conceptions of ideology may make intuitive sense, but they have yet to eclipse the unidimensional conception in terms of popularity or scientific validity. Liberalism and conservatism may have distinctive priorities, but they are almost never orthogonal (i.e., uncorrelated) in empirical tests; typically, multidimensional theories sacrifice parsimony while gaining relatively little in terms of explanatory power (Jost, Federico, & Napier, 2009). For the time being at least, the left–right distinction appears to be useful and convincing enough to stimulate meaningful and productive research in the social and behavioral sciences.

TOP-DOWN PROCESSES

Top-down processes in the context of ideology refer to the ways in which political elites (including party leaders, politicians, media representatives, and others) strategically influence the attitudes of ordinary citizens. Examples include President Lyndon B. Johnson's role in urging the Democratic Party to embrace civil rights legislation in the mid-1960s, and the media's role in framing US military involvement in Vietnam and, later, Iraq. Much of the money and effort expended by electoral campaigns and political parties and administrations is dedicated to influencing public opinion through top-down processes of communication and agenda-setting.

However, it seems improbable that social and political attitudes are shaped only by top-down influences. We know from several decades of research in social and personality psychology that the effects of persuasive messages are moderated by the receiver's motivations and cognitive abilities. Individuals who are highly sophisticated when it comes to politics are more likely to receive, process, and use political information that was acquired in a top-down fashion. Similarly, individuals with a strong need or motivation to evaluate social stimuli are more likely to be receptive to political messages because of their desire to form opinions about a wide range of topics. A focus on bottom-up processes, which are emphasized in psychological research, helps to explain why specific individuals or groups may be more susceptible to certain ideological messages than others.

IDEOLOGY AND PSYCHOLOGY: BOTTOM-UP PROCESSES

Research in social and personality psychology over the past 50 years has demonstrated that ideological outcomes are not solely the result of mass communication and information transmission from elites to ordinary citizens. The cognitive and motivational needs of an individual message recipient (as well as his or her personality characteristics and mental states) influence the degree of receptiveness to various ideologies and opinions. These are sometimes referred to as political predispositions.

Beginning with Adorno, Frenkel-Brunswik, Levinson, and Sanford (1950), research has demonstrated that basic personality characteristics are connected to one's ideological proclivities. For instance, conservatives tend to be lower on the trait of Openness to New Experiences in comparison with liberals but higher in terms of Conscientiousness. Studies show that childhood differences in personality are predictive of ideological opinions in adulthood. Research comparing monozygotic and dizygotic twins suggests that as much as 40–50% of the variability in political orientation may have a genetically heritable component. Presumably, there are some (partially heritable) psychological predispositions that make an individual more or less prone to liberal or conservative ideas, assuming that he or she is exposed to the full "menu" of ideological options.

Ideologies, including political and religious belief systems, are thought to satisfy various epistemic motives by offering subjective certainty. Some ideologies may satisfy these and other motives more efficiently or thoroughly than other ideologies. For instance, people who exhibit relatively strong needs for order, structure, and cognitive closure are significantly more likely to hold conservative (vs. liberal) beliefs. These findings and others suggest that a special affinity exists between political conservatism and epistemic motives to reduce uncertainty. Existential motives to achieve psychological security by minimizing threat are also linked to ideological processes. Various experimental paradigms have revealed that threats of death, violence, or terrorism often produce higher levels of conservative responding among research participants. Relational motives, too, appear to contribute in a bottom-up fashion to ideological outcomes. Beliefs, values, and opinions are transmitted by strongly connected family members and friends, especially during the end of adolescence and into early adulthood.

In summary, then, a given individual's ideological belief system reflects the interaction of top-down processes of persuasive communication (or propaganda) and bottom-up phenomena such as personality traits and epistemic, existential, and relational needs (i.e., political predispositions). Presumably, these two sets of processes meet in the "middle" to bring about specific ideological outcomes. Exploring the intersection of top-down and bottom-up processes through experimental methods is a promising future direction for the social psychological study of ideology.

IDEOLOGIES OF CONFLICT AND PEACE

Orientations concerning military conflict (or aggression) and peace can also be thought of as ideological in nature. The distinction, for instance, between "hawks" and "doves" is an ideological distinction that is generally correlated with the left–right political distinction. Support for aggressive foreign policy plays a significant role in "right-wing authoritarianism," and orientations toward conflict and peace are often incorporated into political ideologies. Bar-Tal, Raviv, Raviv, and Dgani-Hirsh (2009) have proposed that in societies that are mired in seemingly intractable conflicts (such as the Israeli–Palestinian conflict), citizens develop an "ethos of conflict," which functions as an ideology. Accordingly, an individual's ethos of conflict produces cognitive biases (such as selective attention, distortion, and reconstructive memory) and affects how information is expressed as well as processed. (See CONFLICT, ETHOS OF.)

SEE ALSO: Authoritarian Personality; Conflict, Ethos of; Social Dominance Theory.

REFERENCES

Adorno, T. W., Frenkel-Brunswik, E., Levinson, D. J., & Sanford, R. N. (1950). *The authoritarian personality.* New York, NY: Harper.
Bar-Tal, D., Raviv, A., Raviv, A., & Dgani-Hirsh, A. (2009). The influence of the ethos of conflict on Israeli Jews' interpretation of Jewish–Palestinian encounters. *Journal of Conflict Resolution, 53,* 94–118.
Converse, P. E. (1964). The nature of belief systems in mass publics. In D. Apter (Ed.), *Ideology and discontent* (pp. 206–226). New York, NY: Free Press.
Freeden, M. (2003). *Ideology: A very short introduction.* New York, NY: Oxford University Press.
Jost, J. T. (2006). The end of the end of ideology. *American Psychologist, 61,* 651–670.
Jost, J. T., Federico, C. M., & Napier, J. L. (2009). Political ideology: Its structure, functions, and elective affinities. *Annual Review of Psychology, 60,* 307–338.
Kerlinger, F. (1984). *Liberalism and conservatism: The nature and structure of social attitudes.* Hillsdale, NJ: Erlbaum.

Image Theory

REZARTA BILALI

The concept of image was introduced by Boulding (1959) as "the total cognitive, affective, and evaluative structure of the behavioral unit, or its internal view of itself and its universe" (pp. 120–121). This definition is inclusive of images of self and others. Each state might be motivated to project a positive self image by portraying itself in a positive light while avoiding negative portrayals. For instance, policymakers might take actions such as saving face or showing good will and prestige to present their nation in a positive light (Jervis, 1970). Images of others, on the other hand, can be considered as mental representations of those nations. As such, an image is a belief about the goals, intentions, and character of an actor in international relations. The function of international images is to simplify a complex international environment and guide perceptions and responses toward other nations. Knowledge of images serves to help us to understand and predict states' behavior. Due to the importance of images in predicting foreign policy decisions, most work in this area has examined images of masses and elites of one nation about another, rather than images of one's own nation.

Until the end of the Cold War, the literature focused primarily on images of the enemy which were used to explain the United States' and Soviet Union's mirror perceptions of each other during the Cold War. (See PEACE PSYCHOLOGY: CONTRIBUTIONS FROM NORTH AMERICA.) The enemy image is viewed as a necessary precondition for undertaking aggressive actions toward other nations. However, a single image is not sufficient to explain the variety of relations between nations in the international arena. Other international images have been identified and include the ally, the imperialist, the barbarian, the colony, the rogue, and the degenerate (Cottam, 1977). These images do not refer only to concepts used in academia, they are also used widely by policymakers, leaders, and masses to justify policies and actions taken toward other nations.

IMAGE AS A PSYCHOLOGICAL CONSTRUCT

The concept of image is analogous to the notion of schema and stereotype in cognitive and social psychology. (See STEREO-TYPES.) Schemas are cognitive structures that organize knowledge about different concepts and stimuli in our environment. They help us deal with complexity of information by influencing the way we select, interpret, memorize, and retrieve information. Similarly, stereotypes are schemas that serve the function of explaining, rationalizing, and justifying behavior. Similar to schemas, each image provides information regarding a set of attributes. Specifically, a description of each image reflects evaluation of the other actor's capability, motivation, leadership, and decision-making processes. Similar to stereotypes, images serve to rationalize and justify behavioral tendencies toward the other country as well as to maintain a moral image of self. For example, the endorsement of an enemy image is useful to justify attacking another country, a behavior which otherwise might constitute an immoral act. As such, images demonstrate how a nation's characteristics are shaped by the perceiver's motives, goals, and interests.

A description of each image and their attributes is included below.

The *enemy image* characterizes the other nation as evil and as nourishing harmful motives. The leadership is viewed as complex and highly capable, especially of carrying out evil intentions.

By contrast, an *ally* is perceived to have benign intentions, is driven by positive forces, and run by a moral and highly capable leadership.

A *barbarian* state is characterized as having aggressive intentions, uncontrollable power, and is led by irrational and dangerous elites.

The *imperialist* is perceived as having highly sophisticated institutions, capable of carrying out complex operations, but motivated to exploit the resources of the perceiver's own country. An imperialist is controlling, dominating, and exploitative.

A *degenerate* lacks strong will, and has an uncertain, confused, and fractured leadership. The degenerate has high power capability, but is not capable of using his/her power effectively.

The *colonial* image portrays the other nation as being weak, childlike, inefficient, and unable to make rational decisions. Its elite is viewed as divided and consisting of destructive, extreme, and moderate elements.

The *rogue* image is similar to the colonial, but in addition to its inefficiency the rogue nation is also perceived as being led by a small aggressive elite having harmful intentions.

Herrmann, Voss, Schooler, and Ciarrochi (1997) experimentally demonstrated that images are schemas. Participants in the experimental condition were provided with specific, manipulated images about a fictitious nation while participants in the control condition did not receive any treatment. Afterwards, all participants read scenarios about the country's military actions, speeches on economic and human rights, etc. As predicted, information in the scenarios was memorized and interpreted consistently with the previously induced images in the experimental but not in the control condition. Components of schemas are interrelated such that even abstract or partial information can be used to derive more detailed and additional information that constitutes the relevant schema. To test these predictions, in experimental studies participants were exposed to one of the aforementioned attributes of an image of a fictitious country and subsequently were asked to infer other attributes. Supporting the hypotheses, participants in the experimental but not control conditions rightly inferred the other attributes of the respective image.

IMAGE THEORY PROPOSITIONS

Image theory makes predictions regarding the relationship among four constructs: (1) perceptions of structural relations between nations; (2) emotions; (3) images; and (4) behavioral tendencies. Specifically, image theory claims that perceptions of structural relations between states elicit emotions which in turn determine images and behavioral tendencies toward another country (Herrmann & Fischerkeller, 1995). The perceived structural relations are a function of three dimensions: perceived goal compatibility between states, assessment of relative power capability, and evaluation of relative cultural status. The first dimension, goal compatibility, refers to the threat or opportunity posed by the other actor. Assuming that the actors' goals are interdependent, there are three alternatives: another actor may pose a threat, may pose an opportunity for exploitation, or provide a chance for mutual gain. Judgments of power capability and cultural status are relative. The other actor may be superior, equal, or inferior in each dimension. A judgment of relative power in combination with the opportunity or threat posed determines alternative

courses of action. For example, if the adversary is more powerful and poses a threat, then a strategy of containment might be the best course of action; whereas if the other country is more powerful but poses an opportunity for gain, then the best strategy is cooperation. Perceived cultural differences affect the norms that will be relevant in the relations between two actors. Judgments of cultural status provide information on the type of action the adversary is most likely to choose given its motivation and power capacities and whether the actor will hold to an agreement.

A description of the relationship between perceived structural relations, emotions, and behavioral tendencies is provided for each image below (for more detailed descriptions see Cottam & Cottam, 2001, pp. 96–121).

Enemy. Enemy image emerges when two nations are perceived as highly competitive but similar in capability and cultural status. This pattern of interaction elicits feelings of threat to both actors about each other, thus leading them to view each other in similar ways. In the enemy condition, the dominant emotional experience is anger. However, perceived equal power and cultural status also trigger respect. A combination of these characteristics with perceived threat triggers fear and distrust. The feelings of threat and insecurity arouse inclinations to eliminate the threat by attack. However, because the enemy is perceived as having equal power, the most feasible strategy is containment.

Ally. The ally image arises when an actor sees the other as having equal power and similar cultural status. The two actors also perceive each other to share mutual goals and interests. A relationship with an ally is an opportunity for mutual gain. An ally evokes feelings of trust, respect, and admiration, which in turn lead to inclination to cooperate.

Barbarian. When the goals of another nation are viewed as incompatible, its power as superior, and its culture as inferior, the typical image will be the barbarian. The perceived cultural inferiority of the barbarian in combination with high power infers that the barbarian uses its power uncontrollably and unpredictably, thus making it capable of carrying out brutal acts and atrocities. The best strategy to deal with the threat posed by the barbarian's destructive potential would be to ensure one's security by insulating oneself or making powerful allies. Fear, intimidation, and disgust mediate the relation between structural perceptions and self-protection responses.

Imperialist. The imperialist image is the image that a person has about another country perceived as superior in capability and culture and motivated to exploit the resources of the perceiver's country. The difference between an imperialist and a barbarian rests on the perception of their cultural status. The perceived superior culture of the imperialist elicits feelings of jealousy, envy, and resentment. If the dominance of the imperial power is seen as illegitimate, the perceived threat combined with perceived lower power and culture inferiority of one's own nation will produce anger and shame, which in combination with jealousy leads to hostile actions such as resistance or rebellion.

Colony. The colonial image arises from a perception of the other as inferior in both power capability and culture but as posing an opportunity for increasing one's own gains. Such an interaction leads the more powerful country (the imperialist) to exploit the weaker one (the colony). A colonial image – that is, viewing the other as weak, inefficient, and child-like – evokes feelings of disgust, contempt, and pity. The imperial power might feel the need to "civilize" the colonial group; thus intervention becomes a duty and exploitation becomes legitimate and moral.

Rogue. A rogue is a country viewed as lower in power capabilities and cultural status but as threatening and nourishing harmful motives. Whereas the colony poses an opportunity for personal gain, the rogue is threatening. Rogue states are perceived as "bad seed." The rogue evokes anger, disgust, and contempt which in combination with the threat posed arouse the desire to reform the rogue by punishing it.

Degenerate. A degenerate is a country with similar or superior power capability and cultural status, but having harmful intentions. What makes the degenerate different from the enemy is its weak-willed political culture and elites. The degenerate is viewed as lacking discipline and a strong leadership which undermines its potential power. The emotions that associate with this image are disgust and contempt combined with anger and scorn. This emotion profile leads to tendencies to attack the degenerate.

CURRENT AND FUTURE DIRECTIONS IN IMAGE THEORY RESEARCH

The literature on international images consists mostly of retrospective research conducted by qualitative methods and content analysis to explain nations' foreign policy choices. A few experimental studies have provided support for the internal validity of the theory. Few studies have empirically tested image theory propositions (i.e., the interrelation between its components) in real-world settings, and consequently there is mixed evidence for its propositions. More research is needed to clarify the relationship between images, emotions, and behavioral tendencies.

Recently, Alexander, Brewer, and Livingston (2005) applied image theory to race relations in the United States, demonstrating the usefulness of the theory as a generalized model of intergroup relations. Attempts have been made to incorporate individual level factors such as ingroup identification and social dominance orientation in the image theory, as well as to establish links with relevant theories of intergroup relations (e.g., the stereotype content model). In order to develop the full potential of this theoretical framework as a useful tool in predicting and understanding intergroup and international relations, further efforts should be made to develop links with the social psychological literature of intergroup relations. (See SOCIAL IDENTITY THEORY; SOCIAL DOMINANCE THEORY; PEACE, OVERCOMING PSYCHOLOGICAL–COGNITIVE BARRIERS TO.)

Finally, images of one's own nation have received almost no attention in the research literature. How people perceive their nation should be an important factor in determining how they view the strategic relations with other nations, their place in the international arena, and the types of responses toward other groups' actions. Images of one's own nation or group should be explored and taken into account in combination with images of the adversary to achieve a better understanding of the dynamics of intergroup conflict.

SEE ALSO: Peace, Overcoming Psychological–Cognitive Barriers to; Peace Psychology: Contributions from North America; Social Dominance Theory; Social Identity Theory; Stereotypes.

REFERENCES

Alexander, M. G., Brewer, M. B., & Livingston, R. W. (2005). Putting stereotype content in context: Image theory and interethnic stereotypes. *Personality and Social Psychology Bulletin, 31*, 781–794.
Boulding, K. (1959). National images and international systems. *Journal of Conflict Resolution, 3*, 120–131.
Cottam, R. (1977). *Foreign policy motivation: A general theory and a case study.* Pittsburgh, PA: University of Pittsburgh Press.
Cottam, M., & Cottam, R. (2001). *Nationalism and politics: The political behavior of nation states.* Boulder, CO: Lynne Rienner Publishers.
Herrmann, R. K., & Fischerkeller, M. P. (1995). Beyond the enemy image and spiral model: Cognitive-strategic research after the Cold War. *International Organizations, 49*, 415–450.
Herrmann, R. K., Voss, J. F., Schooler, T. Y. E., & Ciarrochi, J. (1997). Images in international relations: An experimental test of cognitive schemata. *International Studies Quarterly, 41*, 403–433.
Jervis, R. (1970). *The logic of images in international relations.* Princeton, NJ: Princeton University Press.

ADDITIONAL RESOURCE

Psychologists for Social Responsibility (PsySR). (1989). *Dismantling the mask of enemy: An educational resource manual on the psychology of enemy images.* Brookline, MA: PsySR. Retrieved from www.psysr.org

Interfaith Dialogue

NORAINI M. NOOR

Interfaith dialogue as a contemporary movement can be traced back to the decision of some churches at the beginning of the twentieth century to extend cooperation and build relations with non-Christians. This initiative came from the Christian missionaries' need to adapt to conditions of work in Asia, and the first few world missionary conferences (Edinburgh in 1910, Jerusalem in 1928, and Tambaram, India, in 1938) paved the way for the initial discussions. But the Christians remained divided on how they should approach other religions.

The concept of dialogue was first brought up at the assembly of the World Council of Churches (WCC) in 1961 when the church had to consider the experience of the younger churches in the newly independent countries in Asia that have to deal with people of different religions in nation-building. Together with the Roman Catholic Church, the WCC conference in Kandy, Sri Lanka, in 1967 affirmed dialogue as the most appropriate approach in interfaith relations. Of course, there were also those within the Christian traditions who opposed dialogue, raising fears that such activity would lead to syncretism or that it would compromise the faith (Ariarajah, 2002).

Within this general framework, some see dialogue as a new and creative relationship in which to learn about and to respect others, and as a witness to one's own faith. Others see it as an important historical moment in the development of religious traditions, where the different faiths are challenged and transformed by encounters with other faiths. Still others view dialogue as a common journey towards the truth, within which each faith tradition shares with the others the way in which it has come to perceive and respond to that truth (Ariarajah, 2002).

At present, while interfaith dialogue remains controversial, there is increasing recognition that it is important in developing positive and friendly relations with people of other religions. Since the 9/11 attacks on the United States, efforts to promote interfaith dialogue as a form of religious peacemaking and peacebuilding have increased. This is as a result of the recognition that many modern conflicts are caused by issues that have traditionally belonged in religious domains. Furthermore, in spite of the marginalization of religion by many secular states, religion continues to be significant in individual lives, in the formation of collective identities, and even in political mobilization. Thus, the value of interfaith dialogue to counter negative conditioning, stereotypes, and fanaticism, and in the process open the door to listening, communication, respect, and hopefully acceptance for one another, cannot be underestimated.

DEFINITION

Interfaith dialogue can be understood as an encounter between people of different faith traditions, in an atmosphere of mutual trust and acceptance. In the encounter, people talk and listen to one another to try to appreciate each other's faith (and also culture). A dialogue does not require one to give up or to invalidate one's religious convictions; rather one is expected to hold on to one's faith while trying to be informed of and to understand another's faith. In such a setting, Muzaffar (2002) recommends an emphasis on shared religious values, that is, certain standards or principles upheld in common that can bring groups together and reduce hostility and conflict rather than focusing on the theologies, philosophies, and doctrines of the religions. These common values include attitudes and orientations which have both positive and negative impacts on the individual and on society (e.g., the positive values of honesty and compassion, and the negative values of greed and corruption); values associated with institutions or the human being's larger environment which serve to enhance the moral aspect of human existence (e.g., institutions such as the family, marriage, and community); visions associated with the meaning of life and life processes (e.g., while the rites and rituals to some of life's major milestones may differ, there are similarities in the meanings attached to them); and finally, the human bond, where people all go through similar life processes.

At the same time, religious (and cultural) differences must also be understood to dispel fear, suspicion, and distrust of the other. The goal is not to eliminate differences of opinion and conviction, but to gain an understanding and acceptance of those differences. In an interfaith forum, by emphasizing the common religious attributes of compassion, empathy, love, kindness, and forgiveness, people are more likely to be open to hear and listen, and to respect the other side. While there are differences in the belief and practice of other faiths, the objective is not to "correct" but to hear and listen and to understand each other. These shared religious attributes can also be used to find a solution to an existing conflict and to foster understanding between groups.

The aim of an emphasis on shared values in interfaith dialogues is to modify people's perceptions of their differences and to expand the level of category inclusiveness, which is consistent with the cognitive perspective in social psychological research on intergroup relations (Dovidio, Gaertner, Saguy, & Halabi, 2008). When people of different faiths meet, religious (and ethnic) identities become salient, and this condition can amplify social identity differences. However, self-categorization is a dynamic process, and people at any one time possess the potential for many different group identities and are capable of focusing on different social categories. Therefore, an emphasis on shared values can alter the way people think about members of the ingroup and the outgroup, enlarging category inclusiveness (see COMMON INGROUP IDENTITY MODEL). Hence, group members may be moved toward recategorization, in which a superordinate category of common values is most salient, or members of one group may view members of another group as individuals, through a process of decategorization (Dovidio et al., 2008). In either case, reducing the salience of the original group boundaries is assumed to decrease conflict between the groups.

LEVELS OF INTERFAITH DIALOGUE AND SOME GUIDELINES

There are different levels of interfaith dialogue: (1) formal theological discussions between scholars or religious leaders; (2) social exchanges and action between members of different faith traditions which promote interfaith friendships; and (3) joint problem-solving where people of different faiths get together to deal with specific local concrete problems.

Dialogue between scholars and religious leaders is growing as they look for new solutions to the increasing divisions between adherents of different religions. Topics of dialogue may vary but the focus is usually on religious understanding of one another's belief systems. In addition, their roles as religious leaders also provide them with some authority to try to address structural and cultural issues that underlie many grievances in society. For example, Varshney (2002) showed that dialogue between influential religious and secular leaders of the community resulted in peace between Hindus and Muslims because economic disparities between the groups were reduced. If they are not addressed, structural problems such as economic inequality can escalate into religious conflict. Because these religious leaders command the respect of their community, they can act as peacebuilders by discussing these issues at the formal level.

The second kind of dialogue is usually between ordinary members of different religions which typically focus on organizing and promoting various interfaith activities such as religious-social activities like interfaith gatherings over a meal, visits to each other's place of worship to get a better understanding of each other's religion, and so on. These interfaith friendship activities can be seen as the necessary first step to acquiring a better understanding of other religions, and though they may seem trivial, the power of such activities should not be underestimated. Many strangers have become friends through such partnership programs as open houses and picnics.

The final level, where people of different traditions get together over concrete problems, may be the easiest and most productive because the shared common problems (e.g., transportation, safety, and so on) may force people to reconsider their differences. Here again, religious leaders of the community can be instrumental in facilitating the dialogue. As Varshney (2002) demonstrated, Indian cities with interethnic networks where Hindus and Muslims are connected through civil society organizations, and united in mutual concern about spiritual welfare, are much less likely to suffer from communal riots. In this case, friendships are formed and trust is built through everyday interactions and collaboration on peace committees and in business associations.

Good manners are essential foundations for interfaith dialogue. Swidler (1983) offers the following 10 guidelines for carrying out an interfaith dialogue.

- The purpose of dialogue is to learn and to increase one's knowledge.
- Participants should be engaged in dialogue within their own religious community and, at the same time, with other religious communities.
- Participants should be honest and sincere.
- Participants are asked not to compare their religious ideals with the other faith's practice, but to compare their ideals with

the other's ideals and their practice with the other's practice.
- Each dialogue partner has a right to define his or her religion and beliefs. Others can describe only what it looks like to them from the outside.
- Participants should abandon all their preconceptions in order to listen to others with sincerity and openness.
- Dialogue can take place only between equals; therefore, one side should not dominate or treat the other as inferior.
- Dialogue must take place in an atmosphere of mutual trust.
- Participants entering into dialogue must be willing to reflect upon themselves and their own religious tradition.
- Participants in dialogue should attempt to experience how others' traditions affect them holistically.

Similar guidelines are also offered by others.

MECHANISMS UNDERLYING INTERFAITH DIALOGUE

Interfaith dialogue, then, works to bring people of the different faiths together through contact. Because dialogue is a process, contacts and discussions are increased and, through joint activities, people may come to a better understanding of and grow in respect for other faiths in the hope of gaining trust and building a more lasting relationship. Such contacts between different religious groups are important because these differences can often be potential sources of conflict. In contrast to many faith-based interventions that are not properly grounded in research, there is abundant literature on intergroup contact that can be used to reinforce the importance of bringing conflicting groups together to reduce prejudice. In its original formulation proposed by Allport (1954) in the context of intergroup prejudice and racism in the

United States, intergroup contact theory attempted to specify the practical conditions which needed to be met before contact could be expected to lead to changes in intergroup attitudes as a result of increased contact:

- The intervention should be supported by relevant authority figures.
- Individuals should be of equal status within the contact situation.
- Group situations should be characterized by cooperation and interdependence.
- Individual contacts should allow friendships to develop across groups.

These basic requirements are also included in the guidelines mentioned earlier (see CONTACT THEORY, INTERGROUP).

A number of explanations have been forwarded to explain why change might occur under these contact conditions. A dissonance theory explanation has been proposed, where positive social contacts with outgroup members who are negatively viewed may force individuals to re-evaluate their attitudes as a result of dissonance between their negative expectations and positive experiences. Contact may also work because it provides knowledge about the outgroup, induces empathy and perspective taking, creates more inclusive group representations, diminishes intergroup anxiety and the perception of threat (for a review, see Tausch, Kenworthy, & Hewstone, 2005). Research has also shown that just the mere exposure to outgroup members (e.g., living in mixed neighborhoods, going to mixed schools) can reduce the implicit negative associations with an outgroup. These findings can be put to good use by interfaith practitioners to bring conflicting groups together.

CONCLUSION

While the short-term goal of interfaith dialogue is to open the door to listening, communication, and respect for others' religions (and cultures), the long-term goal would be to have a pluralistic and peaceful society which includes all people irrespective of religion. Of course, interfaith dialogue as a form of religious peacemaking and peacebuilding is by no means a solution to many conflicts. But because it touches on people's spiritual dimension it can provide access to the more deep-seated, affective base for their behavior, enabling them to examine their own attitudes and actions critically. It is therefore useful in cases where the conflict is perceived to be rooted in religion, and where religious actors and institutions are seen as legitimate and are recognized by the people in the conflicting communities. However, interfaith dialogue on its own may not be sufficient to improve intergroup relations. In such cases, it may be more effective when used alongside other forms of traditional diplomatic approaches.

SEE ALSO: Common Ingroup Identity Model; Contact Theory, Intergroup.

REFERENCES

Allport, G. W. (1954). *The nature of prejudice.* Cambridge, MA: Addison-Wesley.

Ariarajah, S. W. (2002, January). *Dialogue, interfaith.* Retrieved from http://www. wcc-coe.org/wcc/who/dictionary-article1.html

Dovidio, J. F., Gaertner, S. L., Saguy, T., & Halabi, S. (2008). From when to why: Understanding how contact reduces bias. In U. Wagner, L. R. Tropp, G. Finchilescu, & C. Tredoux (Eds.), *Improving intergroup relations* (pp. 75–90). Oxford, UK: Blackwell.

Muzaffar, C. (2002). *Common values of the religions and faiths in Malaysia.* Retrieved from http://www.just-international.org/article.cfm?newsid=20000243

Swidler, L. (1984). The dialogue decalogue: Ground rules for interreligious dialogue. *Journal of Ecumenical Studies, 20*(1), 1–4.

Tausch, N., Kenworthy, J., & Hewstone, M. (2005). Intergroup contact and the improvement of intergroup relations. In M. Fitzduff & C. E. Stout (Eds.), *Psychological approaches to dealing with conflict and war* (Vol. 2, pp. 67–108). Westport, CT: Prager.

Varshney, A. (2002). *Ethnic conflict and civic life: Hindus and Muslims in India*. New Haven, CT: Yale University Press.

ADDITIONAL RESOURCES

Shafiq, M., & Abu-Nimer, M. (2007). *Interfaith dialogue: A guide for Muslims*. Herndon, VA: The International Institute of Islamic Thought.

Smock, D. R. (Ed.). (2006). *Religious contributions to peacemaking: When religion brings peace, not war*. Retrieved from http://www.usip.org/files/resources/PWJan2006.pdf

Intergroup Conflict, Theories of

RONALD J. FISHER

Destructive intergroup conflict – that is, badly managed differences between distinct identity groups – is the most serious problem facing humankind. It occurs at every social level within and between societies, and usurps resources that are sorely needed for human development and satisfaction. Within organizations, misunderstanding and animosity between different departments and levels reduces motivation and productivity, thus compromising the attainment of overall goals. Within communities, cleavages among different ethnic, racial, and religious groups are expressed in prejudice and discrimination, and at times in violent interactions, such as gang warfare and race riots. Within societies, destructive interactions between such identity groups can escalate to ethno-political war, ethnic cleansing, and genocide. In addition, controversial issues between competing interest groups and ideologies squander resources through conflicts over environmental protection, poverty, or the provision of public services, rather than using dialogue to find common ground on improving the quality of life. At the international level, the costs of war are well known, and while the Cold War threat of nuclear annihilation has abated, future conflicts between major powers could induce Armageddon.

It is thus incumbent upon social scientists, including peace psychologists, to more fully understand this enigmatic dilemma of humankind. With knowledge and understanding, we can then develop methods, strategies, and policies to transform destructive intergroup conflict into constructive interactions and outcomes that foster social change toward greater equity and justice. (See INTERGROUP VIOLENCE AND PSYCHOSOCIAL INTERVENTIONS, CYCLES OF.) This essay is directed toward that understanding by presenting a sample of the most powerful theories about intergroup conflict developed by social psychologists and others, and by identifying some of the commonalities among these that provide a basis for both hope and action. (See IDENTITY-BASED CONFLICTS, THE ARIA CONTINGENCY APPROACH TO; CONFLICT RESOLUTION, INTERACTIVE.)

Conflict can be defined as "a social situation involving perceived incompatibilities in goals or values between two or more parties, attempts by the parties to control each other, and antagonistic feelings by the parties toward each other" (Fisher, 1990, p. 6). Thus, conflict is both an objective and subjective phenomenon – that is, typically based in real differences, but fueled by emotions, perceptions, and other cognitive elements that render it a rather volatile and yet malleable entity. This phenomenological stance maintains that how other parties and differences with them are perceived and experienced sets expectations and affects behavior toward them in ways that can be counterproductive, particularly when the perceiver is under some degree of threat that typically accompanies conflict. At the intergroup level, these subjective elements are collective in nature, shared by most group members, and are linked to norms within the group about how the other group should be perceived and treated. Intergroup conflict thus occurs within the broader context of intergroup relations, which involves all manner of interactions, both positive and negative, between members of different groups behaving in terms of their group identities. Much theorizing and research has occurred in the interdisciplinary field of intergroup relations, encompassing a number of models which help explain ongoing interactions among groups of people. According to Taylor and Moghaddam (1994), the primary focus in their analysis of models of intergroup relations is on conflict between groups, thus underscoring the centrality and importance of the phenomenon in human relations and in social change.

CONTENDING AND COMPLEMENTARY THEORIES OF INTERGROUP CONFLICT

Since the end of the Second World War, Western social psychologists have sought to develop ideas to help understand and then ameliorate the highly destructive tendencies of humankind. Four of the most influential theories are discussed here, with the note that other ones exist and continue to be developed. Although these theories generally attempt to explain the causation, escalation, and resolution of intergroup conflict in a universal manner, they have been developed within a Western social scientific and cultural context and their applicability to other settings needs to be assessed through cross-cultural research. While these theories typically offer competing explanations for the same occurrences, the potential does

exist for them to be merged into more comprehensive and valid representations of social reality in explaining intergroup conflict. The power of the social-psychological approach is that it works to blend the understanding of individual-level variables with elements of the social context, in this case at the group and intergroup levels, to provide integrated explanations which generalize beyond specific cases.

Realistic group conflict theory (RCT) is based in the proposition that real conflicts of interest or issues in the functional relations between groups lie at the heart of intergroup conflict, as opposed to unconscious motives or irrational tendencies (LeVine & Campbell, 1972; Sherif, 1966). Supported by anthropological studies, sociological surveys, as well as field experiments in social psychology, RCT proposes that incompatible goals and competition for scarce resources (i.e., real conflicts of interest) cause real threat (and the perception of threat) which then cause hostility to the source of the threat (i.e., the other group), as well as heightening the awareness of group identity and the sense of ingroup solidarity. These latter points merge into the phenomenon of "ethnocentrism," originating from the anthropological literature, by which each distinct cultural group comes to see itself as superior and more valued, and looks down on other groups as inferior objects of scorn and contempt. Ethnocentrism thus involves increased ingroup loyalty and glorification, coupled with outgroup derogation and discrimination. RCT posits a number of other propositions about the full effects of heightened ethnocentrism such as the ingroup ostracism of deviants and the increased hostility toward the outgroup. Many of these effects were demonstrated in the groundbreaking field experiments by Sherif and his colleagues, which induced intergroup hostility and ethnocentrism between groups with no historical antagonism by bringing them into competitive interactions around incompatible goals. RCT thus concludes that the threat from real conflicts of interest increases ethnocentrism to levels that support negative attitudes and aggressive, destructive behaviors between conflicting groups. (See THREAT, KINDS AND EFFECTS OF.)

An alternative explanation for intergroup conflict came out of the work of Henri Tajfel and his colleagues on the so-called "minimal group paradigm," which demonstrated that the simple fact of social categorization (i.e., the mere perception of belonging to a group) without any conflict of interest or interaction was sufficient to produce intergroup discrimination favoring the ingroup (Tajfel & Turner, 1979). Given that social categorizations are points of self-reference and define an individual's place in society, Tajfel and his colleagues developed social identity theory (SIT) to explain the power of such identifications in influencing relations among groups. SIT posits that individuals strive to achieve or to maintain a positive social identity, to which membership in groups makes a contribution. Further, given that the evaluation of one's groups is based on social comparison with other groups, a positive social identity requires positive comparisons – that is, ones that elevate one's own group while denigrating other groups, thus inducing ethnocentrism. In addition, social categorization research demonstrates that people tend to minimize differences within categories and exaggerate differences between categories, thus adding to the sense of differentiation and ethnocentrism between groups. In line with other thinking in social psychology, ethnocentrism is thus seen as linked to a need for enhanced self-esteem provided by group distinctiveness and invidious comparisons with outgroups. However, there is some question on the degree to which social identity processes drive outgroup discrimination and hostility, as opposed to only ingroup favoritism and affection. Nonetheless, SIT provides a useful complement to RCT in that it highlights the importance of individual-level variables (self-esteem, positive social identity) on the emergence of ethnocentrism and intergroup conflict. Through the effects of social categorization and social comparison, it also augments the role of competition and threat in the etiology of ethnocentrism. (See MINIMAL GROUP PARADIGM; SOCIAL IDENTITY THEORY.)

Social dominance theory (SDT) is a more recent attempt to link individual predispositions with group- and intergroup-level variables in order to explain conflict among groups, particularly that which is based in the inequitable distribution of resources (Sidanius & Pratto, 1999). The theory assumes that there is a human tendency to form hierarchies in society (a controversial tenet in its own right), which results in some groups being advantaged while others are disadvantaged, thus resulting in conflict between groups. The central construct is *social dominance orientation* which measures the degree to which individuals support ideologies and structures that promote group-based hierarchies, and thus legitimize discrimination in favor of more powerful groups. Some of the supporting research indicates that members of majority groups are more likely to exhibit a higher social dominance orientation, which is compatible with their privileged position in society and also supports the status quo of group inequalities. Thus, in comparison to RCT and SIT, SDT more directly addresses group differences in power and status, while still adding to the explanation of individual differences in discrimination and intergroup hostility. (See SOCIAL DOMINANCE THEORY.)

A broader interdisciplinary explanation of destructive intergroup conflict is found in human needs theory (HNT), which has precursors in the work of psychologist Abraham Maslow and sociologist Paul Sites as well as many others. The development and application of HNT in the field of conflict

556 INTERGROUP CONFLICT, THEORIES OF

resolution is generally credited to Burton (1990) who posited that the frustration and denial of the basic human needs of disadvantaged groups by more powerful groups is the primary driving force of destructive conflict, particularly of an ethnopolitical nature. The commonly identified needs include security, identity and recognition of it, freedom or autonomy, distributive justice, and participation. Thus, when minority groups are disadvantaged, oppressed, not recognized, and closed out from decision-making, the common tendency will be to resist this marginalization by whatever means necessary, including the use of violence. Burton and other theorists see the identity group, rather than the state, as the primary vehicle through which basic human needs are expressed and satisfied, thus calling for the creation of pluralistic, decentralized societies in which distinct identity groups have their place in the sun. Given that needs are expressed both at the individual level and the collective level of the identity group, HNT is essentially a social-psychological construction that integrates these levels of analysis. (See HUMAN NEEDS THEORY, CONFLICT, AND PEACE.)

COMMONALITIES IN INTERGROUP CONFLICT

Regardless of the primary theory used to explain intergroup conflict, a number of commonalities distinguish the phenomenon in terms of perceptual processes and group-level factors, both of which drive conflict toward higher degrees of intensity through escalation and intractability. Group categorization initiates differentiation between groups that reduces the perception of outgroups to stereotypes – a set of simplified, inaccurate, derogatory, and rigid beliefs about their attributes. Stereotypes drive insidious processes, such as selective and self-serving perceptions and memories,

self-fulfilling prophecies, discrimination, and dehumanization. Stereotypes develop readily into enemy images, which are often complemented by positive self-images, thus creating a powerful "mirror image" phenomenon involving mutual misperception and hostility. Stereotypes and images are rendered resistant to change through the tendency to maintain cognitive consistency, such that contrary information is ignored, discounted, or assimilated. In addition, errors in making causal attributions ascribe the destructive actions of conflicting groups to their inherent negative characteristics rather than contextual factors. (See STEREOTYPES.)

At the group level, identification with the group goes hand in hand with the development of cohesiveness, which is increased through the effects of outgroup threat. Cohesiveness drives conformity pressures on group members, which support norms of discrimination, hostility, and aggression toward outgroup members. Cohesiveness is also seen as a prime cause of faulty decision-making in groups, identified as "groupthink" in the work of psychologist Irving Janis. In this model, cohesiveness drives concurrence seeking (conformity) in the group to the point that it overrides the realistic and moral appraisal of alternative courses of action. Such processes also tend to support the emergence of aggressive leaders that often gain power in situations of conflict. (See GROUPTHINK.)

All the above factors operate to induce escalation toward greater levels of intensity, hostility, and aggressiveness. Escalation is also grounded in the principle of reciprocity, captured in psychologist Morton Deutsch's "crude law of social relations," in which the characteristic processes and effects elicited by a type of social relationship (competitive or cooperative) tend to elicit that type of relationship. Thus, conflict interaction tends to feed on itself in a self-perpetuating cycle, driving the relationship toward greater levels of destruction. When intergroup conflicts become highly escalated, they have a tendency to become protracted and even intractable. This is caused by a host of resistances at the individual and group levels to de-escalation and resolution brought about by the same processes as fed escalation. In addition to being trapped in this way, parties also experience entrapment in the sense that costs already expended need to be justified by continuing the same destructive course of action in pursuit of victory. (See CONFLICT, INTRACTABLE.)

Theories of intergroup conflict are intended to illuminate and unravel the complex human and social forces that drive the escalation and intractability of destructive conflict. An "eclectic model of intergroup conflict" is offered by Fisher (1990) in an attempt to incorporate RCT, SIT, and HNT, along with individual and group factors, to provide an integrated explanation of the etiology, escalation, and resolution of intergroup conflict. Only by first understanding the phenomenon in systematic and valid ways can humankind then realize and implement the behaviors required to control this insidious threat to our very survival.

SEE ALSO: Conflict, Intractable; Conflict Resolution, Interactive; Groupthink; Human Needs Theory, Conflict, and Peace; Identity-Based Conflicts, The ARIA Contingency Approach to; Intergroup Violence and Psychosocial Interventions, Cycles of; Minimal Group Paradigm; Social Dominance Theory; Social Identity Theory; Stereotypes; Threat, Kinds and Effects of.

REFERENCES

Burton, J. W. (Ed.). (1990). *Conflict: Human needs theory*. New York, NY: St. Martin's Press.
Fisher, R. J. (1990). *The social psychology of intergroup and international conflict resolution*. New York, NY: Springer-Verlag.
LeVine, R. A., & Campbell, D. T. (1972). *Ethnocentrism: Theories of conflict, ethnic attitudes and group behavior*. New York, NY: Wiley.
Sherif, M. (1966). *In common predicament: Social psychology of intergroup conflict and cooperation*. Boston, MA: Houghton-Mifflin.
Sidanius, J., & Pratto, F. (1999). *Social dominance: An intergroup theory of social hierarchy and oppression* New York, NY: Cambridge University Press.
Tajfel, H., & Turner, J. C. (1979). An integrative theory of intergroup conflict. In W. G. Austin & S. Worchel (Eds.), *The social psychology of intergroup relations* (pp. 33–47). Monterey, CA: Brooks/Cole.
Taylor, D. M., & Moghaddam, F. M. (1994). *Theories of intergroup relations: International social psychological perspectives* (2nd ed.). New York, NY: Praeger.

ADDITIONAL RESOURCES

Beyond Intractability Web resource: http://www.beyondintractability.org
Fisher, R. J. (2006). Intergroup conflict. In M. Deutsch, P. T. Coleman, & G. E. Marcus (Eds.), *The handbook of conflict resolution: Theory and practice* (2nd ed., pp. 176–196). San Francisco, CA: Jossey-Bass.
Moghaddam, F. M. (2008). *Multiculturalism and intergroup relations: Psychological implications for democracy in global context*. Washington, DC: American Psychological Association.

Intergroup Hatred: Psychological Dimensions

ERAN HALPERIN

The negative impact of hatred on human life has been widely documented (Sternberg 2003; Opotow & McClelland, 2007). Aristotle perceived hatred as one of the more momentous emotions because of the way it undermines people's sense of judgment. Hatred is also known as one of the most prevalent and destructive affective phenomena in situations of long-term intergroup conflict (Halperin, 2008). It fulfills a fundamentally destructive role in the violent effect it exerts on intergroup relations, potentially impelling people to acts of mass murder and war. Hence, hate makes a huge contribution to the escalation and maintenance of long-term conflicts and it stands as a powerful barrier to conflict resolution. (See AFFECT: ORIGINS AND TARGETS OF HATE.)

But do we really know why intergroup hatred plays such a central role in intergroup conflicts? Interestingly, despite extensive acknowledgment of its potentially destructive impact, there are few contemporary definitions of hatred (for a review, see Royzman, McCauley, & Rosin, 2005). Even more surprisingly, only a few social scientists have undertaken in-depth empirical research on hatred both as a personal and as a collective emotion, and on the role it plays in intergroup conflicts. Thus, a huge gap exists between the prevalence of hatred in the social and political realms, and the paucity of research in the field. It seems that one of the main reasons for the shortage in research and definitions of hatred is the fact that hatred is commonly viewed as an illegitimate social emotion by laymen and scholars alike.

THE NATURE OF INTERGROUP HATRED: DEFINITION AND COMPONENTS

In order to reduce hatred and to minimize its implications, a thorough understanding of the phenomenon is required. Through the years, different scholars have tried to define the concept of hatred. Some of these definitions have been very general and all-inclusive, while others have concentrated on very specific features of hatred. In very general terms, I define intergroup hatred as a secondary, extreme, and continuous emotion which is directed at a particular group, and fundamentally and all-inclusively denounces the group and its members (Halperin, 2008). In further detail, an in-depth review of previous theoretical writings about hatred (Royzman et al. 2005) indicates that two core elements constitute the basis for most definitions.

First, many of the conceptions deal with the appraisal of the hater regarding the nature and the motives of the hated group or object. These conceptions are closely related to some basic insights that were first introduced in the attribution theory. For example, Ben-Zeev (1992) argued that contrary to other emotions that are frequently targeted at specific events or behaviors, hatred is always directed at a defined object or group and denounces that object or group basically and all-inclusively. Others have suggested that hatred is an emotion caused by the judgment that the other person or group is evil by nature and will never change its negative, immoral, or violent ways (Halperin, 2008). In addition, the negative or offensive behavior of the hated group or its members is perceived to derive from a pure motivation to hurt the hater and his/her group and not from some other instrumental or practical motivations of gaining more resources. The almost natural implications of these appraisals are: (a) an in-depth belief that there is no real hope of improving the hated group's behavior and (b) a generalized hostility towards every behavior, action, or trait of the hated group.

Second, a large number of the definitions focus mainly on the behavioral intentions or goals that are associated with hatred. According to these definitions, when people say they "hate" a certain group, what they really mean is that they wish they could hurt members of that group or even that they would really be happy to hear that the group or its members were hurt (or even annihilated) by someone else. In line with that idea, in his classic book *The Nature of Prejudice*, Gordon Allport (1954) suggested that hatred is an "enduring organization of aggressive impulses towards a person or a class of persons" (p. 363).

What follows is that hatred reflects the desire to harm, humiliate, or even kill its object – not always instrumentally, but rather to cause harm as a vengeful objective in itself. These general patterns were recently demonstrated in a study conducted by Halperin (2008), who found that the two main emotional goals of Jewish-Israelis who felt hatred towards Palestinians were to "do evil to the Palestinians" and to "remove, destroy or even annihilate the Palestinian people." In more practical terms, people who felt hatred supported "the use of physical and violent actions towards Palestinians" as well as "the use of different means to ensure exclusion of Palestinians from any social or political rights."

To summarize, hatred is often a direct reaction to protracted harm caused to the "hater" or other members of the ingroup (group-based hatred). The hater perceives this harm as deliberate, unjust, and unmanageable. Hatred toward outgroups includes a wide cognitive spectrum which produces a clear distinction between outgroup members and ingroup members, and consequently rejects the hated outgroup. The affective aspect of intergroup hatred is secondary and thus involves unpleasant physical symptoms, as well as anger, fear, and powerful negative feelings toward outgroup members (Sternberg, 2003). Behaviorally, hatred may lead to the desire to eradicate the hated outgroup (Allport, 1954).

DIFFERENTIATION BETWEEN HATRED AND OTHER EMOTIONS

Despite past suggestions that there is overlap between hatred, anger, and fear or that hatred is an extreme form of anger, recent empirical evidence suggests that hatred is a discrete emotion, particularly in terms of its

unique cognitive appraisals, emotional goals, and response tendencies (Halperin, 2008). Although in some cases hatred syndromes will include some burst of fear or anger (and probably other emotions), the recent empirical evidence indicates that there are qualitative differences between hatred and these other emotions, and not just magnitude differences.

In more detail, while anger results from the perception of the outgroup's actions as unfair or unjust, and fear from the appraisal of high threat and low control, hatred includes a perception of the group as evil and its actions as deliberate and aimed at hurting the hater or members of the ingroup. In addition, haters reject the possibility that the outgroup members can change, whereas the emotional goal associated with anger focuses on correction of the object or the situation and the emotional goal associated with fear focuses on creating a safer environment. Hence, hatred leads to a desire to destroy the object or group, while anger and fear may lead people to much more ambiguous and even constructive reactions (Halperin, Sharvit, & Gross, in press-b).

Hence, unlike fear or anger, which are targeted at specific actions, hatred is targeted at the fundamental characteristics of the individual or the group (Ben-Zeev, 1992). In other words, haters do not believe in any possibility of improving intergroup relations. As a result, hatred gives expression to the dismissal of any attempt to change or to improve relations with the hated individual or group (Halperin, 2008).

HATRED AS AN INTERGROUP EMOTION

In recent decades scholars of emotions have acknowledged the fact that emotions can be experienced on a group level and not only on an individual level. While some of these scholars have focused on group-based emotions, namely, emotions that are experienced "in the name" of other group members, others described a tendency of group members, especially in conflict situations, to experience emotions simultaneously (Halperin et al., in press-b). Yet not all emotions have the same potential to transcend from the individual to the group or collective level.

Hatred can easily go through that transformation and some will even claim that it is the most "group-based" emotion. Aristotle states succinctly that whereas anger is customarily felt toward individuals, hatred is often felt towards groups. In contrast to fear and anger, rather than at specific individual actions, hatred is targeted at the fundamental characteristics of the individual or the group (Ben-Zeev, 1992). Actions are usually conducted by individuals rather than by groups. The generalized attribution of the action to the basic traits and features of members of the outgroup enables a parsimonious explanation of the action. This facile transition of hatred from the interpersonal level to the collective level makes it a pivotal agent in group-based political dynamics in general and in intergroup conflicts in particular.

IS HATRED AN EMOTION OR A SENTIMENT?

Scholars of emotions point to a fundamental distinction between immediate emotion and an emotional attitude, sentiment, or chronic emotion. While immediate emotion is an acute, short-term reaction to stimuli or to a changing environment, the sentiment is a chronic emotional phenomenon which represents a highly emotional standing disposition toward a person, group, or symbol (Halperin et al., in press-b).

Scholars of hatred have continually debated the question of whether hatred is an emotion or an emotional attitude (Royzman et al., 2005). However, in the last two decades, scholars (e.g., Sternberg, 2003; Halperin, 2008) have resolved the dispute by suggesting that hatred can occur in both configurations – immediate and chronic. In-depth interviews with lay people that I have conducted in recent years suggest that more than half of the participants, when requested to describe a hatred experience, chose to relate to an ongoing emotional experience, while the remainder focused on a more acute event (Halperin, 2008).

Hence, it is suggested that there are two types of hatred (Halperin, Canetti, & Kimhi, in press-a). The first is a sentimental, stable, and familiar "hating" emotional attitude (chronic hatred). The second is an emotional, powerful, and "burning" hate (immediate hatred) that occurs in response to significant events. They are related yet distinct. Frequent incidents of immediate hatred may make the development of chronic emotion more probable. Chronic hatred is fertile ground for the eruption of immediate hatred. Chronic haters encountering outgroup members or the consequences of their actions are apt to react with immediate hatred.

DOWN-REGULATION OF INTERGROUP HATRED

Given the destructive implications of hatred in general and especially in the context of intergroup conflicts, one of the most important questions that scholars and practitioners alike should deal with is whether there are ways to reduce levels of hatred or to down-regulate hatred (Halperin et al., in press-a). I'd like to suggest that any attempt to reduce levels of hatred should concentrate on undermining the unique characteristics of hatred, and specifically those characteristics that distinguish it from other (less destructive) negative emotions.

Accordingly, these attempts should emphasize humanness and heterogeneity of the outgroup as well as the ability of individuals and groups to change their characteristics, moral values, positions, and behavior (Halperin et al., in press-b). In addition, strategies of perspective taking can be used in order to increase understanding regarding the motives and goals of the adversary. I propose that such long-term processes, disseminated through education channels, cultural products, and other societal mechanisms, will alter the behavioral manifestations of reactive negative emotions, which are themselves natural and legitimate responses to offensive acts or provocations.

SEE ALSO: Affect: Origins and Targets of Hate.

REFERENCES

Allport, G. (1954). *The nature of prejudice.* Reading, MA: Addison-Wesley.
Ben-Zeev, A. (1992). Anger and hate. *Journal of Social Philosophy, 2,* 85–110.
Halperin, E. (2008). Group-based hatred in intractable conflict in Israel. *Journal of Conflict Resolution, 52,* 713–736.
Halperin, E., Canetti, D., & Kimhi, S. (in press-a). In love with hatred: Longitudinal study on the political consequences of group-based hatred. *Journal of Applied Social Psychology.*
Halperin, E., Sharvit, K., & Gross, J. J. (in press-b). Emotions and emotion regulation in conflicts. In D. Bar-Tal (Ed.), *Intergroup conflicts and their resolution: Social psychological perspective.* New York, NY: Psychology Press. (in press).
Opotow, S., & McClelland, S. (2007). The intensification of hating: A theory. *Social Justice Research, 20,* 68–97.
Royzman, E. B., McCauley, C., & Rosin, P. (2005). From Plato to Putnam: Four ways to think about hate. In R. J. Sternberg (Ed.), *The psychology of hate* (pp. 3–36).

Washington, DC: American Psychological Association.
Sternberg, R. J. (2003). A duplex theory of hate: Development and application to terrorism, massacres and genocide. *Review of General Psychology, 7,* 299–328.

Intergroup Threat Theory

WALTER G. STEPHAN AND
MARISA D. MEALY

Over the past several decades, a growing number of social scientists have become interested in the role that threats play in intergroup conflict. Threats are believed to be a major cause of conflict as well as an impediment to peace and reconciliation. In this essay we explore these two issues using the intergroup threat theory as a framework. We also discuss psychological processes and techniques involved in reducing intergroup threats.

TYPES OF THREAT

Intergroup threat theory proposes four basic types of threats that can cause intergroup conflict. These threats vary along two dimensions. The first dimension concerns whether the threat involves realistic (tangible) or symbolic (intangible) harm to the ingroup. (See THREATS, KINDS AND EFFECTS OF.) Realistic threats include threats to the ingroup's welfare, such as territorial threats, threats to political power, economic threats, and threats of physical harm. Symbolic threats include threats to the ingroup's identity, values, beliefs, norms, and way of life. The second dimension concerns whether the threats are perceived to be directed at the ingroup as a whole or at individual members. In combination, the two dimensions result in four types of threat: realistic group threat, symbolic group threats, realistic individual threats, and symbolic individual threats.

Distinctions between these types of threats are important because different types of threats have different consequences. For example, threats to the group as a whole are more likely to evoke anger than fear, whereas individual threats are more likely to evoke fear than anger. Likewise, symbolic threats are more likely to lead to emotions that involve a moral evaluation of the outgroup (e.g., contempt and disgust), while realistic threats are more likely to cause feelings of insecurity and frustration. Generally, to have an impact on the development of a conflict, threats must be seen as credible. However, threats do not necessarily have to be perceived accurately to have an impact – even inaccurately perceived threats can have real consequences. The magnitude of perceived intergroup threats increases as a function of the size of the stakes and the immediacy of the threatened negative outcomes.

CONSEQUENCES OF THREAT

Intergroup threats contribute to conflict because they influence emotions, perceptions, and behaviors. An appraisal of threat can evoke strong negative emotions, including fear, rage, anger, hatred, resentment, frustration, contempt, and insecurity. In addition, perceptions of threat reduce emotional empathy for members of the outgroup. These negative emotional responses, combined with a lack of empathy for the other group, can bring people to the point of killing their enemies. (See EMOTION.)

Intergroup perceptions are characterized by a wide variety of biases that hinder accurate perceptions of outgroups. These biases include negative stereotyping, distorted perceptions of the outgroup's intentions and motives, dehumanization of its members, an inflated sense of the moral legitimacy of the ingroup's cause, a perception that the outgroup is homogeneous, negative attributions to explain outgroup conduct,

a magnification of perceived intergroup differences, and a heightened belief in the difficulty of resolving conflicts with the outgroup. The arousal and anxiety associated with intergroup emotions can amplify these intergroup perceptual biases. Furthermore, the cognitive demands of coping with threat reduce executive functioning, which can lead to poor decision-making (e.g., groupthink). (See GROUPTHINK.) Intergroup threats can also influence the ingroup's perceptions of itself in relation to the outgroup. For instance, when powerful groups feel threatened they may perceive themselves as vulnerable – as happened to Americans after the terrorist attacks on 9/11/2001 and to many Europeans shortly thereafter. (See TERROR MANAGEMENT THEORY: WHY WAR?)

Negative intergroup emotions and intergroup perceptual biases contribute to the behavioral responses to threat. To some extent, these behavioral responses depend on the power of the threatened group. High-power groups are unaccustomed to being threatened because their power typically insulates them from threat. For high-power groups, feeling threatened is a new and unwanted experience. High-power groups often react more forcefully to being threatened than low-power groups and use their power to take repressive, and often violent, countermeasures. These behavioral countermeasures include warfare, genocide, economic sanctions, deprivation of civil liberties, unlawful detention, torture, discrimination, segregation, exile, prohibition of cultural displays (e.g., minorities speaking their own language or practicing their religion), destruction of property, and negative media campaigns.

Low-power groups may be more accustomed to feeling threatened and usually must be careful to respond in ways that do not risk overwhelming retaliation by the more powerful group. Nonetheless, they, too, have a wide range of behavioral options available to them. These options may include terrorism, riots, street violence, sabotage, dissident media campaigns, cyber attacks, the destruction of outgroup cultural symbols (e.g., flag burning), the formation of local militia, alliances with antigovernment forces, and open rebellion. Dissent may also be expressed in the form of demonstrations, boycotts, nonviolent protests, public violations of the dominant group's moral code, and civil disobedience. It is important to note that low-power groups are also more likely than powerful groups to comply with demands made by the other group.

Even after the cessation of open conflict, intergroup threats create emotional, cognitive, and behavioral responses that can interfere with attempts to foster peace and reconciliation. The threats that are present during conflict resolution may be new or they may be altered forms of threats that existed during open conflict. New threats may be related to apprehensions of being exploited or deceived by the other group during negotiations, losing face, or making too many concessions. Negative behavioral effects associated with these threats can impede peace and derail reconciliation. For example, the perception of threats may lead to a refusal to cease hostilities, reluctance to compromise, lack of creativity in problem solving, as well as argumentation, guile, and false assurances. Perceived threats can also prevent the ingroup from accepting responsibility for injustices perpetrated by its members or from forgiving the outgroup for the offenses committed by its members. Finally, it is worth noting that the effects of threats are not always negative: In some cases, intergroup threats can be beneficial to conflict resolution processes by deterring new violence and encouraging negotiations and reconciliation.

REDUCING THREAT / BUILDING PEACE

When considering how to reduce threats among the general populace, it is important to distinguish between threats to the ingroup as a whole (i.e., group threats) and threats directed at individual members of the ingroup (i.e., individual threats). Those threats which are perceived to be directed toward the group are best addressed at the societal level. Realistic group threats can be reduced by such behaviors as public declarations of peace, prosecuting crimes against humanity, and providing amnesty to low-level combatants. Leaders of both groups can contribute to the reduction of realistic threat by coming together to renounce violence, denounce hate groups, and engage in civil public discourse. In addition, they should establish and promote a set of mutually verifiable steps to intergroup peace, thereby facilitating a public vision of a pathway to a more peaceful future. To address perceptions of symbolic group threats, public displays of divisive or offensive symbols (e.g., flags, graffiti) can be outlawed, media campaigns to support peace and reconciliation can be undertaken, memorials can be erected to those who suffered or died in the conflict, billboards can display messages that promote peaceful coexistence, and social norms and roles that place a greater emphasis on inclusiveness and equality can be encouraged. The media can also play a supportive role by helping to prevent incidents of intergroup violence from spiraling out of control by providing accurate information quickly when incidents arise.

Individual threats may be more difficult to de-escalate than group threats because they often result from individuals' own personal circumstances. Furthermore, evidence indicating that these types of threats have been diminished may not be readily available to, or accepted by, the individuals who feel threatened. Nonetheless, realistic individual threats can be reduced by ensuring that basic human rights are protected and day-to-day security is maintained, passing laws or establishing rules that prohibit intergroup violence, discrimination, and

564 INTERGROUP THREAT THEORY

exclusionary policies, as well as implementing affirmative action policies which ensure the representation of all groups in employment, government, and educational settings. Individual symbolic threats can be reduced through efforts to forge superordinate identities, providing opportunities for intergroup contact under optimal conditions, and creating a sympathetic understanding of cultural differences, values, beliefs, and practices. New educational practices can be introduced in order to counter negative stereotypes, reduce perceived dissimilarity, and increase emotional and cognitive empathy for members of the other group. These practices should also emphasize the decategorization of outgroup members through the use of multiple crosscutting identities (e.g., age, sex, social class, interests, social and work roles). Efforts such as these should foster perceptions of outgroup members as less menacing and more human. (See COMMON INGROUP IDENTITY MODEL; DIALOGUE METHODS; CONTACT THEORY: EXTENDED AND PARASOCIAL; PEACE EDUCATION; CONTACT THEORY, INTERGROUP.)

There are a number of intergroup relations programs currently in existence that can help to reduce intergroup threats and promote peace. These programs include peace education, multicultural education, intergroup dialogues, problem-solving intergroup workshops, intercultural relations training, and conflict resolution training. What most of these programs share in common is intergroup contact under optimal conditions, opportunities to acquire positive, personalized, and accurate information about the outgroup, and an opportunity to learn interactions skills associated with conflict avoidance and resolution. Despite the existence of these programs, there is a pressing need for new programs that take advantage of what is known about the specific psychological processes that reduce threat and promote improved intergroup relations, especially for constituencies that have not been targeted in previous programs.

In sum, although an enormous number of factors contribute to conflict and its resolution, intergroup threats play a particularly prominent role because they are a direct cause of conflict and undermine efforts to create peace. Reducing perceived threats is a complex and often subtle process, but it does hold great promise as a means of promoting and maintaining peace.

SEE ALSO: Common Ingroup Identity Model; Contact Theory: Extended and Parasocial; Contact Theory, Intergroup; Dialogue Methods; Emotion; Groupthink; Peace Education; Terror Management Theory: Why War?; Threats, Kinds and Effects of.

REFERENCES

Greenberg, J., Landau, M. Kosloff, S., & Solomon, S. (2009). How our dreams of death transcendence breed prejudice. In T. Nelson (Ed.), *Handbook of prejudice*, (pp. 309–332). Mahwah, NJ: Lawrence Erlbaum Associates.
Maoz, I., & McCauley, C. (2008). Threat, dehumanization, and support for retaliatory aggressive policies in asymmetric conflict. *Journal of Conflict Resolution*, 52(1), 93–116.
Richeson, J. A., & Trawalter, S. (2005). Why do interracial interactions impair executive function? A resource depletion account. *Journal of Personality and Social Psychology*, 88, 934–947.
Stephan, W. G., & Renfro, C. L. (2002). The role of threats in intergroup relations. In D. Mackie & E. R. Smith (Eds.), *From prejudice to intergroup emotions* (pp. 191–208). New York, NY: Psychology Press.
Stephan, W. G., & Stephan, C. W. (2001). *Improving intergroup relations*. Thousand Oaks, CA: Sage.
Stephan, W. G., Ybarra, O., & Rios Morrison, K. (2009). Intergroup threat theory. In T. Nelson (Ed.), *Handbook of prejudice*

(pp. 43–59). Mahwah, NJ: Lawrence Erlbaum Associates.

Intergroup Violence and Psychosocial Interventions, Cycles of

DANIEL J. CHRISTIE

As the number of interstate wars has diminished in recent years, peace scholars and practitioners have redirected their attention to three kinds of intergroup violence: (1) structural violence, (2) terrorism, and (3) cycles of intergroup violence. Structural violence is a pernicious form of violence that is built into the structure of a society and generates enormous inequalities in power, wealth, and overall well-being. Structural violence occurs when there are enough resources for everyone in a society but some segments of the society remain deprived of need satisfaction. (See PEACE PSYCHOLOGY: DEFINITIONS, SCOPE, AND IMPACT.) The result is disproportionately high levels of infant mortality and shorter life spans for groups that are oppressed. Terrorism has been defined in a number of ways but usually refers to acts committed by nonstate actors who seek to target and kill civilian noncombatants with the purpose of advancing a political, religious, or ideological agenda. (See TERRORISM, PSYCHOLOGY OF.) The current article addresses the third type of violence, cycles of intergroup violence. Three phases of the cycle will be identified and psychosocial intervention strategies that are most appropriate for each phase will be presented.

THE NATURE OF CYCLES OF VIOLENCE

In contrast to structural violence, which is ubiquitous and continuous, violent episodes are geohistorically situated and intermittent. These episodes of violence have antecedent conditions and consequences. Moreover, a complete cycle can be divided into three phases: (1) conflict (antecedent conditions), (2) a violent episode, and (3) post-violence (consequent events). Cycles of violence vary in frequency, intensity, rise time, and duration. For instance, intractable conflicts tend to be marked by cycles of violence that are intense, frequent, and intergenerational, among other characteristics (Bar-Tal, 2007; Coleman, 2003). (See CONFLICT, INTRACTABLE.) In the following sections, three general classes or kinds of interventions that are typically applied to each phase of the cycle will be described (for more details, see Christie, Tint, Wagner, & Winter, 2008).

THE CYCLE OF VIOLENCE

The Conflict Phase: Violence Prevention Strategies

The term conflict is often conflated with violence as, for example, in reference to "post-conflict societies." However, from a psychological perspective, conflict involves perceptual framing and cognitive processes rather than overt forms of organized aggression. Hence, a conflict arises when members of one group perceive the acquisition of their interests or goals as incompatible with members of an opposing group who share the same interests or goals. Cognitive processes in turn affect the selection, interpretation, and memory of information in relation to the conflict. There is no implication that overt acts of violence are inevitable when a conflict arises. In light of the distinction between conflict and violence, the opportunity presents itself to manage conflicts constructively in order to prevent a violent episode.

A common way to manage conflict and prevent violence is through peacekeeping and peacemaking. Traditionally, United

Nations peacekeeping missions consisted of unarmed or lightly armed multinational soldiers who were expected to refrain from fighting and stand between previously warring parties who had signed a ceasefire agreement and consented to have peacekeepers deployed to keep the peace. Peacekeepers monitored the movement and activities of both sides and generally were charged with the responsibility of supporting the terms of the peace agreement. Of course, peacekeeping alone will not resolve a conflict, as evident in deployments that have been in place for more than 50 years in the Middle East, Cyprus, and Kashmir. In recent years, the scope of activities engaged in by peacekeepers has been greatly expanded in an effort to more effectively set the stage for conflict resolution and sustainable peace. (See PEACEKEEPING, PSYCHOLOGY OF.)

The term conflict resolution is sometimes used to describe a process that brings conflicted parties together to discuss the conflict in order to work toward its resolution. The term also refers to the outcome of a process, that is, the arrival at terms acceptable to the conflicted parties. There are many conflict resolution processes: unilateral initiatives, dialogue, negotiation, mediation, interactive problem solving, intergroup contact, and other processes designed to bring parties together and change intergroup attitudes and relations (Deutsch, Coleman, & Marcus, 2006). (See CONFLICT MANAGEMENT, RESOLUTION, AND TRANSFORMATION.) A major challenge for practitioners of conflict resolution is to bring the parties together and keep them focused on resolving the conflict. A number of approaches to bringing parties together have been explored. They include confidence-building measures (CBMs), reframing the conflict, and unofficial diplomacy.

In a psychological sense, CBMs are initiatives that are designed to reduce fear, anxiety, and suspicion while building trust and mutual security between parties in conflict.

CBMs can be unilateral initiatives that signal a willingness to talk or agreements that clarify intentions and make each other's behavior more transparent and predictable. For instance, hot lines can be used to communicate benign intentions and actions (e.g., military maneuvers) that otherwise could be interpreted as menacing. CBMs can lay the groundwork for more predictable and stable diplomatic and political relations. (See DIPLOMACY, PREVENTIVE.)

Another psychological tool for improving relations is reframing, a process in which the view of one or both parties to a conflict is reinterpreted in ways that are more likely to resolve the conflict. Reframing may alter initial assumptions about what the key issues are, what factors led to the conflict, who are the players, and more generally, how to resolve the conflict. Reframing is most useful if it can set in motion a circular relationship between tension reduction, trust development, and cooperation. (See TRUST AND DISTRUST.)

Unofficial diplomacy can be useful in all phases of a cycle of violence. Unofficial diplomacy is usually mediated by a third party that brings together unofficial but influential members of groups in conflict. Mediators can de-escalate tensions, reframe problems for both sides, take care of logistics, offer technical assistance, and generally encourage movement toward the resolution of conflict. (See MEDIATION.) Participants are guided in a problem-solving process that encourages honest disclosure of interests and needs, intergroup empathy, and constructive analysis of the conflict. Relationships are built while participants test faulty assumptions, correct biases, arrive at insights, and develop policies that, under ideal conditions, are adopted by policymakers. (See CONFLICT RESOLUTION, INTERACTIVE.)

Intergroup contact theory suggests that bringing together groups in conflict, under certain conditions, is likely to reduce intergroup prejudice. Moreover, the effects can be amplified if four conditions are met, as outlined in Allport's classic book, *The Nature of Prejudice* (1954): (1) cooperation, on (2) common goals, between (3) equal status groups, in the context of (4) support from authorities. Empathy and perspective taking are important mechanisms for the contact effect; while intergroup anxiety and threat can be substantial obstacles to the contact effect. (See CONTACT THEORY, INTERGROUP.)

In addition to applying the contact hypothesis, it is also possible to improve relations between groups through direct negotiations or conflict resolution processes. Typically, approaches to conflict resolution rely on perspective taking, joint problem solving, generating options for mutual gain, and a host of other "rational" processes that emphasize human cognition. While rationality matters, recent approaches have emphasized the importance of human emotions, noting for example that positive emotions can facilitate the disclosure of information, increase flexibility of thought, enhance creative brainstorming, and yield constructive problem solving. Even when problems are not amenable to mutually satisfying outcomes because they have a zero sum structure in which gains by one side (e.g., land, water, and other limited resources) result in losses to the other side, positive emotions make outcomes seem more fair than negative emotions. (See NEGOTIATION, ROLE OF EMOTIONS IN.) When conflicts cannot be managed effectively, they can be an antecedent of violence.

The Violence Phase: De-escalation Strategies

The rapid de-escalation of violence is important in part because prolonged violence can intensify outgroup antipathy, faulty, rigid, black/white thinking, negative attributions of the other, selective inattention, moral disengagement, and other psychological processes that make it difficult to move toward a constructive dialogue. When episodes of intergroup violence intensify and occur over a long period of time, an "ethos of conflict" may crystallize with both sides generating relatively permanent ideologies that dehumanize the Other while aggrandizing their own group. The ideology represents a substantial barrier to resolving the conflict because incoming information is distorted to fit the ideological frame. (See CONFLICT, ETHOS OF.)

Three common de-escalation strategies are leadership-induced readiness, unofficial diplomacy, and grassroots antiwar activism. These strategies correspond to top-down, middle-out, and bottom-up approaches to de-escalation.

Elites can initiate a top-down approach to de-escalation by attempting to raise the costs of armed conflict to the point where both sides experience a mutually hurting stalemate that in turn creates a sense of ripeness for negotiation. A mutually hurting stalemate occurs when neither side can defeat the other yet both are enduring unacceptable costs and believe a negotiated solution is possible. In a psychological sense, ripeness corresponds to psychological readiness in which there is motivation to escape the situation, followed by optimism about the prospect of reaching a mutually beneficial outcome (Pruitt, 2007). (See RIPENESS THEORY.)

Unofficial diplomacy, a middle-out strategy, brings together unofficial members of conflicted groups who engage in dialogue to deepen mutual understanding and generate new perspectives on problems, thereby laying the groundwork for nonbinding agreements. Although these unofficial diplomats do not represent their governments, they tend to be influential individuals who may have direct access to official negotiators or policymakers (Fisher, 2005). (See CONFLICT RESOLUTION, INTERACTIVE.)

Grassroots antiwar activism, a bottom-up strategy, is likely to take place under certain conditions: namely, when members (1) perceive themselves as sharing a common social identity and concrete goals, (2) view conflict as normal, (3) are driven by anger, and (4) have a commitment to long-term change. (See ACTIVISM, ANTIWAR.)

The Post-Violence Phase: Reconciliation and Development

Psychologists have long been involved in treatment of traumatic stress in the wake of violent episodes and there is growing recognition that a wide range of mental health problems typically arise in post-violent settings. There also has been a growing appreciation for the legitimacy and potential efficacy of intergroup forgiveness and reconciliation. While details are still being worked out, it is clear that a number of psychosocial variables can pose serious barriers to the reconciliation process. Examples of barriers include the intergenerational transfer of trauma, memories of harm, feelings of victimization, and various cultural products such as memorials and commemorations. (See VICTIMHOOD, COLLECTIVE.)

Notwithstanding the barriers to reconciliation, there are some glimmers of hope. Research indicates that positive intergroup contact, particularly contact that promotes cross-group friendships, can reduce tendencies to dehumanize the Other and increase the likelihood of forgiveness. Key mediating variables appear to be the reduction of anger and increases in intergroup empathy, perspective taking, and trust (Nadler, Malloy, & Fisher, 2008). (See FORGIVENESS, INTERGROUP.)

While peace psychologists are engaged in trying more deeply to understand and promote intergroup reconciliation, a key task in the aftermath of violence is to restructure societies so that the conditions that laid the groundwork for violence are not reproduced. Clearly, peace psychologists are well positioned to contribute to a wide range of development tasks that favor sustainable peace: building security both within and between individuals and groups, ensuring the equitable allocation of physical reconstruction resources, encouraging social and community interdependence, and working on the establishment of legitimate governance and economic well-being for all. (See POST-VIOLENCE RECONSTRUCTION.)

Finally, it should be noted that although the phases of violence have been delineated in a neat and tidy way, some intervention strategies are robust (e.g., interactive conflict resolution) and can be applied in two or more phases of a cycle. Moreover, multiple kinds of interventions are sometimes used when a violent cycle has elements of all three phases.

SEE ALSO: Activism, Antiwar; Conflict, Ethos of; Conflict, Intractable; Conflict Management, Resolution, and Transformation; Conflict Resolution, Interactive; Contact Theory, Intergroup; Diplomacy, Preventive; Forgiveness, Intergroup; Mediation; Negotiation, Role of Emotions in; Peace Psychology: Definitions, Scope, and Impact; Peacekeeping, Psychology of; Post-Violence Reconstruction; Ripeness Theory; Terrorism, Psychology of; Trust and Distrust; Victimhood, Collective.

REFERENCES

Allport, G. (1954). *The nature of prejudice.* Reading, MA: Addison-Wesley.

Bar-Tal, D. (2007). Sociopsychological foundations of intractable conflicts. *American Behavioral Scientist, 50,* 1430–1453.

Christie, D. J., Tint, B. S., Wagner, R. V., & Winter, D. D. (2008). Peace psychology for a peaceful world. *American Psychologist, 63,* 540–552.

Coleman, P. T. (2003). Characteristics of protracted, intractable conflict: Toward the development of a metaframework – I. *Peace and Conflict: Journal of Peace Psychology, 9,* 1–38.

Deutsch, M., Coleman, P. T., & Marcus, E. C. (2006). *Handbook of conflict resolution: Theory and practice.* San Francisco, CA: Jossey-Bass.

Fisher, R. J. (2005). *Paving the way: Contributions of interactive conflict resolution to peacemaking.* Lanham, MD: Lexington Books.

Nadler, A., Malloy, T. E., & Fisher, J. D. (2008). *The social psychology of intergroup reconciliation.* Oxford, UK: Oxford University Press.

Pruitt, D. G. (2007). Readiness theory and the Northern Ireland peace process. *American Behavioral Scientist, 50,* 1520–1541.

International Relations, Psychological Perspectives on

JANICE GROSS STEIN

Psychological explanations of international politics focus on the impact of cognition and emotion on choice. Through the analysis of decision-making, political psychologists have explored a wide range of topics that are central to international politics: the onset of war, nuclear strategy, deterrence and reassurance, signaling and bargaining, conflict management and conflict resolution, and peace. Recent neuroscientific research on emotion is changing the analysis of foreign policy decision-making and rational choice. This essay looks first at psychological theories of decision-making. Second, it examines the consequences of new understandings of decision-making for strategic models of interaction. Third, the essay looks at the contribution of psychological explanations to the analysis of collective beliefs and moods on international political issues.

COGNITION AND EMOTION IN DECISION-MAKING

The Cognitive Revolution

Forty years ago, psychologists started a "cognitive revolution" as they rejected simple behaviorist models and looked again at the way cognition shaped the choices people make. Although this was not its original purpose, the cognitive revolution can be understood largely as a commentary on the limits of rational choice. Much of the early work accepted rational choice as the default position and then demonstrated its boundaries. Research has now accumulated to show that people rarely conform to the expectations of the rational model and that these deviations are not random but systematic. (See DECISION-MAKING, PSYCHOLOGICAL DIMENSIONS OF FOREIGN POLICY.)

Cognitive psychology has demonstrated important differences between the expectations of rational decision models and the processes of attribution, estimation, judgment, and choice people frequently use. It explains these differences by the need for simple rules of information processing and judgment that are necessary to make sense of environments that are both uncertain and complex. People have a preference for simplicity, they are averse to ambiguity and dissonance, and they misunderstand fundamentally the essence of probability. And people have risk profiles that depart from what models of rational choice would expect; we are far more averse to loss than we are gain-seeking (Kahneman & Tversky, 1979). Together, these attributes compromise the capacity for rational choice.

Political leaders making decisions about the world need to order their world and make a very complex world somewhat simpler (Jervis, 1976). When they look to the past to learn about the future, political leaders tend to draw simple one-to-one analogies without qualifying conditions. In 1991, President George H. Bush called Saddam Hussein "another Hitler," with little attention to what was different either about the two men or about Iraq in 1990 and Germany in 1938. Yet fitting Saddam into an existing frame through use of analogical reasoning gave the president a readily accessible script about how to respond to Iraq's invasion of Kuwait.

Cognitive psychologists have produced robust evidence that people strongly prefer consistency, that they are made uncomfortable by dissonant information, and that they consequently deny or discount inconsistent information to preserve their beliefs. This drive for consistency impairs the processes of estimation and judgment. The well-established tendency to discount inconsistent information contributes significantly to the persistence of beliefs. Political leaders in the United States were generally resistant to changing their beliefs about the Soviet Union after Mikhail Gorbachev came to power with a reform agenda. Three years after he became general secretary, senior policymakers were arguing that his strategy was to lull the West while the Soviet Union recovered.

Cognitive processes of attribution can also confound policymaking. One of the most pervasive biases is the fundamental attribution error, where people exaggerate the importance of dispositional over situational factors in explaining the disliked behavior of others but explain their own behavior by the situational constraints that they face. When explaining behavior that they like, they simply reverse the pattern of inference. When the government of North Korea makes a concession in the talks about its nuclear program, leaders in Washington see that concession as a function of the situational constraints Pyongyang faces, but explain their own willingness to participate in the talks as evidence of their disposition to search for a peaceful compromise. The double standard in reasoning is clear. (See ATTRIBUTION THEORY, INTERGROUP CONFLICT AND.)

Cognitive psychology has generated robust evidence that loss is more painful than comparable gain is pleasant. Leaders tend to be risk averse when things are going well and relatively risk acceptant when things are going badly, when they face a crisis in which they are likely to lose or have lost something that matters to them (Kahneman & Tversky, 1979). Leaders are also likely to take greater risks to protect what they already have – the "endowment effect" – than to increase their gains. They are also likely to take greater risks to reverse losses, to recapture what they once held, than they would to make new gains. And when decision-makers suffer a significant loss, they are far slower to accommodate to these losses than they would be to incorporate gains. These general findings apply directly to foreign policy choices. President Sadat of Egypt, for example, never "normalized" for the loss of the Sinai to Israel in 1967. Even though Israel had an obvious advantage in military capabilities, Sadat was undeterred and highly motivated to recapture the Sinai; thus, he launched a high-risk war in 1973 that was designed to begin a political process of negotiation with Israel that would restore the Sinai to Egypt.

Emotion, Cognition, and Choice

New research in neuroscience is revolutionizing the understanding of the relationship between emotion, cognition, and decision. Two results stand out. First, many decisions seem not to be the result of a deliberative thought process, but preconscious neurological processes. Second, emotion is primary and plays a dominant role in choice. (See DECISION-MAKING, THE ROLE OF EMOTIONS IN.)

Emotions are adaptive programs of action that have evolved over time to ensure survival and then reproduction. A useful way of thinking about emotion and cognition is to see affective processes as those that address the go/no-go questions, while cognitive processes are those that answer true/false questions. Choice clearly invokes both kinds of processes. Establishing truth claims about states of the world is usually not enough for people to make a choice. What people value is an emotional as well as cognitive process, and both are important in whether they decide to approach or avoid. Hence, emotion carries utility. The new field of neuro-economics is beginning to conceive utility as something one experiences subjectively.

There is an ongoing and vigorous debate among psychologists, neuroscientists, and behavioral economists about the relationship between affect and cognition. Three approaches are particularly relevant. The first is the "somatic marker" hypothesis, the second is the "affect-as-appraisal" hypothesis, and the third is "affect-as-information." Each understands the relationship between emotion and cognition differently (McDermott, 2004).

The first argues that the information people receive through their senses, that they experience physiologically, creates emotions which then cue decision and action. These physiological experiences, or somatic markers, create learned emotional responses which allow people to decide quickly what should be approached and what should be avoided (Damasio, 1994). In the early stages of decision-making, emotions are primary.

The appraisal approach to emotion is quite different. It reflects the long-standing view that cognition precedes emotion. It is thoughts that evoke feelings. The cognitive process of appraising – a treaty, a leader, a new institution – as good or bad elicits an emotion. This approach is inconsistent with those neuroscientists who see emotion as primary and as the carrier of value.

A third approach treats affect as information (Clore & Gasper, 2000). Emotions carry information to people about their unconscious processes which then become conscious thoughts and feelings and an input into the decisions they face. In this sense, emotion does not follow cognitive appraisal but creates appraisals through the information it provides.

Affective and cognitive processes can collaborate or compete. At low levels of intensity, affect appears to play a largely "advisory" role; it provides information which informs cognitive processes. At intermediate levels of intensity, people begin to become conscious of conflict between cognitive and affective inputs and struggle for self-control. At high levels of intensity, affect can be so powerful that it short-circuits thought and moves to action. Emotion precedes cognition and can swamp cognition. Only after the fact can people reflect on the choices that they made.

Emotion and Cognition as Explanations of Strategic Interaction

Emotion is a core driver in theories of decision-making, with significant consequences for the understanding of foreign policy decision-making. Psychological explanations of foreign policy choice have been extended to strategic interaction in international politics. The credibility of signals, an essential component in theories of deterrence, compellence, and bargaining, is not only a property of the sender, as some formal models of signaling suggest, but also a function of the beliefs of the receiver (Mercer, 2005). These beliefs are not only cognitive but emotional as well. The emotional cues that signals evoke – fear, anger – matter insofar as these emotions then prompt beliefs and action in turn. Research demonstrates that fear prompts uncertainty and risk-averse action while anger prompts certainty and risk acceptance. Threats that evoke fear are likely to prompt hesitancy and a risk-averse response; that is the purpose of most deterrent threats. Frightening threats are less likely to be successful, however, when they are designed to compel adversarial leaders to act. And threats that humiliate are likely to evoke anger and provoke the risk-acceptant response that a threat-based strategy is designed to avoid. Threat-based strategies consequently become much more complex and dangerous to design and implement. (See EMOTION.)

Research also demonstrates that credibility, a fundamental component of theories of action in international politics, is emotional as well as cognitive. Credibility is not simply a function of either the cost of the signal or past behavior, as some theories of bargaining claim. It is an emotional belief that is held by its intended receiver. Russia's credibility is not only a function of what its leaders say and do, or have said and done, but what Georgia's leaders believe Moscow will say and do. Psychological explanations call into question reputational models based exclusively on past behavior of states or on the costliness of signals. They give theoretical weight to the pattern of inference leaders make and build in emotion as the primary driver of assessment in the early stages of decision-making.

Emotion, Cognition, and Collective Beliefs

Psychological models explain not only leaders' choices and the interactive sequencing of those choices across a range of domains in international politics, but also collective beliefs and moods. Epidemiological and viral models help to explain the diffusion of emotion from an individual to a larger group. The spread of emotions from one individual to another is similar to other contagious processes.

Trust and confidence are central to the workings of the international order. Confidence and trust are emotional states, an indicator of optimism about the future. They are also cognitive – one person's sense of how confident others are and their perceptions of how confident still others are. An individual's mood is in part a function of the mood of others and, in this sense, it is as reasonable to speak of a collective mood as it is to speak of shared norms. Psychological models speak to both collective beliefs and to collective moods. Emotions, political psychologists argue, constitute feelings and moods that can be powerful spurs to action in international politics or can lead to panic and withdrawal.

Nationalism is an emotional belief, an attachment to one's society that is evoked by emotional cues and expressed through emotional identification with the collective. Mobilizational appeals to nationalist loyalty for both constructive and destructive purposes are emotional, phrased as "love of the motherland [or fatherland]." Milosevic's appeal to Serb nationalism, for example, invoked past humiliations and grievances in an effort to mobilize anger and support for action. (See EMOTIONAL APPEALS, MOBILIZING THROUGH.) The onset of ethnic war in the former Yugoslavia cannot be understood without referencing the "emotional entrepreneurship" of the Serbian political leader. (See PATRIOTISM AND NATIONALISM.)

Psychological models explain both individual and collective behavior in international politics. Research in neuroscience is bringing emotion back in to the analysis of international politics across a wide variety of issues. The research challenge will be to connect psychological processes to political and institutional streams and to identify and explain the amplifying feedback loops.

SEE ALSO: Attribution Theory, Intergroup Conflict and; Decision-Making, Psychological Dimensions of Foreign Policy; Decision-Making, the Role of Emotions in; Emotion;

Emotional Appeals, Mobilizing through; Patriotism and Nationalism.

REFERENCES

Clore, G. L., & Gasper, K. (2000). Feeling is believing: Some affective influences on belief. In N. H. Frijda, A. S. R. Manstead, & S. Bem (Eds.), *Emotions and beliefs: How feelings influence thoughts* (pp. 10–44). Cambridge, UK: Cambridge University Press.

Damasio, A. (1994). *Descartes' error: Emotion, reason, and the human brain*. New York, NY: Putnam.

Jervis, R. (1976). *Perception and misperception in international politics*. Princeton, NJ: Princeton University Press.

Kahneman, D. & Tversky, A. (1979). Prospect theory: An analysis of decision under risk. *Econometrica*, 47, 263–291.

McDermott, R. (2004). The feeling of rationality: The meaning of neuroscientific advances for political science. *Perspectives on Politics*, 2, 691–706.

Mercer, J. (2005). Rationality and psychology in international politics. *International Organization*, 59, 77–106.

Internet Data Collection

MICHAEL R. HULSIZER AND
LINDA M. WOOLF

The Internet has been both an important research tool and an important area of inquiry for peace psychologists. As a tool, the Internet has enabled investigators to research topics through the use of email, online surveys, chat rooms, and electronic focus groups. These methods often enable researchers to access difficult-to-reach populations and build large participant pools and collect data amendable to complex statistical analyses (e.g., factor analysis, structural equation modeling). Anderson and Kanuka (2003) stated that "like any useful tool in the hands of a skilled practitioner, the Net can provide opportunities and techniques that enhance many components of our research practice" (p. 3).

In addition to using the Internet as a tool for research, some investigators have begun examining the activities which take place in cyberspace. For example, hate group researchers have been investigating recruitment strategies used by online hate groups as a means to develop effective counter-techniques (e.g., Gerstenfeld, Grant, & Chiang, 2003). In addition, investigators have researched completely virtual communities (e.g., Second Life), online social networks, massive multiplayer online role-playing games (MMORPG), and other online groups using techniques modified for Internet use such as an online ethnographies (i.e., netnography). Online communities have become increasingly important as the range of behaviors present in these environments often mirror the real world. (See DISPUTE RESOLUTION, ONLINE.) For example, a software glitch caused the uncontrollable spread of a "plague" in the online World of Warcraft (Sydell, 2005). Soon after the virtual outbreak, the Centers for Disease Control (CDC) contacted the game's creators to examine these data to better understand how people might react to a real-world pandemic.

THE INTERNET AS A RESEARCH TOOL

Researchers have been flocking to the Internet as a means to conduct research. For example, Birnbaum (2000) revealed that in 1998 there were just 35 Internet experiments and surveys cited in the American Psychological Society's list of Psychological Research on the Net (maintained by John H. Krantz). By 1999 the list had nearly doubled to over 65 online experiments and surveys. In 2010 there were over 500 current surveys and experiments linked through the site (http://psych.hanover.edu/research/exponnet.html) on a variety of topics including predictors of forgiveness, social attitudes on Facebook, perceptions of global warming, and beliefs about sexual assault. However, the majority of the e-research listed was social psychological in nature. Thus, it comes as no surprise that the Social Psychology Network (maintained by Scott Plous) cited over 196 Web-based experiments and surveys on its Web site in 2010 (http://www.socialpsychology.org/expts.htm).

Much of the enthusiasm regarding Internet data collection is a result of the flexibility associated with this data collection tool. For example, using the Internet, researchers can collect data in synchronous or asynchronous formats. Previously, synchronous data were limited to participants within a specific geographic region. However, readily available video conferencing software (e.g., Skype) enables researchers to run focus groups with participants from across the globe – creating a much more representative participant pool. Similarly, asynchronous bulletin board communications give the researcher access to a detailed log of a specific conversation in which participants were able to take as much time as necessary to formulate an appropriate response to a particular topic.

Peace researchers are uniquely suited to reaping the benefits of the Internet to further advance our understanding of peace psychology. For example, forgiveness researchers can now interact with survivors of mass violence from different conflict regions throughout the world in real time. Hate group researchers can now examine the content of hate-related electronic bulletin boards to determine what strategies are used to recruit new members and perpetuate hateful ideology.

However, despite the allure of the Internet as a means for data collection, there is reason for caution. Anderson and Kanuka

(2003) stated that "the use of the Net in itself adds little intrinsic value to enhancing the quality of research" (p. 3). They suggested that regardless of the medium, good research design is essential. The mere use of the Internet cannot overcome methodological confounds, validity shortcomings, and poor sampling.

ETHICS AND INTERNET DATA COLLECTION

All researchers, regardless of the data collection medium, need to ensure that they collect data in an ethical fashion. (See DO NO HARM.) Unfortunately, much of the regulations surrounding research ethics are grounded in the traditional research setting, not the fluid environment of the Internet. Issues of particular concern for research conducted on the Internet include: (a) informed consent; (b) privacy, confidentiality, and anonymity; and (c) participant risk. For example, when are Internet-based data considered in the public domain? Is there an expectation of privacy on social network sites? Does the researcher need permission to publish online public speech? Do participants understand and recognize the fragility associated with privacy, confidentiality, and anonymity in the online environment? What extra risks are involved relative to online responses collected from participants living in politically repressive contexts?

According to Anderson and Kanuka (2003), ethical concerns associated with online research vary as a function of whether the behavior in question took place in the real world or the online environment. Research on participant behavior, which takes place in the real world but reported through an Internet-based tool (e.g., SurveyMonkey), tends to have fewer ethical concerns unique to the online medium. Typical ethical concerns include questions regarding the best means of obtaining informed consent and the ability to guarantee the privacy, confidentiality, and/or anonymity of the data.

The most apparent means by which consent differs online versus in the real world is the lack of a physical signature to signal that the participant has agreed to take part in the study. For example, in the online environment, participants typically indicate their consent by clicking a radio button. For added security, SurveyMonkey records a respondent time stamp to ensure the researcher knows exactly when consent was given.

Privacy is a major concern given that data may not be completely controlled by the researcher. Often data is collected by a third party vendor and then disseminated to the experimenter. Unfortunately, there are many opportunities for the privacy of participant responses to be compromised during this journey. Data can be intercepted during data collection, stolen from the third party data warehouse, or improperly accessed years after the study. Consequently, researchers need to make participants aware that they cannot guarantee that data will remain private, confidential, or anonymous. Indeed, although SurveyMonkey advises researchers to include a data confidentiality statement in their consent form, they urge researchers not to make guarantees to confidentiality or anonymity. Peace psychology researchers need to be aware of the limits of Internet privacy and the risks associated with participant's use of the Internet when collecting data from individuals living in countries associated with a high degree of control over the Internet.

Anderson and Kanuka (2003) asserted that there is a lack of understanding on the part of the researcher and participant about how safe their data is in an online research project. Similarly, SurveyMonkey recommends that researchers restrict the amount of private data they collect from participants to only that information which is essential to the study. Consequently, Anderson and Kanuka assert that if the data are very sensitive, it may be that the costs outweigh the potential benefits. In other words, it may be unethical to collect the data in the online medium.

Behavior which takes place and is studied in the online environment involves many of the same ethical issues (e.g., consent, privacy) discussed earlier but the online medium adds to the complexity of these concerns. For example, the online environment makes it more difficult to indentify exactly who is taking part in the research study. Proxy servers and online anonymizer tools may disguise a participant's real identity. As a result, researchers may find it difficult to rule out the possibility that participants are misrepresenting themselves. In addition, researchers need to be cognizant of the possibility that vulnerable populations (e.g., children) are taking part in the research. There is a variety of techniques to increase the likelihood that participants are who they claim they are (e.g., use of a witness, providing credit card information); however, there is no foolproof method. Complicating matters, in some countries women may not be legally able to give consent. Consequently, some situations may necessitate greater controls in relation to garnering consent, broader informed consent statements, or the use of traditional consent measures (e.g., face-to-face).

Consent may not be needed when the activity is nonintrusive and takes place in the public domain. This is a relatively simple question to address in the real world. However, the online environment makes this a much thornier issue. For example, Gerstenfeld, Grant, and Chiang (2003) conducted a content analysis of 157 extremist Web sites. The researchers found that these sites were actively recruiting and educating members by including multimedia content, racist symbols and literature, and providing links to similar sites. In addition, some of the sites encouraged violence. Gerstenfeld and colleagues restricted their analysis to static elements of the Web site. Consequently, there were few ethical issues to consider. However, the ethics of the study would have been much more in question had the researchers examined member comments in the site chat rooms. The primary ethical dilemma in this situation concerns the question as to whether online chat rooms are public or private environments.

Researchers investigating behavior in public settings generally do not need to seek informed consent given the fact that data collection is nonintrusive. The American Psychological Association's (APA) *Ethical Principles of Psychologists and Code of Conduct* (2003) exempts psychologists from gaining informed consent when collecting observational data within a public place. However, the APA has not specifically addressed the online environment where the distinction between public and private settings is more fluid. Indeed, Anderson and Kanuka (2003) asserted that "the sense of what is public or private is defined not by the technology, but by the perception of privacy and inclusion that is maintained by the participants" (p. 68). Consequently, researchers should look carefully at the online culture surrounding the use of the chat rooms in question and make conservative decisions regarding the decision to collect online data without seeking the consent of participants.

Lastly, debriefing participants taking part in Internet-based research can also be complicated. Typically, researchers can conduct a face-to-face debriefing addressing any questions and concerns that the participant may raise following completion of the research study. The online environment makes this type of interaction difficult to replicate. Participants can be provided with a written statement explaining the nature of the study, but the lack of nonverbals and other nuances makes true debriefing difficult. The challenges associated with online debriefing are even more apparent when the study involves deception. When conducting research involving deception, the gold standard is to return the participant to the pre-experimental state. This is difficult to achieve in the online environment. Scott Plous commented that "you'll lose control over whether people receive the correction afterwards. It raises serious ethical concerns" (Azar, 2000). Consequently, care should be taken to ensure that a proper debriefing can be achieved when conducting research in the online environment.

CONCLUSION

The Internet has been a wonderful tool for researchers to use when investigating peace psychology. The online environment can be used to collect data on behavior taking place in the real world or can be used to examine the increasingly rich environment which exists solely in cyberspace. Regardless of the medium used, good research trumps bad research. The Internet cannot overcome poor research design. One challenge for conducting research online is the fact that our current code of research ethics seems best suited for research conducted in the real world. At times, the translation to the online environment is smooth. However, in many instances the online environment introduces further complexities when attempting to design an ethical research study and presents additional challenges relative to protecting research participants both in terms of privacy and minimizing risk. Consequently, peace psychologists need to exercise caution when examining behavior which exists solely in the online environment.

SEE ALSO: Dispute Resolution, Online; Do No Harm.

REFERENCES

American Psychological Association (2003). *Ethical principles of psychologists and code of conduct.* Retrieved October 8, 2010, from http://www.apa.org/ethics/code

Anderson, T., & Kanuka, H. (2003). *e-Research: Methods, strategies, and issues.* Boston, MA: Allyn & Bacon.

Azar, B. (2000, April). Online experiments: Ethically fair or foul? *Monitor on Psychology*, *31*(4), 50.

Birnbaum, M. H. (Ed.). (2000). *Psychological experiments on the Internet.* San Diego, CA: Academic Press.

Gerstenfeld, P., Grant, D., & Chiang, C. (2003). Hate online: A content analysis of extremist Internet sites. *Analyses of Social Issues and Public Policy (ASAP)*, *3*, 29–44.

Sydell, L. (2005, October 5). All things considered: "Virtual" virus sheds light on real-world behavior. Washington, DC: National Public Radio. Retrieved October 8, 2010, from http://www.npr.org/templates/story/story.php?storyId=4946772

ADDITIONAL RESOURCE

Woolf, L. M., & Hulsizer, M. R. (2004). Hate groups for dummies: How to build a successful hate group. *Humanity and Society*, *28*, 40–62.

Interrogation, Psychology and

JEAN MARIA ARRIGO, STEPHEN SOLDZ, AND RAY BENNETT

Interrogation refers to the process of state agents questioning captive, often unwilling individuals for state purposes. Historically, state-recognized experts on mind–body relations have often provided the rationales for state methods of interrogation. Aristotle, for example, described the ancient Greek practice of juridical torture from the naturalistic perspective and maintained that slaves, lacking reason, tell the truth to stop the pain, whereas free men can reason to their long-term advantage and give false testimony under torture. European juridical torture in the fifteenth to eighteenth centuries was grounded in the ascetic principle that bodily pain drives out self-will in favor of God's will, thus resulting in true testimony. In the Korean War (1950–1953), Chinese "brainwashing" of United Nations prisoners proceeded as Maoist re-education, wherein prisoners of war confessed their political crimes.

In the post-9/11 (2001) Global War on Terror led by the United States, psychologists adapted psychological and physical stressors to render terrorist suspects pliable to interrogators. Seasoned interrogators disputed the efficacy of these techniques; human rights advocates rejected the techniques as unethical; the American Psychological Association (APA) supported psychologist participation to keep interrogations "safe, legal, ethical, and effective"; and the American Psychiatric and Medical Associations forbade their members to participate on the principles of nondeception and "do no harm." This controversy brought interrogation to the fore for peace psychologists. (See DO NO HARM; ETHICAL CONSIDERATIONS IN PEACE PSYCHOLOGY.)

TYPES OF INTERROGATION

Three overlapping classes of modern interrogation can be distinguished: forensic, political, and military/intelligence.

Forensic Interrogation

In Western legal frameworks, forensic interrogation aims at determination of innocence or guilt of criminal defendants. (Questioning of nonsuspects is an *interview*.) Forensic psychology has made substantial progress in delimiting the usefulness of older deception-detection methods, such as polygraphy, and articulating causes of false confession, such as suggestibility; it has ruled out many once-promising techniques of truth access, such as hypnosis; and it continues to pursue new technologies, now brainwave analysis. Although known in forensic psychology to produce high rates of false confession, police torture is common in many parts of the world, including Brazil, the Middle East, India, and elsewhere. In the United States, police torture is sometimes tolerated against minority group members (Human Rights at Home: The Chicago Police Torture Archive, n.d.).

Political Interrogation

Political interrogation aims not at elicitation of true information but political control. State-sponsored torture interrogation has proven effective worldwide in terrorizing subpopulations, as in the suppression of "communist subversives" under Latin American dictatorships during the "dirty wars" of the 1980s and suppression of Blacks in South Africa under apartheid. Soviet historians estimated that 5–10% of the populace was arrested between 1936 and 1939 to force confessions of treachery, thus justifying totalitarian crackdowns. In this context, peace psychology addresses the development of torturers, effects of torture, identification and rehabilitation of victims, psychosocial processes leading to state-sponsored torture, and the complicity of psychologists.

On a more limited scale, interrogation-like diagnostic and therapeutic procedures can serve to reframe the reality of individuals for state purposes. Soviet psychiatrists diagnosed political dissidents with nonsensical "creeping schizophrenia" in the 1970s to justify incarceration. A US counterintelligence officer expressed a common belief that "the military has always used the nut ward as a hanging sword over each agent." Israeli psychologist David Senesh, who had been interrogated and tortured in Egypt during the 1973 War, described his later experience with mental health examiners for the Ministry of Defense. As a criterion for disability claims, they used interview techniques to check the boundaries of mental stability and "break" the claimants again, thereby limiting payments and precedents.

Military/Intelligence Interrogation

Military/intelligence interrogation aims to extract, from willing or unwilling enemy sources, the maximum amount of accurate information in the minimum amount of time using legal methods. (Questioning of an allied source is a *debriefing*.) The military interrogator seeks not to incriminate the source but to suborn or trick the source into providing "actionable intelligence" for strategic or tactical application elsewhere. Validity, reliability, and timeliness of information are paramount in the national security context. Giving ear to hostile sources creates vulnerabilities, as illustrated by the Japanese capture of a US fighter pilot between the bombings of Hiroshima and Nagasaki. Marcus McDilda "revealed" under torture that the United States would similarly bomb Kyoto and Tokyo, although the atomic arsenal was exhausted.

Hans Scharff, the celebrated World War II German interrogator of Allied pilots, set a standard still emulated: congenial conversation with the source, elicitation of small pieces of information whose significance the source does not know, and mosaic-like reconstruction of the pieces from diverse sources to reveal the information sought. Some best practices for interrogation procedures in the US Army have evolved over time, from emotional manipulations that play on the source's egotism, gullibility, or fears, to straightforward questioning and offers of incentives, to a collection of relationship maneuvers. "Acts of violence or intimidation, including physical or mental torture, or exposure to inhumane treatment as a means of or aid to interrogation are expressly prohibited" (US Army Headquarters, 2006, pp. 5–26). From the social skills perspective, interrogation is a field of expertise requiring, like chess or medical diagnosis, comprehensive training, mentorship, and years of practice to develop the knowledge and self-mastery of a professional interrogator. As recast by a senior interrogator: "Everybody wants to talk to someone. My job is to discover the one you want to talk to and become that one."

An alternate (sometimes concurrent) approach to interrogations, notably pursued by the Central Intelligence Agency (CIA), focuses on disabling the source in order to increase pliability. From 1957 to 1964, CIA-funded psychiatrist Ewen Cameron experimentally developed in Canada the blitz psychoanalytic technique of "psychic driving," with electroshock and drugs, to erase and reconstitute personality. The 1977 US Senate investigation of the CIA Behavioral Modification Project MKULTRA found the CIA had contracted with hundreds of civilian researchers at 80 prominent institutions to explore the viability in the case of drugs to alter personality structure and concussion devices to induce amnesia. A front funding agency also was employed to draw in eminent psychologists, which included the humanist Carl Rogers, as a decoy (Greenfield, 1977). The United States has exported disabling interrogation techniques through covert operations, military advisors, and training programs, an example of which is the program that was used at the former School of the Americas.

Under the George W. Bush administration (2001–2008), contract and military psychologists combined findings from sensory deprivation, extreme environment, and learned helplessness research with experience from military Survival, Evasion, Resistance, and Escape (SERE) training programs to develop interrogation protocols that may psychologically and physically damage the source, thus requiring medical and psychological supervision. Psychologists also helped implement and supervise these protocols. Designated interrogators typically had little training in social skills approaches to interrogation. Political authorities deemed "enhanced interrogations," which included simulated drowning ("water boarding"), essential to national security. Professional interrogators criticized these interrogations as amateurish and ill-informed.

THE CONTROVERSY OVER
PSYCHOLOGY AND
INTERROGATION, 2004–2009

In 2004 the press first reported the involvement of psychologists and psychiatrists in abusive interrogations. Conflict erupted in the American Psychological Association (APA) as two historical trends collided. One trend is the increasing dependence of psychology as a profession on the national security sector. World War I psychologists used aptitude tests to sort out thousands of military recruits for job assignments, thereby becoming competitive with psychiatrists in the military context after decades of inferiority in the civilian context. World War II psychologists improved military training, teamwork, propaganda, communications, intelligence processing, morale, enemy profiling, etc. In 1951 Meredith Crawford, with the encouragement of the army Human Resources Section chief Harry Harlow (famous for social isolation experiments on monkeys), founded the Human Resources Research Organization (HumRRO) to continue psychological research for the army. Crawford combined his 25-year tenure at HumRRO with service as APA treasurer (1958–1967), where he secured the APA's financial success in real estate. Later, Crawford headed the APA Office of Accreditation, remaining active on the HumRRO board of trustees. Since that time, HumRRO personnel and members of the Society of Military Psychology (a division of the APA) have often influenced APA decision-making out of proportion to their numbers.

Representing guild interests, the APA is necessarily attentive to the Department of Defense (DoD) as a major source of funding for psychological research, to the Veterans Administration as a major source of training and employment for clinical psychologists, and to Congress for the government budget for the behavioral sciences. The APA further depends upon the government for guild legislation, such as parity for clinical psychology with medicine in managed healthcare and psychologist prescription privileges for psychiatric drugs – a venture pioneered by the army in the 1990s.

In addition to the trend toward increased government support, the second trend is the rise of social conscience in psychology, as manifested in the founding of the Society for the Psychological Study of Social Issues (1936) and the Society for Community Research and Action (1966–1967) (both divisions of the APA), Psychologists for Social Responsibility (1982), the Ignacio Martín-Baró Fund for Mental Health and Human Rights (1989), and the Society for the Study of Peace, Conflict, and Violence (1990, APA Division of Peace Psychology). (See PSYCHOLOGISTS FOR SOCIAL RESPONSIBILITY.) In North America, there was some investigation of psychologists' involvement in torture (Suedfeld, 1990) and mind control (Greenfield, 1977), but usually well after the alleged events.

Following 9/11, APA officials sought opportunities for psychology to contribute to the rapidly expanding security sector, and security-sector psychologists probed the moral boundaries of interrogation (Ewing & Gelles, 2003). A private APA–CIA Science of Deception conference in 2003 included two former military psychologists, James Mitchell and Bruce Jessen, credited with designing the CIA's "enhanced interrogation" techniques. They adapted the simulated torture techniques of SERE training of US forces to interrogation of terrorist suspects. Intensified psychological stressors were added, such as sexual humiliation. Confirmation much later emerged in documents from the International Committee of the Red Cross, the Inspectors General of the Department of Defense, Justice Department, and CIA, and the Senate Armed Services Committee (SASC).

In 2005 the APA Board created a task force on Psychological Ethics and National Security (PENS) to propose guidelines for psychologists in interrogations. Its report established that "Psychologists have a valuable and ethical role to assist in protecting our nation, other nations, and innocent civilians from harm, which will at times entail gathering information that can be used in our nation's and other nations' defense" (APA, 2005). PENS proponents pointed to the report's firm injunction against psychologists' direct or indirect involvement in torture, to its disavowal of dual-role theory (i.e., the APA Ethics Code applies to psychologists in all roles), and to the importance of psychologists' involvement in keeping interrogations "safe, legal, ethical, and effective." PENS opponents pointed to the surreptitious adoption of this phrase from prior army instructions to interrogation psychologists, to the acceptance of the Bush administration's permissive legal definition of torture, and to the retention of APA Ethical Standard 1.02, which permits psychologists to obey government regulations that conflict with the APA Ethics Code – creating a "Nuremberg defense." Opponents were further inflamed by the discovery that six of the ten-member task force were employed by the military intelligence establishment, and four had served in chains of command accused of detainee abuse. Proponents defended these members as relevant experts, notable for their opposition to torture.

Dissident factions arose, including the group "WithholdAPAdues," energized by psychologists from families with Holocaust victims. Dissidents blogged, wrote open letters of protest, rallied human rights organizations, briefed journalists, investigated APA conflicts of interest, collaborated with anti-torture military personnel, unsuccessfully ran an anti-torture candidate for APA president, filed Ethics Committee grievances against suspect psychologists, sent evidence to SASC, called for an investigation of the APA, and proposed multiple anti-torture resolutions to the Council of Representatives (COR). APA authorities issued positive press releases, cultivated allies in state psychological associations and government offices, successfully ran candidates for president, ignored allegations, dismissed dissidents, issued ever-firmer anti-torture statements without practical consequence, and delayed for further study. APA Division of Peace Psychology representatives served as informal liaisons between APA authorities and dissidents, bearing charges of *naïveté* from both sides.

In 2008 the dissident group Psychologists for an Ethical APA initiated a petition referendum of APA members to forbid psychologists from serving in detention facilities that fail standards of international law or the Constitution (except those psychologists treating military personnel or working directly for detainees). The referendum passed with 59% of the vote but was not implemented to the satisfaction of the dissidents. Under continuing pressure, in 2010 the APA strengthened the Ethics Code against psychologist involvement in human rights violations but left intact some problematic dispensations from psychological

ethics for government-sponsored human subjects research.

As the storm passes over clinical psychologists in interrogation roles, another storm gathers over psychologists as interrogation researchers.

SEE ALSO: Do No Harm; Ethical Considerations in Peace Psychology; Psychologists for Social Responsibility.

REFERENCES

American Psychological Association (APA). (2005, July). Report of the APA Presidential Task Force on Psychological Ethics and National Security. Retrieved from http://www.apa.org/releases/PENSTaskForceReportFinal.pdf.

Arrigo, J. M., & Wagner, R. V. (Eds.). (2007). Torture is for amateurs: A meeting of psychologists and military interrogators [special issue]. *Peace and Conflict, 13*(4).

Ewing, C. P., & Gelles, M. G. (2003). Ethical concern in forensic consultation regarding national safety and security. *Journal of Threat Assessment, 2*(3): 95–107.

Greenfield, P. (1977, December). CIA's behavioral caper. *American Psychological Association Monitor*, pp. 1, 10–11. Retrieved from http://www.cia-on-campus.org/social/behavior.html.

Human Rights at Home: The Chicago Police Torture Archive. (n.d.). Retrieved October 2, 2009, from http://humanrights.uchicago.edu/chicagotorture/timeline.shtml.

Soldz, S. (2009). Closing eyes to atrocities: US psychologists, detainee interrogations, and response of the American Psychological Association. In M. Roseman & R. Goodman (Eds.), *Interrogations, forced feedings, and the role of health professionals* (pp. 103–142). Cambridge, MA: Harvard University Press.

Suedfeld, P. (Ed). (1990). *Psychology and torture*. New York, NY: Hemisphere.

US Army Headquarters. (2006). Field Manual 2–22.3 Human intelligence collector operations. Washington, DC: US Army Headquarters.

ADDITIONAL RESOURCES

Allen, S., Keller, A., Reisner, S., & Iacopino, V. (2009, August). Aiding torture: Health professionals' ethics and human rights violations. Physicians for Human Rights Library [Online]. Retrieved from http://physiciansforhumanrights.org/library/documents/reports/aiding-torture.pdf.

Blanton, T., & Kornbluth, P. (Eds). *Prisoner abuse: Patterns from the past*. National Security Archive Electronic Briefing Book No. 122. National Security Archives, George Washington University [Online]. Retrieved from http://www.gwu.edu/~nsarchiv/NSAEBB/NSAEBB122/.

Miles, S., & Marks, L. (2007). *United States military medicine in war on terror prisons*. Human Rights Library of the University of Minnesota [Online]. Retrieved from http://www1.umn.edu/humanrts/OathBetrayed/index.html.

J

Just War Theory

ALEXANDER MOSELEY

War unleashes deadly violence and destruction and inverts the normal codes and conventions of society: killing, maiming, and injuring become justifiable; damage to land, resources, and buildings a normal occurrence; and the seizure of people and property a regularity. Following a century that has accustomed us to think about war in terms of totalitarian effects and total consequences, of genocidal campaigns, of the obliteration of cities and the threat of mutually assured destruction with atomic weapons, it may seem an arcane proclamation that war's reach and vehemence ought to be restrained. Yet that is what the just war conventions seek to explore and to uphold as guides to human action. While the pacifist rejects war absolutely and thereby contends that all acts within war are immoral and inexcusable and the militarist declares that in war (as in love) all is fair (Holmes, 1989), the just war theorist takes a middle position, acknowledging that should war break out, a range of considerations concerning its justification and the procedures that soldiers follow ought to be maintained as guides to ensure, in effect, that some sanctuaries from war's evils are acknowledged (Clark, 1988; Norman, 1995; Walzer, 1977).

Just war conventions are often held to emanate from the Christian tradition, particularly from the writings of Thomas Aquinas which later scholastics and jurists augmented until a recognizable set of principles and accompanying body of analysis emerged (Cook, 2004). While the philosophical critique often has a Western bias, the conventions themselves are easily identified in practically all cultures that have waged war: indeed, it would appear that warring societies possess a strong incentive to restrain the violence that war unleashes either to avoid perpetual recriminations and vengeance or to restrict actions that are inimically prohibited by all sides of the conflict. For example, religious sanctuaries are typically deemed off-limits as a moral injunction, while the targeting of noncombatants such as children is heavily restrained, perhaps for avoiding the escalatory consequences that may ensue following a breach. The interplay between the absolutist or deontological approaches and the consequentialist or utilitarian approaches to analyzing just war

The Encyclopedia of Peace Psychology, First Edition. Edited by Daniel J. Christie.
© 2012 Blackwell Publishing Ltd. Published 2012 by Blackwell Publishing Ltd.

conventions naturally provides much discussion in the literature, with researchers providing useful examples of known infringements of putative boundaries for further reflection. (See MORAL EXCLUSION.)

The first criteria of the just war conventions are known as the requirements of *jus ad bellum* or the justice of going to war. War, it is held, should be fought for a just cause; it should be a last resort; it should be properly proclaimed by the proper authority; its aims should be proportional to the ends for which war is waged; the ends themselves should be morally justifiable or the war must be fought with the right intentions; there must be a reasonable chance of success; and the peace conditions should also be morally comprehensible.

Each guide in turn provokes much debate. For instance, what is meant by a just cause? The concept of justice is inextricably complicated and often is perceived to suit the demands of the victorious party in war: theorists have tended to reject claims of honor or of imperial aggrandizement, but divergent political philosophies present their own claims to justice which inevitably color reasons for waging war. Why should war be a last resort if an attack halts an enemy's aggressive threats or policies against its own or other peoples? (See HUMANITARIAN MILITARY INTERVENTIONS, SUPPORT FOR.) A timely intervention may, it could be argued, deter greater future bloodshed, but that raises complex moral concerns (Norman, 1995; Walzer, 1977). Possessing the proper authority to wage war seems a reasonable principle; however, it begs examination: what makes a political representative the "proper authority"? In an age of nation states, it would seem that that the nation state is the right authority, but nation states are relatively new institutions and in turn are subject to other supranational entities such as the UN Security Council (Cook, 2004). On the other hand, asserting the need for a "proper

authority" can lead to a pragmatic political maneuver in which the perpetrator avoids calling war "war" (Elshtain, 2003). Calling something a conflict or a peace operation may dissolve the temerity of the action in the minds of citizens or onlookers, while enemy action may be termed an insurrection (rather than a liberation war) or terrorism, thereby demeaning the moral stance of the opposing party. What nature the peace takes is similarly controversial – should it aim to deter future war or merely claim for the damages the war has caused, or should it accept territorial gains as the rightful trophy of war?

The second criterion involves how war is pursued. Once war is unleashed by whomever and for whatever goals, the *jus in bello* conventions act as guides for soldiers' behavior. There are two principles here: the principle of proportionality and the principle of discrimination. Proportionality guidelines concern the breadth and intensity of the fight and, in the modern era particularly, involve guidelines on what kinds of armaments, quality, and quantity, ought to be proscribed in war. For instance, dumdum bullets were banned by the Hague Convention IV(3) in 1899, and forms of chemical warfare were banned by the 1925 Geneva Gas Protocol (Green, 1993). Since the American attacks on Hiroshima and Nagasaki, there have been numerous attempts to curtail the expansion of atomic weapons as well as political maneuvers to restrict ownership to a select group of nations. While the policy to curtail the expansion of atomic warheads is more readily understood as a deep and perhaps universal moral reaction to the threat of weapons of mass destruction and total warfare – "terror must never be answered with terror," as Caleb Carr notes (cited in Elshtain, 2003) – the policy to limit ownership to a few countries is often criticized as self-serving political partiality and hence not supportable by just war theories. However, no international conventions (as against moral proclamations) have yet been generated to restrain the use of nuclear arms, whose remit for countries such as the United States and the United Kingdom remain under the jurisdiction of the conventional military manuals on appropriate use and deployment – that is, nuclear weapons may "justly" be used according to the military, so long as their use is proportional and discriminatory, a position that just war theorists find unsettling.

The existence of a legal treaty is, of course, no strong reason to constrain disproportionate acts within war, for military complexes may seek to act first and explain later, preferring that an advantage be gained or held rather than succumb to equivocating moralizing. In war, it may be claimed, violence begets violence, a fact that is often lost on postbellum examinations of moral conduct: violence is dehumanizing and acts in turn to distort judgments. However, that is to ignore the overt role that deliberation and planning do have in warfare – not all soldiers, and especially not those taking momentous decisions on strategies, are acting under fire. International treatises or moral conventions often are ignored by those who are free to make alternative plans, and from a just war theory perspective, they are thus deemed more culpable for breaching the rules governing engagement than the soldier acting under fire.

The principle of discrimination in war is often the most understandable convention, for it seeks to prohibit or to severely curtail the use of violence against people who are held to be morally innocent of the war's claims or are merely noncombatants. Herein lies much debate, though: it may begin with the premise that human life is somehow sanctified or morally special such that an act of violence by one against another is by definition immoral and

perhaps deserving of punishment or at least self-defense (Norman, 1995). In ethics, the term "person" is used to describe one fitting the criterion of moral autonomy that no other may violate; however, in war, there are some persons who are armed and trained to kill, and other persons who are not armed and trained; there are some persons, who, while not being armed, may wholly support the war morally or financially, while others who are armed may not give their moral support to the war. In other words, the concept of personhood fragments in war. On one hand, there are those who claim that war itself removes all moral boundaries and hence the concept of personhood becomes redundant: all are targets or should be, either definitionally so, or for the purpose of superior military ends. The latter assumes that the justice of the war, or military action in itself, removes any requirements to discriminate. This is the ethos of total warfare – there are no sanctuaries or boundaries that need respecting and so the warrior may kill and injure indiscriminately. However, most societies have rejected the blanket dissolution of personhood in favor of some form of conditional standing: those incapable of self-defense such as children, or those upon whose lives humanity's future depends such as women or technological experts or farmers, are accordingly deemed to possess inviolable moral status and should not be targeted by the military.

In asserting the principle of discrimination, theorists have, generally speaking, abandoned the notion of innocence, which assumes that personhood is dependent upon inaccessible conscience, in favor of the more readily observable noncombatant status. The lack of arms immediately, on this argument, retains a civilian's moral status as one to be protected or not fired upon, or returns a soldier to the civilian state despite the uniform and training. That is, the cry for "no quarter" is unsupportable: soldiers in combat ought to avoid targeting or using noncombatants for military ends, and in turn surrendering soldiers, or those who are off-duty, return to a form of civilian status deserving respect or nominal rights.

The controversies here, though, are legion. A nefarious tactic employed by soldiers is to use civilian cover to arrange military adventures, which necessarily compromises the noncombatant status of those within whose midst they operate (Walzer, 1977). In turn, this typically leads opposing forces to explore the boundaries of excusing a violation of the principle of discrimination, a move that is generally not supported by just war theorists. Few battles may now take place on prescribed fields and operate within the area's confines for a given time, for soldiers may use the architectural cover of towns and the moral cover afforded by civilians to effect their aims: however, some theorists prefer that the onus remain on the attacking side to avoid inflicting unnecessary civilian casualties, arguing that legitimate targets ought to be specified and any action taken against noncombatants be severely restricted. Otherwise, it may be claimed that the presence of civilians amidst soldiers incidentally militarizes the civilians and thereby brings them into the realm of justifiable (or excusable) targets – just as a nonsupportive civilian who is conscripted into the army becomes militarized and thereby a traditionally accepted target.

An alternative approach stems from the Thomist doctrine of double effect (Holmes, 1989): Thomas Aquinas noted that an act remains within moral acceptance so long as the intention (to target enemy combatants) is pure and the outcome (to remove the threat of the enemy combatants) is what is aimed for, then any civilian casualties can be deemed incidental ("collateral damage" in modern parlance); their deaths and injuries are thereby morally excused. Compare this to asserting a military "need"

to target civilians, which was upheld in World War II by those in charge of the aerial bombing of densely population civilian centers.

Between the two general principles of *jus ad bellum* and *jus in bello* we find a debate on whether the justice of a cause may be said to overrule the ethical parameters of how war is fought: if, the argument goes, the cause is just, then all restraints on the conduct of the war can be removed. Proposals fall into the category of making a better, more just world, or of abolishing war forever.

Beyond the commonly understood zone warfare, of combatants targeting combatants, there are plenty of issues that warrant inclusion in ethical discussions of war. Is the use of psychological manipulation through propaganda acceptable, or the forcible cleansing or imprisonment of an area's ethnic population excusable (even if it reduces the numbers killed by military operations)? Do crowd control measures tip over into the realm of military action, particularly if they involve weaponry, or is the analysis of policing inextricably entwined with the moral status of the incumbent regime?

A host of awkward problems thus arise for the definitions and applicability of the just war conventions. However, when we look at war, we find that even in the bloodiest of disputes some forms of restraint remain or emerge, and that that portends well for the conventions.

SEE ALSO: Humanitarian Military Interventions, Support for; Moral Exclusion.

REFERENCES

Clark, I. (1988). *Waging war: A philosophical introduction.* Oxford, UK: Clarendon Press.

Cook, M. L. (2004). *The moral warrior.* Albany, NY: State University of New York Press.

Elshtain, J. B. (2003). *Just war against terror*. New
York, NY: Basic Books.

Green, L. C. (1993). *The contemporary law of
armed conflict*. Manchester, UK: Manchester
University Press

Holmes, R. L. (1989). *On war and morality*.
Princeton, NJ: Princeton University Press.

Norman, R. (1995). *Ethics, killing & war*.
Cambridge, UK: Cambridge University Press

Walzer, M. (1977). *Just and unjust wars*. New
York, NY: Basic Books.

ADDITIONAL RESOURCES

http://www.iep.utm.edu/justwar/: Alexander
Moseley's introduction to just war theory.

http://www.justwartheory.com/: Mark Rigstad's
introduction to the history of just war theory
and an overview of contemporary issues and
debates.

http://plato.stanford.edu/entries/war/: Brian
Orend's introduction to just war theory.

L

Laboratory Experiments

MICHAEL R. HULSIZER AND
LINDA M. WOOLF

Laboratory experimentation is an important technique in the array of research tools available to peace psychologists. Unlike other categories of research (e.g., archival research, naturalistic observation), laboratory experimentation, if done correctly, can enable the researcher to make causal inferences when explaining the relationship between variables of interest. (See EXPERIMENTATION, DESIGN, AND ANALYSIS.) Specifically, the laboratory environment is uniquely situated to establish causality by enabling the researcher to manipulate variables of interest, examine the impact on outcome variables, and eliminate or minimize extraneous variables. However, the usefulness of laboratory experiments hinges on the degree to which the research results can be generalized from the artificial confines of the lab to the outside world. The challenge for any laboratory researcher is to design a research paradigm that can enable the researcher to make causal inferences (i.e., internal validity) and still maintain maximum generalizability (i.e., external validity).

INTERNAL VALIDITY

Internal validity is the extent to which the covariation between the independent and dependent variables reflect an underlying causal relationship (Shadish, Cook, & Campbell, 2002). In other words, a study has high internal validity when the researcher can conclusively demonstrate that changes in one variable caused the changes in the outcome variable. Shadish et al. noted that "causal conclusions are limited to the context of the particular treatments, outcomes, times, settings, and persons studied" (p. 54). To achieve high internal validity, the researcher needs to utilize a design which eliminates or minimizes all threats to internal validity.

Threats to internal validity are those extraneous factors which may have produced the observed changes in the dependent variable. Shadish et al. (2002) described nine threats to internal validity. Many of the threats to internal validity can be addressed using random assignment to condition,

The Encyclopedia of Peace Psychology, First Edition. Edited by Daniel J. Christie.
© 2012 Blackwell Publishing Ltd. Published 2012 by Blackwell Publishing Ltd.

including a similar control or comparison group, and treating groups equivalently across all elements of the experiment (except the independent variable manipulation). Threats which respond best to these design safeguards include: (1) *selection* – the possibility that there may be systematic differences between conditions due to pre-existing characteristics of participants; (2) *history* – events which occur between the beginning and end of the experiment may influence the results; (3) *maturation* – natural changes (e.g., cognitive development, boredom) that may differentially impact participants; and (4) *attrition* – a subset of the sample may leave the study at a different rate than other participants.

Some of the threats to validity cited by Shadish et al. (2002) can be addressed only by creating a laboratory experiment specifically designed to meet each particular threat: (5) *testing* – problems associated with giving participants a pre- and posttest; (6) *instrumentation* – the means by which a variable is measured may change with the passage of time; (7) *regression artifacts* – extreme scores tend to regress to the mean over time; (8) *ambiguous temporal precedence* – unclear which variable occurred first; and (9) *additive and interactive effects* – the above eight threats will likely occur in combination, resulting in more pronounced confounds.

The threats cited by Shadish et al. (2002) are most pronounced in quasi-experimental studies in which participants are not randomly assigned to the experimental conditions resulting in systematic differences between participants (in addition to any differences that may be attributed to the independent variable). Consequently, true (non-quasi) experimental studies are most likely to have high internal validity when there is random/representative sampling of the population of interest, a proper control or comparison group, random assignment of participants to conditions, and equivalent treatment between experimental groups.

EXTERNAL VALIDITY

External validity refers to the extent to which the results of the study are generalizable from the lab environment to the outside world. More specifically, can the research results generalize to other populations, in different settings, across treatments and outcomes? Ideally, experimental research should be high in both internal validity and external validity. Unfortunately, it is difficult to achieve both in experimental designs. Researchers are often reluctant to sacrifice internal validity for the sake of external validity given the value placed on causality within the psychological sciences (Chang & Sue, 2005).

According to Chang and Sue (2005), the importance of causality in psychological research has led to: (1) an overabundance of college students as research participants, (2) the assumption that research conducted on one population (e.g., White, middle class, US citizens) can be generalized to other groups, (3) a devaluing of research designed to explore cross-cultural differences versus explaining such differences, (4) the tendency of journal reviewers to insist that a White control group is needed when conducting research on minority groups, and (5) the formation of aggregate, presumed homogeneous, non-White populations to obtain a large enough sample size for statistical analysis. These practices result in psychological research which may not reflect the diversity of human experience.

The laboratory environment lends itself to experimental designs which are very high in internal validity. However, such designs are meaningless if they cannot be used to understand real-world situations – particularly in the field of peace psychology. Therefore, it is imperative that researchers work to design experiments that can be generalized to a variety of situations.

ADDITIONAL VALIDITY CONSIDERATIONS

In addition to internal and external validity, research needs to achieve high construct validity – the degree to which the operational definition of the variable accurately reflects the underlying abstract concept. A research paradigm with high internal and external validity is meaningless without the confidence that the variables are measuring what they purport to measure. The same can be said for having high statistical conclusion validity – the most well-designed research paradigm is useless if it cannot be tested for statistical significance.

All participants need to be given informed consent regarding the lab procedures. Participants should be able to withdraw from the study at any time without penalty and should be properly debriefed. Deception should be limited to situations in which no other approach would be sufficient. It goes without saying that all research should be approved by an institutional review board to determine if the study is ethical. This protects the participants, the experimenter, and the institution.

EXAMPLE: LABORATORY INVESTIGATION OF AGGRESSIVE BEHAVIOR

There are numerous methods available to study aggressive behavior (Krahé, 2001). The use of archival records, such as crime statistics, can be troublesome owing to sampling biases, unreliable police observations, and underreporting. (See ARCHIVAL RESEARCH.) Naturalistic observation methods have been employed by some researchers concerned about the artificiality of the lab environment. However, this research approach is especially difficult with human participants given aggression has a low base rate in natural settings. In addition, it is impossible to control for potential confounds such as disposition, environmental conditions, and expectations which may influence study results.

One popular method is to examine aggression using self-report measures. Often, researchers examine the relationship between a variable of interest (e.g., personality measure, attitudinal measure) with aggression (e.g., State–Trait Anger Expression Inventory). Although this approach can provide useful information, there are significant problems associated with this methodology. Specifically, people tend to be reluctant to reveal such personal, socially undesirable, and potentially incriminating information. Furthermore, it is difficult to ascertain causal relationships from such data.

The most well-accepted means to investigate aggressive behavior is using laboratory experiments (Krahé, 2001). Versions of the Taylor Competitive Reaction Time paradigm have been used for decades to investigate the effects of a number of variables (e.g., video games, psychoactive drugs, personality scales) on human aggressive behavior (Anderson & Bushman, 1997; Taylor & Hulsizer, 1998). The paradigm used in these laboratory experiments provides the participant with the opportunity to aggress against a fictitious opponent while competing in a reaction time task. Prior to each competitive trial, the participant receives a signal to select the intensity of the noxious stimulus (e.g., shock, white noise) the participant wishes to administer their opponent. Participants can select shock or white noise intensities ranging from 1 (barely noticeable) to 10 (definitely unpleasant) for their opponent. The participant and fictitious competitor (i.e., computer) then compete on a reaction time trial. The person with the slower reaction time receives the noxious stimulus that had presumably been selected by the competitor. Regardless of who wins or loses, the participant is shown the intensity of noxious stimuli his/her competitor had set. The measure of aggression used in this paradigm is the intensity of noxious stimuli the participant selects for the opponent.

In comparison to other approaches to studying aggression, the experimental paradigm randomly assigns participants to conditions, disguises the true nature of the experiment by suggesting it is a competitive reaction time task, controls the levels of the independent variable, and obtains a behavioral measure of aggression under controlled conditions (Taylor & Hulsizer, 1998). The reaction time paradigm has been demonstrated to provide a valid measure of aggressive behavior (Krahé, 2001). Specifically, Bernstein, Richardson, and Hammock (1987) established the construct validity of the Taylor paradigm. Using a meta-analysis, Anderson and Bushman (1997) established the external validity of laboratory experiments of aggression such as the Taylor paradigm. (See META-ANALYSIS.)

CONCLUSION

Aggression is a phenomenon which is of critical importance to peace psychologists. The laboratory research paradigm associated with this area of inquiry has been demonstrated to have high internal, construct, external, and statistical conclusion validity. However, it is important to note that the best means to examine any area of interest is to use all available research approaches. For example, Anderson and Dill (2000) examined the relationship between violent video games and aggressive behavior. (See VIOLENT VIDEO GAMES AND AGGRESSION.) They conducted two studies to address this question. The first study examined the relationship between exposure to violent video games and several outcome variables (aggressive behavior, worldview) using a correlational design. The second study

employed a modified version of the Taylor Competitive Reaction Time paradigm using white noise as the aversive stimulus. The results of both studies demonstrated that exposure to violent video games increased aggressive behavior. Using different methodologies bolstered the researcher's claims – which have since been replicated in subsequent research findings (Anderson & Bushman, 2001).

SEE ALSO: Archival Research; Experimentation, Design, and Analysis; Meta-Analysis; Violent Video Games and Aggression.

REFERENCES

Anderson, C. A., & Bushman, B. J. (1997). External validity of "trivial" experiments: The case of laboratory aggression. *Review of General Psychology*, 1, 19–41.

Anderson, C. A., & Bushman, B. J. (2001). Effects of violent video games on aggressive behavior, aggressive cognition, aggressive affect, physiological arousal, and pro-social behavior: A meta-analytic review of the scientific literature. *Psychological Science*, 12, 353–359.

Anderson, C. A., & Dill, K. E. (2000). Video games and aggressive thoughts, feelings, and behavior in the laboratory and in life. *Journal of Personality and Social Psychology*, 78, 772–790.

Bernstein, S., Richardson, D., & Hammock, G. (1987). Convergent and discriminate validity of the Taylor and Buss measures of physical aggression. *Aggressive Behavior*, 13, 15–24.

Chang, J., & Sue, S. (2005). Culturally sensitive research: Where have we gone wrong and what do we need to do now? In M. G. Constantine & D. W. Sue (Eds.), *Strategies for building multicultural competence in mental health and educational settings* (pp. 229–246). Hoboken, NJ: John Wiley & Sons, Inc.

Krahé, B. (2001). *The social psychology of aggression*. Philadelphia, PA: Psychology Press.

Shadish, W. R., Cook, T. D., & Campbell, D. T. (2002). *Experimental and quasi-experimental designs for generalized causal inference.* Boston, MA: Houghton Mifflin.

Taylor, S. P., & Hulsizer, M. R. (1998). Psychoactive drugs and human aggression. In R. G. Geen & E. Donnerstein (Eds.), *Human aggression: Theories, research, and implications for social policy* (pp. 139–165). New York, NY: Academic Press.

ADDITIONAL RESOURCES

Baron, R. A., & Richardson, D. R. (1994). *Human aggression* (2nd ed.). New York, NY: Plenum Press.

Kirk, R. E. (1995). *Experimental design: Procedures for the behavioral sciences* (3rd ed.). Pacific Grove, CA: Brooks/Cole.

Woolf, L. M., & Hulsizer, M. R. (2011). Why diversity matters: The power of inclusion in research methods. In K. D. Keith (Ed.), *Cross-cultural psychology: Contemporary themes and perspectives* (pp. 56–72). Oxford, UK: Wiley-Blackwell.

Language, Violent and Peaceful Uses of

ADRIANA BOLÍVAR

The importance of language and its effects for preserving or damaging peace has been acknowledged in psychology and other disciplines for a long time. However, there has been little attention to the problem from a linguistic perspective because language is often taken for granted – more or less in the same way as the air we breathe is taken for granted. We all know by experience what violent and peaceful uses of language look like, and we also know that in the private space (and in some public spaces too) words may be accompanied with gestures, screaming, yelling, and more intense bodily actions such as throwing things, kicking, bumping, breaking objects, etc. We have been warned that verbal violence often leads to physical violence and, perhaps, death. However, our interest is to call attention to the fact that language is above all a social practice in which we all participate with rights and duties and that, as speakers of a language, we are responsible for choosing the words and acts of discourse that may either mitigate or intensify conflicts and promote peaceful dialogue or not. (See POSITIONING THEORY.)

Because the use of language is what makes us human, we need to become more conscious of how we use it in social interaction in order to understand better why we talk about violent uses of language or peaceful uses of language. As humans we share the universal need to live in peace. We also share other needs, such as the need for having (1) a face and (2) to be treated with consideration. "Face" is an abstract cultural notion "which consists of two kinds of desires ('face wants'): the desire to be unimpeded in one's actions (negative face), and the desire (in some respects) to be approved of (positive face)" (Brown & Levinson, 1987, p. 13). "Consideration" is a sociocultural notion that lies at the root of every interaction. Similarly, "Cooperative social interaction and displaying consideration for others seem to be universal characteristics of every sociocultural group" (Watts, 2003, p. 14).

In addition to considering universals, we need to focus on language in a more detailed manner because language is used for a variety of purposes: to construct our identities and that of others, to engage in relationships with others, to represent the world, and to build our value systems (Halliday, 2004). It is only by focusing on language use that we may discover how humans interact in everyday conversations and in more complex interactions in a wide range of contexts that include the family, work, and institutions (Schiffrin, Tannen, & Hamilton, 2001). Therefore, it is fundamental to keep in mind at least two things: (1) the uses of language are never devoid of context and culture, and (2) verbal violence arises in conflicts whose nature varies fundamentally for three reasons: poverty, social injustice, and political oppression, which materialize in the discourse of despair, anger and frustration, discrimination, exclusion, and abuse of power. This implies that we shall come across a great variety of linguistic forms of aggression in every language and culture. These forms can be detected as words that hurt, offend, or destroy others.

THE LINGUISTIC EXPRESSION OF VIOLENT LANGUAGE

While we cannot speak of universal forms of verbal violence because the notions of "consideration" and "violence" vary in each culture and acquire their meaning in the discursive struggle where moral judgments and ideological reasons combine, it is possible to say that all languages have resources to express violent meanings. Independently of whether the same language event may be evaluated as violent or nonviolent, we can assume that in general verbal violence is characterized by the use of language that affects another person negatively in his/her self-esteem, identity, integrity, and value as a member of a group. Depending on the cause of the conflict, the aggression may be unintentional or intentional. It is often unintentional for emotional reasons; it is intentional when it is strategically used to destroy others and keep absolute control of power. What we must not forget is that verbal violence is born out of conflict and attack and that it is always destructive in some way.

In order to identify verbal violence, it is important to understand that this can be conveyed at all levels of language: phonology, grammar, semantics, pragmatics, and discourse. Violence can be expressed phonologically by means of loudness and tone of voice, also by rhythm and intonation. It can be expressed grammatically by words that

hurt feelings and cause emotional and mental unrest. The words used serve as weapons whose target is to destroy the esteem of individuals, groups, and nations who are discredited in their personal, professional, intellectual, moral, political, and cultural dimensions. While in every culture there is agreement that some words are more offensive than others (such as insults), the decision on how offensive they are rests on the offended, and the evaluation depends on situational and cultural factors such as who the persons involved are, their roles, their aims, the nonverbal elements that accompany the verbal acts, the duration of the offense, and whether or not mediators participate. The semantics of violence may include a wide range of topics including personal appearance, skin color, intellectual capacity, social class, religious beliefs, political affiliation, etc. The pragmatics of violence is expressed by the use of linguistic impoliteness, that is, language that transgresses the tacitly agreed norms of consideration or "politic behavior" (Watts, 2003), including threats, insults, complaints, accusations, and other face-threatening acts. Verbal violence is expressed at the discourse level when only one speaker takes all the turns at talk and intentionally does not allow equal opportunities to all. The speaker repeatedly interrupts the other, refuses to talk about the same topic, and makes use of repetition, exaggeration, sarcasm, irony, and other rhetorical resources that destabilize the other emotionally and mentally. Discursive violence focuses on conflictive dialogue and avoidance of dialogue.

Violent words may be uttered as the result of anger or frustration (out of despair when things are not going well), but they can also be pronounced intentionally to harm someone's self-esteem and so gain or maintain control over individuals or groups (gender or race discrimination, power abuse and oppression in political discourse, etc.). People tend to associate violent verbal

actions with swearing, insults, and directness, but we must be cautious because different cultures make different uses of these
resources and they can even be perceived as
positive (Mills, 2003) or may be simultaneously celebrated or rejected by people from
the same culture for political reasons
(Bolívar, 2008). Research has shown that
impoliteness is more "normal" than expected
in certain contexts such as army training,
court rooms, family discourse, adolescent
discourse, doctor–patient interaction, therapeutic discourse, political discourse, and
everyday conversation. However, the fact
that it is apparently accepted does not
make it less violent. The problem is for each
culture to know where the limits of the
acceptable are.

LINGUISTIC RESOURCES FOR
PEACEFUL USES OF LANGUAGE

As for peaceful uses of language, we cannot
list formulas that can be universally described
as peaceful, but we can claim that when we
opt for peace as opposed to war, discrimination, and exclusion, we choose dialogue, that
is, cooperation and interactions that recognize and accept the other (*you form part of
my life*), give him or her equal opportunities
to talk (*I talk/you talk*), and agree to work
toward common aims (*we, joint efforts*). We
also favor the semantics of cooperation (*we
talk and work together*), negotiation (*let us see
what you think and what we can do*), respect
(*you are worth my consideration*), equality (*we
are equals and have the same rights and duties*),
freedom (*you are free to think, talk, and do*),
tolerance (*I accept that you are different*), love
and affection (*we have positive feelings for each
other*). (See HUMILIATION AND DIGNITY; COM-
MUNICATION, LISTENING, AND CONFLICT RESO-
LUTION SKILLS.)

One way of avoiding conflict and friction
and, eventually, promoting peaceful uses of
language is politeness, either viewed from a
linguistics and/or pragmatic perspective
(Brown & Levinson, 1987) or from a wider
scope that takes into account the perspective
of the members of a society, their evaluations and arguments (Mills, 2003; Watts,
2003; Bolívar, 2008). This is so because
politeness is "basic to the production of
social order, and a precondition of human
cooperation, so that any theory which provides an understanding of this phenomenon
at the time goes to the foundations of human
social life" (Brown & Levinson 1987, p. xiii).
It has been agreed by researchers in many
countries that while politeness is a universal
phenomenon, the linguistic expressions of it
are not. Brown and Levinson's original theoretical proposal has been extended from a
concern for the individual's face to the construction of identities in relational work in
the discursive struggle, which makes room
for the relations between discourse and ideology (van Dijk, 2005).

In spite of the enormous variety of linguistic forms to indicate politeness and/or
consideration, the search for some universal
formulas has not stopped. In general, we can
at least distinguish between conventional
formulas such as "Thank you" to show
appreciation, "I am sorry" to apologize for
an offense, and "Please" to accompany
requests. We can identify the linguistic indicators of mitigation of the illocutionary
force of utterances in hedges (such as choice
of lexical items, diminutives, modal verbs
that lower the force of the proposition, the
semantics of verbs, etc.) and face-flattering
acts. In English it is assumed that utterances
such as "Bring me the car keys" are more
direct and consequently less polite than, for
example, "Will you bring me the car keys?"
Or "Will you please bring me the car keys?"
However, an utterance such as "I wonder if
it would be possible for you to bring me the
car keys," which might be perfectly suitable
and accepted by speakers of English in
certain contexts, would be evaluated as
not sincere or even threatening by persons

from other cultures who value directness. However, if the utterance is accompanied by name calling, epithets, insults, yelling, an angry face, kicking, or other forms of intensification of aggression, we would easily agree that we have come across an instance of violent language, linguistic and nonlinguistic.

Violent and peaceful uses of language coexist in many contexts in our society. Although some kind of verbal aggression is needed in order to compete with others, the problem is how to keep the equilibrium and not transgress the limits of what is accepted as appropriate by a community. When the community we are talking about concerns the global world then our concern and the task ahead are even bigger. This task requires the joint effort of linguists, discourse analysts, psychologists, sociologists, social communicators, politicians, and others in order to give more attention to the role of language in peace processes, as words have the power to construct as well as to destroy people in their self-esteem, identity, and physical integrity.

SUMMARY

Violent and peaceful uses of language coexist in our society in many contexts, but verbal violence is always destructive. Verbal violence materializes in words often motivated by emotional states, but can also be used intentionally to gain and maintain power and control. In order to mitigate the uses of violent language and promote peace, it is necessary to call attention to the causes of conflict and do more research on the linguistic behaviors that each culture evaluates as appropriate, considerate, and peaceful.

SEE ALSO: Communication, Listening, and Conflict Resolution Skills; Humiliation and Dignity; Positioning Theory.

REFERENCES

Bolívar, A. (2008). Dialogue and confrontation in Venezuelan political interaction. In T. A. van Dijk (Ed.), *Discourse studies* (Vol. 1, pp. 261–274). London, UK: Sage.

Brown, R., & Levinson, P. (1987). *Politeness: Some universals in language usage*. Cambridge, UK: Cambridge University Press.

Halliday, M. A. K. (2004). *An introduction to functional grammar* (3rd ed.). London, UK: Hodder Education.

Mills, S. (2003). *Gender and politeness*. Cambridge, UK: Cambridge University Press.

Schiffrin, D., Tannen, D., & Hamilton, H. (Eds.). (2001). *The handbook of discourse analysis*. Cambridge, UK: Cambridge University Press.

van Dijk, T. A. (2005). *Ideology. A multidisciplinary approach*. London, UK: Sage.

Watts, R. (2003). *Politeness*. Cambridge, UK: Cambridge University Press.

ADDITIONAL RESOURCES

http://www.reference-global.com/loi/jplr (*Journal of Politeness Research: Language, Behavior, Culture*)

Levels of Analysis Problem

PETER SUEDFELD, RYAN W. CROSS, AND MICHAEL STEWART

Peace and war (and intermediate conditions) are states or events that can involve the lives or deaths of hundreds of millions of people and most of the world. The debate about how to explain, predict, and influence their occurrence has engaged political leaders as well as scholars for centuries. Substantial progress in this enterprise could enable us to forecast when the peace is imperiled or when the end of war approaches, understand the gradations and differences between different kinds of peace and of war, and perhaps to develop strategies for averting, limiting, ameliorating, or ending armed conflict.

Of the many variables involved, one of the thorniest to resolve is just what to study. Appropriate levels of analysis range from the individual (head of state, advisor, cabinet minister, demagogue) to a small group (cabinet, junta, cabal, revolutionary cell), the voice of the masses in whole or in part, and the economic and sociopolitical structures. Depending on the topic, relevant aspects of these structures can include the domestic and international system of alliances and rivalries, governmental and nongovernmental institutions, bureaucracies, economies, ethnic and religious groups, and the traditions, rules, norms, and laws that govern the behavior of all of these linked components. These are interactive, not independent, levels: clearly, individuals and groups function within a macrolevel system; equally clearly, the functioning of the system depends on the psychology and behavior of individuals and groups.

The levels of analysis question arises in many areas of political psychology, from election outcomes to intergroup attitudes and interactions. However, it is probably most compelling in the context of leader behavior, where proponents of "Great Man" theories have traditionally clashed with believers in the inexorable march of history. Would World War II have been averted if Adolf Hitler had been killed during his military service in World War I, or would the same events have happened because the conditions of Germany and her neighbors in the interwar period would have inexorably led to the same policies regardless of the identity of the leader?

Such a complex and dynamic puzzle can probably be approached only in a selective fashion. No theory or research has emerged that can satisfactorily include both personality and the macro-system in a comprehensible fashion. As a result, social scientists have tended to focus either on the decision-making "agents" – individual leaders or small leadership groups – or on the systemic variables that govern or guide decision-making in the particular situation ("structure"). Although with many exceptions, there is a general disciplinary split: political scientists tend to emphasize structural influences; political psychologists tend to focus on the level of individual or small-group agents.

In studying the progress of intergroup confrontations to their resolution by negotiation or by force, social scientists who work at the structural level have attempted to find the warning signs of large-scale internal or international violence in structural components. These systemic factors obviously bear on political outcomes (and hence on the agent–structure debate), but there has been a relative lack of research that would connect the literature with research on the individual or microlevel.

Other scholars have developed theoretical systems and methods that bear upon the understanding of peace and war based on the functioning of such variables as personality characteristics, small-group dynamics, intergroup attitudes and experiences, biases, and the processes of information search, information processing, and decision-making. For the most part, political psychology research has not embedded the individual agent in the macrolevel structure and ignored or at best de-emphasized the externally imposed limitations and opportunities within which the person must function.

In comparing the usefulness of macro- vs. microlevel approaches, it is important to recognize a significant difference between domestic and foreign policy. The former is created, legislated, and administered within the normal structures and negotiations among the power centers of the country. The latter, especially in times of crisis – as is usually the case with decisions about going to war – is much more under the influence of individual leaders and their circle (Maranto & Redding, 2009). Therefore, when studying decisions that lead to peace or war, paying extra attention to leader personality is a good strategy. (See DECISION-MAKING, PSYCHOLOGICAL DIMENSIONS OF FOREIGN POLICY; DECISION-MAKING, THE ROLE OF EMOTIONS IN FOREIGN POLICY.) Bearing that in mind, let us consider what tools political psychologists have to study questions of peace and war.

Relatively few studies have examined the psychological factors that precede a decision to *end* a war. Rather, microlevel analyses in the area of peace psychology typically address the crucial decisions that leaders and leadership groups make, which – sometimes unwittingly or unexpectedly – lead to either a peaceful or a bellicose outcome to international confrontations. High-level political leaders are seldom accessible for interviews, questionnaires, or psychological experiments; therefore, almost all of this research is so-called "assessment at a distance," using biographical, archival, or other publicly available materials. (See ARCHIVAL RESEARCH.) Additionally, this strategy eliminates such problems of face-to-face communication as language comprehension, and opens the subject pool to include leaders who may have been dead for centuries. Methods of analysis range from the application of psychodynamic concepts of unconscious motives influenced by childhood experiences and Freudian drives (psychohistory and psychobiography) to the computerized count of how frequently particular words, phrases, or themes are found in the oral, written, or recorded utterances of the individuals of interest. (See QUALITATIVE METHODS AND CODING.)

Assessment at a distance can be divided between profiling and tracking approaches. Profiling strategies aim either at assessing personality traits or other stable characteristics that the researcher considers relevant, or at developing a holistic portrait of the individual's personality, and inferring the subject's general tendency to behave in certain ways across a range of situations and problems. Theoretical linkages between personality profiles and leader decisions can be tested in two ways:

1. *Retrospectively*, generating profile measurements of one or more historic leaders and then interpreting what those measurements imply in terms of the leader's known foreign policy decisions. This can be done without scorer bias because the personality measures can be applied to verbal materials without the scorers' knowledge of whose characteristics they are scoring or of the source's foreign policy actions. Different experts, who have no knowledge of these scores, independently assess the leader's decisions. A good fit between the personality profile and the expert assessments of the leader's decisions would affirm the validity of the method.

2. *Prospectively*, creating a profile of one or more current leaders, using that profile to make predictions about the leader's decisions in a current or imminent situation, and then, as history unfolds, confirming or disconfirming those predictions. This is more rigorous than retrodiction, because there is no possibility of biasing either the profile or its implications by the knowledge of what actually happened. Obviously, if the predictions turn out to be correct, it is also more useful; and if they do not, the findings can be used to adjust how profiles are generated and/or how they are applied to the forecasting of decisions. With contemporary leaders, there may be possible bias among scorers who are aware of the identity of the individual(s) and event they are scoring. It is necessary here, and in other "assessment at a distance" research, to take all feasible steps to minimize this confound by removing from the database

information that would serve as identification of the source, and to use scorers who are not informed of the context or hypotheses of their task.

Among profiling approaches that use trait-like characteristics to explain past decisions is operational code analysis, a widely used technique that draws inferences concerning the subject's belief system to support conclusions about his or her strategic decisions (e.g., Schafer & Walker, 2006). Among leaders studied through this system have been Woodrow Wilson, Henry Kissinger, and George W. Bush. A number of less well-known methods also use biographical and personality assessment at a distance data for a wide variety of purposes, including explanations of political leadership.

With holistic profiling, the methodological warning about minimizing scorer bias cannot be followed. The researcher, studying the biography of a particular leader, may conclude that early family constellation and the child–parent relationship might incline him or her toward a need to prove himself as strong and superior, and lead to a relatively high willingness to risk or even initiate violence to support that need (Post, 2007). A similar conclusion may be reached by comparing the frequency of phrases appearing in several leaders' verbal output denoting, for example, an expectation of positive outcomes brought about by a particular leader's ability to shape events, leading him to take risks in the expectation that they will lead to success (Hermann, 1993).

Another approach is to track leaders' statements as a particular problematic situation develops and predict the outcome from changes in measures of cognition and motivation. Tracking methods do not attempt to assess levels of "trait" variables; rather, they look at how the individual's "state" characteristics related to decision-making change over the course of the event and what these changes may portend concerning the outcome. For example, as international confrontations develop, different outcomes have been shown reliably to be associated with changes in such aspects as open-minded, flexible thinking, or the desire to impose one's will on others (Smith, 1992).

Given that "behavior is the function of personality interacting with environment" is one of the clichés of modern psychology, a fusion between theories at the two levels is likely to improve both research and application, the latter including policy analysis and formulation as well as the forecasting of the outcomes of political dilemmas and confrontations. The incorporation of important psychological (microlevel) components into macrolevel theories and research programs is not new. It has cropped up repeatedly, from Harold Lasswell's (1930/1960) analyses of the relationship between stages of development of revolutions and the prominence of different "political types" (actually, personalities), to Alexander George's (1980) studies of leaders and to contemporary studies of individual as well as environmental factors as predictors of group violence and combinations of systemic and psychological components, used to predict the outcome of threatening confrontations.

The approaches reviewed here have shown significant power in identifying variables that are compatible with explanations of past events and have high reliability in forecasting crisis outcomes. As has been pointed out, they are arguably more significant in international than domestic crises. Nevertheless, the final word should rest with the argument in favor of the ideal, i.e., of looking at both levels of analysis: "The study of individuals can only be part of a larger whole. Ignoring their role is foolish, but so too is ignoring the influence of other forces such as systemic factors, domestic politics, and bureaucratic pressures" (Byman & Pollack, 2001, p. 146).

SEE ALSO: Archival Research; Decision-Making, Psychological Dimensions of Foreign Policy; Decision-Making, the Role of Emotions in Foreign Policy; Qualitative Methods and Coding.

REFERENCES

Byman, D., & Pollack, K. (2001). Let us now praise great men: Bringing the statesman back in. *International Security*, 25, 107–146.

George, A. (1980). *Presidential decisionmaking in foreign policy: The effective use of advice and information*. Boulder, CO: Westview Press.

Hermann, M. G. (1993). Leaders and foreign policy decision-making. In D. Caldwell & T. J. McKeown (Eds.), *Diplomacy, force, and leadership: Essays in honor of Alexander L. George* (pp. 77–94). Boulder, CO: Westview Press.

Lasswell, H. D. (1930/1960). *Psychopathology and politics*. New York, NY: Viking.

Maranto, R., & Redding, R. E. (2009). Bush's brain (no, not Karl Rove): How Bush's psyche shaped his decision making. In R. Maranto, T. Lansford, & J. Johnson (Eds.), *Judging Bush* (pp. 21–40). Stanford, CA: Stanford University Press.

Post, J. M. (2007). *The mind of the terrorist: The psychology of terrorism from the IRA to al-Qaeda*. New York, NY: St. Martin's Press.

Schafer, M., & Walker, S. (Eds.). (2006). *Beliefs and leadership in world politics: Methods and applications of operational code analysis*. New York, NY: Palgrave Macmillan.

Smith, C. P. (Ed.). (1992). *Motivation and personality: Handbook of thematic content analysis*. Cambridge, UK: Cambridge University Press.

Liberation Psychology

MARITZA MONTERO

Liberation psychology was introduced into psychology during the mid-1980s and since then has continued to develop not as a new branch for the discipline, but as an ethical and political way to do psychology. Although liberation psychology in Latin America was originally considered a politically oriented social psychology, it has been mainly developed as a way to practice psychology which acknowledges the political implications permeating all aspects of the psychological profession. This is due to its concern for social change and economic problems traceable to inequality, oppression, and exclusion within societies. Specifically, it has been developed as an answer to the necessity to study psychological processes and conditions that oppress and liberate people.

Liberation psychology's main antecedents are the theology and philosophy of liberation, and the critical movement that denounced the insufficiency of mainstream science, not only in Latin America, but across the world. The so-called crisis of social sciences, with psychology among them, was acutely and simultaneously felt all over America, triggering a critique of conventional theories and ways to apply psychology. Liberation psychology is a way to carry out and to think about psychology and its role in society and in science, part of a critical movement developed in social sciences in Latin America at the beginning of the 1960s, and developed in other parts of the world since the 1970s. The theory of dependency, the movement of alternatives to psychiatry, and the need to include the voice of the oppressed were parts of this zeitgeist. (See CRITICAL AND RADICAL PSYCHOLOGY; CRITICAL SECURITY STUDIES.)

Ignacio Martín-Baró pioneered liberation psychology. He was a Jesuit priest and social psychologist of Spanish origin who studied psychology first in El Salvador, his country of adoption, and later at the University of Chicago, where he obtained his MSc (1977) and PhD (1979) in social and organizational psychology. The name "liberation psychology" was coined in a paper published by him in 1986 (Martín-Baró, 1986/1994) in the *Bulletin of Psychology* of the Universidad

Centroamericana "José Simeón Cañas" (El Salvador), where he was vice-rector and where he was murdered by a military death squad in 1989.

The main theoretical influences in Martín-Baró's work, and in liberation psychology as it has been developed after his death during the past two decades, come from the work of Brazilian educator Paulo Freire (1970); from critical social sciences (Barreiro, Bourdieu, Fals Borda, and Foucault, among others), and from philosophy (Marx, Levinas, Dussel, Scannone).

From Freire's work come the main theoretical concepts of liberation psychology. Freire was the first to introduce the term liberation as part of a praxis (practice informing theory, theory generating practice) that could transform social conditions. Along with that term came the concepts of naturalization, denaturalization, de-ideologization, de-alienation, problematization, and conscientization, which he used in an applied way in connection with adult literacy programs. (See CONSCIENTIZATION; PROBLEMATIZATION.)

Naturalization is a learned and habitual mode of understanding daily events and circumstances as if they were the natural and essential way for things to be; therefore, accepting them as inevitable and part of life. Problematization is the process that starts denaturalizing unequal and oppressive situations. Ideologization refers to the ways through which ideas serving the interests of the oppressors are induced in the oppressed in order to have them accepted. It is a way of blocking sectors of people's consciousness. Alienation explains the phenomenon of people's submission to ideas, practices, and their products, which although being created by the people, are considered as separated from their creators, who feel distant, alien, and inferior to them. Thus, the object is considered more important than the person who crafted it. The person is objectified whereas the object is attributed more value.

De-ideologization is the process of making people aware of the sources of oppression, the interests fostering a certain ideology, and the character of the power relationships sustaining it. De-alienation consists of the mobilization of people's consciousness in order to understand that the relation in which things are considered worthier than people is a form of exclusion and of oppression. These processes lead to conscientization.

Conscientization refers to the consciousness that allows both individuals and groups to understand the circumstances they are in and to react, transforming them while transforming themselves. Conscientization facilitates processes through which people develop consciousness about their life circumstances as well as the strength to transform such conditions. Transforming power relations and one's own roles and actions in them ends various forms of oppression and exclusions within society. Liberation processes should be worked both with the oppressed and excluded as well as with the oppressors and excluding, for they also need to work on their own liberation from their oppressive behavior.

Educators and social scientists adopted Freire's technique and orientation to social transformation in Brazil. His ideas and method spread throughout several Latin American countries, Africa (Tanzania, Guinea-Bissau, Angola, Mozambique), and Asia (India and the Philippines). Scholars in several European countries also adopted his perspective (among them Heinz Moser, Guy Le Boterf, and Marja Liisa Swantz).

Although Martín-Baró's writings on liberation psychology were few, they received the attention of many researchers not only in Latin America, but in other parts of the world. Soon liberation psychology expanded to South Africa, the United Kingdom,

Australia, the United States, and southeast Asia. Today it is a movement, and a paradigm for theory, research, and action that continues to be applied around the world.

In Martín-Baró's papers of 1986 and 1990 he outlined the following central ideas for a liberation-oriented psychology:

1. To work with the oppressed population among which truth could be found; for as he said, their voice is the voice of God (Martín-Baró, 1986, 1990), an idea strongly influenced by the theology of liberation. The idea of truth was made objective by incorporating, as Freire did, the people's knowledge, and disseminating the verifiable results of public opinion polls produced at the Institute of Public Opinion created by Martín-Baró in 1987.
2. To give a different meaning to psychology so that it can empower people to develop positive forms of social identity, and find in themselves the capacities to change their lives.
3. To decenter psychology from its concern about its scientific status and put its knowledge at the service of the people suffering inequality, exclusion, and oppression in Latin American societies.
4. To view liberation as a de-alienating process that is simultaneously individual and collective.
5. To incorporate the Freirean concept of conscientization (i.e., critical awareness) about one's role and living conditions and relating it to people's potential for change.
6. To empower people in order to develop their capacities to overcome oppressions and produce a redistribution of power, thus working on their own liberation.
7. To retrieve the people's cultural and historic memory in order to achieve a de-ideologized social identity, as they obtain their liberation.

According to Martín-Baró, liberation is a historic experience, a condition reflecting the influence of the critical movement and Freire's work. It is also characterized by being conflictive, since it generates a rupture with dominant oppressive social conditions. Liberation has a collective nature directed to overcoming oppressive, exploitive, and unequal relations, and build a positive social identity. But it should not be mistaken with warfare. It is a peaceful confrontation producing a transformation carried out in daily life.

During the past two decades the liberation paradigm has been applied to a wide variety of psychological concerns, with a large presence in the field of political psychology and topics such as racism, social movements, citizenship construction, political polarization, displaced groups, and human, civil, and social rights (Montero & Sonn, 2009). There is also a politics of liberation (McLaren & Lankshear, 1994). Gender issues, community development, and education, as well as other specialties and fields, have made important contributions to the liberation perspective.

The concept of liberation is defined as an ethical, critical, and political praxis whose focal points are the oppressed and excluded. Liberation is also a democratizing process, fostering the potentials and resources of those who are oppressed for the purpose of social transformation. Social, cultural, and historic conditions tend to make such potentials and resources invisible among social victims. The idea of liberation is related to the concepts of self-determination and free will, and refers to social and political freedom. It struggles for autonomy, well-being, inclusion, rights, peace, and conditions of mutual respect, in order to be free from oppression.

The definition of liberation needs to be complemented by the definition of oppression, a concept that changes across time and space, so new parameters of oppressive practices have to be established (McLaren & Lankshear, 1994). While there are many faces of oppression, it invariably involves a power relation characterized by domination of some people, and complemented by the submission of those upon whom the dominance is exerted. Disempowerment, exploitation, marginalization, and different forms of violence are suffered by the oppressed. Those effects are complemented by alienation and ideologization in order to obtain the blind acceptance of the victims, but whenever and wherever there is oppression, liberation movements have emerged.

From the episteme of relatedness, developed in psychology during the 1990s, liberation psychology has taken the idea of relation as the ontological unit. This displaces the individual as the center of every action, making psychology aware of the individualistic bias dominant in its theories. But individuality is not proscribed; it is constructed within relationships allowing the people belonging to them to be acknowledged as diverse subjects with rights and voice. Liberation, according to this perspective, opposes what Levinas (1961/1969) called ontology of egotism, which privileges possession and reduces the Other to an object belonging to the One. That is a form of oppression and also a form of rejection, since in that way, as a thing, the Other is alienated and excluded from social opportunities and benefits, developing self-deprecating feelings and negative forms of social identities. Exclusion of the Other also empties the One, who, according to Levinas, tries to fill the void with the Other's submission or his/her annihilation. As Freire said: "No one is if [he, she] forbids others to be." Therefore, liberation is a way to introduce peace in the daily struggle for freedom.

Epistemologically, liberation psychology maintains that knowledge is not the exclusive outcome of science, for there are other forms of knowledge, including knowledge-producing relationships that are characterized by the incorporation of people as knowledge producers rather than being seen as known objects. People know about their lives and also contribute with popular knowledge and ideas. The concept of relatedness also goes back to Paulo Freire, and to European philosophers Emmanuel Levinas and Martin Buber.

From the ethic of liberation (Dussel, 1998) comes the liberation principle, consisting of the critical–ethical duty for every human being to collaborate in the social transformation of laws, social norms, actions, microstructures, institutions, and ethical systems for the victims of oppression and exclusion in order to create conditions that support the viable development of human life for all.

The liberating process does not imply a successive chain of events, since the processes leading to conscientization may happen simultaneously. Liberation occurs within the group relation while happening at the same time within each person participating in that relationship, at different moments and with different rhythms, degrees of intensity, and understandings. In addition to the Freirian influences of reflective dialogue and the action–reflection–action model, liberation psychology likewise employs with a critical perspective a variety of methods already in use in social sciences. Hermeneutics, analectics, and the current development of methods for consciousness (Montero & Sonn, 2009) are ways to facilitate the application of liberation psychology.

To summarize, the main aspects developed by liberation psychology are:

- An active conception of the subject. Every human being is a social actor and his/her actions affect the world that person lives in. As Freire said, "No one liberates no one, no one is self-liberated. People are liberated in communion"

(1970, p. 29), meaning that liberation is not given but produced by each one within liberating relations.

- Incorporation of the people's knowledge, ideas, opinions, and participation in the liberating processes.
- Social transformation.
- Development of a variety of resources of which people may not be aware because of their situation, to be used in their search for liberation from oppression.
- Opposition to asymmetrical power relations, using unexpected forms of strategic power to oppose domination.
- Construction of positive and empowered social identities that can carry out the task of eliminating oppressive and excluding circumstances.

SEE ALSO: Conscientization; Critical and Radical Psychology; Critical Security Studies; Problematization.

REFERENCES

Dussel, E. (1998). *Ética de la liberación en la edad de la globalización y de la exclusión [Ethics of liberation in the age of globalization and exclusion]*. Madrid, Spain: Trotta.
Freire, P. (1970). *Pedagogy of the oppressed*. New York, NY: Continuum.
Freire, P. (1973 / 1988). *Extension or communication? Conscientization in the rural environment* (16th ed.). Montevideo, Uruguay: Siglo XXI.
Levinas, E. (1961 / 1969). *Totality and infinity: An essay on exteriority*. Pittsburgh, PA: Duquesne University Press.
McLaren, P. L., & Lankshear, C. (1994). Introduction. In P. L. McLaren & C. Lankshear (Eds.), *Politics of liberation: Paths from Freire* (pp. 1–11). London, UK: Routledge.
Martín-Baró, I. (1986 / 1994). Towards a psychology of liberation. In A. Aron & S. Corne (Eds.). *Writings for a liberation psychology* (pp. 17–32). Cambridge, MA: Harvard University Press.
Martín-Baró, I. (1990) Retos y perspectivas de la psicología en América Latina [Challenges and perspectives for psychology in Latin America]. In G. Pacheco & B. Jiménez-Domínguez (Eds.), *Ignacio Martín-Baró. Psicología de la Liberación para América Latina* (pp. 51–80). Guadalajara, Mexico: University of Guadalajara-ITESO.
Montero, M., & Sonn, C. C. (Eds.). (2009). *The psychology of liberation*. New York, NY: Springer.

Lucifer Effect

PHILIP G. ZIMBARDO

By the 1970s, social psychologists had conducted a series of studies establishing the social power of groups, and of situational forces to influence individual behaviors. They showed, for example, that groups of strangers could persuade people to believe statements that were obviously false (Asch, 1955) by endorsing the false value as if it were correct. Others found that the presence of three or more people who did not respond to an emergency created a definition of that situation as one in which it is appropriate not to intervene or give aid to those in need (Darley & Latané, 1968). Dissonance theory researchers revealed that rational people could justify virtually any irrational decision they had taken in order to make it appear that their behavior was consonant with their attitudes and values (Festinger, 1957; Tavris & Arsonson, 2008). Milgram (1974 / 2009) and other psychologists had also found that research participants were often willing to obey authority figures even when doing so violated their morality and conscience. (See OBEDIENCE; OBEDIENCE TO AUTHORITY.)

These and a host of other social psychological studies were showing that human nature was more pliable than previously imagined and more responsive to situational pressures than we acknowledged. Missing from the body of social science research at the time was the direct confrontation of good versus evil, of good people pitted against the forces inherent in bad situations. I decided that what was needed was to create a situation in a controlled experimental setting in which we could array on one side a host of variables, such as role-playing, coercive rules, power differentials, anonymity, group dynamics, and dehumanization. On the other side, we lined up a collection of the "best and brightest" of young college men in collective opposition to the might of a dominant system. Thus in 1971, the Stanford prison experiment was launched. Unlike the Milgram studies, there was no authority ordering antisocial behaviors; rather, it was all part of an institutional framework in which roles, rules, power, and control were exercised as natural aspects of a prison-like setting.

First we established that all 24 participants were physically and mentally healthy, with no history of crime or violence, so as to be sure that initially they were all "good apples." They were paid $15 a day to participate. Each of the student volunteers was randomly assigned to play the role of prisoner or guard in a setting designed to convey a sense of the psychology of imprisonment (in actuality, a mock prison set up in the basement of the Stanford psychology department). Palo Alto City Police agreed to "arrest" the prisoners and book them at the local station, and, once at our prison, they were given identity numbers, stripped naked, and deloused. The prisoners wore large smocks with no underclothes and lived in the prison 24/7 for a planned two weeks; three shifts of guards patrolled eight-hour shifts each. Throughout the experiment, I served as the prison "superintendent," being assisted by graduate students Craig Haney and Curtis Banks, and by the "warden," undergraduate student David Jaffe.

Initially, nothing much happened as the students awkwardly tried out their assigned roles in their new uniforms. However, all that changed suddenly on the morning of the second day following a rebellion, when the prisoners barricaded themselves inside their cells by putting their beds against the door. Suddenly, the guards perceived the prisoners as "dangerous." With their new definition of the situation, the guards determined that they had to deal more harshly with these rebels, to demonstrate who was boss and who was powerless. At first, guard abuses were retaliation for taunts and disobedience. Over time they became ever more abusive, some guards even delighting in sadistically tormenting their prisoners. Though physical punishment was restricted (by my orders), the guards on each shift were free to make up their own rules, and they invented a variety of psychological tactics to demonstrate their dominance over their powerless charges. Nakedness was a common punishment, as was placing paper bags over prisoners' heads, chaining their legs, repeatedly waking them up throughout the night for hour-long counts, and forcing them into humiliating "fun and games" activities.

PRISON LOG: FIFTH NIGHT

On the fifth night, the prisoners who had not yet broken down emotionally under the incessant stress the guards had subjected them to since their aborted rebellion on day two wearily line up against the wall, to recite their ID numbers and to demonstrate that they remembered all 17 prisoner rules of engagement. It is the 1 a.m. count, the last one of the night before the morning shift comes on at 2 a.m. No matter how well the prisoners do, one of them gets singled out for punishment. They are yelled at, cursed out, and made to say abusive things to each other. "Tell him he's a prick," yells one guard. And each prisoner says that to the next guy in line. Then the sexual harassment that had started to bubble up the night before resumes, as the testosterone flows freely in every direction.

Our toughest guard (nicknamed John Wayne by the prisoners) and his sidekick buddy confer and devise a new sexual game. "OK, now pay attention. You three are going to be female camels. Get over here and bend over, touching your hands to the floor." When they do, their naked butts are exposed because they have no underwear beneath their smocks. Guard John Wayne continues with obvious glee, "Now you two, you're male camels. Stand behind the female camels and *hump* them."

The guards all giggle at this double entendre. Although their bodies never touch, the helpless prisoners begin to simulate sodomy by making thrusting motions. They are then dismissed back to their cells to get an hour of sleep before the next shift comes on, and the abuse continues.

By day five, five mock prisoner-students had been released early because of extreme stress reactions. Recall that each of them was physically healthy and psychologically stable less than a week before. Most of those who remained adopted a zombie-like attitude and posture, being totally obedient to any and all of the guards' escalating demands.

TERMINATING THE TORMENT

I was forced to terminate the projected two-week-long study after only six days because it was running out of control. Dozens of people had come down to our "little shop of horrors," saw some of the abuse or its effects, and said nothing other than how realistic the simulation was. A prison chaplain, parents, and friends had visited the prisoners, and psychologists and others on the parole board saw a realistic prison simulation, an experiment in action, but did not challenge me to stop it. The one exception was a former doctoral student of mine, Christina Maslach, then a new assistant professor at the University of California at Berkeley. When she saw the prisoners lined up with bags over their heads, their legs chained, and guards shouting abuse at them while herding them to the toilet, she got emotionally upset. "It is terrible what YOU are doing to those boys!" she yelled at me. Christina made evident in that one statement that human beings were suffering – not prisoners, not experimental subjects, and not paid volunteers. And further, I was the one who was personally responsible for the horrors she had witnessed (and which she assumed were even worse when no outsider was noticing). She also made it clear that if this person I had become – the heartless superintendent of the Stanford prison – was the real me, and not the caring, generous person she had come to like, she wanted nothing more to do with me.

That powerful jolt of reality snapped me back to my senses. I agreed we had gone too far, that whatever was to be learned about situational power was already indelibly etched on our videos, data logs, and minds; there was no need to continue. I too had been transformed by my role in that situation, made to become a person that under any other circumstances I detest – an uncaring, authoritarian boss man. In retrospect, I believe that the main reason I did not end the study sooner resulted from the conflict created in me by my dual roles as principal investigator, and thus guardian of the research ethics of the experiment, and as the prison superintendent, eager to maintain the stability of my prison at all costs. I now realize that there should have been someone with authority above mine, someone in charge of overseeing the experiment, who surely would have blown the whistle earlier.

GOOD APPLES IN BAD BARRELS AND BAD BARREL MAKERS

The situational forces in that "bad barrel" had overwhelmed the goodness of most of those who came to be infected by their viral power. Thus, this little experiment added further substance to Milgram's earlier demonstration of the power of situations to influence individual and group behavior. But something more is added, beyond the call to appreciate what people bring into situations and what situations bring out of people. We need to understand the usually nontransparent systems that create and maintain those situations of control. Systems are where the power emanates from, the legal, economic, institutional, cultural, and historical. We need to know who the makers of those bad barrels are and to expose them as such.

CURRENT RELEVANCE

The Stanford prison experiment is now more popular then ever in its 40-year history. Some of this recent interest comes from the apparent similarities of the experiment's abuses with the images of depravity in Iraq's Abu Ghraib prison – of nakedness, bagged heads, and sexual humiliation. Indeed, I became part of the expert defense team for one of those military police guards to try to minimize the severity of his guilty plea by illustrating the degree to which his behavior was under situational control in that dungeon.

Among the dozen investigations of the Abu Ghraib abuses, the one chaired by James Schlesinger, former secretary of defense, boldly proclaims that the landmark Stanford study "provides a cautionary tale for all military detention operations." In contrasting the relatively benign environment of the Stanford prison experiment, the report makes evident that "in military detention operations, soldiers work under stressful

combat conditions that are far from benign." The implication is that those combat conditions might be expected to generate even more extreme abuses of power than were observed in our mock prison experiment. The report continued: "The potential for abusive treatment of detainees during the Global War on Terrorism was entirely predictable based on a fundamental understanding of the principles of social psychology coupled with an awareness of numerous known environmental risk factors. Findings from the field of social psychology suggest that the conditions of war and the dynamics of detainee operations carry inherent risks for human mistreatment, and therefore must be approached with great caution and careful planning and training." (See INTERROGATION, PSYCHOLOGY AND.)

The implications of this research for law are considerable, as legal scholars are beginning to recognize. The criminal justice system, for instance, focuses primarily on individual defendants and their "state of mind" and largely ignores situational forces. If the goals of the criminal system are simply to blame and punish individual perpetrators, then focusing almost exclusively on the individual defendant makes sense. If, however, the goal is actually to reduce the behavior that we now call "criminal" (and its resultant suffering), and to assign punishments that correspond with the degree of culpability, then the criminal justice system is obligated, much as I was in the Stanford prison experiment, to confront the situation and our role in creating and perpetuating it. By recognizing the situational determinants of behavior, we can move to a more productive public-health model of prevention and intervention and away from the individualistic medical and religious "sin" model that has never worked since its inception during the Inquisition.

The Lucifer Effect is a term I created to depict the ease with which good people can fall from grace, as did Lucifer, God's favorite angel, through his act of disobedience (Zimbardo, 2008). The Lucifer Effect is a detailed presentation of the social psychological processes engaged when ordinary, even good people, start down the slippery slope of evil. When confronted with situational and systemic power, human character is transformed. The Lucifer Effect removes the comfort zone from those who believe that the line between good and evil is impermeable, and thus they are protected by having been on the right side. That line is permeable, allowing almost any of us to be seduced across to the dark side by pervasive situational forces.

The critical message then is to be sensitive about our vulnerability to subtle but powerful situational forces and, by virtue of such awareness, to be better able to resist and overcome these forces. Group pressures, authority symbols, dehumanization of others, imposed anonymity, dominant ideologies that enable spurious ends to justify immoral means, lack of surveillance, and other situational forces can work to transform even some of the best of us into Mr. Hyde monsters, without the benefit of Dr. Jekyll's chemical elixir. We must be more aware of how situational variables can influence our behavior, but further, that veiled behind the Power of the Situation is the greater Power of the System, which creates and maintains complicity at the highest military, governmental, and other institutional levels by means of evil-inducing situations, like those at Abu Ghraib and Guantánamo prisons.

SEE ALSO: Interrogation, Psychology and; Obedience; Obedience to Authority.

REFERENCES

Asch, S. E. (1955). Opinions and social pressure. *Scientific American, 193,* 31–35.
Darley, J., & Latané, B. (1968, December). When will people help in a crisis? *Psychology Today, 2,* 54–57, 70–71.
Festinger, L. (1957). *A theory of cognitive dissonance.* Stanford, CA: Stanford University Press.
Milgram, S. (1974/2009). *Obedience to authority: An experimental view.* New York, NY: Harper Perennial.
Tavris, C., & Arsonson, E. (2008). *Mistakes were made (but not by me).* Orlando, FL: Harcourt.
Zimbardo, P. G. (2008). *The Lucifer Effect: Understanding how good people turn evil.* New York, NY: Random House.

ADDITIONAL RESOURCES

www.LuciferEffect.com
www.prisonexp.org

M

Markov Chain Models of Negotiators' Communication

MARA OLEKALNS, PHILIP L. SMITH,
AND LAURIE R. WEINGART

Negotiators' communication can be analyzed at several levels: the frequency with which strategies are used, how negotiators sequence strategies, and how strategies evolve over time. Each level of analysis provides us with different kinds of information about the negotiation process. An important difference between these approaches is that analyses focusing on how often negotiators use a specific strategy assume that the negotiation process is static over time whereas analyses that focus on sequences or phases allow for the possibility that, as negotiators learn about each other, they redefine the negotiation and change their strategy preferences. (See also QUANTITATIVE METHODS AND CODING.) The analysis of sequences enables us to answer questions that cannot be answered by focusing solely on the frequency with which negotiators use particular strategies. By analyzing sequences, we

are able to assess how negotiations unfold over time and how negotiators influence each other and transform the negotiation. Understanding how the negotiation is transformed is especially important because it helps us to identify the most important mechanisms for building mutually beneficial solutions across a range of questions. In this entry, we describe the use of Markov chain models to represent and analyze strategy sequences (Bakeman & Gottman, 1986; Smith, Olekalns & Weingart, 2005; Thomas, 1985).

At its simplest, a strategy sequence describes an action–reaction pattern which represents the strategy used by one negotiator (Negotiator A) and the response from the other negotiator (Negotiator B). Thus, a basic sequence looks like this: $\text{strategy}_{\text{Negotiator A}} \rightarrow \text{strategy}_{\text{Negotiator B}}$. Researchers might start by asking about the basic structure of sequences: do negotiators match or mismatch each other's strategies? At this level of analysis, sequences can be described as reciprocal, complementary, or structural. When negotiators reciprocate, they match each other's strategies exactly ($\text{threat}_{\text{Negotiator A}} \rightarrow \text{threat}_{\text{Negotiator B}}$). However, they may also loosely match each other's strategies, maintaining a broad strategic approach in which they respond with similar, but not identical, strategies (threat_{Negotiator A} → argumentation_{Negotiator B}). Finally, negotiators may mismatch strategies, so that a cooperative behavior is followed by a competitive one, or vice versa (threat_{Negotiator A} → problem solving_{Negotiator B}). Although some research questions may be answered by focusing on this very general categorization of sequences, it is more revealing to focus on both the form and the content of sequences. This allows researchers to answer questions such as: What is the likelihood that cooperative tactics will be reciprocated? Is the reciprocation of cooperative tactics related to the quality of negotiated outcomes? Does the relationship between integrative reciprocity and outcome quality hold irrespective of the negotiating context?

DATA PREPARATION

Answers to these kinds of questions require that we first decide on the number of strategies to be included in the analysis. We may choose to use a very broad classificatory scheme, for example, by coding strategies as either "integrative" or "distributive"; or we may choose instead to undertake a more fine-grained classification of strategies, breaking down the broad integrative–distributive categories into more distinct behaviors such as process management, priority information, argumentation, proposal management, and contention. Once the strategies are coded, we construct a contingency table that summarizes the number of strategy sequences of each kind in the negotiation. At its simplest, the sequences can be represented in a 2×2 contingency table in which one dimension, or margin, of the table shows Negotiator A's strategy (cooperative or competitive) and the other dimension shows Negotiator B's response (cooperative or competitive). The entries in

the table represent the frequency of each of the possible strategy-response pairs, that is, of each possible strategy by Negotiator A followed by each possible response by Negotiator B.

Contingency tables become more complex as we add dimensions for variables such as negotiators' outcomes and the negotiation context. We may, for example, create a four-dimensional contingency table to represent each negotiator's strategy (cooperative or competitive), their joint outcome (low, moderate, high), and the level of power within a dyad (equal or unequal). As we add dimensions to a contingency table, the number of cells rapidly increases, creating very sparse data for subsequent analysis. For this reason, it is important to consider how many categories will be used to code the data. Choosing broad categories has the advantage that, in subsequent analyses, researchers have many observations in each cell of their contingency table. However, they may miss subtle nuances in negotiators' interactions. Conversely, using many categories creates sparse tables with many empty cells. In our analyses, we have found that using between four and seven strategy clusters creates sufficiently well-populated contingency tables while adequately capturing the emerging negotiation process.

MARKOV CHAINS

Markov chain analyses are based on a representation of the negotiating dyad as a system, which can be in one of a finite number of states at any time, each with some probability. The states describe the propensity or disposition of each member of the dyad to use each of the strategies available to them. The sequencing of strategies, conceived of as a sequence of transitions between states, is described by a simple probability model. Markov chain analyses recognize that, at any given time, negotiators can choose to use one of several strategies. The probability that they will prefer one strategy over others is determined by their opponent's preceding strategy. Specifically, Markov chain models allow us to determine the probability that Negotiator B will use a particular strategy from the set of strategies we have defined, based on the strategy used by Negotiator A: If Negotiator A uses a cooperative strategy, what is the probability that Negotiator B will respond with a cooperative strategy or a competitive strategy?

An important question is how far back in the negotiation we need to look in order to determine the probability that Negotiator B will at this point in time choose a specific strategy, X_n. Is it sufficient to know Negotiator A's immediately preceding strategy or do we need to trace the process back through several turns? The Markov assumption states that the probability of X_n (Negotiator B's strategy choice at *this* point in time) depends on only a fixed number of the set of preceding X values (strategies). How far back in time do we need to go to determine the level (order) of the Markov chain? If we need to look only at the preceding strategy used by Negotiator A to predict Negotiator B's strategy choice, we are representing the sequence as a *first-order* Markov chain, $X_{n-1} \rightarrow X_n$. It may, however, be that Negotiator B's current strategy choice is predicted by both Negotiator A's immediately preceding strategy and Negotiator B's own earlier strategy. To predict Negotiator B's strategy we need to go back two steps in time and represent the sequence as a *second-order* Markov chain, $X_{n-2} \rightarrow X_{n-1} \rightarrow X_n$. In addition to being important conceptually, the order of a Markov chain is important statistically. The order of the chain determines the minimum size of the contingency table needed to render successive parts of a sequence of strategies conditionally independent of one another. Conditional independence is required in order to analyze the

data using widely available log-linear models. In our research, we have found that second-order Markov chains are usually sufficient to capture the structure of negotiation. To represent the dependencies between consecutive strategies, we construct a transition matrix from our contingency table. The transition matrix expresses the conditional probability that each of the set of possible strategies will be reciprocated by each of the others. The simplest analysis that we can conduct is to code strategies as either cooperative or competitive and to restrict our analysis to first-order Markov chains, that is, sequences of two strategies, $X_{n-1} \rightarrow X_n$. In this case, a transition matrix might look like this:

		Time n	
		Cooperative	Competitive
Time n−1	Cooperative	0.6	0.4
	Competitive	0.3	0.7

This table shows that the probability of reciprocating a cooperative strategy is 0.6, whereas the probability of reciprocating a competitive strategy is 0.7.

LOG-LINEAR ANALYSIS OF MARKOV CHAIN MODELS

Because the data are a multi-way contingency table, log-linear analysis provides a convenient and readily accessible technique for analyzing Markov chain models (Agresti, 1990). A difference between other applications of log-linear models and their application to Markov chains is that the unit of analysis changes from the individual to the strategy or speech act. The first step in using log-linear models is the creation of a contingency table. In this table, the margins are formed by strategies at consecutive steps in time. Again, the simplest model would be two-dimensional, cross-classifying the strategies used at Time n and Time $n-1$ $(X_{n-1} \rightarrow X_n)$. The number of dimensions in the contingency table is thus determined by the expected order of the underlying Markov chain. A two-dimensional table is required to represent a first-order Markov chain whereas a three-dimensional table is required to represent a second-order Markov chain, and so on. In this analysis, sequential dependencies appear statistically as interactions between strategies: A first-order chain emerges as an interaction between strategies at Time n and Time $n-1$ $(X_{n-1} {}^\star X_n)$, whereas a second-order chain would appear as an interaction between strategies at Time n, Time $n-1$ and Time $n-2$ $(X_{n-2} {}^\star X_{n-1} {}^\star X_n)$.

To understand which sequence structure best captures the underlying data, we use the likelihood ratio test statistic, G^2, to test for model fit. Typically, we start by testing whether an independence model, comprising simple frequencies with no interactions, fits the data. We do this in the largest nonsparse contingency table we can form using the available data. We then add model terms of increasing complexity (two-way interactions for first-order chains, followed by three-way interactions for second-order chains, and so on), testing whether the inclusion of these terms improves the fit of the model to the data. To test this, we look for significant changes in G^2 at each step.

ADDING DIMENSIONS

So far, we have described relatively simple models that will help us answer the question "Can we predict Negotiator B's strategy at a given point in time, if we know what Negotiator A (and Negotiator B) did in the immediately preceding moments of the negotiation?" While this question is interesting in its own right, we are able to ask considerably more complex questions that increase our understanding of the negotiation process by adding other variables to the model. We might choose to compare different subgroups based, for example, on their goals. We might compare negotiating dyads or groups who both have cooperative goals to dyads with competitive or mixed goals (i.e., one negotiator has a competitive goal, the other has a cooperative goal; see Weingart, Brett, Olekalns, & Smith, 2007). This *prospective* classification of our sample allows us to compare how negotiators' goals shape the strategy sequences that dominate a negotiation. In past research, researchers have tested how negotiators' goals, tactical knowledge (present/absent) and power (low/high) affect the emergence of dominant strategy sequences. Alternatively, we might *retrospectively* classify subgroups based on their outcomes (e.g., low, moderate, and high joint gain.) This kind of classification allows us to ask whether there are unique sequences that are associated with each kind of outcome. Past research has shown that negotiators who use competitive–competitive sequences are more likely to obtain low joint gain whereas those who use cooperative–cooperative sequences are more likely to obtain high joint gain. A different kind of retrospective classification is based on time. By subdividing the negotiation into halves (or even smaller units), we can examine whether negotiators use different sequences in difference stages of a negotiation. Any one of these classifications (goals, outcomes, time) adds another dimension to the contingency table. We can expand the contingency table further to ask even more complex questions, linking prospective and retrospective classifications of negotiation strategies. Examples of such complex models can be seen in Olekalns and Smith's (2003) research linking negotiators' goals, strategies sequences, and outcomes.

SEE ALSO: Quantitative Methods and Coding.

REFERENCES

Agresti, A. (1990). *Categorical data analysis*. New York, NY: John Wiley & Sons, Inc.

Bakeman, R., & Gottman, J. M. (1986). *Observing interaction: An introduction to sequential analysis*. Cambridge, UK: Cambridge University Press.

Olekalns, M., & Smith, P. L. (2003). Testing the relationships among negotiators' motivational orientations, strategy choices and outcomes. *Journal of Experimental Social Psychology, 39*, 101–117.

Smith, P. L., Olekalns, M., & Weingart, L. (2005). Markov chain analyses of communication processes in negotiation. *International Negotiation, 10*, 97–113.

Thomas, A. (1985). Conversational routines: A Markov chain analysis. *Language and Communication, 5*, 177–188.

Weingart, L., Brett, J., Olekalns, M., & Smith, P. L. (2007). Conflicting social motives in negotiating groups. *Journal of Personality and Social Psychology, 93*, 994–1010.

Media and Peace: Emerging Technologies

JUDY KURIANSKY AND
CATHERINE MOUNTCASTLE

While traditional forms of media have been useful in promoting peace, the current article examines advances in technology and instant digital communication that have greatly expanded platforms for mass media. (See MEDIA AND PEACE: TRADITIONAL OUTLETS.) As a result, there is greater communication between individuals and groups, and new possibilities for public awareness, social movements, and peace efforts. Internet and computer technologies are being applied to peace efforts through formats like dialogue forums, grassroots movements, and educational training programs, allowing people to interact and comment, and to form virtual communities. Greater accessibility to information and educational tools for intercultural cooperation is shifting power from political and corporate elite to grassroots civil society, and giving disenfranchised people a greater voice while motivating activism. At the same time, some potential dangers must also be recognized.

PROGRAM APPLICATIONS OF TECHNOLOGY

Programs for intergroup cooperation are increasingly using Internet resources and technology for teaching and communication. The Middle East Education through Technology (MEET) educational program teaches technological, leadership, and professional skills to Israeli and Palestinian teens while fostering positive social exchanges (Brandenburg, 2007). The non-profit organization Soliya uses Internet technology to promote understanding among university students from diverse backgrounds; its flagship initiative, called Connect Program, links university students from the United States, Europe, the Middle East, and north Africa through web-based video-conferencing, making it possible to dialogue about relationships in the regions, and cooperate in evaluating and producing media products. Interactive Management (IM) uses electronic messaging, web-conferencing, and systems supporting complex decision-making and conflict resolution (e.g., between Greeks and Turks in Cyprus) and online dispute resolution (ODR) is an approach that similarly applies Internet technology to facilitate resolution between disputants in the Asia Pacific region (e.g. China, Malaysia, the Philippines, Singapore, Australia, and Malaysia), walking people through online filings and discussions in order to peacefully resolve problems relating to land, refugee resettlement, and disaster management, as well as business disputes and even marital separation. Professionals and individuals can connect freely through Skype (calls) and web mailing list management systems (e.g., Listserv). (See DISPUTE RESOLUTION, ONLINE.)

Live interactive web-conferencing bridges vast geographic distances to allow groups to communicate as if they are in the same room. In one such recent event, members of peace-oriented nongovernmental organizations gathered at the United Nations headquarters in New York and were connected to a group of female leaders gathered around a conference table in the Democratic Republic of the Congo. Through videoconferencing, the groups had a live discussion on the role of women in peacekeeping, sex discrimination on the job, and the need for accountability where there is abuse and violence against women.

EMERGING TECHNOLOGIES

Social networking sites include MySpace and Facebook, where over 300 million users create and update personal or group-oriented profiles and pictures, add friends, send messages, and link to other sites. While these are widely used by individuals, groups with a specific mission can set up their own site designed for their purpose and connect with specific members. Access to parts of sites can be open to anyone or limited to invitees. World leaders, nonprofit organizations, and grassroots activists have harnessed these resources to communicate policies and to organize events related to conflicts (e.g., in Venezuela, Sri Lanka, Egypt, and Honduras). In 2009 the use of Facebook was instrumental in organizing a grassroots march against Columbia's FARC leftist guerrillas. And US President Barack Obama's 2008 presidential campaign was cited particularly as a blueprint for the successful use of Facebook and other Internet resources to make his policies known and to rally supporters.

Blogs, or online versions of diaries, record personal reflections that are posted on the Internet. These can be set up free of charge through certain services, and can be managed by individuals or others given necessary passwords.

Microblogging allows even simpler and quicker communication services like Short Message Service (SMS), cell phone applications, or Twitter (short sent and received messages called "tweets" transmitted via the Twitter website which is increasingly popular among politicians, celebrities, and the public). Using a limited number of letters, messages can be sent any number of times about any subject, with the sender inviting others to "follow" their messages. Twitter was used by civilians in Moldova to communicate about events and protests in the aftermath of the 2009 contested presidential elections.

Wikipedia is a Web 2.0 technology which allows the public to post encyclopedia-like entries on the Web, covering any topic, with definitions, examples, and even citations. These can cover innumerable peace and antiviolence topics, experts, or events.

Online video sharing can be done through sites like YouTube, launched in 2005, and the newer Google Video, websites that allow users to upload, view, and comment on visual materials, videos, movies, music, TV clips, and amateur content (video-blogs) free of charge. Content can also be easily uploaded and viewed on other web pages outside the site or embedded in and used in accordance with other websites such as social networking websites and blogs. Individuals and groups can set up their own channels with their own video-messaging. This is clearly an opportunity for peace activists.

THE CASE OF THE UNITED NATIONS DISARMAMENT CAMPAIGN

Various social networking sites were linked in 2009 for the United Nations Secretary General's multiplatform campaign, WMD-We Must Disarm (http://www.un.org/en/events/peaceday/2009/). The public awareness campaign supporting peace and disarmament, targeted especially at youth, consisted of a 100-day countdown leading up to the International Day of Peace. The campaign included public exhibits promoting the websites and reasons for nuclear disarmament, a competition for the best three-minute videos on nuclear disarmament, and support from media celebrities like UN Messenger of Peace Michael Douglas and actor Rainn Wilson (featured in the TV series *The Office*). At the 2009 United Nations Department of Public Information NGO conference in Mexico City on "Disarm Now: For Peace and Development," the Secretary General further harnessed media for the peace initiative by making personal appearances at various events and signing a student-constructed conference symbol, a plant growing out of a grenade (Kuriansky & Daisey, 2010). (See ACTIVISM, ANTIWAR.)

A COORDINATED SITE FOR DISRUPTIVE SITUATIONS

Advanced technology is also making possible sites through the Internet and hand-held devices that can record needs in the community either preventively or postdisaster. These devices record epidemiological information about populations and can also track cohorts affected by violent events and consequent needs and availability of services. One model being developed is a collaborative venture between a private company and an Argentinean psychiatrist who is an expert on disruptive situations (Benyakar & Collazo, 2009).

Civic journalism and news forums have made it possible for citizens to become actively involved in providing news content. (See PEACE JOURNALISM.) Reporters are going beyond their traditional role as objective observers through active participation in community issues and debates. This movement of citizen journalism has had a positive impact on some peace efforts, as it did years ago in the aftermath of the Rodney King race riots. Many broadcast media are actively encouraging audiences to submit their content to their websites; with these submissions at times becoming the subject of entire shows. The photo agency website Demotix connects freelance and amateur journalists with mainstream media, facilitating democratization of information, since anyone anywhere can upload articles and photos to market for others to view. Over eight thousand members in more than a hundred countries have provided real-time images of local and international conflicts (e.g., in Israel, Turkey, and Egypt) to outlets like *The New York Times*, *The Huffington Post*, and *The Daily Telegraph*.

Positive news is making an appearance. While traditional media have focused mainly on sensational stories of conflict, an increasing number of Internet sites, online news forums, and even entire webcasts are offering alternative content more oriented towards promoting peace efforts and "good news." The *Good News Broadcast* (http://www.goodnewsbroadcast.com) offers such programming, including information about international peace efforts, interviews with peace pioneers and peace-related events. A TED Prize given to scholar and author Karen Armstrong led to the November 12, 2009, launching of an Internet site (http://www.charterforcompassion.org) inviting people to affirm the Charter for Compassion – a document calling upon the global community to refrain from violence and instead to appreciate cultural and religious diversity – and to post individual acts of compassion on the website. With the website able to be viewed in four different languages (Arabic, Hebrew, English, and Spanish) and the Charter downloaded in 26 languages, over 125 partner organizations worldwide have spread the word about peace in synagogues, churches, schools, and other public places. Word about the movement could be further shared by embedding the Charter for Compassion widget (via a code on a "share" tab) into a site or a blog post.

THE MEDIA CASE IN IRAN

The 2009 presidential elections in Iran and ensuing allegations of electoral fraud led to popular uprising and public demonstrations. A heavy-handed government response and considerable political repression followed. Protesters, who came to be called the Green Movement (made up mainly of youth who represented 70% of Iran's population) used modern technologies, such as blogging (Twitter), social networking websites (Facebook), SMS messaging, and other Internet-based services (Demotix) to communicate messages and images to each other and to the world in real time. As a result, rallies and gatherings were organized worldwide; they included prominent peace activists like Nobel peace laureate Archbishop Desmond Tutu, author Noam Chomsky, and rock stars Madonna and U2. This constituted a pioneering effort of citizen activism and a grassroots movement for freedom. By using extensive web services and communication technologies, citizen activists quickly gained global attention and support.

Video and online gaming is a recently emerging genre of simulations that provide engaging and entertaining ways to expose users (especially youth) to complex scenarios requiring critical thinking, perspective taking, and conflict resolution skills. In the interactive video game "Global Conflicts: Palestine," designed by a Danish research-based gaming company, players explore the Israeli–Palestinian conflict by role-playing a journalist faced with settlements, human rights issues, checkpoints, suicide bombs, and biased information. Another simulation, the popular MTV-created narrative-based online video simulation "Darfur is Dying," led thousands of players to send email messages to politicians to urge action over the genocide. (See SIMULATION: LEARNING THROUGH ROLE PLAYING AND DESIGN.)

DANGERS

Easily accessed and anonymous information available through technological sources can be unreliable and invalid or can distort the size, influence, and representation of viewpoints, especially when targeted at people in less developed nations by more educated and web-savvy groups. Moreover, the privacy and security of websites are not ensured, as sites can be altered, impounded, filtered, susceptible to glitches, and vulnerable to hacking. Governments can impose censorship without transparency, as happened for example, when the government of Kazakhstan slowed down website access speed. These dangers suggest that media technologies should not replace the relationship building and dialoguing allowed by face-to-face contact.

Internet sites and technological devices have been used to disseminate discriminatory and violent messages in what is being called "cyberhate," or cyberbullying: willful and repeated harm inflicted through the use of computers, cell phones, and other electronic devices (Hinduja & Patchin, 2009). The use of these devices has amplified the reach and frequency of malicious messages and slanderous photos or videos that can be sent anonymously and spread virally to a limitless number of people in a short period of time through temporary email accounts, instant messaging, and postings to websites or social networking sites. More dangerous yet, these cannot be erased once they are posted and/or virally transmitted. (See CYBERBULLYING.)

A 2009 Unlearning Intolerance Seminar at the United Nations on "Cyberhate: Danger in Cyber space" highlighted pitfalls of the virtual world, including the spread of hatred with disastrous results especially to youth. In one tragic case, postings about a teen led to his committing suicide. The seminar was part of the Unlearning Intolerance Seminar Series, to promote respect and understanding and to examine how intolerance can be "unlearned" through education, inclusion, and positive example (United Nations Department of Public Information, 2009, p. 10).

In other examples, racial and ethnic violence, and hate against Jews, Blacks, and others, were posted on an anti-Semitic website called *The Holy Western Empire* of the 88-year old White supremacist mass shooter at the Washington D.C. Holocaust Museum in June 2009, and pro-jihadist postings were reportedly made by the psychiatrist who murdered and injured many service personnel at Fort Hood, Texas, in November 2009. A 48-year-old gunman who committed mass murder-suicide in a fitness center class filled with women in August 2009 reportedly kept a web page on which he recorded innumerable rejections by women and details of an earlier failed shooting attempt, ending his entries with the words "Death Lives!" Inattention to such Internet postings and warnings of violence has led to contested issues concerning the policing of such Internet outlets.

CONCLUSION

Formats and platforms on the Internet and other technological devices have expanded vastly, leading to user-generated content.

These emerging telecommunications and information technologies present invaluable methodologies for peace efforts that are easily accessible and economical, and that accelerate exchanges between people worldwide, enabling populations to skirt repressive bureaucracies and be more informed and involved in conflict resolution at a grassroots level. Sophisticated and integrated technology strategies should be considered in peace efforts, but caution must still be exercised because of the lack of content validation and policing.

SEE ALSO: Activism, Antiwar; Cyberbullying; Dispute Resolution, Online; Media and Peace: Traditional Outlets; Peace Journalism; Simulation: Learning Through Role Playing and Design.

REFERENCES

Benyakar, M., & Collazo, C. (2009). Salud mental en disastres: problemáticas, paradojas u perspectivas Clínicas. In J. T. Thome, M. Benyakar, & I. H. Taralli (Eds.), *Intervention in destabilizing situations: Crises and traumas* (pp. 37–99). Rio de Janeiro, Brazil: Associação Brasileira de Psiquiatria.

Brandenburg, R. (2007). Young leaders on the front lines for Palestinian–Israeli peace. In J. Kuriansky (Ed.), *Beyond bullets and bombs: Grassroots peacebuilding between Israelis and Palestinians* (pp. 155–165). Westport, CT: Praeger.

Hinduja, S., & Patchin, J. W. (2009). *Bullying beyond the schoolyard: Preventing and responding to cyberbullying*. Thousand Oaks, CA: Sage.

Kuriansky, J., & Daisey, R. (2010). Youth efforts for peace at the United Nations DPI NGO conference on Disarmament. *Peace Psychology Newsletter, 19*(1), 17–18.

United Nations Department of Public Information (2009, June). "Cyberhate" topic of unlearning intolerance seminar at United Nations Headquarters 16 June. Retrieved from http://www.un.org/News/Press/docs/2009/note6207.doc.htm

ADDITIONAL RESOURCES

http://www.apa.org/divisions/div46/ Website of the Media Division of the American Psychological Association. See, particularly, the division newsletters, called the Amplifier.

http://www.apa.org/divisions/div48/ Website of the Peace Division of the American Psychological Association. See, particularly, the division newsletter *Peace Psychology*, and the division journal *Peace and Conflict: The Journal of Peace Psychology*.

Benyakar, M., Michel Farina, J. J., & Collazo, C. (n.d.). *IBIS: International Bioethical Information System. Preparedness and intervention in disasters: Mental health guide [CD-ROM]*. Buenos Aires, Argentina: Ibero-American Ecobioethics Network for Education, Science and Technology. See also http://www.desastres.org

http://www.un.org/en/unlearningintolerance/

Media and Peace: Traditional Outlets

JUDY KURIANSKY AND
CATHERINE MOUNTCASTLE

While emerging technologies continue to offer new opportunities for peacebuilding, the current article focuses on the use of traditional forms of mass media that has greatly aided individuals, mental health professionals, and societies to communicate about peace and to deal with conflict. (See MEDIA AND PEACE: EMERGING TECHNOLOGIES.) Messaging through broadcast (television and radio programming), film, print (newspapers and magazines), and live events (artistic efforts and music festivals) informs and educates the public and empowers communities by facilitating awareness about peace and healing processes, and by presenting solutions to conflict by stimulating dialogue and increased government transparency and accountability. (See PEACE JOURNALISM.) Entertaining and informative programming has also reached rural communities of marginalized and less educated people. While such outlets have pro-social advantages for humanitarianism and good practice, some risks exist in that media coverage can inflame conflict, as happened in places like Somalia and Bosnia (Adam & Holguin, 2003).

RADIO

Radio is a particularly useful media for making information available to large numbers of people, including the underserved and undereducated, worldwide, particularly with prosocial programming (Gigli, 2004). Radio soap operas have successfully addressed issues related to peacebuilding in conflict zones like Colombia, Albania, Afghanistan, and innumerable African nations including Rwanda and Kenya. The Sabido Method, created in the 1970s, formalizes the use of serial dramas to present compelling and dramatic storylines reflecting real-life situations that address social issues and influence pro-social behavior changes in areas like family planning and AIDS prevention (Barker, 2009). Also, the Washington, DC-based nonprofit organization Search for Common Ground (SFCG) has developed many radio news programs and dramas worldwide promoting community participation and discussion of conflict issues (Bell, 2007). Shows from the *Talking Drum Studio* in Sierra Leone address topics like the rehabilitation of child soldiers, and their program, *The Golden Kids News*, engages youth as producers, reporters, and actors to identify and to discuss issues for broadcast aimed at supporting tolerance and understanding. A radio soap opera series (*Naya Bato Naya Paila* or *New Path New Footprints*), in partnership with the local media nongovernmental organization (NGO) Antenna Foundation Nepal, depicts families coping with a decade-long conflict between Maoist insurgents and the government (recently resolved through a peace agreement). Despite Taliban media proscriptions, a mid-1990s BBC radio soap opera, *New Home New Life*, aired in war-torn Afghanistan, addressing forced marriage, blood feuds, landmines, and opium addiction. More recently, a weekly radio program (entitled *Da Pulay Poray*, or *On the Borderline*) was broadcast on independent stations in Afghanistan and Pakistan covering issues that affect people on both sides of the border region, emphasizing cooperation, harmony, and coexistence. The program, produced by Internews, was also one of the first to address women's issues in such a conservative region.

TELEVISION

While broadcast television presents many entertainment shows (e.g., for escapism) and news that often focuses on conflict (following the precept "If it bleeds, it leads"), it offers a potentially powerful medium for disseminating information about peace. For example, SFCG's TV series *The Team*, set in postconflict Côte d'Ivoire, focuses on themes of ethnic tensions, poverty, disease, and governance through the story of a local football (soccer) club. Music Television (MTV) has consistently teamed up with organizations to present pro-peace public service campaigns, as early as 1999 in the "Fight for Your Rights: Take a Stand Against Violence" campaign with the American Psychological Association, which gave warning signs of violence, in response to a poll where 40% of youth said they were concerned about a potentially violent classmate.

FILM

The international NGO Human Rights Watch (HRW) hosts an annual highly acclaimed international film festival of documentaries and films that raise awareness about conflict and constructive means of dealing with human rights violations. The documentary *Flowers of Rwanda* confronts the horrors of the 1994 genocide. Animated films, in particular, reach a youth audience; for example, *The Story of Baba*, about a young elephant that loses its father in a jungle war, has been shown in conflict-ridden countries such as Sierra Leone, Afghanistan, and Colombia to help children cope with realities of war and disease. The Israel Film Festival offers forums and screenings of films about the trials and tribulations of cooperation projects between Palestinians and Jews (e.g., *Men on the Edge: Fishermen's Diary*, about Palestinian and Israeli fishermen living and working together until the Intifada divides them) and the Other Israel Film Festival showcases the lives of Arab citizens (e.g., an Arab journalist working for a Jewish newspaper). Increasingly, students produce independent documentaries; for example, *A Chance for Peace* depicts the political, social, and economic realities of Kenya following violence that erupted after the 2007 contested elections.

VIDEOS AND DVDS

The DVD *Peacemakers: Palestinians and Jews Living Together at Camp* (available free of charge from LTraubman@igc.org) follows Muslim, Jewish, and Christian families' exchanges while participating in a camp. The video dialogue project in South Africa, *Simunye* (Zulu for "We are one"), had former warring leaders make films of the conflict that were then discussed by communities, which led to a collective commitment to peace. DVDs of the award-winning documentary *The Day After Peace* (http://peaceoneday.org/en/film/the-day-after-peace) are available for showing in small screenings and even private gatherings, and the viewing is meant to be followed by discussion on the recorded 10-year journey of the filmmaker to galvanize countries of the world to observe an official day of ceasefire and nonviolence.

EXPRESSIVE ARTS

Projects involving the expressive arts (e.g., dance, music festivals, drama, poetry) bring individuals and institutions together to collaborate, create, and communicate messages of peace, antiviolence, and healing after trauma (e.g., http://www.towersoflightsong.com). The Drum Café music festival in Nairobi, Kenya, aimed to heal ethnic tensions after the December 2007 presidential elections that left more than 1,000 people killed and 3,000 displaced. Peace Charity Concerts have been performed in Japan, at anniversaries of the Hiroshima bombings and 9/11 terrorist attacks, and at UN NGO conferences, with Japanese and American musicians promoting peace and disarmament (Kuriansky, 2008a). In the "Journeys for Peace" programs of the Mexican-based NGO, youth participate in painting workshops, photography, music, theater, publishing, and encounters with world leaders and Nobel Peace Prizewinners to promote human rights, tolerance, and nonviolence (Kopeliovich & Kuriansky, 2009). Graffiti art throughout war-torn regions displays public grief and pain but also resilience, for example, the Liberian experiences as depicted by award-winning photographer and filmmaker Tim Hetherington.

MEDIA SKILLS, PEACE JOURNALISM, AND DANGERS TO JOURNALISTS

Programs are increasingly being developed to train journalists in covering disasters and conflicts in a humane way, for the benefit of the parties involved in the conflict, of the general public, and of journalists themselves. Organizations like the Dart Center for Journalism and Trauma, the International Association of Women in Radio and TV, and the International Women's Media Foundation, train journalists covering conflicts to report sensitively, to cope with psychological distress, and to avoid becoming victims of violence themselves (e.g., as happened in the 2009 assassination of award-wining activist Natalia Estemirova, while she was investigating abuses by government-backed militias in Chechnya). Individuals are also being educated about how to be better consumers of media, with peaceful perspectives. Responding to worldwide violence that affects the press as well as the public, the International News Safety Institute (INSI), an NGO, provides an information service covering all aspects of ensuring safety for journalists and news gatherers, including an extensive program of risk awareness training for journalists and media staff in regions where news gatherers are routinely under pressure.

Internews Network (http://www.internews.org) is an international nonprofit organization that has trained over 80,000 people in over 70 countries in media skills, and given the public news and information, an ability to connect, and ways to make their voices heard so as to participate in their communities and to effect positive social change. The organization also documents ways in which local media can make more effective humanitarian responses (e.g., by bringing together African journalists and humanitarian groups to discuss cases), rebuilt media capacity to aid victims after the earthquake in Pakistan, and made specific efforts to support female journalists in order to diversify voices in the media.

DANGERS

Mass media can distort or derail peacebuilding efforts and advance conflict, through manipulation and "spin" that facilitates corruption, rallies violent mobs, and disseminates hate. Entertainment content can also negatively impact nondiscerning youth, by highlighting violence and focusing on glamorous, unrealistic stereotypes that conflict with the values of education and peace. (See MEDIA VIOLENCE, EFFECTS OF; VIOLENT VIDEOGAMES AND AGGRESSION.) Less developed countries without media resources may rely on outside media that may clash culturally or contain violent imagery or discriminatory content (Gigli, 2004).

PSYCHOLOGISTS USING MASS MEDIA

Mental health professionals play an important role in helping individuals and communities deal with and recover from conflict and disruptive situations, work collectively on peace initiatives, communicate with the public about violence and peace, and train local helpers to become trainers themselves. These activities constitute a field of *media psychology*, which is a division of the American Psychological Association. Psychologists have harnessed the media to explain profiles of violent perpetrators, to calm public fears, and to promote public resilience after tragedies and disasters (Kuriansky, 2009). Such traumas include environmental events (floods, Hurricane Katrina, the Indian Ocean tsunami), manmade terrorism (the 9/11 attacks on the World Trade Center and the Pentagon), mass shootings (e.g., in schools and at the Holocaust Museum in 2009), interpersonal violence (e.g., murders, rapes), and other emotionally disruptive public events (e.g., celebrity deaths like that of Michael Jackson). Mental health professionals have even given public advice on the air after traumas, on government-controlled television, for example, on Chinese TV after the devastating earthquakes in Sichuan province in 2008 and the trapping of the Chilean miners in 2010. Models of delivering advice on the media in a viewer-friendly and clear manner must be devised and followed, offering necessary steps for recovery and safety, for example, through the "reassure model" (Kuriansky, 2008b).

Peace activists need to overcome several resistances to using mass media for peace messages, including (1) fear of how the media may distort or misinterpret their message, because of inadequate time, attentiveness, understanding, or even prejudice; (2) inadequate knowledge about how the media works (e.g., requires personal stories, clear jargon-free statements); (3) insecurity about expertise in a subject; (4) concern about criticism from the public or from colleagues. These can be overcome with training, support, and experience, and by using referral sources.

Professionals also need to educate the media to cover positive stories about peace by making these more appealing, by providing positive examples that include compelling stories, and by promoting newer concepts in the peace field like post-traumatic growth and resilience. Mental health professionals must also be proactive in offering stories about reconciliation and resolution (instead of just reacting to media requests), in adapting pitches to the needs of the media outlet (e.g., on news or talk shows), as well as keeping important stories newsworthy, for example on anniversaries of disruptive situations.

CONCLUSION

The media play an important role in peacebuilding and conflict resolution, including the promotion of positive messages, the mobilization of large groups, and the education of wide and diverse publics. As such, media strategies should be incorporated into any peace efforts in order to increase their reach and influence. Just as the psychological community has long campaigned to make "psychology" a household word with many educational and training programs and organizational initiatives (such as those for the American Psychological Association), the peace community can harness similar media strategies and traditional media outlets to promote peace and to emphasize the negative impact of violence and war.

SEE ALSO: Media and Peace: Emerging Technologies; Media Violence, Effects of; Peace Journalism; Violent Videogames and Aggression.

REFERENCES

Adam, G., & Holguin, L. (2003). The media's role in peace-building: asset or liability? Paper presented at the Media 3 Conference, Barranquilla, Colombia. Retrieved from http://129.11.76.45/papers/pmt/exhibits/1769/mediainpeace.pdf

Barker, K. (2009). Sex, soap, and social change: The Sabido methodology for behavior change communication. In E. Schroeder & J. Kuriansky (Eds.), Sexuality education: Past, present and future (Vol. 2, ch. 10). Westport, CT: Praeger.

Bell, J. (2007). Media and the search for common ground on the Middle East. In J. Kuriansky (Ed.), Beyond bullets and bombs: Grassroots peacebuilding between Israelis and Palestinians (pp. 327–336). Westport, CT: Praeger.

Gigli, S. (2004). Children, youth and media around the world: An overview of trends and issues. Report for the Fourth World Summit on Media for Children and Adolescents, Rio de Janeiro, Brazil, April 2004. Retrieved from http://www.unicef.org/videoaudio/intermedia_revised.pdf

Kopeliovich, S., & Kuriansky, J. (2009). Journeys for peace: A model of human rights education for young people in Mexico. Counselling Psychology Quarterly, 22(1), 83–102.

Kuriansky, J. (2008a). Americans and Japanese commemorate 9/11 together. Peace Psychology Newsletter, 17(2), 13.

Kuriansky, J. (2008b). A clinical tool box for counseling training and intervention. In U. P. Gielen, J. G. Draguns, & J. M. Fish (Eds.), Principles of multicultural counseling and therapy. New York, NY: Taylor & Francis/Routledge.

Kuriansky, J. (2009). Communication and media in mass trauma: How mental health professionals can help. In J. T. Thome, M. Benyakar, & I. H. Taralli (Eds.), Intervention in destabilizing situations: Crises and traumas (pp. 195–232). Rio de Janeiro, Brazil: Associação Brasileira de Psiquiatria.

ADDITIONAL RESOURCES

Kuriansky, J. (2005, Fall). Disaster and the media: Experiences and advice. The Amplifier, 7. Retrieved from http://www.apa.org/divisions/div46/AmpFall05.pdf

Kuriansky, J. (2007). Efforts in education, media and mental health. In Beyond bullets and bombs: Grassroots peacebuilding between Palestinians and Israelis (pp. 243–353). Westport, CT: Praeger.

Kuriansky, J., & Alladin, W. J. (Eds.). (2009). Models of mental health and human rights: In celebration of the 60th anniversary of the United Nations Declaration of Human Rights for All [special issue]. Counselling Psychology Quarterly, 22(1), 1–145.

Media Violence, Effects of

MARKUS APPEL AND SUSANNE JODLBAUER

Research on the impact of violence in the mass media dates back to the Payne Fund Studies in the 1930s which focused on the effects of motion pictures on children. Public and scientific interest in this topic has increased with the widespread accessibility of TV in the 1950s and 1960s and the rise of computer games in the 1980s and 1990s. (See VIOLENT VIDEO GAMES AND AGGRESSION.) A number of content analyses conducted throughout the years indicate that the depiction of physical violence is widespread in mass media, e.g., in feature films, comics, animation series, TV news, popular music, and computer games. Compared to statistics about real-life incidents, violence is by far overrepresented in various media products.

MEDIA VIOLENCE AND AGGRESSION: MAJORITY CONSENSUS

Studies on mass media content, however, do not answer questions on media effects. Most media effect studies conducted so far examine the impact of media violence on aggressive thoughts and behavior. A consensus about the interpretation of the scientific evidence is shared by a majority of academic researchers (AAP, 2000). This consensus has two parts:

1. Media violence increases the likelihood of aggressive thoughts, feelings, and behavior among the audience, short term and long term. The effects on aggression are considered substantial when effect size is compared to other causal relationships reported in the social and medical sciences. The magnitude of the effect depends on person, product, and situation characteristics.
2. Media violence is not the only – and likely not the most important – factor contributing to aggressive thoughts, feelings, and behavior. Other factors include school, family, and peer influences, as well as the availability of weapons.

Although this consensus is widespread among academic researchers from different disciplines (e.g., psychology, communication studies, pediatrics) and from different world regions, this interpretation of scientific

evidence is a matter of ongoing debate. Theory and empirical evidence are reviewed in this article before the criticism on this majority consensus is briefly considered.

MEDIA VIOLENCE AND AGGRESSION: THEORY

A number of theories and concepts have been employed to deepen our understanding of the link between media violence and aggression. According to Albert Bandura's social learning theory, media characters may serve as models for aggressive behavior. Imitation of violent behavior is supposed to be more likely when aggressive models are rewarded (e.g., they obtain money, love, or respect). When aggressive behaviors are penalized (e.g., violent characters lose respect or get arrested) imitation of violent behavior is supposed to be less likely.

A second approach is focused on desensitization. Repeated exposure to media violence is supposed to weaken negative responses to violence such as anxiety, disgust, or repulsion. As a consequence, real-life violence may appear more common and acceptable.

The concept of priming suggests that violent media stimuli make aggressive thoughts more easily accessible. Thus, ambivalent situations and behavior by others may be perceived as aggressive and hostile. Moreover, aggressive thoughts may activate behavioral systems linked to aggression. Although priming effects are short term, they are supposed to contribute to longer-term effects.

Based on the excitation transfer theory put forward by Dolf Zillmann, it has been assumed that violent media increase an individual's arousal, which amplifies any emotional and behavioral tendency. The arousal is supposed to be unspecific; thus it may intensify anger and aggressive behavior or joy and non-aggressive behavior depending upon the context present after violent media exposure.

Much recent research on media violence is based on the General Aggression Model (GAM), which aims at integrating different theories to explain and predict both short-term and long-term effects (Anderson & Bushman, 2002). Regarding short-term effects, the GAM is a process model that illustrates (a) the *inputs* and (b) the *routes* through which these input variables are working in order to explain (c) aggression-related *outcomes* which involve the interplay of appraisal and decision processes. In this model, violent media are considered aggressive cues that are part of the situation encountered. Other situational factors are the current levels of provocation, frustration, or pain. The situation variables are supposed to interact with person variables such as traits, values, or gender to determine the aggression-related internal state. Related research showed that violent movies are more influential when trait hostility is high rather than low, leading to more aggressive thoughts, more aggressive affect, and more aggressive behavior. Affect, cognition, and arousal are considered as the three routes that transfer input variables (situation and person) to aggression-related outcomes. According to the long-run perspective of the GAM, the repeated use of violent media leads to aggressive knowledge structures, including aggressive beliefs and attitudes, aggressive perceptual and expectation schemata, aggressive behavior scripts, and aggression desensitization. These long-term effects are seen as changes in personality which in turn affect the *input* variables in a situational episode, as expressed in the short-term process model. Repeated violent game playing, for example, is expected to produce trait aggressiveness (person factor) and a situational context that fits this personality (e.g., change in peer group).

MEDIA VIOLENCE AND AGGRESSION: EMPIRICAL EVIDENCE

The main empirical evidence on the detrimental effects of media violence is based on survey designs or experiments. Surveys were employed to investigate the relationship between violent media use and a person variable such as aggressiveness. A large number of studies reported the results of data that were gathered at one point in time (i.e., a cross-sectional design). The majority of available meta-analyses conclude that the more often individuals watch violent TV or play violent games, the more aggressive cognitions and behaviors are reported (average effect size around $r = .20$) (Paik & Comstock, 1994; Anderson, 2004). (See META-ANALYSIS.)

Fewer studies reported the results of data that were gathered at two or more points in time (i.e., a longitudinal design). In one of the most prominent longitudinal studies (Huesmann, Moise-Titus, Podolski, & Eron, 2003), researchers examined children aged 6–9 years old (1977–1978) and then again when they were 21–23 years old (1993–1995). The authors found that children's amount of TV-violence viewing, children's identification with aggressive same-sex TV characters, and children's perceptions that TV violence is realistic predicted their adult aggression.

In order to investigate claims about the causal impact of media violence, experiments were conducted in laboratories and in the field. In these studies, the researchers typically prepare a violent media condition and one or more control conditions with lower-violent media or no media use at all. Participants are randomly assigned to one of these groups. During and/or after media exposure participants' aggressive thoughts, feelings, or actions are assessed. Dependent variables may include the amount of aversive noise administered to a fellow participant in a staged educational setting (noise blast paradigm) or the number of aggressive actions outside the lab (e.g., during a game of hockey). Available meta-analyses on computer game use and TV use point at higher scores on aggressive outcomes for groups that were exposed to violent media as compared to the control conditions. Average effect sizes reported in meta-analyses vary between $r = .10$ and $r = .40$. Effect sizes tend to be smaller under more natural circumstances in the field than under more highly controlled circumstances in the lab.

Time-series field studies compare violence rates or any other data of interest before and after a specific mass mediated occurrence. This method has been used to estimate the impact of highly publicized news of a violent occurrence such as a kidnapping, a terrorist attack, or a suicide. There are only a few studies on the notion that news stories of aggressive events affect imitative or "copycat" behavior. Evidence indicates that mass mediated suicides of celebrities (e.g., Marilyn Monroe, Kurt Cobain) may be a risk factor for imitative suicides. National authorities and organizations of journalists provide guidelines about how to report about a suicide (e.g., avoid details of suicide methods). Anecdotal evidence suggests that also a fictional character's suicide may provoke imitation effects. The phenomenon of copycat suicides is sometimes referred to as the Werther Effect, based on an eighteenth-century novel by J. W. Goethe.

MEDIA VIOLENCE AND AGGRESSION: CRITICISM

Despite the widespread expert consensus that media violence is one substantial factor (among other factors) that contributes to aggressive thoughts, feelings, and behavior, the media violence–aggression link is still a controversial issue at least in the news, in popular science books, and in Internet weblogs (for the critical perspective, see Freedman, 2002). Media violence research has been criticized for a number of reasons. Prominent points of critique are:

1. The dependent variables in the lab experiments have low external validity (e.g., the noise blast paradigm).
2. Demand characteristics (i.e., participants' expectations about how to behave) invalidate the results of many experimental studies.
3. Null-findings are obtained when aggressive crime is the dependent variable.
4. Correlational data are interpreted as a causal influence.
5. Effects are exaggerated – only highly vulnerable individuals are influenced by violent media, the great majority of viewers/users are not.
6. The effect sizes are too small to have real-life relevance.

It is beyond the scope of this article to elaborate on the media violence controversy. The majority of experts contend that the weight of the evidence for a link between media violence and aggression is more compelling than the objections that have been associated with this research.

OTHER EFFECTS OF MEDIA VIOLENCE

Most of the research on violent acts in the media has focused on the extent to which they may evoke similar thoughts, feelings, and behavior in the observer. However, when violent acts are followed by harm, pain, and sadness of victims, audience members may process media violence from a victim perspective and not exhibit aggression.

Research in the tradition of the cultivation hypothesis found that heavy TV viewers overestimated real-world violence rates, and showed less interpersonal trust and more fear of violence. The specific impact of real-world violence presented in nonfictional formats such as newspapers or TV news has also been investigated. Television coverage, for example, had a profound impact on children after the *Challenger* explosion, the first Gulf War, and the Oklahoma City bombing. The terrorist attacks on 9/11 have been related to clinically relevant fears and stress symptoms for individuals who had not been directly exposed to danger. Audience members may experience fear and stress after watching the news about incidents that happened in distant parts of the world. Finally, another important avenue of research has explored the impact of violator ethnicity (e.g., African American) on thoughts, feelings, and behavior regarding this group.

SEE ALSO: Meta-Analysis; Violent Video Games and Aggression.

REFERENCES

AAP (2000). American Academy of Pediatrics (AAP), American Psychological Association (APA), and four other prominent academic organizations: Joint statement on the impact of entertainment violence on children. Congressional Public Health Summit. Retrieved August 19, 2009, from http://www.aap.org/advocacy/releases/jstmtevc.htm.

Anderson, C. A. (2004). An update on the effects of violent video games. *Journal of Adolescence, 27*, 133–122.

Anderson, C. A., & Bushman, B. J. (2002). Human aggression. *Annual Review Psychology, 53*, 27–51.

Freedman, J. L. (2002). *Media violence and its effect on aggression: Assessing the scientific evidence.* Toronto, Canada: University of Toronto Press.

Huesmann, L. R., Moise-Titus, J., Podolski, C.-L., & Eron, L. D. (2003). Longitudinal relations between children's exposure to TV violence and their aggressive and violent behavior in young adulthood: 1977–1992. *Developmental Psychology, 39*, 201–221.

Paik, H., & Comstock, G. (1994). The effects of television violence on antisocial behavior: A meta-analysis. *Communication Research, 21*, 516–546.

ADDITIONAL RESOURCES

Anderson, C. A., Berkowitz, L., Donnerstein, E., Huesmann, L. R., Johnson, J., Linz, D., Malamuth, N., & Wartella, E. (2003). The influence of media violence on youth. *Psychological Science in the Public Interest, 4*, 81–110.

Sparks, G. G., Sparks, C. W., & Sparks, E. A. (2009). Media violence. In J. Bryant & M. B. Oliver (Eds.), *Media effects: Advances in theory and research.* New York, NY: Routledge.

Mediation

SAMANTHA HARDY

Generally speaking, mediation is a process that involves two or more people in conflict who are assisted by a third person, who does not determine the outcome of their conflict (Wall, Stark, & Standifer, 2001). This third person is called the mediator. The mediator's main role is to assist the people to communicate with each other in relation to the conflict between them. (See CONFLICT RESOLUTION, INTERACTIVE; RIPENESS THEORY.)

In Western society, mediation is often seen as a new form of dispute resolution; however, the practice of mediation in some form or another has existed in almost all parts of the world and across different cultures and religions for hundreds, if not thousands, of years. China and Asia have a strong history of mediation based on the Confucian emphasis on conflict resolution and on moral persuasion and agreement rather than coercion. In Japan, intermediaries are often used to assist in ensuring that business relationships are productively managed. In collectivist cultures, cooperation is fundamentally important and conflicts are often mediated by a respected elder, a religious or political leader, or a wise and respected member of the community.

Mediation is used in a wide range of contexts, including: family law disputes; parent and adolescent disputes; workplace conflict; commercial disputes; construction and building disputes; personal injury disputes; environmental and planning disputes; consumer disputes; industrial disputes; healthcare disputes; community disputes; administrative law disputes; international conflicts; testamentary disputes over deceased estates; residential and retail tenancy disputes; maritime disputes; public sector disputes; and criminal justice matters.

Mediation is quite difficult to define because the term encompasses a very wide variety of practices. As Menkel-Meadow (1995) points out, "mediation literature and practice abound with differences and inconsistencies in descriptive and prescriptive propositions." Studies have also shown that there is a great deal of confusion in mediation practice arising from the lack of agreement about how various approaches are described (Charkoudian, de Ritis, Buck, & Wilson, 2009).

There are many different classification schemes for the variety of mediation models that exist. For example, Bush and Folger (2005) classify models according to whether they are problem-solving, relational, or harmony models. Models can be distinguished by how they define the problem to be mediated, the goal of the process, and the mediator's role in the process. Different models of mediation that have been identified by a wide range of authors include: evaluative, settlement, facilitative, problem-solving, narrative, therapeutic, mindfulness, insight, mandatory, wise-counsel, community, traditional, transformative, expert-advisory, court-annexed, co-mediation, victim–offender, child-focused, and child-inclusive.

In Western society mediators are specially trained to understand conflict and to manage a process in which they facilitate interaction between parties in conflict. Mediation is seen as a constructive conflict intervention, with an emphasis on process as a means of managing the content of a conflict.

Mediation is seen as a private method of dispute resolution since most of what is said during the process is confidential. Broadly speaking, this means that nothing discussed during the mediation can be revealed outside the mediation without the consent of the parties. However, there are a number of exceptions to the principle of confidentiality – some imposed by law, practice standards, or organizational guidelines, and others agreed to by the parties in a confidentiality or mediation agreement signed prior to the mediation.

Mediation processes are generally more flexible than other dispute resolution processes such as litigation and arbitration. However, the mediation process and its flexibility differ according to which model is used. In facilitative mediation the mediator is seen as the "process controller" and will guide the parties through a fairly structured process that usually includes identifying issues, exploration and discussion of those issues, developing and evaluating a range of options, and considering alternatives, before making choices about future steps. In contrast, transformative mediation is a much less structured process and a transformative mediator will seek guidance from the parties and adapt to their needs about which process steps might best support them throughout the mediation. Across the various models the mediator may be more or less directive about the process used at any given time during the mediation (Riskin, 2003–2004).

Mediation may involve more than just two parties in conflict and the mediator. Other participants may include disputants' support people (e.g., lawyers or advocates), expert advisors, and other interested stakeholders. Mediation can also take place with multiple parties. There can also be more than one mediator. Co-mediation involves two mediators who jointly facilitate the process. There are many benefits to a co-mediation model, including balancing gender, age, or culture.

The purpose of mediation varies according to the different models of mediation. Most commonly, mediation is seen as a process that supports parties to resolve conflict between them. However, not all models of mediation are focused on settlement of the conflict. For example, the transformative model aims to improve the conflict interaction between the parties. While resolution of the conflict may well occur when the interaction is improved, this is not the aim of the process.

What most models of mediation have in common is the premise that the process can assist the parties to uncover the hidden layers to their conflict which will then allow them to constructively manage it. In the facilitative model, identifying this hidden layer is expressed as identifying the parties' underlying interests, needs, and concerns. The transformative model assumes that what the parties really need to say to each other is hidden beneath the language of weakness and confusion, and that parties need support to be able to communicate clearly about what is really important to them.

Most definitions of mediation include reference to a "neutral" or "impartial" third party who assists the parties through the process. In other words, the mediator is not an advocate for either side and does not become involved in any negotiations towards an outcome. (See NEGOTIATION, PRINCIPLED.) However, it can be difficult for a mediator to be entirely neutral or impartial. In some models of mediation, such as narrative mediation, the mediator is acknowledged not to be neutral or impartial, and to be an active participant in any outcome. Recent discussions about the impossibility of real neutrality or impartiality have led to a move away from those terms towards notions of the mediator aspiring to maximize party self-determination, practicing according to professional and ethical standards, and incorporating reflective mediation practice.

Another premise of mediation is that the parties attend voluntarily. However, again in practice this is not always the case, with many jurisdictions around the world establishing mandatory mediation schemes through their court systems. The concept of voluntariness has, in these contexts, been interpreted to mean self-determination in terms of any outcome reached in the mediation, in that parties have a choice about what they do or do not agree on. While most mediation models in practice support party choice in this way, in practice there are some exceptions.

Mediation is usually distinguished from other dispute resolution processes by the fact that the mediator acts as a facilitator and does not have any determinative power in relation to the outcome of the dispute. (See ALTERNATIVE DISPUTE RESOLUTION; DISPUTE RESOLUTION, ONLINE.) However, there are some hybrid models of mediation used in practice in which a mediator may provide information or advice to the parties about the outcome of their dispute, sometimes referred to as conciliation. In many court-connected mediation schemes the mediator may evaluate the strengths and weaknesses of each party's case and make suggestions or recommendations for the resolution of the conflict (this is often known as evaluative mediation). Although the mediator's role is not determinative, the parties will often be greatly influenced by the mediator's comments and this may have some impact on parties' choice. Taking this a step further, in med-arb (a hybrid between mediation and arbitration) the mediator may determine the outcome if, in certain circumstances, the parties are not able to agree.

In most mediation models it is assumed that the parties are participating in good faith. In some contexts parties are required to have attempted mediation in good faith before they will be allowed to take their dispute to court. In practice it is difficult to assess whether or not a party is acting in good faith. Parties may have many reasons for behaving in a way that, to the mediator, appears to be unhelpful to a constructive conflict interaction. Despite some agreements to mediate having clauses requiring respectful behavior, full disclosure, and a genuine effort to collaborate, the notion of good-faith participation also creates tension when mediation is mandatory, as it seems almost impossible to *require* people to participate in good faith.

In recent years there has been a move towards the accreditation of mediators. For example, in Australia in 2007 the National Mediator Accreditation Standards were introduced. These standards regulate the process for approval of mediation practitioners as accredited mediators and also set out practice standards with which accredited mediators agree to comply. However, the standards are voluntary and mediators are not required to obtain accreditation in order to practice. Since 2009 under the Australian Family Law Act there is a separate accreditation regime for Family Dispute Resolution Practitioners which involves family-specific training. This training includes theoretical and psychological understanding about separation, family violence, child developmental needs, parenting plans, family law regulations, and so on. There are also international mediator competency standards developed by the International Mediation Institute.

The future of mediation appears to be moving beyond its role in resolving conflict towards using mediation theory and skills for the prevention and management of conflict. Mayer (2009) suggests that the future role of conflict specialists involves building people's capacity for constructively engaging with conflict, rather than facilitating its resolution. (See CONFLICTS, CONSTRUCTIVE.) Mayer (2004) explains that some conflict is long term and ongoing, and that conflict specialists have an important role to play beyond a neutral facilitator working towards resolution. Processes such as conflict coaching are gaining popularity, either as a premediation intervention or as an alternative to third-party facilitation. Lawyers have also developed different approaches to managing conflict based on mediation principles, such as collaborative law.

SEE ALSO: Alternative Dispute Resolution; Conflict Resolution, Interactive; Conflicts, Constructive; Dispute Resolution, Online; Negotiation, Principled; Ripeness Theory.

REFERENCES

Bush, R. A. B., & Folger, J. P. (2005). *The promise of mediation: Responding to conflict through empowerment and recognition.* San Francisco, CA: Jossey-Bass.

Charkoudian, L., de Ritis, C., Buck, R., & Wilson, C. L. (2009). Mediation by any other name would smell as sweet – or would it? The struggle to define mediation and its various approaches. *Conflict Resolution Quarterly, 26*(3), 293–316.

Mayer, B. (2004). *Beyond neutrality.* San Francisco, CA: Jossey-Bass.

Mayer, B. (2009). *Staying with conflict: A strategic approach to ongoing disputes.* San Francisco, CA: Jossey-Bass.

Menkel-Meadow, C. (1995). The many ways of mediation: The transformation of traditions, ideologies, practices and paradigms. *Negotiation Journal, 11,* 217–242.

Riskin, L. L. (2003–2004). Decisionmaking in mediation: The new old grid and the new grid system. *Notre Dame Law Review, 79*(1), 1–53.

Wall, J. A., Jr., Stark, J. B., & Standifer, R. L. (2001). Mediation: A current review and theory development. *Journal of Conflict Resolution, 45,* 370–391.

ADDITIONAL RESOURCES

http://www.imimediation.org
http://www.mediate.com

Meta-Analysis

DAVID M. FISHER AND
ALICE F. STUHLMACHER

Meta-analysis is the process of integrating findings from primary research studies in order to estimate true values in a population. While multiple primary studies on a topic may produce conflicting findings, combining these estimates through meta-analyses can help resolve conflicts in the literature and direct future research. Importantly, a meta-analysis is more than a statistical method for integrating research data across studies; it involves a research process with several distinct steps requiring subjective judgments (Arthur, Bennett, & Huffcutt, 2001) that must be delineated.

A principal goal of science is to develop theories that not only describe, but also explain phenomena. To achieve this goal, the vast majority of research in psychology attempts to estimate values or relationships that exist within a target population, whether it is individuals in a specific community, a particular minority group, or all of humankind. Primary research studies are conducted with samples of the chosen population in which to examine the relationship of interest. However, each of these samples is much smaller than the actual population and is subject to sampling error, such that the values or relationships being examined will vary from the true population levels. In some samples the values or relationships will be higher than those in the population, while in other samples the values or relationships will be lower than those in the population. A key characteristic of sampling error is that it is often random and thus typically forms a normal distribution around zero. By combining the findings across a large number of primary studies (i.e., meta-analysis), the sampling errors tend to be cancelled out across studies. The process of meta-analysis, therefore, allows for a more stable estimate of population values of interest.

Meta-analysis is an indispensable tool for creating accurate descriptions of results as they occur in a body of research as compared to a single sample. Through reducing the noise of sampling errors, meta-analysis can clarify inconsistencies in research findings. Additionally, in collecting primary studies to conduct a meta-analysis, gaps in the literature become readily apparent. Therefore, meta-analyses also help to identify areas for future research.

There are two distinct types of meta-analysis, with the major distinction being the type of metric that is integrated across studies. In a meta-analysis of effect sizes, the common metric is an effect size (d), which refers to the standardized difference between two group means. The primary studies used in a meta-analysis of effect sizes typically represent experimental or quasi-experimental research designs in which a treatment group is compared to a control group. In such studies, the effect size (d) represents the standardized difference between the treatment group mean and control group mean on the dependent variable of interest. In other words, the effect size quantifies the impact (or effect) of an experimental treatment on a dependent variable. This type of meta-analysis is exemplified in the procedures described by Glass (1976) and Hedges and Olkin (1985). Not all meta-analyses of effect sizes, however, necessarily examine an experimental manipulation. Rather, such meta-analyses are appropriate whenever the focus is on the extent of differences between two groups. As an example, Walters, Stuhlmacher, and Meyer (1998) meta-analyzed gender differences in competitive behavior in negotiation. Summarizing across 62 studies clarified disparate findings, revealing that men were on average slightly more competitive than women; they also tested contextual factors that moderated the effect.

For a meta-analysis of correlations, on the other hand, the common metric of interest is the correlation coefficient (r), which refers to the standardized covariance between two variables. In other words, the correlation coefficient quantifies the extent of co-occurrences of two variables. Accordingly, the primary studies used in a meta-analysis of correlations typically represent the associated relationship between two variables in a single sample, as opposed to the difference between groups. As a relevant example, Pettigrew and Tropp (2006) examined how intergroup contact corresponds to intergroup prejudice. In this instance, the meta-analysis focused on the strength of association between intergroup contact and intergroup prejudice across a variety of samples to inform estimates about the population level (see CONTACT THEORY, INTERGROUP).

Regardless of the type of meta-analysis (i.e., effect sizes, correlations), there are several key steps to follow when conducting any meta-analysis (Huffcutt, 2002). These steps, as described below, highlight an important point about meta-analysis in general. Because meta-analysis is both a research method and a set of statistical procedures, it is critical that researchers clearly document and report their activities and decisions so that the quality of the meta-analysis can be evaluated.

The first step in conducting any meta-analysis is to choose the topic to be examined. While it may seem unnecessary to touch upon this step, the choice of topic is important in that the researcher must clearly define what characteristics or relationships to examine. As will be seen below, this has implications for subsequent steps in the meta-analytic process.

Once a topic has been chosen and clearly defined, a second step is to locate relevant studies through a literature search. Good starting places for searches are databases such as *PsycINFO* or *EBSCSO* in which keywords can be used to locate relevant articles. While databases are starting points, it is often necessary to tap other sources such as the reference lists of major articles on the topic, conference presentations, dissertations, and technical reports. Furthermore, it is advisable to contact researchers in the area in order to acquire unpublished work on the topic. The search for, and inclusion of, unpublished research can reduce a publication bias towards certain findings in the meta-analysis. The question of where specifically to obtain articles will likely depend on the topic and how the topic is defined. Therefore, the choice of where to obtain articles represents a subjective judgment and must be clearly documented (Arthur et al., 2001).

Once an initial set of articles has been obtained, a third step is to establish specific inclusion criteria that determine the set of usable articles. For example, a researcher might want only to examine research based on certain participant demographics or operationalization of variables. The inclusion criteria determine which of the initial set of articles should be retained for the actual analysis. Again, the choice of inclusion criteria depends on the specific research questions being examined and how relevant constructs are defined. Therefore, the choices of inclusion criteria also represent subjective judgments that should be documented (Arthur et al., 2001).

Following the determination of a final set of articles to be analyzed, a fourth step is to extract the relevant information from the final set of articles. This typically involves reading the articles and recording the necessary information. At an absolute minimum, it is necessary to record information on the sample size and the common metric to be integrated (i.e., effect sizes, correlations). In some cases, the common metric will be directly reported, while in other cases it can be calculated from other information provided such as means, standard deviations, t statistics, and F statistics. Common conversion formulas for both effects sizes and correlations are available (e.g., Hunter & Schmidt, 2004). At this stage, coders, or those extracting the information, should be thoroughly trained on the coding process. Further, it is advisable to have multiple coders, at least in a subset of the research reports, in order to refine categories, enhance accuracy, and assess coding agreement.

A final step is to actually integrate the extracted information mathematically. This is typically done by calculating the mean value of the metric of interest (i.e., effect sizes, correlations). However, as mentioned previously, small sample sizes are more subject to sampling error than larger sample sizes, meaning that larger sample sizes are expected to provide more stable estimates of the values or relationships of interest. Therefore, when combining the common metric, the metric from each individual study is often weighted by the sample size of that study, such that studies with larger sample sizes are given more weight in determining the mean value. The resulting mean value becomes a direct estimate of the corresponding population value (Arthur et al., 2001).

The above steps outline what some have called a basic or "bare bones" meta-analysis (Hunter & Schmidt, 2004). Beyond a bare-bones meta-analysis, however, it is often of interest to record additional information, such as the types of measures used and their reliability, characteristics of the sample, study setting, and additional contextual information. This information becomes relevant in the assessment of statistical artifacts and the examination of moderators. In particular, it is often extremely important to assess the variability across the studies (Hunter & Schmidt, 2004). One useful piece of information is the confidence interval around the mean value. The more variability there is, the larger the width of the confidence interval, indicating a lower accuracy of the estimate. It becomes important to determine the source(s) of this variability. Generally speaking, there are two types of variability. Unsystematic variability is caused by various statistical artifacts, such as sampling error. Systematic variability, on the other hand, can be caused by the presence of moderator variables.

In terms of unsystematic variability, Hunter and Schmidt (2004) outline several statistical artifacts that represent sources for variability in research findings. The most commonly examined artifacts include sampling error and measurement error. These two artifacts are frequently addressed because they are present in any research design. Other artifacts include dichotomization of a continuous variable, range restriction, attrition artifacts, imperfect construct validity, and transcriptional/clerical errors (Hunter & Schmidt, 2004). Once the variance attributable to these artifacts is calculated, it can be subtracted from the variance observed in the initial meta-analysis. As a general guideline, if one or two of the statistical artifacts, namely sampling error and measurement error, account for 75% or more of the observed variance, then it is assumed that the remaining artifacts account for the rest of the variance, suggesting that the value or relationship of interest is consistent throughout the population (Hunter & Schmidt, 2004).

In terms of systematic variance, any variance that is not accounted for by statistical artifacts typically suggests the presence of moderator variables. As indicated above, the

75% rule is one means of determining the possible presence of moderators. Other means for assessing the presence of moderators are possible (Arthur et al., 2001). Note, however, that one does not necessarily need to assess the amount of variance attributable to statistical artifacts before examining moderators. Rather, a researcher may have a theoretical reason for examining the presence of moderators. By examining the values or relationship of interest at different levels of a moderator, an even more precise estimate of population values may be achieved, as indicated by reduced variability within levels of the moderator variable.

Meta-analysis has emerged as an influential research technique and is likely to remain important for social and behavioral sciences in general, and for psychology in particular, for many years to come. Accordingly, a basic understanding of meta-analysis is becoming a requirement for modern researchers and policy-makers. The references below offer further resources for those interested in conducting a meta-analysis.

SEE ALSO: Contact Theory, Intergroup.

REFERENCES

Arthur, W., Jr., Bennett, W., Jr., & Huffcutt, A. I. (2001). *Conducting meta-analyses using SAS*. Mahwah, NJ: Lawrence Erlbaum.

Glass, G. V. (1976). Primary, secondary and meta-analysis of research. *Educational Researcher, 5*, 3–8.

Hedges, L. V., & Olkin, I. (1985). *Statistical methods for meta-analysis*. Orlando, FL: Academic Press.

Huffcutt, A. I. (2002). Research perspectives on meta-analysis. In Steven G. Rogelberg (Ed.), *Handbook of research methods in industrial and organizational psychology* (pp. 198–215). Oxford, UK: Blackwell.

Hunter, J. E., & Schmidt, F. L. (2004). *Methods of meta-analysis: Correcting error and bias in research findings* (2nd ed.). Thousand Oaks, CA: Sage.

Pettigrew, T. F., & Tropp, L. R. (2006). A meta-analytic test of intergroup contact theory. *Journal of Personality and Social Psychology, 90*, 751–783.

Walters, A. E., Stuhlmacher, A. F., & Meyer, L. L. (1998). Gender and negotiator competitiveness: A meta-analysis. *Organizational Behavior and Human Decision Processes, 76*, 1–29.

Militarism and Who Benefits

MARC PILISUK AND GIANINA PELLEGRINI

When psychologists hunt for the basic cause of military conflicts, we tend to stress psychological constructs. This emphasis detracts from a contextual explanation that likely goes further to explain modern war than any other. This latter viewpoint gained visibility in the 1961 farewell address by President Dwight D. Eisenhower, who foresaw grave implications of the conjunction of the military establishment and the arms industry, which he labeled the military–industrial complex. Eisenhower warned against the military–industrial complex acquiring too much influence, whether it was sought or unsought. He saw the potential for a disastrous rise of misplaced power and the likelihood that it would persist. Nikita Khrushchev in the former Soviet Union labeled a comparable collaboration the "metal eaters," an alliance of industrial bureaucrats and military leaders in the USSR (Barash & Webel, 2008). But the concept is typically considered American. (See MILITARISTIC ATTITUDE.)

Since Eisenhower's warning, the complex has grown. Wars are more dependent on military equipment for surveillance and for delivering and targeting of weapons. Corporate military equipment suppliers have grown financially dependant on government contracts. Contracts provide employment in many communities, making it difficult politically to cut even useless programs. In order to guarantee government demand for their services, corporations maintain close contact with Defense Department officials. They market their wares by hiring former military and government officials as lobbyists and provide corporate personnel to governmental decision-making bodies.

Today, a network of US corporate elites is positioned to constrain policies of development such that corporate growth will continue even when such growth destroys habitats and displaces people. Security for such arrangements requires the application of military force. The United States is the world's specialist in weapons: it is the sole dissenting vote on a United Nations General Assembly resolution for a global arms trade treaty, the only nation to oppose a UN Agreement to Curb the International Flow of Illicit Small Arms, and one of seven nations to oppose the International Criminal Court (ICC) Treaty. The US Congress has exempted US military from ICC jurisdiction (Pilisuk, 2008).

MILITARY–INDUSTRIAL PROFITS

Defense Department contracts are attractive because they provide corporations with opportunities for risk-free investments. The US government is the major customer for these corporations and often the only one. Cost overruns in which profits increase when the contractor spends (or wastes) more than the estimate of the original bid are covered by these contracts. In addition, destroyed, defective, or used military equipment is replaced by extending contracts. Work that is subcontracted to subsidiaries also adds profits for the prime contractor.

Over the six-year period between fiscal year 1998 through 2003, the Center for

Public Integrity examined more than 2.2 million defense contract actions totaling $900 billion in authorized expenditures (Makison, 2006). The investigation showed that half of the Defense Department's budget went to private contractors. Close to 60% of Pentagon contracts fell under the category of no-bid contracts. Out of tens of thousands of contractors, the biggest 737 collected nearly 80% of the contracting dollars; the top 50 contractors got more than half of all the money. The list for this fiscal period included Lockheed Martin ($94 billion) and Boeing ($82 billion). By 2003, 56% of the Defense Department's contracts paid for services rather than goods. Some cover the logistics of serving a vast army. Some are awarded to firms like Xe (formerly Blackwater) which serve as mercenaries who are less constrained by military codes for the harm they inflict.

Many companies have been accused of overcharging. Auditors discovered that Kellogg, Brown, & Root, then a Halliburton subsidiary, was overpaid $208 million to transport oil in Iraq; also that government employees doing the same job (in this case, the Defense Energy Support Center) were much more efficient. Particularly troubling is that after the discrepancy was revealed, the US Army paid nearly $204 million of the $208 million overcharge (Makison, 2006). The revolving door in which industry officials play government roles could be a factor. The powerful former vice-president Dick Cheney was the former head of Halliburton. Moreover, high-level Army personnel are often hoping to find work with these companies after retiring from duty.

Among numerous efforts to define this complex, some have argued that this was not a sector of American society competing with other parts of society but rather a network of powerful military, political, and industrial leaders who were able to create a permanent war economy with tentacles that reach out into every sector of society: education, housing, computer technology, and healthcare. Its presence is felt in contracts in communities in every state and most countries (Pilisuk, 2008).

A close connection between the US military and industry began with World War II and expanded through the years of the Cold War. After profitable mobilization of industrial production for war, Charles Wilson, a CEO of General Motors and subsequent secretary of defense, emphasized the desirability of a semi-command economy run mostly by corporate executives and geared toward military production. The Cold War and a nuclear arms race helped bring about such an economy.

In 1949 the United States Department of War changed its name to Department of Defense. The change reflected potential new roles, largely in support, often clandestine, of counterrevolutionary activities in those less developed countries with popular protest against US-based corporations. The new title came to cover a costly and dangerous race in nuclear weapons and missiles and permanent bases. Today, the Pentagon's ever-expanding empire of over 6,000 domestic bases and 725 overseas bases is among the largest organizational structures in the world (Pilisuk, 2008).

PSYCHOLOGY AND THE MILITARY–INDUSTRIAL COMPLEX

Psychology plays a role in the military–industrial complex. Psychologists help in the recruitment, selection, and training of personnel. We contribute to teaching them how to become motivated warriors, how to develop team identities with their unit, how to break down prisoners in interrogations, and how to return traumatized soldiers to combat. Psychologists also have an important role in helping us to understand the mindset of those central to the complex and those who corporations and government have hired to be strategic planners.

Such defense planning strategists define their goals as gaining competitive advantage for their own side and are often preoccupied with strategies that enable them to outsmart or coerce adversaries. The defense intellectuals, however, display behavior suggesting that their work meets deep psychological needs. Among themselves they speak with a dry technocratic language that distances their reality from the cost in lives. The nuclear weapons laboratories develop the most lethal of all weapons. But human suffering is not part of their discussion. They exist in a culture in which bigger is better, in which rationality prevails over intuition and feelings, in which the culture of macho bravado is provided a sophisticated form of expression and a beneficent rationale – the honorable pursuit of security. (See SECURITY.)

But closer studies of this elite group of men (they are almost all male) reveal that the vocations also provide gratification for masculine identities that play with a God-like power sufficient to destroy the planet. Such activities are often pursued without conscious awareness of an underlying preoccupation with the subjugation of the weak and the feminine. (See SOCIAL DOMINANCE THEORY.) Images of bullying and domination of women creep through the outward rationality of their emotionless technical language (Cohn, 1987).

The policy effects were visible in the sending of US weapons, aerial bombardments, or marine occupations in proxy wars (fought in other countries for US interests) that occurred in the 1950s and into the Vietnam War. Even the public aversion to war following Vietnam did not stem the pattern of weapons flow and military incursions into Latin America, Indonesia, Africa, Southeast Asia, and the Middle East. The complex was extending its role from global policeman to an engine of empire.

SHAPING THE AGENDA

The demise of the Soviet Union might have offered an opportunity for major disarmament and cooperative security agreements. But the complex lobbied for new wars, first on drugs, then on terror. After the tragedy of 9/11, the United States chose not to seek international assistance to apprehend supporters of the hijackers but rather to pay (and bribe) informants to justify an invasion and military occupation of Afghanistan and of Iraq (Boyle, 2004). The decision revealed a power that the complex had acquired to shape the media messages of what citizens consider to be reality. The Pentagon provided large "perception management" contracts with firms such as Lincoln and the Rendon Group whose expertise lies in "the ability to influence their target audience" (Pilisuk, 2008). A "war on terror" was marketed and Congress approved massive military plans including contracts for missiles and missile defense, new nuclear weapons, missile-launching submarines, military aircraft, privatized intelligence gathering, private mercenary armies, reconstruction plans, and the arrest and torture of suspects who were held without charge (Scheer, 2008).

Military media infiltration was highlighted in a *New York Times* article titled "Behind TV Analysts, Pentagon's Hidden Hand," which found that "military analysts" from Fox News, NBC, CNN, CBS, and ABC had ties (not revealed) to military contractors who were vested in the same Iraq war policies they were asked to publicly evaluate. As in most military–industrial links, profits and potential business relationships played a decisive role in the analysts' willingness to present a biased view. According to the *New York Times*,

> Many analysts were being paid by the "hit," the number of times they appeared on TV. The more an analyst could boast of fresh inside information from high-level Pentagon "sources," the more hits he could expect. The more hits, the greater his potential influence in the military marketplace, where several analysts prominently advertised their network roles. (Barstow, 2008)

The power to control the public image of reality derives from the power to amass great wealth from government contracts. The positive assessment of a military response in Iraq by paid "military analysts" made it easier for business interests to operate without checks and harder for individuals to question war conduct. The control of information, the dispersion of large contracts to many communities, and the heroic image of soldiers defending their country all emanate from a military–industrial power elite. Hence the reaction to 9/11 was not simply a tough but misguided response but rather a product of a military–industrial system with more pervasive power than is generally understood.

Companies like Bechtel, Carlyle, Halliburton, and Blackwater are strategically placed to help write the contingency plans that will be needed when certain crises occur, plans that will include their services in the response. Many US military and political officers move between positions in government and the private sector. The transition from positions in governing bodies to the companies soliciting contracts creates substantial conflicts of interest. But it is the connections between the officers of government agencies and the defense industry that are most egregious. With their connections to the upper echelons of government, these companies have had a major impact on foreign policy.

There are consequences of a centralization of power and its many tentacles. It directs foreign policy in a way that assumes the legitimacy and the inevitability of armed conflict and the absolute requisite of military spending. Nonviolent alternatives are typically left unexplored and tragic casualties and costs of warfare are rarely taken into account. The complex creates a society in which people live in fear, feel dependent upon militant leaders for protection, and forego their hopes for peace.

SEE ALSO: Militaristic Attitude; Security; Social Dominance Theory.

REFERENCES

Barash, D. P., & Webel, C. P. (2008). *Peace and conflict studies*. London, UK: Sage.

Barstow, D. (2008). Behind TV analysts, Pentagon's hidden hand. *New York Times*, July 22.

Boyle, F. A. (2004). *Destroying world order: US imperialism in the Middle East before and after September 11th*. Atlanta, GA: Clarity Press.

Cohn, C. (1987). Sex and death in the rational world of the defense intellectuals. *Journal of Women in Culture and Society*, 12, 687–718.

Makison, L. (2006). *Outsourcing the Pentagon: Who benefits from the politics and economics of national security?* Retrieved August 12, 2006, from http://usgovinfo.about.com/od/thepoliticalsystem/a/aboutpacs.htm.

Pilisuk, M. (2008). *Who benefits from global violence and war: Uncovering a destructive system (with Jennifer Achord Rountree)*. Westport, CT: Greenwood/Praeger.

Scheer, R. (2008). *The pornography of power: How defense hawks hijacked 9/11 and weakened America*. New York, NY: Little, Brown.

ADDITIONAL RESOURCES

The history and current evolution of the military–industrial complex are covered in the following recommended books:

Caldicott, H. (2004). *The new nuclear danger: George W. Bush's military–industrial complex*. New York, NY: New Press.

Johnson, C. (2004). *The sorrows of empire: Militarism, secrecy and the end of the republic*. New York, NY: Metropolitan Books.

Klein, N. (2008). *The shock doctrine: The rise of disaster capitalism*. New York, NY: Picador.

Lapp, R. E. (1968). *The weapons culture*. New York, NY: Norton.

http://www.peace-action.org (Peace Action: Practical, Positive Alternative for Peace)

http://www.publicintegrity.org (Center for Public Integrity: Investigative Journalism in the Public Interest)

http://www.stopcorporateabuse.org (Corporate Accountability International)

Militaristic Attitude

J. CHRISTOPHER COHRS AND
LINDEN L. NELSON

INTRODUCTION

Current figures for military expenditure documented by the Stockholm International Peace Research Institute show that across the planet in 2008, states spent US$1,464 billion towards military expenses (with the United States, China, France, the United Kingdom, and Russia being the "top five"). The Heidelberg Institute for International Conflict Research reports 39 high-intensity violent conflicts worldwide in 2008, plus 95 crises with sporadic violence. The militaries of many Western democracies are deployed in many different places in the world, and there have been several aggressive military interventions in recent years. While, against this background, there is a lot of public criticism of militarization and the use of military force to pursue political goals, many people believe in the necessity of a strong military and in the usefulness and legitimacy of the use of military force.

This article deals with the structure and determinants of "militaristic attitude" – the attitudes and beliefs that support militarism. Support for militarism is an important topic in peace psychology. If militaristic attitudes are widespread in a culture, they represent a form of cultural violence because they serve to legitimize and facilitate direct violence (i.e., the use of military force) as well as

MILITARISTIC ATTITUDE 637

structural violence (i.e., militarization). (See PEACE PSYCHOLOGY: DEFINITIONS, SCOPE, AND IMPACT.) We will describe several components of militaristic attitude, along with brief illustrations of how they are measured. We will then discuss the determinants of militaristic attitude, and conclude with open questions for future research.

COMPONENTS OF MILITARISTIC ATTITUDE

Researchers have been interested in measuring militaristic attitude or related constructs since the beginnings of attitude measurement after World War I. Later, research distinguished between several components of militaristic attitude, which will be reviewed in the following.

Beliefs about Human Nature

According to the seventeenth-century philosopher Thomas Hobbes, human beings are self-interested and motivated to invade others to take control of their resources. From such a perspective, human nature would result in a dog-eat-dog world, with groups being prepared for self-defense and tempted to strike against their enemies preemptively. Recognizing that a belief in the evilness of human nature reflects and perpetuates militarism, in 1986 an international group of scientists criticized the notion that humans are predetermined to make war in the Seville Statement on Violence. (See SEVILLE STATEMENT ON VIOLENCE.) Scales that measure militaristic attitudes often include items about beliefs about human nature such as "War is unavoidable due to human nature."

Beliefs about the Efficacy of Military Force

Related to a belief in the evilness of human nature is a belief in deterrence. According to

this view, because wars are thought to result from potential aggressors not being kept in check, projecting a strong and credible military threat is necessary to protect national security, resolve international conflicts, and keep peace. A contrasting view is that wars result from the escalating spiral of rearmament driven by mutual threat perceptions, and international agreements and institutions, disarmament treaties, and cooperative problem solving are more effective strategies because of their potential for reducing threat perceptions. Accordingly, militaristic attitude scales include items tapping beliefs about the relative efficacy of the military such as "Cooperation and negotiation are more effective than military force for dealing with international conflicts" (reverse-scored).

Ethical Beliefs about War

Another component of militaristic attitude relates to beliefs about the moral legitimacy of militarism. People differ in terms of their beliefs about what is required to render the use of military force, as well as killing of others, morally acceptable. These beliefs range from general moral advocacy of force, to acceptance of force for self-defense, to absolute rejection of force for any purpose. This component is measured in militaristic attitude scales with items such as "War should be morally condemned as a matter of principle" (reverse-scored).

Emotional Reactions toward the Military

In addition to the cognitive components mentioned above, militaristic attitude can have affective aspects, just like other attitudes. Affective aspects can include positive feelings such as liking, pride, admiration, and respect for the military and military values such as strength, bravery, loyalty, and patriotism, as well as negative feelings such as rejection, detestation, and disgust. Accordingly, militaristic attitude scales

contain items such as "Somehow, I am fasci-
nated by the possibilities of modern military
technology."

Military Policy Preferences

Another component of militaristic attitude
refers to concrete policy preferences with
respect to national security and foreign
affairs, without making assumptions about
the underlying cognitive or affective sources
of these preferences. This component
includes, for example, opinions about the
development of new weapon systems,
increases or cuts in the military budget, and
specific military operations. Accordingly,
militaristic attitude scales contain items such
as "Spending money on the development of
advanced military weapons is a waste of
national resources" (reverse-scored). Many
studies focus specifically on support for military interventions as a particularly important aspect of militaristic attitude, although
a distinction between aggressive and humanitarian intervention may be useful here.
(See HUMANITARIAN MILITARY INTERVENTIONS,
SUPPORT FOR.)

An Integrative Conceptualization

The five components of militaristic attitude
reviewed above, while conceptually distin-
guishable, form an internally consistent attitudinal dimension (Cohrs, Göritz, & Brähler,
2009). Several militaristic attitude scales
have been developed that are based on
combinations of these components or on
similar additional ones (e.g., Nelson &
Milburn, 1999; Bliss, Oh, & Williams, 2007).
The validity of these scales has been
demonstrated in various ways, such as predicting opinions about real and hypothetical
military actions, discriminating between
military personnel and control samples, and
reporting correlations with a large number
of conceptually related personality and
sociopolitical characteristics.

One issue to be investigated is whether
militaristic attitudes and cooperative attitudes (as reflected in beliefs in the goodness
of human nature, belief in the efficacy of
international cooperation, moral rejection
of military force, detestation of the military, and conciliatory policy preferences)
should be conceptualized and measured
as separate dimensions or opposite poles
of a single dimension. It may be possible to
simultaneously hold both militaristic and
cooperative attitudes, and one could be
antimilitaristic without being cooperative.
However, because militaristic attitudes are
often relevant for situations in which military and cooperative actions would be
incompatible, it seems useful to argue for a
single dimension. Whether one approach
can generally make better predictions is an
empirical question that has not been
resolved.

DETERMINANTS OF
MILITARISTIC ATTITUDES

Why do people hold militaristic attitudes?
This question can be approached at different
levels. At the collective level, militaristic attitude may be influenced by enduring aspects
of the political system or culture, as well as
by more immediate political events. At the
individual level, militaristic attitudes seem to
be influenced by personality traits, personal
values, and ideological orientations. Finally,
a developmental perspective examines
how attitudes are transmitted within cultures from one generation to the next and
helps explain the origins of individual
differences.

Collective Influences

Cultural factors that may affect militaristic
attitudes include nationalism, patriotism,
and political norms favoring national military strength and eschewing military weakness. (See PATRIOTISM AND NATIONALISM.) In

contrast, a culture of peace works against militaristic attitudes. (See CULTURE OF PEACE.) Gender norms that require males to be strong and dominant support militaristic attitudes, and there is evidence showing an association between popularity of contact sports and warfare (Winter, Pilisuk, Houck, & Lee, 2001). Religion is another cultural influence that may affect militarism, as in the examples of the Christian Crusades and some manifestations of Islamic Jihad.

Collectives are also influenced by threats and violent events that provoke fear and anger. In many circumstances these emotions elicit tendencies toward self-defense and aggression. Studies comparing attitudes before and after a violent event (e.g., the Japanese attack on Pearl Harbor in 1941; the terrorist attacks on the United States in 2001), as well as experimental studies, have demonstrated such increases in militaristic attitudes.

Situational norms also affect people's attitudes. Bystanders who were surveyed during a demonstration against the Vietnam War in the United States had less militaristic attitudes than pedestrians surveyed when there was no demonstration. More generally, people are influenced by observing the words and actions of respected national leaders, relatives, and friends.

Individual Differences

Most research on militaristic attitudes has looked at their correlates at the level of individual differences (Eckhardt & Lentz, 1967; McCleary & Williams, 2009). Because men have generally been found to be more militaristic than women, it is reasonable to suggest that masculinity and femininity relate to militaristic attitude (Winter et al., 2001). D'Agostino (1995) reported that militaristic men, compared to less militaristic men, described themselves as more competitive, aggressive, and ambitious, and as less feminine, rebellious, and idealistic. In

contrast, militaristic women described themselves as more cautious, conventional, and guileful and less rebellious, sympathetic, and erotic.

A number of traits describing interpersonal orientations and behaviors have been shown to correlate with militaristic attitude. General distrust of other people, competitiveness, and acceptance of negative reciprocity norms correlated positively with militaristic attitude. Cooperativeness, nonviolence, empathic concern, perspective taking, ethnocultural empathy, universal orientation (seeing others as similar to oneself), and agreeableness correlated negatively. (see PEACEFUL PERSONALITY.)

The relationship of cognitive traits to militaristic attitude has also been investigated. Intelligence, scholastic aptitude, college course grades, conflict-related problem-solving abilities, and knowledge about current international conflict issues did not correlate with militaristic attitude. However, closed-mindedness correlated positively.

Personal values correlated with militaristic attitude in several studies. The following value types correlated positively in at least two studies: power, security, hedonism, achievement, and conformity. Universalism and benevolence correlated negatively. The highest correlations were with universalism, power, and security values. It may be concluded that militaristic attitude relates to low relative importance of self-transcendence values (universalism, benevolence) and to high relative importance of self-enhancement values (power, achievement) and conservation values (security, conformity). (See VALUES, NONVIOLENCE, AND PEACE PSYCHOLOGY.)

Finally, national goals as well as sociopolitical attitudes and ideologies have been shown to relate to militaristic attitude. Ratings of the importance of national strength goals were positively correlated and ratings of the importance of humanitarian goals were negatively correlated with militaristic attitude. Militaristic attitude correlated positively with nationalism, (blind) patriotism, ethnocentrism, conservatism, social dominance orientation, religious fundamentalism, support for one's political system, religious/moral imposition, opposition to gun control, various forms of authoritarianism, and punitiveness. Militaristic attitude correlated negatively with internationalism, worldmindedness, respect for civil liberties, and tolerance of dissent. (See CONSERVATIVE IDEOLOGY; SOCIAL DOMINANCE ORIENTATION; AUTHORITARIAN PERSONALITY.)

Attempting to integrate the evidence on individual differences, McCleary and Williams (2009) suggested that militaristic people take a simplistic worldview. However, as we have noted, some studies did not find links between militaristic attitude and problem-solving competencies, intelligence, academic grades, or political knowledge. Rather, various factors such as interpersonal attitudes, closed-mindedness, personal values and goals, and sociopolitical ideologies are important for explaining individual differences in militaristic attitude. The psychological dynamics underlying militaristic attitude seem to mainly involve reactions to feelings of insecurity and uncertainty, needs for status and dominance, as well as relatively low concern for others.

Developmental Factors

Little is known about development of militaristic attitude except that there is a positive correlation between attitudes of parents and their college-aged children. Perhaps the most common speculation is that parental neglect, punitiveness, rigidity, or inconsistent care may affect attachment processes and lead to insecurity, distrust of other people, or hostility. Although these conditions might promote militaristic attitudes, there is little evidence for this. Modeling of peer and adult attitudes as well as political socialization more generally are probably better explanations.

DIRECTIONS FOR FUTURE RESEARCH

There are a number of methodological shortcomings of existing research and several issues that are not well understood. Virtually all research has been conducted in (mainly Western) democracies using cross-sectional questionnaire methods, often without examining the potential influence of social desirability bias. We need longitudinal and intervention studies to examine whether changes in the correlates of militaristic attitude will in turn produce changes in militaristic attitude. Also, there is a need for comparative studies, both across countries and within countries across time, that look into the role of collective influences on militaristic attitude in a more controlled way. Such research could also investigate how militaristic attitudes of the public and militaristic vs. conciliatory decisions of political leaders influence one another.

There are also conceptual issues that need to be addressed. It is not only the case that women generally score lower on militaristic attitude than men, but the correlates of militaristic attitude are often different for men and women. Researchers should report and try to understand these gender differences. (See WOMEN AND PEACE HYPOTHESIS.) Another issue relates to the differentiation between use of military force for humanistic purposes and use of military force for self-serving purposes. It may be useful, accordingly, to distinguish between two factors of militaristic attitude. (See HUMANITARIAN MILITARY INTERVENTIONS, SUPPORT FOR.) We look forward to future studies addressing these and other methodological and conceptual challenges.

SEE ALSO: Authoritarian Personality; Conservative Ideology; Culture of Peace; Humanitarian Military Interventions, Support for; Patriotism and Nationalism; Peace Psychology: Definitions, Scope, and Impact Peaceful Personality; Seville Statement on Violence; Social Dominance Orientation;

Values, Nonviolence, and Peace Psychology; Women and Peace Hypothesis.

REFERENCES

Bliss, S. L., Oh, E. J., & Williams, R. L. (2007). Militarism and sociopolitical perspectives among college students in the US and South Korea. *Peace and Conflict: Journal of Peace Psychology*, *13*, 175–199.

Cohrs, J. C., Göritz, A. S., & Brähler, E. (2009). *Dimensions and determinants of (anti-) militaristic attitudes*. Paper presented at the 32nd Annual Scientific Meeting of the International Society of Political Psychology, Dublin, Ireland, July 14–17.

D'Agostino, B. (1995). Self-images of hawks and doves: A control systems model of militarism. *Political Psychology*, *16*, 259–295.

Eckhardt, W., & Lentz, T. F. (1967). Factors of war/peace attitudes. *Peace Research Reviews*, *1*(5), 1–102.

McCleary, D. F., & Williams, R. L. (2009). Sociopolitical and personality correlates of militarism in democratic societies. *Peace and Conflict: Journal of Peace Psychology*, *15*, 161–187.

Nelson, L. L., & Milburn, T. W. (1999). Relationships between problem-solving competencies and militaristic attitudes: Implications for peace education. *Peace and Conflict: Journal of Peace Psychology*, *5*, 149–168.

Winter, D. D., Pilisuk, M., Houck, S., & Lee, M. (2001). Understanding militarism: Money, masculinity, and the search for the mystical. In D. J. Christie, R. V. Wagner, & D. D. Winter (Eds.), *Peace, conflict, and violence* (pp. 139–148). Upper Saddle River, NJ: Prentice-Hall.

ADDITIONAL RESOURCES

http://www.sipri.org/research/armaments/milex (Stockholm International Peace Research Institute's research on military expenditure)

Military Psychology

DEANNA BEECH

Military psychology is most often assumed to mean the use of psychology in the effort to treat the wounds of war. However, this application is only the most visible aspect of a fertile and multifaceted field. Over the course of its history this discipline has expanded to the extent that it is now described as the application of all forms of psychology to the military context (Society for Military Psychology, 2009). Historically, the concept of "military context" was clearer. War was fought between two or more governments and, for the most part, it was fought by soldiers. However, with the Global War on Terrorism (GWOT) the scope of the military context has been stretched and psychological applications are rapidly stretching with it.

The historical roots of military psychology can be traced back to the Napoleonic and Crimean wars of the early 1800s, where the French and British found that it was better to treat the wounded close to the battlefield and return them back to duty, rather than send them to the rear (out of the warzone) for treatment (Department of the Army, 2006). These lessons were later shared among allies and used on the battlefields in World War I. Additionally, psychological assessment was catapulted into a mainstream of psychological knowledge at this time, as the US Army initiated a mass administration of capacity testing known as the Army Alpha and Beta Tests, the results of which were used for job classification (Society for Military Psychology, 2009).

In World War II the contributions of psychologists to the military mission expanded. Psychological testing was advanced as the Army and Navy General Classification Tests were developed. And it was during the war, as psychiatric services were overrun with cases of "shell shock," that clinical psychologists were brought directly onto military service. By the end of the war one out of every four psychologists were working for or with the military (Society for Military Psychology, 2009). Social psychology was also popularized as "people all over the world became desperate for answers to . . . questions about what causes violence, prejudice and genocide, conformity and obedience" (Brehm, Kassin, & Fein, 1999, p. 12). Even the field of engineering psychology was developed to address issues such as the design of weapons and the placement of controls in aircraft.

Post-World War II the number of disabled veterans was staggering. In the United States alone, there were more than 15 million veterans in need of services and approximately half of these individuals suffered with psychological trauma (shell shock) as their primary diagnosis. To address the overwhelming number of people in need of services, the Veteran's Administration rapidly built hospitals, increased staff, and called on clinical psychology to help. They invested considerable funds in the development of training programs for doctoral candidates, which resulted in the development of the first formal internship programs in clinical psychology (Reisman, 1991). Similar developments took place in postwar England as they also developed the field of clinical psychology in the efforts to treat British veterans.

Treating the effects of war on soldiers and their families continues to be the largest demand facing military psychologists across the globe. What was once a poorly understood cluster of symptoms known as shell shock has become the more clearly defined diagnosis of post-traumatic stress disorder (PTSD). (See TRAUMA – FROM AN INDIVIDUAL AND A GROUP PERSPECTIVE; POST-TRAUMATIC STRESS DISORDER AND PEACE.) The prominent treatments that are showing evidence-based results include Eye Movement Desensitization and Reprocessing, Prolonged Exposure, and Somatic Experiencing. The

Department of Defense focuses considerable resources on training psychologists in the current treatment techniques for PTSD, and has recently moved to trying to prevent PTSD, and other psychiatric difficulties related to military service, by developing programs aimed at building resiliency (Comprehensive Soldier Fitness Program). In fact, the military is the single largest employer of psychologists in the United States (Society for Military Psychology, 2009).

The persisting widespread conflict of today's GWOT requires that military psychology continue to expand its scope and application. More recent developments include Combat Stress Control Units, operational psychology, and the highly controversial role psychologists play in the interrogation of prisoners at US detention centers. (See INTERROGATION, PSYCHOLOGY AND.)

Combat Stress Control Units (Department of the Army, 2006) have evolved from the early World War I doctrine of providing psychological care in the battlefield (proximity) as soon as symptoms start to appear (immediacy) with the expectation that the soldier will return to duty (expectancy). This process is known as PIE. More recently, the concept has been expanded to PIES by adding that the interventions should be simple (simplicity). Currently, these units move around in the battlefield providing care to those on the frontlines. They are a much more fluid system that is no longer tied to medical treatment facilities, as the older model of Medical Detachment Psychiatry was in the Gulf War, and they no longer just treat individuals suffering with combat stress reactions. The mission of these units has evolved to include Unit Needs Assessments, management of traumatic events, and consultation with command groups (Department of the Army, 2006).

Operational psychology can generally be described as the use of psychological knowledge to impact military operations. Traditionally, this impact was indirect and included activities such as psychological evaluations on personnel as a means for selecting individuals for elite training programs like sniper school, or to determine whether or not a soldier is fit for duty. However, with the GWOT, this field is rapidly expanding and psychologists are taking a more and more active role in how the military engages in warfare. Psychologists now use their knowledge "to attain strategic goals in a theater of war or theater of operations by leveraging and applying their psychological expertise in helping to identify enemy capabilities, personalities, and intentions" (Kennedy & Zillmer, 2006, p. 194). This active participation in the combat process takes these psychologists out of the Geneva Convention and moves them into the role of combatant (Staal & Stephenson, 2006), crossing the line of "do no harm" and raising significant ethical concerns.

The best-documented ethical controversy in this field is between the ethical guidelines on patient–provider confidentiality and the reduced limits of confidentiality for soldiers. Problems with the reduced limits occur when soldiers report information in therapy that could compromise their ability to perform their duties or could compromise the effectiveness of the mission. In these situations, military psychologists have the obligation to inform the commander of the unit about the difficulties, thus breaching that patient's confidentiality. These situations illustrate the inherent dual roles of the military psychologist. Specifically, they straddle the fence between the needs of the patient and the needs of the service, and it is accepted doctrine that the needs of the service come first.

Presently, the "slippery ethical slopes" are even steeper (Staal & Stephenson, 2006, p. 280). This has been most evident in the creation of Behavioral Science Consultation Teams (BSCT – pronounced "Biscuit") by

the US Army, whose entire function is to make interrogations more productive. Since this type of position did not exist in the past, the first psychologists tasked with this function had little or no training in facilitating interrogations. The blurry line that this created has been well documented in the numerous accounts of how psychologists unintentionally contributed to the abuses that were perpetrated at Abu Ghraib and other detention facilities (James, 2008); thus, in these vague new situations, due to the "lack of proper guidance or training, psychologists may unintentionally break international laws or guidelines" (Staal & Stephenson, 2006, p. 280).

In today's changing geopolitical and military context psychologists are again called upon to respond to urgent situations that can affect the welfare of many. Therefore, it is essential that we act cautiously and consider the possible uses and outcomes of applying our skills in new contexts. We must be vigilant to guard the high ethical standards that psychology holds as a profession.

SEE ALSO: Interrogation, Psychology and; Post-Traumatic Stress Disorder and Peace; Trauma – from an Individual and a Group Perspective.

REFERENCES

Brehm, S., Kassin, S., & Fein, S. (1999). *Social psychology* (4th ed.). Boston, MA: Houghton.
Department of the Army. (2006). Combat and operational stress control (Field Manual 4–02.51). Washington, DC: http://www.fas.org/irp/doddir/army/fm4–02–51.pdf.
James, L. (2008). *Fixing hell: An army psychologist confronts Abu Ghraib*. New York, NY: Grand Central Publishing.
Kennedy, C., & Zillmer, E. (2006). *Military psychology: Clinical and operational applications*. New York, NY: Guilford Press.
Reisman, J. (1991). *A history of clinical psychology* (2nd ed.). New York, NY: Brunner Routledge.

Society for Military Psychology. (2009). *Military psychology overview*. Retrieved November 24, 2009, from www.apadivision19.org/overview.htm.

Staal, M., & Stephenson, J. (2006). Operational psychology: An emerging subdiscipline. *Military Psychology, 18*(4), 269–282.

Mindfulness

HERBERT H. BLUMBERG

Being mindful may help people who are embedded in a variety of situations related to peace psychology. Instructive publications by Thich Nhat Hanh and others explain the view that nonviolent social action and personal growth focused on behavioral and contextual awareness can readily potentiate each other rather than being incompatible choices or at best independent ones. Experimental research by Langer and colleagues supports the idea that mindfulness training can lessen prejudicial behavior against outgroups. Principles of mindfulness are, moreover, potentially applicable to all of the major areas of peace psychology. (See BUDDHISM AND PEACE PSYCHOLOGY.)

SOCIAL ACTION AND BEING MEDITATIVE

A holistic understanding of mindfulness is provided by "Eastern" approaches. Thich Nhat Hanh (English pronunciation: Tik N'yat Hawn) has explained the importance of combining nonviolent social action with personal meditative awareness of the present moment, even (or perhaps especially) in extraordinarily trying circumstances. As a Vietnamese Buddhist monk (and also a poet), during the Vietnam War in the 1960s he organized peacebuilding efforts such as re-establishing infrastructure and rebuilding destroyed homes. At the same time, the "engaged buddhism" movement that he founded urged people to practice a meditative mindful awareness of one's immediate tasks and surroundings. This awareness extends to one's mundane activities such as washing dishes or eating a tangerine.

In regard to the question of activism, Thich Nhat Hanh put it this way: "Should we continue to practice in our monasteries or should we leave the meditation halls in order to help the people who were suffering under the bombs? We decided to do both – to go out and help people and to do so in mindfulness" (Nhat Hanh, 1995, p. 91). His work stresses various reminders for facilitating awareness, suggestions for breaking what Morton Deutsch has called the vicious negative spiral of aggression, and the importance of replacing mere hope with constructive remedies.

An experimental counterpart of Nhat Hanh's advice can arguably be found in Tetlock's work on integrative complexity and Janis's on avoiding groupthink. Ironically, groupthink represents a group's attempts to avoid conflict but by uncritically suppressing dissent. By contrast, being receptive to a nuanced understanding of events and having a flexible approach may be particularly important in times of crisis, when – often unfortunately – unipolar thinking is particularly common. (See COGNITIVE COMPLEXITY; GROUPTHINK.)

Classic research on social facilitation by Zajonc and others posits that when a drive is strong, habitual dominant responses come to the fore regardless of whether they are "right" or, as may be especially likely in complex situations, "wrong." In those international crises where just one major party does avoid the pitfalls of groupthink, the outcome is typically better for all concerned. At least, the evidence points in this direction, though meta-analysts find that, as one might imagine, it has not (yet) been possible to control all of the main relevant contextual factors within the same study. Mindfulness, seemingly paradoxically, requires a focus on the immediate situation but openness to the panoply of factors impinging on it.

MINDFULNESS TRAINING CAN REDUCE PREJUDICE

A research tradition established by Langer and colleagues has shown that general or specific mindfulness training can, for example, attenuate schoolchildren's bias against people with disabilities (Langer, 1989). The rationale is that by being *more* mindful of others' disabilities one will realize that limitations are function-specific rather than whole-person-specific. This field experiment's components seem particularly enlightening with regard to a way of reducing ingroup–outgroup prejudices which underlie many conflicts. The details of this particular study, therefore, help one to understand how mindfulness can help in conflict prevention.

Training of schoolchildren from primary grade 6 took place for just 40 minutes a day for five days and consisted of various exercises – for example, naming several different ways in which a pictured person could run a race without bumping into others (general training) or the same question asked about a blind person (specific training). Pupils in a control condition followed similar exercises requiring the same overall time and number of responses but, for instance, needed only to name one way or explain *whether* the problem could be solved, responses that most people can provide fairly mindlessly.

Participants were then shown photographs of pupils said to be from a nearby school that was planning a joint picnic, and were asked to nominate those whom they would choose to have on their teams. Students who had received either form of mindfulness training (but especially the specific training) were more likely to choose people with disabilities (where the disability was irrelevant or positive for the task at hand) and, perhaps even more importantly,

were less likely to avoid the disabled others altogether. In a world where mindless automatic behavior runs rife, as Langer and her colleagues have demonstrated, a readiness to engage in mindful tracking will frequently reap dividends for everybody concerned.

APPLICATIONS TO PEACE PSYCHOLOGY

Principles of mindfulness are potentially applicable to all of the main areas of peace psychology delineated by Christie and colleagues (Christie, Tint, Wagner, & Winter, 2008). Potential examples follow, organized according to the scheme used by Blumberg, Hare, and Costin (2006), looking in turn at interdisciplinary practice, psychological areas, and some core topics in peace and environmental studies. The actual extent of applicability to some of these areas remains to be developed empirically.

Although the roots of mindfulness research go back at least to the 1960s, a literature search in late 2009 revealed only about a dozen mindfulness publications especially relevant to peace psychology in each of the 1980s and 1990s, but well over 50 since 2000, most of them since 2007. (See Additional Resources below).

INTERDISCIPLINARY PRACTICE

The psychology of mindfulness as described above has relevance to a variety of disciplines, some of which are as follows. In the context of government policy and international relations, recommendations would again favor relatively high integrative complexity and appropriate steps for countering groupthink, but applicability would extend in particular to major policymakers.

- *Education*: including general or specific mindfulness training as part of peace education should lead to more informed awareness of relevant issues and, where applicable, better decision-making. Orr (2002) discusses the value of mindfulness practices within anti-oppressive pedagogies.

- *Feminist approaches*: to take one example, the salutary effects of attributes amounting to empathetic mindfulness are evident in the work of Annie Howell, Peggy DesAutels, Margaret Urban Walker, Susan McKay, Cheryl de la Ray, and others.
- *Philosophy, ethics, and religion*: in addition to the above-described principles put forward by Thich Nhat Hanh, it is a corollary of existing experimental research that mindfulness training would be expected to diminish unthinking acceptance of plausible or widespread but potentially suboptimal beliefs and behavior.

THEORY AND APPLICATION RELATED TO SOME PRIMARY PSYCHOLOGICAL TOPICS

Psychological research on mindfulness covers a full spectrum from neuropsychology to humanistic approaches, though the present focus is necessarily selective, with an emphasis of course on areas most relevant to peace psychology.

- *Measurement*: mindfulness has five facets, according to factor analyses bringing together a variety of measures: describing one's thoughts and feelings with words; acting with awareness and nondistraction; being nonjudgmental, at least temporarily; nonreactivity to inner experience; and – at least among people who have meditated – observing and attending sensations, feelings, and thoughts. Although cognition underlies all of these, applicability to peace and conflict resolution relates to a variety of major psychological areas.

- *Developmental issues*: essentially the same comments are applicable as for peace education, above. At its best, being mindful represents a life-long endeavor.
- *Attitudes*: most notably, mindfulness fosters diminished prejudice against outgroups, as documented in Langer's work. Implicitly, however, it also entails efforts toward unbiased consistency – or at least awareness of discrepancies – among one's thoughts, feelings, and actions.
- *Psychodynamics*: in addition to fostering richer awareness and better decision-making, mindfulness training would be expected also to have psychotherapeutic applications, as in Joanna Macy's work in converting despair into constructive personal and social activity even among people who have endured extreme hardship. Indeed, mindfulness may be integrated into virtually all of the helping professions, as delineated by Shapiro and Carlson (2009).
- *Cognition and images* have apparently been little researched explicitly in the present context, but nevertheless people's cognitions underlie and mediate most of the positive findings described above for the advantages of being mindful. Mindfulness may best be understood as a cognitive style, though it also has characteristics of a cognitive ability and of a personality trait.
- *Aggression*: Horton-Deutsch and Horton (2003) have posited mindfulness as inducing diminished aggression as a result of improved communication, even with regard to apparently intractable conflict.
- *Language and communication*: Burgoon, Berger, and Waldron (2000) give numerous examples of potentially improved communication applicable to conflict situations such as workplace problems, detecting scams and hoaxes, "reducing stereotyping and cross-cultural misunderstanding, managing interpersonal

conflict, and constructing effective public . . . campaigns" (p. 105).

CORE TOPICS IN PEACE AND ENVIRONMENTAL STUDIES

- *Conflict resolution*: a variety of explicit applications have been discussed above with regard to the work of Nhat Hanh, Janis, Burgoon et al., and Horton-Deutsch and Horton.
- *Emergency decisions, crisis management, and the effects of conflicts*: work mentioned so far – including that of Langer, Tetlock, and Janis – emphasizes the importance of enhanced mindfulness. Langer and others acknowledge, however, that automatic mindless behavior may sometimes – indeed, perhaps often – be advantageous, especially when a quick over-learned response is wanted. Fred Fiedler has suggested that fire-fighters, for instance, should generally not be overly hesitant and deliberative.
- *Peacemaking, wars, and crises*: once again the work of Tetlock and Janis is relevant – but also that of Gardner and Moore, who have described interventions for enhancing human performance in organizational and domestic settings, with exercises facilitating a sequence of mindfulness–acceptance–commitment.
- *Sustainable development*: putting forward an experimental parallel, as it were, to a crux of Nhat Hanh's work, in 2005 Brown and Kasser described the empirical concordance of psychological and ecological well-being. In this correlational research, the two were found to be positively associated and hence, at the very least, compatible.
- *Terrorism*: for countering terrorist threats, the "lessons" from mindfulness research are implicitly applicable – for instance, having a flexible approach and avoiding presumptions of prejudice against entire outgroups. Instead of acting simplistically, one of course often needs to foster both mindful evaluation of threats and also constructive ways of dealing with them. As regards dealing with victims of terrorism, which is the other major area of psychological research on terrorism, as noted above, victims are likely to benefit from mindfulness training, fostering empowerment as a way of escaping from "learned helplessness."

CONCLUSION

There is a strong case for teaching enhanced mindfulness in dealing with conflictual and many everyday situations. It is less clear that withholding judgment and focusing on the present moment and surroundings will automatically increase empathy. Langer and her colleagues have experimentally demonstrated not only people's readiness to act mindlessly – for example, by obeying minor requests without paying proper attention – but also a variety of personal, social, and task benefits from interventions that encourage or provide training for mindfulness. Thich Nhat Hanh describes the interconnectedness of everything in the universe, the joy of the present moment, and the realization that even the worst evils will fade – but he effectively warns against such appreciation being used to support fatalism rather than efforts toward constructive transformation of conflicts.

SEE ALSO: Buddhism and Peace Psychology; Cognitive Complexity; Groupthink.

REFERENCES

Blumberg, H. H., Hare, A. P., & Costin, A. (2006). *Peace psychology: A comprehensive introduction*. Cambridge, UK: Cambridge University Press.

Burgoon, J. K., Berger, C. R., & Waldron, V. R. (2000). Mindfulness and interpersonal communication. *Journal of Social Issues, 56*, 105–127.

Christie, D. J., Tint, B. S., Wagner, R. V., & Winter, D. D. (2008). Peace psychology for a peaceful world. *American Psychologist, 63*, 540–552.

Christie, D. J., Wagner, R. V., & Winter, D. D. (Eds.). (2001). *Peace, conflict, and violence: Peace psychology for the 21st century*. Upper Saddle River, NJ: Prentice-Hall.

Horton-Deutsch, S. L., & Horton, J. M. (2003). Mindfulness: Overcoming intractable conflict. *Archives of Psychiatric Nursing, 17*, 186–193.

Langer, E. J. (1989). *Mindfulness*. Reading, MA: Addison-Wesley.

Nhat Hanh, T. (1995). *Peace is every step: The path of mindfulness in everyday life*. London, UK: Rider.

Orr, D. (2002). The uses of mindfulness in anti-oppressive pedagogies: Philosophy and praxis. *Canadian Journal of Education, 27*(4), 477–497.

Shapiro, S. L., & Carlson, L. E. (2009). *The art and science of mindfulness: Integrating mindfulness into psychology and the helping professions*. Washington, DC: American Psychological Association.

ADDITIONAL RESOURCES

http://eprints-gro.gold.ac.uk/2391/ and www.learn.gold.ac.uk [select Psychology, then Small Group Research, then login as a guest] (a brief bibliography by Blumberg, "Psychological literature related to mindfulness")
www.ellenlanger.com (Langer's ongoing work)
www.joannamacy.net and www.plumvillage.org (mindful activism combined with ecological awareness)

Minimal Group Paradigm

SABINE OTTEN

"Can discrimination be traced to such origin as social conflict or a history of hostility? Not necessarily. Apparently the mere fact of division into groups is enough to trigger discriminatory behavior." These sentences, with which Tajfel (1970) opened his first report on what is now known as the minimal group experiments, provide in a nutshell both the main research question that led to the development of the Minimal Group Paradigm (MGP), and the main conclusion from its results. When this publication – and later the better-known piece by Tajfel, Billig, Bundy, and Flament (1971) – came out, the authors probably weren't expecting how much impact their research on the minimum conditions for eliciting ingroup favoritism and relative outgroup derogation would have on both theory and research in the field. In fact, MGP as designed by Tajfel and his co-workers quickly became, and still is, a widely used and extremely useful approach, allowing researchers to investigate basic processes in people's behavior as group members in a highly controlled setting. Moreover, the findings on so-called minimal groups inspired the development of one of the most relevant theories on intergroup behavior: social identity theory (Tajfel & Turner, 1979). (See SOCIAL IDENTITY THEORY.)

THE PARADIGM

The procedure that became famous as MGP was originally designed by Tajfel et al. (1971) as a sort of baseline control condition to be pitted against situations that would elicit intergroup behavior. Yet, the 1971 studies and many others that followed (e.g., Brewer, 1979; Hewstone, Rubin, & Willis, 2002) revealed that mere categorization, that is, assigning people to an arbitrary category as opposed to another arbitrary category, can result in ingroup bias. According to Tajfel et al., the following features characterize the minimal group situation:

- People are categorized into groups that are arbitrary: There are no previous experiences with group membership, nor a group history (such as a previous conflict or relations of negative interdependence with the other group), nor any preexisting stereotypes that might directly feed in and possibly justify evaluation or allocation decisions at stake.
- The categorization is anonymous; people know only which group they themselves are in. By keeping the categorization of the other group members concealed, it is assured that only group membership *per se* and not interpersonal liking can guide responses.
- There is no direct individual self-interest involved: people do resource allocations for other ingroup and outgroup members, but not for themselves.

In the study by Tajfel et al., for example, a group of schoolboys was categorized allegedly based on their preference for a certain painter, Klee or Kandinsky. This preference was determined by a fake test, in which participants were presented several pairs of pictures from which they had to choose the one they liked best. After a short delay, the schoolboys were randomly and anonymously categorized as member of either the Klee or the Kandinsky group. Next they filled in a series of allocation matrices in order to distribute money between several pairs of recipients, who were differentiated only by a code number and their group membership (i.e., Klee or Kandinsky). Importantly, their own code number was not included in any of the matrices to ensure that self-interest did not influence how they allocated money to the groups. The allocation matrices allowed the schoolboys to pursue several allocation strategies, namely:

- Fairness (ingroup and outgroup get exactly the same).

- Maximum ingroup profit (trying to allocate such that the ingroup gets maximum resources).
- Maximum joint profit (seeking an allocation option that implies the highest profit for the two groups together, irrespective of which group gets more).
- Maximum difference (a distribution in which the positive difference between ingroup and outgroup is maximized, without necessarily implying maximum ingroup profit).

It would exceed the scope of this article to describe the allocation matrices and the way they are analyzed in more detail, or to summarize the heated debate about its validity and about alternative methods of measurement. In fact, in later studies many different variables have been measured in minimal group settings, with intergroup allocation decisions, intergroup evaluations, and measures of group identification being the most popular options. Also, a whole variety of arbitrary categorization criteria have been used, varying from categorization characteristics that have the appeal to be plausible and potentially meaningful (such as perceptual styles, concentration curves, artistic preferences) to criteria that are fully meaningless (such as distinguishing a blue from a red group, and tossing a coin in order to determine who would end up in which group). Moreover, in some variations of the experiment, the criterion of anonymous categorization has been given up in order to allow for investigating, for example, interaction processes in completely novel groups. The most important point is that the lack of a group history and the arbitrariness of the categorization can be identified as the key features characterizing minimal groups.

FINDINGS

The findings by Tajfel et al. became famous as the mere categorization effect: Merely categorizing members into two distinct, but fully arbitrary, novel groups can be sufficient to elicit intergroup behavior, i.e., favoritism for one's own group relative to the other group. Surprisingly, even in the absence of any conflict relation or negative interdependence between the groups, people showed a strong interest to differentiate between their own and other group, and they were inclined to treat and evaluate their own group better than the other group. These findings turned out to be very robust, and have been replicated in numerous studies (for surveys, see Brewer, 1979; Hewstone, Rubin, & Willis, 2002). Probably the most striking finding in the original group experiment was that people's interest to establish a – positive – difference between own and other group was so strong that it was even pursued at the expense of maximizing ingroup profit. As will be outlined below, this phenomenon was specifically inspiring for theories on intergroup behavior.

Interestingly, when measures are used that allow us to differentiate between ingroup and outgroup treatment, it turns out that – compared with allocations or evaluations directed at uncategorized recipients – introducing a distinction between us and them, however trivial the underlying reasoning is, will especially affect reactions to fellow ingroup members: those who belong to the own group are treated and evaluated significantly better than anonymous uncategorized targets. Importantly, however, a basic minimal group situation does *not* easily lead to outgroup derogation. Based on only an arbitrary categorization and in the absence of any negative interdependence, reactions to outgroup members are as neutral (or slightly positive) as those to uncategorized recipients (Brewer, 1979). One's increased valuing of the ingroup does not mean that there will be a commensurate devaluing of the outgroup.

More recently, the basic minimal group was also used to demonstrate ingroup favoritism on implicit measures. For example, Otten and Wentura (1999) categorized participants into one of two groups (allegedly based on "concentration styles") and immediately afterwards asked them to do an evaluation task at the computer: adjectives had to be classified as quickly as possible as either positive or negative. Importantly, each adjective was preceded by a subliminally presented prime, either the ingroup or the outgroup label. The results showed that response latencies for pairings of an ingroup prime with a positive adjective were indeed fastest, signaling ingroup bias also on this very subtle measure. As the categorization used in the experiment was minimal, the finding implies that positive bias towards own groups can be perceived as an automatic response and a sort of default option from which people only deviate when reality forces them to do so.

RELEVANCE

The findings obtained in MGP were of utmost relevance for the development of theories on intergroup behavior. The fact that people were even willing to sacrifice material benefits for the sake of creating more distance between own and other groups did challenge the idea that intergroup conflict is fully determined by the nature of interdependence between groups. As long as a group is not hindered by an outgroup in getting its relevant resources, there should be harmony rather than tension. This idea, however, is challenged by the mere categorization effect. Obviously, not only realistic conflict of interests, but also other psychological motives can instigate intergroup differentiation and discrimination. In a first attempt to understand this finding, Tajfel (1970) postulated a generic norm of intergroup discrimination behavior as underlying the process for the mere categorization effect; yet such explanation turned out to be rather circular and, accordingly, of relatively little predictive value. In 1979, however, Tajfel and Turner published their social identity theory (SIT), which offered a much more convincing and elaborated account for the findings in MGP, and which up to now is extremely relevant in theories and research on ingroup favoritism and intergroup discrimination. (See SOCIAL IDENTITY THEORY.)

The basic assumption of SIT is that an individual's self-concept is comprised of both a personal and a social identity, with the latter being determined by the social categories a person belongs to. Once social identity becomes salient, people will define themselves and act in terms of that group membership, thereby attenuating intragroup differences and accentuating intergroup differences. Therein, the differentiation from other groups serves, on the one hand, a cognitive function, as it helps in structuring the social world, and, on the other hand, a motivational function: positive distinctiveness of the own group as compared to other groups provides the individual with positive self-regard, whereas disadvantageous intergroup comparisons (negative social identities) will elicit coping mechanisms, either cognitively or behaviorally.

Importantly, the idea of a striving for positive ingroup distinctiveness – irrespective of material conflict of interests – offers an account for ingroup favoritism and intergroup discrimination in MGP, which is, at least by many, still considered convincing. Moreover, and more importantly, SIT does justice to the idea that is demonstrated so impressively by the findings on minimal groups: When group membership becomes salient, this brings in specific cognitive and motivational factors, and, therefore, intra- and intergroup behavior deserve to be studied in their own right. While this was still a controversial statement in the early 1970s, it is now a commonplace idea. Clearly, MGP has its share in this development.

CONCLUSION

The observation that the very minimal conditions that Tajfel and his collaborators developed were sufficient to elicit ingroup bias was and still is certainly fascinating, and the value that this paradigm had for developing theories on intergroup behavior cannot be overestimated. But, of course, MGP and the conclusions derived from its results have also elicited criticism. Obviously, the paradigm provides a highly arbitrary setting, thereby creating doubts about the generalizability to intergroup behavior in the "real" world. Nonetheless, such criticism does not question the idea that this paradigm offers the researcher a highly controllable and thus very useful environment to test basic processes in situations wherein people's group membership is salient.

SEE ALSO: Social Identity Theory.

REFERENCES

Brewer, M. (1979). Ingroup bias in the minimal intergroup situation: A cognitive–motivational analysis. *Psychological Bulletin*, 86(2), 307–324.

Hewstone, M., Rubin, M., & Willis, H. (2002). Intergroup bias. *Annual Review of Psychology*, 53(1), 575–604.

Otten, S., & Wentura, D. (1999). About the impact of automaticity in the Minimal Group Paradigm: Evidence from affective priming tasks. *European Journal of Social Psychology*, 29(8), 1049–1071.

Tajfel, H. (1970). Experiments in intergroup discrimination. *Scientific American, 223*, 96–102.

Tajfel, H., Billig, M., Bundy, R., & Flament, C. (1971). Social categorization and intergroup behaviour. *European Journal of Social Psychology, 1*(2), 149–178.

Tajfel, H., & Turner, J. C. (1979). An integrative theory of intergroup conflict. In W. G. Austin & S. Worchel (Eds.), *The social psychology of intergroup relations* (S. 33–47). Monterey, CA: Brooks/Cole Publishing.

Mobilization: Peaceful and Violent

JOSE F. VALENCIA

There is agreement among the scholars of democracy, from Rousseau and J. S. Mill to Tarrow and Putnam, that mass participation is essential for the life of a representative democracy. Political participation is the critical link between the citizenry and the governing process and "provides the mechanism by which citizens can communicate information about their interests, preferences, and needs and generate pressure to respond" (Verba, Schlozman, & Brady, 1995, p. 1). (See ACTIVISM, PSYCHOLOGY OF SOCIAL.)

After World War II, studies on conventional behavior began with the "legitimacy perspective" of participation: actions like working for a party and contacting authorities reflected satisfaction and support for the political system. Protest actions like taking part in demonstrations or strikes reflected dissatisfaction with the political system. Individual rational theories were the main explanatory devices for action: efficacy, value-expectancy theories, individual background factors, identification with the party and the leaders, etc.

The objective political and economic changes that happened during the 1960s and 1970s, however, led to the legitimacy perspective which distinguished between people who supported and those who protested the political system being challenged. An alternative perspective was offered: the "strategic resources perspective." According to the latter perspective, different issues and different times require alternative strategies. Moreover, political mobilization was no longer divided between people who support and people who oppose the political system: activists were shown to choose to participate in both forms of political mobilization.

In addition, survey research was demonstrating a rise in nonconventional forms of political mobilization (Barnes & Kaase, 1979). Comparing the Political Action Survey of 1974 with the World Values Survey of 2000 in eight Western countries, 32% vs. 63% of the population said that they had signed a petition, 9% vs. 21% had taken part in a demonstration, 2% vs. 4% had taken part in an unofficial strike, and 2% vs. 3% had occupied buildings. At the same time, according to the World Values Survey, in the 1980s and 2000 in most European countries, membership of political parties had decreased from 4.9% to 3.8% by 2000. In other words, the traditional citizen-oriented strategy – mainly related to elections and parties – was being complemented with a cause-oriented strategy – mainly related to boycotting, petitioning, demonstrations, and protest.

Today, the term political participation refers to any type of behavior carried out by an individual or group for the purpose of affecting public matters. Hence, political mobilization is *active* engagement by individuals and groups with the governmental processes that affect their lives. This encompasses involvement both in decision-making and in acts of opposition. Acts of active engagement include conventional political participation (such as voting, standing for office, and campaigning for a political party) and unconventional acts, which may be legitimate (such as signing a petition and attending a peaceful demonstration), or illegal (such as violent protest and refusing to pay taxes).

THEORIES OF MOBILIZATION

The literature on social mobilization started from the very beginning by analyzing the relationship between grievances and political protest. From the point of view of social movements theory, three main views have been offered. According to the first view, the mass society theory, collective behavior is based on grievances and the irrational image of the actor is the main theoretical feature. During the 1970s, with improvements in different forms of political protest, a change of paradigm appeared with two versions: resource mobilization theory (RMT) in the United States and new social movements (NSM) in Europe.

According to the RMT version, theorists stopped asking why people felt frustrated enough to engage in collective protest, and instead they asked when and how people secured the resources to combat their exclusion from those channels. Collective actors' "interests" were implied by the formulation, with people mobilizing to gain access to the stable structure of political bargaining. Collective interests were taken to be long-standing: RMT assumed an already existing collective actor able to recognize the opening of political opportunities and to mobilize their resources for political purposes, having thus a rational image of the actor. In short, RMT attempts to explain social mobilization by viewing individuals as rational actors engaged in instrumental actions and using formal organizations to secure resources and foster mobilization (Zald & McCarthy, 1987). Because individual participation in social mobilization is explained only by a cost–benefit analysis of resources, cultural tools such as grievances and mechanisms for the social cohesion of groups are not the deciding factors for when social mobilization will arise. Grievances are considered to be more a background factor always present in a society, but with no explanatory power for predicting social mobilization. In fact, grievances may be created and manipulated by issue entrepreneurs to form social movement organizations for personal resource gain (Zald & McCarthy, 1987).

This assumption was challenged by scholars of the second version: NSM theory. Compared to RMT, NSM is based to a great extent on social constructionism, which looks at framing processes and identity formation. NSM theory conceptualizes changes in identity formation as manifestations of macro-social changes in industrial societies (Melucci, 1980). These changes in identity formation and framing processes result in NSMs, which is why framing processes and identity formations are given prime consideration in determining when individuals will join NSMs. Here grievances are closely linked with the frame and identity of the individual, and so NSM theory considers grievances to be important.

In recent decades, the objective transformations of our societies have also produced changes in the cognitive systems of actors motivated towards the change of political conditions. On the one hand, social conflict and deviation are the basic analytical tools of this theory. On the other hand, and in relation to the characteristics of social actors, cognitive changes refer to: (1) the loss of legitimacy on the part of the political system, (2) the disappearance of fatalism on the part of the citizens, and (3) an increase in the sense of political efficacy.

Constructionism within the theory of NSM now has a broad literature, the perspective of "frame analysis" being one of the most widely used in the analysis of the production of meaning (Klandermans, 1997). The perspective of frame analysis is based on the idea that political protest does not depend only on the existence of inequality and grievances, structural changes, political opportunities, resources of the organization, and cost–benefit calculus, but also on the way in which those variables are framed, to the extent that they are related to the goals of mobilization. This perspective emphasizes the way in which the actors translate the macro-structural conditions into a predisposition to mobilize. (See NON-VIOLENT DEMOCRATIC TRANSITIONS.)

Three specialized frames are important in the social construction of protest, the first two being the "injustice frame" and the "identity frame," through which certain events or situations are defined as problematic, and diverse agents are regarded as responsible for causing the problem. However, for the social actors to apply themselves in mobilization it is necessary to develop the conviction of the existence of urgency, as well as a sense of efficacy to proceed in a collective manner: this is known as the "efficacy frame." (See SELF-EFFICACY.)

TYPES OF MOBILIZATION

To the extent that political mobilization establishes links between the public and political decision-makers, a wide range of activities are included: voting in elections, giving money or devoting time to political campaigns, writing petitions, boycotting, organizing social movements (whether old or new), demonstrating (whether legally or illegally), occupying buildings, physical violence against the forces of order, blockades, using political violence, etc. (See PEOPLE POWER.) These loosely related activities have traditionally been classified as two main modes of mobilization: conventional and nonconventional.

Under the first umbrella – conventional or peaceful political mobilization – are behaviors related to campaigns, voting, discussing politics, convincing people to vote, contacting politicians, and working to solve community problems. In regard to nonconventional or violent political mobilization, the question of how many and what kinds of dimensions underlie it are contested. Nonconventional political mobilization includes behaviors related to taking part in demonstrations (whether legally or illegally), taking part in strikes, signing petitions, blocking roads, boycotting products, occupying buildings, spraying graffiti,

damaging property, physical violence against the forces of order, using political violence, etc. Political protest has usually been used as an index consisting of the sum of items either for theoretical reasons or for practical reasons (Barnes & Kaase, 1979). However, some studies in this area have distinguished two main dimensions: illegal versus radical forms. New strategies of analysis such as smallest space analysis have found two other dimensions (Cohen & Valencia 2008): availability and involvement. In contrast, large surveys (i.e., World Values Surveys) have used factor analyses and have shown only one dimension.

Engaging in political protest – a less popular form of political participation than voting behavior – is problematic because of both the costs levied on participants and the benefits that might be expected from the protest. There is more uncertainty related to political protest than in conventional participation in both costs and impact. The uncertainty of taking part in protest, however, depends on the expectation of how many people will take part. Generalized trust fosters movement participation, and "trusters" are able to make guesses about the likelihood of success in protest with more confidence than "nontrusters," because trust allows them to form expectations about the actions of others. The likelihood of taking part in protest has been related in the literature to the individual's resources for participation, to the grievances toward the regime, to the tolerance displayed by the regime, to social networks, and to interpersonal trust.

INTERNET AND MOBILIZATION

Finally, the rapid growth of new information technologies and especially the Internet has allowed the emergence of new forms of political mobilization. Behaviors related to replying to or sending a petition by short messaging service (SMS) which may, for example, use cell phones, or using web chatrooms and/or forums, or spreading information by email, or setting up websites, are all becoming popular ways of communicating. Two perspectives have been posited in this area: optimistic and pessimistic perspectives. According to the optimistic view, Internet use increases levels of political participation, suggesting that the Internet positively affects political information gathering and political activities (Norris, 2002). According to the pessimistic view, theorists argue that the Internet has no effect on political participation in general, because the Internet itself does not transform people into politically interested people. Recent research testing the competing views has shown that given equality of access, the Internet does show genuine potential towards political participation.

SEE ALSO: Activism, Psychology of Social; Nonviolent Democratic Transitions; People Power; Self-Efficacy.

REFERENCES

Barnes, S., & Kaase, M. (1979). *Political action*. Beverly Hills, CA: Sage.

Cohen, E., & Valencia, J. F. (2008). Political protest and power distance: Towards a typology of political participation. *Bulletin de Méthodologie Sociologique, 99*, 54–72.

Klandermans, B. (1997). *The social psychology of protest*. Oxford, UK: Blackwell.

Melucci, A. (1980). The new social movements: A theoretical approach. *Social Science Information, 19*, 199–226.

Norris, P. (2002) Revolution? What revolution? The Internet and US elections, 1992–2000. In J. S. Nye & E. C. Kamarck (Eds.), *Governance. com: Democracy in the information age*. Cambridge, UK: Cambridge University Press.

Verba, S., Schlozman, K., & Brady, H. (1995). *Voice and equality*. Cambridge, UK: Cambridge University Press.

Zald, M., & McCarthy, J. D. (1987). *Social movements in an organizational society*. New Brunswick, NJ: Transaction.

ADDITIONAL RESOURCES

http://www.europeansocialsurvey.org/ (European Social Survey, with available data from 30 countries on political participation from 2002 on)

http://www.socialpsychology.org/ (Social Psychology Network, with searchable links to many topics on political mobilization)

Monitoring Human Rights in Educational Settings

MICHAEL B. GREENE

Education is both a human right in itself and an indispensable means of realizing other human rights.

United Nations Economic and
Social Council

The first internationally recognized statement of modern-day human rights is embodied in the Universal Declaration of Human Rights (UDHR). Ratified without objection by the United Nation General Assembly in 1948, the UDHR recognizes the "inherent dignity" and "equal and inalienable rights" of all persons. The UNHR and two subsequently adopted international human rights documents – the International Covenant on Civil and Political Rights (1966) and the International Covenant on Economic, Social and Cultural Rights (1966) – comprise the International Bill of Rights (IBR). In addition, the Convention on the Rights of the Child (CRC), adopted by the United Nations General Assembly in 1989, incorporates an unprecedented array of civil, political, social, cultural, and economic rights that accrue specifically to children. Together, the IBR and the CRC, supplemented by official commentaries, represent

656   MONITORING HUMAN RIGHTS IN EDUCATIONAL SETTINGS

the most widely endorsed set of articulated fundamental human rights that can serve and have served to inform and direct educational policies and practices. (See CHILDREN AND HUMAN RIGHTS; HUMAN RIGHTS AND HUMAN RIGHTS VIOLATIONS, PSYCHOLOGICAL ASPECTS OF.)

At the outset, it must be noted that international human rights covenants and conventions must be ratified by each nation state in order to attain the status of domestic law. When ratified, it is each nation's responsibility to ensure that rights are monitored and enforced. Moreover, nations have the option to ratify human rights documents with reservations, an option that typically weakens a nation's human rights obligations. Nevertheless, the UDHR, while universally endorsed and often described as an international moral compass, does not obligate nation states to monitor or to enforce the 30 articles contained therein.

Furthermore, any reading of the international landscape reveals widespread violations of fundamental human rights among nations that have and have not ratified international human rights documents. Monitoring and enforcement of human rights treaties by individual nations, as well as the United Nations, are simply very weak. Indeed, it is nongovernmental human rights organizations that have produced the most rigorous reports of human rights violations.

If the international community does a poor job of monitoring and enforcing human rights, why is it important, or even reasonable, for educational institutions to take on this burden? The most straightforward answer is that the IBR and the CRC provide the only set of internationally endorsed standards that focus on "the best interests of the child," a focus much needed and much abused in educational institutions throughout the world. Moreover, most nations have promulgated educational laws and regulations that overlap significantly

with specific human rights articles, including laws and regulations regarding mandatory education, bullying and sexual harassment, equity standards and disability rights, and corporal punishment (Stone, 2002). Similarly, many components of existing curricula focus directly or indirectly on human rights, for example, holocaust studies, the study of the American Bill of (Civil) Rights, the French Revolution, and the history of slavery and civil rights movements.

In addition, many of the precepts embraced in the IBR and the CRC have been independently endorsed as best practices within a large body of educational research. For example, the CRC requires that children be listened to and participate actively and meaningfully in their education. A great deal of research has demonstrated superior educational outcomes with active or participatory versus passive engagement of children in their own schooling (Davis, 2007). Similarly, the CRC's emphasis on a holistic approach to development, embracing the child's physical, mental, spiritual, moral, psychological, and social development is widely endorsed by developmental psychologists and progressive educational leaders.

HUMAN RIGHTS OBLIGATIONS PERTAINING TO EDUCATIONAL INSTITUTIONS

The most fundamental human rights obligation with respect to education is the requirement to provide free, compulsory, accessible, and nondiscriminatory education for all individuals at the elementary school level and the requirement to progressively introduce free and compulsory education at the secondary and higher educational levels. Furthermore, education must be provided in settings that provide adequate sanitation facilities, safe drinking water, appropriate heating and cooling systems, and appropriate teaching materials.

The IBR and the CRC, and corresponding commentaries, also have much to say about the aims of education (Office of the United Nations High Commissioner for Human Rights, 2001). To wit, education must:

- be directed to the full and harmonious development of the child's personality, talents, and mental abilities;
- prepare the child to live and participate responsibly in a free society in the spirit of understanding, peace, respect, and dignity for all;
- be relevant to the circumstances of the societal and cultural context in which students are educated;
- promote among children respect for the their parents and their cultural identities;
- formulate and implement policies and practices based upon the dictum "best interests of the child";
- ensure that children have the skills to make sound decisions, resolve conflicts, establish healthy relationships, and think critically; and
- instill a lifelong respect for human rights, diversity, and fundamental freedoms.

In addition to specifying the fundamental aims of education, human rights documents and commentaries outline three types of obligations: protection of children, direct provision of rights, and promotion of participatory rights. Educational institutions must first and foremost protect the child from harm, including psychological harm. Intimidation, bullying, and other forms of victimization are anathema to a human rights education. Some types of protection, however, cannot be fully guaranteed by educational institutions alone, for example, freedom of movement within a country, the right to asylum in case of persecution, and the right to practice a religion. On the other hand, educational institutions can educate children about these and other fundamental rights and provide time and space to discuss and analyze the rationale for such rights. Furthermore, programs, class exercises, and processes to identify and redress human rights violations can be provided as part of the educational endeavor. And, of course, a sound education is perhaps the clearest way to promote economic human rights for all.

The provision of human rights by educational institutions takes several forms, including but not limited to pedagogical practices, educational polices, curricular materials, and the establishment of rules and sanctions. Pedagogical practices must reflect the democratic and participatory processes that are articulated in all human rights documents. Inflexible and hierarchical structures and authoritarian practices are contrary to human rights education. Instead, education must be organized as a flexible, exploratory, experiential, participatory, and nondogmatic endeavor. Rules must be experienced as fair and just by students and staff and sanctions must be consistently applied. A restorative justice model should be promoted, dictating that corporal punishment and shaming techniques are inappropriate practices. Similarly, an ethos of caring should be promoted, encouraging all members of the school community to do their best to be supportive of one another.

Respect for students and for children's rights also dictates that students should have the right to express themselves and their points of view and that their perspectives are taken seriously. It requires that students – based upon their evolving cognitive and affective capacities – are provided with appropriate and meaningful opportunities to participate in decision-making about policies and procedures that affect their lives.

The curricula must also mirror the core principle of nondiscrimination. Educational materials cannot convey, through omission or commission, gender, class, cultural, ethnic, disability, and religious biases.

Similarly, fundamental human rights documents, the history of human rights movements, and methods to identify and remedy human rights violations must be included in the curricula. As importantly, educational processes must be designed to sensitize students to human rights violations wherever they may occur and to promote a commitment to act to redress such violations when such violations are identified (Johnny, 2005). In this sense, human rights education is empowering and transformative.

While this sounds daunting, much work has already been done in reforming educational practices to embrace a human rights orientation. Programs that incorporate the principles and processes described above, such as "Communities that Care" and "Facing History and Ourselves," have been developed, comprehensive human rights curricula have been written, and human-rights-oriented service learning projects and classroom activities have been described (Stone, 2002).

MONITORING HUMAN RIGHTS OBLIGATIONS

Monitoring, as used herein, refers to a continuous feedback mechanism or quality improvement process through which schools can increasingly implement a human rights framework (Carvalho, 2008). As such, the monitoring process requires assessments over time in order to identify where and how improvements need to be made and whether such improvements are secured as a result of appropriate corrective action. Monitoring also must be a collaborative endeavor, a process shared by all members of the educational community, that is, students, staff, parents, community members, and nongovernmental organizations (NGOs). Indeed, participation of NGOs in the monitoring process is mandated by the CRC. It is

also important to note that monitoring activity must be comprehensive and holistic. Because human rights are indivisible and intrinsically interdependent (Hunt, 2007), the monitoring process cannot cherry-pick specific rights for monitoring.

Monitoring human rights can broadly be divided into "monitoring in principle" and "monitoring in practice." *Monitoring in principle* involves a comparative analysis of human rights obligations with existing educational laws, regulations, and standards. This kind of monitoring is time consuming and requires a thoroughgoing knowledge of human rights standards as well as federal and state laws and regulations. Rather than examining state and federal laws, it is more efficient and effective to utilize local educational policies and regulations as the fundamental documents that should be examined with regard to human rights adherence. Local policies and regulations generally incorporate the vast array of state and federal laws and regulations, for example, equity plans, special education policies and procedures, sexual harassment policies, codes of conduct, and curricular standards and requirements. With these documents in hand, checklists, matrices, and benchmarks derived from relevant articles of the IBR and the CRC, and official commentaries can be used to assess human rights compliance. Models for doing this kind of work have been developed (Landman, 2004).

Monitoring in practice is even more daunting in that it is designed to examine the degree to which human rights principles and practices are implemented and accorded to all. Different sets of data are needed and different methodologies must be used. For example, while core curriculum standards and required texts may be useful in assessing rights in principle, monitoring rights in practice requires an examination of what is taught and practiced in the classroom.

Methods to conduct these types of analyses include surveys of all key stakeholders, interviews and focus groups, classroom observations, reviews of archival materials documenting past instances of and responses to rights violations, and ethnographies (Landman, 2004).

Multiple dimensions must be examined to monitoring rights in practice, including pedagogical methods (hierarchical versus participatory, power sharing, and democratic), educational content (including the history of human rights movements and fundamental human rights documents), opportunities to promote human rights and remedy human rights violations, interpersonal relationships (dismissive versus respectful and supportive), restorative justice practices, safety (programs and practices to reduce bullying and intimidation), and opportunities to engage in dialogues and discussions about human rights (utilizing such methods as class debates and peer education) (Stone, 2002). As with protocols to monitor human rights in principle, many survey instruments, focus group protocols, and observational checklists have been developed to monitor rights in practice (Carvalho, 2008).

In order to determine whether human rights are provided to all, data pertaining to the provision of human rights must be disaggregated, minimally by race, gender, and ethnicity, in order to determine whether discriminatory practices exist (Carvalho, 2008). Specific instances of human rights violations, systematic practices related to human rights (omissions and commissions), and structural underpinnings that facilitate human rights violations (inequities in educational funding, building maintenance, and equipment) must be monitored. Strategies to remedy each type of violation must be discussed and developed, an ongoing task that is the responsibility of all stakeholders.

CONCLUSION

An education system that incorporates and infuses a thoroughgoing human rights framework ensures that our future generations understand the meaning and importance of civil, political, cultural, social, and economic rights and that they have the knowhow and will to advocate and pursue these rights within their own communities and in the world at large. Monitoring how these rights are accorded, taught, and implemented in the school setting provides a critically important mechanism for promoting and continuously improving the ways these tasks are accomplished. If it does nothing else, the monitoring endeavor promotes an inward look by the professional educational community, students, parents, and citizens at large about how the key human rights values that have been articulated and internationally embraced are conveyed to our children and youth.

SEE ALSO: Children and Human Rights; Human Rights and Human Rights Violations, Psychological Aspects of.

REFERENCES

Carvalho, E. (2008). Measuring children's rights: An alternative approach. *International Journal of Children's Rights*, 16, 543–563.

Davis, J. M. (2007). Analysing participation and social exclusion with children and young people: Lessons from practice. *International Journal of Children's Rights*, 15(1), 121–146.

Hunt, L. (2007). *Inventing human rights: A history*. New York, NY: Norton.

Johnny, L. (2005). UN Convention on the Rights of the Child: A rationale for implementing participatory rights in schools. *Canadian Journal of Educational Administration and Policy*, 40, 1–20.

Landman, T. (2004). Measuring human rights: Principle, practice and policy. *Human Rights Quarterly*, 26, 906–931.

Office of the United Nations High
Commissioner for Human Rights. (2001).
General Comment 1: The aims of education.
Geneva, Switzerland: Office of the United
Nations High Commissioner for Human
Rights. Retrieved from http://
www.unhchr.ch/tbs/doc.nsf/(symbol)/
CRC.GC.2001.1.En?OpenDocument
Stone, A. (2002). Human rights education and
public policy in the United States: Mapping
the road ahead. *Human Rights Quarterly, 24,*
537–557.

ADDITIONAL RESOURCES

Human Rights Resource Center, at http://
www.hrusa.org/default.htm: provides a
wealth of free information, curricula, and
resource materials regarding human rights
education.
National Center for Human Rights Education,
at http://www.pdhre.org/index.html: a
treasure trove of information and documents
about human rights education.
Office of the High Commissioner for Human
Rights, at http://www.ohchr.org/EN/Pages/
WelcomePage.aspx: offers a wealth of
information about human rights, including
virtually every UN-sponsored human rights
document, official commentaries, model
human rights curricula, current activities, and
additional literature.

Moral Conviction

G. SCOTT MORGAN AND LINDA J. SKITKA

A theme that cuts across many societal debates is that at least one side defines its position in moral terms. For example, some people's positions on legalized abortion, same-sex marriage, or healthcare reform are vested with moral conviction (i.e., these positions are based on beliefs about fundamental right and wrong, good and bad). The recognition that some attitudes seem to be imbued with particular moral fervor led to a program of theory and research designed to investigate whether there is anything special about attitudes held with strong moral conviction ("moral mandates"). This article will briefly review the integrated theory of moral conviction, which distinguishes moral mandates from otherwise strong but nonmoral attitudes. In addition, we will review some research that clarifies some potentially unsettling and reassuring implications of moral conviction for peace and conflict.

THE INTEGRATED THEORY OF MORAL CONVICTION

Moral mandates have a number of defining characteristics that theoretically distinguish them from otherwise strong but nonmoral attitudes, including perceived universality, perceived objectivity, autonomy, and ties to strong emotions. These factors provide moral mandates with considerable motivational force, and therefore higher degrees of consistency between attitudes and behavior.

Perceived Universality

People perceive their moral mandates as more universally applicable than other kinds of attitudes such as preferences or normative conventions. In contrast to moral mandates, personal preferences are subject to individual discretion and are not socially regulated; one's preference to vacation at the beach instead of the mountains is a matter of taste. Attitudes rooted in normative convention reflect socially or culturally shared notions about the way things are normally done in one's group, and differ from moral imperatives because people outside of the group are not required to adhere to them. (See NORMATIVE INFLUENCE, THEORIES OF.) For example, people will say it is "wrong" to drive on the left side of the street in the United States, but that it is perfectly fine to do so in the United Kingdom. In contrast to preferences and conventions, moral mandates are absolute standards of truth that people perceive as applying to everyone: right is right and wrong is wrong. People may realize that there are differences of opinion on issues they see as moral, but seem to believe that if they could explain the "facts" to those who disagree, these others would certainly see the light and adopt the "correct" point of view.

Perceived Objectivity

Closely related to the proposition that moral mandates are perceived as universals, people also perceive their moral mandates as objective facts about the world. For example, if one asks a person with a moral mandate about female circumcision to explain why it is wrong, that person is likely to declare, "Because it's just wrong!" The "fact" that female circumcision is wrong is as psychologically self-evident as $2 + 2 = 4$.

Autonomy

Moral mandates represent something different from and independent of people's concerns about authority or group acceptance. When people's moral convictions are at stake, they are likely to believe that duties and rights follow from the greater moral purposes that underlie rules, procedures, authority dictates, or group norms rather than from these things themselves. Moral mandates are not by definition anti-authority or anti-group; they simply reflect personal and autonomous concerns rather than authority or group dependent concerns.

Motivation and Justification

Another characteristic that distinguishes moral mandates from otherwise strong but nonmoral attitudes is the degree to which the former motivate behavior. (See EMOTIONAL APPEALS, MOBILIZING THROUGH.) Nonmoral preferences – even very strong

preferences – may be easily overwhelmed by factors that prevent people from translating those preferences into action. In contrast, the anticipated negative consequences of failing to live up to one's own moral beliefs (e.g., shame, guilt, and regret) may be more severe than failing to do something one would prefer. Similarly, the anticipated positive consequences of taking a stand for what is "right" (e.g., pride, gratification, elevation, and self-affirmation) may be more uplifting than the satisfaction of doing something one would prefer. People experience emotions in conjunction with moral mandates more strongly than they do with preferences or conventions – people do not become angry when others disagree with their vacation tastes but may become enraged by those who violate their moral mandates. In short, the emotional intensity of moral mandates is associated with stronger motivations to take action. (See EMOTION.)

In addition to having a strong motivational component, moral mandates are self-justifying. People tend to describe their moral mandates with statements such as "It's just right!" or "It's just wrong!" The question, "Why is it right or wrong?" is perceived as odd: The notion that one's position is simply right or simply wrong *is* sufficient justification for taking a stand.

IMPLICATIONS OF MORAL MANDATES FOR PEACE AND CONFLICT

The psychological characteristics of moral mandates have both negative and positive implications for peace and conflict. On one hand, our understanding of moral mandates provides some insights into when and why people sometimes become mired in intractable conflict. (See CONFLICT, INTRACTABLE.) When people hold a moral mandate, they (a) are more intolerant of and likely to discriminate against attitudinally dissimilar others, (b) experience difficulty developing or agreeing to procedures to resolve conflict, (c) are more resistant to the power of authority or rule of law, (d) are inoculated against majority group influence, and (e) are more willing to accept any means, including violence, to achieve preferred ends. On the other hand, moral mandates also provide the courage for people to stand up for what they believe is right and provide the motivational impetus for prosocial behaviors and activism. (See PROSOCIAL BEHAVIOR; ACTIVISM, PSYCHOLOGY OF SOCIAL.)

Moral Conviction as a Potential Barrier to Conflict Resolution

Intolerance   When moral mandates are at stake, tolerance of differing viewpoints has little or no room at the table: right is right and wrong is wrong. (See TOLERANCE FOR DIVERSE GROUPS.) Accordingly, stronger moral convictions predict increased intolerance of attitudinally dissimilar others. People do not want to live near, be friends, share resources with, or even sit too close to someone who does not share their moral convictions (e.g., Skitka, Bauman, & Sargis, 2005; Wright, Cullum, & Schwab, 2008).

Barriers to conflict resolution   Moral mandates impede people's ability to find procedural solutions to conflict. For example, Skitka et al. (2005) examined the interactions of people within attitudinally heterogeneous and homogeneous groups who were asked to develop a procedure to resolve an assigned issue. Some groups had members with strong but nonmoral attitudes whereas other groups had members with moral mandates about the issue at hand. Results indicated that group processes and climate were strikingly different in these types of groups. Compared to other groups, attitudinally heterogeneous groups that discussed procedures to resolve a morally mandated issue were (a) lowest in reported good will and cooperativeness toward their fellow group members, and (b) perceived as most

defensive and tense by third party observers who were blind to details about group composition. Furthermore, groups that worked to develop procedures to resolve a morally mandated issue (regardless of whether groups were attitudinally heterogeneous or homogeneous) were the least likely to successfully develop a procedure to resolve their assigned issue. Many forms of social conflict are rooted in deep moral cleavages and different assumptions about fundamental questions of right and wrong; these results reveal some of the inherent barriers that moral mandates pose for conflict resolution. (See CONFLICT RESOLUTION, SOCIOPSYCHOLOGICAL BARRIERS TO; PEACE, OVERCOMING PSYCHOLOGICAL–COGNITIVE BARRIERS TO.)

Resistance to authorities and majority group influence   People often do not know the "right" answer to various decisions or conflicts and therefore frequently rely on authorities, rules, or laws to provide solutions. However, when people have a moral mandate about what outcome authorities and institutions should deliver, they become much more invested in decision outcomes than whether decision-making authorities or institutions are legitimate or procedurally fair. "Right" decisions indicate that authorities are appropriate and work as they should. "Wrong" decisions signal that the system is somehow broken. In short, when moral mandates are at stake, people are less concerned about complying with authorities or the law, and they use whether authorities "get it right" as an important test of the authorities' fairness and legitimacy. Consistent with the authority independence hypothesis, whether decisions are consistent or inconsistent with people's morally convicted outcome preferences has repeatedly emerged as a stronger predictor of outcome fairness judgments and decision acceptance than whether procedures were fair or authorities were perceived as legitimate (for a review, see Skitka, Bauman, & Mullen, 2008).

People may also appeal to majority opinion to resolve conflict. Nonetheless, when a morally mandated issue is at stake, people are relatively immune to majority group pressure (Aramovich, Lytle, & Skitka, under review) and consensus information (Hornsey, Smith, & Begg, 2007). Even under substantial pressure to conform, people with moral mandates persist in defending their point of view.

Violence Finally, people also are more willing to accept violence when it supports a morally mandated end. Skitka and Houston (2001) presented participants with newspaper articles that were ambiguous about defendant guilt or innocence, or indicated whether a defendant in a capital murder case appeared to be truly guilty or truly innocent. The articles also indicated whether the defendant was executed by the state following a fair trial or killed by a vigilante before the trial began. When participants lacked moral clarity about defendant guilt or innocence, participants' fairness judgments were shaped by whether the outcome was the result of a fair process: the defendant's death was fair if it was a consequence of a full trial and unfair if it was a result of vigilantism. However, when people had moral clarity about guilt or innocence, they perceived the death of a guilty defendant to be fair and the death of an innocent defendant as unfair regardless of whether the death was the outcome of a full trial or an act of vigilantism. The defendant's death – regardless of how it occurred – was perceived as morally right if he was guilty and morally wrong if he was innocent.

Moral Convictions Could Promote Peace

Much of our research on moral mandates has revealed a potential "dark side" of moralized attitudes. That said, moral mandates have prosocial implications as well. For example, moral convictions provide people with the courage to stand up for their ideals, and to work for a better and more just world. Likewise, moral conviction motivates civic participation (which is generally seen as a social good). For example, people with stronger moral convictions about issues of the day or political candidates are consistently higher in intentions to vote and actual voting behavior (Morgan & Skitka, under review). Moreover, moral mandates are equal opportunity motivators of political engagement for those on the political right and left – liberals and conservatives are equally likely to express moral mandates about preferred candidates and societal issues, and these moral mandates similarly predict voting intentions and actual voting behavior. Some of our ongoing research indicates that moral mandates are also associated with other constructive forms of political activism such as willingness to collect signatures for petitions or to donate money to a cause. Accordingly, morally convicted activists for peace and other prosocial agendas are more likely to become politically engaged and active in these causes. In sum, moral mandates motivate constructive political engagement and willingness to fight for one's conception of the good.

CONCLUSION

There is considerable individual variation in the degree that people report that their attitudes on specific issues reflect their core moral convictions. Knowing whether someone vests their position with moral conviction has a number of positive and negative implications for peace and conflict. On one hand, moral mandates facilitate intolerance of those with different positions, encourage rejection of the rule of law, and provide a motivational foundation for the acceptance of violence. On the other hand, moral mandates provide people with a willingness to stand up for what is perceived as right and motivate prosocial behaviors such as activism and civic engagement. In short, moral convictions act as double-edged swords – both as a barrier to conflict resolution and provide people with the courage to work for a more just world. Just as having too much moral conviction can lead to potentially horrific consequences (e.g., suicide bombings), too little can lead to inaction and apathy rather than a willingness to take a stand for peace and justice.

SEE ALSO: Activism, Psychology of Social; Conflict, Intractable; Conflict Resolution, Sociopsychological Barriers to; Emotion; Emotional Appeals, Mobilizing through; Peace, Overcoming Psychological–Cognitive Barriers to; Prosocial Behavior; Normative Influence, Theories of; Tolerance for Diverse Groups.

REFERENCES

Aramovich, N. P., Lytle, B. L., & Skitka, L. J. (under review). *Supporting torture: The morally convicted defy and the religiously convicted defer to majority-group influence.*

Hornsey, M. J., Smith, J. R., & Begg, D. I. (2007). Effects of norms among those with moral conviction: Counter-conformity emerges on intentions but not behaviors. *Social Influence, 2,* 244–268.

Morgan, G. S., & Skitka, L. J. (under review). *Moral and religious convictions and intentions to vote in the 2008 presidential election.*

Skitka, L. J., Bauman, C. W., & Mullen, E. (2008). Morality and justice: An expanded theoretical perspective and review. In K. A. Hedgvedt & J. Clay-Warner (Eds.), *Advances in group processes* (Vol. 25, pp. 1–27). Bingley, UK: Emerald Group Publishing.

Skitka, L. J., Bauman, C. W., & Sargis, E. G. (2005). Moral conviction: Another contributor to attitude strength or something more? *Journal of Personality and Social Psychology, 88,* 895–917.

Skitka, L. J., & Houston, D. (2001). When due process is of no consequence: Moral mandates and presumed defendant guilt or innocence. *Social Justice Research, 14,* 305–326.

Wright, J. C., Cullum, J., & Schwab, N. (2008). The cognitive and affective dimensions of moral conviction: Implications for attitudinal and behavioral measures of interpersonal tolerance. *Personality and Social Psychology Bulletin, 34,* 1461–1476.

Moral Development

NEIL FERGUSON

Human morality has been the focus of philosophical debate and anguish since Socrates asked "what is a virtuous man, and what is a virtuous school and society which educates a virtuous man?" Many philosophers have puzzled over this proposition and psychologists have attempted to study and analyze the moral person.

Psychology has approached this issue from two distinct perspectives. Either morality is expressed in behavior and thus is a result of tendencies to perform the moral action, or morality is directed by moral beliefs and cognitive processes. In the former case individuals have a number of behavioral traits which cause a number of behaviors. Therefore, the behaviors we perform or inhibit (aggression, cooperation, etc.) are simply dependent on the strength of our behavioral traits or tendencies.

A number of popular psychological theories deal with behavioral traits or tendencies, two major ones being psychoanalysis and behaviorism. Psychoanalysis explains morality as a result of conflict between the guilt-inducing superego and the other dimensions of personality. The behaviorist and social learning theories characterize moral behavior as moral socialization resulting from environmental contingencies, schedules of reinforcement, and situational learning through modeling. These theoretical perspectives are moral-relativist, as they perceive morality to be a product of the predominant values and norms within a particular culture or community at a particular time. (See SOCIALIZATION.)

Another proponent of this strand of moral reasoning involves evolutionary theory where moral behavior is seen as the product of preprogrammed genes, which promote the survival of the species through adaptation to our environment. Morality is simply a function that promotes human survival. (See EVOLUTIONARY PSYCHOLOGY.)

The second and predominant approach considers that moral behavior is essentially the result of underlying moral reasoning and meaning constructed by the cognitive processes which categorize the personal and social world. Morality is to be found in the individual's internal processes which achieve the moral actions visible to other actors. Thus, reasoning is emphasized over the actual moral, immoral, or morally neutral actions performed by the individual. In other words, it is the why, not the how, that is important in moral development.

This approach to the study of human morality is characteristic of cognitive developmentalism, as found in the theories of Jean Piaget (1932/1997), Lawrence Kohlberg (1984), and neo-Kohlbergians such as John Gibbs (Gibbs, Basinger, & Fuller, 1994) and Georg Lind (Lind & Wakenhunt, 1985). It is characterized by a universalistic view of morality, with moral reasoning and behavior being judged by a collection of timeless and universal principles, common to all of humanity, in terms of which the values of any culture may be judged. This universalistic cognitive-developmental approach has received the greatest research and theoretical attention and will provide the theoretical backdrop for this article.

Piaget's research investigating lying, rules of the game, clumsiness, and stealing provided the framework for Kohlberg and others to build upon. Piaget proposed that

"morality consists of a system of rules, and the essence of all morality is to be sought for in the respect which the individual acquires for those rules" (Piaget, 1932/1997, p. 1). He explored childhood reasoning of morality through the "moral realities" of the game of marbles and by employing what have become known as Piaget's short stories.

This research led Piaget to develop a stage model of the practice of rules and the consciousness of rules in which the child develops from heteronomy (being under the control of an outside authority) to autonomy (independent in will and action). This upward progression is an evolution from conformity to individualistic cooperation, with initial conformity arising from a unilateral respect for age and power, with cooperation following from mutual respect arising from the lessening of adult supervision as the child grows older and engages in greater peer-to-peer interactions.

Piaget did not see this progression in terms of separate stages. He visualized it as two moralities following on from each other. The moral constraint characterized by unilateral respect of the adult leads to heteronomy and moral realism, while autonomy arises out of cooperation with peers. Cooperation with peers in play allows the development of mutual respect through equality and these peer relationships are the driver for moral development. It is important to remember that autonomy does not grow out of heteronomy; instead, the two moralities are in conflict. Both these moralities are grounded in two different styles of social relationships (parents vs. peers) and social experiences (unilateral respect vs. mutual respect). Therefore, the development from heteronomous morality to autonomous morality is a gradual movement caused through the process of a child growing older and engaging in additional relationships based on mutual respect and solidarity between equals which generates more autonomous morality and a decline in unilateral respect and heteronomy. However, although unilateral respect and heteronomy are diminished, even in adulthood they linger. For example, many adults demonstrate heteronomous reasoning when dealing with their physicians or religious leaders.

Lawrence Kohlberg complemented and expanded the pioneering work of Piaget by integrating the philosophies of Socrates, Kant, Dewey, and a program of research evolving over three decades. Between 1958 and 1970 his work elaborated on the philosophy of moral development, and during the 1970s and 1980s there was a stronger focus on his theory and methodologies. This evolution was combined with a continual revision of the theory and methods and a movement from dealing specifically with the moral development of the individual to a more sociological approach exploring the interaction between the individual and his or her environment.

Like Piaget, Kohlberg concentrated on the moral reasoning behind moral behavior, as he believed more could be gained from the reasoning than the final outcome. For example, imagine two women, one aged 16 and the other aged 40, refuse a stranger's sexual advances. By refusing, both women make a moral action. Yet the 16-year-old girl's reasoning of "my mother told me it's wrong" is only acceptable in her case. If the mature woman had offered this in defense of her actions it would be viewed as immature and inappropriate. Thus, without the correct moral reasoning, the judgment, no matter how beneficial, cannot be judged as a moral act.

Kohlberg and his colleagues carried out a series of longitudinal studies and identified six qualitatively different stages grouped into three moral levels in the development of moral reasoning. He proposed that every individual moved through the same sequence of moral stages, although with differing rates of development, without every individual proceeding to the highest stages of moral development. His methodology was centered on the use of a structured interview based on the presentation of a hypothetical dilemma followed by a series of questions designed to uncover the reasons used in the recommendation of a certain course of action.

These three levels can be seen as three different styles of relationship between the individual and society's rules and expectations. At the pre-conventional level, rules and social expectations are external to the self; at the conventional level the individual has internalized the rules and expectations of others, and at the post-conventional level the individual has differentiated him or herself from the rules and expectations of others and now defines his or her own terms.

Kohlberg viewed development through these stages as invariant. By this he meant that individuals must progress through the stages in order and a higher stage cannot be obtained without the complete consolidation of the stage immediately preceding it. Therefore, consolidation of stage 2 is necessary before there can be transition to stage 3. There is also no backwards movement through the stages of development, except in extreme conditions, such as regression induced by stress or damage.

These developmental stages relate to the sociomoral perspective taken at these stages, or the extent of the view the individual holds of the social system in which they live. As we develop through the stages, we decenter our thinking from dwelling on the concrete and most colorful aspects of the dilemma (stealing the car and going to jail) and begin to consider factors which are not discernable to the senses, such as relationships (what about the victim?) and role in community and society (stealing cars isn't very neighborly). Movement from stage to stage or level to level is the result of gaining a different perception of others and groups and one's relationship to these groups and wider society.

This development through the stages is fueled by optimal role-taking opportunities or encounters in which the individual is exposed to moderately more advanced thought. Individuals are cognitively attracted to reasoning one level above their own predominant level, as this higher reasoning is cognitively more adequate than the reasoning of the lower stage, since it resolves moral dilemmas in a more satisfactory way, as it takes account of more of the factors at work in the social environment. As reasoning at one stage higher is intelligible, makes more sense of the situation, reduces more difficulties, and is a more attractive solution to life's moral challenges, we are attracted to it. However, individuals cannot fully comprehend moral reasoning more than one stage above their own.

Kohlberg's theory and research evidence explain how an individual moves through the stages of moral development. Upward movement comes about when cognitive disequilibrium is created – that is, when an individual's cognitive outlook is not adequate to cope with a given moral dilemma. When an individual finds him or herself in this situation, he or she will attempt to adjust to another cognitive framework which can solve the dilemma. Unless the individual's cognitive orientation is disturbed there is no reason to expect moral development.

Thus a person's moral development is linked to their development of logical reasoning. Additionally, the environment the individual lives in needs to provide optimal role-taking opportunities which they can encounter to cause disequilibrium and push moral development. So moral development is heavily influenced by the moral atmosphere of the society with which the individual interacts.

Kohlberg's ideas were not static – his stage definitions were developed over 25 years and accompany an evolution in the style of assessment methodology which fueled a redefinition and refinement of the theory. These refinements included the introduction of stage 4.5, moral types A and B, the soft stage 7, and the eventual removal of stage 6. Although Kohlberg's theory received wide acceptance from the academic community, it has not been without its critics. Criticisms of Kohlberg have been leveled on various fronts, some holding objections to the entire theory on either philosophical or psychological grounds, while others have singled out certain areas of his theory for criticism while accepting it's general principles. Kohlberg acknowledged these and revised and expanded his theory to accommodate some of the criticisms.

His critics tend to focus on key areas of his theory, namely, the general philosophy and politics behind his theory, and the relationship between moral judgment and actual moral action, in addition to accusations of gender and cultural bias. Kohlberg's theories have also inspired others to develop and reformulate his ideas to build their own neo-Kohlbergian approaches.

SUMMARY

Theories of moral development attempt to explain what is a morally mature person and how we develop or educate people to act and reason in a morally mature way. The principal psychological approach developed to understand moral development takes a universalistic view of morality, with moral reasoning and behavior being judged by a collection of universal principles. This cognitive developmentalist approach views moral behavior as the result of individual logical reasoning combined with interaction amid the moral atmosphere in the individual's personal and social world. This approach has been pioneered by Jean Piaget and

Lawrence Kohlberg, who developed stage theories to explain how individuals mature morally through their interaction with other individuals, groups, and wider society as they deal with the various moral problems they face in their social environment. This interaction with more diverse individuals and groups causes the individual to develop more abstract conceptions of society, its groups and institutions, and the relationships that link the individual to these social agents. Thus, by taking more aspects of the situation into consideration, the individual will formulate a more extensive, balanced, and mature moral reasoning.

SEE ALSO: Evolutionary Psychology; Socialization.

REFERENCES

Gibbs, J. C., Basinger, K. S., & Fuller, D. (1992). *Moral maturity: Measuring the development of sociomoral reflection.* Englewood Cliffs, NJ: Erlbaum.

Kohlberg, L. (1984). *Essays in moral development, Vol. 2: The psychology of moral development: Moral stages, their nature and validity.* San Francisco, CA: Harper and Row.

Lind, G., & Wakenhunt, R. (1985). Testing for moral judgment competence. In G. Lind, H. A. Hartmann, & R. Wakenhunt (Eds.), *Moral development and the social environment: Studies in the philosophy and psychology of moral judgement and education.* Chicago, IL: Precedent.

Piaget, J. (1932/1997). *The moral judgement of the child.* New York, NY: Free Press.

ADDITIONAL RESOURCES

http://www.amenetwork.org/ (Association of Moral Education)

http://www.tandf.co.uk/journals/titles/03057240.asp (*Journal of Moral Education* is an interdisciplinary forum for consideration of all aspects of moral education and development across the lifespan)

http://tigger.uic.edu/~lnucci/MoralEd/index.html (Larry Nucci's Studies in Social and Moral Development and Education website)

http://www.uni-konstanz.de/ag-moral/home-e.htm (Georg Lind's Psychology of Morality and Democracy & Applications in Education website)

Moral Disengagement

ALBERT BANDURA

The moral standards people adopt serve as guides for conduct and deterrents for detrimental activities. They do things that bring them satisfaction and a sense of self-worth, and refrain from violating their moral standards because such conduct begets self-condemnation. Self-sanctions keep conduct in line with internal standards. However, moral standards do not function as an unwavering regulator of moral conduct. There are many psychosocial maneuvers by which people selectively disengage moral self-sanctions from inhumane conduct. This enables them to do cruel things with freedom from the restraints of self-censure. Indeed, large-scale inhumanities are often perpetrated by people who are compassionate in other aspects of their lives. They can even behave compassionately and cruelly at the same time depending on whom they include and exclude in their category of humanity. (See MORAL EXCLUSION; GENOCIDE AND MASS KILLING: ORIGINS AND PREVENTION.)

Figure 1 shows the point in the process of moral control at which the disengagement can occur (Bandura, 1999). There are eight such mechanisms of moral evasion. Three of them change harmful conduct into benign or worthy conduct. This is achieved by sanctifying harmful means with worthy ends; enlisting exonerative comparisons that make harmful practices appear benign or even righteous; using sanitizing and convoluted language that disguises the harm being done. Two of the mechanisms reduce accountability for detrimental practices by

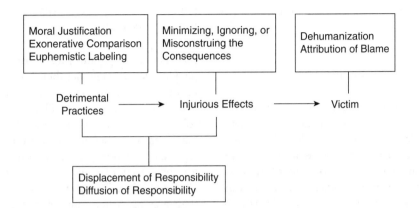

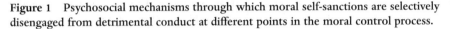

Figure 1 Psychosocial mechanisms through which moral self-sanctions are selectively disengaged from detrimental conduct at different points in the moral control process.

displacement and diffusion of responsibility. Another form of moral evasion is to ignore, minimize, distort, or even dispute that one's activities cause any harm. The disengagement may also include dehumanizing and blaming the victims for bringing the harm on themselves. The following sections review the eight mechanisms of moral disengagement in greater detail. These psychosocial mechanisms operate at both the individual and social system levels.

SOCIAL AND MORAL JUSTIFICATION

The prime mode of moral disengagement operates by cognitive reconstrual of the detrimental behavior itself. In this process of moral justification, such conduct is made personally and socially commendable by portraying it as serving socially worthy or moral purposes. People then act on a moral imperative. Through moral justification of violent means, they see themselves as protecting cherished values, fighting ruthless oppressors, preserving peace, saving humanity from subjugation, or honoring righteous commitments. Voltaire put it well when he said, "Those who can make you believe absurdities can make you commit atrocities."

Over the centuries, much inhumane conduct has been perpetrated by ordinary decent people in the name of righteous ideologies, religious principles, and nationalistic imperatives (Reich, 1990). The politicization of religion, for example, has produced a long bloody history of holy terror. Among the set of mechanisms, moral justification is uniquely powerful. This is because it serves dual functions. It enlists ardent moral engagement in the worthy cause, but moral disengagement in its injurious and destructive execution.

ADVANTAGEOUS COMPARISON

How behavior is viewed is colored by what it is compared against. By exploiting the contrast principle, reprehensible acts can be made righteous. For example, terrorists see their behavior as acts of selfless martyrdom by comparing them with widespread cruelties inflicted on the people with whom they identify (Bandura, 2004). The more flagrant the contrasting inhumanities, the more one's destructive conduct appears benevolent. Exonerating comparison relies heavily on moral justification by the utilitarian standard. Violence is made morally acceptable by claiming that one's injurious actions will prevent more human suffering than they cause.

EUPHEMISTIC LANGUAGE

Language is widely used to make detrimental conduct socially and personally acceptable. Gambino (1973) identifies three linguistic forms that serve a neutralizing function. The first is sanitizing language. Consider, by way of example, aerial bombardment. Bombers drop "vertically deployed anti-personnel devices." We call them bombs. Bombing missions are described as "servicing the target," in the likeness of a public utility, or as "visiting a sight," in the likeness of a social call. The airplanes are "force packages," as though propelled non-agentically. The attacks become "clean, surgical strikes," arousing imagery of curative activities. Bombing errors that kill civilians are characterized as "outside current accuracy requirements." The civilians the bombs kill are linguistically converted to "collateral damage." Collateral damage takes on a different appearance if one puts a human face on it. Sanitizing language pervades most organizational practices that have adverse effects. The *Quarterly Journal of Doublespeak* records the linguistic cleansing practiced by diverse occupations. People behave more cruelly when detrimental practices are sanitized than when they are called aggression.

The agentless passive voice serves as another self-exonerative linguistic tool. It creates the appearance that detrimental acts are the work of nameless forces rather than people. The specialized jargon of a legitimate enterprise can also be exploited to lend an aura of respectability to an illegitimate one. The detrimental schemes concocted by ill-doers are "game plans," and the dutiful functionaries are "team players" conjuring up admirable qualities befitting the best of champions.

DISPLACEMENT AND DIFFUSION OF RESPONSIBILITY

Moral control operates most strongly when people acknowledge that their actions cause harm. The second set of disengagement practices obscures or minimizes the agentic role in the harm one causes. People will behave in ways they normally repudiate if a legitimate authority accepts responsibility for the effects of their injurious activities. Under displaced responsibility they view their actions as stemming from the dictates of authorities rather than being personally responsible. This spares them self-condemning reactions. They are merely carrying out orders, as Adolf Eichmann claimed in his 1961 Nazi War Crimes trial in Jerusalem.

As shown in Milgram's (1974) research, the more legitimate the authority giving the injurious orders, the higher the obedient aggression. However, in real life the authorization of cruelty differs in two important ways from Milgram's authorization practice. The authority was present, pressured participants when they resisted the orders, and publicly accepted responsibility for any harm done when they refused to escalate their punitiveness. In real life, authorities usually sanction harmful practices surreptitiously. This enables them to remain intentionally uninformed about what is going on. They create schemes of deniability that leave the higher echelons blameless. Surreptitious sanctioning provides self-protection from social criticism for failed policies. However, authorizers have to live with themselves. They do not want blood on their hands. Surreptitious authorization of human cruelty spares them loss of self-regard. When harmful practices are publicized they are dismissed as isolated incidents resulting from misunderstanding of what was authorized. The blame usually gets shifted to subordinates who are portrayed as mistaken, overzealous, or irresponsible freelancers.

Displacement of responsibility requires obliging functionaries. If they cast off all responsibility they would be quite unreliable, obeying only when the authority is present. One must distinguish between two levels of responsibility. The best functionaries have a strong sense of duty to honor their obligations to authorities, but no personal responsibility for the harm caused by carrying out the orders.

Moral control is also weakened through diffusion of responsibility for detrimental behavior. (See DIFFUSION OF RESPONSIBIITY.) Kelman and Hamilton (1989) identify three ways in which responsibility is dispersed. Tasks are subdivided so the parts seem harmless in detached isolation. Group decision-making is also self-exonerative because the faceless collectivity becomes the agent. Where everyone is responsible, no one feels personally responsible. Collective action further weakens moral control by providing anonymity and making it easy to discount the significance of one's contribution in the aggregate mix of activities. People behave more cruelly under group responsibility than when they hold themselves accountable for their actions.

DISREGARDING AND DENIAL OF INJURIOUS EFFECTS

Other ways of weakening moral control operate by minimizing, disregarding, or disputing the harmful effects of one's actions. As long as the harmful effects are out of sight and out of mind, there is little reason for self-censure to be activated. When people see and hear the suffering they cause they find it difficult to behave destructively.

We are now in the era of satellite and laser-guided hardware wars. These technologies have become highly lethal and depersonalized, with mass destruction delivered remotely via satellite-guided systems with no restraining human contact. For example, officers operate pilotless drones from a control center in Nevada. The cameras aboard the drones identify possible suspects in Iraq or Afghanistan. The operator fires rockets that blow them up. This remotely implemented faceless warfare underscores the extraordinary flexibility of moral regulation of conduct. The operators switch their moral control off and on daily between their military working hours and their off-duty life.

DEHUMANIZATION AND ATTRIBUTION OF BLAME

The final set of disengagement practices operates on the recipients of detrimental activities (Bandura, 1999; Zimbardo, 2007). Blaming one's foes for bringing the suffering on themselves by their provocative behavior is another form of self-exoneration. Injurious actions toward provocateurs or compelling circumstances are not only excusable, but one can even feel self-righteous in inflicting harm.

The strength of moral self-censure also depends on how the perpetrators regard their foes. To perceive another as human activates empathetic reactions through a sense of common humanity. It is difficult to mistreat humanized persons without self-condemnation. Hence, self-censure for harmful conduct can be disengaged or blunted by stripping people of human qualities. If dispossessing one's foes of humanness does not weaken self-censure, it can be eliminated by attributing demonic or bestial qualities to them. They become "satanic friends," "degenerates," "vermin," and other bestial creatures. It is easier to brutalize people when they are viewed as low animal forms. (See DEHUMANIZATION, INFRAHUMANIZATION, AND NATURALIZATION.)

Psychological analyses tend to emphasize how easy it is to bring out the worst in people through dehumanization. However, the power of humanization to counteract cruelty is equally striking but receives relatively little attention. The affirmation of common humanity can foster peaceable relationships among people (Bandura, 1999).

Given the easily enlisted psychosocial mechanisms for disengaging moral self-sanctions, societies cannot rely solely on individuals, however righteous their standards, to ensure a civil society. Humane life requires, in addition to ethical personal standards, effective safeguards built into social systems that uphold compassionate behavior and curb human cruelty. Regardless of whether inhumane practices are executed individually, organizationally, or institutionally, it should be made difficult for people to remove humanity from their conduct.

SEE ALSO: Dehumanization, Infrahumanization, and Naturalization; Diffusion of Responsibility; Genocide and Mass Killing: Origins and Prevention; Moral Exclusion.

REFERENCES

Bandura, A. (1999). Moral disengagement in the perpetration of inhumanities. *Personality and Social Psychology Review, 3,* 193–209.

Bandura, A. (2004). The role of selective moral disengagement in terrorism and counterterrorism. In F. M. Mogahaddam & A. J. Marsella (Eds.), *Understanding terrorism: Psychological roots, consequences and interventions* (pp. 121–150). Washington, DC: American Psychological Association Press.

Gambino, R. (1973, November–December). Watergate lingo: A language of non-responsibility. *Freedom at Issue, 22,* 7–9, 15–17.

Kelman, H. C., & Hamilton, V. L. (1989). *Crimes of obedience: Toward a social psychology of authority and responsibility.* New Haven, CT: Yale University Press.

Milgram, S. (1974). *Obedience to authority: An experimental view.* New York, NY: Harper and Row.

Reich, W. (Ed.). (1990). *Origins of terrorism: Psychologies, ideologies, theologies, states of mind.* Cambridge, UK: Cambridge University Press.

Zimbardo, P. G. (2007). *The Lucifer Effect: Understanding how good people turn evil.* New York, NY: Random House.

Moral Exclusion

SUSAN OPOTOW

Morton Deutsch has defined the scope of justice as follows: "The narrower one's conception of one's community, the narrower will be the scope of situations in which one's action will be governed by considerations of justice" (Deutsch, 1985, p. 37).

This definition suggests that the scope of justice can change, and this change has implications for justice (Opotow, 1990). Empirical research on the scope of justice indicates that inclusion in the scope of justice (or moral inclusion) means that a social unit (i.e., an individual, a group, an institution, or a nation) is willing to apply considerations of fairness to another, allocate resources to them, and willing to make sacrifices to foster their well-being (Opotow, 1995). Stated negatively, moral exclusion occurs when one social unit views another as outside their scope of justice and therefore as undeserving of fairness, resources, or sacrifices. Those excluded are then seen as appropriate targets for exploitation, oppression, and harm. While excluding some kinds of people from the scope of justice can seem morally odious, groups have their own boundaries for justice. Seeing some kinds of people as outside the scope of justice can set in motion a vicious cycle, in which those excluded are debilitated by degrading treatment and seem increasingly unworthy. Severe forms of moral exclusion are characteristic of conflicts in which some groups are derogated as inferior. (See MORAL DISENGAGEMENT.)

Table 1 Three dimensions of moral exclusion

Severity: From rude, degrading behavior to mild injury, severe injury, torture, irreversible injuries, mutilation, and murder.
  Mild: Inadequate housing, schools, and healthcare (structural violence)
  Severe: Torture, death, destruction of homes, businesses, crops, schools, hospitals, and communities (direct violence)

Extent: From narrowly focused to widely prevalent in a society.
  Narrowly focused: Directed at racial or ethnic minorities such as "guestworkers" or the Romany people in Europe
  Widespread: Engulfs an entire society, such as during inquisitions and dictatorships when human rights violations are pervasive

Engagement: From unawareness to ignoring, allowing, facilitating, executing, and devising moral exclusion.
  Passive: People with intellectual, financial, or social resources to hinder harm remain aloof, uninterested, or uninformed
  Active: Architects of genocide such as Hitler, Stalin, and Pol Pot

Moral exclusion can be mild or severe, narrowly focused or widespread, and active or passive (see Table 1). It can occur as mild, ordinary, and institutionalized inequality as well as in brutal forms of harm-doing characterized by direct and structural violence. Regardless of its phenotypical presentation, moral exclusion is a social psychological orientation in which those who are advantaged view those who are excluded from their scope of justice as psychologically distant, unconnected with themselves, undeserving of constructive obligations, and eligible for harms that would be unacceptable for those inside the scope of justice (Opotow, 1990, 1995). (See DELEGITIMIZATION.)

Gender, ethnicity, religious identity, age, mental capacity, sexual orientation, and political affiliation have, in various places and times, justified excluding some kinds of people from the scope of justice. Excluded people can be invisible and expendable or hated as enemies. Fairness and deserving may seem irrelevant when applied to excluded people. Indeed, harm befalling those outside the scope of justice may not elicit remorse, outrage, or demands for restitution. Instead, harm they experience can

seem acceptable and even celebrated as fostering the greater good. (See SOCIAL INJUSTICE.)

Moral exclusion can rationalize the injustices of everyday life, such as illnesses and deaths of workers who were knowingly exposed to dangerous working conditions. It can also rationalize larger and more blatant injustices, such as violations of human rights. Although these are harms that differ in type and degree, psychologically they are similar in that those who are advantaged have an orientation that (1) views those excluded as psychologically distant and unconnected with oneself; (2) lacks constructive obligations or responsibilities toward those excluded; (3) views those excluded as nonentities, expendable, and undeserving of fairness or community resources and sacrifices that could foster their well-being; and (4) condones procedures and outcomes for those excluded that would be unacceptable for those inside the scope of justice.

The capacity of moral exclusion to render harm-doing and injustice as normal is important. Once normalized by moral exclusion, harm-doing can be institutionalized in formal rules and informal mores that foster disparate outcomes between groups that can then be widely accepted as the way things are or ought to be. Because moral exclusion can veil injustice, it is easier to detect and deplore when it occurred long ago or far away, but it can be unacknowledged in one's own society in the present.

Moral exclusion has relevance for individuals as well as for groups. Both want to see themselves as good, fair, and morally upstanding and therefore they rationalize, justify, and ignore structural inequalities that may benefit themselves or their group at the expense of others. Shared rationalizations for injustice can make it difficult to detect exclusionary conventions, norms, and practices within a society.

SYMPTOMS OF MORAL EXCLUSION

Symptoms of moral exclusion can aid its detection. These include symptoms that are common in everyday life and those that are more ominous (Opotow, 1990; Opotow & Weiss, 2000). Some everyday symptoms include psychological distancing, displacing responsibility, group loyalty, and normalizing and glorifying violence. These symptoms can be a normal aspect of work in societal institutions. Normalizing violence, for example, is common in the military; transcendent ideologies are common in religious organizations; and technical thinking is common in business organizations. Many societal institutions routinely employ euphemisms to discuss sensitive topics associated with harm. Although ordinary symptoms of moral exclusion can occur without necessarily perceiving others as outside one's scope of justice, those who habitually employ them can distance themselves from some kinds of people and increasingly see those people as less human. (See IDEOLOGY; SYSTEM JUSTIFICATION THEORY.)

Some ominous symptoms of moral exclusion include dehumanizing others, fearing contamination from social contact, and reducing one's moral standards. (See DEHUMANIZATION, INFRAHUMANIZATION, AND NATURALIZATION.) Although these symptoms can occur in everyday relations, they can signal that interpersonal or intergroup conflict is taking a destructive and violent turn. In his Crude Law of Social Relations, Morton Deutsch (1973) states that the "characteristic processes and effects elicited by a given type of social relationship tend also to elicit that type of relationship" (p. 365). This law applies as well to these potent symptoms of moral exclusion. There can be a reciprocal relation between symptoms and effects. Symptoms that provoke moral exclusion can be triggered by moral exclusion initiating a vicious cycle.

ASSESSING THE SCOPE OF JUSTICE

An empirically derived Scope of Justice Scale consists of three items: (1) believing that considerations of fairness apply to another, (2) willingness to allocate a share of community resources to another, and (3) willingness to make sacrifices to foster another's well-being (Opotow, 1990). This scale defines inclusion in the scope of justice as extending fairness and resources to others and being concerned about their well-being. These three attitudes that operationalize moral inclusion are often an implicit aspect of controversial social issues that concern allocating public resources. Examples of such social issues are developing educational programs to foster school completion for school dropouts, providing health insurance for illegal immigrants, and providing assistance to people who are homeless, substance abusers, or vulnerable in a variety of ways. Controversies about these issues essentially hinge on a moral and ideological stance about who is inside the scope of justice and is therefore deserving of societal resources as well as who is outside and deserves less even if it leads to suffering and disadvantage.

THE CHANGING SCOPE OF JUSTICE

The scope of justice does not remain static. What seems right, acceptable, proper, and fair may appear immutable, but as lives, social contexts, and social conventions change, the scope of justice changes too. Research on factors that modify the scope of justice indicates that decreases in a sense of connection to others and increases in conflict can shrink the scope of justice (Opotow, 1995). War, disaster, or economic recession can shrink the scope of justice and reduce resources available to those who are not securely within it. Immigration is one example. Although immigrants can benefit a country by bringing their talents and willingness to work, during times of recession or conflict immigrants can be viewed as a threat to a shaky economy. Rather than labeling immigrants as "newcomers" who are welcome and bring skills that can enliven a community, they can instead be labeled a "dangerous refugee flow," describing them as a form of effluent. During World War II, refugees from Germany and Eastern Europe were refused admission to some countries, and recent wars have resulted in strict immigration policies and quotas.

DENIAL AND MORAL EXCLUSION

Denial, a psychological defense mechanism, is selective inattention toward threat-provoking aspects of a situation that protect a person from anxiety, guilt, or other threats to one's well-being (Corsini, 1999). Denial can occur in individuals as well as in groups. Research on moral exclusion in environmental conflict concerning air quality indicates that three kinds of denial can foster moral

exclusion (Opotow & Weiss, 2000). The first kind of denial minimizes harms that others experience, indicating a disinterest in their well-being. The second kind of denial devalues others and their needs, with unflattering between-group comparisons that trivialize others' needs for a healthy environment to live and work. (See ATTRIBUTION THEORY, INTERGROUP CONFLICT AND.) The third kind of denial minimizes one's own role in harming others, exonerating one's role by locating blame for air pollution elsewhere. Together, these three kinds of denial justify the moral exclusion and the harm it can inflict.

FOSTERING MORAL INCLUSION

What can effect a shift from a culture of moral exclusion to a culture of moral inclusion? What would reduce morally justified harm-doing and increase the applicability of justice in a society? These questions link research on moral inclusion to research on peacebuilding. Both seek to institutionalize a culture of mutual respect, human rights, and intergroup harmony. (See CULTURE OF PEACE.) Achieving a stable peace may indeed require a shift from moral exclusion to moral inclusion. As Betty Reardon (2001) argues, peace is possible "when society agrees that the overarching purpose of public policies is the achievement and maintenance of mutually beneficial circumstances that enhance the life possibilities of all" (p. 5).

Moral inclusion can serve as a fundamental and strategic principle of peace in its emphasis on nurturing a willingness to extend fairness to others and the willingness to allocate resources to others and make sacrifices that would foster their well-being. For moral inclusion to increase and endure, particularly after societal calamities such as war (Opotow, 2001), it needs to be understood as a project occurring (1) at all levels of society, from grassroots to state-level; (2) across all subpopulations, including people who are vulnerable or excluded because they are women, children, elderly, infirm, survivors of physical and psychological trauma, illiterate, or from remote areas; and (3) across time – not only in the short term but as a long-term project worthy of significant resources and cooperation.

SEE ALSO: Attribution Theory; Intergroup Conflict and; Culture of Peace; Dehumanization, Infrahumanization, and Naturalization; Ideology; Moral Disengagement; Social Injustice; System Justification Theory.

REFERENCES

Corsini, R. J. (1999). *The dictionary of psychology.* Philadelphia, PA: Bruner/Mazel.
Deutsch, M. (1973). *The resolution of conflict.* New Haven, CT: Yale University Press.
Deutsch, M. (1985). *Distributive justice: A social psychological perspective.* New Haven, CT: Yale University Press.
Opotow, S. (1990). Moral exclusion and injustice: An overview. *Journal of Social Issues, 46*(1), 1–20.
Opotow, S. (1995). Drawing the line: Social categorization, moral exclusion, and the scope of justice. In B. B. Bunker & J. Z. Rubin (Eds.), *Conflict, cooperation, and justice* (pp. 347–369). San Francisco, CA: Jossey-Bass.
Opotow, S. (2001). Reconciliation in times of impunity: Challenges for social justice. *Social Justice Research, 14*(2), 149–170.
Opotow, S., & Weiss, L. (2000). Denial and exclusion in environmental conflict. *Journal of Social Issues, 56*(3), 475–490.
Reardon, B. (2001). *Educating for a culture of peace in a gender perspective.* Paris, France: UNESCO.

ADDITIONAL RESOURCES

Couteau, C., Hastier, D., Sasson, A., & Willemont, L. (Producers), Panh, R. (Director). (2003). *S-21: The Khmer Rouge killing machine [French: S-21, la machine de mort Khmère rouge] [Documentary].* France: Institut National de l'Audiovisuel.
Jacobs, H. A. (1860/1987). *Incidents in the life of a slave girl: Written by herself* (L. M. Child & J. F. Yellin, Eds.). Cambridge, MA: Harvard University Press.
Kanstroom, D. (2007). *Deportation nation: Outsiders in American history.* Cambridge, MA: Harvard University Press.

Mortality Salience in Peace and Conflict

IMMO FRITSCHE & EVA JONAS

Intergroup conflicts which involve severe violent measures such as warfare or terrorist threat might increase people's awareness of the fragility of their life and may cause a state of existential threat. Tragically, appraisals of existential threat might significantly contribute to both conservation and escalation of such conflicts. Since the late 1980s, social psychologists have been systematically investigating the effects of the awareness of one's own mortality on social thinking and behavior, revealing a broad range of subtle processes. In this article we will first describe the basic phenomenon of mortality salience effects and then illustrate how these effects may contribute to processes of peace and conflict.

THE MORTALITY SALIENCE PARADIGM

In a mortality salience experiment (e.g., Greenberg, Solomon, & Pyszczynski, 1997), participants are randomly assigned to either a mortality salience (MS) or a mortality not salient (MNS) condition. Most typically, participants in the MS condition are asked to imagine their own death and to write down some thoughts about how it will be when they have died and how they feel about that. In the MNS condition participants are also asked to write down their thoughts but about a different self-related negative event, for instance, suffering dental pain. Then, after a distracter task, researchers measure people's social thinking and behavior. Comparing the reactions of MS and MNS participants revealed that MS has a reliable influence on a multitude of phenomena indicating social defensiveness, as it increased punishment of norm violations, compliance with social norms (Jonas et al., 2008), identification with and favoritism towards social ingroups (Castano & Dechesne, 2005), the derogation of outgroups, social consensus estimates, and the liking of stereotypical others. In addition, MS increases self-esteem striving (for reviews on MS effects, see Greenberg et al., 1997; Burke, Martens, & Faucher, 2010).

Interestingly, for MS effects to occur, death thoughts must be made increasingly accessible to people but not conscious. This is why the explicit manipulation described above is followed by a distracter task. Without any distracter, the above-mentioned MS effects on social defensiveness and self-esteem striving only occur for subtle manipulations of MS (e.g., subliminal priming or interviewing participants in front of a cemetery). Besides distraction from conscious thoughts, MS effects depend on the increased accessibility of death-related cognitions in memory, which has been shown immediately after subtle reminders of death but only after a distracter if MS had been manipulated explicitly. Obviously, effects of MS are driven by largely unconscious processes.

To explain this pattern it has been proposed that people may cope with threatening thoughts about death on either a direct and proximal level or on an indirect and distal level (for a summary, see Greenberg et al., 1997; Burke et al., 2010). Direct defenses, such as avoiding self-awareness, denying vulnerability, or suppressing death-related thoughts, are supposed to occur

when people have been confronted with explicit reminders of death. However, indirect defenses, such as social defensiveness and self-esteem striving, only occur if the death reminder is outside of conscious awareness and thus people are not able to suppress death-related thoughts.

EXPLANATIONS OF MORTALITY SALIENCE EFFECTS

The interest in the consequences MS has for socially and personally defensive behavior has emerged with the formulation of terror management theory (Greenberg et al., 1997). (See TERROR MANAGEMENT THEORY: WHY WAR?) The theory proposes that people need to prevent the paralyzing terror which awareness of mortality might potentially cause in everyday life. This is said to be achieved by the validation of cultural worldviews as well as self-esteem, both working as anxiety buffers. Other researchers have proposed additional anxiety buffers, which include romantic relationships, one's own offspring, or self-categorization as an ingroup member (e.g., Castano & Dechesne, 2005). At the same time, alternative accounts of mortality salience effects have been suggested, such as uncertainty reduction, coalition building, or control restoration (for an overview, see Fritsche, Jonas, & Fankhänel, 2008). In these approaches, it is assumed that MS is just a special case of a more general kind of threat (e.g., uncertainty or threat to sense of control) and that reactions to MS thus reflect efforts to reduce uncertainty or to restore a global sense of control rather than a unique reaction to threats to existence. Supporting this assumption Fritsche et al. (2008) showed that MS effects on social defensiveness were eliminated if partial controllability of death had been made salient by letting people think about the possibility of self-determined death. Although there is an actual debate about the motivational

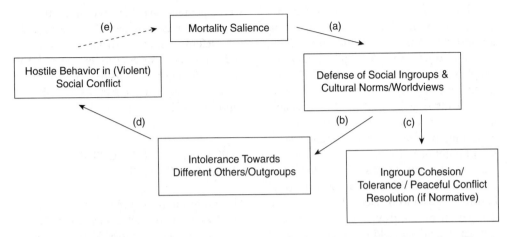

Figure 1 Schematic model of the role of mortality salience in processes of peace and conflict.

foundations of MS effects there is broad consensus in the literature that defending social ingroups and their cultural norms/worldviews is a means to cope with the terror of mortality.

MORTALITY SALIENCE IN PROCESSES OF PEACE AND CONFLICT

Mortality salience might both be an antecedent as well as an outcome of social conflict and has thus been proposed as a candidate variable for explaining the escalation of violent social conflicts (Niesta, Fritsche, & Jonas, 2008). At the same time, MS might foster peace by increasing people's compliance to social norms. These possible relationships are displayed in Figure 1.

Path (a) represents the above-mentioned findings that MS leads people to cling more strongly to their social ingroup and to increase their readiness to support and defend the ingroup and its norms. This should lead to increased levels of intolerance and derogation towards different others or members of outgroups whose mere existence might threaten either group status or the validity of cherished cultural worldviews (Path b).

Interestingly, research has shown that increased compliance with cultural norms following MS can result in different and sometimes even contradictory reactions. This should depend on which of the various possible social norms a culture may offer is salient in a situation. For example, Jonas et al. (2008) showed that whereas MS decreased approval of pacifist organizations and nonviolent conflict solutions if no specific norm was salient, reminding people of the pacifism norm by hiding in a word-search task pacifism-related words such as peace, reconciliation, mediation, or harmony led to a reversed effect. In this condition, MS *increased* people's pacifist attitudes. Path (c) highlights this possibility of MS increasing compliance to ingroup norms of peaceful conflict resolution or tolerance (Greenberg et al., 1997). In addition, MS has been shown to increase prosocial behavior and forgiveness within groups, which might foster peace within certain social boundaries. However, to dampen optimism, *intra*group peace does not preclude severe *inter*group conflict and such conflict can be expected to foster norms that oppose pacifism or intergroup tolerance.

Increased intolerance towards different others as a consequence of MS can elicit hostile behavior or aggravate existing aggressive interactions between individuals and groups (Path d). For the interpersonal level this has been demonstrated in studies by McGregor and colleagues (for a summary, see Greenberg et al., 1997), who showed that MS increased participants' aggressive behavior towards other participants who were opposing their political worldviews. In addition, there are also examples of MS strengthening approval of violent behavior in intergroup conflicts. Pyszczynski et al. (2006) have investigated the impact of existential threat on attitudes on both sides of the ongoing conflict between Western countries such as the United States and Muslim countries such as Iran. In both countries, MS increased attitudes towards violent conflict measures, such as the use of extreme military force (in US participants) or suicide bombing (in Iranian participants).

In these studies it has been shown that MS can catalyze processes of interpersonal and intergroup conflict. Moreover, MS might also contribute to the self-perpetuating tendency of violent intergroup conflict. This is because violent social conflict might itself create the conditions under which mortality is increasingly salient (Path e). This becomes obvious in research on the consequences of terrorist threat (e.g., Landau et al., 2004). Here it has been shown that reminding US citizens of the attacks on the World Trade Center in New York in 2001 increased their cognitive accessibility of death-related thoughts. This effect might be explained in two ways: (1) reminders of terrorist threat might be directly associated with death concerns; or (2) a serious threat to one's own nation might weaken the belief in the validity of the cultural worldview which has been shown by Jeff Schimel and colleagues to have the capacity of increasing the accessibility of death-related thoughts. More so, reminders of 9/11 or the Word Trade Center elicited the same

effects as a context-neutral reminder of MS on increased support for former US president George W. Bush and his counterterrorism policies. Obviously, death concerns have the potential to change people's political opinions and the potential to influence voters' decisions about conflict-enhancing policies. Recent studies in other parts of the world (e.g., by Peter Fischer and colleagues in Germany) also demonstrate that the salience of terrorist threat can lead to increased social defensiveness, such as more severe punishment intentions towards norm breakers.

Summing up, being involved in violent intergroup conflict can elicit MS and thus creates the conditions for escalating conflict by increasing ethnocentric tendencies and violent conflict measures. (See ETHNOCENTRISM.)

CONCLUSION

Knowing about the effects of mortality salience can improve the understanding of escalation dynamics in violent intergroup conflict. Moreover, it also helps to predict the conditions under which nonviolent conflict resolution and peace might be possible. Although there seems to be a general increase of ethnocentric cognition and behavior under conditions of MS, existential threat also has the potential to foster peace processes. Here, the interaction of existential threat inherent in a situation and salient social norms seems to play a critical role. As a rule, MS may energize any norm which is represented in the repertoire of a social ingroup. If violent norms are both shared within society and salient in a situation, existential threat might obstruct the way to peace and reconciliation. However, if norms of pacifism and nonviolent conflict resolution are both shared and salient, increased threat may foster peaceful solutions of social conflict.

SEE ALSO: Ethnocentrism; Terror Management Theory: Why War?

REFERENCES

Burke, B. L., Martens, A., & Faucher, E. H. (2010). Two decades of terror management theory: A meta-analysis of mortality salience research. *Personality and Social Psychology Review, 14,* 155–195.

Castano, E., & Dechesne, M. (2005). On defeating death: Group reification and social identification as immortality strategies. *European Review of Social Psychology, 16,* 221–255.

Fritsche, I., Jonas, E., & Fankhänel, T. (2008). The role of control motivation in mortality salience effects on ingroup support and defense. *Journal of Personality and Social Psychology, 95,* 524–541.

Greenberg, J., Solomon, S., & Pyszczynski, T. (1997). Terror management theory of self-esteem and cultural worldviews: Empirical assessments and conceptual refinements. In M. P. Zanna (Ed.), *Advances in experimental social psychology* (Vol. 29, pp. 61–141). San Diego, CA: Academic Press.

Jonas, E., Martens, A., Niesta Kayser, D., Fritsche, I., Sullivan, D., & Greenberg, J. (2008). Focus theory of normative conduct and terror management theory: The interactive impact of mortality salience and norm salience on social judgment. *Journal of Personality and Social Psychology, 95,* 1239–1251.

Landau, M. J., Solomon, S., Greenberg, J., Cohen, F., Pyszczynski, T., Arndt, J., Miller, C. H., Ogilvie, D. M., & Cook, A. (2004). Deliver us from evil: The effects of mortality salience and reminders of 9/11 on support for President George W. Bush. *Personality and Social Psychology Bulletin, 30,* 1136–1150.

Niesta, D., Fritsche, I., & Jonas, E. (2008). Mortality salience and its effects on peace processes: A review. *Social Psychology, 39,* 48–58.

Pyszczynski, T., Abdollahi, A., Solomon, S., Greenberg, J., Cohen, F., & Weise, D. (2006). Mortality salience, martyrdom, and military might: The great satan versus the axis of evil. *Personality and Social Psychology Bulletin, 32,* 525–537.

ADDITIONAL RESOURCES

http://www.flightfromdeath.com/index.htm (website of the documentary movie)

http://www.tmt.missouri.edu/index.html (overview of research and literature on terror management theory and mortality salience effects)

Multidimensional Scaling Methods in Peace Psychology

ROBIN L. PINKLEY

Multidimensional scaling (MDS) is a data-reduction technique that explores *how* and *why* variables are related and, thus, the spatial representation or "hidden structure" that underlies and defines behavioral data (Kruskal & Wish, 1978). As sense-makers, people compare the objects around them to determine the extent to which they are similar or different. The objective of MDS is to create a geometric map of similarity–dissimilarity judgments to illustrate the underlying structure of complex psychological phenomena, such that the smaller the distance between stimuli, the greater the similarity. In doing this, MDS illuminates the "hidden structure" or underling dimensions that distinguish one category of stimuli from another. For example, Chinese citizens are certain to have beliefs about how their country and others are related to one another, although they may not fully recognize the criteria they are using to make such judgments. MDS techniques provide a mechanism for uncovering and labeling the perceived attributes or "dimensions" that account for correlations between these judgments.

MDS has been used throughout the social sciences to explore a wide range of topics ranging from perceptions of conflict (Pinkley, 1990), to attitudinal differences and similarities between ethnic groups (Bakke, Cao, O'Loughlin, & Ward, 2010), but it is underutilized in the study of peace psychology and related topics. This is unfortunate, for MDS is ideally suited to research of this kind. Like factor analysis, it can be applied to any matrix of data concerning the relationships between perceptions regarding objects, events, or behaviors, but unlike factor analysis it does not rely on metric data (interval or ratio). With MDS it is also feasible to utilize nonmetric (ordinal) data. Because data concerning people's attitudes and cognitions are nonmetric in nature, MDS techniques have great appeal in the social sciences. Further, since MDS is an inductive approach, it allows investigators to uncover the beliefs and perceptions of those they seek to understand without contamination by preconceived ideas or existing theory. (See GROUNDED THEORY.)

This essay will differentiate MDS from factor analysis and then summarize the various multidimensional scaling techniques, highlighting methods for collecting, analyzing, and interpreting proximity data.

MULTIDIMENSIONAL SCALING (MDS) VERSUS FACTOR ANALYSIS (FA)

Although factor analysis (FA) and MDS use very different sets of statistics, the principle that underlies each of them is quite similar. Both techniques are based on the assumption that variables found to correlate with each other have something in common. In FA that "something" is a *factor* while in MDS it is a *data cluster* or *category*. In all cases the "something" is a latent variant that subsumes a number of variables (or stimuli) into fewer, broader variable classes. Thus, both FA and MDS identify the *structure* or

interrelationships among these super variables to explain the variance in the dependent variable with a smaller number of independent variables (Young & Hamer, 1987).

While the principle that underlies the two statistical techniques is the same, there are a number of important differences. First, with MDS a single respondent's data is sufficient (although rarely used), since individuals rather than attributes are the unit of analysis. This is not the case for FA which determines the number of factors that explain the relationships between a larger set of attributes across individuals. Second, MDS can use both attribute-based and attribute-free approaches for obtaining stimuli assessment data from participants, while FA uses only an attribute-based approach (Young & Hamer, 1987).

Attribute-Based Approaches

With an attribute-based approach participants evaluate stimuli on a set of attributes predefined by researchers. FA techniques rely on an attribute-based approach, and are therefore deductive in nature; they are open to possible distortion by investigator preconceptions, because subject responses are limited by preset criteria.

Attribute-Free Approaches

An attribute-free approach provides participants with no guidelines as to what criteria to use for making similarity judgments between stimuli. For example, Pinkley (1990) asked respondents to sort conflict descriptions into categories based on similarity, with free rein as to what criteria to use for doing so. Thus an attribute-free approach inductively detects, quantitatively categorizes, and labels people's mental models and preferences, even when the criteria people use to make such judgments are implicit or are cognitively unavailable.

DIFFERENT TYPES OF MDS

Both homogeneous and heterogeneous samples can be used with MDS. When a sample is assumed to be homogeneous or individual differences are of no interest, a two-way matrix (i.e.., in-group scaling) procedure is most appropriate. In the case of a large or heterogeneous sample size, however, a three-way matrix (i.e., individual differences scaling) procedure is more appropriate since the pattern of each respondent's or subgroup's perception of the stimuli can be examined. This is important because it allows homogeneity to be uncovered through analysis rather than mandated through assumption, leading to an aggregation of data.

The most widely used three-way MDS procedure, the INDSCAL model (Carroll & Chang, 1970), develops a common or "group" space (similar to a two-way MDS method) and a set of respondent weights so that each respondent point of view is related to every other respondent point of view. Differences in dimension saliency (i.e., points of view) can be correlated with individual differences and other variables to test for hypothesized relationships. A three-way MDS can be used to make intergroup as well as intragroup comparisons. The INDSCAL model can also be used to evaluate the *goodness of fit* for each respondent stimulus configuration (i.e., the amount of variance in respondent judgments explained by the multidimensional solution).

A number of additional computing programs exist for MDS and other related tasks such as cluster analysis. One notable example, ALSCAL (Takane, Young, & Deleeuw, 1977), is included in the SPSS 10.0 Base package and available in the SAS ALSCAL procedure, performs metric and nonmetric MDS, has a number of individual difference scaling options, and allows investigators to compare the differences of several individual or group matrices. As an alternative to ALSCAL, PROXSCAL (Young & Hamer, 1987), which is also available in the SPSS 10.0 Categories package, offers several improvements upon ALSCAL, including algorithmic strategies that ensure better convergence, a wider range of data transformations, and a number of different options for fitting models to the data.

DATA COLLECTION METHODS

Regardless of which type of stimuli respondents receive (e.g., descriptions, objects, events), the data used for MDS are the similarity judgments or *proximity data* provided by subjects. MDS is designed to handle all types of proximity data including metric or nonmetric, complete matrices or those with missing proximity data, rectangular (i.e., two-way) or square matrices and unequally replicated matrices (Young & Hamer, 1987).

Sundry methods can be used for converting stimuli into proximity data. The most commonly used method is to collect direct, pair-wise comparisons by asking respondents to judge the degree to which each stimulus is similar to every other stimulus on a Likert-type scale (see Gelfand, Triandis, & Chan, 1996 for an example). A second method is to randomly select a subset of "target" stimuli (e.g., 10 out of a set of 40) and then present a subset of respondents with each of the target stimuli against which they are to rank-order the remaining stimulus (the remaining 39 out of 40) in ascending or descending order of similarity (see Pinkley, 1990 for example). For the third method, (i.e., subjective clustering method) respondents are asked to sort stimuli into however many piles they feel distinguish them in terms of similarity (see Gelfand et al., 2001 for an example).

INTERPRETING THE MDS CONFIGURATION AND LABELING THE DIMENSIONS

There are two issues that scholars face when interpreting MDS configurations: (1) determining the number of dimensions and (2) labeling each dimension. Each is discussed in turn below.

Determining Dimensionality

In most cases, three criteria are used to determine the number of dimensions that best describe the stimulus space. First, a *STRESS index* or "goodness of fit" is used to determine to what extent the distances displayed in the configuration reflect the actual proximities in the similarities data and, thus, how much of the variance *is unaccounted for* by the model (Kruskal & Wish, 1978). Technically speaking, the STRESS index is the square root of a normalized "residual sum of squares." While measurements of STRESS vary from analysis program to analysis program, the meaning of stress does not. In all cases, the larger the number of dimensions, the smaller the STRESS index and the better the fit, with good fit nearing 0 and poor fit nearing 1. A number of factors can affect the STRESS value, so a good rule of thumb is to use at least four times as many stimulus items (I) as the number of dimensions (R) likely to underlie the stimulus space (i.e., $I > 4R$).

A second criterion for arriving at the optimum number of dimensions is the *RSQ index* or squared multiple correlations between the proximities in the similarities data and the distances plotted by the MDS model. As the flip side of the Stress index, the RSQ index indicates how much of the variance in the proximity data *is accounted for* by the MDS model, with 1 indicating a perfect fit and 0 indicating no fit at all. Researchers often designate the appropriate

number of dimensions in terms of an *elbow* or bend, designated by a sudden rise in RSQ and fall in STRESS (Young & Hamer, 1987), along with an examining of the amount of variance that is accounted for by the MDS procedure. If an elbow is not found, however, the third criteria should be used for selecting dimensionality.

A third criteria for selecting dimensionality is the interpretability of the dimensions, with the goal being to "select the space with the fewest dimensions and the richest interpretation" (Young & Hamer, 1987, p. 205). Even when an elbow test is successful, it is beneficial for investigators to couple that approach with the interpretability test since all dimensions must be interpreted and labeled.

Labeling Dimensions

The first step when attempting to assign labels to the dimensional space is to search for possible patterns that distinguish the stimuli clustered at one end of the continuum from those falling at the other end. The insights that can be derived from "living" with the data are irreplaceable even when combined with more formalized, rigorous methods.

Empirical techniques can be coupled with the more subjective approach described above. One approach is to use multiple regressions to regress the unidimensional attributes provided by those who made the proximity judgments (on which they rated the stimuli) onto the coordinate values in the multidimensional space. An attribute can be said to adequately label a dimension when it has: (1) a significant multiple correlation and F value – which shows that the configuration "explains" the attribute well, and (2) a significant Beta weight or normalized regression coefficient on a dimension – which shows that the attribute corresponds well with the multidimensional space (Kruskal & Wish, 1978). The more the labels are found to load on only one dimension, the greater the confidence the investigator can have on the dimensions (Pinkley, 1990).

A second and more inductive method for labeling the dimensions is to ask those who originally made the proximity judgments to list the criteria that have been used for making those judgments and then asking a second set of participants to evaluate the original set of stimulus objects on the criteria list provided by the first set of participant, on a Likert-type scale.

CONCLUSION

MDS is a marvelous set of procedures for inductively uncovering the hidden structures that underlie people's implicit mental models of the world around them, without distortion by the preconceived notions of the investigator. Compared to other multivariate techniques such as FA, it is grossly underutilized in the social sciences. This is unfortunate since MDS enables researchers to translate qualitative experience into quantifiable categories for future study. Hopefully this article demonstrates the important theoretical and practical application of MDS in the study of peace psychology and related topics.

SEE ALSO: Grounded Theory.

REFERENCES

Bakke, K. M., Cao, X., O'Loughlin, J., & Ward, M. D. (2010). Social distance in Bosnia-Herzegovina and the North Caucasus region of Russia: Inter and intra-ethnic attitudes and identities. *Nations and Nationalism, 15,* 227–253.

Carroll, J. D., & Chang, J. J. (1970). *A quasi-nonmetric version of INDSCAL, a procedure for individual differences in multidimensional scaling.* Paper presented at Meetings of the Psychometric Society, Stanford, CA.

Gelfand, M., Nishii, L., Holcombe, K., Dyer, N., Ohbuchi, K., & Fukuno, M. (2001). Cultural influences on cognitive representations of conflict: Interpretations of conflict episodes in the U.S. and Japan. *Journal of Applied Psychology, 86,* 1059–1074.

Gelfand, M., Triandis, H., & Chan, D. (1996). Individualism versus collectivism or versus authoritarianism? *European Journal of Social Psychology, 26,* 397–410.

Kruskal, J. B., & Wish, M. (1978). *Multidimensional scaling.* Quantitative Applications in the Social Sciences, no. 07–011. Beverly Hills, CA: Sage.

Pinkley, R. L. (1990). Dimensions of conflict frame: Disputant interpretations of conflict. *Journal of Applied Psychology, 75*(2), 117–126.

Takane, Y., Young, F. W., & De Leeuw, J. (1977). Nonmetric individual differences in multidimensional scaling: An alternating least squares method with optimal scaling features. *Psychometrika, 42,* 7–67.

Young, F. W., & Hamer, R. M. (1987). *Multidimensional scaling: History, theory and application.* Hillsdale, NJ: Lawrence Erlbaum.

N

Narrative Analysis

CHERYL DE LA REY

Narrative analysis does not fit neatly within any one scholarly field; it is intrinsically interdisciplinary. Narrative research is conducted across disciplines such as psychology, sociology, and history. Generally, the term "narrative analysis" refers to the interpretation of some form of storytelling derived from long interviews, biographies, journals, and diaries. (See NARRATIVE PSYCHOLOGY.)

Riessman (1993) was one of the first scholars who attempted to develop narrative analysis as a systematic research method. She identified some general features to which the majority of scholars using this method seemed to subscribe.

Some level of sequence is a necessary feature of narratives. This may be sequencing by time or theme. Narratives may take a variety of forms and not all are stories in the sense of having protagonists, a plot, events, complications, and an ending. Riessman pointed to habitual narratives when events happen over and over again, hypothetical narratives which depict events that did not happen, and topic-centered narratives, described as snapshots of past events that are linked thematically.

A significant feature of a narrative is that it tells about not only how we understand past deeds and events, but also how the self is constructed. Narrative analysis is about systematically interpreting how people construct meaning – meanings of themselves, of others, and of events. In psychology the idea of self as narrative was developed initially by Gergen and Gergen (1984). In simple terms, the idea is that we make sense of our lives and our relationships through constructing stories – stories about childhood, our school days, our families, sexual relationships, and working experiences. Through these stories we make ourselves intelligible to self and to others.

Narratives always imply an audience, either real or imaginary. As such these stories are products of interacting persons, not products of an autonomous individual mind. This means that narratives are social and that they are grounded in social interaction and practice.

Another feature of narratives is that they are culturally and historically situated. The lives and selves we construct develop in response to present circumstances and also

The Encyclopedia of Peace Psychology, First Edition. Edited by Daniel J. Christie.
© 2012 Blackwell Publishing Ltd. Published 2012 by Blackwell Publishing Ltd.

assume meaning from the historical circumstances that give shape to the culture in which the person is positioned. (See SOCIAL REPRESENTATIONS OF HISTORY; NATIONAL POLITICAL CULTURES.)

Through narrative we are given an account of the person in process. In a narrative an event is typically located temporally by being placed in a context of preceding and subsequent events. Through this, connections between life events are constructed and reference is made to the past, the present, and the future.

In addition, Gergen and Gergen suggested that a narrative usually has a valued endpoint, purpose, or goal that would inform the selection and arrangement of events. In building on this idea, they identified three prototypical narrative forms – a progressive narrative in which there is movement towards the goal, a regressive narrative in which achievement of the goal is impeded, and a stability narrative where no change occurs.

Sample sizes in narrative studies are generally small. In deciding on sample size the researcher needs to consider a balance between the need for generalization on the one hand, and close attention to narrative detail on the other. If the aim is to show variation and to make comparisons across cases, then several narratives must be studied.

Narratives are frequently derived through interviews which are transcribed. But the researcher may use narratives that are already documented in written form such as in diaries, journals, and biographies.

There is a range of approaches to the analysis of narratives. Studies using larger samples tend either to present key substantive themes that cut across all the narratives or to select and concentrate on a few key individual narratives.

A commonly used technique when presenting narratives is to reduce them to core narratives, or to summaries derived through a process of close listening to audio transcripts and/or repeated readings of the transcriptions. Core narratives are reductions of the full narratives that comprise basic content and plot line but numerous parts are excluded, such as descriptions, evaluations, and explanations. Even though core narratives are reductions, they can be usefully deployed for presenting the substantive content of a large number of narratives. Commonalities and variations across participants are detectable, even though they are reductions. Although the emphasis is on content, features of narrative such as directionality and movement through time are still evident in the configuration of the core. The analysis and interpretation may, however, go beyond the core narratives by including quotations and material from full transcripts.

A distinctive feature of narrative analysis is that the researcher can extend the interpretation beyond content *per se* by looking at other features of the narrative such as structure, form, and function. The analysis can examine commonalities and differences across narratives in terms of both content and form.

Narrative forms can be categorized, for example, by assessing whether a certain prototype is evident. Is it a progressive narrative, defined as a narrative in which there is progressive movement towards a goal state or valued endpoint? Are events described and positioned in relation to how they contribute to or detract from the movement towards an endpoint? Or is it a regressive narrative whereby events are positioned as regressive, that is, incidents or events are construed as retreats or digressions along the path to a particular endpoint? These are some of the ways in which narratives may be categorized in terms of their form.

By analyzing the form and content of narratives we can derive information about the meaning imbued in the actions of others and in events and about how these meanings may be shaped by specific historical and cultural contexts. For example, much has been learned about gender through analysis of narratives. Overall, it has been shown that in narratives of women, the actions of men as fathers, husbands, and lovers play a pivotal part in shaping the movements and key events in the women protagonists, whereas in men's narratives the self is given centrality.

There is much debate about the truth value of narratives. Are narratives to be regarded as truth? Many scholars believe that narratives have the potential to bear truth, while others argue that all narratives do not reflect truth, but construct it. The former view is consistent with empiricism, a perspective that would argue that the truth value of narratives is subject to systematic observation. In other words, a narrative could be systematically tested to assess whether it is true. The other view is consistent with the social constructionist approach which holds that narratives do not reflect truth but create what is understood to be true. However, there is agreement across approaches that narratives are always limited accounts. Narratives may be limited by context, by the communicative competencies of the narrator, and/or by cognitive processes such as memory.

Coffey and Atkinson (1996) suggested that metaphor could be a useful means for examining how individuals and groups organize and express their experiences. Here metaphor refers to all forms of figurative speech such as similes, analogies, and imagery. Values, beliefs, and shared knowledge within a specific cultural group are often conveyed through the use of idiomatic language and imagery. The analysis of idiomatic speech forms may reveal insights into the cultural context of a narrative. Furthermore, narratives are a useful means for accessing the myths and folklores of different cultures.

There are no recipes or formulae to be followed in analyzing narratives. It is a qualitative, interpretive method which has been systematized by researchers but there are no set procedures. The researcher is able to be creative in narrative analysis. What matters is that the researcher is able to give a clear, credible account of the analytic procedures used and that within any study these procedures are used consistently and systematically.

SEE ALSO: Narrative Psychology; National Political Cultures; Social Representations of History.

REFERENCES

Coffey, A., & Atkinson, P. (1996). *Making sense of qualitative data: Complementary research strategies*. Thousand Oaks, CA: Sage.

Gergen, M. M., & Gergen, K. J. (1984). The social construction of narrative accounts. In K. J. Gergen & M. M. Gergen (Eds.), *Historical social psychology*. Hillsdale, NJ: Lawrence Erlbaum.

Riessman, C. K. (1993). *Narrative analysis*. Newbury Park, CA: Sage.

ADDITIONAL RESOURCES

Daite, C., & Lightfoot, C. (2004). *Narrative analysis: Shaping the development of individuals in society*. Thousand Oaks, CA: Sage.

Labov, W., & Waletzky, J. (2003). Narrative analysis: Oral versions of research experience. In C. B. Paulston & G. R. Tucker (Eds.), *Sociolinguistics: The essential readings*. Oxford, UK: Blackwell.

Schedloff, E. A. (2003). "Narrative analysis" thirty years later. In C. B. Paulston & G. R. Tucker (Eds.), *Sociolinguistics: The essential readings*. Oxford, UK: Blackwell.

Narrative Psychology

JÁNOS LÁSZLÓ

Narratives are generally conceived as accounts of events which involve some temporal and/or causal coherence. This minimal definition is usually amended with criteria according to which storiness requires some goal-directed action of living or impersonated actors taking place in time. A full-blown narrative involves an initial steady state which implies the legitimate order of things including the characters' normal wishes and beliefs, a trouble which disturbs this state, efforts for re-establishing the normal state, a new, often transformed state, and a concluding evaluation, which draws the moral of the story.

Narratives – whether oral, written, or pictorial – are bound to narrative thinking. It is a natural (i.e., universal, innate) capacity of the human mind. Evolutionary arguments for narrative thinking stress its capacity to encode deviations from the ordinary and its mimetic force. Paul Ricoeur derived humankind's concept of time from narrative capacity. Recently, brain mechanisms of narrative thinking have been traced by sophisticated brain-imaging devices. Nevertheless, as with time concepts or languages, narrative forms show wide cultural variations. This variation provides ground to sociocultural theories of narrative, which stress the cultural evolution of narrative forms. According to these theories, narrative genres model characteristic intentions, goals, and values of a group sharing a culture.

Narrative thinking can be contrasted with paradigmatic or logico-scientific thinking (Bruner, 1986). When we think in terms of a paradigmatic or logical–scientific mode, we work with abstract concepts and construe truth by means of empirical evidence and methods of formal logic, and while doing so, we seek causal relations that lead to universal truth conditions. When we use the narrative mode we investigate human or human-like intentions and acts, as well as the stories and consequences related to them. What justifies this mode is life-likeness rather than truth, and it aspires to create a realistic representation of life. Bruner (1986,

pp. 11–12.) illustrates the two types of causality as follows: "The term then functions differently in the logical proposition 'if x then y' and in the narrative 'The king died, and then the queen died.' One leads to a search for universal truth conditions, the other for likely particular connections between two events – mortal grief, suicide, foul play." In other words, narrative thinking aspires to make sense or to establish coherence.

Narratives do not depict events as they "find" them out there in the world, but construe these events by narrative forms and categories in order to arrive at the *meaning* of the events. Narrative theories are *constructivist theories*.

Narrative theories and approaches have spread out in various disciplines. Historiography, for instance, became susceptible to this approach very early. A true historical text recounts events in terms of their inherent interrelations in the light of an existing legal and moral order, so it has all the properties of narrative. As a consequence, the reality of these events does not consist in the fact that they occurred. Rather, it depends on remembering (i.e., they are remembered) and on their capacity of finding a place in a chronologically ordered sequence. "The authority of the historical narrative is the authority of reality itself; the historical account endows this reality with form and thereby makes it desirable, imposing upon its processes the formal coherency that only stories possess" (White, 1981, p. 19).

To intensify a sense of reality and truthfulness to real life, a historical account makes use of rhetorical figures and relies heavily on the dimension of consciousness; that is, on what historical figures might have known, thought, and felt. The origin of modern historical science itself is also closely related to the national history that was demanded by nineteenth-century nationalism.

The narrative approach reached psychology in the late 1980s. The term narrative psychology was introduced by Theodor Sarbin (1986), who claimed that human conduct can be best explained through stories, and this explanation should be done by qualitative studies. Narrative accounts are embedded in social action. Events become socially visible through narratives, and expectations towards future events are, for the most part, substantiated by them. Since narratives permeate the events of everyday life, the events themselves become story-like too. They assume the reality of "beginning," "peak," "nadir," or "termination." According to Sarbin, a proper interpretation of narratives gives the explanation social action.

Another book from the same year, Jerome Bruner's *Actual Minds, Possible Words* (1986), explored the "narrative kind of knowing" in a more empirical manner. Around the same time, Dan McAdams (1985) developed a theoretical framework and a coding system for interpreting life narratives in the personological tradition. It builds on the Eriksonian tradition which assumes a close relationship between life story and personal identity. Accordingly, it derives various characteristics of identity from the content and structure of life stories. Whereas earlier psychological studies were directed to story production and story comprehension in the cognitivist tradition, the new narrative psychology has turned to the issues of identity construction and functioning. The narrative meta-theory has become particularly influential in self- and identity theory, where, based on the life story, it offers a nonessentialist solution for the unity and identity of the individual self. The conception of narrative as a means of identity construction is summarized by Polkinghorne (1988, p. 150) as follows:

> The tools being used by the human disciplines to gain access to the self-concept are, in general, the traditional research implements designed for formal science to locate and measure objects and things. We

achieve our personal identities and self-concept through the use of the narrative configuration, and make our existence into a whole by understanding it as an expression of a single unfolding and developing story. We are in the middle of our stories and cannot be sure how they will end; we constantly have to revise the plot as new events are added to our lives. Self, then, is not a static thing or a substance, but a configuring of personal events into a historical unity, which includes not only what one has been but also anticipations of what one will be.

Recently, a new direction of narrative psychology has emerged, which draws on the scientific traditions of psychological study, but adds to the existing theories by pursuing the empirical study of psychological meaning construction (László, 2008). Scientific narrative psychology takes seriously the interrelations between language and human psychological processes or narrative and identity. This is what distinguishes it from earlier psychometric studies, which established correlations between language use and psychological states. It assumes that studying narratives as vehicles of complex psychological contents leads to empirically based knowledge about human social adaptation. Individuals in their life stories, just like groups in their group histories, compose their significant life episodes. In this composition, which is meaning construction in itself, they express the ways in which they organize their relations to the social world, or construct their identity. Organizational characters and experiential qualities of these stories tell about the potential behavioral adaptation and the coping capacities of the storytellers.

Another remarkable novelty comes from the recognition of correspondences between narrative organization and psychological organization, namely from the fact that narrative features of self-narratives (e.g., the characters' functions, the temporal characteristics of the story, or the speakers' perspectives) will provide information about the features and conditions of self-representations. Similarly, the stories about the world will disclose the psychological features of social representations.

NARRATIVE ANALYSIS

Traditionally, narratives are analyzed in social sciences in three distinct ways. *Formal–structural analysis* initiated by the Russian formalists focuses on the role that linguistic and discourse structures play in conveying meaning. In psychology this approach prevails in cognitive studies of story production and comprehension. *Content analysis* is directed to the semantic content and tries to quantify it. In psychology, of course, psychological contents are classified and measured. Major limits of both analytic tools are, first, the uncertainty of the external validity of the constructs derived from them, and second, blindness to the context where structures or semantic contents occur. This latter flaw prevents formal–structural analysis and content analysis to reconstruct the pragmatic or psychological meaning of texts However, the third type of narrative analytics, *hermeneutic analysis*, embraces the social, cultural, and textual context of the narrative and interprets its meaning against this background. In psychology it mostly means interpretation of personal narratives with reference to identity. Validity of the interpretation, however, is not amenable to empirical testing. The interpretation is performed against a possible wide cultural, social, and historical background and extends to issues of authority, dialogicity, and voice, as well as positioning. Some authors emphasize that qualitative narrative psychology even need not deal with narrative texts. The principal requirement is the narrativity of the interpretation of the data coming from any

source. In other words, discussion should be a "storied account." (See NARRATIVE ANALYSIS.)

The positivism versus hermeneutics or the sciences versus humanities controversy is clearly reflected in the above approaches. Whereas content analysis goes bottom-up, attempting to construct meaning from elementary pieces of narrative discourse, hermeneutics adopts a top-down strategy in which the interpretation horizon has absolute primacy.

Scientific narrative psychology strives toward concerted application of top-down and bottom-up methodologies, because it studies highly complex issues of personality, culture, and society. In order to study the experiential organizations and qualities of life narratives and group narratives, the methodology of narrative psychological content analysis has been developed. This methodology is based on narratological concepts and on social psychological theories of language use. Narratology has described the limited number of elements and the limited number of variations of the elements in narrative composition. These compositional factors can be reliably identified in discourse. Narrative components correspond to certain processes or states of experiential organization or psychological meaning construction. For instance, using a retrospective narrative perspective as opposed to experiencing or re-experiencing perspectives when telling a traumatic life event suggests emotional balance, that is, the storyteller has managed to elaborate the negative experience and restore the integrity of his or her identity. In an experiment, Pólya, László, and Forgas (2005) provided evidence supporting the above assumption. Traumatic life events, such as the failure of an *in vitro* fertilization (IVF) treatment, were reported from different perspectives. The use of the different perspectives can be illustrated with the following excerpts: "I was waiting in the doctor's office . . . The doctor entered the room . . . He told me that we had not succeeded . . . " (retrospective perspective); "It was in the doctor's office . . . I see the doctor entering the room . . . I don't remember how it could happen . . . " (re-experiencing perspective). Subjects consistently evaluated the target person as having better emotional control, higher social value, and more stable identity when they read retrospective stories as opposed to re-experienced ones.

Beyond the perspective, narratives contain other compositional devices such as time structure and time experience, characters' agency, characters' mental involvement, coherence, evaluation, spatial and interpersonal relations of the characters, etc. This limited number of compositional "slots" corresponds to a similarly limited number of psychological constructions, whereas the text can be endlessly variable on the surface level (i.e., linguistically). Based on the narrative compositional elements, algorithms have been constructed that are able to automatically detect and quantitatively process the linguistic features of each element (László, 2008).

Narrative psychological content analysis, just as any content analytic research, begins with qualitative decisions, which attribute some meaning to certain textual elements. In psychology this meaning is usually psychological meaning. The analysis does not stop, however, at this qualitative phase. Narrative psychological content analysis treats the content analytical codes as values of psychological variables, which, in turn, will become quantifiable and statistically processible.

The narrative psychological approach has recently been applied to studying relations between social representations of history and identity.

SEE ALSO: Narrative Analysis.

REFERENCES

Bruner, J. (1986). *Actual minds, possible worlds.* Cambridge, MA: Harvard University Press.

László, J. (2008). *The science of stories: An introduction to narrative psychology.* New York, NY: Routledge.

McAdams, D. P. (1985). *Power, intimacy, and the life story: Personological inquiries into identity.* New York, NY: Guilford Press.

Polkinghorne, D. E. (1988). *Narrative knowing and the human sciences.* Albany: State University of New York Press.

Pólya, T., László, J., & Forgas, J. P. (2005). Making sense of life stories: The role of narrative perspective in communicating hidden information about social identity and personality. *European Journal of Social Psychology, 35,* 785–796.

Sarbin, T. R. (1986). The narrative as a root metaphor for psychology. In T. R. Sarbin (Ed.), *Narrative psychology: The storied nature of human conduct* (pp. 3–21). New York, NY: Praeger.

White, H. (1981). The value of narrativity in the representation of reality. In W. J. T. Mitchell (Ed.), *On narrative* (pp. 1–23). Chicago, IL: University of Chicago Press.

National Political Cultures

JAMES H. LIU AND DARIO PAEZ

The global system of sovereign states solidified in the nineteenth century as European peoples engaged in political projects that solidified the boundaries between them and regularized warfare and governance, not as the hereditary prerogative of princes, but the lawful activity of peoples forming "nationalities." European experiences were both emulated voluntarily and exported violently through a process of aggressively military colonization, resulting in the global system of states that govern the political boundaries of the world today. These states may or may not be nationalities (that is, where a majority of the people share common ethnic and linguistic origins), but they are frequently imagined as such (Smith, 1995). States claim the sole prerogative to exercise the legitimate use of violence within their boundaries, and are often the only recognized political entities that other states recognize as having the power to govern. Hence, the multilingual and multi-cultural empires that governed large parts of the world until the nineteenth and twentieth centuries (e.g., the Spanish Empire, the Austro-Hungarian Empire, the Ottoman Turkish Empire) have disappeared, creating many new states but leaving other peoples who aspire to sovereignty but do not have that status.

It is in this context that contemporary cross-cultural psychology has begun a project to characterize psychological features of different societies. In contrast to anthropology, which focuses on tribes and other pre-state groupings, cross-cultural psychology attempts to characterize the national psychologies of states by analyzing survey responses from different countries. Seminally, Geert Hofstede (1980/2001) identified four dimensions of psychological variation on which country-level scores differed across cultures: individualism, power distance, masculinity, and uncertainty avoidance. Inspired by Chinese scholars, a fifth dimension – long-term orientation – was added later. Among these, individualism–collectivism and power distance (acceptance and expectation of inequality) have been the most influential and the best replicated. Each culture (operationalized as the average of survey responses from a state) can be located as a point on a multidimensional space to be compared to other cultures.

The dimensions of cultural variation produced by cross-cultural psychology tend to be based on relatively enduring and largely implicit aspects of culture such as values. They do not focus much attention on elements of culture critical to politics, like

ethnic, religious, or political factions or the political discourses that accompany these within a state, but tend to treat populations within states as homogeneous. A notable sociological project known as the World Values Survey by Ronald Inglehart has demonstrated significant changes in country-level values over the last 30 years, with the world moving away from traditional and towards secular–rational values (e.g., away from religious and authority-based systems), and away from survival towards self-expression values (in most regions), but at rates that have maintained cultural differences between countries and regions and provided no evidence of global convergence. Inglehart and colleagues (e.g., Inglehart & Norris, 2004) have remarked that a society becomes more oriented towards self-expression values as it democratizes, and while it is well documented that the two are associated, it is less certain what the causal path is between the political system a society adopts and the values its people hold.

The domain of value-based support for equality versus inequality in society has been a fertile area for intersection between cross-cultural psychology and the social psychology of intergroup relations. This latter literature has been largely culture-free, individualistic, and dominated by universalistic theories of social, cognitive, motivational, and emotional functions grounded in Western epistemologies. Among these, the social dominance theory of Sidanius and Pratto (1999) fused with contemporary versions of authoritarian personality theory (Duckitt, 2001) show promise as avenues of consolidation between societal and individual-level theories of intergroup relations and political culture. According to Sidanius and Pratto (1999), all human societies are group-based hierarchies that differ primarily in the legitimizing ideology that is used to justify inequality, and the degree to which inequality is subscribed to as a societal value. At the individual level, people high in social dominance orientation (a motivational goal for group-based dominance and inequality) and high in right-wing authoritarianism tend also to be more prejudiced, across a wide range of target populations within a number of societies. It is less well understood how an entire society high in social dominance orientation or right-wing authoritarianism (these two are positively correlated in most societies) should behave internally with respect to prejudice and discrimination to low-status groups in society, and externally with respect to international relations with other countries. There is not necessarily a simple linear relationship between the internal logic of prejudice and discrimination within a society to international relations between societies, nor are the relationships between the same psychological variables analyzed at the individual level and at the country level necessarily identical. However, recent work has found that a hierarchical value system was one factor related to a psychological willingness to fight in future conflicts at both levels. (See AUTHORITARIAN PERSONALITY; SOCIAL DOMINANCE THEORY.)

One avenue to uncover these relations is to analyze the impact of a system of societal beliefs that Bar-Tal (2000) has referred to as a societal ethos. Using Israel as a primary case study, he defined an ethos of conflict as consisting of a configuration of eight themes that provide a dominant orientation toward dealing with prolonged intractable conflict in a society. These societal beliefs are the justness of nationalistic goals, concerns for personal safety and national survival, ethnocentrism with respect to collective self-image, patriotism, unity, portraying the ingroup as a victim, delegitimizing and dehumanizing the concerns of the opponent, and a belief about the ultimate peaceful intentions of the ingroup. This societal ethos then conditions political behavior within society, often perpetuating a cycle of

mistrust and reducing the possibilities for peace. It remains to be seen how widely the holistic and comprehensive ethos of conflict described by Bar-Tal (2000) as characterizing Israel applies to other societies also experiencing prolonged intractable conflict. (See CONFLICT, ETHOS OF.)

It should be noted that one of the most difficult situations for conflict resolution in the contemporary state system is when two or more peoples that have become incompatible both claim a sovereign right to overlapping territory. A less comprehensive and holistic approach to defining national political cultures and claims to sovereignty is an approach using historical representations. Hilton and Liu (2008) describe a historical charter as a "widely shared and iconic representation where selective elements of group history, its causes, and consequences have been elaborated into a quasi-legal form that gives moral and sometimes legal implications for group action." Again, culture-specific logics governing intergroup relations and other issues of social governance are described, this time with reference to foundational historical events and people that are used to justify a prospective political agenda and explain past events in a way that makes sense of the particular historical experience of a society.

This program of research has emphasized cleavages versus consensus between different groups within a society, based on the idea that the degree to which representations are shared across subgroups cannot be assumed, but is a critical feature of the political culture of a state. Generally, it has been found that in all the states surveyed, including several that are young and multi-ethnic (Hungary, New Zealand, the Philippines, Malaysia, and Singapore), the most widely known events and people are consensual across ethnic or regional groups. They provide a set of symbolic resources that can be worked by political elites and major institutions to form a historical charter (Hilton

& Liu, 2008) that influences the society's political behavior in fundamental but culture-specific ways, through the operation of normative (e.g., legitimizing ideologies), cognitive (e.g., analogical transfer, attributional schemas), motivational (e.g., setting national agendas, agenda-driven collective remembering), and social identity functions (e.g., building national identity and prototypical traits).

For instance, in New Zealand, where the Treaty of Waitangi between Maori (first peoples who were subject to a process of colonization) and the British Crown is considered by all groups to be the most important event in New Zealand history, Maori claims for historical redress and self-determination, a pattern of symbolic inclusion (equality in principle, even at the level of implicit associations) and resource-based exclusion (inequality in practice, founded on a resistance to "special privileges" to Maori for past injustices) have emerged. In the Philippines, where the 1986 EDSA "People Power" revolution that toppled the Marcos dictatorship is consensually regarded as the most important event in Filipino history, a pattern of subsequent, less consensual People Power revolutions has troubled the original consensus around the desirability of peaceful revolution to overthrow corrupt government. The military and civilians offer alternative accounts of the EDSA revolution that each warrant different forms of interference in the process of regular elections of the national government. In Taiwan the pattern of historical events leading to local autonomy and the institution of free democratic elections has made reunification with mainland China unpopular, just as the mainland Chinese historical narrative of China's rise from a weak and divided nation preyed upon by foreign powers bent on its dismemberment to its contemporary standing as a strong and indivisible nation will not allow Taiwan to become independent. Each of these "historical charters" appears to condition the political behavior of a people through particular prisms of historical experience that make some political actions likely and others impossible.

Wertsch (2002) has provided an alternative conception for these phenomena by drawing from narrative traditions in sociology and psychology. He identified the following sequence of moves abstracted from Russian history resulting in the schematic narrative template for Russian people: (1) An initial situation where Russians are living in a peaceful setting where they are no threat to others is disrupted by (2) the initiation of trouble or aggression by alien forces, which leads to (3) a time of crisis and great suffering for the Russian people, which is (4) overcome by the triumph over the alien force by the Russian people, acting heroically and alone. This template has been used to provide a Russian account of their actions in signing the Molotov–Ribbentrop Pact partitioning Poland at the beginning of World War II; Stalin can be viewed not as malevolent or aggressive, but as acting defensively to bide time before the inevitable battle with Hitler for the survival of the Russian people.

Both holistic and more analytical approaches have made important contributions to identifying national political cultures and the degree to which different cultures may be differentiated psychologically from one another.

SEE ALSO: Authoritarian Personality; Conflict, Ethos of; Social Dominance Theory.

REFERENCES

Bar-Tal, D. (2000). *Shared beliefs in a society: Social psychological analysis*. Thousand Oaks, CA: Sage.

Duckitt, J. (2001). A dual-process cognitive–motivational theory of ideology and prejudice. In M. P. Zanna (Ed.), *Advances in experimental social psychology* (Vol. 33, pp. 41–113). New York, NY: Academic Press.

Hilton, D. J., & Liu, J. H. (2008). Culture and intergroup relations. The role of social representations of history. In R. Sorrentino & S. Yamaguchi (Eds.), *The handbook of motivation and cognition: The cultural context* (pp. 343–368). New York, NY: Guilford Press.

Hofstede, G. (1980/2001). *Culture's consequences* (2nd ed.). Thousand Oaks, CA: Sage.

Inglehart, R., & Norris, P. (2004). *Sacred and secular: Religion and politics worldwide.* Cambridge, UK: Cambridge University Press.

Sidanius, J., & Pratto, F. (1999). *Social dominance: An intergroup theory of social hierarchy and oppression.* Cambridge, UK: Cambridge University Press.

Smith, A. D. (1995). *Nations and nationalism in a global era.* Oxford, UK: Blackwell.

Wertsch, J. V. (2002). *Voices of collective remembering.* Cambridge, UK: Cambridge University Press.

ADDITIONAL RESOURCES

www.geert-hostede.com
www.vuw.ac.nz/cacr
www.worldvaluessurvey.org

Native Peacemaking

POLLY O. WALKER

"Peacemaking is . . . a way of thinking and living in respectful relations with others." This definition of Navajo peacemaking shared by Robert Yazzie (2004, p. 112), Chief Justice of the Navajo Peacemakers Court, also describes the peacemaking traditions of many other Native peoples in Canada and the United States. Native peacemaking seeks to maintain and restore balance and harmony to vast networks of relationships among living humans, ancestors, generations to come, and the natural world. It also seeks to restore balance within each individual, seeking to bring harmony to the spiritual, emotional, intellectual, and physical aspects

of human experience. Native peacemaking might be described as processes which assist people to live in harmony with the flux and patterns of the natural world.

There are well over 1,000 forms of Native peacemaking in Canada and the United States. Within this diversity there is no single pan-Indigenous peacemaking paradigm. However, there are a number of commonalities based on common principles of the Native worldviews in which these peacemaking processes are embedded. The worldviews of Native peoples demonstrate a number of shared attributes which have been termed "tenets of Native Philosophy" (Cajete, 2000) and the "Native American Paradigm" (Little Bear, 2000). Some of the aspects of the Native American Paradigm which impact on peacemaking are the interrelatedness of all aspects of experience, a universe characterized by harmony in flux, and elders as knowledge keepers. A focus on balanced yet fluid interrelationships among humans, and between humans and the cosmos, is one of the defining characteristics of Native peacemaking. (See PSYCHOSPIRITUAL HARMONY.)

Native peacemaking creates space for exploration of all aspects of human experience: intellectual, spiritual, emotional, and physical. Adverse impact on, or imbalance in, any of these aspects is considered to adversely affect both the individual and the wider community. Peacemaking seeks to restore well-being when and where it has been damaged in any of these aspects.

Native peacemaking is inherently spiritual, based on the values and beliefs of Native peoples, and explicitly addresses spiritual aspects of experience throughout the process (LaResche 1993). Most peacemaking processes begin with prayer and ritual, reminding the participants that they are part of a greater whole which includes ancestors who are present in spirit, as well as relations who are yet unborn. Peacemakers encourage participants to reflect on the wisdom and teachings of their spiritual traditions which may be shared in story, song, or ceremony.

Emotional expression is also an integral part of the Native peacemaking process and peacemakers encourage participants to express their emotions openly. However, participants are reminded to be reflective and considerate of the ways in which their expression might impact on relationships among those involved. For example, in the Navajo Justice and Harmony Ceremony expressions of sadness and regret are considered to be critical indications that the process is moving in a positive direction (Yazzie, 1995). Native peacemakers also describe the importance of working at the *heart level*, of being both authentic and compassionate in expressing emotions.

Embodied, physical aspects of peacemaking are crucial to developing balance and harmony in Native peacemaking, and participants may dance, sing, drum, or engage in other performative rituals. In the Native Paradigm, a person's physical health is considered to be impacted by conflict and peacemaking understood to enhance physical well-being as well as social healing.

Intellectual processing of conflict is also an integral part of Native peacemaking and peacemakers facilitate processes designed to uncover the roots of the conflict, even when it requires going back several generations to understand how the foundations of the conflict were created. The integration of mental experience includes more than developing an understanding of the underlying factors of the conflict; it also includes a multi-party synthesis regarding restoration of a wide range of impacted relationships.

The Native Paradigm principle of living in harmony with the flux of the universe is evidenced in cyclical conceptualizations of time. Native peacemaking processes are designed to be responsive to concepts of time in which past, present, and future coexist and in which time is measured in reference to cycles of natural and social worlds. These conceptualizations of time have been referred to as *right time*, the time at which all things come together to support a particular action or decision. In many cases, due to the extensive networks of relationships among humans and the natural world, Native peacemaking may require an extensive amount of clock and calendar time as peacemakers engage in iterative consensual decision-making processes designed to involve members of the wider community as well as people centrally involved in the conflict. An emphasis on cyclical time is also evidenced in the consideration of generational relationships when peacemakers and participants reflect on how the decisions being made will impact on the next seven generations, as well as how they might integrate the wisdom of the preceding generations.

Communication styles exhibited in Native peacemaking support interrelatedness, which is a central tenet of the Native Paradigm. The range of communication is quite broad, incorporating silence, traditional teachings, stories, song, dance, and dialogue. These forms of communication are designed to strengthen and renew relationships among participants and the wider networks of relationships. For example, in the Cherokee Talking Circle, responses are shaped by the use of a talking stick, which strengthens interrelatedness by encouraging the participants to speak and listen from the heart, rather than from the mind alone. Silent time spent in waiting for one's turn to speak is considered to bring about new understanding of others' experience and perspectives, as listeners have time to reflect on others' points of view (Garrett 1998, pp. 80–83). Stories, both traditional and contemporary, are often shared in peacemaking and serve to strengthen participants' connections with traditional values and beliefs.

Humor is another form of communication that is often used in Native peacemaking. Peacemakers may share contemporary and real-life examples of humorous situations, as well as draw on trickster stories, traditional narratives in which the main character represents the flux of the cosmos. In this way, humor reminds participants to respond in balanced ways to unexpected occurrences, and to remember that in the Native Paradigm the only constant in life is change. Native elders often use humor to lighten a situation, to respond to the heaviness or sadness of conflict in ways designed to bring balance and harmony to all involved.

Native peacemakers are chosen by their communities based on demonstration of wisdom and integrity in the way the peacemakers live, speak, and move in harmony with traditional values and teachings. Peacemakers are the people to whom others in the community naturally turn for leadership in times of conflict. Native peacemakers are also known for their ability to strengthen and restore relationships in the broadest sense of the term, including relationships with the more-than-human community: the plants, animals, landforms, and processes which make up the natural world.

Native peacemaking does not function in isolation. Native communities are affected by colonization, globalization, and climate change, and Native peacemakers are facing new conflict situations both within their communities and within the nation-states in which they currently find themselves. There is not sufficient space in this article to explore the differences in Native and non-Native peacemaking, or the impact of Westernization on Native peacemaking. Nevertheless, there are some important issues that need to be mentioned as vital considerations in appropriate and respectful engagement with Native peacemaking: (1) Native and Western worldviews are starkly different in ways which impact significantly on peacemaking

among and between these peoples; (2) within Western governance, Indigenous/ Western worldview differences are seldom understood or respected, and Western dispute resolution models are often presented as the most effective processes for dealing with contemporary conflicts involving Native peoples; (3) when Native peacemaking is acknowledged by Western peacebuilders and conflict resolution specialists, there is a tendency to codify Indigenous processes, remove them from place and people, and implement the processes in new ways and settings.

Peacemaking between Native and non-Native peoples is affected by worldview differences. For example, the cyclical time evidenced in Native peacemaking contrasts starkly with the linear, time-urgent processes of Western dispute resolution. Native concepts of right time, of exploring the generational antecedents of the conflict, and examining the impact of decisions on future generations, are often interpreted by Western third party interveners as obfuscation. The dominant society's failure to engage respectfully with these and other differences in worldview continues to create and exacerbate conflicts involving Native peoples.

At times when Western scholars and dispute resolution practitioners have acknowledged Native peacemaking processes, they have failed to respect the interrelationships honored and valued by Native peoples. In these cases, Native peacemaking processes have been appropriated and codified by non-Indigenous peoples. In such applications the processes no longer fully belong to Indigenous peoples, and indeed are no longer able to fully effect peacemaking because the people, values, stories, and ceremonies that comprise an integral part of Native peacemaking are no longer present in the institutionalized form. Furthermore, the rigidity exhibited in codification does not allow for the flux of relationally responsive processes which are a characteristic of the Native Paradigm.

Throughout the colonization of North America, Native peacemaking ceremonies and rituals were marginalized and suppressed. In many cases, Canadian and US governments forcibly replaced Native peacemaking processes with Western legal and dispute resolution systems. Nevertheless, Native peoples continue to practice their peacemaking traditions even when they have been adversely impacted. Currently, there is a resurgence of a fuller expression of, and support for, Native peacemaking processes. One of the most widely known and widely researched examples of such revitalization is the 1982 introduction of Navajo peacemaking into the formal Navajo justice system. This process, which has been largely successful, was based on a careful examination of Navajo values, ways of knowing, and Navajo-specific cultural values (Yazzie, 2004).

Revitalization of Native peacemaking does not, however, require a wholesale rejection of Western peacemaking and dispute resolution processes. There are a number of Native peoples who have approached dispute resolution through an integration of their traditional peacemaking processes with Western dispute resolution. These processes honor Native peoples and their worldviews while achieving appropriate and sustainable outcomes. One example of such collaboration is outlined by Elmer Ghostkeeper (2004), who describes the practice of *Wechewehtowin*, or "partnershipping" between "Aboriginal and Western concepts and values," a process which assisted in resolving a number of conflicts over Metis land. Collaborative processes such as these recenter Native ways of knowing, reducing the epistemic violence evidenced in colonial suppression and contemporary appropriation of Native peacemaking processes.

SUMMARY

Native peacemaking processes are embedded in a worldview which emphasizes the interrelatedness of humans, ancestors, coming generations, and the natural world. Within this relational network, Native communities select peacemakers based on demonstrated ability to speak and live in balance and harmony within extended webs of relationships. The peacemaking processes themselves seek to bring health and well-being to the emotional, mental, spiritual, and physical aspects of individuals, their communities, and their relationships with the natural world. Although impacted by colonization and at times appropriated by contemporary Western scholars and practitioners, Native peacemaking continues to be practiced and is experiencing a revitalization in a number of Native nations. Developing respectful and appropriate engagement between Indigenous and Western peoples and their peacemaking processes requires ongoing and iterative processes of developing deeper understanding of, and respect for, Indigenous peoples, their worldviews, and their peacemaking processes.

SEE ALSO: Psychospiritual Harmony.

REFERENCES

Cajete, G. (2000). *Native science: Natural laws of interdependence*. Santa Fe, NM: Clear Light Publications.

Garrett, M. (1998). *Walking on the wind*. Santa Fe, NM: Bear.

Ghostkeeper, E. (2004). *Weche* teachings: Aboriginal wisdom and dispute resolution. In C. Bell & D. Kahane (Eds.), *Intercultural dispute resolution in Aboriginal contexts* (pp. 161–175). Vancouver, Canada: University of British Columbia Press.

LaResche, D. (1993). Native American perspectives on peacemaking. *Mediation Quarterly, 10*(4), 321–322.

Little Bear, L. (2000). Foreword. In G. Cajete, *Native science: Natural laws of interdependence* (pp. ix–xxii). Santa Fe, NM: Clear Light Publications.

Yazzie, R. (1995). Traditional Navajo dispute resolution in the Navajo Peacemaker Court. *NIDR FORUM* (Spring).

Yazzie, R. (2004). Navajo peacemaking and intercultural dispute resolution. In C. Bell & D. Kahane (Eds.), *Intercultural dispute resolution in Aboriginal contexts* (pp. 107–115). Vancouver, Canada: University of British Columbia Press.

ADDITIONAL RESOURCES

Bluehouse, P., & Zion, J. W. (1993). Hozhooji Naat'aanii: The Navajo Justice and Harmony Ceremony. *Mediation Quarterly, 10*(4), 327–337.

Ross, R. (1996). *Returning to the teachings: Exploring Aboriginal justice.* Toronto, Canada: Penguin.

http://www.ecr.gov/Resources/NativeNetwork/NativeNetwork.aspx (Native Dispute Resolution Network, a division of the US Institute for Environmental Conflict Resolution, Udall Foundation)

Negotiating Strategies and Processes, Psychological Aspects of

MARA OLEKALNS AND PHILIP L. SMITH

One of the first decisions a negotiator makes is whether to adopt a broadly cooperative or broadly competitive approach. This decision is critical because it affects the boundaries that negotiators set (the range of acceptable outcomes), where they start the negotiation and their willingness to make concessions. It also shapes how negotiations unfold because it shifts negotiators' tactical preferences to more heavily emphasize either problem-solving, collaborative behaviors or contentious, power-oriented behaviors.

In making this strategic choice, individuals are faced with the negotiator's dilemma. On the one hand, a cooperative strategy is the most effective approach for creating value and maximizing both parties' outcomes. However, if only one negotiator behaves cooperatively, he or she opens the way to exploitation. While behaving competitively might provide protection against exploitation, this strategic approach also has limitations. Among these is the possibility that negotiators fail to create value and bargain over the division of a smaller resource pool. An even greater risk occurs if both negotiators choose the competitive path because they are likely to become locked in a contentious cycle, consequently failing to resolve the negotiation.

FACTORS THAT SHAPE STRATEGIC CHOICE

Because most negotiations are mixed motive, individuals need to juggle both cooperation and competition. What varies across individuals and situations is the relative weight that negotiators give to one or other of these broad approaches. According to Pruitt's dual concern model, negotiators are most likely to employ a competitive strategy when they are highly concerned about their individual outcomes but unconcerned about maintaining the relationship with the other party. Negotiators shift to a more collaborative, problem-solving approach when they place equal weight on their own and the other party's outcomes, recognizing the importance of preserving their relationship with the other negotiator. A central question for negotiation researchers is the identification of factors that shift the weights assigned to economic and social outcomes. In this section, we review the factors that influence negotiators' strategic choices. (See MEDIATION; RIPENESS THEORY; CONFLICT, ESCALATION AND DE-ESCALATION OF; COMPARATIVE CASE STUDIES.)

Cognitive Biases

Cognitive biases affect negotiators' representations of their outcomes. Perhaps the most investigated of those biases is the negotiators' frame. Research focusing on framing effects shows that negotiators are more likely to behave competitively if they view their outcomes in terms of losses than in terms of gains. Compared to gain-framed negotiators, loss-framed negotiators set higher minimum acceptable outcomes, make higher opening offers, and give smaller concessions to the other party. Because they are more contentious, they take longer to reach settlement. Negotiators may also behave more contentiously because the fixed-pie error leads to the assumption that negotiators' outcomes are negatively correlated: An improvement for one person is necessarily a loss for the other person.

Social Motives

Social motives determine negotiators' preferences for resource allocation, that is, whether negotiators focus on maximizing collective (prosocial social motive) or personal (proself social motive) outcomes. These different outcome goals can occur because of dispositional differences (social value orientation) or situational differences (motivational orientation). Although negotiators have a personal preference for cooperation or competition, strategic preferences can be primed to explicitly encourage negotiators to maximize their own or both parties' outcomes. Factors such as time pressure, accountability to others, and no expectation of future interaction all prime a more competitive, proself orientation. Prosocial

negotiators adopt a softer bargaining style than proself negotiators, show greater concern about the well-being of the other party, and are more likely to express support of the other party (De Dreu, Weingart, & Kwon, 2000).

Power

In negotiation it is important to consider each negotiator's power and the distribution of power across negotiators. High-power negotiators set both higher targets and higher resistance points. To meet their limits, high-power negotiators are more likely to engage in put-downs and threats, to use more persuasive arguments, and to ask fewer diagnostic questions. Counterintuitively, when faced with a high-power counterpart, low-power negotiators do not respond submissively. Instead, they increase their level of contentiousness by matching the competitive behaviors of the high-power negotiator.

Gender

Men and women differ in how they approach negotiations. Overall, women adopt a somewhat less competitive approach and obtain poorer economic outcomes than men. These differences can be traced back to differences in women's willingness to engage in negotiation, as well as their goal-setting processes. Compared to men, women set lower targets and are more likely to settle as soon as their resistance point (lower limit) is met. They are more willing to accept the first offer and, compared to men, receive less generous offers. Finally, women are less willing to persist in the face of difficulties and setbacks in a negotiation.

Culture

Individuals from collectivist, high-context cultures place greater emphasis on social outcomes than those from individualistic cultures. As a result, many of their strategy choices reflect their greater emphasis on preserving social harmony. They are more indirect in their communication style and are less likely to give explicit information about their underlying preferences and priorities. Negotiators from these cultures are also more likely to appeal to sympathy and the common good in order to influence other negotiators.

Other Intrapersonal Variables

How negotiators feel plays a crucial role in their strategy choices (Druckman & Olekalns, 2008). Negotiators who report positive affect are more honest, more cooperative, and more concessionary than negotiators who report negative affect. Emotion can be used strategically by negotiators to elicit concessions from the other party: Individuals make more concessions to angry others than to happy others. However, in disputes, expressing anger triggers an escalatory cycle that blocks problem solving and resolution. Impressions of the other person, especially their perceived trustworthiness, also affect strategy choices. Negotiators are more likely to share information and problem-solve when they view the other party as trustworthy. However, when one party is perceived as benevolent, it is likely to elicit deception from the other party. (See NEGOTIATIONS AND TRUST.)

NEGOTIATIONS AS DYNAMIC PROCESSES

The variables that we have described so far influence how individuals approach their negotiation. However, negotiation is a dynamic process. As we start to negotiate with others we learn more about the context, their goals and intentions, as well as our relative power. All of this might cause negotiators to reassess their initial strategies. In short, we need to understand not just how

the factors at the start of a negotiation shape strategic preferences, but also how negotiators adapt and change their strategies in light of new information (Putnam, 1990; Weingart & Olekalns, 2004). This means that, as well as considering how often negotiators use competitive and cooperative strategies, we need to focus on when those strategies are used.

Strategy Sequences

Negotiations shape how negotiators respond to the other party's tactics. Responses can either confirm a dominant strategic approach or initiate a shift to a different style. For this reason, negotiation researchers focus on strategy sequences, chains of two (or more) strategies. Negotiation researchers have identified three kinds of strategy sequences: reciprocal, complementary, and transformational. Reciprocity occurs when negotiators match each other's tactics exactly, for example responding to a threat with a threat. Reciprocity reinforces and maintains the dominant strategic approach. Complementary sequences, sometimes also described as heteromorphic reciprocity, describe tactical chains in which negotiators respond in-kind without the strict matching observed in reciprocal sequences. For example, a negotiator might respond to a threat with a demand. Both tactics are competitive, but they are not identical. A benefit of this "looser" kind of reciprocity is that it does not lock negotiators into an increasingly rigid strategic approach. Negotiators may also try to break a dominant strategic approach by mismatching strategies. Transformational sequences describe tactical chains of cooperation–competition or competition–cooperation. Research shows that the variables we described above influence not only the tactics that negotiators choose but also the kinds of sequences that characterize their negotiations and lead to high joint gains (Olekalns & Smith, 2000).

Strategic Adaptation

How negotiations develop over time also provides important information about each individual's intentions. Communication theorists describe two interaction patterns, convergence and divergence. Convergence occurs when the interaction patterns of two people become increasingly similar over time, whereas divergence occurs when interaction patterns become increasingly dissimilar over time. Whereas convergence is interpreted as signaling similarity and reducing social distance, divergence is interpreted as signaling dissimilarity and increasing social distance. In negotiations the interpretation of convergence is more complex because negotiators can converge to either a cooperative or a competitive strategy – and it is unlikely that convergence to competition reduces social distance. Convergence is most evident in negotiating dyads that start with different approaches to the negotiation. When this occurs it is negotiators who start with the more cooperative, accommodating approach who shift their strategies to be like those of their counterparts: Negotiators with a prosocial orientation, a gain-frame, or low power shift to a more competitive style of negotiating when faced with proself, loss-framed, or high-power counterparts.

Phases and Interruptions

Strategy sequences focus on how negotiators react to each other on a moment-to-moment basis. However, it is possible to observe broader patterns over time. Both phase and stage models of negotiation focus on larger-scale shifts in strategies as negotiations move from beginning to end. These models differ in how they identify strategic shifts. Phase models are more organic, determining phase shifts inductively by looking for shifts in dominant strategy. In comparison, stage models divide negotiations into a predetermined number of segments and assess dominant strategies in each segment. Stage models suggest that negotiations begin with competition and positioning, shift to information search, and conclude with the generation and selection of a settlement option. They leave open the question of how negotiators move from one stage to the next, a question better addressed by phase models.

Negotiations do not unfold smoothly over time. Instead, the negotiation process is punctuated by critical events, or turning points. Turning points mark a change in the negotiation process, either for better or worse. They can be triggered by external events such as policy and leadership changes and third-party interventions or by the actions of negotiators themselves. When negotiators make an unexpected tactical move, they pave the way for a major reassessment of what is possible in the negotiation. When such surprise moves are better than expected – cooperation after prolonged competition – the negotiation process is redirected towards collaboration and settlement. However, when surprise moves are worse than expected they inhibit settlement and may trigger an escalatory spiral that results in impasse.

SEE ALSO: Comparative Case Studies; Conflict, Escalation and De-escalation of; Mediation; Negotiations and Trust; Ripeness Theory.

REFERENCES

Brett, J., Weingart, L., & Olekalns, M. (2004). Baubles, bangles and beads: Modeling the evolution of negotiating groups over time. In S. Blount, B. Mannix, & M. Neale (Eds.), *Research on managing groups and teams: Time in groups* (Vol. 6). Greenwich, CT: JAI Press.

De Dreu, C. K. W., Weingart, L. R., & Kwon, S. (2000). Influence of social motives on integrative negotiations: A meta-analytic review and test of two theories. *Journal of Personality and Social Psychology, 78,* 889–905.

Druckman, D., & Olekalns, M. (2008). Emotion in negotiation: Introduction to special issue. *Group Decision and Negotiation, 17,* 1–11.

Olekalns, M., & Smith, P. L. (2000). Negotiating optimal outcomes: The role of strategic sequences in competitive negotiations. *Human Communication Research, 26,* 527–557.

Putnam, L. L. (1990). Reframing integrative and distributive bargaining: A process perspective. *Research on Negotiation in Organizations, 2,* 3–30.

Weingart, L., & Olekalns, M. (2004). Communication processes in negotiation. In M. Gelfand & J. Brett (Eds.), *Handbook of negotiation and culture.* Stanford, CA: Stanford University Press.

Negotiation, Principled

DANIEL L. SHAPIRO

Principled negotiation, also known as interest-based negotiation, is a non-adversarial method of dealing with differences between individuals or groups ("parties"). The aim of this method is to reach an agreement that serves each party's interests. The core ideas were developed at the Harvard Negotiation Project and introduced in the classic book *Getting to YES* (1991), coauthored by Roger Fisher, William Ury, and Bruce Patton. Principled negotiation has proven useful in innumerable large-scale conflicts and negotiations, including the original Camp David negotiations between Egypt and Israel, the South Africa constitutional negotiations, and the 1998 Peru–Ecuador boundary dispute. (See MEDIATION; NEGOTIATIONS AND TRUST; NEGOTIATING STRATEGIES AND PROCESSES, PSYCHOLOGICAL ASPECTS OF; NEGOTIATION, ROLE OF EMOTIONS IN.)

HISTORY OF PRINCIPLED NEGOTIATION

Principled negotiation has its roots in the work of numerous scholars of management and negotiation. Mary Parker Follett pioneered ideas on integrative negotiation (1924, 1940). She differentiated between three approaches for dealing with difference: domination, compromise, and integration. In domination, one side wins; the other loses. In compromise, each side concedes to reach a settlement acceptable to all. In integration, all sides have their interests met. Follett describes how she was sitting in the Harvard library and wanted the window closed; another person wanted it open. They agreed to open a window in an adjacent room. As she explains, this was not a compromise, because everyone satisfied their interests: The other person wanted more air, and Follett did not want the breeze blowing directly on her. A second giant leap in the field of negotiation emerged with the publication of *A Behavioral Theory of Labor Relations* (1965), coauthored by Richard Walton and Robert McKersie. These negotiation scholars highlight four key aspects of negotiation: integration, distribution, attitudinal restructuring, and intraorganizational bargaining. Integrative bargaining focuses on how to expand the pie and create options that serve everyone's interests; distributive bargaining focuses on how to "divide the pie" and distribute value; attitudinal restructuring deals with building good relations; and intraorganizational bargaining focuses on alignment of expectations between principals and agents of the negotiation.

THE NEGOTIATOR'S DILEMMA

Principled negotiation is a way of addressing the "negotiator's dilemma." In short, this dilemma suggests that negotiators must choose between two opposing motives:

Shall I cooperate or compete with my counterpart? On the one hand, there is incentive to cooperate with the other party: The more information parties share, the more effective they will be at structuring an agreement that meets each party's interests. On the other hand, there is incentive to compete. The more information any single party reveals, the more vulnerable they become to exploitation by the other. Imagine a company seeking a loan from a lender. If the lender discovers that the bank is desperate for capital, the lender may decide to hike the interest rate on the loan. Thus, negotiation also involves a motivation to withhold information. Negotiation is not just about expanding the pie, but also about distributing the value that has been created. This, then, puts the negotiator in a dilemma of strategy.

Two common approaches to the negotiator's dilemma each have significant drawbacks. *Soft bargaining* focuses on building a good relationship with the other side. Concessions are made for the sake of the relationship. While this approach demonstrates to all parties a valuing of the relationship, it comes at significant substantive cost and can easily lead to exploitation. In a second approach, *hard bargaining*, parties view one another as adversaries, and the negotiation is viewed as a zero-sum contest in which one party's win comes at the expense of the other. Hard bargainers typically start with an extreme position, concede stubbornly, and compete to demonstrate a greater willingness to walk away from the negotiation. This method is epitomized by the fact that each party starts with a position – a preformulated commitment – and concedes value to the approximate degree that the other side concedes value. While hard bargaining can be an efficient approach to the distribution of resources, it has at least three major drawbacks. First, strict hard bargaining fails to engage parties in

value creation. Rather than trying to expand the pie, parties relentlessly focus on value distribution. Second, because hard bargaining focuses on haggling over positions, little information about interests is shared, hampering parties from identifying creative options for mutual gains. Third, hard bargaining puts the relationship at risk by pitting parties against one another. The party who is more effective at using force, threats, and demands tends to reap greater concessions, but often at short- or long-term cost to the quality of the relationship.

KEY INSIGHTS OF PRINCIPLED NEGOTIATION

Principled negotiation attempts to address key problems of soft bargaining and hard bargaining. Building upon the work of Follett, Walton and McKersie, and other scholars, it addresses drawbacks of hard bargaining while also capturing the benefits of soft bargaining, value creation, low-risk information exchange, and relationship enhancement. The process has several key elements (Fisher, Ury, & Patton, 1991):

1. *Look behind positions for interests.* A *position* is what a party states they want. An *interest* is the reason why. Whereas positional bargaining focuses on each party's position, principled negotiation casts attention to each party's underlying motivations, desires, and needs. The information learned through this process can help parties craft an agreement that serves their mutual benefit. The classic example involves two sisters fighting over an orange. Each clings to the position that the orange is "hers." By looking beneath positions at underlying interests, the principled negotiator discovers that the one child wants to eat the inside of

the orange, while the other wants use of the rind for a pie.

2. *Seek options for mutual gain.* As parties learn each other's interests, they are better situated to invent options for mutual gain. Consider the negotiations between Israel and Egypt over the Sinai. Egypt claimed the land had belonged to it since the time of the Pharaohs and resisted conceding any of it. At the same time, the Israelis feared that conceding the land would heighten their security risk. International mediation led to a creative option for mutual gain. Israel agreed to Egyptian sovereignty over the Sinai. In return, Egypt granted Israel a demilitarized zone along the border, assuaging Israeli security concerns.

3. *Insist on using objective criteria.* Hard bargainers attempt to gain as much of the pie as possible through a battle of wills. The party who is more forceful tends to reap greater concessions, but often at major cost to the relationship and to the potential for value creation. The principled negotiator, in contrast, insists on using objective criteria to facilitate value distribution. Objective criteria are standards of fairness external to the individual, such as industry standards, expert opinion, and international law. By drawing on objective criteria, parties can persuade one another while maintaining a positive relationship conducive to cooperation and value creation.

4. *Only commit to an agreement better than your BATNA.* A party's BATNA is its *best alternative to a negotiated agreement.* It is the party's walk-away alternative. Principled negotiation suggests that a party commit to an agreement only when it satisfies its interests better than its BATNA. In the jargon of principled negotiation, both an *option* and a *BATNA* are ways of having a party's interests satisfied. An option is a way for the party to satisfy its interests through agreement *with* its negotiating counterpart. An alternative is a way for a party to satisfy its interests *independent* of its negotiating counterpart.

THE NEXT FRONTIER OF NEGOTIATION: DEALING WITH EMOTIONS

Over the years, principled negotiation has been criticized on numerous grounds. Some scholars argue that principled negotiation is "too Western," failing to account for cultural variations of dispute resolution that are more relational and contextually driven. A related criticism is that principled negotiation is "too rational," failing to account for the emotional and relational dimensions of negotiation. These kinds of criticisms point to the need for a more comprehensive theory of negotiation that accounts for the emotional and relational complexities of negotiation and conflict.

Roger Fisher and I developed the core concerns framework as a methodology to help negotiators address the emotional dimension of negotiation. This method supports the efforts of the interest-based negotiator. In *Beyond Reason* (Fisher & Shapiro, 2005), we begin by acknowledging the fact that there exists a lack of good advice for dealing with the emotional dimensions of negotiation. We note that parties commonly try either to get rid of emotions, as if that were humanly possible, or to deal directly with the overwhelming number of emotions that arise. We suggest that a more effective approach is to turn attention to a handful of relational motives (what we call "core concerns") that stimulate emotions. These five core concerns are appreciation, affiliation, autonomy, status, and role. By addressing constructively the core concerns, parties can stimulate positive emotions, consequently improving relationships, enhancing information sharing and problem solving, and boosting the overall effectiveness of principled negotiation. (See NEGOTIATION, ROLE OF EMOTIONS IN.)

SUMMARY

Principled negotiation is a cornerstone of the modern field of negotiation and mediation. It has had remarkable success as a method of negotiation, and its key tenets have been supported through laboratory experimentation, as well as real-world application in political, business, and family negotiations and mediations.

SEE ALSO: Mediation; Negotiating Strategies and Processes, Psychological Aspects of; Negotiation, Role of Emotions in; Negotiations and Trust.

REFERENCES

Fisher, R., & Shapiro, D. (2005). *Beyond reason: Using emotions as you negotiate*. New York, NY: Penguin.
Fisher, R., Ury, W., & Patton, B. (1991). *Getting to YES: Negotiating agreement without giving in*. New York, NY: Penguin.
Follett, Mary Parker. (1924). *Creative experience*. New York, NY: Longmans, Green and Co.
Follett, Mary Parker. (1940). *Dynamic administration: The collected papers of Mary Parker Follet*. (H. C. Metcalf & L. Urwick, Eds.). New York, NY: Harper & Brothers.
Walton, R., & McKersie, R. (1965). *A behavioral theory of labor negotiations: An analysis of a social interaction system*. Ithaca, NY: ILR Press.

ADDITIONAL RESOURCES

Program on Negotiation at Harvard Law School (PON); the PON Clearinghouse has a vast number of negotiation simulations for teaching principled negotiation: www.pon.harvard.edu

Negotiation, Role of Emotions in

DANIEL L. SHAPIRO

Scientific inquiry into the role of emotions in negotiation has transformed from a quiet niche to a major field of scholarly study. During the early years of scholarship on negotiation, game theory, decision analysis, and behavioral theories of negotiation consumed widespread attention. As the cognitive revolution struck, a new genre of negotiation study examined cognitive biases, heuristics, framing, and "rational" approaches to negotiation.

It was only in the 1990s that the systematic study of the role of emotions in negotiation gained scholarly and popular traction. The seeds of this line of inquiry were planted in 1986, when Peter Carnevale and Alice Isen conducted a seminal study demonstrating that a positive mood is associated with creative problem solving in negotiation. By the late 1990s, researchers were investigating such varied topics as the role of anger and compassion on negotiation performance (Allred, Mallozzi, Matsui, & Raia, 1997) and the differential impact of affective and instrumental satisfaction during a negotiation on long-term relationship quality (Shapiro, 1999). (See NEGOTIATIONS AND TRUST; NEGOTIATING STRATEGIES AND PROCESSES, PSYCHOLOGICAL ASPECTS OF; NEGOTIATION, PRINCIPLED.)

In 1998, Daniel Goleman's bestseller, *Emotional Intelligence*, catapulted emotional intelligence from an isolated concept of parochial study to a widespread field of critical importance for conflict resolution, business, politics, and education. Research programs such as Columbia University's "Human Dignity and Humiliation Studies" and the Harvard International Negotiation Program emerged with an explicit mission to explore the role of emotions in negotiation and conflict resolution. In 2005, Roger Fisher and I published *Beyond Reason: Using Emotions as You Negotiate*, offering a systematic, practical framework for dealing with the emotional dimensions of negotiation. This book received substantial international attention by the media, businesses, and government, bringing additional attention to the role of emotions in negotiation.

Several fundamental insights can be distilled from the burgeoning literature on the role of emotions in negotiation:

1.   *We are in a state of "perpetual emotion" (Shapiro, 2001)*. We are constantly experiencing emotions of one kind or another, and these emotions impact a negotiator in four specific ways. First, they impact physiology. When angry or anxious, our heart rate increases and we may sweat more than when calm. Second, emotions affect cognition. Frustration, for example, primes negative thoughts, whereas happiness primes positive thoughts. Third, emotions impact behavior. Emotions prepare our body and mind to respond to the world around and within us. When angry, for example, we prepare to attack through words or action. Fourth, emotions affect subjective feelings. A physical sensation tends to be associated with most emotions, such as the experience of "butterflies in your stomach" when we feel nervous.

2.   *Positive emotions can improve relationships*. Positive emotions are an important tool for building a good working relationship between negotiating parties. A reservoir of positive emotions can offset the destructive impact of negative feelings, facilitate the honest exchange of information, and increase loyalty toward one's counterpart and toward the final agreement. Without the mutual expression of positive emotions, a relationship may suffer. John Gottman has discovered that marital couples are more likely to divorce if the ratio of their positive

to negative interactions during a disagreement is approximately one to one; those marriages that last over time tend to have a ratio of approximately five to one (Gottman, Murray, Swanson, Tyson, & Swanson, 2005). This finding underscores the importance of positive emotions to relational success.

3.   *Positive emotions can facilitate acquisition of substantive goals*. Negotiators who feel positive emotions tend to collaborate more than negotiators who feel negative emotions. Positive emotions motivate parties to trust one another, share information, understand each other's perspective, and seek agreements for mutual gain. All of these behaviors enhance the quality of the substantive outcome. Furthermore, how each party feels in their current negotiation often affects how they feel and act toward one another in future negotiations. If two negotiators build trust, future negotiations will tend to be more efficient and constructive. On the other hand, if either negotiator deceives the other and is caught, distrust may hamper future substantive success. Perhaps more troubling, deception and other forms of emotional violation may establish a norm that such behavior is acceptable for everyone in the negotiation, further impeding the maximization of mutual gains. (See NEGOTIATIONS AND TRUST.)

Positive emotions tend to be most beneficial when a situation involves not only distributive issues, but also the potential for creating options that meet each side's interests. Positive emotions elicit numerous behaviors that contribute to effective value creation, including empathy for the perspective of others, creative brainstorming of ideas, and constructive problem solving. A negotiator in a positive mood is more likely than a negotiator in a negative mood to see areas for value creation. For example, a negotiator in a positive mood is more likely to realize that issues such as security and respect are not purely distributional, but can be enhanced for each party. Countries in the midst of a border dispute need not argue over security as though more for one means less for the other. Through creative problem solving, they can invent options that grant a high degree of security for each country. That said, even in purely distributive negotiations, positive emotions can prove useful. Parties can work jointly on designing a process each deems fair for dividing the pie.

4. *Negative emotions have benefits and costs.* Scholars have debated the value of expressing negative emotions in a conflict situation. In some situations, venting can "release" the toxicity of negative emotions. In other situations, the expression of anger or other negative emotions actually may amplify negative emotions. As parties discuss their anger in an uncensored, unmoderated fashion, they create new arguments that justify their behavior and diminish the legitimacy of the other's perspective. The confusion around the value of venting stems from the observation that venting can be both a *sign of distress* and a *possible means of coping with that distress* (Kennedy-Moore & Watson, 1999). Venting is adaptive in problem-solving negotiations to the degree that it reduces distress and increases attention toward cooperation and mutual gains.

A party who tries to produce negative emotions in another negotiator – such as through scare tactics or the induction of guilt – may be able to influence the other party to make substantive concessions (van Kleef, De Dreu, & Manstead, 2004). The expression of anger, for example, can communicate the gravity of one's demands and one's apparent seriousness in exiting the negotiation if those demands are not met. The other party may be more likely to agree to one's demands.

The use of negative emotions, however, comes at a cost. Anger may reduce a negotiator's motivation to understand and empathize with the other side, leading to an agreement that fails to meet each side's interests to the extent possible. Negative emotions also can lead a party to act counter to their own substantive goals, such as by rejecting an agreement that is superior to their best alternative to a negotiated agreement (Fisher & Shapiro, 2005). Furthermore, rational thinking may take a backseat when strong negative emotions ignite, putting parties at risk of saying or doing actions they may later regret.

Given both the risks to using negative emotions and the benefits to drawing on positive ones, the best general advice for a negotiator is to stimulate positive emotions in oneself and in those with whom one negotiates. Few negotiators complain that their negotiations are in trouble because everyone is "too happy." To the contrary, positive emotions facilitate the maximization of value creation, value distribution, and relationship enhancement.

5. *Negotiators can induce positive emotions.* Negotiators are not just victim to the whims of emotion. They can take action to induce emotions that help them satisfy their interests. While emotions can result from automatic biological or physiological processes, negotiators have a great deal of power to stimulate positive emotions in others and in themselves.

One approach to stimulate positive emotions is to satisfy each negotiator's "core concerns" (Fisher & Shapiro, 2005), relational motives that tend to stimulate many of the emotions that arise in a negotiation. Roger Fisher and I have identified five such core concerns: appreciation, autonomy, affiliation, status, and role. A negotiator can stimulate positive emotions in another by: (1) appreciating the other's perspective, feelings, thoughts, or efforts, (2) respecting the other's autonomy – their freedom to make decisions without undue imposition, (3) turning the affiliation between the parties from that of adversaries to partners working on a shared problem, (4) respecting the other's status where deserved, and (5) inviting the other to play fulfilling roles. As a result, parties feel increased positive emotions toward one another and are more likely to collaborate to reach mutual gains.

CONCLUSION

Emotions have a substantial impact on the process and outcome of negotiation. While positive and negative emotions each can help a party reach a desired outcome, positive emotions generally have greater benefits than their negative counterparts. By addressing five core concerns constructively, negotiators can stimulate positive emotions conducive to value creation, fair distribution, and relationship enhancement.

SEE ALSO: Negotiating Strategies and Processes, Psychological Aspects of; Negotiation, Principled; Negotiations and Trust.

REFERENCES

Allred, K. G., Mallozzi, J., Matsui, F., & Raia, C. P. (1997). The influence of anger and compassion on negotiation performance. *Organizational Behavior and Human Decision Processes*, 70, 175–187.

Carnevale, P. J. D., & Isen, A. M. (1986). The influence of positive affect and visual access on the discovery of integrative solutions in bilateral negotiation. *Organizational Behavior and Human Decision Processes*, 37, 1–13.

Fisher, R., & Shapiro, D. L. (2005). *Beyond reason: Using emotions as you negotiate*. New York, NY: Penguin.

Gottman, J. M., Murray, J. D., Swanson, C., Tyson, R., & Swanson, K. R. (2005). *The mathematics of marriage: Dynamic nonlinear models*. Cambridge, MA: MIT Press.

Kennedy-Moore, E., & Watson, J. C. (1999). *Expressing emotion*. New York, NY: Guilford Press.

Shapiro, D. L. (1999). *The extended nature of conflict: The varying impact of instrumental and affective satisfaction during conflict on working and post-conflict relationship quality*. Dissertation. University of Massachusetts, Amherst.

Shapiro, D. L. (2001). A negotiator's guide to emotions: Four "laws" to effective practice. *Dispute Resolution Magazine*, 7(2): 3–8.

van Kleef, G. A., De Dreu, C. K. W., & Manstead, A. S. R. (2004). The interpersonal effects of anger and happiness in negotiations. *Journal of Personality and Social Psychology*, 86(1), 57–76.

ADDITIONAL RESOURCES

www.humiliationstudies.org (Humiliation and Dignity Studies, Columbia University)
www.internationalnegotiation.org (Harvard International Negotiation Program)

Negotiations and Trust

MARA OLEKALNS AND PHILIP L. SMITH

Trust is commonly defined as a confident, positive expectation about the actions of another person. When we trust someone, we assume that she will meet those expectations by considering our welfare and honoring her obligations towards us. This assumption enables us to coordinate activities in interdependent relationships, that is, relationships in which an individual's outcomes are influenced by another party's actions. However, while trusting others is essential for maintaining our relationships, trusting also increases our vulnerability. While we assume that others will meet our positive expectations and behave in a trustworthy way, there is no guarantee that this will be so (Lewicki, Tomlinson, & Gillespie, 2006). (See TRUST AND DISTRUST.)

Negotiations pose many dilemmas for individuals, including a trust dilemma. Like other interdependent relationships, negotiations are characterized by dependency and vulnerability. To create value, integrate interests, and find mutually beneficial solutions, negotiators need to coordinate their actions. Willingness to solve problems, provide information, and offer concessions is based on the expectation that the other party will reciprocate. (See MARKOV CHAIN MODELS OF NEGOTIATORS' COMMUNICATION.) However, the kinds of behaviors that enable successful coordination also increase negotiators' vulnerability to exploitation. If the other party withholds information or does not match concessions, negotiators are disadvantaged (Ross & LaCroix, 1996). (See NEGOTIATING STRATEGIES AND PROCESSES, PSYCHOLOGICAL ASPECTS OF.)

Like other impressions, our judgments of trustworthiness can occur rapidly at the start of a negotiation. While these initial impressions may change as a negotiation unfolds, they create a powerful frame for interpreting the other party's behavior and also provide a heuristic for guiding negotiators' strategy choices. As a result, the initial impressions that negotiators form about the other party's trustworthiness are critical to how a negotiation unfolds. If initial impressions suggest the other party is trustworthy, negotiators are more willing to cooperate. This in turn is likely to elicit cooperation from the other party, establishing a virtuous cycle of increasing trust and cooperation. Conversely, if initial impressions suggest the other party is untrustworthy, negotiators are likely to take self-protective action and behave competitively, thereby establishing a vicious cycle of mistrust and competition. (See COOPERATION AND COMPETITION.)

In assessing trustworthiness, negotiators can focus on the competence or values of the other person. Competence-based trust focuses on the skills, abilities, and reliability of the other party. Determining that the other party is capable of keeping his promises and commitments gives negotiators "good reason" to trust. This form of trust is

relatively easy to establish, but also relatively easy to violate. It invites a trust-calculus, in which we determine another person's trustworthiness based on the costs and benefits the other party obtains by keeping commitments. Competence-based trust is a kind of trust that requires close monitoring of the other person's behavior: Trust is violated when the other party reneges on commitments and promises. In comparison, affect-based trust focuses on the attributes and intentions of the other person. It develops when we believe that the other person is genuinely concerned about our welfare, is benevolent and well-intentioned, and shares our values. Affect-based trust gives the trustee greater behavioral latitude. When this form of trust is high, negotiators assume that the other party is working towards the same goals. Negotiators need to amass more evidence about failures of affect-based trust than failures of competence-based trust before revising their assessment of another party's trustworthiness (Lewicki et al., 2006).

Judgments of trustworthiness are shaped by the context in which negotiations take place. The outcome goals that negotiators hold at the start of a negotiation affect their perceptions of the other party's trustworthiness. Outcome goals may be cooperative, emphasizing mutual gain, or individualistic, emphasizing personal gain. Negotiators who start with a cooperative orientation are more trusting of the other party than negotiators who start with a competitive orientation. Perceived power also affects negotiators' judgments of other parties' trustworthiness: Negotiators who have high power are perceived as less trustworthy than negotiators who have low power (Giebels, De Dreu, & Van de Vliert, 1998). As the negotiation setting becomes more complex, so do judgments about trustworthiness. In multiparty negotiations, relative trust is more critical to outcomes than absolute trust: The person who is trusted the most by the other negotiators also obtains the best outcomes. However, the overall trust climate is affected by the least trustworthy person: The overall level of trust in a group negotiation converges to equal the level of trust in the least trusted person.

One of the most critical activities that negotiators engage in is information exchange. Without accurate information about the other party's priorities, negotiators are unable to craft mutually beneficial agreements. Research shows that high levels of trust enable the exchange of information about underlying needs, interests, and priorities. Moreover, negotiators who are oriented to in-depth information processing also report higher levels of trust in the other party. The converse is that low levels of trust encourage negotiators to conceal or misrepresent information, that is, to deceive the other party. This is the case when negotiators assess the other party's competence-based trust to be high. Counterintuitively, research shows that high affect-based trust elicits deception: Negotiators are more likely to deceive others whom they perceive to be trustworthy. The decision to give accurate information – or not – is shaped by a combination of initial levels of trust and the negotiating context. Factors such as outcome goals and power combine with initial assessments of trustworthiness to shape negotiators' decisions to deceive the other party.

The descriptions of competence- and affect-based trust above also give important insight into how negotiators can build trust. To establish competence-based trust, negotiators need to demonstrate that they are able to keep commitments. These kinds of guarantees can be provided by past history, especially negotiators' reputation. We don't need direct experience of another person's ability to keep commitments – just knowing their reputation provides important information. Indeed, negotiators with a bad reputation are more likely to trigger the vicious

cycle we described above, eliciting higher levels of competition and finding it difficult to successfully conclude negotiations. In negotiations, individuals can take concrete actions to confirm their competence by reciprocating concessions and information and by keeping the promises that they make. To establish affect-based trust, negotiators need to demonstrate that they are well-intentioned towards the other party. Relationship-building activities such as expressions of liking and positive affect, flattery, and the identification of similarities all help to establish common ground and build affect-based trust. Empathy with the other person's perspective signals a concern about the other person that further strengthens the emotional bond at the heart of affect-based trust. (See EMPATHY.)

Because negotiation is a dynamic process, it is possible for negotiators to violate trust through what they say and do as a negotiation unfolds. Trust violations occur when trust is not fulfilled, resulting in either tangible (e.g., monetary) or intangible (e.g., loss to self-esteem) harm to the trusting party. They elicit both a cognitive and an emotional reaction which results in a negative reassessment of the other person's trustworthiness. Cognitive reactions reflect the severity of the trust violation, which describes individuals' perceptions that they have suffered harm as a result of the trust violation. As the perceived severity of trust violations increases, so the willingness to forgive the violator decreases. Trust researchers consistently argue that violations of competence-based trust (ability) are less serious than violations of affect-based trust (integrity, benevolence), suggesting that violations of benevolence and integrity will be perceived as more severe than violations of ability. Emotional reactions reflect the negative affect that individuals experience following a trust violation: Individuals are likely to experience anger at the person who violated trust and sadness that the relationship was betrayed.

Independent of the level of trust at the outset of negotiations, negotiators' actions shape how trust develops over time. Research shows that negotiators' attention is drawn to events that stand out from the flow of behavior and interrupt the negotiation process. These turning points punctuate negotiations, either eroding or building trust over time. Actions that trigger negative attributions, causing negotiators to question the other party's motives and intentions, reduce competence-based trust. However, actions that draw attention to underlying interests, in some way improve the process or trigger positive attributions about the other party, and help build competence-based trust. Research also shows the presence of a virtuous cycle in relation to affect-based trust: High affect-based trust at the start of negotiations draws negotiators' attention to the other party's positive characteristics, which in turn build affect-based trust (Olekalns & Smith, 2005).

In order to repair trust, individuals need to acknowledge the trust violation, admit culpability, admit harm, and accept responsibility for the consequences of their actions. This four-step process has encouraged researchers to focus on the role that apologies play in mitigating trust violations. Apologies are at their most effective when paired with sincerity. When paired with an internal attribution for the trust violation, they effectively repair violations of competence, whereas when paired with an external attribution they effectively repair violations of integrity (Kim, Ferrin, Cooper, & Dirks, 2004). Apologies clearly target the harm done to the underlying relationship. However, trust violations can also cause material harm. Research suggests that under these circumstances apologies may be less effective than more tangible repair mechanisms such as offering financial compensation. In negotiation, trust can be re-established if the trust violator displays consistent trustworthiness after the violation. However, if trust is violated because negotiators uncover deception by the other party, it is exceedingly difficult to restore: even apologies, promises not to deceive again, and consistent trustworthy behavior are insufficient to restore deception-based violations (Schweitzer, Hershey, & Bradlow, 2006). (See APOLOGIES AND FORGIVENESS.)

SEE ALSO: Apologies and Forgiveness; Cooperation and Competition; Empathy; Markov Chain Models of Negotiators' Communication; Negotiating Strategies and Processes, Psychological Aspects of; Trust and Distrust.

REFERENCES

Giebels, E., De Dreu, C., & Van de Vliert, E. (1998). Social motives and trust in negotiation: The disruptive effects of punitive capability. *Journal of Applied Psychology, 83,* 408–422.

Kim, P., Ferrin, D., Cooper, C., & Dirks, K. (2004). Removing the shadow of suspicion: The effects of apology versus denial for repairing competence- versus integrity-based trust violations. *Journal of Applied Psychology, 89,* 104–118.

Lewicki, R. J., Tomlinson, E. C., & Gillespie, N. (2006). Models of interpersonal trust development: Theoretical approaches, empirical evidence and future directions. *Journal of Management, 32,* 991–1022.

Olekalns, M., & Smith, P. (2005). Moments in time: Metacognition, trust and outcomes in negotiation. *Personality and Social Psychology Bulletin, 31,* 1696–1707.

Ross, W., & LaCroix, J. (1996). Multiple meanings of trust in negotiation theory and research: A literature review and integrative model. *International Journal of Conflict Management, 7,* 314–360.

Schweitzer, M., Hershey, J. C., & Bradlow, E. T. (2006). Promises and lies: Restoring violated trust. *Organizational Behavior and Human Decision Processes, 101,* 1–19.

Nonviolence, Psychology of

DANIEL M. MAYTON II AND
CRYSTAL A. BURROWS

While examples of nonviolent action can be traced back at least to the ancient Greeks (Sharp, 1973), much of our current understanding of the psychology of nonviolence begins with the life and writings of Mohandas K. Gandhi. Gandhi's view on nonviolence had three major facets: *ahimsa, satyagraha,* and *tapasya.* (See NONVIOLENT DISPOSITIONS; PACIFISM, PSYCHOLOGY OF; VALUES, NONVIOLENCE, AND PEACE PSYCHOLOGY.) *Ahimsa* is an ancient Hindu word literally meaning the absence of injury and generally translated to mean nonviolence. In practice *ahimsa* is more than noninjury, as it encompasses a loving relationship of doing good to an evil-doer (Bondurant, 1965). *Satyagraha* is a concept developed by Gandhi to reflect the process of pursuing truth within any situation. Seeking wisdom and understanding of all sides of a conflict situation is an important and continuous process for a nonviolent person from Gandhi's perspective. *Tapasya,* Gandhi's third component of nonviolence, prescribes the use of self-suffering as needed to break the cycle of violence. When a self-suffering response is chosen over a violent one, the nonviolent person will penetrate the heart of the perpetrator, thereby encouraging empathy and ameliorating any urge for retaliation or revenge by the perpetrator.

It is from the three nonviolent principles outlined by Gandhi that much of the psychology of nonviolence has emerged over the last century. Nonviolence means more than the absence of violence. Nonviolence is an action designed to influence others so one can reach a goal without direct injury to the person or persons working against the achievement of a goal. Nonviolence may be a pragmatic action or a principled one. An individual using pragmatic nonviolence believes that nonviolent behavior is an effective method to resolve conflict, does not maintain a philosophy of life consistent with principled nonviolence, and engages in nonviolent behaviors that confront a conflict situation without using direct violence. A person using principled nonviolence believes that violent behavior and retaliations are to be avoided, desires to understand the truth within a conflict, accepts the burden of suffering to break the cycle of violence, believes in noncooperation with evil, and engages in behaviors that confront injustice with the intention of increasing social justice in a manner consistent with the above-mentioned beliefs without using direct violence. Thus, nonviolence is not a passive absence of violence but can be viewed as having cognitive, affective, and behavioral components (Mayton, 2009).

PSYCHOLOGICAL THEORIES OF NONVIOLENCE

The father of American psychology, William James, was the first peace psychologist and also spoke about nonviolence. James (1910/1995) believed that war serves a moral function as it can provide discipline to societies and can produce heroes and honorary people within a society. James acknowledged the ugliness of war but he also saw how war provided a positive cohesiveness in a society. Seeing both the positive and negative benefits of war, James encouraged people to create new, nonviolent ways to challenge and resolve conflicts that might also fulfill the needs of a society by producing cohesiveness and creating heroes.

While this challenge has not been addressed to date, many psychologists have developed theories of nonviolence to assist our understanding and to locate positive applications. These include Blumberg's

utility model of nonviolent mass demonstrations, Hare's social psychological perspectives on nonviolent action, Kool's theory
of nonviolence, Teixeira's holistic model of
nonviolence, and Brenes' model of peaceful
selfhood (Mayton, 2009).

Herbert Blumberg created his three-step
utility model of nonviolent mass demonstrations in the late 1960s. The first step is
the evolution of the process or tactics of
demonstrators. A number of activities are
tried until the demonstrators find the most
effective activity for their goal. The second
step involves contagion, where the best
form of protest is spread throughout the
group and the group is cohesive about the
aims, methods, and conduct of the group.
The third step is reinforcement. This is
when the rewards for the group's protest are
received.

A. Paul Hare developed his exchange
theory of nonviolent action in the 1960s. His
theory views nonviolence as a human activity that might result in possible rewards
exchanged between people. Both the costs
and benefits of action are measured against
each other. For the action to take place, the
benefits should be considered greater than
the negative consequences. Hare's three-
dimensional model also predicts when nonviolence will precipitate positive nonviolent
responses or violent ones depending on the
communication of empathy and love toward
those persons working against the achievement of goals.

V. K. Kool differentiates acts of nonviolence from nonviolent acts within his theory
of nonviolence. Acts of nonviolence resolve
conflict in situations where either aggression
or violence might be a reasonable response.
A boycott or demonstration would be an
example of acts of nonviolence. A nonviolent act does not use violence, as these are
normative patterns of behavior within a
culture. Examples of nonviolent acts would
be nurturing and caring for children.
Nonviolent acts are everyday actions that

have positive consequences and are socially
desirable, whereas acts of nonviolence
may have some negative consequences, for
example a boycott of a merchant would
reduce profits which in turn affects salaries.

Kool places nonviolence within a three
dimensional space defined by moral concerns, power, and levels of aggression.
Nonviolence is projected as high on the
moral dimension that involves both the
justice perspective and the caring perspective. Someone who relies heavily on the
justice perspective follows rules like equity
and equality and someone who relies heavily
on the caring perspective follows supreme
compassion. A person who uses high
amounts of both justice and caring in their
moral reasoning acts in ways that are both
fair and compassionate. Nonviolence is
reflected as low on aggression in Kool's
model of nonviolence. Along the dimension
of power, Kool emphasized the concept of
integrative power. This concept is derived
from the trust and good will given to those
in positions of power by their followers.
Nonviolence is manifested in actions that
reflect shared power with others and not
power based on self-gratification alone.
Thus, within Kool's three-dimensional
model, low levels of aggression and high
moral concerns along with other-oriented
power represent nonviolence.

Bryan Teixeira is another key theorist in
the psychology of nonviolence. His holistic
approach to nonviolence focuses on actions
void of harmful intent and requires congru-
ence between the means and ends of an
action. Teixeira recognizes that nonviolence
is a worldwide occurrence across time and
cultures, value-based, and a practical way to
deal with real conflicts in pluralistic societies
that are multiethnic, multicultural, and mul-
tifaith. Teixeira's holistic theory encompasses macro- and microlevel perspectives
that address cognitive, affective, and spiritual
dimensions of psychological experience and
behavior.

Abelardo Brenes developed a model of peaceful selfhood that integrates the psychology of nonviolence from both secular and religious traditions. Brenes' integral model centers on the universal responsibility of peace at the community level and includes the threads of peace with oneself, peace with others, and peace with nature. The psychology of nonviolence within this model focuses on three value levels for the expression of peace in the mind (self-regard, self-realization, autonomy), peace in the heart (harmony, love and compassion, tolerance), and peace in one's body (psychosomatic harmony, consciousness of needs, right use of satisfiers).

PSYCHOLOGICAL UNDERPINNINGS OF NONVIOLENCE

Nonviolence may exist at the intrapersonal, interpersonal, societal, or world level and the psychological variables relevant shift as different levels are addressed (Mayton, 2009). At the intrapersonal and interpersonal levels the personality traits of agreeableness, anger control, cooperativeness, empathy, forgivingness, materialism, need for cognition, optimism, spirituality, and trust are relevant, along with higher priority on benevolence values and lower priorities on the values of power and hedonism. (See NONVIOLENT DISPOSITIONS; PEACEFUL PERSONALITY.) Selected religious beliefs, teachings, and values within all major religions – including Hinduism, Buddhism, Judaism, Christianity, and Islam – are consistent with nonviolence. At the societal and world levels the components of cultures of peace including social justice, gender equity, human rights, education, and environmental sustainability are relevant. (See CULTURE OF PEACE.) While many prominent people like the Dalai Lama and the Oglala Sioux medicine man Black Elk make the compelling assertion that intrapersonal peace is necessary before interpersonal,

societal, and world peace can be attained, there is no definitive research to support these views.

The effectiveness of nonviolent action may be explained by many psychological concepts. (See NONVIOLENT DEMOCRATIC TRANSITIONS.) Attribution theory explains how people develop explanations for the causes of behavior in their everyday lives. When followers of Gandhi in India refused to obey an unjust law and were treated violently by the British, their nonviolent responses were uncharacteristic. This forced the British and observers from around the world to think hard about the plight of the Indian people and to try to understand why this was happening. Since the nonviolent activists behaved in a positive way and did not resort to violence, they could be seen as doing so only because of internal reasons, since the normal response to an attack by the British would be a violent retaliation. Understanding the harsh British behavior then becomes problematic. Why would the British treat nonviolent people so brutally? If one assumes that the British are a moral and reasonable people, then the situation must be the cause of their violent acts and therefore the focus is on the unjust law that subjugates the Indian people. Since the British, like many people, are susceptible to the self-serving bias and take less credit for failures, each nonviolent act of civil disobedience would accentuate their belief that these unjust laws needed to be repealed or remain unenforced. Before nonviolent noncooperation was used, the unjust laws were routinely obeyed and accepted as a part of normal society. However, once nonviolent noncooperation or intervention was employed, a conflict provoked serious in-depth thought about the situation in ways that did not occur before the accepted normative behavior was challenged. This deep processing of arguments is an important aspect of persuasion that results in more long-term attitude change (Mayton, 2000).

Characteristics of the social situations that people find themselves in are powerful factors that determine much of human behavior. Nonviolent behavior is no exception. While nonviolent action has successfully been used in a wide variety of contexts from democracies to dictatorships in countries all across the world, there has been little research on the situational factors that influence nonviolence. Certain cultural norms, like the norm of reciprocity (an eye for an eye) or the culture of honor (violence expected to protect one's reputation), create situations where nonviolence is less likely (Fiske, 2004). Societies that value the norms of equity, social responsibility, and cooperation are more likely to encourage nonviolent behavior. Currently, the prominence of the military–economic–governmental–news complex in many societies works against nonviolent responses to conflict (Mayton, 2009). Communities and societies that reflect the values inherent in a culture of peace as compared to a culture of violence will stimulate more nonviolent responses to conflict. Individuals often act in accordance with internalized scripts that inform us how to act in a normative way in a particular situation. Given the preponderance of aggressive content in popular television programs and movies, most people have many more violent scripts than nonviolent ones to choose from when deciding how to resolve a conflict. This may be reflected in their behavior.

SEE ALSO: Culture of Peace; Nonviolent Democratic Transitions; Nonviolent Dispositions; Pacifism, Psychology of; Peaceful Personality; Values, Nonviolence, and Peace Psychology.

REFERENCES

Bondurant, J. V. (1965). *Conquest of violence: The Gandhian philosophy of conflict* (rev. ed.). Berkeley, CA: University of California Press.

Fiske, S. T. (2004). *Social beings: A core motives approach to social psychology.* New York, NY: Wiley.

James, W. (1910/1995). The moral equivalent of war. *Peace and Conflict: Journal of Peace Psychology, 1,* 17–26.

Mayton, D. M. (2000). Gandhi as peacebuilder: The social psychology of satyagraha. In D. Christie, R. Wagner, & D. D. Winter (Eds.), *Peace, conflict, and violence: Peace psychology for the 21st century* (pp. 307–313). Englewood Cliffs, NJ: Prentice-Hall.

Mayton, D. M. (2009). *Nonviolence and peace psychology: Intrapersonal, interpersonal, societal, and world peace.* New York, NY: Springer.

Sharp, G. (1973). *The politics of nonviolent action.* Boston, MA: Porter Sargent Books.

Nonviolent Democratic Transitions

CRISTINA JAYME MONTIEL

Nonviolent democratic transition refers to the use of peaceful means to dismantle an authoritarian structure and create a more open political system by increasing the distribution of political power among larger human pluralities. The nonviolent collective action generates political pressure through successful organization and mobilization of large numbers of prodemocracy groups, making manifest previously latent, hidden, or underground mass movements that challenge the status quo power arrangement. Antigovernment initiatives are thus able to remain contentious and coercive vis-à-vis the authoritarian state (Bond, Jenkins, Taylor, & Schock, 1997) without the employment of direct violence.

For instance, in 2006, Nepal's Jana-Aldolan-II engaged hundreds of thousands of citizens to protest the royal takeover of King Gyanendra and the implementation of martial law. On April 24, 2006, King Gyanendra publicly announced the restoration of the political power to the people and the re-establishment of the Nepali House of

Representatives that was dissolved four years earlier (Dahal, 2006). Similar examples of nonviolent transitions may be seen throughout the world, like in the Philippines (1986), Estonia, Lithuania, and Latvia (1987), East Germany (1989), South Africa (1994), Indonesia (1998), and Pakistan (2008).

PEACE AND VIOLENCE ACROSS STAGES OF DEMOCRATIZATION

Nonviolent democratic transition develops along five stages: (1) control by an authoritarian regime, (2) toppling an authoritarian regime, (3) power shift, (4) state building, and (5) nation building. Each stage is marked by varying forms of direct and structural violence. Each stage likewise requires different nonviolent collective actions.

Control by an Authoritarian Regime

Nonviolent democratic transitions occur in situations where power in a political structure is initially extremely skewed in favor of one person or one political party, who controls state resources. Direct state violence supports the oppressive political system. For example, firearms are used to silence political opposition, or massive human rights violations are used in order to maintain public order. The peacebuilding response at this stage is the employment of nonviolent means to fight the strong rule, as for example nationwide boycotts of companies owned by the ruling family and its cronies, and offering flowers to state police during massive street protests. This may be accompanied or paralleled by attempts by political opposition forces to wrest power from the dominant group through already established avenues within the state (i.e., legislation).

Toppling an Authoritarian Regime

Nonviolent democratic transitions necessitate the overthrow of authoritarian rulers. The toppling of a regime is often preceded by the internal weakening of groups in power, and the growth of political potency among prodemocracy forces. The former may entail fragmentation, disagreement, or unrest within the dominant political group. On the other hand, the strengthening of prodemocracy forces is marked by the emergence of charismatic leaders, the unification of various protest movements, and the global support of sympathetic groups, especially through transnational logistical support and media coverage. Apart from generating social pressure, toppling an authoritarian regime may also include participating and winning in elections. The electoral process provides an opportunity for the opposition to assert its political will and for the people to mobilize against an oppressive regime.

Peacebuilding responses at this stage of the nonviolent democratic transition require the production of nonviolent social forcefulness through effective networking, mobilization, and consciousness raising. The successful overthrow of a regime, however, is rarely achieved through either purely violent or purely peaceful means, and often occurs as a mix of both peaceful and violent forms of opposition. (See PEOPLE POWER.)

Power Shift

The removal of an authoritarian leader, although pivotal in the transition process, is insufficient in itself as a democratization process. If the lead forces in the toppling of a regime come solely from the financial elite, without real concern for the majority of the populace, or if international intervention meddles with political matters without proper understanding of indigenous concerns, the "toppled" authoritarian regime may simply be replaced by another one, without significant change to the unequal distribution of political power.

Thus, following the removal of an authoritarian leader, nonviolent democratic transition requires attending to the immediate aftermath of the struggle. The victorious groups must now consolidate their hold on the new state, dismantle the authoritarian structure by removing its key backers, and prevent fellow opposition forces from realizing any nondemocratic agenda. New forms of negotiated power-sharing may evolve at this stage of democratization.

State Building

After the political instability that accompanies transition between power groups, the new democracy must attend to state building. In other words, they must ensure that the new government's executive, legislative, and judicial sections genuinely serve and improve the lives of the greater population. They must also keep military institutions (that may still have a large influence in matters of the state) from backing the interests of another small group, such as a family or political party.

The issue of direct violence at this stage may come in the form of human rights abuses from a restless military or maybe even in the form of some opposition parties taking up arms again when personal or collective agendas are not satisfied during the transition from authoritarian rule. Structural violence, on the other hand, may take the form of the creation of political structures that distribute wealth and power in an essentially vertical configuration where there is inequitable access to material resources. Structural violence may also take the form of foreign companies that take advantage of the instability of the situation to create contracts with the government that are exploitative and oppressive to the citizenry. Nonviolent democratic transition, in order to be successful, should address all these forms of direct and structural violence. Legislation in the new state must block political dynasties or a re-monopolization of power by the military. Wealth distribution and economic development must likewise attend to the well-being of impoverished sectors of society. (See PEACE, POSITIVE AND NEGATIVE.)

Nation Building

A nation refers to the people or peoples within a state, usually bound together by a common culture. A nation is not necessarily equal to the people of a state (Linz & Stepan, 1996). Nation building addresses the group well-being of ethnic aggregations. It is especially challenging to countries with heterogeneous ethnic groups, or where a country's boundaries have been defined by former colonizers without regard to ethnic groupings.

During nation building, direct violence may take the form of a territory based armed struggle between the state and movements seeking territorial autonomy. Violence may also take the form of marginalization or the silencing of weaker ethnic clusters in favor of the politically dominant ethnic group. Nonviolent democratic transition may address cultural inequities through the employment of indigenous conflict resolution strategies, the creation of fair intergroup relations, and the exploration of political structures like federalism that may better accommodate cultural and ethnic heterogeneity.

A caveat must be offered regarding democratization processes in developing societies. In pursuing democracy, a new state has to be careful about Western attempts to impose imported forms of democracy. Although this policy has had beneficial effects (Shattuck & Atwood, 1998), it may cause a local people to doubt their own capacities or silence their indigenous decision-making processes in favor of fashionable Western practices, thus increasing the global inequality of power. Foreign-aid benefits make these propositions more enticing, especially to the developing countries.

NONVIOLENT DEMOCRATIC TRANSITION AND PEACE PSYCHOLOGY

Understanding nonviolent democratic transition contributes to the conceptual and pragmatic growth of peace psychology in various ways. First, because the main avenue of assertion within nonviolent democratic transition is by definition peaceful and nonviolent, political actions that challenge authoritarian regimes are powerfully agentic and pose opportunities for structural changes to the political system. Thus, it could be understood as a structurally framed mode of transition that demonstrates human agency in a collective and socially potent form. Second, as nonviolent democratic transitions are mass based with networking, organization, and mobilization occurring across heterogeneous groups, the transition itself may facilitate a transformative identity process, wherein national identities become more inclusive and disparate groups may come to share feelings of belongingness and a common sense of who they are, and where they are as people of a state. Third, a nonviolent democratic transition, carried out "by the people" in mass movements, generates its coerciveness from indigenous social power rather than armed and foreign forces.

Instead of talking about democratization as a single process, nonviolent democratic transition favors illustrating a plurality of democratization processes. In other words, because nonviolent democratic transition is peaceful and mass based, yet contentious and structurally framed, it can challenge the violent approaches that characterize authoritarian systems, while offering viable alternatives that do not return to armed struggle or fall into the danger of foreign imposition. Such a strategy demonstrates peace by peaceful means, in the political world of developing societies. Psychology can contribute significantly to the success of nonviolent democratic transition by illuminating aspects of democratization processes related to liberated indigenous consciousness, collective empowerment, egalitarian political structures, participative social identities, and the development of democratic collectives and selves.

SEE ALSO: Peace, Positive and Negative; People Power.

REFERENCES

Bond, D., Jenkins, J. C., Taylor, C. L., & Schock, K. (1997). Mapping mass political conflict and civil society: Issues and prospects for the automated development of data. *Journal of Conflict Resolution, 41,* 553–579.

Dahal, D. R. (2006). Nepal's difficult transition to democracy and peace. *Friedrich Ebert Stiftung Kathmandu.* From http://www.nepaldemocracy.org/conflict_resolution/KBNepal2006.pdf.

Linz, J., & Stepan, A. (1996). *Problems of democratic transition and consolidation: Southern Europe, South America and post-communist Europe.* Baltimore, MD: Johns Hopkins University Press.

Shattuck, J., & Atwood, J. (1998). Defending democracy. *Foreign Affairs, 77,* 167–170.

ADDITIONAL RESOURCES

Montiel, C. (2006). Political psychology of nonviolent democratic transitions in southeast Asia. *Journal of Social Issues, 62,* 173–190.

Montiel, C., & Christie, D. (2008). Conceptual frame for a psychology of nonviolent democratic transitions: Positioning across analytical layers. In F. M. Moghaddam, R. Harré, & N. Lee (Eds.), *Global conflict resolution through positioning analysis* (pp. 261–282). New York, NY: Springer.

Montiel, C. J., & Wessells, M. (2001). Democratization, psychology, and the construction of cultures of peace. *Peace and Conflict: Journal of Peace Psychology*, 7(2), 119–129.

Nonviolent Dispositions

DANIEL M. MAYTON II AND
CHRISTINA N. BROWNE

Nonviolence seems like a very simple construct but it is actually fairly nuanced and quite complex (Mayton, 2009). At its most basic level, nonviolence may be construed as refraining from a violent or aggressive act. From a peace psychologist's point of view, however, this definition is far from complete, as this definition claims that an individual's failure to act in a certain situation is enough to qualify him/her as nonviolent, even if that failure to act is a result of that individual's apathy or cowardice. However, there is no consensus among peace psychologists on what the exact definition of nonviolence should be. Sharp (1979) defined nonviolence as "non-injury in thought, word, and deed to all forms of life" (p. 134). Bondurant (1965) believes it to be "the exercise of power or influence to reflect change without injury to the opponent" (cited in Mayton, 2009, p. 7). Mayton provides an integrated definition of nonviolence as "an action that uses power and influence to reach one's goal without direct injury or violence to the person or persons working to thwart one's goal achievement" (p. 8). One element that these three definitions have in common is that they conceptualize nonviolence as a behavior or action rather than a state of being. One individual who firmly believed in and practiced nonviolent action was Mohandas Gandhi, whose writings and views of nonviolence focused on the underlying philosophy possessed by nonviolent activists.

THE NONVIOLENT PHILOSOPHY OF GANDHI

Nonviolence played an integral role in Gandhi's general philosophy of life, especially in terms of conflict resolution, and this philosophy was based on three main concepts reflected in the Indian-based words of *satyagraha*, *ahimsa*, and *tapasya*. (See NONVIOLENCE, PSYCHOLOGY OF.) All of these are interconnected and have provided the inspiration and foundation for much of past and present research on nonviolence (Mayton, 2001, 2009).

Satyagraha is derived from Sanskrit roots and means "holding on to the truth." This particular word was created by Gandhi to demonstrate that *satyagraha* is an action and does not imply passive resistance. However, as Nahkre (1982) pointed out, in order to hold on to the truth, one must discover it first. According to Gandhi, though, only God knows the absolute truth, thereby rendering man's search as one for relative truth. Because this relative truth is based on subjective perceptions, a person must be willing to change his/her conception of the truth if opposing views seem more convincing (Mayton et al., 2002). In other words, *satyagraha* requires one to be open-minded and continually searching for the truth, even if it means admitting that one's beliefs may have been previously wrong

While the goal of *satyagraha* is to discover truth, *ahimsa* provides the means to achieve this discovery (Nakhre, 1982). This word literally means "noninjury" and emphasizes the belief in the sacredness of life. With *ahimsa*, there is absolute refusal to inflict harm or injury on others, as well as the refusal to allow harm or injustice to exist anywhere in the world. This particular concept emphasizes the belief that each individual life is precious and of value and that no one has the right to damage that sacred life except God. This concept can also be taken to mean active goodwill and love towards humankind, even towards those who relish doing evil things (Mayton, 2009).

The third principle of Gandhi's philosophy, *tapasya*, is translated as "self-suffering" (Nakhre, 1982). People who follow this principle are more likely, and more willing, to endure hardship or suffering personally than to inflict it upon others who thwart their goals. *Tapasya* is intertwined with *satyagraha* as nonviolent individuals realize that their ongoing pursuit of the truth is coupled with an awareness that they may be further from the truth than their opponents are, thereby making it inappropriate to inflict harm on someone who may be closer to the truth. The nonviolent person also believes that because violence begets violence, the willingness to endure self-suffering instead of inflicting suffering on others can result in the least amount of suffering and the least total loss of life (Mayton, 2001).

MEASURING NONVIOLENT
DISPOSITIONS

Because of Gandhi's enormous influence, his three principles have provided the foundation for a great deal of the subsequent research and assessment of the dispositions of nonviolent individuals. Mayton et al. (2002) reviewed five different measures of nonviolence in order to help shed more light on some of the important aspects of nonviolent dispositions. These five measures are the Pacifism Scale, the Gandhian Personality Scale, the Nonviolent Test, the Teenage Nonviolent Test, and the Multidimensional Scales of Nonviolence. The first measure, the Pacifism Scale, was developed by Elliott in 1980 and consists of three components: physical nonviolence, psychological nonviolence, and active value orientation. This scale measured *ahimsa* at the physical and psychological levels as well as a belief in the importance of open and direct communication in the resolution of conflicts.

The second measure, the Gandhian Personality Scale (GPS), was developed in 1983 with six subscales. While the GPS was psychometrically weak, it was based on some aspects of the Gandhian philosophy of nonviolence and attempted to assess *ahimsa*, openness to experience, self-disclosure, self-control, and self-suffering. The following year yielded the Nonviolent Test (NVT), which was published by Kool and Sen, and this scale proved to be both reliable and valid. While only reporting an overall score, the NVT measures self-control, rational problem-solving approaches in conflict resolution, and tendencies to use communication in a manipulative manner.

The fourth measure, the Teenage Nonviolence Test (TNT), which was developed and validated by Mayton and his colleagues between 1998 and 2005, followed the lead of Elliott in measuring *ahimsa* with both physical and psychological nonviolence subscales. The two other TNT subscales are based directly on the Gandhian principles of *satyagraha* and *tapasya* and the fifth subscale measures levels of helping/empathy. The fifth and final measure, the Multidimensional Scales of Nonviolence (MSN), was developed by Johnson and her colleagues in 1998 to assess direct nonviolence, systems-level nonviolence, compassion and connection, indirect oppression, nonviolence toward the planet, and spirituality. The MSN assumes nonviolent individuals are courageous, compassionate, spiritual, and have a high respect for all forms of life.

PERSONALITY CORRELATES OF
NONVIOLENT DISPOSITIONS

A small but growing body of research has used the measures of nonviolence and known groups to determine the personality characteristics of people with nonviolent dispositions (Kool, 1990; Mayton, 2009). The correlates of nonviolence have been identified for human values, the "big five" personality factors, and selected personality constructs. (See PEACEFUL PERSONALITY.)

Values are an integral part of Gandhian philosophy of nonviolence. Several research studies have correlated ten value types with nonviolent dispositions. (See VALUES, NONVIOLENCE, AND PEACE PSYCHOLOGY.) By and large, nonviolent dispositions have been found to be associated with high priorities on the self-transcendent values of benevolence (concern about preservation and enhancement of the welfare of people close to you) and universalism (concern about protecting all of humanity and nature), as well as conformity values (the restraint of actions and impulses that might upset or harm others or violate expectations or norms). People with nonviolent dispositions have also been shown to place low priorities on power values (concern about status and dominance) (Mayton, 2009).

The "big five," or the five-factor model of personality, is a well-established and widely accepted theory of personality that pinpoints five main traits (neuroticism, extraversion, openness to experience, agreeableness, and conscientiousness) that underlie an individual's personality. There is strong support across three studies that agreeableness correlates positively with nonviolence (Mayton, 2009). People scoring high on agreeableness are described as being altruistic, sympathetic, and confident that they will be helped in return and also score high on psychological nonviolence, helping/empathy, *satyagraha*, and *tapasya* (Heuchert, 2003, cited in Mayton, 2009). There is new data that show a positive correlation between the big-five trait of conscientiousness and psychological nonviolence, helping/empathy, and *satyagraha*. People who score high on conscientiousness are

more self-disciplined and would prefer to plan than to be spontaneous. In addition, individuals with nonviolent dispositions are more agreeable and more conscientious.

Mayton and his colleagues have administered the TNT and various other measures to young adults in three separate studies in order to assess additional personality characteristics of nonviolent individuals (Mayton, 2009). These personality constructs were selected because they related either to Gandhi's philosophy of nonviolence or Nelson's model of a peaceful person. (See PEACEFUL PERSONALITY.) In three separate studies, nonviolent dispositions, as measured by the TNT, were positively correlated with a need for cognition. People with nonviolent dispositions engage in and take pleasure in cognitive activities and simply enjoy thinking through issues. In addition, empathy, meaningfulness of life, life satisfaction, self-control, and mindfulness were positively correlated with subscales of the TNT in the two studies that included these measures. People with nonviolent dispositions are more empathetic, have more self-control, are more satisfied with their lives, and report that their lives are more meaningful. They also report living in the present more or having higher levels of mindfulness. Serenity, desire for control, self-acceptance, and inner peace were also positively correlated with TNT scores in the only study that investigated these relationships. People with nonviolent dispositions are more serene, have stronger desires for control, accept themselves more, and have more inner peace.

On the other hand, materialism and anger were measured in two studies and were negatively correlated with nonviolent scores on TNT subscales in both studies. People with nonviolent dispositions are less materialistic and do not look for happiness through the acquisition of possessions and material goods. They also report lower levels of anger. One study investigated dogmatism and found a significant negative correlation between dogmatism and nonviolence. People with nonviolent dispositions are less dogmatic and more open-minded.

Several other variables were investigated to see if they were correlated with nonviolence but these relationships were not found to exist. Two such variables are happiness and self-esteem and, as of now, no significant correlations have been discovered. And on three separate occasions, spirituality was measured using three different measures but this yielded mixed results. Sometimes spirituality was positively associated with nonviolence but other measures demonstrated negative correlations. Therefore, much more research needs to be done in order to better understand how religion and spirituality relate to nonviolent dispositions.

It has also been hypothesized that there exists a direct relationship between moral reasoning and nonviolence. However, Kool and Keyes (in Kool, 1990) and Mayton, Diessner, & Granby (1993) failed to identify significant relationships using the NVT. While the study of morality seems critical to understanding the nonviolent personality, individuals who are predisposed to nonviolent conflict resolution have not been shown to exhibit higher levels of moral reasoning. Kool and Keyes posit that this can possibly be attributed to the complexity of morality and the concern of justice versus concern for love and compassion.

CONCLUSION

Individuals with nonviolent dispositions are more agreeable, more conscientious, more empathetic, and more desirous of control than their more violent peers. They also show higher levels of satisfaction with life, higher levels of self-acceptance, higher levels of serenity and inner peace, and higher levels of concern for the welfare of people

close to them and for all of humanity and nature. Individuals with nonviolent dispositions also exhibit more self-control, more optimism, and more meaningfulness in their lives and are less materialistic, less dogmatic, less angry, and less concerned about status and power.

SEE ALSO: Nonviolence, Psychology of; Peaceful Personality; Values, Nonviolence, and Peace Psychology.

REFERENCES

Kool, V. K. (Ed.) (1990). *Perspectives on nonviolence*. New York, NY: Springer.
Mayton, D. M. (2001). Nonviolence within cultures of peace: A means and an ends. *Peace and Conflict: Journal of Peace Psychology, 7*(2), 143–155.
Mayton, D. M. (2009). *Nonviolence and peace psychology: Intrapersonal, interpersonal, societal, and world peace*. New York, NY: Springer.
Mayton, D. M., Diessner, R., & Granby, C. D. (1993). Nonviolence and moral reasoning. *Journal of Social Psychology, 133*(5), 745–746.
Mayton, D. M., Susnjic, S., Palmer, B. J., Peters, D. J., Gierth, R., & Caswell, R. N. (2002). The measurement of nonviolence: A review. *Peace and Conflict: Journal of Peace Psychology, 8*(4), 343–354.
Nakhre, A. W. (1982). *Social psychology of nonviolent action: A study of three satyagrahas*. Delhi, India: Chanakya Publications.
Sharp, G. (1979). *Gandhi as political strategist*. Boston, MA: Porter Sargent.

Normative Influence, Theories of

WINNIFRED R. LOUIS

Norms are defined as group-based rules or standards for perception, attitudes, or action. In psychological research, norms may be explicit or implicit. In sociological research, the term is more likely to be reserved for implicit rules communicated nonverbally (e.g., "folkways"), in contrast to explicitly stated rules or "black-letter" laws ("state-ways"). A central distinction in psychological theories of normative influence is between *models of compliance*, in which normative influence changes behavior or expressed attitudes for extrinsic motives but private perceptions or attitudes are unaffected; and *models of conformity*, in which people internalize norms so that both private attitudes and public actions change. (See also SOCIAL INFLUENCE.)

In early work, Deutsch and Gerard (1955) proposed the most widely known theoretical model of this distinction, contrasting *informational influence* (which leads to conformity) and *normative influence* (which leads to compliance). Both types of influence involve perceived norms, confusingly! In informational influence, the behavior and views of other group members are unthinkingly adopted, because others are seen as relevant guides to appropriate perceptions, attitudes, and actions. Internal attitudes change as well as behaviors, and individuals are often unconscious of their conformity. For example, informational influence takes place when we observe others engage in cooperative problem solving and we imitate it without conscious choice because that is what is appropriate.

Informational influence varies with geohistorical context. For the most part, citizens of modern cities refrain from killing citizens of neighboring cities when resource disputes arise. However, this is not because they consciously choose to eschew violence; instead, all accept a negotiated political resolution as the appropriate alternative. In contrast, in another geohistorical context, such as ancient Greece, a more powerful city might routinely attack a weaker target. Norms often act in this manner to limit the contexts in which violence is a psychologically

permissible alternative, and to define the targets against which violence is permissible. (See also PREJUDICE REDUCTION, APPROACHES TO; DEHUMANIZATION, INFRAHUMANIZATION, AND NATURALIZATION.) One modern theoretical successor to the notion of "informational influence" is found in Bandura's social cognitive theory. The models stress nonverbal observation and imitation, and emphasize that we conform to norms because we infer conformity is appropriate – "the right thing to do." (See also MORAL DISENGAGEMENT.)

In contrast, in Deutsch and Gerard's original model, the term "normative influence" was reserved for compliance motivated by needs for interpersonal approval – when behavior changes to avoid disapproval or to gain approval, despite personal views. The focus on the need for approval has a modern successor in the *subjective norm* of the theory of planned behavior (Ajzen, 1985). In these models, norms introduce compliance, changing behavior or expressed attitudes while internal attitudes are unaffected. Individuals' action is motivated *either* intrinsically, by their attitude toward the behavior ("I attend a peace rally because I view the rally positively myself") or *extrinsically* by norms ("I attend peace rallies because important others want and expect me to do so; I want them to approve of me").

Recent theories have tried to understand *when* norms create internal attitude change versus only changing external behavior. Some distinguish *prescriptive norms*, where deviance is morally stigmatized and evokes social disapproval or punishment (e.g., "jewelers do not steal from clients"), from *descriptive norms*, where deviance may be morally neutral (e.g., "jewelers wear glasses"). Two new directions of research have been especially important in understanding the underlying psychological processes: theories of group processes, and norm focus theory.

THEORIES OF GROUP PROCESSES

According to the social identity perspective, people can identify not just as a unique individual ("I," a personal identity) but also as social and collective ("we," a social identity). (See also SOCIAL IDENTITY THEORY.) According to *referent informational influence*, the social identity theory of normative influence (Turner, Wetherell, & Hogg, 1989; see also van Zomeren, Postmes, & Spears, 2008), intrinsic change is produced by ingroup norms (norms for groups with which one identifies). In contrast, extrinsic change is produced by outgroup norms (norms for groups to which one does not belong psychologically). The model proposes that norms attach to particular social categories or groups, and individuals identify more or less strongly with the source of a norm (or referent group) in the context of the decision. When identification is strong, the ingroup norm is internalized (behavior *and* attitudes both change intrinsically) because the norm defines what is appropriate in that context: this is referent informational influence. But when individuals do not identify with the referent group, they will ignore the norm – or, at best, comply because of extrinsic motives based on the referent's power to deliver social or material rewards and punishments.

This referent informational influence model is valuable because it is able to predict when different types of normative influence will occur, and also which norm referents are salient and influential for which decisions. For example, an individual who identifies as politically left-wing in a right-wing family may conform to family norms for where to spend the holidays, but reject family norms on whether to support peace versus war. The holiday decision makes salient family identities, producing conformity to family norms ("Our family always goes to mom's house"), but for the same individual the peace versus war decision makes salient *political identities*, so the family's right-wing norms are ignored and, instead, other left-wing referents' norms guide behavior. Whether or not a group identity is salient for a particular behavior or attitude depends, according to social identity theory, on the prototypicality of the behavior or attitude for the group, which depends on how common it is within the group, and whether or not it is implicated in core group values. Prototypicality in turn is determined by the meta-contrast ratio: an identity becomes salient because it most meaningfully captures a small degree of within-group variability compared to a larger degree of between-group variability. So religious or political identities may become salient in peace and conflict decisions because those dimensions of social categorization subjectively identify the pro- versus antiwar camps within a society. Put differently, if I identify with a religious group that is prototypically pro-peace (e.g., Quakers), and I perceive other religions to be relatively pro-war, then because my group is homogeneous and other groups are different, my group identity should be salient when I make peace decisions. If my religion has mixed views on peace, then all other things being equal my religious identity won't be salient for that decision.

In most group models, norms from groups to which one does not belong psychologically (outgroup norms) are thought to be ineffective: the outgroup norm will be ignored when the ingroup identity is salient. Communicating an outgroup norm may even provoke a backlash of rejection, called *group polarization*, by making salient the social identities on which group differences are constructed. For example, showing a Michael Moore antiwar film to conservative Republicans could strengthen the latter's pro-war views by making salient the left/ right divide and associating peace with a source perceived as outgroup. In contrast, if a common or shared identity can be sustained (e.g., as fellow humans), the *minority influence* literature indicates that both public and private change can occur. The minority influence literature has argued that ingroup majorities elicit more shallow compliance from group members motivated to gain approval or avoid disapproval. Ironically, dissenting minorities may sway group members' attitudes more deeply, as individuals infer that a consistent minority which is braving the stigma of deviance must have a good reason for it and the minority exerts informational influence.

Even where a salient intergroup distinction is observed, outgroup normative influence is possible according to the *agentic normative influence* model (e.g., Louis, 2009). This model proposes that group members may *choose* to comply with outgroup norms as a conciliatory gesture, or to violate outgroup norms deliberately as a gesture of provocation or defiance. Whether group members choose conciliation or confrontation, it is proposed, depends in turn on expectations about how outgroup members will react – for example, whether conciliation will be seen as weakness eliciting exploitation, or as cooperation eliciting reciprocity. The agentic normative influence model proposes that decision-makers infer the costs and benefits of conflict choices such as peace versus war from perceived ingroup and outgroup norms (what the ingroup and outgroup want me to do; what they will do if I support peace vs. war; etc.). This type of model stresses the importance of social learning from both ingroups and outgroups, with feedback loops of own and collective experience linking in with learned perceptions so that "rational" decision-making is shaped by normative expectations. (See also COLLECTIVE EFFICACY.)

DISTINGUISHING WHAT PEOPLE DO FROM WHAT THEY THINK SHOULD BE DONE

A second important direction of normative research, *norm focus theory* (Cialdini, Kallgren, & Reno, 1990), has distinguished between *injunctive norms* (what others think should be done; what is morally right or desired) and *descriptive norms* (what is commonly done; what others do). In some contexts, injunctive and descriptive norms overlap, and the distinction is unimportant: for example, one would expect that Quakers oppose war both morally and behaviorally (negative injunctive *and* descriptive norms for war). But what occurs when the norms are in conflict, for example if Canadians are perceived to oppose war, but to be waging war?

Some approaches suggest that injunctive norms always prevail. As seen above, some have argued that the descriptive norm is morally unweighted, so dissent is tolerated, in contrast to prescriptive norms or injunctive norms, which threaten social penalties for norm violation. Another rationale for injunctive primacy defines injunctive norms as more generalizable and abstract, as opposed to descriptive norms, which are argued to be salient only in the context in which others' behavior may be observed (e.g., I could think of an injunctive norm for war in any context, but I will see only a descriptive norm for war if I observe a battle). But it does not seem to be true that descriptive norms cannot be salient outside the actual context of observation; both descriptive and injunctive norms can be inferred or remembered. Empirically, research by Cialdini and colleagues has shown that communicating contradictory injunctive and descriptive norms (e.g., a message against widespread theft, for example, or against pervasive energy wastage) can actually increase the problem behavior, rather than motivating change. Similarly, when injunctive and descriptive norms are manipulated from the same source, people do not always conform to the injunctive norm (see Smith & Louis, 2008). Negative descriptive norms can erase or even reverse the positive impact of injunctive norms (e.g., if you tell me that Americans disapprove of war but wage war, I may be *more* likely to support war in some contexts). Some researchers have found that a discrepancy can even suggest a group meta-norm of hypocrisy for that behavior (what is "normal" is that I espouse *attitudes* in favor of peace while continuing to support war *behaviorally*). And other researchers have found that communicating any injunctive norm can imply a negative descriptive norm ("If you tell us to make love not war, that must mean our group is militarist; why else would you say so?").

INTEGRATING THEORIES OF NORMATIVE INFLUENCE

Integrating the study of group processes with studying the difference between injunctive and descriptive norms is a hot area of emerging research. The diversity of conceptualizations of normative influence makes it difficult to draw one overarching conclusion for students or researchers regarding when social rules will be followed versus when they will be broken, but it is safe to say that norms are vital in understanding support for peace and war, and that studies of normative influence play a vital role in peace psychology.

SEE ALSO: Collective Efficacy; Dehumanization, Infrahumanization, and Naturalization; Moral Disengagement; Prejudice Reduction, Approaches to; Social Identity Theory; Social Influence.

REFERENCES

Ajzen, I. (1985). From intentions to actions: A theory of planned behavior. In J. Kuhl & J. Beckmann (Eds.), *Action control: From cognition to behavior* (pp. 11–39). New York, NY: Springer.

Cialdini, R. B., Kallgren, C. A., & Reno, R. R. (1990). A focus theory of normative conduct: Recycling the concept of norms to reduce littering in public places. *Journal of Personality and Social Psychology, 58,* 1015–1026.

Deutsch, M., & Gerard, H. B. (1955). A study of normative and informational influences upon individual judgement. *Journal of Abnormal and Social Psychology, 51,* 629–636.

Louis, W. R. (2009). If they're not crazy, then what? The implications of social psychological approaches to terrorism for conflict management. In W. Stritzke, S. Lewandowsky, D. Denemark, F. Morgan, & J. Clare (Eds.), *Terrorism and torture: An interdisciplinary perspective* (pp. 125–153). Cambridge, UK: Cambridge University Press.

Smith, J. R., & Louis, W. R. (2008). Do as we say and as we do: The interplay of descriptive and injunctive group norms in the attitude–behavior relationship. *British Journal of Social Psychology, 47,* 647–666.

Turner, J. C., Wetherell, M. S., & Hogg, M. A. (1989). Referent informational influence and group polarization. *British Journal of Social Psychology, 28,* 135–147.

van Zomeren, M., Postmes, T., & Spears, R. (2008). Toward an integrative social identity model of collective action: A quantitative research synthesis of three sociopsychological perspectives. *Psychological Bulletin, 134,* 504–535.

ADDITIONAL RESOURCES

International Society of Political Psychology: http://ispp.org/

Society for the Psychological Study of Social Issues: http://www.spssi.org/

Society for the Study of Peace, Conflict, and Violence: Peace Psychology Division of the American Psychological Association: http://www.apa.org/about/division/div48.html/

O

Obedience

LINDA M. WOOLF AND
MICHAEL R. HULSIZER

Following the Holocaust, scholars from a range of disciplines began to question how one of the most civilized countries in the Western world, noted for exemplary educational, scientific, and cultural pursuits, could have carried out the systematic mass murder of millions. One of the answers provided at Nuremberg and later by Eichmann during his trial in Israel was that those responsible were just following orders. Similar justifications have been provided in response to the My Lai massacre in Vietnam, crimes committed at Abu Ghraib, and other destructive actions that have occurred during wartime. However, destructive obedience extends beyond the military to other contexts such as terrorist organizations (e.g., international terrorist organizations and domestic hate groups), corporations, and cults. The litany of "I was just doing what I was told" spans across cultural contexts with the ramifications ranging from the benign to the horrific.

Stanley Milgram (1974) conducted the most noted example of research concerning obedience and recently Burger completed a modified replication of the original study. (See OBEDIENCE TO AUTHORITY.) Within this research paradigm, participants were instructed to give increasingly higher levels of electric shock (note that no shocks were actually delivered) to a "learner" in response to every incorrect answer. In the most commonly cited of Milgram's studies, 65% of the participants went all the way to the highest level of shock, well beyond the levels where the "learner" made exclamations of pain, demands of "Let me out of here!," expressions of alarm about a heart condition, and then silence. Milgram, hoping to examine differences between Germany and the United States, instead found that obedience to authority is a bond shared by most individuals.

Although Milgram's research is significant, it only paints a partial picture of the factors involved in obedience. Obedience is best understood as a dynamic gestalt between culture, leaders, followers, and a host of social psychological factors – all of which enhance the power of the social situation. It is important to note that a change to one of these features (each discussed below) can substantially alter the group

The Encyclopedia of Peace Psychology, First Edition. Edited by Daniel J. Christie.
© 2012 Blackwell Publishing Ltd. Published 2012 by Blackwell Publishing Ltd.

dynamic and either foster or inhibit destructive obedience.

CULTURAL FACTORS

Although the impulse towards obedience
appears to be a fundamental trait within all
humans, the regard placed on obedience
varies within and between cultures. Within
many societies, cultural rituals and standards, whether in religious, educational, corporate, or community structures, help to
perpetuate compliance. The existing cultural milieu may include severe penalties for
non-adherence to norms, ranging from
ostracism and verbal aggression to physical
violence. The pressure to comply, conform,
or obey becomes even more salient upon
the introduction of an authority figure.
Typically, those cultures noted for a history
of violence, an ideology that one group is
superior to another, a low tolerance for
diversity, and the tendency for authoritarian
forms of government, tend to be more at
risk for destructive forms of obedience
(Staub, 1989; Woolf & Hulsizer, 2005).
Indeed, most genocides and democides (i.e.,
death by government, such as Stalin's
purges) that occurred during the twentieth
century were committed by militaries
serving at the hand of an authoritarian
leader, within countries dominated by a
history of violent conflict, and a monolithic
belief system often marked by clear opposition to those who were different.

    Cultures at risk for destructive forms of
obedience are typically propelled down a
path to mass violence by crisis (e.g., war,
political instability, economic crises, terrorist
attacks). Rarely do populations set out to
commit an atrocity but rather "learn by
doing" as these cultures move down a path
of destructive obedience and violence
(Newman & Erber, 2002, p. 22). The path to
mass violence is marked by stages exemplified by increasing levels of destructiveness,

dehumanization of the victim group, and
resocialization of both the military and the
general society. Actions that would have
been defined as previously unacceptable
(e.g., torture, genocide) become accepted as
policy and perhaps even defined as honorable action (Woolf & Hulsizer, 2005).

LEADERS

Leaders are a necessary component within
the constellation of factors associated with
destructive obedience. However, leaders
who promote a high level of obedience
within governments, terrorist groups, or
cults cannot be defined simply in relation to
a specific personality type (Woolf & Hulsizer,
2005). Indeed, researchers have found only
modest correlations between leadership
success and a variety of variables such as
charisma, morality, desire for power, and
social dominance. Ironically, personality
characteristics tend to be poor predictors of
leadership abilities. What is most important
is the leader–follower gestalt – a complementary system whereby a good leader
learns to effectively strengthen the bonds
between the individual and the group.
Effective leaders are in tune to the needs and
abilities of their followers and as such can
maximize their manipulation of the group
to achieve higher levels of commitment and
organizational success.

    Leaders often manipulate highly destruc-
tive groups by creating an atmosphere of "us
against them" (Woolf & Hulsizer, 2005).
Terrorist groups, cults, many military and
quasi-military groups, and other destructive
organizations often push individuals to
isolate themselves from those not associated
with the groups and conform to group
norms. Within destructive groups, leaders
generally work to maintain environmental
control so as to manage what followers see,
hear, and experience. Terrorist groups, cults,
and military organizations may become a

follower's sole source of identity and life activity, which enables leaders to maintain authority and control over the group. (See TERRORISTS, PSYCHOLOGY OF.) Moreover, destructive leaders often work to develop a military, quasi-military, or organized cell structure with unique jargon and rituals for the group. With uniforms and clearly identifiable prescribed rules for behavior, followers become more willing to commit destructive acts because of enhanced deindividuation, conformity, and diffusion of responsibility. (See DIFFUSION OF RESPONSIBILITY; SOCIAL INFLUENCE.) Whereas a civilian might never dream of torturing someone as part of their daily life, they might willingly engage in such actions while wearing a uniform.

Finally, destructive leaders are able to promote destructive ideologies or religious codes within their own cultures. Such ideologies often are presented as moral, highly idealistic, and for the greater good. Thus, although leaders may or may not necessarily believe their own espoused ideologies, they are able to create fanatical followers who exhibit a high degree of obedience.

FOLLOWERS

Destructive groups not only need leaders but they need recruits. The reasons behind individuals' decisions to join groups grounded in enmity are complex but rooted in an interaction of personality and situational factors. Adorno, Frenkel-Brunswik, Levinson, and Sanford (1950) hypothesized that authoritarian personalities were cultivated in children raised in households characterized by strict and punitive disciplinary practices and rigid belief systems. Unable to rebel against such authoritarian patterns, children project their unacceptable impulses, anger, and frustrations on others less able to defend themselves – a highly psychoanalytic approach. Altemeyer (1996) revised the concept of the authoritarian personality by focusing on individuals with a high level of deference to authority (authoritarian submission), aggressiveness toward those identified as different (authoritarian aggression), and strong adherence to group norms, traditions, and rituals (conventionalism). This personality type, labeled right-wing authoritarianism (RWA), has provided evidence suggesting that individuals with a high degree of authoritarianism are more likely to become authoritarian leaders and blind followers. (See AUTHORITARIAN PERSONALITY.)

Individuals may also self-select to join groups that require high levels of obedience (Staub, 1989; Woolf & Hulsizer, 2005). Greek men who became torturers, Nazi doctors, and men who volunteered as Einsatzgrüppen (i.e., mobile killing squads) include individuals who have been identified as possessing characteristics that made them uniquely qualified to fill destructively obedient roles. Although the examples and variables involved may differ, the premise is that individuals who are destructively obedient in a particular context often have opted for a particular role. Individuals may join organizations that require a high level of obedience because of a need to belong, a need for structure, for idealist reasons, cultural disillusionment, or to fulfill a need for control, aggression, and/or status. Terrorist organizations, cults, and military organizations actively recruit vulnerable populations with promises of belonging, identity, stability, self-worth, excitement, and direction. Leaders can manipulate these needs to foster a high degree of conformity, compliance, and obedience.

SOCIAL PSYCHOLOGICAL FACTORS

One of the most powerful tools available to a government or leader is the ability to manipulate how the group thinks about, influences, and relates to each other

(Newman & Erber, 2002; Staub, 1989; Woolf & Hulsizer, 2005). Therefore, the identification of social psychological factors most amenable to distortion and manipulation is critical to developing an understanding of destructive obedience.

Milgram (1974) demonstrated how the mere presence of an authority figure increases the risk of destructive obedience. However, obedience to authority involves additional social psychological factors. For example, the foot-in-the-door technique (moving from minor acts of compliance to increasingly greater levels of involvement) is a proven technique that has been used to facilitate an escalation of destructive obedience and violence. Hate groups will often have new members engage in relatively innocuous activities such as simply setting up a literature table at a group event before moving on to greater levels of commitment. Each level of acceptance is met with approval and reward. Eventually, recruits increasingly become committed to the hate group's ideology and activities, identified solely as a group member, and loyal to those in positions of authority.

Leaders can work to fuel prejudice, discrimination, and violence against those identified as different. Humans have the tendency to divide the world into "us" and "them" (i.e., ingroups and outgroups). (See US AND THEM: MODERATING DICHOTOMOUS INGROUP/OUTGROUP THINKING.) This distinction between "us" and "them" is far from trivial, as we tend to view our ingroup positively and hold the outgroup in less esteem. (See SOCIAL IDENTITY THEORY.) This bias can be manipulated by leaders as justification of violence against the outgroup by fomenting prejudice, discrimination, and, ultimately, moral exclusion of those targeted for atrocity. (See MORAL EXCLUSION.) Leaders can design propaganda to increase the "otherness" of the object of derision. For example, leaders can use caricatures of the enemy (e.g., in cartoons, literature, symbols, and media images) with concomitant dehumanization to facilitate obedience in soldiers and the acceptability of violent actions during times of war. Ultimately, as we tend to believe that we live in a just world and that a victim's plight is largely due to dispositional causes (e.g., personality flaws, low intelligence, innate evil) rather than situational factors, perpetrators and bystanders may assume that the victim of violent actions is responsible for their own fate – we blame the victim. Destructive leaders can also push for conformity within groups, leading towards groupthink and the polarization of beliefs and ideologies, and hence foster obedience. (See GROUPTHINK.)

CONCLUSION

Obedience exists in a dynamic gestalt of cultural factors, leaders, followers, and the manipulation of social psychological factors. Although obedience can exist in any context, terrorist organizations (domestic and international), cults, quasi-military organizations (e.g., militias), and military units all represent nexuses whereby all of these factors come together to create situations ripe for destructive obedience. Moreover, passive bystanders (e.g., those who remain silent in the face of genocide or torture) provide fuel for increased obedience and cultural acceptance of the actions taken within and by these organizations. Ultimately, any intervention attempts (primary, secondary, or tertiary) directed towards preventing or reducing destructive obedience need to incorporate the entire constellation of factors involved in the dynamic gestalt of obedience.

SEE ALSO: Authoritarian Personality; Diffusion of Responsibility; Groupthink; Moral Exclusion; Obedience to Authority; Social Identity Theory; Social Influence; Terrorists, Psychology of; Us and Them:

Moderating Dichotomous Ingroup/ Outgroup Thinking.

REFERENCES

Adorno, T. W., Frenkel-Brunswik, E., Levinson, D., & Sanford, R. N. (1950). *The authoritarian personality*. New York, NY: Harper and Row.
Altemeyer, B. (1996). *The authoritarian specter*. Cambridge, MA: Harvard University Press.
Burger, J. M. (2009). Replicating Milgram: Would people still obey today? *American Psychologist, 64*, 1–11.
Milgram, S. (1974). *Obedience to authority*. New York, NY: Harper and Row.
Newman, L. S., & Erber. R. (2002). *Understanding genocide: The social psychology of the Holocaust*. New York, NY: Oxford University Press.
Staub, E. (1989). *The roots of evil: The origins of genocide and other group violence*. New York, NY: Cambridge University Press.
Woolf, L. M., & Hulsizer, M. R. (2005). Psychosocial roots of genocide: Risk, prevention, and intervention, *Journal of Genocide Research, 7*, 101–128.

ADDITIONAL RESOURCES

Haritos-Fatouros, M. (1988). The official torturer: A learning model for obedience to the authority of violence. *Journal of Applied Social Psychology, 18*, 1107–1120.
Opotow, S. (Ed.). (1990). Moral exclusion and injustice [Special issue]. *Journal of Social Issues, 46*(1).
Woolf, L. M., & Hulsizer, M. R. (2004). Hate groups for dummies: How to build a successful hate group. *Humanity and Society, 28*, 40–62.

Obedience to Authority

JERRY M. BURGER

Between August 1961 and May 1962, Yale psychologist Stanley Milgram (1963, 1965, 1974) conducted a series of investigations on the psychology of obedience. Under the guise of a learning experiment, participants were placed in a situation in which they were instructed to deliver what they thought were increasingly painful and dangerous electric shocks to another individual. The point of the studies was to see how long participants would follow the experimenter's instructions before they refused to administer any more shocks. Milgram found that the average person continued to shock the innocent victim far longer than anyone had anticipated. The findings have implications for the worst of human behavior, including massacres, atrocities, and genocide. (See OBEDIENCE.)

Although Milgram conducted more than a dozen variations of the basic procedure, the version most people are familiar with (Experiment 5) consisted of one male participant, one male confederate posing as a real participant, and a male experimenter. Participants were men, ages 20 through 50, recruited through newspaper ads and flyers to be part of a study on "memory and learning." Through a rigged drawing, the real participant was always assigned the role of the teacher, while the confederate was the learner. The learner's task was to learn a series of 25 word-pairs (e.g., *blue–girl*). The teacher's job was to administer the test and punish incorrect answers by delivering electric shocks to the learner.

The teacher sat in front of a large machine identified as a shock generator. In addition to lights and gauges, 30 switches spanned the front of the machine. Each switch was identified with the number of volts it delivered, starting with 15 volts and moving in 15-volt increments up to 450 volts. Labels above the switches at the high end of the generator warned DANGER: SEVERE SHOCK and XXX. For each test item, the teacher gave the first word of the pair and four options for the correct pairing by speaking into a microphone. The learner was strapped into a chair on the other side of the wall from the teacher. He had an electrode attached to one wrist. With the other hand, he could reach four buttons that allowed him to respond to the test items. The buttons were connected to lights on the teacher's side of the wall. The teacher was instructed to start with the 15-volt switch for the first wrong answer and to move one step up the shock generator for each successive wrong answer.

In reality, the learner received no shocks. But he gave many wrong answers, which caused the teacher to deliver what he believed to be increasingly strong shocks. Whenever the teacher expressed a reluctance to continue, the experimenter encouraged him with a verbal prod. If the learner continued to resist, the experimenter responded with a second prod. The sequence continued until the teacher resumed the test or until he had resisted each of four prods. In order, the prods were: *Please continue* or *continue*; *The experiment requires that you continue*; *It is absolutely essential that you continue*; and *You have no other choice, you must continue.* If the teacher continued with another test item, the experimenter started over with the first prod the next time the teacher expressed reluctance.

After pressing the 75-volt switch, the teacher heard through the wall a muffled *Ow!* From that point on, the learner's response became louder with each shock. After 150 volts, the learner yelled out that he could not stand the pain, that his heart was bothering him, and that he wanted to be released. His cries of pain and his protests became more vehement with each shock. At 300 volts, the learner refused to give any more answers, which the experimenter instructed to consider a wrong answer. The anguished screams and demands to be released continued until the teacher pressed the 330 volt switch. At that point, the teacher heard only silence, suggesting that the learner was no longer physically capable of participating. Nonetheless, the experimenter instructed the teacher to continue the test and the shocks.

Most people hearing about the obedience studies for the first time predict that few if any participants would continue to press switches after hearing the participant's demands to be released. And it is a rare individual who does not believe that he or she would stop very early in the process. Yet Milgram found that 65% of the participants in the basic procedure continued all the way to the 450 volt switch. Milgram conducted 19 variations of the experiment, each time altering the procedure slightly to better understand the effect. He found obedience decreased when the learner was in the same room as the teacher, when the teacher saw two other "teachers" refuse to continue, when a second experimenter expressed reservations about continuing, and when the role of the experimenter was given to a man who appeared to be just another participant. However, no change in obedience levels was found when the location of the lab was moved off campus or when the participants were women.

Milgram's research also triggered a great deal of discussion about the ethical treatment of research participants. Many psychologists argued that the procedures exposed participants to unacceptable levels of stress with the possibility of long-term emotional consequences. In his defense, Milgram pointed to data from follow-up questionnaires indicating that the vast majority of his participants had no problem with being part of the study. Moreover, most participants believed more research of this kind should be conducted. Nonetheless, by the 1970s, professional and legal standards effectively prevented researchers from replicating Milgram's procedures. As a result, many questions about obedience were left unanswered, and many interpretations of the findings were left untested.

Among the unanswered questions was whether Milgram's findings could be replicated today. To address this concern, Burger (2009) conducted a partial replication of Milgram's basic procedure. In addition to several added safeguards, the replication stopped the procedure after observing the participants' reaction following the administration of the 150-volt shock. This is the point at which the learner first says that he is suffering and that he demands to be released. In Milgram's original study, 79% of the participants who continued past this point continued all the way to 450 volts. Thus, by stopping after 150 volts, a reasonable guess could be made about what the participants would have done if allowed to continue. Seventy percent of the participants in the replication continued the procedure after pressing the 150 volt lever, not significantly different from the 82.5% who continued past this point in Milgram's study.

Psychologists and scholars have been engaged in a decades-long discussion about how to interpret Milgram's findings. Individuals first encountering Milgram's work sometimes misinterpret the results as a pessimistic comment on human nature. However, most social psychologists argue that the findings actually suggest the opposite. The obedience studies are a dramatic demonstration of a phenomenon known as the fundamental attribution error, i.e., that people typically fail to appreciate the extent to which situational factors influence behavior. Participants in Milgram's studies were not sadistic or brutal individuals. Rather, they were ordinary citizens who found themselves in a situation that made it extremely difficult to do anything but go along with the experimenter's instructions. The sometimes unwelcome implication of this interpretation is that most of us would continue to press the shock levers if we were in the same situation.

Milgram's interpretation of the findings focused on the relationship between the authority figure and the individual taking the orders. The research participants were said to fall into an "agentic state" in which they relinquished their judgment to the authority figure (Milgram, 1974). The authority figure did not need to be charismatic or threatening, but rather only needed to be seen as legitimate. Most researchers agree that the personal manner of the experimenter had little impact on whether participants went along with the instructions. However, the notion of an agentic state was never embraced by psychologists and is rarely mentioned today.

Decades of social psychological research have identified several situational variables that may have led Milgram's participants to administer seemingly dangerous shocks. One of these variables is the incremental nature of the task. Participants started by administering a relatively mild 15-volt shock and continued in small increments as the study progressed. Researchers now know that this approach is an effective way to change attitudes and behaviors. Consistency needs and changes in self-perception make it difficult for people to not take the next step in the sequence. This observation explains why the 150 volt lever was a critical turning point in Milgram's studies. Pressing the shock levers after hearing the learner's demands to be released is qualitatively different than pressing the levers before. After participants passed 150 volts, there was no obvious stopping point.

Another situational variable that contributed to the high obedience levels was the absence of information about how one should act. Participants had never been in a situation like the obedience study before and had no idea of what was expected of them. In these kinds of settings, people often turn to experts. The expert in Milgram's study was the experimenter, who presumably knew all about the shock generator and had seen many other participants in this same situation. The experimenter's manner and words indicated that he saw nothing alarming and that the proper response for the teacher was to continue with the procedure.

A third situational variable built into Milgram's procedure that made it easy for participants to continue giving shocks was the removal of personal responsibility. Milgram reported that most participants expressed in post-session interviews an absence of responsibility for harming the learner. They instead placed responsibility on the experimenter who gave the instructions or on Milgram or the university for designing and allowing the study. When participants expressed a concern during the study about responsibility for harming the learner, the experimenter replied, "I am responsible." Researchers find that diffused or removed responsibility often increases the likelihood of antisocial and aggressive behavior.

One reason the obedience studies remain an important part of social psychology nearly a half century after they were conducted is the implications they have for understanding the most disturbing of human behaviors. Milgram frequently pointed to his findings to explain why so many German citizens went along with the atrocities committed during the Holocaust. Milgram's work is often invoked when news stories about atrocities and blind obedience surface. Examples include the My Lai massacres during the Vietnam War and the Abu Ghraib incident during the Iraq War.

However, many psychologists have accused Milgram of overstating the connection between the obedience studies and the Holocaust (Miller, 2004). These critics point to several important elements present in Nazi Germany that could never be replicated in a laboratory experiment. Perhaps most noteworthy of these missing elements are the decades of widespread prejudice and dehumanization of the victims. Nonetheless, there is general agreement that the obedience studies provide at least one piece of the puzzle in understanding the psychology behind the unsettling and seemingly inexplicable behavior of otherwise decent people during the Holocaust.

Along with other research conducted in the relatively new field of social psychology at the time, the obedience studies changed the way psychologists looked at the atrocities in Nazi Germany. In the 1950s, research was often focused on the personal characteristics that allowed individuals to engage in these kinds of behaviors. Many studies examined the "authoritarian personality" that was said to have been prevalent in Germany during the first part of the twentieth century. Milgram's work took psychology's focus away from the characteristics of the perpetrators and placed it on situational variables.

SEE ALSO: Obedience.

REFERENCES

Burger, J. M. (2009). Replicating Milgram: Would people still obey today? *American Psychologist*, 64, 1–11.
Milgram, S. (1963). Behavioral study of obedience. *Journal of Abnormal and Social Psychology*, 67, 371–378.
Milgram, S. (1965). Some conditions of obedience and disobedience to authority. *Human Relations*, 18, 57–76.
Milgram, S. (1974). *Obedience to authority: An experimental view*. New York, NY: Harper and Row.
Miller, A. G. (2004). What can the Milgram obedience experiments tell us about the Holocaust? Generalizing from the social psychology laboratory. In A. G. Miller (Ed.), *The social psychology of good and evil* (pp. 193–239). New York, NY: Guilford Press.

ADDITIONAL RESOURCES

Blass, T. (2000). *Obedience to authority: Current perspectives on the Milgram paradigm* (pp. 35–59). Mahwah, NJ: Erlbaum.

Blass, T. (2004). *The man who shocked the world: The life and legacy of Stanley Milgram*. New York, NY: Basic Books.

Occupation

DANIEL BAR-TAL AND NIMROD ROSLER

Occupation of a geographical area and its inhabiting population can be the deliberate or accidental product of a militarized intergroup conflict. Such a state of affairs carries military, political, economic, societal, and legal consequences for both the occupying and occupied societies. But when an occupation persists for a long period, it creates major human, material, psychological, and moral consequences for each of the involved societies and for their relations, affecting all aspects of individual and social life, as well as their image, set of beliefs and values, and codes of behavior.

LEGAL ASPECTS OF OCCUPATION

Definitions for occupation can be commonly found in the field of international law, with important contributions by Adam Roberts and Eyal Benvenisty. These definitions deal with situations where international law considers occupation as a formal procedure that has implications for the relationship between the occupying force and the occupied population. The most prominent characteristic of occupation, according to these definitions, is its temporary nature. Hence, the occupant is forbidden from taking actions that introduce permanent changes in the occupied territory (Benvenisty, 1993). In addition, the legal definitions reveal that occupation is usually seen as a possible unplanned byproduct of military activities, which result in the conquering party ruling a territory that is recognized as belonging to the defeated party. Therefore, such a situation is usually regarded as "belligerent" or "military" occupation. However, the history of the last two

centuries has demonstrated that occupation may also be a long-term outcome of a threat to use force, of agreement and status quo, or may even be created on the basis of peace agreements (e.g., the German occupation of Bosnia in 1939 and of Denmark in 1940). These changes have shifted the emphasis from warlike acts that result in occupation to the phenomenon and its mechanisms.

Accordingly, Benvenisty (1993) defines occupation as "effective control of a certain power (be it one or several states or an international organization), over a territory which is not under the formal sovereignty of that entity, without the volition of the actual sovereigns of that territory" (p. 4). Edelstein (2008) adds that this act refers to temporary control of the territory by a state that does not claim the right of permanent sovereignty over the territory. This addition distinguishes occupation from colonialism or annexation, where the occupant does not necessarily intend to vacate the territory in the future.

Roberts distinguishes between 17 types of military occupation that vary in terms of the circumstances in which they occur, the degree of consent of the occupied society to this action, the identity of the occupying entity, and the former status of the occupied territory. Another important aspect that he notes is the duration of the occupation, which may reflect its essence as well as the goals of the occupant. If the occupation is perceived – by both occupier and occupied – as temporary from the outset, intended to protect the military interests of the occupier and to prevent the occupied territory from becoming a source of instability, then both the occupier and the occupied will likely strive to end it as quickly as possible (Edelstein, 2008).

PROLONGED OCCUPATION

Roberts argues that the legal definition of occupation is based on an implied assumption that it is a temporary state that may end or change status within a short period of time. Accordingly, he suggested that "prolonged occupation" must be regarded as a category that is entirely distinct from temporary military occupation. He defined prolonged occupation as lasting more than five years and continuing even when military hostilities subside or cease. In addition, prolonged occupation raises legal questions concerning the aims of the occupier, who may intend to change the status of the occupied territory. This type of occupation, which has extensive legal, behavioral, and sociopsychological implications, often leads to pressure from the occupied society as well as from the international community to terminate it.

IMPLICATIONS OF OCCUPATION

Looking at history, in most cases of occupation the occupied societies resist the occupation. The resistance can be manifested in political action, civilian disobedience, or other forms of peaceful protest. But in many cases it may also turn to violent actions, such as attacks against the occupying military forces, as well as against the occupying civilian population. The occupier always attempts to prevent the resistance and punish its initiators. Preventive measures take the form of curfews, restrictions, and prevention of free movement by using roadblocks and checkpoints, as well as extensive arrests, torture, and killings. The preventive measures might also reflect the will to punish the resisting occupied groups, which may lead to other retributive measures, such as imprisonment without trial, collective punishment, deportation of individuals and/or mass forcible transfer, demolishing houses, and the use of excessive force against the civilian population that can lead to mass killing and even ethnic cleansing.

In addition, especially during prolonged occupation, the occupying power often

takes different actions that serve its ideological, political, economic, military, and social interests (Gordon, 2008). Examples of these direct actions may include confiscation of land, placement of civilian settlers from the occupying state in the occupied territory, utilization of natural and economic resources of the occupied land, economic exploitation of the occupied population, institutionalized discrimination of the occupied population – the list goes on. In addition, the occupying force might also strive to maintain its superiority and domination by exercising control and surveillance over the local population. In order to accomplish such domination, the occupant may control the occupied population's political, social, economic, educational and health systems, other systems, and movement and migration, as well as preventing their social, economic, and cultural development. These actions cause significant offense to the occupied population as a collective and as individuals. Individuals living under prolonged occupation and its consequent vicious circle of coercion, resistance, and violence, not only suffer physically but also may suffer from complex chronic post-traumatic symptoms, as well as pessimistic personal and national future orientation (Lavi & Solomon, 2005). On the collective level, the occupation and its consequent circle of violence may cause dramatic demographic changes in the occupied society, put difficult constraints and eventually harm its economic situation, social structure, education system, and cultural heritage (Aruri, 1983).

In addition, an occupation cannot operate in isolation from the occupying society, which cannot seal itself from it. Occupation as a military–political–societal–economic–cultural system, which inherently includes both the occupied and occupying societies, has interactive features that influence both societies. This premise receives special support in cases in which the occupation is prolonged and when the occupier not only penetrates the spaces of the occupied territories but also settles in these spaces, which are perceived as a continuation of the homeland territory. Despite the occupying force's belief that it can control the occupied society and the territory, in reality it begins to lose its grip, and processes gradually evolve and extend into the occupying society that are beyond control. These processes touch upon every aspect of the collective life of the occupying society, including the military, political, societal, economic, and cultural domains. In most cases they have negative effects (Bar-Tal & Schnell, 2010).

Finally, the offensive actions commonly taken by the occupier are intolerable on the international, societal, and individual levels in terms of basic moral codes that developed in the last century (Rosler, Bar-Tal, Halperin, Sharvit, & Raviv, 2009). On the international level, they contradict the principles of self-determination, political independence, and territorial integrity that gained worldwide acceptance as basic moral principles of states and collectives. On the societal and individual levels, they violate various moral principles that are the bases of universal human rights, such as the dignity of human life, and the right of individual and collective freedom and independence. All these principles are well anchored in various international declarations, agreements, and conventions.

PSYCHOLOGICAL ASPECTS OF OCCUPATION

Halperin and his colleagues (Halperin, Bar-Tal, Sharvit, Rosler, & Raviv, 2010) proposed that a comprehensive analysis of occupation must include a sociopsychological perspective in addition to the formal–legal aspect. This approach regarding the psychology of the occupation adopts a contemporary Western view of this reality, which is informed by liberal–moral values and norms that have developed since the end of World War II. Therefore, from a psychological perspective, the term occupation has negative connotations: it indicates an inherent conflict of interest between occupier and occupied; it means that the context is characterized by violence; it reflects wrongdoing, injustice, and immorality; it involves a large degree of empathy toward the occupied and a negative attitude toward the occupier, and it conveys an expectation that the situation is temporary and will be terminated.

In most cases the occupied group objects to occupation, does not accept it, and experiences negative feelings, believing that it violates its basic rights. At the same time, occupation also poses great challenges to the occupying society regarding how to cope with the situation. The occupying society tends to avoid using the term occupation as a reference to its own acts because of its psychologically negative meaning. The central sociopsychological challenge that an occupying group faces is resolution of the discrepancy between the positive manner in which the group members perceive themselves, on various levels, and their role as occupier with all its negative implications. This discrepancy may induce a psychological state of cognitive dissonance, which creates discomfort and subsequently a drive to reduce the inconsistency between the group members' behaviors and their perceptions of themselves. An emotional experience of guilt is yet another possible result of the self-discrepancies between the "actual self" – occupying group members' perceptions of their behavior – and the "ought self" – their perception of their responsibilities and obligations according to moral values. (See GUILT, PERSONAL AND COLLECTIVE.) Although only some members of the occupying group are directly involved in actions that violate moral standards, many of the group members potentially may experience negative feelings. Thus, one of the challenges that an occupying society faces is coping with the evoked negative feelings in attempts to reduce them.

In order to cope with such challenges, Halperin and his colleagues suggest that individuals and societies may develop and use a set of psychodynamic mechanisms such as repression, denial, avoidance, projection, intellectualization, and rationalization. In addition, members of an occupying society develop a system of societal beliefs, which provides justification for its goals and actions, constructs a positive collective self-image of the occupying group, and delegitimization of the occupied nation. (See DELEGITIMIZATION; SYSTEM JUSTIFICATION THEORY.)

SUMMARY

Occupation is usually defined in legal terms and considered a temporary state following belligerent actions. Of special importance is the fact that it inherently involves actions breaching basic moral principles concerning the occupied society by agents of the occupying society, especially when it becomes prolonged. Thus, it has important sociopsychological implications for the occupied and the occupying societies. On the one hand, occupation leads to rejection of and resistance by the occupied population; on the other hand, it often has negative effects on the occupying society in many spheres of life. It also poses a challenge to the occupying society of how to explain this situation in view of the need to maintain positive self-image and be accepted by the international community.

SEE ALSO: Delegitimization; Guilt: Personal and Collective; System Justification Theory.

REFERENCES

Aruri, N. A. (Ed.). (1983). *Occupation: Israel over Palestine*. Belmont, MA: Association of Arab-American University Graduates.

Bar-Tal, D., & Schnell, I. (Eds.). (2010). *Impacts of occupation on occupiers: Lessons from the Israeli occupation of the West Bank and Gaza Strip*. Book submitted for publication.

Benvenisti, E. (1993). *The international law of occupation*. Princeton, NJ: Princeton University Press.

Edelstein, D. M. (2008). *Occupational hazards: Success and failure in military occupation*. Ithaca, NY: Cornell University Press.

Gordon, N. (2008). *Israel's occupation*. Berkeley: University of California Press.

Halperin, E., Bar-Tal, D., Sharvit, K., Rosler, N., & Raviv, A. (2010). Social psychological implications for an occupying society: The case of Israel. *Journal of Peace Research, 47,* 59–70.

Lavi, T., & Solomon, Z. (2005). Palestinian youth of the Intifada: PTSD and future orientation. *Journal of American Academy of Child and Adolescent Psychiatry, 44,* 1176–1183.

Rosler, N., Bar-Tal, D., Halperin, E., Sharvit, K., & Raviv, A. (2009). Moral aspects of prolonged occupation: Implications for an occupying society. In S. Scuzzarello, C. Kinnvall, & K. Monroe (Eds.), *On behalf of others: The morality of care in a global world* (pp. 211–232). New York, NY: Oxford University Press.

ADDITIONAL RESOURCES

Bornstein, A. (2008). Military occupation as carceral society: Prisons, checkpoints, and walls in the Israeli–Palestinian struggle. *Social Analysis, 52,* 106–130.

Othering of People and Phenomena

HÉLÈNE JOFFE

This article delineates the role played by "othering" in the formation of people's identities and in their responses to mass threats. Cultural theory, most notably that of the modernist theorist Edward Said, utilizes the notion of othering to explain Western ways of subordinating certain peoples and thereby constructing superior identities. Drawing on psychoanalytic and social psychological theories, this article demonstrates that the process by which people buttress their own sense of identity by locating undesirable qualities in others is not necessarily culture specific. Such processes lie at the root of identity formation.

The concepts "the other" and "othering" are central to a theory of identity and identity formation. This article adopts, but later critically reflects upon, the definition of the other prevalent in modernist cultural theory. Here the other signifies those outside of, and implicitly subordinate to, the more dominant groups. The other includes groups lacking in power within a particular society (such as women), identified outgroups (such as gay people), and "foreigners." Othering is the location of negative aspersions, and often blame for societal problems, with the other.

A crucial means by which people forge their identities lies not merely in what they affiliate with (such as gender or ethnic categories), but also by comparisons with other groups, in which they emerge as the superior party. Gaining a positive sense of identity through comparison with negatively valued groups is common in contemporary and earlier Western societies alike (Said, 1978). A fifth-century BCE Athenian was as likely to gain his sense of identity from being defined as a non-Barbarian as from positively feeling like an Athenian. Similarly, a nineteenth-century bourgeois person continually defined the self through the exclusion of what (and who) was marked out as "low" in terms of being dirty, repulsive, noisy, or contaminating. This exclusion, which still prevails in the middle classes, is constitutive of identity (Stallybrass & White, 1986).

Africans have provided a prototypical example of the lowly, "uncivilized" other for Europeans who have buttressed their

positive sense of identity by way of this representation. The written work of psychiatrists in Africa in the first half of the twentieth century shows that the African was described in terms of everything that the European was not: savage, lazy, violent, and sexually promiscuous (McCulloch, 1995). These qualities were the very antithesis of the order, reason, moral standards, discipline, sexual continence, self-control, and altruism attributed to the European. This emphasis on the virtues of Europeans and the supposed vices of others has a long history. It reflects and perpetuates a representation in which culture and civilization are associated with white races, and nature with black races.

These examples demonstrate that Western understandings of "others" contain a particular set of interrelated features. First and foremost, the other is construed as fundamentally different from the European. Second, the other is viewed in terms of two extremes: highly debased but also, perhaps less obviously, extremely admirable and enviable; as a corollary of their association with nature, others are invested with excessive sexuality, emotionality, and spirituality (Said, 1978); having not kept pace with Western notions of progress they are seen to possess animal eroticism (Fanon, 1992). Thus, others are imbued with, and lauded for, the very qualities that are surrounded by taboo in the rational climate of Western culture. While such qualities may be admired, those associated with them can, simultaneously, be the objects of debasement. The other can excel in activities regarded as peripheral to the workings of civilized society, such as sport and dance, without threatening a sense of Western superiority. (See ETHNOCENTRISM.) Westerners do their "identity work" (Crawford, 1994), they mark out what it is to be a "good" and upright citizen precisely by way of devaluing certain qualities. Thus, a third feature of Western understandings of the other is that cultures think of themselves in terms of hierarchies in which some elements are "high" and others "low." The low elements are associated with the other, the high with dominant groups. (See SOCIAL DOMINANCE THEORY.)

While such theorization provides a valuable way into key processes that underpin identity work, the centrality of the European/non-European dichotomy has given way to a less centralized notion of intergroup relations in late modernist thought. In the multicultural environments in which people live, they do their identity work via construction of differences between their ingroup(s) and a range of others, whom they associate with a mixture of debased and enviable qualities. However, the process is not solely a relativist one in which each group projects onto groups less powerful than themselves. Ideological processes still constrain who and what can be regarded as superior and who and what inferior.

OTHERING AND CRISES

Representations of others' difference, their debased and low qualities, form a constant feature of society. They leave those in whom debased aspersions are lodged with stigmatized identities. However, the focus on the negative and threatening features becomes intensified in periods of potential threat and crisis. One only has to think of the amplification of anti-Semitism in the German economic crisis of the 1920s and 1930s to be reminded of the salience increasingly accorded to Jews as debased (and envied) others. (See AUTHORITARIAN PERSONALITY.) Or, indeed, with less severe consequences, of the escalation of anti-gay sentiment from the time when AIDS began to affect the West in the 1980s. A multitude of past and contemporary instances could be added to this. However, caution is called for in relation to framing the litany of "hate

crimes" or acts of genocide as responses to crises. Rather, a sense of threat and imminent crisis can sometimes be engineered in order to justify the harsh treatment of others.

In periods where crisis is seen to loom on the horizon, when anxiety is raised, those associated with undesirable qualities move from being represented as mildly threatening, a challenge to the core values of the society, to being linked to the root of the crisis. Thus, while the other is defined in terms of difference and inferiority in relation to normative values in an ongoing sense, the representations that arise at times of crisis intensify this distinction. They reflect a powerful division between a decorous, righteous "us" and a disruptive, transgressive "them." Representations that declare which groups and practices pollute the order and decorum of the community proliferate (Douglas, 1992). They are motivated by communities' impetus to maintain their safety and comfort. The decorum and positive sense of identity of "us" is sustained by imbuing others with devalued properties. Such representations can lead to the desire for the removal of this polluting force. The prototypical act which aims to rid a community of impure elements is scapegoating, a ritual that transfers evil from inside to outside the community (Douglas, 1992). The other occupies a similar role to the scapegoat.

THE ROOTS OF OTHERING

A psychoanalytically informed social psychological theory (Joffe, 1999) can elucidate the psychological counterpart and psychic roots of scapegoating or othering and its consequences for the people who scapegoat. While the emphasis has been on the function of othering in Western contexts, this allows for a broader, nonculture-specific perspective on the phenomenon.

A development of Freudian ideas in the work of Melanie Klein illustrates that infantile representations are oriented towards protection of the self from anxiety. To accomplish this, the other becomes the repository of material that the individual seeks to push out from its own space, to locate externally. These early building blocks of what is to be associated with others, rather than the self, leave their mark on the developing identity. When changes in the social environment make for insecurity, thereby raising levels of anxiety, forms of this early representational activity in which the other can be fantasized in terms of one's own unwanted thoughts re-emerge. The early pattern of representation, by which the infant handles anxiety, is thereby reproduced in adult life.

Thus, from infancy to later life, when faced with anxiety-provoking situations, people rearrange their representations of themselves and of others unconsciously. People organize their representations in accordance with the struggle for a sense of a boundary between a pure inner space and a polluted outside world. The subjective management of anxiety springs from a relational process in which the self continually strives for protection from negative feelings evoked in it, by projecting unwanted material onto others at the level of representation. Ascribing to othering representations in relation to threatening phenomena relates to a self-protective motivation, but such representations are constituted by the values and ideologies that circulate in the particular communities, cultures, and societies of which all individuals form a part.

Individuals enter a world of existing representations from the very start of life. Representations that circulate in a particular social group prior to the individual being born into it influence identity. Thus identity positionings – such as gender, ethnicity, and sexuality – are imposed upon people via the shared thinking of others. Broader communication systems, such as the mass media, also relay ongoing representations concerning certain identities, which constantly construct and reconstruct identities. Of course, more active processes of affiliation and distancing also build identities.

Identity relates not just to the traditional social categories such as ethnicity, nationality, religion, gender, and sexuality. It is also informed by more nuanced aspects of the sense of self, which can relate to core values in the culture. One core value in Western cultures, for example, is that of self-control, in particular, over the body, mind, and destiny (Joffe & Staerklé, 2007). Those who violate the core values of a particular society are often chosen for othering. This value accounts for several categories of others, ranging from the obese to the poor, from addicts and welfare recipients to "mad" people. Such others tend to symbolize the counterpoint of what dominant groups would like to be constituted by in the West – selves in control of body, destiny, and mind.

In the ideas passed down through the generations, social groups store not only a sense of who their disfavored others are, but what aspersions are to be linked to such groups. Thus the particular set of features that Western understandings of others contain – difference, debasement/ admiration, and polarization into high and low – are driven by core values such as self-control.

While there is strong evidence in Western culture for the pattern of othering mapped out in this article, does it generalize beyond the West? Othering and its function as an identity-buttressing process for dominant groups is well established in the feminist literature that pertains to Western and non-Western contexts alike. Similarly, such processes are at work in Western and non-Western stigmatization of people with AIDS. Thus, despite differences across societies and historical periods in the contents of the core values that define who is other, others are objectified in unwelcome qualities well beyond Western cultures, particularly at times of crisis.

In summary, a major foundation of identity formation lies in the human unconscious response to anxiety. This may well be universal. From infancy to later life there is a tendency to strive for protection from negative feelings by making the other the repository for them. However, rather than gaining a firm sense of safety and comfort from othering, those casting the negative aspersions come to experience the other as a threat by way of its association with polluting, contaminating qualities. One comes to fear that which one gets rid of in the project of identity construction. In accordance with the psychoanalytic concept of projective identification, the bad qualities projected onto the other threaten to "leak" back into the space of the self.

CONCLUDING COMMENTS

Othering is a way of protecting self and ingroup; it is defense by way of representation. It also serves the function of status quo maintenance in that each society perpetuates its core values by the ways in which it represents others. The way that a culture defines the other discloses how it characterizes itself (Said, 1978).

However, the use of the other to buttress a sense of superiority is not inevitable. Even if proclivities towards certain patterns of representation are forged in the early years, this in no way diminishes the role played by the slowly unfolding social world in constraining or exacerbating such proclivities. Projection of unwanted aspects of the self onto others can be constrained by laws, norms, and other aspects of the social environment, including upbringing. This lends hope for those who aim to diminish processes of social exclusion. It also challenges pervasive psychological theories concerning the inevitability of negative stereotyping and prejudice.

SEE ALSO: Authoritarian Personality; Ethnocentrism; Social Dominance Theory.

REFERENCES

Crawford, R. (1994). The boundaries of the self and the unhealthy other: Reflections on health, culture and AIDS. *Social Science and Medicine, 38*(10), 1347–1365.

Douglas, M. (1992). *Risk and blame: Essays in cultural theory*. London, UK: Routledge.

Fanon, F. (1992). The fact of blackness. In J. Donald & A. Rattansi (Eds.), *"Race", culture and difference* (pp. 220–240). London, UK: Sage.

Joffe, H. (1999). *Risk and "the Other"*. Cambridge, UK: Cambridge University Press.

Joffe, H., & Staerklé, C. (2007). The centrality of the self-control ethos in western aspersions regarding outgroups: A social representational analysis of stereotype content. *Culture and Psychology, 13*(4), 395–418.

McCulloch, J. (1995). *Colonial psychiatry and "the African mind"*. Cambridge, UK: Cambridge University Press.

Said, E. W. (1978). *Orientalism: Western conceptions of the Orient*. London, UK: Penguin.

Stallybrass, P., & White, A. (1986). *The politics and poetics of transgression*. Ithaca, NY: Cornell University Press.

ADDITIONAL RESOURCES

Joffe, H. (2006). Anxiety, mass crisis and "the other". In A. Treacher & C. Squire (Eds.), *Public emotions* (pp. 161–180). Basingstoke, UK: Palgrave Macmillan.

Joffe, H. (2007). Identity, self-control and risk. In G. Moloney & I. Walker (Eds.), *Social representations and identity* (pp. 197–214). Basingstoke, UK: Palgrave Macmillan.

P

Pacifism, Psychology of

DANIEL M. MAYTON II AND
JONELLE C. MCCOY

The term pacifism is relatively new. It was not in the 1904 edition of *The Complete Oxford Dictionary*. The word popped into common usage not long after, though, to connote antiwar-ism and is attributed to the French, who originated the terms *pacifisme* and *pacifiste* from the French *pacifique*, which generally means to "make peace" or "calm." The 2005 *Merriam-Webster's Collegiate Dictionary* defines pacifism as "opposition to war or violence as a means of settling disputes; *specifically*: refusal to bear arms on moral or religious grounds." This simplistic definition belies the very complex and nuanced incarnations of pacifism.

It's no coincidence that pacifists are oftentimes mistaken for passivists. The mishap is especially understandable among English speakers, as "passivist" is nearly a homonym for "pacifist." Some pacifists certainly take issue with this association. Rather than thinking of pacifists as submissive or passive, pacifists should be characterized as actively resisting violence. In fact, some people use the terms pacifism and nonviolence interchangeably. Little (1995) considers pacifism to be a theory about the use of nonviolence in a specific situation.

Yoder (1992) has catalogued over two dozen distinct types of pacifism. Little (1995) places all these types of pacifism into two major underlying themes: (1) pragmatic or situational and (2) principled or absolute. Pragmatic pacifism is characterized by resisting violence up to a point, but allowing for a justification of violence or war in certain prescribed circumstances. Principled pacifism is a stricter form whereby violence and war are not permitted and may be based on religious beliefs or on humanistic moral reasoning (Mayton, 2009).

PRAGMATIC PACIFISM

The first of these two overarching types of pacifism is pragmatic pacifism and one form is the "pacifism of the honest study of cases" (Yoder, 1992). This type of passive – also called just-war – pacifism is an excellent example of pragmatic pacifism as it dictates "that war might sometimes be justifiable"

The Encyclopedia of Peace Psychology, First Edition. Edited by Daniel J. Christie.
© 2012 Blackwell Publishing Ltd. Published 2012 by Blackwell Publishing Ltd.

and follows the principle that "every ethical decision must be made concretely" (p. 23). In other words, there can be no absolute stance of nonviolence for all situations because particular cases or situations should be studied and evaluated on the merit of their cause, the authority under whose name it is undertaken, and the methods used. Yoder notes "there is nothing new about the fundamental principles behind this position. The doctrine of the just war has been the official position of all western Christian communions since the Crusades, with the exception of a few tiny 'peace churches' and a few solitary prophets" (p. 24). Indeed, many people believe there are certain circumstances in which a justification of a particular war is warranted, especially in relation to defensive purposes. (See JUST WAR THEORY.)

Another prominent variation of pragmatic pacifism is seen in many self-proclaimed pacifists who reject all war but consider violence used for personal self-defense or the defense of an innocent third party as reasonable and appropriate (Yoder, 1992). The idea of war and violence can seem vague and impersonal, but the argument can be framed in an immediate and personal way by asking what would someone do if a loved one was being threatened by someone else. Generally, a person instinctively wants to protect them and this would be appropriate for this type of pragmatic pacifist. Because people do not like to feel helpless or unhelpful, it follows that people, even pacifists, might leap to defend her/himself or help someone who cannot help or defend themselves. Pragmatic pacifists could still reject war by saying war is not only different in scale to self-defense but it creates a culture of hostility because of the necessity to prepare for it in advance through societal institutions, budgets, and professions (Yoder, 1992).

The "pacifism of prophetic protest" considers pacifistic behavior as a form of communication. From this perspective what a pacifist's action says to the oppressor is as important as the rightness or wrongness of the act itself. The implicit moral meaningfulness of pacifism from this perspective is both the rationale and what is to be communicated. Other types of pragmatic pacifism include "pacifism of programmatic political alternatives" and "pacifism of nonviolent social action." These approaches claim either that war is not a viable solution to any conflict or problem or that nonviolent social action is a better and more just path to follow when confronting a challenge to one's goals. Practicality is the major determinant in choosing a pacifist position in both of these varieties of pacifism (Yoder, 1992).

PRINCIPLED PACIFISM

Principled pacifists believe nonviolence is a moral imperative that allows for no situational exceptions. Their position may be derived either from religious beliefs or humanistic moral reasoning. Yoder describes a typical principled pacifism in the "pacifism of absolute principle." This form of pacifism holds that the sanctity of human life is an inviolate principle. The underlying belief is that human beings "have to be guided, by meaningful general directives, received from beyond [them] selves, and bearing authority over [them]" (Yoder, 1992, p. 34).

Other types of pacifism are driven by principles and provide various criteria and mechanisms that determine why and when war is to be avoided. The "pacifism of absolute consciousness" presumes that the determination of the appropriateness of a war lies within the individual and that the individual will know immediately whether it is right or wrong. Since this type of pacifism is void of any religious or moral criteria to determine the characteristics of a particular war, its reliance on an individual's subjective sincerity has been noted as a serious shortcoming. The "pacifism of categorical imperative" uses a society based criterion to determine how best to respond to a war. Specifically, how would a situation turn out if a pacifistic approach became public policy and everyone followed it? While the argument in favor of this type of pacifism has elements within the "golden rule," this view also has logical limitations (Yoder, 1992).

Notably, traditions of principled pacifism (with and without some exceptions to principle) exist in Hinduism, Jainism, Buddhism, Judaism, Christianity, and Islam (Mayton, 2009; Smock, 1995). For these religions, principled pacifism supports the idea that humankind's earthly reality is transitory or an illusion and nonviolence will be rewarded and/or violence will be punished by a higher power.

An integral part of Hinduism and Jainism is *ahimsa* or nonviolence. (See NONVIOLENCE, PSYCHOLOGY OF; NONVIOLENT DISPOSITIONS.) *Ahimsa* is a virtue that renounces the everyday violence of the real world. In these traditions violence and war come from attachment to the material world and so nonattachment and nonviolence bring the practitioner closer to a larger truth, to enlightenment. *Ahimsa* is also linked to the idea that all sentient beings are interdependent. For Jains, this implies that by hurting any other sentient creature, you are in some way hurting yourself – though it may not be immediately apparent. Thus, Jains are principled vegetarians (Mayton, 2009).

While all the major Abrahamic religions (Judaism, Christianity, and Islam) speak to the correctness of violence in certain situations, each also supports some level of pacifism in their teachings and doctrine. For instance, Christianity holds a person's life on earth is short and should be modeled on God's commandments as related by Jesus. Since Jesus espoused "blessed are the peacemakers" in his Sermon on the Mount

(Matthew 5:9), and then went on to nonviolently resist his trial and crucifixion, it follows that principled pacifism is a way to be like Jesus and therefore closer to God. Christianity also holds that God will provide strength to endure worldly suffering and a reward for those committed to principled pacifism. Christianity as a whole has not always followed principled pacifism. Indeed, from the Crusades to now, pragmatic "just war" Christians have both tolerated and perpetrated violence in the name of God. However, there are also certain historic peace denominations of Christianity that strictly follow principled pacifism and reject all war and violence, such as the Religious Society of Friends (Quakers), Church of the Brethren, and Mennonites (including Amish) (Smock, 1995).

While Western and Eastern traditions have separate histories, the dawn of the twentieth century saw the convergence of their ideas. Communication and travel enabled distant thinkers like Thoreau and Tolstoy to influence Gandhi. In turn, Gandhi was an inspiration to Western pacifists including Albert Einstein, Bertrand Russell, and later Martin Luther King, Jr. Like Gandhi, King claimed that the most important underlying idea of pacifism is love – specifically *agape*, the Greek New Testament term which refers to disinterested brotherly love. King elaborates on the connection between *agape* and *ahisma* by saying: "In the final analysis, *agape* means recognition of the fact that all life is interrelated. All humanity is involved in a single process, and all men are brothers. To the degree that I harm my brother, no matter what he is doing to me, to that extent I am harming myself" (King, 1986, p. 20).

The tradition of practicing principled pacifism for entirely nonreligious reasons has a long history, extending back to Greek thinkers like the Stoics and Socrates. Stoics believed that life was full of pain, and that the best way to deal with life is through disciplined tranquility. The Stoic Epictetus lived most of his life as a slave enduring terrible abuse from his master, but upon achieving his freedom he espoused tolerating with dignity the abuses of an unjust world and love for one's enemies. In the *Crito* Socrates states that one "ought not retaliate or render evil for evil to anyone, whatever evil we may have suffered from him" (Plato, 1961, 49d). When Socrates was condemned for poisoning the minds of youth, he resisted aid from those who would have helped him flee to safety, instead choosing to stay and drink a cup of poisonous hemlock. Like many religious martyrs, Socrates so believed in his principles that he would rather die than break them.

In more recent history nonreligious principled pacifism has been practiced by humanists. In 1793 the French philosopher the Marquis de Condorcet proclaimed, "Once people are enlightened . . . they will gradually learn to regard war as the most dreadful of scourges, the most terrible of crimes." Nall (2009), founder of Humanists for Peace, calls for the protest of war based on the assertion within the *Humanist Manifesto III* that people have a responsibility to lead ethical lives that both enable personal fulfillment and the greater good for humanity.

Whether the pacifist is pragmatic or principled, humanistic or religious, the beliefs of pacifists are against war and violence at some level. In some cases pacifists are fervently against all war and all forms of violence; however, there are many types of pacifism that make exceptions to this absolutist position.

SEE ALSO: Just War Theory; Nonviolence, Psychology of; Nonviolent Dispositions.

REFERENCES

King, M. L. (1986). *A testament of hope: The essential writings of Martin Luther King Jr.*

(J. M. Washington, Ed.). San Francisco, CA: Harper and Row.

Little, D. (1995). Introduction. In D. R. Smock (Ed.), *Perspectives on pacifism: Christian, Jewish, and Muslim views on nonviolence and international conflict* (pp. 3–9). Washington, DC: United States Institute of Peace Press.

Mayton, D. M. (2009). *Nonviolence and peace psychology: Intrapersonal, interpersonal, societal, and world peace.* New York, NY: Springer.

Nall, J. (2009). *Saving the soul of secularism.* From http://www.americanhumanist.org/HNN/details/2009–11–saving-the-soul-of-secularism.

Plato. (1961). *The collected dialogues of Plato.* Princeton, NJ: Princeton University Press.

Smock, D. R. (Ed.). (1995). *Perspectives on pacifism: Christian, Jewish, and Muslim views on nonviolence and international conflict.* Washington, DC: United States Institute of Peace Press.

Yoder, J. H. (1992). *Nevertheless: The varieties and shortcomings of religious pacifism.* Scottdale, PA: Herald Press.

Participatory Action Research, Community-Based

SUSAN MCKAY

In researching complex problems such as armed conflict, social injustice, and seemingly intractable health problems, multiple perspectives, including the voices of those who are directly affected, are often marginalized or ignored. Instead, outsiders usually create research questions, develop methodologies, and conduct studies with little or no involvement from the people who are affected. Or the affected population may participate as informants for researcher-constructed surveys and interviews to gather data that the researcher then interprets without "insider" input. Consequently, valuable cultural knowledge and insights are lost when analyzing data, discussing results, and formulating recommendations.

> Community-based participatory action research (CBPAR) offers a contrasting model. Beginning with concerns that exist within a community, CBPAR seeks "to generate knowledge and practice that is of genuine benefit to all co-researchers" (Lykes & Coquillon, 2006). Thus CBPAR is highly-collaborative, bringing cultural insiders together with expert outsiders to develop all phases of the research. Common elements of CBPAR include jointly identifying research priorities within the community; promoting social change; guiding partnerships across sites; generating instrumental and practical knowledge; increasing focus on process (as compared with pre-designated tangible outcomes); and power sharing between the researcher and community. (RTI International, 2004, p. 6)

In addition, decisions are made about who retains ownership of the data and how it will be disseminated. In the context of this discussion, "community" refers to an entity with a sense of shared identity and not necessarily a geographic location. As observed by Lykes and Coquillon (2006), community is a fluid concept that typically is experienced affectively by a "sense of belonging" by insiders. In contrast, outsider researchers tend to define community using descriptive categories because they seek to study "it" or to engage with "it." A core value of CBPAR, which has been strongly influenced by the work and writings of Pablo Freire which emphasize tapping into and engaging local knowledge (Freire, 1970), is meaningful participation, that is, "Nothing about us without us" (Ball, 2005). The focus, therefore, is upon working *with* communities rather than *in* communities (RTI International, 2004). Meaningful participation eschews tokenism such as asking people in the community to share information that furthers the researcher's goals and yet not involving them once

data are obtained or sharing research results. When participation is meaningful, communities are supported in mobilizing on their own behalf (empowerment) rather than outsiders "doing" for them. Furthermore, effective CBPAR recruits study participants though a community focus, utilizes the expertise of community-based staff, discusses study results with community partners, and incorporates community interpretations in disseminating findings and conducting future analyses. (See also CONSCIENTIZATION; PROBLEMATIZATION; LIBERATION PSYCHOLOGY.)

Insiders and outsiders may decide the study design, questions to be asked, measurement tools employed to collect data, interventions used, and how results will be documented and disseminated (Minkler & Wallerstein, 2008). In CBPAR, surveys and questionnaires and other typical social science methods may be used; what may differ is that outsiders work with insiders in designing these, and community members may be responsible for their administration and the interpretation of findings. CBPAR may also use research methodologies such as dramas, poetry, diaries, photography, community murals, videotapes, risk-mapping, Delphi surveys, and other creative methods of tapping into community knowledge and generating cultural data.

A number of models exist for how CBPAR can be structured and implemented – for example, the community may choose to do the research themselves, with researchers facilitating their work; they may engage outside researchers to collect data or to investigate a problem that they have identified but which they do not have the time or inclination to research themselves. Regardless of the model that best fits the community's needs, CBPAR emphasizes relationships and building community capacity which may challenge both researchers and agency partners who may be unaccustomed to sharing power and decision-making. Developing relationships requires significant time, self-disclosure, and care in preparing for the actual research that will be conducted (Ball, 2005).

The process of discovery is an important component of CBPAR. A process-oriented focus can be in opposition to insistence by funders that there be predetermined "outputs." In addition, a concern for sustainable social change is intrinsic to CBPAR – that is, the research is not simply a scholarly exercise but aims to create action that will improve people's lives. This is the reason why, in this essay, I use the abbreviation CBPAR (rather than CBPR, PR, or AR), to emphasize taking *action*. With CBPAR, locally identified concerns become an impetus for research, and key goals are to develop social action and to advocate for change.

Ethical research is central to CBPAR. A key principle is to protect confidentiality and "do no harm" (Wessells, 2009). (See DO NO HARM.) Grounded in relationships of trust and inclusion between researchers and community members, ethical research can be seen in practices such as choosing research questions that have meaning for the people involved, following cultural protocols, and resonating with indigenous ways of knowing when collecting data. Ethical research also emphasizes culturally fair and transparent data measurement and decision-making about the frames of reference that will be used in interpreting and communicating results (Ball, 2005).

CBPAR: A CASE STUDY

Here is a case example of a CBPAR study of girl mothers who returned from armed groups in three African countries – Liberia, Sierra Leone, and Uganda. This study is multi-tiered and involved academics (both cultural outsiders and academics partners who were "insiders" to the culture), partners

in 10 nongovernmental agencies that have child protection programs as a focus of their work, CBPAR personnel at 20 field sites, community advisers, and girl mother participants.

The CBPAR was developed to deepen understanding of how participatory methods may be instrumental in changing the lives of young mothers and of their children through a focus upon the mothers' social transformation and through their empowerment in tackling deep-seated cultural attitudes that stigmatized them. Most of these girls and young women had been abducted and raped or forced to marry bush "husbands" and had consequently become pregnant and given birth to children during their capture. When they returned to their communities pregnant or with children, they were marginalized (Burman & McKay, 2007). Over 650 girls and young women and over 1,200 of their children were enrolled in this CBPAR. Just over 70% of the mothers were formerly associated with armed groups and the remainder were other vulnerable young mothers from the community (Worthen, Veale, McKay, & Wessells, 2010). (See also GIRLS IN ARMED GROUPS.)

In recognition of the widespread marginalization of these girl mothers, a meeting was convened at the Rockefeller Study and Conference Center in Bellagio, Italy, in April 2005 which brought together international experts on child soldiers, policy-makers, national staff of nongovernmental organizations (NGOs) carrying out programs for child soldiers, and researchers. Together we examined concerns about girl mothers and their children and made recommendations. (See also CHILD SOLDIERS.)

A second meeting was held at Bellagio in October 2006 to act upon several of the research recommendations generated from the first meeting, and we decided to use a CBPAR framework. Participants at the second meeting included representatives from various child-protection agencies in sub-Saharan Africa, UNICEF, independent consultants, and four Western academics. We spent the week designing the study, practicing roles that would be useful at our field sites, and building relationships between academics and agency partners. Initially planned for one year, the CBPAR grew into a project that took over three years because of the complexities of implementation and the requirement of adequate time for the girl mother participants to organize and to develop their capacity. In addition, because the CBPAR was unfamiliar to agency staff, capacity-building was integral throughout the study.

The major responsibilities of the Western academics were to provide oversight for the CBPAR, seek funding, secure institutional review board approval, develop a process for assuring confidentiality, consult with country teams in the three countries, work at field sites with agency personnel, and participate in external evaluation of the CBPAR at its conclusion and in the months after funding ended. Western academics also worked in collaboration with an African academic from each country who, in turn, met with girl mother participants and collected data.

Importantly, the girls were always at the center of the CBPAR which began with girls coming together as a group at each site and meeting regularly for mutual support and to develop their social action plans. Most social action centered on education, livelihoods, and health. NGOs learned to trust the girls to make decisions – even if these were sometimes bad decisions. Agency personnel provided counseling, encouragement, funding, and logistical assistance such as training in business skills and health education. Because of varying organizing approaches, cultural distinctions, and decisions made by the girls themselves, the PAR structure differed in each field site and country, although the underlying principle was understood by all: "If the girls aren't doing it, it's not PAR" and "No research without action."

The leadership of the CBPAR project (academics, consultants, and agency partners) met annually for three years to assess learning outcomes and to plan dissemination of study findings.

From this brief description, some key components of this CBPAR emerge:

1. Highly collaborative relationships developed over time as cultural insiders were brought together with expert outsiders to develop all phases of the research. From its beginning, Western outsiders and African insiders learned from each other. The relationship-building and collaboration took place during yearly meetings of the research team, during site visits by Western and in-country academics to speak to the girl mothers, agency implementers at the sites, and community members, and through regular e-mail communication.

2. Recruitment and enrollment of girl mother participants were based on a community focus. To elicit interest in participating, African NGO personnel identified field sites and talked to leaders, stakeholders, and community members – especially women elders – about the CBPAR and its goals. When support was obtained, community members helped identify girl mothers – both those formerly associated with armed groups and other vulnerable girl mothers. In some sites, girl mothers participated in recruiting other girl mothers.

3. Ethical processes were established to assure confidentiality and informed consent. Through a standard protocol that was witnessed by an adult, each girl was informed of how confidentiality would be maintained and of her right to leave the study if she chose. The Institutional Review Board at the University of Wyoming approved the process for the protection of subjects in the study.

4. The focus of the work was on the process of participation and empowerment through social action initiated by the girl mothers. Groups chose their social actions; for instance, some participated in literacy training or farming while others maintained individual small businesses or enrolled in school.

5. Data-gathering methods were creative, using nontraditional approaches to capture data, and included the involvement of girls in the generation of data at each site. The girls were trained in research skills, at their level. For example, in many sites (where girls were literate) they took meeting notes which were full of rich detail. Others videotaped dramas or songs that they had created. These data were retained by the girls and kept in secure places at each site. There was recognition that CBPAR is a process and doesn't lend itself well to pre-established outcome criteria. Over time, funders who had initially requested concrete outputs shifted their focus to how the outcomes evolved from the CBPAR process itself.

6. Survey instruments were created based upon indicators identified by the girls and pilot-tested by in-country academics. Instruments were created using indicators the girls themselves had established. They were field-tested by in-country academics with feedback on wording provided by all team members. Finally, they were administered by teams of African academics in each country and analyzed by a Western epidemiologist who was one of the CBPAR academics.

7. Dissemination was a collaborative effort of the entire team. A final report of the CBPAR was disseminated with all members of the CBPAR team listed as authors. The report was written by Western academics based upon data collected from all sites and at meetings. Team members provided feedback before the final edited version was distributed via the Internet. Individual team members also authored their own papers according to dissemination principles established early in the development of the CBPAR.

SEE ALSO: Child Soldiers; Conscientization; Do No Harm; Girls in Armed Groups; Liberation Psychology; Problematization.

REFERENCES

Ball, J. (2005). Restorative research partnerships in Indigenous communities. In A. Farrell (Ed.), *Ethical research with children* (pp. 81–96). Maidenhead, UK: Open University Press.

Burman, M., & McKay, S. (2007). Marginalization of girl mothers during reintegration from armed groups in Sierra Leone. *International Nursing Review, 54*, 316–323.

Freire, P. (1970). *Pedagogy of the oppressed.* New York, NY: Continuum.

Lykes, M. B., & Coquillon, E. (2006). Participatory and action research and feminisms: Towards transformative praxis. In Sharlene Hesse-Biber (Ed.), *Handbook of feminist research: Theory and praxis.* Thousand Oaks, CA: Sage.

Minkler, M., & Wallerstein, N. (Eds.) (2008). *Community-based participatory research for health: From process to outcomes* (2nd ed.). San Francisco, CA: Jossey-Bass.

RTI International. (2004, July). *Community-based participatory research: Assessing the evidence.* Evidence Report/Technology Assessment No. 99, University of North Carolina, Durham.

Wessells, M. (2009). Do no harm: Toward contextually appropriate psychosocial support in international emergencies. *American Psychologist, 64*, 839–854.

Worthen, M., Veale, A., McKay, S., & Wessells, M. (2010). "I stand like a woman": Empowerment and human rights in the context of community-based reintegration of girl mothers formerly associated with fighting forces and armed groups. *Journal of Human Rights Practice, 2*, 49–70.

ADDITIONAL RESOURCES

For Participatory Action Research see http://
www.PARGirlMothers.com and http://
www.uwyo.edu/girlmothersparsupport/
docs/PAR%20Final%20Report%20June%20
30%202010%20doc.pdf
http://www.ids.ac.uk/go/research-teams/
participation-team
http://www2.bc.edu/~lykes/research.htm

Patriotism and Nationalism

PAUL R. KIMMEL

Patriotism is when love of your own people comes first; nationalism, when hate for people other than your own comes first.

Charles de Gaulle

George Washington cautioned Americans about patriotism in his Farewell Address: "A fire not to be quenched, it [patriotism] demands a uniform vigilance to prevent its bursting into a flame, lest, instead of warming, it should consume." There has been a resurgence of patriotism and nationalism in the United States since 9/11 and the ensuing war on terrorism, which increased a sense of fear and vulnerability in Americans. As Unger (2006) noted: "The events of September 11 were closely followed by enhanced perceptions of oneness with other Americans and a decline in perception of similarity to other people. . . . This pattern of enhanced ingroup identification and disparagement of outgroups is characteristic of nationalism and some forms of patriotism" (p. 83). Christie (2006) wrote "a nationalistic climate was further inflamed by the rhetoric of the US president" (p. 33), mentioning that Bush did not distinguish patriotism from nationalism. This climate resulted in aggression against those identified as threatening us and negative feelings and actions toward those not with us.

In a less threatening time, before World War I and between the world wars, essays written by US psychologists and philosophers made distinctions between patriotism and nationalism, pointing out potential positive and negative connotations of these concepts. Patriotism could be a healthy love of country or a jingoistic cause of war. Nationalism could encompass the civic ties among citizens or be negative internationalism based on a sense of superiority to other nationalities. During and after World War II, however, the healthy and functional aspects of patriotism and nationalism were ignored by social scientists and the more negative implications were highlighted. Early US research on patriotic attitudes in the 1940s and early 1950s gave a jingoistic connotation to patriotism and often equated it with nationalism. The nationalistic fervor of the Axis, especially the Nazis, affected the initiation of studies and the interpretation of their results in this era. For example, a renowned study of authoritarianism was motivated by a desire to understand the rise of Nazi Germany. The ethnocentrism scale of the authoritarian personality measures negative nationalism. During this era there was little interest among social scientists in studying positive aspects of patriotism or nationalism in America. (See AUTHORITARIAN PERSONALITY; ETHNOCENTRISM.)

As the threat and memories of World War II lessened, research on these concepts became more detached. After examining the psychological foundations of patriotism and nationalism, Doob (1964) wrote: "There is no reason to suppose that the personality traits associated with love of country are the same as those connected with hostility toward foreign countries or foreigners" (p. 128). Laboratory and field studies by US psychologists of ingroup attachment and outgroup hostility led to and then supported Doob's conclusion. More nuanced studies of patriotism and nationalism and their correlates culminated in a survey by Kosterman and Feshbach (1989). This study used questions from nine previous US surveys plus 58 original items to generate a 120-item Patriotism/Nationalism Questionnaire. This instrument was administered to 194 students at UCLA, and 24 high school students and 21 building contractors in Washington State. Kosterman and Feshbach's analysis of all their responses found six factors, the first three of which are relevant to this article: Patriotism (affect for America, 12 items), Nationalism (American superiority, 8 items), and Internationalism (global welfare, 9 items). Tests of these factors for reliability and independence showed that patriotism, nationalism, and internationalism are more complex and multidimensional dispositions than earlier researchers had assumed. They also found that these factors were related to differences in country of birth, income, political party, and occupation/student status. These findings were intuitively consistent and suggested that future research should use separate measures of patriotism, nationalism, and internationalism.

Following this advice, Schatz, Staub, & Lavine (1999) found a difference between blind and constructive patriotism. Blind patriots gave unquestioning positive evaluations of and unfaltering allegiance to the United States, while constructive patriots exhibited a more critical loyalty, questioning current group practices that did not promote positive social change. Language idealizing Americanism heightened the nationalistic aspects of blind patriotism. Christie (2006) noted that after 9/11 many political speeches framed the attack in apocalyptic terms and portrayed the US responses as a crusade against evil. This rhetoric elicited blind patriotism and negative nationalism in the American public. It was these feelings and beliefs that made aggressive actions in the Middle East more acceptable, limited civil liberties in the United States, and stifled constructive patriotism.

In 2002 Unger predicted:

> Patriotism and nationalism are double-edged swords. At the same time as they unite us in a common purpose, they make it easy to see others as the enemy – as unlike ourselves. It is possible that the "war against terrorism" will increase "normative" levels of authoritarianism, social dominance, and positivist ideation. It might "just" make people who think in these ways more influential than they have been in recent years. Or, it may give such individuals permission to act against those they perceive to be different from themselves. None of these are positive developments. (Unger, 2002, p. 49)

Unger documented the influence of these factors on students immediately after 9/11. Students who scored higher on positivist ideation (trust in external reality and the legitimacy of external authority rather than their subjective reality) were more likely to endorse militant patriotism than those who scored lower. Moreover, this relationship between positivism and militant patriotism was even stronger six months after 9/11. She concluded: "Once the initial shock of the attacks had worn off, individual differences in worldview became a more important influence on patriot militancy" (Unger, 2006, p. 89). Christie (2006) also called attention to worldview and its defense after the 9/11 attacks, citing Kosterman and Feshbach's (1989) findings on patriotism and nationalism.

Given the importance of worldview in understanding and influencing patriotism and nationalism during periods of personal and national vulnerability, there is surprisingly little theory or research on different worldviews in the patriotism and nationalism literature. An early peace psychologist, William James, suggested such a theory in his address on pacifism in 1906. Like General Washington, he believed that patriotism was necessary, but that in a militarized nation patriotic pride and ambition could lead to war. He theorized that since there were no peaceful countries, evolution had resulted in innate pugnacity and fascination with the horrors of war. As a pacifist, he sought a moral equivalent of war to instill the civic passion and sense of national honor that military discipline provided without war's violence and subjugation of others. He recommended conscription of youth into a national service to battle against nature, an idea that took shape in the Civilian Conservation Corp of the 1930s. Ironically, this successful program was ended by the US entry into World War II, its funding and properties going to the War Department. Are our initiatives for constructive patriotism and civic pride always destined to vanish in times of national threat? (See PEACE PSYCHOLOGY: CONTRIBUTIONS FROM NORTH AMERICA.)

James did not mention the fundamental cause of blind patriotism and negative nationalism in his address: the mindset of the American people (Kimmel, 2006). He realized that "preparation for war is the real war, permanent and unceasing," but living in the US culture of war, he could not envision a culture that did not have a military budget or a negative sense of nationalism. What might peace psychologists suggest to change the mindset of Americans, moving them toward a culture of peace? (See CULTURE OF PEACE.)

One idea that goes back at least to McDougall – who in 1899 saw canoe races used to reduce intertribal war in New Guinea – is to use sports to get those favoring a militant patriotism to let off steam. International competitions such as the World Cup and the Olympics come to mind. While such competitions may reduce blind patriotism and negative nationalism in some of the participants and even postpone or reduce ongoing violence, recent World Cup matches show that they can also lead to increased nationalism (especially among the victors) and violence among the fans. The problem is that the win–lose model of sporting events is not compatible with the empathy and cooperation that are keys to relationships in a culture of peace. Sports cannot provide the moral equivalent of war.

Another suggestion is to use the arts to promote constructive patriotism. The arts have the advantage of engaging people since they are emotional and perceptual. But if the performances that bring peoples together are mainly perceptual (as in dance and instrumental music) it is unlikely that peace cultures that are also conceptual will evolve. The new norms, values, and codes of ethics that must be constructed and externalized require language. So shall we look more toward drama and the cinema and television to move our citizens from a culture of war toward a culture of peace?

At the moment, most of the movies and TV shows in the United States are more likely to increase militant patriotism and nationalism than they are to provide a moral equivalent to war. The action films, programs, and plays reinforce enemy images, black-and-white thinking, the use of violence to solve problems, and other confrontational features of the culture of war. Even films like The Hurt Locker (2008) that won a peace psychology media award in 2010 emphasize heroism and bravado and use the rhetorical framing of our culture of war. The hero had the "most dangerous job in the world" and was seen as fearless and extraordinary by his senior officers and as "a crazy man" by his comrades. It is not surprising that many youth are attracted to the military by such images rather than repelled by war, especially when the enemy absorbs most of the devastation.

Perhaps the most famous antiwar film, All Quiet on the Western Front (1930), works better as a check on blind patriotism and national superiority because it makes the audience more aware of the culture of war's influence on the protagonist as he is recruited into the army and after he returns home from World War I. It also has more emphasis on the inhumanity of war, for example showing the lead character with a soldier that he shot dying in his trench as he tries to save his life. The film, based on a novel by a pacifist, came out in 1930 and was remade in 1979. It was said that Hollywood wanted a more up-beat ending in the remake. But the story is about a German youth and the soldier he shoots is an American. Since they could not let Germany win the war, there was no patriotic ending. It may be that the best antiwar dramas are about the wars of others against us that they lose. But even these dramas do not provide audiences with a moral equivalent to war and may increase their sense of nationalism.

If a culture of war like that of the United States cannot (or will not) use the dramatic arts to change the mindsets of citizens, where else can peace psychologists turn? Perhaps we should consider the noncompetitive and noncommercial use of film, video, and drama, since – as clinicians, teachers and trainers – we are better equipped to work creatively with individuals than with audiences. I have described the use of dramatic role plays with videoed feedback to train individuals and small groups in intercultural exploration (Kimmel, 1995). I have used this engaging training technique to increase thousands of Americans' sensitivity to their cultural assumptions and shown them how to raise their cultural awareness in unfamiliar situations. If we could train and educate more citizens with dramatic techniques like these, we could move beyond our culture of war and find its moral equivalent. The use of intercultural exploration would enable Americans to work together as constructive patriots in a civic culture of peace. William James would be proud, probably recommending a war on climate change.

SEE ALSO: Authoritarian Personality; Culture of Peace; Ethnocentrism; Peace Psychology: Contributions from North America.

REFERENCES

Christie, D. J. (2006). 9/11 aftershocks: An analysis of conditions ripe for hate crimes. In P. R. Kimmel & C. E. Stout (Eds.), *Collateral damage: The psychological consequences of America's war on terrorism* (pp. 19–44). Westport, CT: Praeger.

Doob, L. W. (1964). *Patriotism and nationalism: Their psychological foundations.* New Haven, CT: Yale University Press.

Kimmel, P. R. (1995). Facilitating the contrast-culture method. In S. M. Fowler & M. G. Mumford (Eds.), *Intercultural sourcebook: Cross-cultural training methods* (pp. 69–79). Yarmouth, ME: Intercultural Press.

Kimmel, P. R. (2006). Culture and conflict. In M. Deutsch, P. T. Coleman, & E. C. Marcus (Eds.), *The handbook of conflict resolution: Theory and practice* (2nd ed.) (pp. 625–648). San Francisco, CA: Jossey-Bass.

Kosterman, R., & Feshbach, S. (1989). Toward a measure of patriotic and nationalistic attitudes. *Political Psychology, 10,* 257–274.

Schatz, R. T., Staub, E., & Lavine, H. (1999). On the varieties of national attachment: Blind versus constructive patriotism. *Political Psychology, 20,* 151–174.

Unger, R. K. (2002). Them and us: Hidden ideologies – differences in degree or kind? *Analyses of Social Issues and Public Policy, 2,* 43–52.

Unger, R. K. (2006). Untangling the web: Threat, ideology and political behavior. In P. R. Kimmel & C. E. Stout (Eds.), *Collateral damage: The psychological consequences of America's war on terrorism* (pp. 79–108). Westport, CT: Praeger.

ADDITIONAL RESOURCES

http://plato.stanford.edu/entries/nationalism (Stanford Encyclopedia of Philosophy)
http://scholiast.org/nations/natbiblio.html (a bibliography of nationalism)

Peace, Overcoming Psychological–Cognitive Barriers to

IFAT MAOZ

An important phenomenon in ethnopolitical intergroup conflict is the sides' lack of rationality. Deutsch, a major researcher in the area of conflict, asserts that the great tension that is associated with conflict diminishes intellectual resources for dealing with information and leads to perceptual distortions. Such perceptual distortions and biases can contribute substantially to the maintenance and escalation of conflict (Deutsch, 1973). This article will describe major psychological–cognitive barriers to peace in ethnopolitical conflict and will discuss ways to overcome these barriers. (See CONFLICT RESOLUTION, SOCIOPSYCHOLOGICAL BARRIERS TO.)

NEGATIVE PERCEPTIONS AND IMAGES OF OPPONENTS

A basic cognitive bias in situations of ethnopolitical conflict is that of negative representations and images of opponents, so that they are perceived as having evil intentions, low morality, and inferior traits. Such negative perceptions are manifested in the phenomenon of the diabolical image of the opponent and in the mirror-image phenomenon, where one side's negative images of its opponents reflect, in a mirror image, similar negative images that its opponents have of it. Thus each of the sides in ethnopolitical conflict tends to attribute positive traits to itself and to see itself as moral, fair, and peace-seeking, while attributing negative traits to the opponent and seeing it as immoral, unfair, and aggressive.

In addition to the negative image of the opponent, studies that dealt with ethnopolitical conflicts have also found consistent biases of negative evaluation of behavior ascribed to the opponent. For example, studies of US–Soviet relations demonstrated the use of a double standard where American students evaluated the same actions as more negative when they were attributed to the Soviets and as less negative when they were attributed to the United States.

Similar biases also were found in the arena of the Israeli–Arab conflict. In a series of studies, Heradstveit (1974) interviewed members of the political elites of the two sides to the conflict (members of the Israeli elite and of the Egyptian, Lebanese, and Syrian elites). He found that the sides had a greater tendency to mention and emphasize hostile and extreme behavior of the opponent, with indications of extreme intentions that were low in their credibility taken as indicators of the opponent's belligerent intentions in general. On the other hand, the sides belittled the value of positive indications and moderate actions of the opponent, expressing lack of trust in the "real moderacy" of its intentions.

In addition, the respondents demonstrated a characteristic self-serving attributional bias in conflict. Specifically, respondents used two different norms of attribution, one toward themselves and one toward the opponent. Whereas they tended to explain their own friendly and moderate behavior in terms of internal traits, and their aggressive behavior in terms of external factors, they used an opposite norm of attribution toward the opponent, with its moderate or friendly behavior perceived as imposed on it by the situation and thus as temporary and not reflecting its real inclinations, while its hostile behavior was attributed to internal, and therefore stable, factors.

A similar bias also was demonstrated in studies by Rosenberg and Wolfsfeld (1977). These studies showed that Israeli Jews tend to attribute successes and moral acts of

Israeli Jews to internal factors, while attributing immoral acts of Arabs to internal factors. The Arabs, for their part, attributed failures of Israeli Jews to internal factors. (See ATTRIBUTION THEORY, INTERGROUP CONFLICT AND.)

THE INGROUP FAVORABILITY BIAS

These biases of perception and attribution are characterized in the research literature as manifesting the ingroup favorability bias, with identical behaviors of the ingroup and outgroup being perceived, judged, and given explanations that favor the ingroup.

Evidence of ingroup bias also was found in studies focusing on violent or aggressive behavior. It has been repeatedly demonstrated that people involved in ethnopolitical conflict tend to evaluate given violent or aggressive behavior as more grave and less justified when it is attributed to the opponent than when it is attributed to one's own side. In addition, people involved in ethnopolitical conflict were found to manifest attributions that favor the ingroup, with aggressive behavior of the opponents being attributed to personality factors, while aggressive behavior of one's own group is attributed to situational factors.

Thus, groups involved in a protracted ethnopolitical conflict tend to develop simplistic dichotomous perceptions of "us versus them," in which one's own side is construed as good and just and the other side is viewed negatively, delegitimized, and dehumanized (Bar-On, 2008). These images and perceptions are further disseminated through the educational system and the mass media (Bar-Tal, 2000). Negative images that sides in conflict hold of each other escalate and perpetuate the conflict and impede its peaceful resolution. (See DELEGITIMIZATION; DEHUMANIZATION, INFRAHUMANIZATION, AND NATURALIZATION.)

DEVALUATION OF PROPOSALS FOR THE RESOLUTION OF CONFLICT

Negative perceptions of the other side in conflict underlie another important psychological–cognitive barrier to conflict resolution. The "reactive devaluation" bias refers to the tendency of each side in a conflict to devalue proposals made by the opponents, so that the very fact that the opponent offered a compromise or a peace plan makes it devalued in the eyes of the receiver. In a series of studies on this phenomenon, Maoz, Ward, Katz, and Ross (2002) showed Israeli Jews authentic compromise proposals that were actually exchanged between the sides in the Israeli–Palestinian negotiations. In some of the cases the proposals were presented as offered by the Palestinian official delegation to the negotiations. In other cases, the *same* peace plans were presented as offered by the Israeli official delegation to the negotiation. Interestingly, Israeli Jews evaluated compromise proposals as less fair, less effective, and less beneficial to Israel when presented as Palestinian proposals than when the *same* proposals were presented as coming from Israeli negotiators. Clearly, this bias in evaluation of peace proposals constitutes a serious barrier to the ability of sides in conflict to agree on proposals aimed at the resolution of the conflict. When sides in conflict tend to nearly automatically devalue proposals or peace plans that are offered by the other side, the chances of reaching a mutually acceptable agreement are considerably reduced.

OVERCOMING PSYCHOLOGICAL– COGNITIVE BARRIERS TO PEACE

How can the cognitions and perceptions of each of the sides involved in ethnopolitical conflict be moderated so as to counteract negative images and evaluations and enable a shift towards understanding, agreement, and peaceful relations?

Clearly, cultivating compassion towards the other is a most important step in overcoming the psychological barriers to conflict resolution and fostering peace in disputes between religious, national, and ethnic groups (Bar-On, 2008). Organized dialogue workshops in which the sides meet and discuss their experience and opinions of the conflict have been shown to transform negative images and perceptions and create more positive attitudes towards the other and towards the possibility of resolving the conflict (Kelman, 1999). However, the question remains as to what extent such a positive perceptual transformation endures. How can this effect of organized meetings between the sides be preserved after people return to the harsh reality of the conflict?

Evidently, overcoming psychological–cognitive barriers to peace requires a deeper and more extensive transformation in the messages communicated by the educational system and the media about the other side and about the importance of reaching peace and reconciliation (Bar-Tal, 2000). Such messages should focus on rehumanizing and getting to know the other side better, and encourage each side to learn about the narratives and suffering of the other.

SEE ALSO: Attribution Theory, Intergroup Conflict and; Conflict Resolution, Sociopsychological Barriers to; Dehumanization, Infrahumanization, and Naturalization; Delegitimization.

REFERENCES

Bar-On, D. (2008). *The Others within us: Constructing Jewish-Israeli identity.* New York, NY: Cambridge University Press.

Bar-Tal, D. (2000). From intractable conflict through conflict resolution to reconciliation: Psychological analysis. *Political Psychology, 21,* 761–770.

Deutsch, M. (1973). *The resolution of conflict: Constructive and destructive processes.* New Haven, CT: Yale University Press.

Heradstveit, D. (1974). *Arab and Israeli elite perceptions.* Oslo, Norway: Oslo University Press and Humanities Press.

Kelman, H. (1999). Transforming the relationship between former enemies: A sociopsychological analysis. In R. Rothstein (Ed.), *After the peace: Resistance and reconciliation* (pp. 193–205). London, UK: Lynne Rienner.

Maoz, I., Ward, A., Katz, M., & Ross, L. (2002). Reactive devaluation of an Israeli and a Palestinian peace proposal. *Journal of Conflict Resolution, 46*(4): 515–546.

Rosenberg, S., & Wolfsfeld, G. (1977). International conflict and the problem of attribution. *Journal of Conflict Resolution, 21,* 75–103.

ADDITIONAL RESOURCES

Ross, L. (1995). Reactive devaluation in negotiation and conflict resolution. In K. Arrow, R. Mnookin, L. Ross, A. Tversky, & R. Wilson (Eds.), *Barriers to the negotiated resolution of conflict* (pp. 26–33). New York, NY: Norton.

Ross, L., & Stillinger, C. (1991). Psychological barriers to conflict resolution. *Negotiation Journal, 7,* 389–404.

Staub, E. (2000). Genocide and mass killing: Origins, prevention, healing, and reconciliation. *Political Psychology, 21,* 367–382.

Peace, Positive and Negative

JOHAN GALTUNG

Any concept of peace includes the absence of direct violence between states – engaged in by military and others – in general and the absence of massive killing of categories of

Table 1 Matrix of key terms about positive and negative peace

Violence	Direct violence *Intended harming, hurting*	Structural violence *Unintended harming, hurting*	Cultural violence *Intended or unintended, justifying violence*
NEGATIVE PEACE	[1] absence of = ceasefire	[2] absence of = no exploitation; or no structure = atomie	[3] absence of = no justification; or no culture = anomie
POSITIVE PEACE	[4] presence of = cooperation	[5] presence of = equity, equality	[6] presence of = culture of peace, and dialogue
PEACE	negative + positive	negative + positive	negative + positive

humans in particular. All these absences of types of violence add up to negative peace; as by mutual isolation, unrelated by any structure and culture. This situation is better than violence, but it is not fully peaceful because positive peace is missing in this conceptualization. Indeed, peace would be a strange concept if it did not include relations between genders, races, classes, and families, and did not also include absence of structural violence, the nonintended slow, massive suffering caused by economic and political structures of exploitation and repression (Galtung, 1985); and if it excluded the absence of the cultural violence that legitimizes direct and/or structural violence (Galtung, 1990). Table 1 provides an overview of key terms about positive and negative peace.

This gives us six peace tasks: eliminating the direct violence that causes suffering, eliminating the structures that cause suffering through economic inequity – or, say, walls once placing Jews, now Palestinians, in ghettos – and eliminating cultural themes that justify one or the other. The task known as ceasefire is only one-sixth of a complete peace process. But then come the three tasks of building direct, structural, and cultural peace. The parties exchange goods, not "bads," not violence. The structural version of that builds cooperation and sustainability into the structure, with equity for the economy, and equality for the polity.

The goal is to build a structure based on reciprocity, equal rights, benefits, and dignity – "what you want for yourself you should also be willing to give the Other" – and a culture of peace, confirming and stimulating an equitable economy and an equal polity. (See CULTURE OF PEACE.) Economic equity stands as a very weak, undeveloped field in economic theory and practice, with the social, economic, and cultural rights of the Human Rights Convention (December 16, 1966) not yet ratified by a leading state in the state system, the United States. Political equality covers issues of democracy (one person one vote) and human rights, not only within countries, but also among them. Political scientists have been far ahead of economists in giving meaning to equity.

Applying the concepts of positive and negative peace to a couple, violence can be physical (e.g., spouse-battering) or verbal; negative peace is the absence of all that, passive coexistence; positive peace is active love, the union of body, mind, and spirit. Thus, negative peace is like a point, neither violence, nor positive peace. Violence is a region of actors exchanging "bads," and positive peace another region of actors exchanging "goodies."

This idea can be developed further, with two actors, X and Y, avoiding suffering (Sanskrit *dukkha*) and pursuing fulfillment (Sanskrit *sukha*). X and Y can now relate to each other in three ways: (1) they go up or

```
                    Y
Quadrant IV        +9      Quadrant I
                   +8
                   +7
                   +6
                   +5
                   +4
                   +3
                   +2
                   +1
X -9 -8 -7 -6 -5 -4 -3 -2 -1  0 +1+2+3+4+5+6+7+8+9 X
                   -1
                   -2
                   -3
                   -4
                   -5
                   -6
                   -7
                   -8
Quadrant III       -9      Quadrant II
                    Y
```

Figure 1   Reference diagram on which to map the concepts of coupling, decoupling, recoupling.

down the *dukkha–sukha* gradient together; (2) when one goes up the other goes down, and vice versa; or (3) there is no relation between X and Y. In other words, high positive correlation, high negative correlation, or little or no correlation. The correlations are diachronic, not synchronic, identifying trajectories; or symbiosis, antibiosis, abiosis.

Figure 1 presents a diagram with an X axis and a Y axis, each axis running from −9, extreme suffering ("I want to leave this life") to +9, extreme fulfillment ("I want to stay here forever"), crossing each other in the origin of neither–nor.

The diagram has a main diagonal from −9,−9 through the origin to +9,+9 where the two parties enjoy maximum fulfillment, singly or jointly in positive harmony (in

Quadrant I), and maximum suffering, singly or jointly in negative harmony (in Quadrant III). "Harmony," then, does not mean joy, happiness, but "attuned," for good as also for bad.

However, on the diagram's bi-diagonal, from −9,+9 in Quadrant IV to +9,−9 in Quadrant II, the dyad, singly or jointly, experiences the disharmony of fulfillment for one and suffering for the other, with origin as neither–nor.

Let us now tilt the diagonals toward the X axis, starting with the main diagonal. X and Y still grow or suffer together. But a great gain for X is now a small gain for Y; and a great loss for X is a small loss for Y. There is asymmetry, inequity, parasitism. For the bi-diagonal, a great gain for X is only a small loss for Y, and vice versa. So also for Quadrant III: tilting links a great-suffering increase for one to a small one for the other, and in the asymmetric Quadrants II and IV even more so.

If we focus on the main diagonal in Quadrant I we get the "peace diagonal" in the transcend method, with 0,0 as negative transcendence (neither–nor), passing through compromises to +9,+9, positive transcendence (both/and in terms of goal fulfillment). The bi-diagonal in Quadrant I is the "war diagonal" of the either/or: at +9,0 X prevails, at 0,+9 Y prevails, with stalemate in the middle, on the peace diagonal known as compromise. To this can then be added curvilinear trajectories telling more complex stories. In short, this intellectual space can accommodate "grand" peace theory, and *dukkha/sukha* enables us to identify and locate its components.

But we need a concept bridging the singly vs. jointly divide above; coupling, showing up as diachronic correlation, X and Y tracing a trajectory in this diagram jointly, like a couple, in harmony or not. High covariation means strong coupling, low means weak and zero/no coupling. Decoupling is the process from high to no coupling, the reverse process is recoupling; like a married couple separating, divorcing, and then remarrying.

A couple breaking up decouples, explicitly or implicitly, telling each other that "my *sukha/dukkha* is now mine, yours is yours, should they coincide it is by chance only." They may delude themselves and each other, and in the despair over their inability to produce joint fulfillment produce joint suffering, negative instead of positive harmony. Alternatively, they may recouple, or hope for a better coupling to come with the help of "time." But "time" is no substitute for hard work on the relationship. An adolescent leaving the parental home to go his/her own way is obviously decoupling. This may last forever, but with sufficient maturity on both sides, recoupling at higher levels may happen.

Here is one image of coupling, not only in marriage, from daoism: "Share in the suffering of others. Delight in the joy of others. . . . View the good fortune of others as your good fortune. View the losses of others as your own loss." Another is in the Zulu *ubuntu*: "I am in you, you are in me, we are in each other." Both tap definitions of a strong spiritual coupling in a we-culture. The unit of suffering and joy is a we, not two I's.

Compare this to the Golden Rule, positive (or negative): Do (not do) unto others what you (do not) want them to do unto you. The subject for *sukha*, and for *dukkha* avoidance, is an individual, "you." The rule is egocentric, an ethical device for self-satisfaction, highly compatible with abrahamitic individualism. The ethical budget is individual, I-culture, not collective, we-culture oriented. It may not even be very smart; as G. B. Shaw pointed out: "their tastes may be different."

Something of the same applies to the Kantian dictum, *Handle so dass die Maxime deines Willens jederzeit zugleich als Prinzip eines allgemeines Gesetzgebung gelten könne* (Always act so that the thesis underlying your will could serve as a general law). What Kant introduces here is not a we-culture but a traffic rule for individualist coexistence: the validity of an act is linked to its generalizability. Kant wants a multilateral normative umbrella; the Golden Rule is more bilateral. That rule may be useful, if attention is paid to individual and cultural differences, for positive coexistence in an I-culture, but does not produce the *sui generis* union of a we-culture in the daoist sense above, as exemplified in the definition of love.

So far we have degree of coupling, strong versus weak, as illustrated by the perfect versus worn-out clutch, and positive versus negative coupling. But how does coupling come about? Using the pillars of peace studies – nature, culture, and structure – there are three types of answers. Nature produces coupling, the extreme case being Siamese twins, or one-egged twins in general, and siblings; in short, genetic sharing. Being of the same species is already a (weak) coupling. Culture produces coupling as internalized harmony, like in friendship and love. Primary relations (family, school) produce stronger internalization, but also stronger disharmony "when things go wrong." Structure produces coupling as institutionalized cooperation, in secondary relations (school, at work), and in tertiary relations (belonging to the same category, gender, generation, race, class, nation, territory).

Thus, there is inner versus outer coupling, steering us from within by good and bad conscience, and from without by reward and punishment. We-cultures would produce very strong inner couplings. But I-cultures, guided by the Golden Rule and/ or Kantianism, also produce inner couplings, only of a different nature. Love is based on inner we- and I-cultures, and a marriage on an outer social pact, triggering sanctions from all kinds of structures. If one fails, the other coupling devices may still be there.

We can now reap the harvest of all this by linking the concepts of positive and negative peace to the idea of coupling, using the quadrants in Figure 1. Quadrant I is positive peace when there is coupling, positive harmony, and symbiosis; and the more symmetric, equitable, the closer to the diagonal. Quadrant III is violence when there is coupling, negative harmony, and symbiosis; and more symmetric, equitable, the closer to the main diagonal. Quadrants II and IV are fulfillment for one and suffering for the other, negative coupling, disharmony, antibiosis; and more asymmetric, inequitable, the closer to the bi-diagonal, a good illustration of structural violence. The origin is negative peace with both X and Y at the "no peace, no war" point of no coupling–indifference–abiosis.

Quadrant I accommodates not only direct, intended, but also structural, institutionalized peace. Quadrant IV accommodates direct and structural violence. In Quadrants II and IV there must be something strong on the side of the party extracting benefit: structural violence. But the structural elements in Quadrants I and III should not be underestimated: a ritualized marriage may be good for both; wars may be institutionalized like vendettas.

From this we can already draw some conclusions. Positive peace and violence–war are similar in having positive inner or outer (or both) couplings in common, in other words a joint project like a European community, or a world (meaning European) war. Conflict and structural violence are similar in having negative inner or outer (or both) couplings in common, in other words a joint anti-project. Negative peace, like a ceasefire, is a limited and limiting category suitable for dualist minds: violence vs. its absence. Thus, the road from war to positive peace may not be that difficult to travel. Joint projects buoyed by passion are in both, only the content has to be changed. But in negative peace there is little passion, abstention from any joint project, and withdrawal into mutual indifference.

Peace theory and practice are about getting out of Quadrant III direct violence, of Quadrants II and IV structural violence, and into Quadrant I direct and structural, positive peace, beyond bland, negative peace. But how? Gandhi's answer: by decoupling in Quadrants III and II–IV, using nonviolence instead of violence in Quadrant II; using noncooperation, even civil disobedience, in Quadrants II and IV; using constructive action, recoupling, building peace, for Quadrant I.

Gandhi's theory and practice went far beyond Western security theory and practice, the latter with clearly paranoid features. To Gandhi, the level of coupling was the key variable, as opposed to praising peace and blaming violence. The work for positive, or as a minimum negative, peace implies changing interaction relations more than actor attributes, and that is exactly what decoupling and recoupling are about. Great. A genius.

SEE ALSO: Culture of Peace.

REFERENCES

Galtung, J. (1985). Twenty-five years of peace research: Ten challenges and some responses. *Journal of Peace Research*, *22*(2), 141–158.

Galtung, J. (1990). Cultural violence. *Journal of Peace Research*, *27*(3), 291–305.

ADDITIONAL RESOURCES

Galtung, J. (1992). *The way is the goal: Gandhi today*. Ahmedabad, India: Navajivan, Gujarat Vidyapith.

Galtung, J. (1998). *Peace by peaceful means*. London, UK: Sage.

Galtung, J. (2004). *Transcend and transform*. Boulder, CO: Paradigm Press.

Peace and Coexistence Programs in the Israeli–Palestinian and Middle East Context

MOHAMMED ABU-NIMER

In the context of the Middle East, the majority of the peace psychology studies focus on the grassroots and elite intervention efforts to bring peace between Palestinian Arabs and Jews in Israel and in Palestine. Few studies have addressed the psychological factors related to peace in the Arab or larger Middle Eastern societies. Thus this essay will examine some of the possible contributions of these studies to a better understanding of Arab–Jewish relations in the region.

ARAB-JEWISH ENCOUNTERS: FROM DOMINATION TO PARTNERSHIP

In Israel the majority of peace psychology studies since the 1960s have focused on methods of stereotype reduction and, later in the mid-1970s, moved to examine the contact hypothesis and its potential to bring change to Arab–Jewish relations. (See STEREOTYPES; COEXISTENCE EDUCATION; PREJUDICE, TYPES AND ORIGINS OF; CONTACT THEORY, INTERGROUP.) Until the late 1980s, these studies were carried out by Israeli and Jewish American researchers who, in most cases, supported the contact hypothesis and its assumptions about the conflict. Some of these included:

1. overemphasis on the psychology of Arab–Jewish relations and the conflict in general. By focusing the studies and intervention on sorting out interpersonal and individual relations as well as mutual negative images, researchers contributed to the framing of the Arab–Jewish conflict as a case of miscommunication, misunderstanding, and other dimensions of the human relations theories or frameworks.

2. avoidance of structural aspects of the conflict. The majority of the studies that examined Arab–Jewish relations in Israel and Palestine neglected in their analysis to identify the impact of the occupation system and its implications on peace and coexistence programs. The contextual analysis of peacebuilding through dialogue and education for democracy programs was rarely applied by researchers and interveners.

3. acceptance of certain ideological parameters. Arab–Jewish peace programs in Israel accepted the basic definition of the Jewish state without any mutual basic recognition of the rights of Palestinians to the same land as an indigenous population. Researchers who examined these programs followed the same pattern established by the organizers and never questioned the relations between Jewishness of the state and effectiveness of these programs in promoting genuine peace between Arabs and Jewish in Israel or Palestine.

4. the illusion of symmetrical realities. During this period, both peace programs and researchers failed to recognize the asymmetrical nature of the conflict. Researchers of peace and coexistence in Israel failed to recognize the different contextual situations, despite the fact that Palestinian Arabs in Israel and Palestinians in general had lived in different realities than the Israeli Jews (less access to resources, restrictions on movements, militarized zones, deep sense of deprivation of human dignity, etc). These studies made no distinction between a Palestinian, who had been living with no state protection and under an occupation system that produced constant threat to physical survival, and an Israeli citizen, threatened by

the conflict but being served and protected by a powerful state system.

In spite of the above shortcomings, these studies made a significant contribution to the understanding of the psychological dynamics that governed the encounters between Arabs and Jews, both in the peace programs and in public domains. Fear, insecurity, denial, ignorance, and defensiveness were clearly identified as factors that contributed to ongoing destructive Arab–Jewish conflict dynamics.

Since the early 1990s a new wave of studies on Arab–Jewish peace programs began emerging in which some Palestinians and Israeli researchers began identifying the shortcomings of the pure psychological approach in studying Arab–Jewish relations (Rouhana, 1995; Abu-Nimer, 1999; Halabi, 2004; Bekerman & McGlynn, 2007).

Basic conflict analysis tools that examined Arab–Jewish power relations in the context of group identity began emerging as an alternative model to the pure individualized psychological approach to peace and coexistence. Such studies were theoretically situated in both social psychological frameworks and critical theories. These studies asserted that, first, Arabs and Jews have a different set of conflict assumptions and needs; thus peace programs have to be designed differently in order to respond to these nationally distinct needs and expectations. Second, in responding to the root causes of the conflict, Arab–Jewish peace programs need to focus on both individual psychological factors and collective national group identity. The overemphasis on the psychologization and individualization of the parties' identity contributes to the Arab–Jewish asymmetric power relations that exist outside and inside the peace and coexistence programs. Third, confronting conflict issues and differences in perceptions is a necessary step to accomplish deeper understanding of the conflict and between Arab and Jewish

participants. The harmony model of focusing on individual and collective similarities and the basic common human experience is effective as a first step, but it cannot be an end by itself. In the past decade, studies of Arab–Jewish encounters assert that encounter experiences with a process designed to explore both similarities and differences in perceptions of core conflict issues have proven to be more meaningful and effective for the participants (Nadler, Malloy, & Fisher, 2008). (See RECONCILIATION: INSTRUMENTAL AND SOCIOEMOTIONAL ASPECTS.)

BETWEEN LISTENING TO PAIN AND ADVOCATING NONVIOLENT RESISTANCE

Another set of studies that have been examining Israeli–Palestinian conflict is reflected in those peace programs that promote mutual empathy. Such studies have reported on the power of nonjudgmental listening. Similar to the above shortcomings of the Arab–Jewish encounters in Israel, the compassionate listening programs are based on the assumption that listening and deeper understanding can bring healing and change to the situation on the ground. Mostly run by American Jewish nongovernmental organizations (NGOs), the international delegates visit the "Holy Land" for 1–3 weeks with the intention of developing deeper understanding of the conflict and bringing change to troubled areas. The majority of these groups tend to be run within the parameters of the mainstream political ideologies of the two-state solution, countering and eliminating Palestinian terrorism, and countering the narrative of Islamic political religious forces in the region.

An alternative peace program has organized delegations to Israel–Palestine with the intention of gaining a deeper understanding of the conflict from the perspective of the indigenous Palestinian population and with the objective of mobilizing wider awareness among US policymakers; the International Solidarity Movement is a prime example of such a peace and solidarity group that has operated for the past decade in Palestine.

There are no solid studies or research that have examined the psychological dimensions of these peace programs in the region. However, in their edited volume Stohlman and Aladin (2003) captured some of the psychological dynamics associated with international activism in support of nonviolent resistance. There are other nonviolent resistance programs in Palestine operating on the ground and confronting the occupation policies and rules, especially around the issue of the wall. For the past decade, Holy Land Trust and other Palestinian NGOs have conducted training in nonviolent resistance for young activists (see, for example, www.holylandtrust.org).

Nevertheless there are major questions that can be examined in such research – for example, what are the psychological barriers that face peace delegates throughout their exploration of the conflict? When returning to their home environment, how do the delegates handle change in perception as a result of their journey into the conflict? What effect do these delegations have on the American public perception of the conflict?

The nonviolent resistance movement in Palestine will always be limited in its impact if peace programs inside Israel do not engage in a similar active and direct nonviolent resistance. If the bulk of the Israeli peace movement continues to be limited to a camp clustered around its mainstream Zionist ideology (especially Peace Now protest ideology), the effect of nonviolent resistance will be limited. Thus, Palestinians and Israelis who support the nonviolent resistance model need to further coordinate and establish sustainable linkages with each other to enhance their capacity to affect the deep rooted conflict's structural systems.

PROBLEM-SOLVING WORKSHOP

Another major contribution to the understanding of the psychological dimensions of peace in Israel–Palestine is documented in problem-solving workshops, a process that has been mostly practiced and described by Herb Kelman (2001) and other scholars since the early 1970s. In the past three decades, there have been many other studies that have explored the process and impact of the problem-solving workshop model. (See CONFLICT RESOLUTION, INTERACTIVE.) Kelman's social psychological analysis of Arab–Jewish problem-solving encounters conducted in his Harvard lab (dynamics of fear, denial, and recognition) were ground-breaking processes and led to many new studies in the international relations field. Also relevant is the work of Volkan (2001), a psychiatrist who introduced the concept of "chosen trauma" and its impact on deep-rooted conflict dynamics. Volkan's work has focused on Cyprus, Israel–Palestine, and Turkey.

Several conclusions can be made regarding this process of intervention and its effect on conflict dynamics. First, addressing the psychological barriers is a necessary step to establish interpersonal trust among the participants. Without shared and mutual acknowledgement of the victimized identity, participants are unable to shift their adversarial relationships. Second, there is a great deal of scholarly evidence in support of the immediate or short-term impact of these workshops on participants; however, evidence for long-term impact remains lacking. Third, although the participants are often semi-officials who have links to the decision-makers of both sides, problem-solving workshop designers and implementers face major challenges in transferring the impact and change from the individual micro-workshop level to the macro- and collective policy levels. Studies on such mechanisms and on psychological coping mechanisms facing participants in their home environment in the post-workshop phase remain limited. Fourth, the asymmetrical power relations in the design, implementation process, and outcomes of problem-solving workshops have been another limitation for the success of these workshops. Asymmetrical power relations in the problem-solving workshop can be detected when various aspects such as the language, facilitation roles, process, and criteria of success are closely examined to check whether they equally meet the Palestinian and Israeli participants' expectations and realities. (See CONFLICT RESOLUTION, PSYCHOLOGICAL BARRIERS TO; PEACE, OVERCOMING PSYCHOLOGICAL–COGNITIVE BARRIERS TO.)

RELIGIOUS IDENTITY
AND PEACEMAKING

Finally, there are several other areas in which psychological contributions to peace in the larger Middle East context in general and in the Israel Palestinian context in particular have not been explored. Religious peacemaking programs have been carried out, especially after September 11, 2001, events. Christian, Jewish, and Muslim peace workers have launched interfaith peacebuilding programs in countries such as Egypt, Jordan, Lebanon, Turkey, Israel, and Palestine. (For a review of these studies, see Abu-Nimer, Khoury, & Welty, 2007). Despite these efforts, very few studies have focused on the psychological processes associated with religious identity and peace. On the contrary, the majority of the psychological studies that have explored religion in the Middle East have focused their analysis on the connection between religious identity and violence and terrorism (studying the psychological processes and profiles of the suicide bombers, membership and loyalty to terrorist groups, etc.).

More research is needed in regard to the emerging field of religious peacemaking in the Middle East. A few tentative conclusions are: First, interreligious peacebuilding programs are effective in changing individual participant perceptions and attitudes to be more pluralist and less exclusionist. Second, most of the participants in such programs are already willing to meet the other and reach out beyond their religious identity groups (although the motivation for reaching out and attending these programs varies based on the individuals and their group status in the society and conflict). Third, similar to dialogue encounter models in the Israeli–Palestinian context, interfaith dialogue programs in the Middle East are dominated by the members of the majority, and often influenced or shaped by the political regimes' ideology of focusing on harmony, similarities, and avoidance of genuine conflict issues and differences. Fourth, due to lack of coordination, small organizational capacities, and ideological constraints, interreligious peacebuilding efforts remain disconnected from the wider and larger forces of social and political change in these societies and the region in general.

Despite the limitations of the emerging field of interreligious peacemaking, a psychology of peace research agenda in the Middle East context needs to include questions such as: what are the psychological factors that affect the shift in perceptions and attitudes among religious individuals from an exclusionist into a pluralist perspective? What are the most effective processes and strategies to overcome the barriers of fear and denial that characterize many of the interreligious relations, especially in crisis situations? How can the constructive message of interreligious pluralism be institutionally disseminated in the existing religious structures of each faith group?

CONCLUSION

Various psychological frameworks have developed diverse models and strategies to address the complex and deep-rooted aspects of Israeli–Palestinian conflict; however, their impact can be seen mainly on the individual microlevel of perceptional and attitudinal changes. Recently, other identity-based conflict models, such as religious peacemaking frameworks, have emerged as a way to create a space for people from different sides to explore creative possibilities for peaceful coexistence.

SEE ALSO: Coexistence Education; Conflict Resolution, Interactive; Contact Theory, Intergroup; Peace, Overcoming Psychological–Cognitive Barriers to; Prejudice, Types and Origins of; Reconciliation: Instrumental and Socioemotional Aspects; Stereotypes.

REFERENCES

Abu-Nimer, M. (1999). *Dialogue, conflict resolution, and change.* New York, NY: SUNY Press.
Abu Nimer, M., Khoury A. I., & Welty, E. (2007). *Unity in diversity: Interfaith dialogue in the Middle East.* Washington, DC: United States Institute of Peace.
Bekerman, Z., & McGlynn, C. (Eds.). (2007). *Addressing ethnic conflict through peace education: International perspectives.* New York, NY: Palgrave Macmillan.
Halabi R. (Ed.). (2004). *Israeli and Palestinian identities in dialogue.* New Brunswick, NJ: Rutgers University Press.
Kelman, H. C. (2001). The role of national identity in conflict resolution: Experiences from Israeli–Palestinian problem-solving workshops. In R. D. Ashmore, L. Jussim, & D. Wilder (Eds.), *Social identity, intergroup conflict, and conflict reduction* (pp. 187–212). Oxford, UK: Oxford University Press.
Nadler, A., Malloy, T., & Fisher, J. (Eds.). (2008). *The social psychology of intergroup reconciliation* (pp. 345–368). Oxford, UK: Oxford University Press.
Rouhana, N. N. (1995). The dynamics of joint thinking between adversaries in international conflict: Phases of the continuing problem solving workshop. *Political Psychology, 16,* 321–345.
Stohlman, N., & Aladin, L. (Eds.). (2003). *Live from Palestine: International and Palestinian direct action against the occupation.* Cambridge, MA: South End Press.
Volkan, V. D. (2001). Transgenerational transmissions and chosen traumas: An aspect of large-group identity. *Group Analysis, 34,* 79–97.

ADDITIONAL RESOURCES

Saunders, H. H., Diamond, L., Kelman, H. C., Marks, J., Montville, J., & Volkan, V. D. (2000). Interactive conflict resolution: A view for policymakers on making and building peace. In P. C. Stern & D. Druckman (Eds.), *International conflict resolution after the Cold War* (pp. 251–293). Washington, DC: National Academy Press.

Peace and Conflict Studies versus Peace Science

JULIE L. CLEMENS

Grasping the full extent of peace scholarship, given its wide-ranging areas of research and pedagogy, can be quite challenging. Indeed, peace scholarship consists of several academic cultures, which, though related, remain distinct and distant from each other. These separate cultures that have emerged within higher education present obstacles to contemporary peace scholars, who typically have little knowledge about the genealogies of the individual academic peace communities outside their own bailiwick. As Dunn (2005) observes, many participants have "no direct experience of, or memory of, the circumstance in which [the field] developed" and "those who may know of events and context may not be aware of, or misunderstand, the interplay of events, and the consequent effect upon the research agenda and research dynamic" (p. 9). In this article, I explain how peace scholarship came to have disparate communities through a brief historical account of critical events in its growth and development. To that end, the article describes and compares the present-day characteristics of two distinct academic cultures of peace scholarship: "peace and conflict studies" and "peace science."

Peace scholarship was not always balkanized. It began as a loosely organized, but somewhat unified, research endeavor shortly after World War II, when a diverse group of scholars set out to explore how their individual disciplinary specialties and methodological preferences could contribute to the reduction of war. Though divided in their academic disciplines (such as psychology, mathematics, anthropology, and economics), these scholars shared the view that contemporary research on the causes of war conducted by international relations (IR) theorists did not serve their purposes, which were a commitment to "peace" and a deep concern about the threat of nuclear holocaust. Moreover, they believed that their methodological approaches to the study of international conflict, which were mainly positivistic, behavioralist, and empirically driven, would provide a fresh and useful perspective on the matter. Thus, "peace research," as this endeavor came to be formally known, arose among academics who sought to build "a closer bond between social ethics and the scientific method and between the policy process and reproducible evidence" (Singer, 1990, p. 1). Though some IR scholars with similar research methods joined them, these academics were specialists in non-IR fields who believed that their individual disciplinary frameworks and combined commitment to applied science could shed new light on the topic.

In due course, peace research became established as an academic field with several professional outlets, including the Peace Research Society (International), the International Peace Research Association,

the *Journal of Conflict Resolution*, and the *Journal of Peace Research*. Nevertheless, the field, like any organization struggling to develop an identity during its formative years, was not without its share of internal dissent. One significant disagreement centered on whether the field's primary object of study should be conflict or peace. In the United States most peace researchers studied conflict because it "was less controversial (less blatantly normative) than the term 'peace'" (Kelman, 1981, p. 98). Conversely, in Europe (specifically, in Scandinavia) many peace researchers made a conscious decision to analyze the concept of peace, which they believed meant far more than simply the absence of physical violence and war (negative peace) but also a commitment to basic human needs (positive peace). (See PEACE, POSITIVE AND NEGATIVE; PEACE PSYCHOLOGY: DEFINITIONS, SCOPE, AND IMPACT.) This dispute, though simmering for many years, did not boil over or cause serious antagonisms within the field until the late 1960s, when controversy over the Vietnam War triggered two critical events: (1) the "radical critique of peace research" and (2) the "two cultures problem."

The radical critique of peace research was a series of heated debates that began in Copenhagen at the Sixth European Conference of the Peace Research Society in 1969. There, a "radical" group of mostly young European peace scholars issued a declaration criticizing "traditional" peace research for its conservative bias and kowtowing to US policymakers. The spark that lit the powder keg was the publication of a series of nonjudgmental papers regarding the role of the United States in the Vietnam conflict presented at the Conference on Vietnam organized in 1967 by the Peace Research Society in Cambridge, Massachusetts. The impassioned discourse that followed led to a re-examination of the field's epistemological and methodological foundations and brought to the surface deep divisions over the conceptualizations of "peace," "violence," and "research."

According to the "radical" view, peace researchers have a normative obligation to condemn unjust systems and advocate for necessary change. Thus, the goal of peace research should not be merely the prevention of war or the maintenance of peace, but also the *creation* of cooperative structures and systems in which there is a harmony of interests and all members of society are equally rewarded. At the time of the radical critique, Galtung (1969) was already expanding the idea of positive peace to include a social-democratic commitment to universal human rights. The key innovation was what Galtung called structural violence, that is, indirect violence caused by repressive social orders that produce enormous differences between potential and actual human self-realization. More specifically, structural violence refers to chronic, historically entrenched political–economic oppression and social inequality, ranging from exploitative international terms of trade at the macrolevel to exploitative labor markets, marketing arrangements, and the monopolization of services at the microlevel.

After the radical critique, two surveys were conducted during the early 1970s which indicated that the peace research community was divided between two cultures: "humanists" and "scientists." The humanists favored traditional (nonquantitative) and sometimes legal methods and analysis of values and alternative futures, whereas the scientists employed statistical and data-based approaches oriented toward the analysis of observable facts. This divide between the prescriptive/normative approach and the descriptive/analytical approach has been called the "two cultures problem" (Vasquez, 1976). More than 30 years later, peace scholarship remains divided along this central fault line. Today, however, the cultures are rarely referred to as humanist or scientist but rather by the less revealing

monikers of "peace and conflict studies" and "peace science," with humanists working primarily in the former area and scientists in the latter one. A brief discussion of these two distinct areas of peace scholarship follows.

Peace and conflict studies is a transdisciplinary field dedicated to analysis of the causes and consequences of violence, the methods for mediating, reducing, or eliminating it, and the conditions necessary for creating global well-being and peace. The field is organized around three main objectives: to research, educate, and, in varying degrees, actively pursue (or advocate for) peace. Moreover, these objectives are to be accomplished: (1) at all levels of analysis (individual, group, local, regional, global, etc.), (2) across nearly all academic disciplines (political science, history, psychology, sociology, etc.), and (3) in all forums (school systems, communities, organizations, etc.). In short, peace and conflict studies seeks to attain global well-being and expects to achieve this goal through the practical application and advocacy of research developed from a critical examination of multiple frameworks. (See PEACE STUDIES, PSYCHOLOGICAL CONTRIBUTIONS TO.)

Peace science highlights the scientific method in the development of peace analysis and conflict management. Borrowing from relevant work in the social and natural sciences, peace science has as its primary goals the mitigation of armed conflict and the improvement of social science theory as it relates to international relations. In their teaching, peace scientists focus on theory construction, data-making, and hypothesis testing. While mostly associated with quantitative–behavioral research, peace science has recently embraced formal theory, which, though highly mathematical, is embedded in a purely deductive preoperational logic that has been criticized for its nonempirical approach to theory construction and validation.

The contrasting intellectual goals of peace and conflict studies and peace science (prescriptive/normative vs. descriptive/analytical) emerge from and are easily explained by the different research traditions of the two fields. Consistent with the humanist tradition, peace and conflict studies, following the events of the radical critique and the two cultures problem, became the academic community that chose first to appraise and then establish values and norms that would meet the overall needs of society and eliminate violence. Alternatively, peace science became the academic community that continued the tradition of peace research, which was originally motivated by a scientific framework that focused on analyzing issues of war and large-scale conflict to supply reproducible and cumulative evidence.

Although both of the fields have a normative element (viz., each values the discovery of solutions to the scourge of war and violence), they disagree about whether and to what extent this interest should influence and guide peace research. Peace science, for instance, does not let the goal of "finding a solution to war" affect its research designs and strategies. The field stops short of advocating for peace from a political or ideological standpoint and instead champions a removed and detached style of research that seeks to understand causal relationships of conflict. An example of this present-day contrast in intellectual goals is indeed exemplified on the website of the Peace Science Society (formerly, the Peace Research Society), which states that the organization "avoids social, religious, or national bias" and "does not promote political action or polemical discussion" (PSS[I], 2009).

Consistent with their radical tradition, scholars in peace and conflict studies would respond that peace science's detached approach is no way to run "this" railroad. (See CRITICAL AND RADICAL PSYCHOLOGY; CRITICAL SECURITY STUDIES.) The privileging of

science over values and the complete separation of peace research from political action is not only counterproductive, but trivializes a subject of great importance. Moreover, the scientific method is not well suited to issues of positive peace, structural violence, and the need implied by these conditions to achieve social justice and gender, class, and racial equality. Instead, a broader view of peace requires recognition that ideas and social structures, not material forces, drive history. Like the former practices of slavery and dueling, war is a socially constructed institution that should be contextualized and historicized. The critical methodology of peace and conflict studies offers a useful and necessary approach to examine the social, linguistic, and ideological constructions of violence/nonviolence and war/peace. The danger, however, as peace scientists would point out, is that such an approach can quickly evolve from an academic endeavor to a political movement, moving away from research and embracing sloganeering and pamphleteering (Singer, 2006).

In summary, peace science is motivated by a scientific and "objective" framework focused on "negative peace" or the absence of physical violence; whereas, peace and conflict studies is driven by a prescriptive and explicitly value-based framework focused on "positive peace" or the absence of physical and structural violence and the presence of life-affirming structures in society. Peace research began with the mission of combining the scientific method with social ethics to find solutions to the threat of nuclear holocaust. The radical critique of the late 1960s introduced structural violence, strong rejectionist and activist components, and a view of peace as something to be created rather than maintained or restored. In addition, the radical critique characterized those doing applied research as tools of the establishment. Surveys conducted in the early 1970s confirmed that the field of peace research was composed of two fairly hostile academic cultures, mirroring the humanistic vs. scientific divide, that could not work together given their contrasting research traditions and intellectual goals. This two cultures problem largely explains the emergence and development of peace and conflict studies and peace science as relatively isolated fields.

Over the years, peace scholarship has had its share of internal debates and schisms that surfaced at critical junctures over epistemological and methodological concerns. These periods of instability transformed the terrain of peace scholarship. The question arises: Do the various academic communities that comprise peace scholarship recognize and appreciate the significance of the field's genealogy? This matters because, as the saying goes, "it's hard to know where you're going, if you don't know where you've been." Given the markedly contrasting intellectual goals and different research traditions of the two academic cultures of peace and conflict studies and peace science, it is difficult to see how cross-cultural dialogue among peace scholars can emerge in the absence of a broad historical and contextualized understanding of peace scholarship.

SEE ALSO: Critical and Radical Psychology; Critical Security Studies; Peace, Positive and Negative; Peace Psychology: Definitions, Scope, and Impact; Peace Studies, Psychological Contributions to.

REFERENCES

Dunn, D. J. (2005). *The first fifty years of peace research: A survey and interpretation.* Burlington, VT: Ashgate.
Galtung, J. (1969). Violence, peace, and peace research. *Journal of Peace Research, 6*(3), 167–191.
Kelman, H. (1981). Reflections on the history and status of peace research. *Conflict Management and Peace Science, 5*(2), 95–110.
Peace Science Society (International). (2009). Organization: History of the society. Retrieved August 13, 2009, from http://pss.la.psu.edu/2007–History.htm.
Singer, J. D. (1990). *Models, methods, and progress in world politics: A peace research odyssey.* Boulder, CO: Westview Press.
Singer, J. D. (2006, November). *Origins and history of the Peace Science Society.* Paper presented at the annual meeting of the Peace Science Society (International), Columbus, OH.
Vasquez, J. A. (1976). Toward a unified strategy for peace education: Resolving the two cultures problem in the classroom. *Journal of Conflict Resolution, 20*(4), 707–728.

ADDITIONAL RESOURCES

Boulding, K. (1970/1982). Limits or boundaries of peace research: *Proceedings of the IPRA Third General Conference – Volume 1.* In G. Pardesi (Ed.), *Contemporary peace research* (pp. 76–92). Atlantic Highlands, NJ: Humanities Press.
Isard, W. (1992). *Understanding conflict and the science of peace.* Cambridge, MA: Blackwell.
Lawler, P. (1995). *A question of values: Johan Galtung's peace research.* Boulder, CO: Lynne Rienner.

Peace Education

LINDEN L. NELSON

The idea that public education has an essential role in creating a more peaceful world has a long history. It was not until the twentieth century, however, that peace education programs were created. They were originally designed to teach about causes of war and approaches to preventing war, and later in the century they were developed to teach about social conflict, violence, and peace at all levels from interpersonal to international. While definitions of peace education vary in regard to the range of topics and methods that are included, contemporary definitions tend to be very broad. For example, a statement released by educators from 27 nations at a conference convened by the Hague Appeal for Peace on October 20–23, 2004, in Tirana, Albania, defined peace education as including "teaching for and about democracy and human rights, nonviolence, social and economic justice, gender equality, environmental sustainability, disarmament, traditional peace practices, international law, and human security" (Hague Appeal for Peace, 2004). In line with this very broad conception, peace education is defined here as teaching and learning that is intended to facilitate development of peaceful people.

Harris (1999) delineated five types of peace education, most of which are discussed in other essays of this encyclopedia. Global peace education includes international relations, holocaust studies, and nuclear weapon issues. (See COEXISTENCE EDUCATION.) Conflict resolution education provides training in mediation, negotiation, and communication skills. (See CONFLICT RESOLUTION IN SCHOOLS; ALTERNATIVES TO VIOLENCE.) Violence prevention programs address domestic violence, drug abuse, anger management, and prejudice. (See ANTI-BIAS EDUCATION; PREJUDICE REDUCTION, APPROACHES TO.) Development education is concerned with human rights, environmental studies, and emphasizes power and resource inequities and structural violence. (See SOCIAL JUSTICE EDUCATION; MONITORING HUMAN RIGHTS IN EDUCATIONAL SETTINGS.) Nonviolence education is based on the ideas of Gandhi, King, and other great peacemakers. (See NONVIOLENCE, PSYCHOLOGY OF; VALUES, NONVIOLENCE, AND PEACE PSYCHOLOGY.)

Peace education probably occurs most often in schools, at every level from preschool to university. It is sometimes presented as a subject matter or learning method separate from other subjects or courses, but it is often integrated into traditional subjects and courses. For example, it might be found in the social science curriculum at the K-12 level or in a social psychology course at a university. When courses at the college level focus on the academic study of war and peace, they are frequently referred to as peace studies (see PEACE STUDIES, PSYCHOLOGICAL CONTRIBUTIONS TO), and when the emphasis is on application of principles of conflict resolution to all levels of conflict, course titles generally include the words "conflict resolution."

Peace education, as broadly defined, also takes place in homes, churches, counseling centers, clinics, prisons, and many other contexts, and it may be included as part of marriage training, parenting education, character education, and many other programs for developing social competencies. (See SOCIAL AND EMOTIONAL LEARNING.) Specific objectives and content for peace education may vary considerably depending on location, historical period, age, and other attributes of participants. For example, the challenges and goals of peace education differ between areas experiencing intractable conflict, ethnic tension, or relative tranquility. (See PEACE EDUCATION: LESSONS LEARNED IN ISRAEL/ PALESTINE, RESEARCH ON.)

Major psychological contributions to peace education have included: (1) clarifying educational objectives; (2) developing peaceful pedagogy; (3) generating theory and knowledge about conflict, violence, and peace; and (4) assessing outcomes and evaluating peace education programs. Each of these will be discussed in turn and then followed by comments on major challenges for peace education and the potential contributions of peace psychology.

CLARIFYING EDUCATIONAL OBJECTIVES

Without clear objectives, peace educators would lack guidance for selecting the content and methods for their programs and would have a weak foundation for identifying criteria for evaluating programs. Although the specific goals of peace education depend on the targeted population, psychologists have identified objectives that seem essential for fulfilling the general promise to facilitate the development of peaceful people. Nelson and Christie (1995) proposed that peace educators should address the values and expectancies that motivate peaceful actions in addition to the knowledge and competencies that enable peaceful behavior. Both the history of warfare and psychological research has shown that possessing problem-solving competencies and having knowledge about conflict do not correlate very strongly, if at all, with support for peaceful actions. Therefore, psychologists have identified specific educational objectives and offered suggestions for fulfilling them in the categories of "attitudes and values" and "efficacy and outcome expectancies" as well as "knowledge" and "competencies" (Nelson, Van Slyck, & Cardella, 1999). For example, values that promote peaceful action include equality, social justice, democratic decision-making, and preferences for nonviolent social influence and cooperative problem solving. Efficacy and outcome expectancies that promote peaceful behavior include beliefs that one is capable of negotiating effectively and that negotiation will result in outcomes that will meet one's needs.

A related approach for identifying educational objectives studies the values, attitudes, and personality characteristics of peaceful people and assumes that fostering within a person the dispositions that characterize peaceful people will influence the individual to become more peaceful. (See NONVIOLENT DISPOSITIONS; PEACEFUL PERSONALITY.) Results from this research imply that peace education should foster perspective taking, empathic concern, open mindedness, and benevolent and universal values; and it should discourage the acquisition of power

and dominance values, and negative reciprocity norms.

Another approach to determining the specific goals of peace education is based on an analysis of objective indicators for assessing the degree to which nations possess a culture of peace and the presumption that peace education should prepare students to live in a culture of peace (de Rivera, 2010). (See CULTURE OF PEACE.) The analysis of objective indicators revealed four dimensions to the peacefulness of cultures, and each dimension poses a particular psychological tension. The dimensions and tensions are as follows: liberal development (the tension between competitive individualism and cooperative harmony), equality (the tension between compassion and aggressive assertion for justice), state nonviolence (the tension between authority and responsible anarchy), and nurturance (the management of tension among people with different perspectives, and between the real and the ideal). Peace education, according to de Rivera, should provide the knowledge, competencies, and values that appear to be necessary in order to support each of the dimensions of a culture of peace as well as guidance to assist students in their efforts to come to terms with the tensions associated with each dimension.

DEVELOPING PEACEFUL PEDAGOGY

Psychologists have made significant contributions to peace education by developing methodologies for teaching people to be peaceful. Cooperative learning is probably the most widely used and extensively researched of these methods. (See COOPERATIVE LEARNING.) Different approaches to cooperative learning have been developed by Elliot Aronson, David and Roger Johnson, Spencer Kagan, and Robert Slavin; but all of them structure the learning experience so as to promote cooperative interactions between students. Studies show that compared to traditional methods, cooperative learning enhances peaceful dispositions (e.g., interpersonal attraction, positive ethnic attitudes, perspective taking, empathy, cooperativeness) as well as academic achievement.

Cooperative learning is a form of active learning and peace educators prefer active over passive learning because people tend to learn better by doing and because social psychologists have demonstrated that peaceful attitudes and values develop as a result of perceiving that one has voluntarily behaved in peaceful ways. Psychologists have also emphasized that peaceful activities can provide opportunities for students to acquire conflict resolution skills, to gain confidence in their own abilities to behave peacefully, and to develop positive outcome expectations regarding peaceful actions. Therefore, peace education often includes student involvement in simulations, role playing, and analysis of case studies; and students are encouraged to participate in peer mediation programs, service learning, and internships with organizations and agencies working for peace and social justice. (See ACTION TEACHING.)

Psychologists have also developed methods for teaching critical thinking, problem solving, and conflict resolution. For example, the constructive controversy procedure teaches problem-solving skills, perspective taking, rational argumentation, and decision-making. (See CONSTRUCTIVE CONTROVERSY.) Social and emotional learning is a related area of peace education where psychologists have made important contributions to pedagogy. (See SOCIAL AND EMOTIONAL LEARNING.) Psychologists have written many books and teaching manuals on social and communication skills, social problem solving, assertiveness training, and anger management.

Finally, psychologists have contributed to the development of peaceful pedagogy by stressing the importance of school and classroom climate, student participation in democratic decision-making, effective disciplinary techniques, and the role of teachers as models of peaceful behavior. Because optimal learning environments are safe and tolerant of individual and group differences, psychologists also have designed programs to teach respect for diversity, create a cooperative school climate, prevent bullying and other forms of violence, and manage behavior problems in the classroom. For example, "win-win discipline" involves identifying and empathizing with students, working collaboratively with students to create solutions, and teaching positive, responsible behaviors (Kagan, Kyle, & Scott, 2004). Perhaps the most important aspect of peaceful pedagogy is the role of the teacher in modeling democratic behavior, practicing conflict resolution skills, and manifesting peaceful values.

GENERATING THEORY AND KNOWLEDGE ABOUT CONFLICT, VIOLENCE, AND PEACE

Psychologists have generated a considerable literature of theory and knowledge about conflict, violence, and peace that is relevant for the content of peace education. This encyclopedia summarizes much of that literature. The difficult task for educators is selecting the particular theories, information, and principles from this vast literature that would be most helpful for a given target group. Psychologists have occasionally offered suggestions for peace educators regarding appropriate psychological content for adolescents (Nelson, Van Slyck, & Cardella, 1999) and for college students (Christie & Wagner, 2010; Nelson & Christie, 1995). Textbooks by psychologists on peace psychology, conflict resolution, and peace studies can also be seen as efforts to select the psychological concepts and knowledge most relevant for peace education.

ASSESSING AND EVALUATING PEACE EDUCATION PROGRAMS

Efforts to promote peace education programs in schools have benefited from evidence showing that some programs (1) reduce violence, discipline referrals, prejudice, and conflicts at home and school, and (2) increase problem-solving and conflict resolution skills, positive attitudes toward school, and academic achievement. However, given the wide variety of programs that can be considered to be types of peace education, it is not very meaningful to ask whether peace education in general is effective. Rather, effectiveness will vary depending on the type of peace education employed, the particular target group, and the kinds of outcomes assessed.

Psychologists and educators have investigated outcomes for some of the types of peace education described in this encyclopedia essay, and positive results are reported in other encyclopedia essays (e.g., COOPERATIVE LEARNING; CONFLICT RESOLUTION IN SCHOOLS; CONSTRUCTIVE CONTROVERSY). Psychologists have also evaluated peace education curricula published for high school students using subjective ratings of expected outcomes based on content analyses (Nelson, Van Slyck, & Cardella, 1999). The research tools of psychology relevant to development of assessment instruments and for program evaluation are needed in order to demonstrate the benefits of peace education and to provide information essential for improving peace education programs.

PEACE EDUCATION CHALLENGES AND POTENTIAL CONTRIBUTIONS OF PEACE PSYCHOLOGY

A major challenge for educators concerned about the development of peaceful people is to discover the kinds of interventions that most effectively create peaceful dispositions and motivation to support peaceful policies. This requires research both to identify the particular knowledge, competencies, values, and expectancies that influence peaceful behavior, and to learn how best to facilitate the development of these dispositions. Both of these research tasks call for experimental methodology, and psychologists have only just begun to apply their research skills to address these issues.

Because modeling is so important to the development of competencies, values, and expectations, it is essential to teach peaceful behavior to teachers. That is, teachers must learn conflict resolution skills, peaceful methods of discipline, and how to create peaceful classrooms. Psychologists can help promote and design teacher training programs that will develop peaceful teachers.

In order to achieve its universal goals, peace education will probably need to be school-based, compulsory, comprehensive, and implemented across age levels. Psychologists and educators should work with citizen groups to promote legislation that mandates peace education by convincing legislators that peace education in public schools is necessary to fulfill civil needs and to optimize academic learning.

Finally, psychologists have often noted that basic principles of conflict resolution can be applied widely across life situations and across levels of conflict from interpersonal to international. Unfortunately, however, instruction in the schools about interpersonal conflict resolution is often segregated from teaching about international relations, war, and peace. Conflict resolution and peace psychology principles should be integrated into the curriculum and into classroom management practices as broadly as possible in order to promote the generalization of peace psychology concepts and the development of peaceful people.

SEE ALSO: Action Teaching; Alternatives to Violence; Anti-bias Education; Coexistence Education; Conflict Resolution in Schools; Constructive Controversy; Cooperative Learning; Culture of Peace; Monitoring Human Rights in Educational Settings; Nonviolence, Psychology of; Nonviolent Dispositions; Peace Education: Lessons Learned in Israel/Palestine, Research on; Peace Studies, Psychological Contributions to; Peaceful Personality; Prejudice Reduction, Approaches to; Social and Emotional Learning; Social Justice Education; Values, Nonviolence, and Peace Psychology.

REFERENCES

Christie, D. J., & Wagner, R.V. (2010). What does peace psychology have to offer peace education? Five psychologically informed propositions. In G. Salomon & E. Cairns (Eds.), Handbook on peace education (pp. 63–74). London, UK: Psychology Press.

de Rivera, J. H. (2010). Teaching about culture of peace as an approach to peace education. In G. Salomon & E. Cairns (Eds.), Handbook on peace education (pp. 187–198). London, UK: Psychology Press.

Hague Appeal for Peace. (2004). The Tirana call for peace education. Retrieved November 18, 2009, from http://www.haguepeace.org/index.php?action=history&subaction=Tirana conf.

Harris, I. M. (1999). Types of peace education. In A. Raviv, L. Oppenheimer, & D. Bar-Tal (Eds.), How children understand war and peace: A call for international peace education (pp. 299–317). San Francisco, CA: Jossey-Bass.

Kagan, S., Kyle, P., & Scott, S. (2004). Win-win discipline: Strategies for all discipline problems. San Clemente, CA: Kagan Publishing.

Nelson, L. L., & Christie, D. J. (1995). Peace in the psychology curriculum: Moving from assimilation to accommodation. Peace and Conflict: Journal of Peace Psychology, 1,161–178.

Nelson, L. L., Van Slyck, M. R., & Cardella, L. A. (1999). Peace and conflict curricula for adolescents. In L. Forcey & I. Harris (Eds.), Peacebuilding for adolescents: Strategies for educators and community leaders (pp. 91–117). New York, NY: Peter Lang.

ADDITIONAL RESOURCES

Peace Psychology Resource Project: http://www.clarku.edu/peacepsychology/ppresourceproject.html

Psychologists for Social Responsibility peace education resources: http://www.psysr.org/about/programs/education

Peace Education: Lessons Learned in Israel/Palestine, Research on

GAVRIEL SALOMON

The variant of peace and coexistence education in Israel between Israeli Jews and Israeli Arabs and between the former and Palestinians is typical of such programs in regions of intractable conflict and prolonged intense interethnic tension: Northern Ireland ("Education for Mutual Understanding"), Bosnia-Herzegovina ("Education for Peace"), Kosovo, Congo (International Peace Education Development), and such. Some see this brand of peace education as the prototype of the field entailing all that makes peace education what it is, much in line with the 1998 United Nation's Resolution on the Culture of Peace: ". . . an integral approach to preventing violence and violent conflicts, and an alternative to the culture of war and violence based on education for peace" (p. 1). Central to this brand of peace education, and the attribute that makes it seen as the prototype, is the desire to change minds and hearts between real adversaries who pose a perceived collective threat to each other. Programs of this kind are not designed primarily to resolve a conflict, leaving it to political and social forces, but to mainly change attitudes toward, perceptions of, attributions to, stereotypes of, and the prevailing dehumanization and delegitimization of the collective adversary.

Peace education programs in Israel/Palestine are mainly, but not exclusively, based on the well-known contact hypothesis whereby Jewish and Palestinian youngsters meet for planned dialogue workshops. (See CONTACT THEORY, INTERGROUP.) These range from an interpersonal emphasis aiming at mutual understanding to a focus on the conflict aiming at deeper understanding of the prevailing power relations. Another approach, intermediate between the two approaches, is the narrative-based "story telling" approach whereby personal lives are revealed within the context of the collective narrative. Other approaches, less direct, are binational activities such as joint soccer, theater, archeology, or music clubs. However, despite the large number of programs, the number of actual participants is relatively small. Maoz (2010) found in her survey that no more than 16% of Jewish Israelis have ever participated in any peace education program, and of those 56% reported to have experienced a positive attitude change toward West Bank Palestinians and 38.5% toward Israeli Palestinians.

The context within which peace education in Israel/Palestine takes place, also typical of other such contexts, is characterized by grave inequalities between the 80% Jewish majority and the 20% Israeli Arabs who feel discriminated against and excluded, and between the former and the West Bank Palestinians who are under Israeli occupation. This asymmetry contradicts one of the basic tenets of the contact hypothesis. Establishing equality, if even only during dialogue encounters, is one of the major challenges facing peace education programs and, as Maoz (2010) shows, can be achieved by structuring the encounters. Still, Jewish dominance is felt in many cases, as is the fact that once the Arab or Palestinian participants return to their homes the general inequality and experienced injustice are felt full force.

Grave inequalities are not the only hurdle that faces peace education. Other barriers consist of conflicting painful histories, deeply rooted, collectively held beliefs about the conflict, and about "us" and "them," and a belligerent social climate which makes peace education into a subversive activity. Nevertheless, peace education programs in Israel/Palestine have their positive effects on a substantial number of participants. Participation in programs leads to at least a modicum of more positive attitudes toward the adversary, reduces stereotypes, prejudices, and negative emotions, increases willingness for contact, and leads to some greater legitimization of the other side's collective narrative (for summaries see Salomon, 2004; PEACH, 2010).

But this is only half the story. First, the positive findings of research on peace education programs contradict reasonable predictions that should follow from an analysis of the barriers mentioned above. It is either that the barriers are not severe or that the findings are not very valid. Second, not all participants in peace education programs are positively affected. Some 25% are negatively influenced. Third, the effects, as we shall see, are often short-lived. Fourth, the effects are not uniform: Arabs and Jews respond very differently to the programs. And fifth, the effects, even if somewhat sustainable, do not spread to nonparticipants; there is hardly any social "ripple effect." These issues, then, lead to some important lessons that need to be learned and to formulation of the main challenges that face peace education in regions of intractable conflict. To four of these we turn next.

CONTRADICTION BETWEEN THE BARRIERS AND THE FINDINGS

As pointed out above, peace education programs have positive effects, even if limited and short-lived. How can this repeated observation fit with the list of grave barriers facing it? How can the contradiction between barriers and findings be reconciled?

A hypothesis based on the theory of attitude strength (Petty & Krosnick, 2005) was empirically studied. According to this hypothesis attitudes that are held with great conviction and are central to one's attitude and belief system are not subject to change by peace education programs (e.g., "The Palestinian's lands have been forcefully taken from them"; "The Jews have the right to return to their ancestral homeland"). On the other hand, peace education can affect less strongly held, more peripheral attitudes (e.g., "Not all Jews are anti-Palestinian"; "The Palestinians can be trusted"). Thus, while the barriers mentioned above appear to pertain to strongly held attitudes and beliefs, the positive findings hold in relation to more peripheral attitudes and beliefs. A number of controlled studies bear this out very clearly (Bar-Tal, Rosen, & Netz-Zehngut, 2010). The conclusion is that peace education has its built-in limits: It cannot (and perhaps should not) affect the backbone of a group's belief system; it can affect more peripheral ones. One may call this "good enough peace education."

THE TEMPORARY NATURE
OF THE EFFECTS

Much too often program effects are studied only immediately following the completion of a program. However, when measures are taken a while later, one finds that many of the effects tend to have become eroded; measures return to their initial values. Why the erosion? In the Israeli–Palestinian context where consensually held feelings are often filled with hatred, distrust, anger, frustration, and fear, the newly acquired attitudes, perceptions, attributions, and legitimizations stand a poor chance of surviving.

Indeed, in a series of studies (see Arnon, Bar-Natan, Rosen, and Jaussi, in PEACH, 2010) it was found that positive program effects measured "the morning after," were not detected any more 3 or 6 months later.

In series of attempts to revive changes that became eroded over a short span of time it was found that one of three intervention methods could restore the changes. The three methods were: (1) dissonance-based induced compliance whereby participants presented the other side's point of view to their critical peers; (2) peer teaching of what has been learned in the peace education workshop; and (3) reflection of the workshop experiences (see the summaries on Rosen, Jaussi, and Arnon in PEACH, 2010). As can be seen in Figure 1, the method of induced compliance not only revived the changes but also maintained them for another 3 months.

Of course, the possibility exists that the erosion of effects is more apparent than real as it may apply only to the explicit expression of effects. Changes can "go underground" and become implicit ("implicit attitudes") and might surface a while later under certain conditions. While this may be a (still undocumented) possibility, we still need to address the "morning-after effect." It faces us with the major challenge of finding ways not just to *change* minds and hearts but to *sustain* the changes over time and in the face of adverse sociopolitical forces.

THE DIFFERENTIAL NATURE OF
PEACE EDUCATION EFFECTS

Because of individual, cultural, ethnic, and economic differences, no educational intervention can possibly be equally effective with all. The case of peace education in Israel/Palestine is no exception. Indeed, in the studies mentioned above it was repeatedly found that given well-known

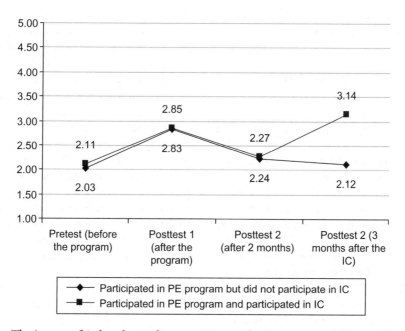

Figure 1   The impact of induced-compliance activity on the importance of the peripheral beliefs from the Palestinian narrative – Jewish participants.

differences, Jews, Arabs, and Palestinians respond very differently to dialogue workshops and to binational joint projects. Thus, for example, Husseissi (see PEACH, 2010) found that while Jews responded to a year-long school-based program by giving greater legitimacy to the Palestinian narrative, Palestinians increased their adherence to their *own* collective narrative. Rosen (Bar-Tal et al., 2010) found that while the application of the induced compliance method did revive changes among the Jewish participants, it did not have any effect on the Arabs.

Applying a needs-based theory, Shnabel, Nadler, Canetti-Nisim, and Ullrich (2008) suggested that the weak side (the alleged victim: Arabs in Israel) and the strong side (the alleged perpetrator: Jews) face different threats and thus approach reconciliation attempts with different needs: The weaker side experiences a threat to its status and power while the stronger side experiences a threat to its image as a moral and socially acceptable entity. Thus, reconciliation processes need to address these differential needs by empowering the weaker side, giving it "a voice," and restoring the public moral image of the stronger side. A series of studies supports this theory.

It follows that programs ought to be differential. However, so far, this becomes a challenging task since the contact hypothesis assumes, even requires, that all parties meet each other face–to-face, which actually means that one program should fit all. It does not, and hence the challenge is to find ways (and some have been found already) to combine the differential with the common approach to peace education. One exception that allows differential programs follows from the extended contact hypothesis (Pettigrew, Christ, Wagner, & Stellmacher, 2007) whereby even knowing somebody from another group might change attitudes toward that group. (See CONTACT THEORY: EXTENDED AND PARASOCIAL.)

THE ABSENCE OF A SOCIAL RIPPLE EFFECT

Another challenge facing peace education is the fact that its effects are limited to those who actually participate in peace education programs and curricula but do not spread to others. Examination of the effects of peace education in Northern Ireland corroborates this observation: Peace education programs had no detectable effect on the political life and atmosphere there. There is no solid evidence about the existence or absence of a social ripple effect in Israel/Palestine, and judging from public opinion surveys, relations between Arabs and Jews in Israel are not improving and the existence of the many peace education programs and projects seem to have no effect on binational relations.

This is where peace education in Israel/Palestine faces one of its major challenges. Being what may be called a subversive activity, it must find its way into the mainstream of education, becoming part of regular school curricula. But this, while perhaps necessary, is insufficient. As long as only children and youth are involved in peace education activities, participants of no political power and social influence, the effects of peace education, even if sustainable, cannot possibly spread to wider circles of society. Revival of what used to be called the "people-to-people" movement where adults, not just school-age children, are involved would be of great importance in this respect. The challenge, then, is to involve communities, not just classrooms.

As the accumulated experience in Israel/Palestine suggests, for peace education to be effective it must be able to successfully face the challenges discussed here. Uniform programs where deeply rooted differences exist, short programs with no follow-up that have only short-lived effects, and programs that do not involve communities but children only, cannot be very successful. A lesson can be learned from the other route to reconciliation: binational clubs where participation is long-term and continuous, where the goal is not dialogue but the attainment of common and very important goals (to win a match, to perform well), and where the whole community can be involved. Our research shows this to be a very effective route to peace education and much can be applied from it to dialogue workshops. There is more than one way to reach mutual understanding and reconciliation among adversaries.

SEE ALSO: Contact Theory: Extended and Parasocial; Contact Theory, Intergroup.

REFERENCES

Bar-Tal, D., Rosen, Y., & Netz-Zehngut, R. (2010). Peace education in societies involved in intractable conflict: Goals, conditions, and directions. In G. Salomon & E. Cairns (Eds.), *Handbook on peace education* (pp. 21–44). New York, NY: Psychology Press.

Maoz. Y. (2010). Education for peace through planned encounters between Jews and Arabs in Israel: A reappraisal of effectiveness. In G. Salomon & E. Cairns (Eds.), *Handbook on peace education* (pp. 303–314). New York, NY: Psychology Press.

PEACH. (2010). Retrieved from. http://peach.haifa.ac.il/index.php?title=Research_Summaries

Pettigrew, T. F., Christ, O., Wagner, U., & Stellmacher, J. (2007). Direct and indirect inter-group contact effects on prejudice: A normative interpretation. *International Journal of Intercultural Relations*, 31, 411–425.

Petty, R. E., & Krosnick, J. A. (2005). *Attitude strength: Antecedents and consequences.* Mahwah, NJ: Lawrence Erlbaum Associates.

Salomon, G. (2004). Does peace education make a difference in the context of an intractable conflict? *Peace and Conflict: Journal of Peace Psychology, 10*(3), 257–274.

Shnabel, N., Nadler, A., Canetti-Nisim, D., & Ullrich, J. (2008). The role of acceptance and empowerment in promoting reconciliation from the perspective of the needs-based model. *Social Issues and Policity Review, 2*, 159–186.

United Nations. (1998). *Resolution on the culture of peace*. Resolution 52/13. Geneva, Switzerland: United Nations.

ADDITIONAL RESOURCES

Rotberg, R. I. (2006). *Israeli and Palestinian narratives of conflict: History's double helix*. Bloomington: Indiana University Press.

Salomon, G. (2006). Does peace education *really* make a difference? *Peace and Conflict: Journal of Peace Psychology, 12*(1), 37–48.

Salomon, G. (2011). Four major challenges facing peace education. *Peace and Conflict: Journal of Peace Psychology, 17*, 46–59.

Peace Journalism

WILHELM KEMPF

Since Galtung (1998) and Kempf (1996) outlined their first ideas of an alternative to mainstream war reporting, their models of peace journalism (PJ) have stimulated a broad debate among peace researchers and journalists, as well as practical thought about how to achieve this type of journalism, and a large body of basic theoretical and empirical research.

In particular, Galtung's famous table which contrasts PJ with conventional war journalism motivated both a huge discipleship and harsh criticism among journalists and media researchers. Critics of the PJ project like David Loyn and Thomas Hanitzsch (in Kempf, 2008) interpreted the PJ approach as an active participation that is simply not the role of a journalist. According to Loyn, there is no need for PJ, since most of the legal framework, and the codes of

conduct for journalists, written by trade unions and responsible employers, provide a sufficient framework which prescribes what journalists can and cannot do. What was proposed by advocates of PJ, however, would be a prescription, defining a way of working which demands that reporters artificially seek out peacemakers (Loyn), actively contribute to peaceful conflict resolution, and overstep the borderline between journalism and public relations (Hanitzsch).

However, the peace mandate of the media is not just an arbitrary claim of peace researchers and journalists who subscribe to the "peace journalism philosophy" (Hanitzsch, cited in Kempf, 2008, p. 69); it is anchored in numerous international treaties and documents like the United Nations (UN) *Universal Declaration of Human Rights* of 1948, the UN *International Covenant on Civil and Political Rights* of 1966 and the UNESCO Mass Media Declaration of 1978. In addition, countless empirical studies have demonstrated that conventional war reporting does not live up to the professional norms of quality journalism like objectivity, detachment, and truthfulness.

The PJ project should, therefore, be better understood as an approach which aims at putting into practice the very norms which Loyn refers to. According to this understanding, PJ is *not* a variant of advocacy journalism (and thus the "opposite of good journalism," as Loyn maintains; cited in Kempf, 2008, p. 53), but an attempt to achieve good journalism even under the delicate conditions of war and crisis.

The legal anchoring of the media peace mandate in international law and its practical implementation are two different things. Compared with the enormous expenditure that has been made to optimize propaganda strategies, military-media management, and psychological warfare, efforts to utilize the media as instruments for constructive conflict management and peacekeeping have taken a back seat. Despite the vast amount of literature that critically examines the exploitation of the media for war propaganda, not only by dictatorial regimes, but also by democratic states, it was not until the end of the twentieth century that peace researchers, media scholars, and journalists focused their attention on the question of how the media could be used as a catalyst for the de-escalation of conflicts and for peaceful dispute settlement. (See MEDIA AND PEACE: EMERGING TECHNOLOGIES; MEDIA AND PEACE: TRADITIONAL OUTLETS.)

One of the first scholars to investigate the significance of the media as a form of modern diplomacy was Yoel Cohen in 1986. In her book *Media Diplomacy* she distinguished three types of relationships between media and diplomacy: media as information sources, media as communication channels between decision-makers, and media as a means to secure public support.

Other authors followed a similar line of argument. Wolfsfeld mentioned that the media enable the political elites that control them to influence peoples' convictions and resulting actions. Lumsden concluded that in peacekeeping, the international community must not limit itself to efforts to promote satisfactory social and economic conditions. It must also offer citizens ways of interpreting the world that make possible enduring peace, and for Roach this means primarily containing the readiness to go to war by reducing enemy images, a task for which the media are an indispensable instrument. (See IMAGE THEORY.)

According to the current state of media effects research, the media contribute to the social construction of reality, for one thing, by introducing specific topics into public discourse (agenda setting) and, for another, by the way they treat these topics (framing).

The *agenda-setting* theory was founded by McCombs and Shaw in 1972 and attributes the influence of the media to decisions about which stories are newsworthy and what importance and how much space

should be assigned to them. Negativism, personalization, and elite orientations are regarded as prominent news factors that make events worth reporting. As Galtung (1998) shows, already these news factors form a cognitive frame in which an image of reality arises that divides the world into elite and peripheral countries – and at the same time into good and evil. No less fateful is the widespread belief among journalists and media producers in the necessity of simplifications that literally make a norm out of the black-and-white stereotyping of a polarizing "we against them" journalism. (See US AND THEM: MODERATING DICHOTOMOUS INGROUP/OUTGROUP THINKING; STEREOTYPES.)

Consequently, it is above all the news factors placed by Galtung at the center of his PJ model which Lynch and McGoldrick (2005) summarize with the formula: "Peace Journalism is when editors and reporters make choices – of what stories to report, and how to report them – which create opportunities for society at large to consider and to value non-violent responses to conflict" (p. 5). (See ALTERNATIVES TO VIOLENCE.)

While some media researchers have criticized Galtung's approach with the argument that the above-named news factors were fixed constants of journalism in general and conflict coverage in particular, there is empirical evidence that this is not the case. As Susanne Jaeger (in Kempf, 2010) has shown with the example of the German press coverage of France after World War II, the media may well diverge from the conventional routines of news selection, and they do so if peace is on their agenda.

The concept of *framing* was originally introduced by Goffman in 1974. According to Entman (1993), it means to select some aspects of a perceived reality and make them more salient in a communicating text, in such a way as to promote a particular problem definition, causal interpretation, moral evaluation, and/or treatment recommendation for the item described.

Depending on the type of mental model used to interpret them, the same situations can be placed in a completely different light. The escalation dynamics of conflicts are, according to Morton Deutsch, decisively influenced by whether a conflict is interpreted as a competitive (win-lose model) or as a cooperative process (win-win model). Competitive conflicts have a tendency to expand and escalate and go together with typical perceptual distortions that become a motor of conflict escalation. (See COOPERATION AND COMPETITION.)

Correspondingly, it is the cognitive-emotional framework which corresponds to the various levels of conflict escalation that Kempf placed at the center of his PJ model. In empirical studies of the coverage of the Gulf War, the civil wars in former Yugoslavia, and other conflicts, Kempf and his research group at the University of Konstanz analyzed the increasingly radicalized mental models according to which escalating conflicts are interpreted by the media along the dimensions of:

1. the conceptualization of the conflict as a win–win, win–lose or lose–lose process;
2. the uneven assessment of the parties' rights and aims;
3. the double standard used in the evaluation of actions and behavior; and
4. the emotional consequences of these interpretations, which ultimately transform outrage at war into outrage at the enemy and disengage group members from moral control of violence. (See MORAL DISENGAGEMENT.)

Finally, in ASPR, Kempf (2003) integrated this approach with Galtung's PJ model. Introducing the concept of constructive conflict coverage, he suggested a two-step strategy to counteract the bias of traditional war reporting: deconstruct war discourses, and gradually transform them into peace and, ultimately, reconciliation discourses.

According to this model, a peace or reconciliation discourse does *not* mean a discourse *about* peace or reconciliation, and especially not a discourse that harmonizes contradictions or suppresses conflicts, etc. It is a matter of *how* to deal with conflict. Correspondingly, the best way to characterize the various discourse forms is by the questions they focus on. In a *war* discourse, it is a matter of "Who is guilty?" and "How can he be stopped?" A *peace* discourse asks "What is the problem?" and "How can it be solved?". And when a *reconciliation* discourse is appropriate, the focus is on questions such as "Who is the other?" and "How can we meet each other with mutual respect?"

The choice of a suitable discourse form is essential for the developmental dynamics of peace processes, and – as Lea Mandelzis (in Shinar & Kempf, 2007) has shown in case of the Oslo Process – mistakes in choosing a discourse form can easily create overly optimistic expectations. Their disappointment provokes ill feeling in the population and ultimately has the consequence that the discourse turns into a renewed war discourse. The danger is even greater in long-lasting, intractable conflicts, where the biased conflict perception has become part of a society's ethos and solidified into what Daniel Bar-Tal calls societal beliefs. (See CONFLICT, ETHOS OF.)

Therefore, during the "hot" phase of a conflict, it is appropriate to limit peace journalism efforts to de-escalation-oriented coverage: objective, detached, fair, and respectful to all sides. Coverage should not fan the conflict, but rather take a critical distance from the belligerents of every stripe and make the public aware of the high price that violent conflict resolution imposes on all participants. Proposals for solutions would not be appropriate at this stage of a conflict. At this point, there is a risk that the conflict parties will rashly dismiss coverage as implausible or as hostile counterpropaganda. Therefore, in this phase the chief aim can only be to find a way out of the fixation on violence and mutual destruction and to alert the public to an external viewpoint that can deconstruct the conflict parties' antagonistic conceptions of reality and their polarization.

In the second phase of the conflict, it is appropriate for journalists to shift to solution-oriented coverage. Here it is a matter of a constructive process following deconstruction. It must work toward the rapprochement of the opponents and seek paths out of the conflict that the parties can take cooperatively. This step can only gain majority support if the conflict has emerged from the hot phase and the parties no longer automatically perceive every voice for moderation as hostile. Thereafter, the phase of conflict management and rapprochement must be initiated and supported urgently – among other things by conflict coverage that actively seeks peaceful alternatives and actors and dedicates itself to the question of how to start peace processes and how to build peace.

Models of peace journalism can, however, only become attractive to a critical mass of journalists if realizable proposals are present for how to get around the impediments that journalists are exposed to in realizing such models in their daily work. Besides journalists' qualifications, there are a great number of structural factors at work in the process of news production that impose constraints on the work of journalists. These factors include, according to Bläsi (in Kempf, 2010), among others: lack of space and time pressure, editorial work routines, deficiencies in cooperation between editors and correspondents, the instrumentalization of the media by the parties to a conflict, the influence exerted on coverage by public relations, propaganda and information management, the hindrances to coverage by censorship, restriction of travel freedom, the personal harassment of journalists by the conflict parties, inadequate access to information,

unsatisfactory infrastructure, and problematic security situations in crisis regions, as well as group-think effects within the community of international correspondents, etc.

Accordingly, the chances of implementing peace journalism are to be evaluated differently depending on the conflict phase and escalation stage (1) during non-violent conflicts, (2) during violently escalated conflicts or wars, and (3) in postwar periods. (See CYCLES OF INTERGROUP VIOLENCE AND PSYCHOSOCIAL INTERVENTIONS.) In concert with other research results that indicate that peace journalism is harder to realize if one's country is acutely involved in a war, Bläsi (as cited in Kempf, 2010) pleads for focusing future implementation efforts on those conflict phases in which conflicts are (still) being conducted nonviolently. The ideas of peace journalism must be firmly anchored in a society and in a media system in peacetime; only then will they have a real chance of having an impact even in wartime. (See PROACTIVE CONFLICT MANAGEMENT.)

SEE ALSO: Alternatives to Violence; Cooperation and Competition; Conflict, Ethos of; Cycles of Intergroup Violence and Psychosocial Interventions; Image Theory; Media and Peace: Emerging Technologies; Media and Peace: Traditional Outlets; Moral Disengagement; Proactive Conflict Management; Stereotypes; Us and Them: Moderating Dichotomous Ingroup/Outgroup Thinking.

REFERENCES

Entman, R. M. (1993). Framing: Toward clarification of a fractured paradigm. *Journal of Communication*, 43, 51–58.

Galtung, J. (1998). Friedensjournalismus: Warum, was, wer, wo, wann? In W. Kempf & I. Schmidt-Regener (Eds.), *Krieg, Nationalismus, Rassismus und die Medien* (pp. 3–20). Münster, Germany: LIT Verlag. English translation: Galtung, J. (2002). Peace

journalism: A challenge. In W. Kempf &
H. Luostarinen (Eds.), *Journalism and the new
world order. Vol. 2: Studying war and the media*
(259–272). Göteborg, Sweden: Nordicom.

Kempf, W. (1996). Konfliktberichterstattung
zwischen Eskalation und Deeskalation.
Wissenschaft und Frieden, 14(2), 51–54. English
translation: Kempf, W. (2008). *News coverage
of conflict: Between escalation and de-escalation*.
In W. Kempf (Ed.), *The peace journalism
controversy* (pp. 11–18). Berlin, Germany:
Regener.

Kempf, W. (2003). Theoretical and empirical
foundations. In ASPR (Ed.), *Constructive
conflict coverage. A social psychological
approach* (pp. 13–123). Berlin, Germany:
Regener.

Kempf, W. (Ed.). (2008). *The peace journalism
controversy*. Berlin, Germany: Regener.

Kempf, W. (Ed.). (2010). *Readings in peace
journalism: Foundations – studies – perspectives*.
Berlin, Germany: Regener.

Lynch, J., & McGoldrick, A. (2005). *Peace
journalism*. Stroud, UK: Hawthorn Press.

Shinar, D., & Kempf, W. (Eds.) (2007). *Peace
journalism: The state of the art*. Berlin:
Regener.

ADDITIONAL RESOURCES

Conflict & Communication Online: http://
www.cco.regener-online.de
Transcend Media Service: http://
www.transcend.org/tms/

Peace Psychology: Contributions from Africa

J. W. P. HEUCHERT

As the cradle of humankind, Africa probably
has the longest history of negotiating human
relationships – including resolving conflicts
and building peace. Over the centuries many
stable communities were established all over
Africa by successful conflict resolution. This
is not to say that there were never any wars
in Africa, but ancient African communities
most often evolved through cooperation
and mutual respect. In most modern African
countries colonial intervention ended the
relative stability and peaceful coexistence
prevalent on the continent. Boundaries were
redrawn to suit the needs of the colonizers
and with little regard of the historic reasons
for the boundaries. Groups were split up, or
artificially combined, rekindling old animos-
ities and creating fresh grievances. Long-
standing traditions that ensured peace and
justice were carelessly abandoned in favor of
new, poorly explained systems thrust upon
societies that were very different from the
colonial society where the laws and practices
evolved. Remnants of indigenous aspects of
peacebuilding have sustained many communities in Africa and some of those will be
offered here as contributions from Africa
to the field of peace psychology. (See CHILD
SOLDIERS, TRADITIONAL HEALING AND.)

Making generalizations in discussing the
contributions from a vast and complex continent is perilous and it is therefore necessary
to recall at the outset that Africa is currently
comprised of about 53 countries and thousands of communities and different languages and ethnic groups. By some estimates
more than 2,000 different languages are
spoken in Africa and with globalization,
group and individual identities are often in
flux. When considering the "contributions
to peace psychology from Africa," it is necessary to remember that such a short discussion as this can only include a very small
sample of the African reality and there are
by necessity generalizations.

Contributions from Africa to the understanding of the psychology of peace can be
considered from different perspectives: from
indigenous or traditional perspectives, from
modern perspectives, from postmodern perspectives, from the perspective of the contribution of women, and from the perspective
of peacemakers recognized by the international community.

INDIGENOUS OR TRADITIONAL PERSPECTIVES

Indigenous African psychology has made strong contributions in several areas of peace psychology such as intergroup relations, peaceful philosophies of life, conflict resolution practices, and peaceful societal traditions and practices. Contributions from the traditional/indigenous perspective include the practice of *ubuntu*, which is a traditional way of life that leads to peaceful coexistence. It is called "a way of life" since it is a combination of a philosophy, cultural practice, worldview, value system, and the underpinning of many traditions and everyday behaviors. *Ubuntu* is an Nguni word that describes the foundation of many African traditions in many African communities. Kamwangamalu (1999) states that some of the tenets of this pan-African concept of *ubuntu* are a focus on interdependence and communalism. These values are expressed in isiZulu as *umuntu ngumuntu ngabantu*, meaning that we are all human by the grace, support, and efforts of others. An acceptance of the resulting responsibility towards, and respect for, the group that ensures your very being, follows. *Ubuntu* informs peace psychology in that it promotes respect for human life, reconciliation when conflict arises, conformity to social norms, an insistence on human dignity, and social obligations of all members of the group. Consequently, those who live by *ubuntu* are more likely to work towards peaceful coexistence and a peaceful resolution of conflicts.

There are several typically African systems of justice operating in the various African communities, ranging from strictly traditional (rare) to a blend of traditional African and Western (British, French, Portuguese, Roman-Dutch, and "universal constitutional"). One often finds both traditional (unofficial in rural areas) and Western (official) systems used in the same country. An example of a blended system is the formal adoption of the traditional *Gacaca* courts in the post-genocide Rwanda. Because *Gacaca* principles are based on conflict resolution, healing, and closure, it serves to promote national reconciliation, empowerment of victims, and expeditious and cost-effective processing of complaints. As with other traditional systems (*Kgotla* – Southern Africa; *Ubuntu* – South Africa; *Mato Oput* – Uganda; etc.), *Gacaca* aims to promote a mediated settlement, but perhaps more importantly, a commitment to peace by the victim, perpetrator, and the spectators (community), thus increasing the likelihood of an ending to cycles of violence and revenge.

Several (traditional) African groups can be described as nonviolent societies. These are societies that have values, traditions, practices, and worldviews that promote peace, cooperation, and nonviolent conflict resolution. Bonta (1997) describes 40 or so peaceful societies and stresses the consequences evident in societies that are based on competition versus societies that stress noncompetitive cooperation (or societies that are opposed to competition). He states that peaceful societies, such as the Fipa (Tanzania), G/wi (Angola, Botswana, Namibia, South Africa), and !Kung (Namibia, South Africa), often equate competition with aggression and violence and therefore shun competition and show a preference for cooperation.

MODERN PERSPECTIVE

Contributions from the modern perspective of psychology include the application of Western (American/European) theories and models of psychology, psychotherapy, trauma, etc., in Africa. Many African psychologists support a liberation psychology that is focused on applying the knowledge and theories accumulated in Western psychology towards developing active strategies to combat oppression and injustice. (See LIBERATION PSYCHOLOGY.) For example, Frantz Fanon (and Hussein Bulhan, who continued with Fanon's work) focused on illuminating the psychological dynamics inherent in oppressive systems that employ direct and structural violence as a means of subjugating people (as was the case during colonialism and apartheid). Bulhan (1985) stresses Fanon's ideas of liberation starting within individuals who must first rid themselves of the internalization of negative stereotypes of their group gained from the views of the oppressors. (See CONSCIENTIZATION.) Once this is achieved, revolt against the structural violence perpetuated by the oppressors becomes a logical next step. Fanon's ideas have been very influential in successful liberation struggles in Africa and elsewhere.

POSTMODERN PERSPECTIVE

Contributions from the postmodern perspective of psychology include critiques of modern psychology in general, and the application of Western (American/ European) theories and models in Africa, in particular. Western psychology practices have been critiqued, noting that the imposition of Western treatment methods on indigenous African practices runs the risk of patronizing complex practices. Dawes (2001) points out that Western psychology is based on a particular ideology that emphasizes individualism, individual autonomy, and particular political values (Western democracy). However, many African societies are more community oriented and when the principles of *ubuntu* are observed, the individual's rights (political and others) and choices are made subordinate to the needs and customs of the society. Dawes warns

that in order to avoid committing ideological violence (when Western values are imposed on other societies), "co-constructing change with, rather than for, communities" should be the approach of Western peace psychologists seeking to work in non-Western societies.

At the same time, the use of traditional African systems of justice is not without its critics, who point out that the procedures are very subjective (although the same can be said of Western-style jury trials), but perhaps more importantly, that the traditional systems can be used, or influenced, by the powers-that-be. For example, there have been criticisms that *Mato Oput* in Uganda is used to provide opportunities for agents of war to escape punishment. *Kgotlas* in South Africa were suspected of punishing young anti-apartheid activists and forcing them to accept traditional justice and apartheid.

WOMEN AS PEACEMAKERS IN AFRICA

Women have much experience in peacemaking and peacebuilding. These experiences are most often utilized informally. McKay and Mazurana (2001) stress the importance of including women, and their unique perspectives and experiences, in formal government and peacebuilding structures. Throughout the world, women play a critical role in times of war and peace. They are often more vulnerable than men since they are often noncombatant, unarmed, targets and victims of violence and exploitation. Women are often the ones to seek an end to war, and try to resolve conflicts and care for the men, women, and children who have been victims of war. This is no different in Africa and as a continent that has often been ravaged by war, colonization, and exploitation, the women of Africa (unfortunately) have much experience in the realities of violent conflict. However, some African countries are leading the way in including women in their parliaments – Rwanda ranks first in the world and South Africa third – for comparison, the United States has 87 countries ahead of it, including 17 African countries – in terms of the percentage of government seats occupied by women (Inter-Parliamentary Union, 2009). It is hoped that these countries, and the pro-peace voices of African women, will rever-berate around the globe and through their collective experiences of violence and con-flict they will set new standards for peace-building, peacekeeping, peaceful conflict resolution, and positive peace.

Wangari Maathai is the first African woman to be awarded the Nobel Peace Prize, only the seventh African and one of only a handful of women from all conti-nents in the more than a hundred years of the existence of the prize. Ensuring equality between women and men is one of Maathai's "seeds of peace." She has faced a lot of opposition to her work, and to herself, as a woman. She rejected the traditional role of subservience and led, by example, the strug-gle for equality for women in Africa, and elsewhere. In South Africa there is a saying, *wathint' abafazi, wathint' imbokodo* (you strike the women, you strike a rock), and when Maathai was struck, a boulder was dis-lodged. She mobilized thousands of women to liberate themselves by being self-reliant. She taught them to create jobs, plant and eat indigenous food crops, and realize that women can, and must, speak for themselves.

OTHER CONTRIBUTIONS TO PEACE FROM AFRICA

Despite tremendous personal sacrifices, the former South African president, Nelson Mandela, committed his life to the ideal of peaceful coexistence and the liberation of the oppressed. Facing a possible death sentence in April 1964 for his role in the struggle against apartheid in South Africa, Mandela spoke these famous words: "I have cherished the ideal of a democratic and free society in which all persons live together in harmony and with equal opportunities. It is an ideal which I hope to live for and to achieve. But, if needs be, it is an ideal for which I am prepared to die." Although Mandela received the Nobel Peace Prize for his work to end apartheid, he will also be remembered for being *the* example of lead-ership for reconciliation after the end of apartheid.

While there was uncertainty about the aftermath of apartheid, a uniquely African ethos led to a peaceful transition and a new interest and investment in the possibilities inherent in reconciliation and successful systems of transitional justice. Another Nobel Peace Prize winner, Archbishop Desmond Tutu, will probably best be remembered for his role in ensuring peace in the post-apartheid South Africa. He chaired the Truth and Reconciliation Commission (TRC) and the success of the TRC in fostering reconciliation in South Africa has widely been lauded not only for contributing to reconciliation, but also for serving as an example to the rest of the world that peace and reconciliation at the national level is attainable. Tutu is widely recognized as the pilot that steered the post-apartheid society through stormy weather to calmer seas. While criticisms of the TRC exist, many contend that the work of the TRC essentially broke the cycle of violence that could have continued after the fall of apartheid. Together with the spirit of *ubuntu* and the leadership and example of Nelson Mandela, Tutu and the TRC showed the world that societies can heal, reconcile, and grow – even after 350 years of violent con-flict. Wangari Maathai was awarded the Nobel Peace Prize for her leadership in bringing peace through development to several African countries. She said: "If we did a better job of managing our resources sustainably, conflicts over them would be reduced. So, protecting the global environment is directly related to securing peace." This was the first time that the Nobel Peace Prize was awarded to someone who is primarily an environmentalist. It signals to the world that peace is inextricably linked to basic human welfare – taking care of our human ecology leads to peace. There are several other African Nobel Laureates for Peace: Albert Luthuli, Anwar Sadat, F. W. De Klerk, Kofi Annan, and Mohamed ElBaradei.

There are many current contributions to peace and reconciliation in Africa. For example, groundbreaking work on reducing intergroup prejudice and conflict in Rwanda by means of radio soap operas shows promising results. However, there are also many remaining challenges to peace in Africa. Inter- and intrastate conflicts are still prevalent and issues such as poverty, natural disasters, and international interference still hamper progress. Issues specific to Africa, such as the rehabilitation, reintegration, and care of former and current child soldiers demand immediate and comprehensive attention. (See CHILD SOLDIERS.) Other issues, such as the continued subjugation of women in some communities, also require urgent attention. (See GENDER INEQUALITY; GENDER-BASED VIOLENCE.)

SEE ALSO: Child Soldiers; Child Soldiers, Traditional Healing and; Conscientization; Gender Inequality; Gender-Based Violence; Liberation Psychology.

REFERENCES

Bonta, B. D. (1997). Cooperation and competition in peaceful societies. *Psychological Bulletin, 121*(2), 299–330.
Bulhan, H. A. (1985). *Frantz Fanon and the psychology of oppression.* New York, NY: Plenum.
Dawes, A. (2001). Psychologies for liberation: Views from elsewhere. In D. J. Christie, R. V. Wagner, & D. D. Winter (Eds.), *Peace, conflict and violence: Peace psychology for the 21st century* (pp. 295–306). Upper Saddle River, NJ: Prentice-Hall. Also available for download at http://academic.marion.ohio-state.edu/dchristie/Peace%20Psychology%20Book.html.
Inter-Parliamentary Union. (2009). *Women in national parliaments.* Retrieved December 2, 2009, from http://www.ipu.org/wmn-e/classif.htm.
Kamwangamalu, N. M. (1999). Ubuntu in South Africa: A sociolinguistic perspective to a pan-African concept. *Critical Arts, 13*(2), 1–7.
McKay, S., & Mazurana, D. (2001). Gendering peacebuilding. In D. J. Christie, D. D. Winter, & R. V. Wagner (Eds.), *Peace, conflict and violence: Peace psychology for the 21st century* (pp. 341–349). Upper Saddle River, NJ: Prentice-Hall. Also available for download at http://academic.marion.ohio-state.edu/dchristie/Peace%20Psychology%20Book.html.

Peace Psychology: Contributions from Asia

CRISTINA JAYME MONTIEL

This essay describes peace psychology in East, South, and Southeast Asia. The first section discusses direct conflict in the region and Asian ways of resolving conflict. The next section analyzes structural violence in Asia and its associated psychological dimensions. The essay closes with a preview of the future of peace psychology in Asia.

DIRECT VIOLENCE IN ASIA

Asian conflicts tend to be intermediate-sized and internal. The disparity is notable: out of 131 violent outbreaks from 1970 until 2001, 19 were interstate, 107 internal in nature, and five were internationalized-internal. Few conflicts in Asia are internationalized – a situation where the government, the opposition, or both sides receive support from other governments. Although internationalized internal conflicts in Asia seldom erupt, these tend to kill more people when they explode. For example, four of the five internationalized internal conflicts erupted into major wars, while only 22 out of 107 non-internationalized internal conflicts grew from intermediate-sized to major wars (Gleditsch, Wallensteen, Eriksson, Sollenberg, & Strand, 2002).

Peacemaking efforts in Asian political conflicts are frequently managed by non-Asian intermediaries, usually from developed societies. However, the initiatives of non-Asians, even in the name of peace, may mirror centuries-old patterns of Western colonization in Asia, as foreign empires worked to "pacify the natives." Intrastate or regional peacemaking may be more acceptable in the Asian region in contemporary times. Examples of regional peacemaking are the hosting by the Indonesian government of peace talks between the government of the Republic of the Philippines (GRP) and the Moro National Liberation Front (MNLF) in Jakarta, and the GRP's negotiations with the Moro Islamic Liberation Front (MILF) in Kuala Lumpur, Malaysia.

Asia-based initiatives to resolve internal conflicts bring to the conflict arena peacemakers culturally attuned to local sensitivities. Cultural orientations mark Asian-style political peacemaking. For example, in Asian conflict resolution, trust is highly personalized, and intermediaries are often monarchic/ spiritual authorities.

In Western societies, the notion of trust is associated with a universalistic, abstract trust, contingent on professional credentials of the intermediary. In most Asian societies, however, trust is particularistic and based on personal knowledge of and affection for the other person. Studies of political cultures in Thailand, India, Malaysia, and the Philippines show that trust-based interactions and loyalties depend on family ties, physical proximity in a village, and personal patronage. In Asian militaries, personalized trust thrives among members of the same graduating class. Intense trust and loyalty among classmates from military academies in Thailand, Indonesia, and the Philippines can partly explain cooperation during militarized political interventions such as coup attempts,

Asian political peacemaking is also marked by a mix of spiritual and secular power. Asian-style spiritual/monarchic authority may come into play during political peacemaking. Spiritual leaders have not only inspired peacemaking efforts, but also participated in pragmatic peace interventions in several southeast Asian internal conflicts; for example, Cambodian Buddhist monk Venerable Maha Gosanda's walk in front of the Dhammayietra (Buddhist walk of peace) during his country's May 1993 elections. Filipino Catholic priests and nuns negotiated for the release of captured civilians caught in the crossfire of coup attempts. In Thai politics, the king has the most *barami* (charisma); he is associated with Buddha. King Bhumipol Adulyadev's intervention in the October 1973 Thammasat University student rallies and May 1992 street violence saved thousands of protesting civilians from harm.

STRUCTURAL VIOLENCE IN ASIA

As a whole, the Asian context is marked by histories and contemporary conditions of structural violence, such as economies of chronic poverty, political histories of colonization and foreign occupations, and culturally homogeneous groups situated in asymmetric power relations. (See PEACE PSY-CHOLOGY: DEFINITIONS, SCOPE, AND IMPACT.)

Economies of Chronic Poverty

With a few exceptions like Japan, China, India, Taiwan, Singapore, and South Korea, the countries of Asia are generally impoverished. Even in improving economies, populations suffer from staggering inequalities between the urban wealthy and the rural poor. Asian peace psychology may thus be concerned with examining how beliefs and value systems can be used to crystallize patterns of economic inequalities, or to create space for economic democratization. Some Asian studies in this area include examining sentiments of the poor towards the rich (Zhou, 2009), people's explanations regarding why poverty persists (Hine & Montiel, 1999), and alternative cultural scripts that may pave the way for changes in unequal economic systems.

History of Colonialism and Foreign Occupation

Except for the Maldives in South Asia, all other Asian countries have been occupied by at least one foreign country. Most Asian societies hold histories of multicolonial occupations. In many cases, full independence was only gained after a World War II marked by Japanese invasions and conquests. During the Cold War, Asia bore the yoke of authoritarian dictatorships, often backed up by state-militarized forces which were perceived as supported by either the United States or the Communist Bloc. These domestic authoritarian regimes employed the use of direct and structural violence to assert their politico-economic will, while silencing their opposition. It was under these oppressive circumstances that, without any space to ventilate social contestations, old group conflicts intensified and degenerated into armed struggles. Some of

these conflicts have harmful repercussions to this day. (See OCCUPATION.)

Asian psychologists have examined how specific histories of colonization have affected contemporary peace in the area. For example, they have looked at how Hindu–Muslim conflicts in India date back to British rule (Khan & Sen, 2009), or how the divide-and-rule policy of colonizers prepared the ground for communal divisions in Malaysia (Noor, 2009) and Indonesia (Muluk & Malik, 2009) today. Other Asian psychologists focus on the dynamics of forgiveness after major conflicts, for instance the role of post-World War II forgiveness in Japan's relations with China (Atsumi & Suwa, 2009). (See FORGIVENESS: INTERGROUP.)

CULTURALLY HETEROGENEOUS GROUPS IN ASYMMETRIC POWER ARRANGEMENTS

Unlike multicultural melting-pot countries such as the United States and European societies, Asian countries are typically host to heterogeneous, nonmigratory, diverse groups. With the exception of the Maldives, all other Asian countries claim multiple mother-tongues, with India having the highest diversity (93 dialects/languages). Asian countries are also typically configured in such a way that one dominant ethnic group holds a majority of the political power. In such structures, minority or low-power groups are often silenced or deprived of social voice.

In relation to these features of Asia, peace psychology has much to offer. Some psychologists have examined how cultural violence can arise when dominant cultures provide popularly accepted scripts that legitimize direct and structural violence. This includes issues that emerge along cultural scripts related to religion, language, and culturally significant symbolisms. Other psychologists have focused on the formation of identity within an asymmetric power structure, as it has been observed that low-power groups internalize negative images of themselves created by the more dominant group. (See SYMBOLS, SYMBOLISM, AND MASS ACTION.)

One highlight of Asian culture is religion. In Asia, religion tends to be part of public space rather than a private affair. Social identities are often deeply rooted in notions of religion. As a result, religious narratives arise along with social conflict. However, it would be a gross oversimplification if a causal relationship between religion and conflict is asserted, as there are instances where religion is blamed as the reason for conflict that is ultimately about unfair material and political power distribution between religion-based groups. Further, religious leaders have been effective mobilizers and mediators in peace-oriented initiatives. One example of this is Indonesia's Kiai Fawa'id, who led his Islam *pesantran* students in rebuilding destroyed Christian churches following a Muslim–Christian violent conflict.

FUTURE OF PEACE PSYCHOLOGY IN ASIA

The expansion of peace psychology in Asia can be seen in the increase of psychology based peace practitioners, international conferences, and academic programs in the region. One may find Asian psychology practitioners like Yayah Khisbiyah doing action research and community based programs among diverse Muslim groups in Indonesia; Ragini Sen, a Mumbai-based social activist, advocating for women's issues in India; Takehiko Ito, facilitating conflict transformation workshops in Japan; and Filipina psychologist Brenda Batistiana, training community based mediators for land and environmental conflicts on the village level. (See PARTICIPATORY ACTION RESEARCH, COMMUNITY-BASED; MEDIATION.)

The Asian region has twice hosted the International Symposium on the Contributions of Psychology to Peace. One was held in Ateneo de Manila in 2001, with People Power's President Corazon Aquino as the keynote speaker. A second Asia-based symposium took place in Indonesia's Universitas Muhammadiyah Surakarta and Universitas Gadjah Mada in 2007.

The continuity of an Asian-based peace psychology may be ensured as the discipline becomes a regular part of academic programs in the region. Recent developments show that peace psychology is growing as an academic discipline. The University of Indonesia has just started an MA in Peace Psychology. In the International Islamic University Malaysia, an MA program in Peace and Conflict Studies that includes peace psychology courses was launched in 2011. A number of other universities may not have a masters program in the field, but offer peace psychology as a course. At the time of this writing, courses in peace psychology are also being taught or developed at the University of the Punjab in Pakistan, Ateneo de Manila University in the Philippines, Wako University in Japan, and Universitas Muhammadiya Surakarta in Solo, Indonesia. The Ateneo de Manila offers a course in Asian Peace Psychology as part of a dual-campus MA Program in Peace Studies of the University for Peace in Costa Rica. Graduate students on this course are composed of around 25 peace practitioners from Asian societies such as Vietnam, China, Mongolia, Japan, Bangladesh, Sri Lanka, Nepal, Indonesia, South Korea, and Kyrgystan.

SEE ALSO: Forgiveness, Intergroup; Mediation; Occupation; Participatory Action Research, Community-Based; Peace Psychology: Definitions, Scope, and Impact; Symbols, Symbolism, and Social Action.

REFERENCES

Atsumi, T., & Suwa, K. (2009). Toward reconciliation of historical conflict between Japan and China: Design science for peace in Asia. In C. J. Montiel & N. M. Noor (Eds.), *Peace psychology in Asia* (pp. 237–247). New York, NY: Springer.

Gleditsch, N. P., Wallensteen, P., Eriksson, M., Sollenberg, M., & Strand, H. (2002). *Armed conflict 1946–2001: A new dataset*. Retrieved January 8, 2003, from http://www.prio.no/cwp/armedconflict/current/conflic_list_1946-2001.pdf.

Hine, D. W., & Montiel, C. J. (1999). Poverty in developing nations: A cross-cultural attributional analysis. *European Journal of Social Psychology, 29*, 943–959.

Khan, S., & Sen, R. (2009). Where are we going? Perspective on Hindu–Muslim relations in India. In C. J. Montiel & N. M. Noor (Eds.), *Peace psychology in Asia* (pp. 43–64). New York, NY: Springer.

Muluk, H., & Malik, I. (2009). Peace psychology of grassroots reconciliation: Lessons learned from the "Baku Bae" peace movement. In C. J. Montiel & N. M. Noor (Eds.), *Peace psychology in Asia* (pp. 85–103). New York, NY: Springer.

Noor, N. M. (2009). The future of Malay–Chinese relations in Malaysia. In C. J. Montiel & N. M. Noor (Eds.), *Peace psychology in Asia* (pp. 161–172). New York, NY: Springer.

Zhou, F. (2009). Income gap, materialism, and attitude toward the rich. In C. J. Montiel & N. M. Noor (Eds.), *Peace psychology in Asia* (pp. 275–286). New York, NY: Springer.

ADDITIONAL RESOURCES

Azar, E. (1990). *The management of protracted social conflict*. Aldershot, UK: Dartmouth Publishing.

Godement, F. (1997). *The new Asian renaissance: From colonialism to the post-Cold War* (E. J. Parcell, Trans.). London, UK: Routledge.

Montiel, C., & Leung, K. (2003). Peace psychology in Asia. Special issue, *Peace and Conflict: Journal of Peace Psychology, 9*.

Peace Psychology: Contributions from Europe

KLAUS BOEHNKE AND MAOR SHANI

As is the case in the entire discipline of psychology, peace psychology as an emerging area of inquiry is relying heavily on research done in North America. (See PEACE PSYCHOLOGY: CONTRIBUTIONS FROM NORTH AMERICA.) The theoretical and empirical study of social conflicts, violence, and peace has, however, been an integral part of European psychology from its beginning as well.

This article will focus on Europe-based research and themes in peace psychology using the discipline's more narrow definition, which refers to conflicts, direct violence, and negative peace, and not to its broader definition, which also includes issues of structural violence and social and economic injustices. For the sake of brevity, the review largely excludes research on interethnic tensions, prejudice, and nationalism, as well as processes of conciliation across the European continent in the context of growing multiculturalism and European integration. Instead, we will offer a brief review of the development of peace psychology in Europe within a particular historical context after World War II, with a glance at major Europe-related themes and topics in empirical research on war and peace. These are related mainly to the East–West antagonism during the Cold War, ethnonational conflicts before and after the fall of the Iron Curtain, particularly in Northern Ireland and former Yugoslavia, and the more contemporaneous threat of terrorism. Throughout this review, particular attention will be paid to peace psychology in Germany, whose institutions and academic facets have developed and gained importance during the final years of the Cold War, and more intensively following German unification in 1990.

EUROPEAN PEACE PSYCHOLOGY
UNTIL THE 1950s

Several prominent early students of psychology in Europe, from Pythagoras to Sigmund Freud, were concerned with wars and their prevention. They developed a number of themes that later constituted the foundations of contemporary peace psychology, such as human rights and social justice, prejudice and outgroup hostilities, and the undesired psychological and sociopsychological consequences of war (Rudmin, 1991). (See PEACE PSYCHOLOGY, PHILOSOPHICAL FOUNDATIONS OF.)

In modern times, peace psychology in Europe has developed in parallel to that in the United States. The establishment of peace psychology as a subdiscipline within psychology occurred in the 1980s, but it extends its roots several decades earlier. Although some psychologies made an effort at establishing that war was undesirable before and during the world wars, the involvement of Western psychologists in matters of peace and conflict was manifested at that time mainly through their work in the service of the fighting armies, as they joined the efforts to win the war. However, in the aftermath of World War II there was a mushrooming of writings in Europe, as well as in other parts of the world, emphasizing the need to apply psychology to prevent war.

EAST–WEST ANTAGONISM DURING
THE COLD WAR

During the 1950s up to the mid-1960s, questions of war and peace were closely tied to Cold War ideologies – in the West peace was closely associated with freedom, while in the East peace was understood in the framework of socialism, and therefore peace research was tied to Marxism-Leninism.

This was the main reason for the relative nonexistence of psychological peace research at that time.

However, in the Détente era (late 1960s and 1970s), due to the arrival of peaceful coexistence, ideological ties loosened. The development in Germany exemplifies a general trend in Central Europe during the 1980s. Both in the West (1983) and in the East (1986) academically rooted peace initiatives were founded by psychologists. Both East and West German peace psychologists dealt with similar issues, mainly enemy images and propaganda, motivation and control beliefs pertaining to activities in the peace movement, war anxiety, and psychological aspects of militarization and rearmament (Boehnke, 1992).

Psychological studies concerning the arms race between the United States and the Soviet Union were of great importance in the 1980s, due to growing worries, particularly among Western Europeans, about the feasibility of nuclear war, following the deployment of US missiles on European land. Nuclear-related psychological research was concerned prominently with psychopolitical aspects of the nuclear annihilation threat and national security issues. Scholars were mainly interested in attitudes toward the arms race and disarmament, and in common psychological reactions to the nuclear threat. They revealed that the prospect of nuclear war resulted in great worries among children and adolescents in both Western and Eastern European countries.

Another major research theme in the framework of Cold War psychology focused on enemy images and perceptions of East–West antagonism. In 1961 Urie Bronfenbrenner coined the term "mirror image" to describe Soviet–American and East–West European relations, referring to a psychological barrier according to which both societies viewed each other as aggressors, and saw their rival's government as one that exploited and oppressed the people, produced policies based on madness, and was therefore untrustworthy and cruel.

POST-COLD WAR AND THE RISE OF ETHNONATIONAL CONFLICTS IN EUROPE

With the fall of the Iron Curtain, the context of war, violence, and conflict in Europe shifted from a bipolar power struggle to ethnopolitics. The dissolution of the Soviet Union and the weakened security assurances gave rise to ethnic and national divisions, and to deteriorating relations between social groups within political units. Consequently, European peace psychology shifted from dealing with global politics to studying particular conflicts, nations, and regions in which problems of war and conflicts had emerged or continued, and to focusing on the prevention of violence and animosity through the promotion of positive intergroup relations.

In Germany, unification gave rise to what might be called psychological conversion research in the early 1990s, which focused on facilitating the sociopsychological transition towards a tolerant society by supporting the conversion of Cold War antagonisms into a culture of peace. Since the breakdown of East–West antagonism did not comprehensively remove enemy images prevailing during the years of division, there was an increasing fear that former enemy images and attitudes resulting from the ideological division would turn towards minority groups and immigrants within society. Maaz (1992) investigated psychosocial aspects of this process, focusing particularly on anxieties and fears of former East Germans who were rapidly subjected to Western conditions, and as a result had developed a psychological defense mechanism in response to the repressive influences of communism. He further argued that the developmental paths of both German states were the result of social maladjustment, resulting from inadequate fulfillment of basic psychosocial needs.

The fall of communism gave rise to an identity crisis and increasing militant nationalism, particularly in Eastern Europe. In this context, Scheye (1991) studied the impact of the post-World War II division of Europe on individual and collective psychic structures. The (Central) European self, he discovered, was split along three dimensions: national–international, civic society–government, and intrapsychical. The divided self prompted Europeans to create inner retreats to protect their true selves. However, with the disappearance of external coercion, intimate bonds dissolved and a European identity crisis emerged.

The splintering of Yugoslavia after the Cold War resulted in growing struggles and negative psychological dynamics between ethnic groups. Studies on the Yugoslav Wars paid attention to the psychological devastations of war and genocide, implications of war crimes, psychological effects of exposure to wartime trauma, motivations for war, and perceptions about war, particularly among Serbs. The culture of conflict in the societies involved and its role in the disastrous events were also analyzed. (See CONFLICT, CULTURE OF.) Scholars have furthermore studied various aspects of peace-building and reconciliation efforts in former Yugoslavia after the wars, such as mental healthcare and programs to facilitate healing of war trauma in postwar Bosnia, and peace education programs in Bosnia and Herzegovina that demonstrated transformative results (Hare, 2006).

For many years the political–religious division in Northern Ireland between the Loyalist/Protestant majority and the Republican/Catholic minority, locally referred to as the Troubles, has been one of the most persistent and intractable conflicts in the world, and has received international research attention. According to Cairns, Wilson, Gallagher, and Trew (1995), studies on the Troubles have dealt with three main themes: (1) behavioral and cognitive consequences of conflict-related events, and particularly the conflict impact on the mental health of children and adults; (2) the complex psychological dynamics of the conflict, particularly from the perspective of social identity theory, emphasizing that categorization and processes of conceptualizing social identity in Northern Ireland play an important role in the conflict; (3) methods of reconciliation and the evaluation of peacebuilding interventions and peace education in the region. (See CHILDREN AND POLITICAL VIOLENCE; SOCIAL IDENTITY THEORY; FORGIVENESS, INTERGROUP.)

Psychological studies on European-based ethnonational conflicts were also dedicated to the role of group identities in Greek–Turkish conflictual relations, conflict resolution training and consultation in Cyprus, group processes in the resolution of conflict in Estonia, trauma-related aspects of the conflict in Macedonia, and indications for a culture of peace in Spain. (See CONFLICT RESOLUTION, INTERACTIVE; POST-TRAUMATIC STRESS DISORDER AND PEACE.)

During the first decade of the twenty-first century, European peace psychology, similar to its American counterpart, has seen an increase in studies on terrorism, aiming particularly at understanding the psychological consequences and emotional reactions of threatened societies. Studies have generally showed that perceptions of threat in Europe have increased following the terrorist attacks in Madrid in 2004 and London in 2005. Scholars in Spain have examined personal emotions, emotional atmosphere, and emotional climate in Spain after the Madrid bombing, and showed how social sharing and participating in secular political rituals (such as demonstrations) helped in coping with the wounds of trauma and enhancing the reconstruction of a positive emotional climate in Madrid after the train bombings.

CONTEMPORARY PSYCHOLOGICAL STUDIES OF PEACE IN GERMANY

During the 2000s, German peace psychology has been preoccupied mainly with understanding macrosocial threats and terrorism, as well as with various aspects of intergroup relations and peace. In 2004, German peace psychology saw the publication of a handbook of peace psychology in German (Sommer & Fuchs, 2004), assembling 46 contributions, mostly by German psychologists.

The Peace Research Group at the University of Konstanz, headed by Wilhelm Kempf, studies conflict communication and its role in the constructive transformation of conflicts, including the contribution of the media to peacebuilding, constructive coverage of conflict, peace journalism, and the construction of national identities in Europe. (See PEACE JOURNALISM.)

The Social Psychology Work Group at Philipps University Marburg studies aspects of intergroup relations, particularly in Germany and in the context of the European Union's expansion. Topics include ethnic prejudice, discrimination, and the effectiveness of prejudice prevention and intervention programs. The interdisciplinary research group "Group Focused Enmity," established in 2004 at the University of Bielefeld, deals with manifestations, causes, consequences, and prevention of group-focused hostile behavior against minority groups in Europe.

Several psychology units at Friedrich Schiller University in Jena investigate topics relating to intergroup relations, conflict, war, and human rights. The research group "Discrimination and Tolerance in Intergroup

Relations" studies, among other topics, cognitive factors of stereotype formation and intergroup judgment, and determinants of rejection and exclusion of outgroups. The research group also evaluates social-cognitive training programs to prevent prejudice and discrimination among children and adolescents.

In 2005 a special issue of *Peace and Conflict: The Journal of Peace Psychology*, edited by Klaus Boehnke, Daniel Fuss, and Angela Kindervater, was dedicated to German peace psychology. It included contributions of contemporary peace psychologists active in Germany on several topics, among them, old and new anti-Semitism and its relations to two personality syndromes, authoritarianism and social dominance; the relations between personal values and war-related attitudes, which included ideological attitudes, threat of terrorism, and concerns for human costs; and the impact of nationality and international conflict on the social identity of young Europeans. (See ANTI-SEMITISM, PSYCHOLOGY OF; AUTHORITARIAN PERSONALITY; SOCIAL DOMINANCE THEORY.)

SUMMARY

This review has merely provided a glimpse of past and present trends and empirical foci of European peace psychology, particularly within a European context of intergroup relations. It has also sought to demonstrate how European and particularly German psychology has played a considerable role in the organizational and academic formation of peace psychology as a respectable subdiscipline of psychology. In the current reality of relative peace across the continent, European peace psychology is expected to continue its scholarly efforts in understanding primary psychological issues in the context of war and peace, as well as in challenging emerging global risks, among them

environmental issues, religious fundamentalism, and terrorism, and in promoting the construction and maintenance of cultures of peace. (See TERRORISM, PSYCHOLOGY OF.)

SEE ALSO: Anti-Semitism, Psychology of; Authoritarian Personality; Children and Political Violence; Conflict, Culture of; Forgiveness, Intergroup; Peace Journalism; Peace Psychology: Contributions from North America; Peace Psychology, Philosophical Foundations of; Social Dominance Theory; Social Identity Theory; Terrorism, Psychology of.

REFERENCES

Boehnke, K. (1992). The status of psychological peace research in East and West Germany in a time of change. *Political Psychology*, 13(1):133–144.
Cairns, E., Wilson, R., Gallagher, T., & Trew, K. (1995). Psychology's contribution to understanding conflict in Northern Ireland. *Peace and Conflict: Journal of Peace Psychology*, 1(2):131–148.
Hare, A. P. (2006). The Middle East, Russia, and other specific areas. In H. H. Blumberg, A. P. Hare, & A. Costin (Eds.), *Peace psychology: A comprehensive introduction* (pp. 162–198). New York, NY: Cambridge University Press.
Maaz, H.-J. (1992). Psychosocial aspects in the German unification process. *International Journal for the Advancement of Counseling*, 15, 91–101.
Rudmin, F. (1991). Seventeen early peace psychologists. *Journal of Humanistic Psychology*, 31(2), 12–43.
Scheye, E. (1991). Psychological notes on Central Europe: 1989 and beyond. *Political Psychology*, 12(2), 331–344.
Sommer, G., & Fuchs, A. (Eds.). (2004). *Krieg und Frieden: Handbuch der Konflikt-und Friedenspsychologie* [War and peace: Handbook of conflict and peace psychology]. Weinheim, Germany: Beltz.

Peace Psychology: Contributions from North America

DANIEL J. CHRISTIE

Peace psychology in North America has been shaped by geohistorical forces emerging during the Cold War, a period when the United States and Soviet Union were engaged in an arms race and competed for global hegemony. But the roots of peace psychology are much deeper. This article will use a historical lens and identify the contributions of North American psychologists to peace psychology. More details can be found in Christie, Wagner, and Winter (2001).

FIRST HALF OF THE TWENTIETH CENTURY

North American psychologists often trace peace psychology back to William James, the founder of modern psychology in North America. James, a pacifist and activist, gave an address at Stanford University in 1906 on *The Moral Equivalent of War*. He argued for the importance of finding a suitable substitute, a moral equivalent of war, which would somehow have the power, attraction, and virtuous aspects of war (e.g., group cohesiveness, loyalty, pursuits beyond self-interest). James' treatise has little bearing on modern peace psychology, though in 1995 when Morton Deutsch served as the first president of the Division of Peace Psychology of the American Psychological Association, he gave tribute to James as the first peace psychologist. A reprint of James' presentation and Deutsch's tribute appeared in the 1995 inaugural issue of *Peace and Conflict: Journal of Peace Psychology*, the flagship journal of peace psychology in North America.

James was an outlier. Throughout most of the twentieth century, psychologists in the United States mostly contributed to war efforts. Contributions during World War I were mainly in two areas: (1) intelligence testing to purge incompetent soldiers and identify "bright" officers, and (2) personnel classification and job placement. There also was concern among the upper echelon in the military about an imminent crisis in morale that might take place when the United States began to sustain casualties comparable to their European allies; hence, psychologists set out to promote morale and motivate men to fight (Keene, 1994).

During the interwar period, psychologists conducted surveys to demonstrate the value of basic military training in an effort to buttress the case for universal military service and a peacetime army, but Congress remained polarized on the issue. During this same period, psychology found a place among courses in the military curriculum with titles like "Morale and Propaganda" and "The Individual Mind in Relation to Military Service." As World War II approached and the cost of medical care for the 2.3 million World War I veterans rose, the economic utility of psychologists became apparent if only to screen conscripts for mental disorders and weed out those who might be most vulnerable (and costly).

World War II gave rise to wider involvement and specialization by psychologists. Clinical psychologists administered intelligence tests, conducted mental health screenings, and selected and trained people for "undercover" intelligence activities. Human factors psychologists contributed to the design of weaponry. Social psychologists engaged in research demonstrating that news headlines could be framed to boost morale if they elicited anger, rather than fear, and could increase recruitment levels by emphasizing Allied losses rather than gains. Based on letters that were written by German citizens, social psychologists were able to infer that only small numbers of surprise bombings were necessary to demoralize the enemy (Johnson & Nichols, 1998), a finding that was lost on the Vietnam War some years later.

BREAKING RANKS: THE SECOND HALF OF THE TWENTIETH CENTURY

Toward the end of World War II, nearly 4,000 North American psychologists signed *The Psychologists' Manifesto: Human Nature and the Peace*, which stated, among other points, that *war is not born in man*. William James had made a similar point in his 1906 address and later, during the Cold War, psychologists and other scientists from around the world issued the *Seville Statement on Violence*, once again noting it was scientifically incorrect to attribute war-making to human nature. Throughout the twentieth century, psychologists have been compelled to remind people repeatedly that the human potential for war does not imply the inevitability of war. (See SEVILLE STATEMENT ON VIOLENCE.)

World War II spawned a great deal of research on the authoritarian personality, which offered a psychodynamic explanation of Germans' attraction to Nazism. (See AUTHORITARIAN PERSONALITY.) At the conclusion of World War II, geopolitical power was configured in a bipolar way and the United States and Soviet Union were poised to wage a Cold War. Both countries were locked in an adversarial relationship, concentrating their resources in an arms race, competing for client states, and pursuing global hegemony. Psychologists continued to support US foreign policy objectives during the Cold War: Survey research indicated that US citizens had little concern about the threat of nuclear war (interpreted as due to "helplessness, deferring to authorities," and the like); clinical psychologists also contributed by, for instance, applying systematic desensitization

procedures to soldiers who were afraid to be near atomic maneuvers.

In the late 1950s and early 1960s, psychologists broke ranks with some Cold War policies and provided a psychologically based critique of the policy of deterrence, US foreign policy, the nuclear arms race, and more broadly the destructive nature of the superpower relationship. Survey research was suggesting Soviet and US citizens shared a *diabolical enemy image* of each other fueled by misperceptions and threats to survival. (See IMAGE THEORY.) Deterrence, the centerpiece of US foreign policy, was scrutinized as a policy that had created a security dilemma in which efforts by one side to increase its own security through the acquisition of more arms inevitably posed a threat to the other side, which in turn ratcheted up its production and deployment of nuclear weapons. A vicious cycle ensued that culminated in the policy of Mutually Assured Destruction (MAD), prompting some psychologists to write about "the madness of MAD." (See SECURITY DILEMMA IN STRUCTURAL INTERNATIONAL RELATIONS THEORY.)

Hope was provided by a raft of concepts and books that offered a way out of the nuclear dilemma. Throughout the Cold War period, the *Journal of Social Issues* (JSI) periodically devoted an entire issue to peace. Meanwhile, the "cognitive revolution" in psychology was being felt in publications like *International Behavior: A Social-Psychological Analysis*, an edited volume by Kelman, about half of which examined "images" of the Other. The revolution also influenced political scientists' analyses, most notable in a widely cited book authored by Jervis entitled *Perception and Misperception in International Politics*.

In the turbulent 1960s, the legacy of slavery in the United States continued to play out as scholars in psychology sought to understand racism and activists took to the streets and demonstrated the power of nonviolence. The literature on intergroup

800 PEACE PSYCHOLOGY: CONTRIBUTIONS FROM NORTH AMERICA

relations has continued to grow in peace psychology, helped along in large part by the landmark publication in 1954 by Allport on *The Nature of Prejudice*. Allport is credited with the development of the contact hypothesis, which specifies conditions that favor the reduction of prejudice between groups. In addition to the contact hypothesis, peace psychologists have continued to explore the nature of nonviolent dispositions, attitudes, and movements. (See CONTACT THEORY, INTERGROUP; NONVIOLENT DISPOSITION; PEOPLE POWER.) The women's movement also continues to reverberate in peace psychology with calls for greater voice and representation of women in the field. (See GENDERING PEACE PSYCHOLOGY.)

As the women's and civil rights movements continued apace, the United States and Soviet Union stepped up the war in Vietnam. Groupthink was proposed to account for the tendency of US policymakers to thoughtlessly seek consensus rather than generating and critically analyzing a wide range of policy alternatives. (See GROUPTHINK.) Effort justification captured policymakers' cognitive dissonance, suggesting that the more they invested in a losing cause (e.g., winning the Vietnam War), the greater they valued the cause. Paradoxically, the goal of winning the war grew in importance with increasing losses in lives and treasure.

As the Vietnam War ended, the Cold War continued in the early 1980s. The United States deployed missiles in Europe and turned up the rhetoric, calling the Soviet Union an "evil empire" and suggesting the possibility of "limited" nuclear war in the European theater. Not even children were spared, as both US and Soviet social scientists demonstrated that the top "worries, concerns, and fears" of children on both sides of the conflict was the threat of nuclear war.

The growing threat of nuclear war ignited a backlash among psychologists who would come to identify themselves as peace psychologists. The tension between advocacy and scientific objectivity was palpable as some psychologists advocated activism and specific policies while others cautioned that taking political positions meant extrapolating far beyond the kind of data psychology had to offer. Scholarship accelerated and benefited from the work emerging in political psychology. The psychological nature of the US–Soviet relationship was captured by the title of Ralph K. White's book, *Fearful Warriors*. A year later, White's (1986) edited volume, *Psychology and the Prevention of Nuclear War*, gave coherence to concepts and perspectives of political psychologists and added a measure of credibility to psychological analyses of the nuclear arms race. Among other points, the book described psychological and political antecedents of a nuclear holocaust within the context of a competitive and unbridled arms race, destructive communication patterns, mutually distorted perceptions, and coercive interactions.

As Soviet influence receded and the Cold War drew down, a complex pattern of conflicts emerged that divided people, not so much by state boundaries, but by ethnicity, religion, and economic well-being. Ethnopolitical conflicts became the focus of many peace psychologists in North America. At the same time, the burgeoning literature on conflict resolution (Deutsch, Coleman, & Marcus, 2006) was brought to bear on the problem of intergroup conflicts, many of which could be subsumed under the rubric of identity based conflicts. (See IDENTITY CONFLICTS, MANAGING INTRACTABLE.)

Promising approaches to conflict resolution were further developed with many falling within two broad categories: interest-based and needs-based approaches. The former provides principles or guidelines for negotiators to seek mutually satisfying solutions to conflicts by dealing with underlying interests rather than taking rigid positions.

The bestselling and highly influential book *Getting to Yes* by Fisher and Ury is an example of the interest-based approach. (See NEGOTIATION, PRINCIPLED.) Also influential were needs-based approaches in which efforts were made to develop intergroup empathy and arrive at outcomes that satisfied the needs of groups in conflict. The needs-based approach could be carried out by policymakers (i.e., official diplomats) or unofficial but influential representatives of the groups who could later feed insights directly to policymakers. (See CONFLICT RESOLUTION, INTERACTIVE.)

These diverse fault lines between ethnopolitical groups laid bare the structural underpinnings of intractable conflicts that often lasted generations and yielded repeated eruptions of violent episodes. Accordingly, peace psychology accommodated to post-Cold War realities by including within its purview the prevention and mitigation of both direct and structural forms of violence as well as the necessity of treating the interplay of direct and structural forms of violence as a system of violence (Christie, 2006). In practice, what this meant was that cycles of intergroup violence presented opportunities for intervention by (1) managing and preventing conflict from turning to violence, (2) de-escalating violent episodes when they occurred, or (3) engaging in reconciliation efforts in post-violent situations, all with due appreciation of the larger structural and cultural context within which intergroup relations were embedded. (See INTERGROUP VIOLENCE AND PSYCHOSOCIAL INTERVENTIONS, CYCLES OF.)

Prior to the 9/11 attacks, few psychologists would claim expertise in the psychology of terrorism; after the attacks, many psychologists retooled and directed their research toward an understanding of terrorism. The evidence from PsychInfo is compelling: Up until 1980 there were only four citations for "terrorism"; from 1980 to 2001, 278; and from 2001 to 2010 there were 3,651.

Of course, some of this work took place outside North America.

Borum provides an overview of the state of psychological research on terrorism. (See TERRORISM, PSYCHOLOGY OF.) He notes that most of the work is quite speculative and certainly not research by any rigorous measure. The early work by psychologists debunked myths about the causes of terrorism (e.g., mental disorder, personality, etc.). Subsequently, the focus has been on how people become radicalized, the role of ideology, how to prevent terrorism, and the structural conditions that favor terrorism. Today, North American psychologists continue to grapple with a world order replete with threats that are ideologically driven and underscore the desirability of embedding a psychological understanding of violence and the pursuit of peace within the broader context of political, economic, social, and cultural forces.

SEE ALSO: Authoritarian Personality; Conflict Resolution, Interactive; Contact Theory, Intergroup; Gendering Peace Psychology; Groupthink; Identity Conflicts, Managing Intractable; Image Theory; Intergroup Violence and Psychosocial Interventions, Cycles of; Negotiation, Principled; Nonviolent Disposition; People Power; Security Dilemma in Structural International Relations Theory; Seville Statement on Violence; Terrorism, Psychology of.

REFERENCES

Christie, D. J. (2006). What is peace psychology the psychology of? *Journal of Social Issues, 62,* 1–17.

Christie, D. J., Wagner, R. V., & Winter, D. D. (2001). Introduction to peace psychology. In D. J. Christie, R. V. Wagner, & D. D. Winter (Eds.), *Peace, conflict, and violence: Peace psychology for the 21st Century* (pp. 1–25). Upper Saddle River, NJ: Prentice-Hall. Available online at http://

academic.marion.ohio-state.edu/dchristie/
Peace%20Psychology%20Book.html.

Deutsch, M., Coleman, P. T., & Marcus, E. C.
(2006). *Handbook of conflict resolution: Theory
and practice*. San Francisco, CA: Jossey-Bass.

Johnson, B. T., & Nichols, D. R. (1998). Social
psychologists' expertise in the public
interest: Civilian morale research during
World War II. *Journal of Social Issues, 54*,
53–77.

Keene, J. D. (1994). Intelligence and morale in
the army of a democracy: The genesis of
military psychology during the First World
War. *Military Psychology, 6*, 235–253.

White, R. K. (1986). *Psychology and the prevention
of nuclear war*. New York, NY: New York
University Press.

ADDITIONAL RESOURCES

http://academic.marion.ohio-state.edu/
dchristie/Peace%20Psychology%20Book.html
(Peace Psychology Book)

http://www.apa.org/about/division/div48.aspx
(Society for the Study of Peace, Conflict, and
Violence: Division of Peace Psychology,
American Psychological Association)

http://www.psysr.org/ (Psychologists for Social
Responsibility)

Peace Psychology: Definitions, Scope, and Impact

DANIEL J. CHRISTIE

Although peace psychology has deep roots in philosophy, peace psychology did not take shape as a coherent area of interest until the second half of the twentieth century. Since then, the growth has been remarkable. In *Peace Psychology: A Comprehensive Introduction*, Blumberg (2007) examined trends in citations to peace psychology using the PsycINFO database and found a large, significant increase in citations between the 1970s and 1980s, and again after the 1990s. These increases were in absolute terms as well as in proportion to the growing number of records. In the current article, some definitions of peace psychology that attempt to delineate the scope of this emerging field are offered. Then, peace psychology is situated in various geohistorical contexts around the world, and finally, some contributions of peace psychology to peace will be discussed.

DEFINITION AND SCOPE OF PEACE PSYCHOLOGY

Despite the growth in literature on peace psychology, few definitions of peace psychology have been advanced. In order to provide a framework for the book *Peace, Conflict, and Violence: Peace Psychology for the 21st Century*, the following working definition was offered:

> Peace psychology seeks to develop theories and practices aimed at the prevention and mitigation of direct and structural violence. Framed positively, peace psychology promotes the nonviolent management of conflict and the pursuit of social justice, what we refer to as peacemaking and peacebuilding, respectively. (Christie, Wagner, & Winter, 2001, p. 7)

The definition recognized the realities of the post-Cold War era in which the prevention of nuclear war between the superpowers was no longer the focal concern. Instead, the problem of structural violence, which kills people slowly though the deprivation of human needs, assumed much greater importance as peace psychologists in the majority world (i.e., the developing parts of the world that comprise two-thirds of the world) began to assert their interests and concerns. Accordingly, a 2 × 2 matrix was proposed that organized topics in the book and captured some of the intellectual currents in peace psychology around the world:

	Direct	Structural
Violence	Direct violence	Structural violence
Peace	Direct peace (Peacemaking)	Structural peace (Peacebuilding)

A similar definition of peace psychology was offered by MacNair (2003):

> Peace Psychology: the study of mental processes and behavior that lead to violence, prevent violence, and facilitate nonviolence as well as promoting fairness, respect, and dignity for all, for the purpose of making violence a less likely occurrence and helping to heal its psychological effects. (p. x)

Moreover, in the post-Cold War period, three major themes could be discerned in peace psychology scholarship and activism around the world: (1) a more differentiated perspective on the meanings and types of violence (i.e., structural, episodic, cultural); (2) a systems view that appreciated the reciprocal links between structurally violent conditions and episodes of violence; and (3) greater sensitivity to the impact of geohistorical context on the manifestations of peace psychology around the world (Christie, 2006). In short, as the Cold War wound down, it became increasingly clear that geohistorical context had a powerful influence on the the meanings and types of peace that were most focal.

THE IMPORTANCE OF GEOHISTORICAL CONTEXT: SOME BROAD TRENDS

Western Geohistorical Context

In the West, some of the earliest concepts in peace psychology appeared during the Cold War, a period when laboratory experiments in psychology on conflict and cooperation in two-person games mirrored the bipolar power configuration in the world. Osgood's GRIT formulation also fit neatly with a bipolar power arrangement and was widely cited as a method for drawing down tensions between groups. (See PEACE PSYCHOLOGY: CONTRIBUTIONS FROM NORTH AMERICA.) GRIT proposed that each side could engage in Graduated Reciprocations In Tension reduction – a reverse arms race in a sense. There is not much evidence that GRIT was ever applied to the US–Soviet relationship but there was a tantalizing resemblance to actions Khrushchev and Kennedy undertook that reduced tensions and resulted in the Limited Test Ban Treaty, which restricted nuclear testing to underground. Also during the Cold War, a number of arms control treaties were negotiated and the field of conflict resolution emerged.

As the Cold War wound down, the dismembering of Yugoslavia challenged peace psychologists to more deeply understand geohistorical and motivational variables that could account for such devastating and widespread violence. Psychologists were dispatched in record numbers in an effort to deal with trauma. Other conflicts, such as the one between the Loyalist/Protestant majority and the Republican/Catholic minority in Norther Ireland, also took center stage as researchers and practitioners applied social categorization theory to the political–religious division in Northern Ireland, studied the impact of the conflict on the mental health of children and adults, and examined the prospects for reconciliation. (See PEACE PSYCHOLOGY: CONTRIBUTIONS FROM EUROPE.) In the aftermath of 9/11 much of the growth in scholarship was on terrorism as scholars sought to understand the causes and consequences of terrorism. (See TERRORISTS, PSYCHOLOGY OF; TERRORISM, PSYCHOLOGY OF.)

Asian Geohistorical Context

While the threat of nuclear annihilation drove much of the content of peace psychology in the West during the Cold War, the dominant peace narratives in much of Asia (and particularly South and Southeast Asia) revolved around the colonial vestiges of occupation. For example, the violent episodes between Hindus and Muslims find their origins in the British partition of India. The British policy of "divide and conquer" in which certain ethnic groups were favored over others continues to find expression in communal divisions in Malaysia and Indonesia. Moreover, when the colonial masters withdrew, the vacuum in political space was often filled by authoritarian rulers. Hence, collective historical memories in much of Asia have been shaped by foreign occupations and dictatorships. Not surprisingly, the problem of structural violence, as reflected in enormous differences in wealth and power, often is the focal concern. In historical contexts where structural violence is focal, the term peace can be viewed with suspicion, implying a pacifist orientation toward the status quo. What matters most are social justice movements (i.e., structural peacebuilding) that ratchet up intergroup tensions and press for a more equitable distribution of material and nonmaterial resources (Montiel & Noor, 2009).

In the post-Cold War world, reactions against authoritarian rule are manifest in collective narratives that fuel nonviolent democratization movements throughout a large swath of Asia, including East Timor, Indonesia, Nepal, the Philippines, South Korea, Taiwan, and Thailand. In contrast to the West, the analysis of People Power movements tends to emphasize religious over secular leadership, collectivism over individualism, and shared subjectivities rather than objective approaches (Montiel & Noor, 2009). (See PEACE PSYCHOLOGY: CONTRIBUTIONS FROM ASIA.) In short, the focal concerns, manifestations of peace, and contributions of peace psychologists in Asia are animated by geohistorical context.

Latin American Geohistorical Context

Latin America has given rise to liberation movements that seek to redress the problem of structural violence. Liberation psychology is typically traced to the contributions of Ignacio Martín-Baró, a social psychologist and Jesuit priest from El Salvador. (See LIBERATION PSYCHOLOGY.) Not unlike peace psychology in Asia, the liberation approach does not always sit comfortably with Western psychology because the tenets of liberation psychology challenge the Western approach to knowledge generation, which embraces an individualistic, decontextualized, and objective view of "the Other." Moreover, liberation psychology shifts emphasis from the practice of helping individuals adjust to difficult life conditions to praxis, which frames problems within the context of oppressors and oppressed and pursues theory development and applications that directly improve the well-being of the oppressed. From the perspective of liberation psychologists, change happens on the personal and political levels and everyone is affected by the liberation process; even the oppressor benefits by becoming emancipated from a sense of alienation. (See PROBLEMATIZATION; CONSCIENTIZATION.)

Liberation psychology also challenges peace psychology's comfort with the technology of conflict management, an approach to human relations that can be a powerful tool of the status quo, reducing tension in conflictual relationships while conveniently leaving the social order uncontested. Clearly, liberation psychology nudges peace psychology to shift emphasis from tension reduction to tension induction and from a reliance on the power of top-down approaches to bottom-up movements for social change (Montero & Sonn, 2009).

Other Geohistorical Contexts: Some Gaps

Africa is a vast and varied continent, comprised of about 53 states and thousands of ethnic groups. There has not been a thoroughgoing history of the contributions of Africa to peace psychology, though some documentation is beginning. Of note are indigenous and traditional approaches to peace, the role of women as peacebuilders, and efforts to work at intergroup reconciliation (See PEACE PSYCHOLOGY: CONTRIBUTIONS FROM AFRICA; TRUTH AND RECONCILIATION COMMISSIONS, PSYCHOLOGICAL IMPACT OF; TRANSITIONAL JUSTICE SYSTEMS, PSYCHOLOGY AND.) There also is a growing literature on the contributions of Australia to peace psychology, a history that overlapped with Western concerns when the threat of nuclear war was salient, but more recently has focused on structural violence in relation to Aboriginal people and recent waves of immigrants. In this context, Australian peace psychologists have elaborated on and applied the concepts of stereotypes, prejudice, and discrimination to the fastest growing immigrant groups: Sudanese, Afghans, and Iraqis. (Bretherton & Balvin, in press). (See PEACE PSYCHOLOGY IN AUSTRALIA.) Finally, at present, there is a lack of scholars in peace psychology from China, though collaborative efforts are beginning to emerge.

HAS PEACE PSYCHOLOGY MADE A DIFFERENCE?

The emergence of peace psychology as an area of interest with its own journal, book series, international conferences, undergraduate courses, and graduate specialties has provided a measure of legitimacy for many psychologists who subscribe to a scholar–activism model in their pursuit of peace and social justice. But overall, it is probably fair to say that psychologists, particularly in the first half of the twentieth century, contributed more to the war-fighting capability of the United States than to peace. (See PEACE PSYCHOLOGY: CONTRIBUTIONS FROM NORTH AMERICA.)

Since then, psychologists have contributed to peace in a number of ways. Behavioral scientists played a key role in the 1951 Supreme Court decision to integrate graduate schools in the United States when scientists offered testimony that segregation was "psychologically damaging." Psychologists also have drawn from Bandura's social cognitive theory as an intellectual scaffolding to produce serial social dramas that have promoted social justice through demonstrable changes in literacy, gender equality, HIV prevention, and family planning. Ignacio Martín-Baró, a social psychologist and Jesuit priest from El Salvador, inspired the liberation psychology movement that swept across Latin America in the 1980s and continues to spawn community based and culturally grounded emancipatory agendas all over the world. Herbert Kelman's Track II diplomacy or Problem Solving Workshops helped create a political atmosphere and ideas that were building blocks for the Oslo Agreement (i.e., the two-state, Israel–Palestine solution) in 1993. Irving Janis' concept of groupthink has made its way into the popular media and is regarded by current members of the executive branch of the US government as an undesirable decision-making style. Hamdi Malik and colleagues at the University of Indonesia used a grassroots and unofficial diplomacy approach to bring Christian and Muslim communities together in a social movement called Baku Bae (reconciliation), replacing violence with the cooperative pursuit of common goals. Anne Anderson, former coordinator of Psychologists for Social Responsibility, provided psychologically informed testimony to the International Criminal Court (ICC) in The Hague which contributed to the Court's decision to increase physical protection and psychosocial support for victims of rape who testified before the ICC. Finally, Brandon Hamber and colleagues in South Africa established Khulumani (Speak Out), a support and self-help group for victims of political violence in South Africa, a group that turned to activism and was instrumental in having the "secrecy clauses" removed from the first draft of the Truth and Reconciliation Commission Act. If the initial draft had been accepted, all TRC hearings would have been behind closed doors, an arrangement that was unacceptable to most victims. These and many other contributions that continue to accumulate attest to the value and promise of peace psychology.

SEE ALSO: Conscientization; Liberation Psychology; Peace Psychology in Australia; Peace Psychology: Contributions from Africa; Peace Psychology: Contributions from Asia; Peace Psychology: Contributions from Europe; Peace Psychology: Contributions from North America; Problematization; Terrorism, Psychology of; Terrorists, Psychology of; Transitional Justice Systems, Psychology and; Truth and Reconciliation Commissions, Psychological Impact of.

REFERENCES

Blumberg, H. H. (2007). *Peace psychology: A comprehensive introduction*. New York, NY: Cambridge University Press.

Bretherton, D., & Balvin, N. (in press). *Peace psychology in Australia*. New York, NY: Springer.

Christie, D. J. (2006). What is peace psychology the psychology of? *Journal of Social Issues, 62*, 1–18.

Christie, D. J., Wagner, R. V., & Winter, D. D. (2001). Introduction to peace psychology. In D. J. Christie, R. V. Wagner, & D. D. Winter (Eds.), *Peace, conflict, and violence: Peace psychology for the 21st Century* (pp. 1–25). Upper Saddle River, NJ: Prentice-Hall. (For online copy, see Peace Psychology Book in section on Additional Resources.)

MacNair, R. M. (2003). *The psychology of peace: An introduction*. Westport, CT: Praeger.

Montero, M., & Sonn, C. C. (2009). *Psychology of liberation: Theory and applications*. New York, NY: Springer.

Montiel, C. J., & Noor, N. M. (2009). *Peace psychology in Asia*. New York, NY: Springer.

ADDITIONAL RESOURCES

Christie, D. J. (2006). Post-Cold War peace psychology: More differentiated, contextualized, and systemic. *Journal of Social Issues, 62*, 1 [entire issue].

http://www.springer.com/ series/7298?detailsPage=titles (Peace Psychology Book Series)

http://academic.marion.ohio-state.edu/ dchristie/Peace%20Psychology%20Book.html (Peace Psychology Book)

Peace Psychology, Philosophical Foundations of

FLOYD W. RUDMIN

Historically, psychology found its roots in philosophy (Hergenhahn, 1997). Modern psychology began to appear in the mid-1800s, primarily in Germany but also in America, Austria, England, France, and Russia. Across the two millennia that psychology was intertwined with philosophy, most writings rarely mentioned peace or war. However, some philosophical psychologists did develop theories on peace and did actively engage in efforts to influence their contemporary politics. Two traditions are evident in this early history of peace psychology, both of which begin with a presumption that humans have a "natural" tendency towards violence and war. (See SEVILLE STATEMENT ON VIOLENCE.)

CHANGING ONESELF

In the first tradition, philosophical psychology conceived that war arises from the perception of whether or not reality is essentially material. If people think their physical, corporeal being is "real," then they become dominated by such selfish emotions as fear, anger, greed, and vengeance. This leads to conflicts and violence, both between persons and between city-states. Peace arises from self-control and from perceiving reality as the pure realm of reason and common divinity. Materialism and its violent consequences are mistakes of perception.

Pythagoreanism

This line of thought was first promoted by Pythagoras in the fifth century BCE (Beck, 2005; Rudmin, 1991; Vogel, 1966; Zalta, 2009). Pythagoras was as much psychologist as mathematician. For example, he discovered that vibration rate was mathematically related to perceived pitch. He argued that illness is not caused by fate or by spirits, but by behavior and diet. He treated grief, anxiety, and depression by music therapy and dance therapy. He proposed a life-span progression in seven stages, with a crisis at each transition. He observed that women are more social and more sharing than are men.

Pythagoras was born on the island of Samos, near the coast of present-day Turkey. He studied with Thales and Anaximander, the most renowned scientists of their day, and then went to Egypt where he studied mathematics as well as Orphic mysticism. He also went to Babylon as a prisoner of war (Vogel, 1966). Around 530 BCE, Pythagoras settled in the Greek city of Croton (also called Krotona, now Crotone) on the south coast of Italy, where he founded a school and began teaching. His students were required to give up all of their worldly possessions to the school. Periods of silence were practiced, as were solitary walks, to encourage calm and gentleness. The diet was vegetarian. The goals were self-control, the development of reason, and appreciation of the divine harmony seen in mathematics and in music.

Pythagoras taught that all living beings shared the same divine godhead. Pythagoras emphasized the essential equality of all living beings, including women, children, slaves, and animals. Pythagoras opposed all killing. Universal friendship was the highest virtue. People should never be abusive towards one another, not even to defend themselves from abuse, and should show themselves to be friendly to their enemies as soon as possible. War arose from lack of self-control and lack of understanding of our common divinity.

The influence of Pythagoras on peace was immediate and was also long lasting. The Greek city-states of south Italy and Sicily had constantly been at war, but under his influence they experienced a period of peace lasting several generations. However, his most enduring influence has been to lay the foundations for the concepts of human rights and international law. Both arise from beliefs that all humans are essentially the same and that we are rational, moral beings.

Stoicism

The Stoics were materialists, conceiving that reality was comprised of the four elements (fire, air, water, and earth), plus "pneuma," a kind of energy that gives form to objects. In humans, pneuma animates us and gives us reason. Thus, Stoicism also argued that humans are essentially the same. Happiness is directing one's life to be in harmony with nature, which means simplicity and moderation in lifestyles, doing one's social duties, and seeking self-control.

The Roman Stoic with the greatest focus on psychology was Seneca (4 BCE–65 CE) (Beck, 2005; Zalta, 2009). He was born in

Spain and lived some time in Egypt. Seneca became a skilled orator in Rome, and served the emperor Tiberius as treasurer. He survived the violent reign of Caligula, and during the reign of Claudius was exiled to Corsica. He was recalled to Rome to serve as tutor to the child emperor, Nero, and later as his advisor. In 62 CE he escaped the political intrigues of Rome by retiring to a life of philosophy, living on fruit and water. In 65, Nero ordered him to commit suicide.

Seneca's psychology focused on emotions. Seneca considered anger to be the worst of the passions and the major cause of war. Anger feeds on itself, is capricious, cannot hear contrary evidence, and never changes its judgment even if wrong. Arrogance and ignorance are preconditions of anger. Seneca said that the three stages of anger are (1) involuntary passion, (2) a will to hurt others, and (3) vengeance. In contexts of anger, decisions should be delayed until reason has returned. Seneca recommended behavior modification: a gentle voice, slow steps, and friendly countenance can calm inner emotions. In moral behavior, Seneca argued that it is better to suffer injury than to do injury, and that friendship creates common interests and good will.

An advisor to a Roman emperor seems an unlikely source of insights about the psychology of peace, but the early reign of Nero, under the advisement of Seneca, had no wars or bloody uprisings. In statecraft, anger is most dangerous because it leads to enmity between states and to war. Violent attempts to destroy enemies only make the enemies multiply. Leaders who are cruel or criminal become worse and worse because crime can only be hidden by more crime. Seneca argued that gentleness enhances security because leaders who consider reasonable requests, disregard insults, and avoid cruel punishments attract the loyalty of the citizens.

There were other philosophical psychologists whose theories led to advocacy of inner peace. For example, Baruch Spinoza (1632–1677) also argued that all humans are essentially the same, and he is often quoted that peace is not an absence of war but is a state of mind, a disposition for benevolence and justice.

CHANGING SOCIETAL INSTITUTIONS

Contemporary with Spinoza was Thomas Hobbes (1588–1679), the British psychologist who argued in his book *Leviathan* that natural human aggression is not constrained by inner virtue and moral effort, but by the power of the government (Hergenhahn, 1997). Subsequent philosophical psychologists made the analogy that an individual state is like an individual person, and hence also needs to be constrained if there is to be peace. This focus on international institutions was also motivated by Europe's experience of the Seven Years' War (1754–1763), which was the first modern world war, with Britain, Prussia, and Portugal against France, Austria, Russia, Sweden, Saxony, and Spain. On land and sea, war was fought in Europe, North America, and India.

Rationalism

Hobbes' psychology of perception and passions was developed by Locke, Berkeley, and Hume, who came to the conclusion that regularities in the world that are studied by science are merely habits of mind, inductive expectations. This inspired Immanuel Kant (1724–1804) to theorize how the mind structures reality by innate categories of thought, for example, time, cause and effect, unity, etc. (Hergenhahn, 1997; Zalta, 2009), thus laying the foundations for physiological psychology, Gestalt psychology, and even psychodynamic psychology, all arguing that the "mind" cannot perceive "reality" beyond the mind's own impositions.

In 1795, when already famous, Kant wrote his essay on "Perpetual Peace" (Beck,

2005). He proposed six "preliminary articles" of peace that rest on rational consistency (Kant, 1795/1963, pp. 85–89):

1. "No treaty of peace shall be held valid in
which there is a tacitly reserved matter
for a future war" because that would be
a contract made in bad faith and would
violate the concept of a peace treaty
which terminates the causes of future
wars.
2. "No independent states . . . shall come
under the dominion of another state"
because by definition a state is "a society
of men whom no one else has any right
to command or to dispose except the
state itself."
3. "Standing armies shall in time be totally
abolished" because they reveal bad faith,
cause distrust, and result in arms races,
which make the cost of peace seem
higher than the cost of a quick offensive
war. Standing armies also degrade the
moral rights of individuals in their own
persons.
4. "National debts shall not be contracted
with a view to the external friction of
states" because that makes an inexhaust-
ible war treasury, that will inevitably lead
to default, bankruptcy, and destruction of
the state.
5. "No state shall by force interfere with the
constitution or government of another
state" because that contradicts the
concept of a state.
6. "No state shall, during the war, permit
such acts of hostility which would make
mutual confidence in the subsequent
peace impossible," including assassins
(terrorism), poisons (biochemical warfare), incitement to treason (subversion),
and breaches of capitulation (killing or
torturing prisoners).

Kant (1795/1963, pp. 93–102) also proposed
three "definitive articles" for perpetual
peace:

1. "The civil constitution of every state
should be republican" because a free citizenry will rarely consent to war since
they suffer the costs. Kant defined despot-
ism to be "the autonomous execution by
the state of laws which it has itself
decreed."
2. "The law of nations shall be founded on
a federation of free states." States, like
individuals, need the rule of law, created
by a freely assembled "league of nations."
International law and international courts
reduce disputes and allow just settlements without resort to war. When disputes are settled by war, a just settlement
is unlikely.
3. "The law of world citizenship shall be
limited to conditions of universal hospi-
tality." This right to immigration is based
on human equality; foreigners must be
treated as citizens.

Kant also argued that trade leads to mutual
interests and less war. Finally, Kant
(1795/1963, pp. 122–128) noted political acts
that lead to war create the conditions for (1)
usurping the rights of the citizenry by bold
actions taken with conviction; (2) when
attacking another nation, claiming that it
was national self-defense; (3) conquering
weaker nations while claiming to protect
them; (4) making decisions in secret. Any
plan that requires secrecy to succeed is by
that fact immoral and irrational.

Utilitarianism

British Empiricism (Hobbes, Locke, Berkeley,
Hume) also inspired Jeremy Bentham (1748–
1832) to initiate Utilitarianism, which is a
school of psychology that presumes that
humans are motivated to seek pleasure
and to avoid pain, both broadly defined
(Hergenhahn, 1997; Rudmin, 1991).
Utilitarianism was an early articulation of
Thorndike's Law of Effect and Skinner's
operant conditioning.

In 1789, six years prior to Kant, Bentham published his *Plan for an Universal and Perpetual Peace*. They were independent works, but had more similarities than just their titles. Both argued that the costs of war paid by the population outweigh any supposed benefit. Both argued that commerce is a counterweight to war. Both argued that international law and a world court would allow states to make concessions without loss of national pride. Both argued for a federation of states. Both argued that secrecy is very dangerous, since it is impossible to stop what one does not know is happening. Both argued for disarmament, but Bentham further specified that this should involve multilateral, balanced, negotiated reductions. Bentham was very aware of colonies, which he said were economic liabilities and increased the opportunity for disputes. Colonial disputes quickly lead to war since people have less opposition to war in foreign lands than to war near to home. Colonies also cause corruption in the civil service and the armed forces.

Bentham noted the cognitive processes of projection, as when one nation frequently violates its own principles of justice and subsequently presumes that injustice is the natural behavior of other nations. A nation with bad intentions perceives that other nations have worse intentions. Measures of defense are then misperceived to be acts of aggression. Finally, Bentham noted that government officials are rarely punished for taking their nation to war. They will argue that war was necessary by principles of justice, and if not, then by principles of patriotism. Thus, injustice, oppression, fraud, lying, and every other kind of crime in the pursuit of personal interests, when done for national interests, is sublimated into patriotic virtue by politicians pursuing war.

SEE ALSO: Seville Statement on Violence.

REFERENCES

Beck, S. (2005). *History of peace* (Vol. 1). Goleta, CA: World Peace Communications.

Bentham, J. (1789/1939). *Plan for an universal and perpetual peace*. London, UK: Peace Books.

Hergenhahn, B. R. (1997). *An introduction to the history of psychology* (3rd ed.). Toronto, Canada: Brooks/Cole.

Kant, I. (1795/1963). Perpetual peace. In L. W. Beck (Ed.), *Kant on history* (pp. 85–135). New York, NY: Macmillan.

Rudmin, F. W. (1991). Seventeen early peace psychologists. *Journal of Humanistic Psychology, 31*, 12–43.

Vogel, C. J. de. (1966). *Pythagoras and early Pythagoreans: An interpretation of neglected evidence on the philosopher Pythagoras*. Assen, The Netherlands: Van Gorcum.

Zalta, E. N. (Ed.). (2009). *Stanford encyclopedia of philosophy*. Retrieved October 12, 2009, from http://plato.stanford.edu/.

Peace Psychology in Australia

DIANE BRETHERTON

Peace psychology in Australia has been influenced by the history of colonization. Before the first fleet arrived from Britain the continent was occupied by a number of Indigenous nations, each with its own territory, language, and culture. The Indigenous people saw themselves not as owners of the land, but rather as custodians born from the land in order to be able to care for it. The creation of the land and its unique plants and animals occurred during the dreamtime, a mystic space which is eternal. Travel through the land of other nations was made possible through knowledge of the stories and songs of the people. In Aboriginal culture the possession of knowledge was of great importance and there are still rules as to who is permitted access to knowledge of particular rituals, sacred sites, and customs.

When the British arrived in Australia they saw the Aborigines as a small number of nomads, who were not really accorded human status. The idea of the land being devoid of human occupation, and hence open for them to settle in, was the legal British doctrine of *terra nullius* or empty land. The actuality was a bloody invasion marked by armed clashes, and in the case of Tasmania, systematic genocide. Australia then has two histories, the one starting about 60,000 years ago with the arrival of Aborigines across a land bridge which is thought to have linked Australia with Asia, and the other starting with the arrival of the British 200 years ago.

Even though history books tended to emphasize the story of white Australia, people of other backgrounds can be seen to have also played significant roles in building modern Australia. While the British were the dominant group in Australia, there were settlers from other places. The exploration of inland Australia relied on the use of camels, and Afghan camel drivers. The discovery of gold attracted people from around the world and cemeteries in the gold field areas had a separate section for the Chinese. Many early Chinese settlers soon gave up the frantic rush for gold and used their skills as market gardeners and traders to supply the needs of the miners.

In recent times the composition of Australia has been changed by a greater proportion of immigrants coming from non-English speaking backgrounds. Currently, almost one in four Australians was born elsewhere. People from the United Kingdom remain the largest group, but in the last decade migration from other regions has increased. Italy, New Zealand, Vietnam, China, South Africa, and India were reported by the Australian Bureau of Statistics to be the most strongly represented birthplaces in

2007. Sudanese-born was the fastest growing immigrant group, followed by settlers from Afghanistan and Iraq. Many migrants come from wartorn areas and need to deal with memories of trauma and dislocation. Multiculturalism adds richness and diversity to Australia, but also poses challenges that are familiar to peace psychology, such as the transmission of stereotypes, the creation of enemy images, and the need to better understand people from other faiths. (See REFUGEES AND ASYLUM SEEKERS: STEREOTYPING AND PREJUDICE.)

The development of psychology in Australia has echoed its colonial past. The first Australian university was established in Sydney in 1850, in a British mold. Psychology was initially seen as part of philosophy. (See PEACE PSYCHOLOGY, PHILOSOPHICAL FOUNDATIONS OF.) It was not until 1929 that the first professor of psychology, Henry Tasman Lovell, was appointed. By 1945 other universities such as Melbourne and South Australia had established departments and psychologists set up their own first professional organization, the Australian Overseas Branch of the British Psychological Society. In the early 1960s this became independent of the parent body and Australian members of the British Psychological Society could transfer their membership across to the Australian Psychological Society. British psychology strongly influenced the development of psychology in Australia to the extent that Brock (2006, p. 5) describes Oceania as an importer of psychology. Because British psychology was itself not static and was increasingly influenced by American empiricism and European schools of thought, the type of product that was imported gradually began to change.

While the 1970s saw a growing concern with social issues among psychologists, it was not until the 1980s that a stream that can be identified as peace psychology emerged. A team of psychologists predominantly based at La Trobe University, and led by Connie Peck, provided the impetus to set up Psychologists for the Prevention of War as an interest group of the Australian Psychological Society in 1984. The idea was to apply the findings of psychology to help prevent war and to resolve conflict without violence. The group liaised with other professional organizations such as the Peace Education Resource Centre that served Victorian schools and the Medical Association for the Prevention of War.

In the 1980s at La Trobe University the chancellor, Richard McGarvie, along with Connie Peck and a number of other colleagues from across disciplines, set up the La Trobe University Institute for Peace Research. First chaired by Connie Peck and subsequently by Margot Prior, members of this institute successfully promoted, taught, and published peace research. The journal they established, which now has the title *Global Change, Peace and Security*, is internationally esteemed. The government of the day became involved with the institute and Connie Peck was seconded from the Psychology Department to the Department of Foreign Affairs and Trade to be a Peace Ambassador to the United Nations, representing Australia. Her influence on the minister of the time can be sensed in Gareth Evans' subsequent publications on cooperating for peace. Connie Peck is now principal coordinator of the Programme in Peace Making and Preventative Diplomacy for the United Nations Institute for Training and Research (UNITAR), through which she has had broad influence on UN preventive diplomacy and peacemaking developments. Psychologists were also politically active in the formation of the Nuclear Disarmament Party, which had Peter Garrett, later minister for the environment and the arts, as one of its leaders.

The Psychologists for the Prevention of War interest group was, and still is, very active in diverse projects at the different levels of the education system. They have developed educational materials and a play that can be used in schools to reinforce conflict resolution training; award prizes for peaceful children's literature and peace-themed art in the secondary schools; and promote peace research in psychology by giving awards to tertiary students who complete outstanding peace-related fourth-year research projects in psychology. Members of the group were vocal in opposing violent toys and television and contributed to the drafting and adoption of government policies in these areas. The work of Eleanor Wertheim deserves particular attention as she has continued to teach conflict resolution, publish curriculum materials, conduct research, and provide leadership in the professional society, having prominence as both a pioneer and a contemporary leader of the field. (See CONFLICT MANAGEMENT STYLES; EMPATHY IN THE PROCESS OF FORGIVENESS; DIPLOMACY, PREVENTIVE.)

A special issue of the *Australian Psychologist* published in 1993, with an introduction by Ann Sanson, on the psychology of peace and conflict, attests to the close relationship between the professional association and the academic psychologists and serves to document achievements made in the area. The influence of peace psychologists within the Australian Psychological Society was not limited to the activities of the special interest group, but came to be integrated into its core functions. The Directorate of Social Issues published position papers on peace-related issues such as race and prejudice (Sanson et al., 1997).

In 1993 the Psychology Department of the University of Melbourne set up the International Conflict Resolution Centre with Diane Bretherton as the director. An important feature of the center was that from its inception it made a link with international peace psychologists. The first speaker in what was to become the center's Conflict Studies Group was Morton Deutsch and the program attracted students from around the world. (See COOPERATION AND COMPETITION.) The center valued the idea of linking theory and practice and its students and interns had strong organizational and people skills, as well as academic strength. (Conley Tyler and Bretherton, 2006). Staff, students, and interns of the center have played significant role in the Committee for the Psychological Study for Peace of the International Union of Psychological Science and can be seen as innovators and creators, not merely importers, of psychology.

The center organized the University of Melbourne's Flagship Conference in 2003, the 150th anniversary of the founding of the university. The theme of the conference was International Perspectives on Peace and Reconciliation. This conference provided an opportunity to showcase some of the accomplishments and contributions to peace not only of the Psychology Department, but also across the other faculties. The program included not only academic papers but also an integrated stream of activities from the performing and visual arts. Indeed, one of the highlights of the conference was a session in which peace academics, negotiators, political leaders, and activists from the region participated in a playback theater performance. Role playing a real-life situation, in which a treaty was signed, but not fully adhered to, provided not only a chance to debrief and learn from the experience, but also a chance to share insights and identify common interests across national boundaries in the Asia Pacific Region. A perusal of the conference themes gives a snapshot of the content of peace psychology and cognate disciplines at that time. Themes included international cooperation for human security; peacekeeping, peacemaking, and peacebuilding; culture and healing; indigenous perspectives; and leadership for reconciliation.

A significant feature of peace psychology in Australia in the last decade has been a shift from the paradigm of applying psychological findings to understanding the need to look more deeply at psychological theory and critically interrogate the assumptions and methods of the discipline itself. (See CRITICAL AND RADICAL PSYCHOLOGY.) For example, research that looks at the relationship between Aboriginal and non-Aboriginal Australians needs to recognize the dynamics of structural violence, and to realize that unless the research process is itself peaceful, the research might reproduce the conditions of colonialism. A number of psychologists have brought a more critical lens to understanding the relationship between Indigenous people and other Australians, using qualitative as well as quantitative methods to ensure that Aboriginal voices are heard and listened to (Bretherton & Mellor, 2006).

The shift in focus in peace psychology has also seen a spotlight on the positive. (See POSITIVE PSYCHOLOGY AND PEACE PSYCHOLOGY.) This is reflected in the change of name in 2005 of the Australian Psychological Society interest group, from Psychologists for the Prevention of War to Psychologists for Peace. This reframing of the task of peace psychology opens up new possibilities for situating peace within the university psychology curriculum. An example is the work of Louis (2008) and her colleagues at the University of Queensland. Their research in social psychology topics such as stereotyping, social identity, conflict management, and decision-making contributes to our understanding of multicultural Australia. Many peace psychologists are concerned with attitudes toward asylum seekers that have allowed harsh government policies such as mandatory detention to prevail. The deeper integration of theory and practice allows the younger psychologists to devote themselves fully to their specialty, rather than forcing them to view peace research as a voluntary extra. A computer search of the names of the earlier peace psychologists will show that while they have been very active in peace organizations many of their psychological publications are in areas other than peace. The conceptual shift has also seen a move from a more individualistic approach to one that also recognizes the importance of studying processes in collectives such as the group, community, or nation.

A key issue, both theoretically and practically, for peace psychology in Australia now is that of climate change. (See CLIMATE CHANGE AND VIOLENCE.) The Australian population continues to grow as migrants flow in from other places, but the natural resources are limited and the ecology is fragile. The pressure on the environment is stark in the central area, which appears on the map to be vast and empty, but the terrain is largely desert. Rising sea levels threaten islands and coastlines around the world, but in Australia there is a particular vulnerability because urban settlement is concentrated in coastal areas. The inland river system is in poor health and the federal government is buying back water from irrigators to try and restore the health of the Murray River. Lack of water has led to restrictions on use by householders, farmers, and businesses in many areas and is already causing competition and conflict between the states. It has become difficult to discuss the limitation of migration on the grounds of environmental sustainability as this quickly becomes conflated with migration debates. These migration debates are about where immigrants come from, how legitimate their path of entry to Australia is, and whether they understand and adhere to Australian values. In this context a person who raises the idea of limiting immigration risks being labeled a racist. There is a need to disentangle the issues and make a space for constructive dialogue.

Psychologists have focused on how people can live together in peace, but now need to turn their attention to how people can live together in peace with each other and the environment. They can learn from the culture of the first Australians, who understood people through their collective connection to the land. Recent psychological research has begun to explore how communities work together to face natural disasters, adapt, remember, and learn from them. This work is creating links with multidisciplinary research on socio-environmental resilience and points to a future direction for peace psychology in Australia and elsewhere. Though there is little attention to psychology in the resilience alliance, the changes that are deemed necessary by the earth scientists are familiar territory to conflict resolution teachers, who aim to move away from the use of domination and force to a more collaborative and flexible approach to creating harmonious relationships with the earth and its people.

SEE ALSO: Climate Change and Violence; Conflict Management Styles; Cooperation and Competition; Critical and Radical Psychology; Diplomacy, Preventive; Empathy in the Process of Forgiveness; Peace Psychology, Philosophical Foundations of; Positive Psychology and Peace Psychology; Refugees and Asylum Seekers: Stereotyping and Prejudice.

REFERENCES

Bretherton, D., & Mellor, D. (2006). Reconciliation between Aboriginal and other Australians: The "stolen generations." *Journal of Social Issues, 62*(1), 81–98.

Brock, A. (2006). *Internationalizing the history of psychology*. New York, NY: New York University Press.

Conley Tyler, M., & Bretherton, D. (2006). Peace education in higher education: Using internships to promote peace. *Journal of Peace Education, 3*(2), 127–145.

Evans, G. (1993). *Cooperating for peace: The global agenda for the 1990s*. Sydney, Australia: Allen and Unwin.

Louis, W. R. (2008). Intergroup positioning and power. In F. M. Moghaddam, R. Harré, & N. Lee (Eds.), *Global conflict resolution through positioning analysis* (pp. 21–39). New York, NY: Springer.

Sanson, A. (1993). The psychology of peace and conflict: An introduction. *Australian Psychologist, 28*(2), i–iv.

Sanson, A., Augoustinos, M., Gridley, H., Kyrios, K., Reser, J., & Turner, C. (1997). Racism and prejudice: Psychological perspectives. An APS Position Paper. Melbourne: Australian Psychological Society. Also published in *Australian Psychologist, 33*, 161–182.

ADDITIONAL RESOURCES

www.abs.gov.au (Australian Bureau of Statistics)

www.psychology.org.au (Australian Psychological Society)

www.resalliance.org (Resilience Alliance)

Peace Studies, Psychological Contributions to

CHARLES P. WEBEL AND VIERA SOTAKOVA

The relationships between psychology and peace studies, often called peace and conflict studies, are, like the disciplines themselves, complex, significant, sometimes contested, and in process. Peace studies emerged after World War II and is largely a response by people in higher education to the nuclear age and the Cold War. It is also a child of peace, antiwar, and social justice movements, and has shifting relationships with peace education, peacekeeping, peace movements, and peace and conflict research. Similarly, what is now known as peace psychology is also a product of the Cold War and its termination, when the perceived threat to global peace posed by nuclear

weapons was at its peak. (See PEACE PSYCHOLOGY: CONTRIBUTIONS FROM NORTH AMERICA.)

The addition of the word "conflict" to "peace studies" is not insignificant. In part, it reflects the fact that much of the earlier history of the field was devoted to understanding war, aggression, violence, and our propensities toward or against them. This occurred to such a degree that two noted figures in the field – Norwegians Johan Galtung and Joergen Johansen – have called peace studies "war studies" and peace research "war research." This is also reflected in the theories, methods, and claims of such distinguished researchers as William James, Sigmund Freud, Konrad Lorenz, and Stanley Milgram, who focused on inner and outer aggression and conflict, not on inner and outer peace. It is only relatively recently that peace studies has examined the roots of peace and peaceful societies, in addition to the reasons for war and violent conflict. (See PEACE AND CONFLICT STUDIES VERSUS PEACE SCIENCE.)

FROM PEACE AND CONFLICT STUDIES TO PEACE PSYCHOLOGY

Since its inception, peace and conflict studies (PCS) has had both theoretical and practical dimensions, and has also drawn upon many human and social science theories and methods, of which psychology is one, but by no means the most dominant. To most students and peacemakers, the heterogeneity of PCS is a distinctive strength; to some academics, a fundamental flaw. As a multidimensional inquiry into the nature of peace and the reasons for human conflict, PCS also has a sometimes conflicted relationship with mainstream social science in general and with the "realpolitik" assumptions undergirding political science and international relations (IR) in particular.

The early history of peace studies is to some degree reminiscent of the struggles a century or so ago by psychology to emancipate itself from philosophy and physiology, as well as by psychoanalysis and public health to separate from clinical and academic medicine and to forge distinct disciplinary and professional identities. Although it is now more than a half-century old, PCS is still marked by academic marginalization, in part due to its theoretical and methodological pluralism and to its explicit value-orientation to nonviolence.

Psychological contributions to PCS, while essential, are usually accompanied by other approaches to understanding peace and conflict. Accordingly, PCS textbooks – Barash and Webel (2009) and Jeong (2000) – incorporate psychological theories, methods, and research findings to varying degrees. Barash and Webel have two entire chapters devoted to the psychological dimensions of individual and collective behavior. And, perhaps reflecting the fact that Barash is a psychologist and Webel a research psychoanalyst, psychological and/or psychoanalytic perspectives inform much of the rest of the text as well. Jeong, whose expertise is in conflict resolution, has one chapter, "Sources of Social Conflict," incorporating psychological materials.

The Handbook of Peace and Conflict Studies (Webel & Galtung, 2009) has a chapter by Sapio and Zamperini called "Peace Psychology: Theory and Practice," and an introductory chapter by Webel called "Toward a Psychology and Metapsychology of Peace." Barash's recent *Approaches to Peace: A Reader in Peace Studies* (2010) has four psychologically oriented selections. Predictably, two peace psychology texts, by MacNair (2003) and Christie, Wagner, and Winter (2001), focus almost exclusively on the psychological dimensions of peace and conflict.

The PCS curriculum in many North American and Western European institutions of higher education, while generally tending to be multidisciplinary and hence inclusive of some psychological perspectives, is still conflict and violence/nonviolence oriented. Psychology is used for the investigation of the causes of war and peace. But, as evidenced in the *Peace, Justice, and Security Studies Curriculum Guide* (McElwee, Hall, Liechty, & Garber, 2009), in contrast with other disciplines, psychology is not yet fully integrated in many North American PCS courses.

Nonetheless, psychological contributions to peace and conflict research are numerous and noteworthy. Only a few can be mentioned here (for more comprehensive overviews, see Barash & Webel, 2009, chaps. 5, 6; Christie, Tint, Wagner, & Winter, 2008). They range from philosophical and metapsychological reflections on war, peace, and the human condition as a whole, to empirical studies of the behavior of individuals and groups in stress-inducing circumstances. And psychological explanations of belligerent and irenic behavior operate on a number of occasionally isolated and often intersecting levels – ranging from the intrapsychic and individual, through the interpersonal and small group, and extending to the sociopolitical and cultural dimensions of human belief, motivation, and interaction. While we acknowledge the limitations of a Western-centered approach, our focus here is mainly on some North American and European psychological contributions to PCS. (See PEACE PSYCHOLOGY: CONTRIBUTIONS FROM EUROPE; PEACE PSYCHOLOGY: CONTRIBUTIONS FROM NORTH AMERICA.)

WAR, AGGRESSION, PERSONALITY, AND SOCIAL SITUATIONS

In 1910 William James, referred to by Morton Deutsch as the first peace psychologist, published his classic article "The Moral Equivalent of War." There, James noted the "militant enthusiasm" of humans to rally around the military flag, and he challenged the simplistic view that war was an inevitable result of human nature. He argued for "the moral equivalent of war" because he claimed that war gives people an opportunity to express their spiritual inclinations towards self-sacrifice and personal honor, and to create peace it is necessary to express these sentiments in another, less bellicose way.

From 1915 until 1932, Sigmund Freud published a series of reflections on aggression, war, and civilization. Like Albert Einstein, with whom he corresponded, Freud was a pacifist. But he postulated the existence of a "death drive" (*Thanatos*) that is ultimately responsible for the deplorable state of the human condition. And while *Thanatos* could not be extinguished, Freud, foreshadowing Lorenz, claimed that aggression might be rechanneled, or sublimated, into nondestructive activities. While Freud was of course better known for his understanding of *inner* conflict, he also contributed significantly to assessing how outer conflicts might be mollified if humanity's destructive propensities could be redirected. In this lay the hope of human civilization, according to Freud.

Konrad Lorenz agreed with Freud that aggression is instinctive. However, he believed that fighting within a species, including humanity, performs species-preserving functions, and he emphasized the role of inhibitions, which control aggression and deter us from killing fellow animals. Paradoxically, Lorenz believed it is the same unique characteristics that elevate humanity above the rest of nature – conceptual thinking and verbal speech – that may cause its extinction. However, many reductionistic theories regard violence as an inherent human (and animal) tendency and ignore its social and cultural roots.

The German philosopher Theodor Adorno and the American social psychologist Nevitt Sanford approached individual inclinations toward violence from a more political perspective. In *The Authoritarian Personality* they connected anti-Semitism, proto-fascism, and other antidemocratic practices with a set of personal traits that predisposes one to act in these ways. The authoritarian personality was negatively associated with peace-supportiveness. Similarly, the Machiavellian personality, as described by Christie and Geis (1970), is likely to be supportive of unjust and violent behavior, if it is profitable for the person. In opposition to the Machiavellian personality stands the altruistic personality – emphatic, moral, and highly peace-supportive.

Dollard, in contrast, assumed that it was individuals' frustration with their environment that causes people to turn violent. According to the frustration–aggression hypothesis, when circumstances disallow people from achieving their goals, individuals are likely to engage in aggressive behavior. Subsequent studies by Milgram showed the importance of situational factors, so Dollard's causal hypthesis has been shown to be too far-reaching, because subjectivity and the possibility of social learning were downplayed. Milgram, in contrast, connected violence with individual obedience to perceived authority figures. His classic experiments demonstrated that specific situations often elicit compliance and aggression.

GROUPS, PREJUDICE, IMAGES OF THE ENEMY, AND HUMAN NEEDS

In *Victims of Groupthink* (1972) Irving Janis focused on the failures of group decision-making. He found that groups sometimes make irrational decisions and authorize extremely dehumanizing activities, such as large-scale bombing, because the core concern is to reach group consensus and not the quality of the decision. Janis named this phenomenon groupthink and claimed that it may result in the group's illusion of invulnerability, while viewing the opponent as weak and stupid. (See GROUPTHINK.)

In *The Nature of Prejudice* (1954) Gordon Allport argued that prejudice is founded on ignorance of others; therefore, less ignorance would mean less prejudice. Allport claimed that conflicts escalate due to ignorance of one's adversaries. According to Allport's contact hypothesis, an increase in social interaction between members of ingroups and outgroups could reduce intergroup prejudice. (See CONTACT THEORY, INTERGROUP.)

Jerome Frank in *Sanity and Survival: Psychological Aspects of War and Peace* (1968) and Ralph White in *Fearful Warriors* (1984) and *Psychology and the Prevention of Nuclear War* (1988) emphasized the dangers of developing diabolical enemy images, which people tend to create, especially when they feel threatened. White developed Uri Bronfenbrenner's theory of mirror images and emphasized their destructive consequences.

Charles Osgood, in *An Alternative to War or Surrender* (1962), proposed "Graduated and Reciprocated Initiatives in Tension-reduction" (GRIT), a method of defusing international tensions by having each side take turns at initiating tension-reducing actions. President Kennedy and Soviet Premier Khrushchev engaged in GRIT when they took a series of initiatives that culminated in a nuclear arms-control treaty in the early 1960s.

John Burton, in *Conflict Resolution and Provention* (1990), claimed that human needs, values, and interests are relevant for understanding the causes of conflicts. Many violent conflicts result from the suppression of human needs. Basic needs, such as security, and core values are not negotiable, unlike interests, which are negotiable and depend on circumstances.

Johan Galtung, perhaps the dean of peace studies, for several decades has also been stressing the primacy of human needs –

especially our needs for security and identity, which, if frustrated, may engender intrastate and destructive identity conflicts. He argues that sustainable peace requires the satisfaction of our needs for security, identity, well-being, and self-determination. For Galtung, psychology has much to say about the causes of intolerance and the way to increase peace and tolerance.

CONCLUSION AND DIRECTIONS FOR FUTURE RESEARCH

Peace and conflict studies in general, and peace psychology in particular, have come very far in a relatively brief period. But they have a great deal more to offer – both for studying and for making peace.

For example, by focusing less on "terrorists" and more on the victims of all forms of political violence, especially that perpetrated by states, PCS might transform the current, constrained terrorism discussion in the West. By developing a cross-cultural political psychology of terrorism, peace psychology might contribute to negotiations between adversaries, instead of violent confrontation, and to reconciliation rather than revenge. In addition, PCS might specify the preconditions and reinforcers of peace and peaceful societies – thus contributing to conflict prevention and transformation, rather than to shortlived conflict "management."

Psychology might contribute to peace and conflict studies and peace research by investigating the inner and intersubjective factors that facilitate or block peace. Minds at peace, and families, small groups, and organizations that practice equitable and nonviolent modes of conflict resolution, are less predisposed to violence. Finally, peace and conflict studies needs both a general theory and a robust methodology. With these, PCS might find itself closer to the center of academic discourse and research.

Peace psychology is indispensable – both to peace studies and to peace.

SEE ALSO: Contact Theory, Intergroup; Groupthink; Peace and Conflict Studies versus Peace Science; Peace Psychology: Contributions from Europe; Peace Psychology: Contributions from North America.

REFERENCES

Barash, D. P. (2010). *Approaches to peace: A reader in peace studies*. New York, NY: Oxford University Press.

Barash, D. P., & Webel, C. P. (2009). *Peace and conflict studies* (2nd ed.). London, UK: Sage.

Christie, D. J., Tint, B. S., Wagner, R. V., & Winter, D. D. (2008). Peace psychology for a peaceful world. *American Psychologist, 63*, 540–552.

Christie, D. J., Wagner, R. V., & Winter, D. D. (2001). *Peace, conflict, and violence: Peace psychology for the 21st century*. Upper Saddle River, NJ: Prentice-Hall.

Christie, R., & Geis, F. L. (1970). *Studies in Machiavellianism*. New York, NY: Academic Press.

Jeong, H.-W. (2000). *Peace and conflict studies: An introduction*. Aldershot, UK: Ashgate.

McElwee, T. A., Hall, B. W., Liechty, J., & Garber, J. (2009). *Peace, justice, and security studies: A curriculum guide*. Boulder, CO: Lynne Rienner.

MacNair, R. M. (2003). *The psychology of peace: An introduction*. Westport, CT: Praeger.

Webel, C., & Galtung, J. (Eds.). (2009). *Handbook of peace and conflict studies*. New York, NY: Routledge.

ADDITIONAL RESOURCES

http://www.rachelmacnair.com/peace-psych-history (Peace Psychology History)

http://www.wcfia.harvard.edu/node/867 (Reflections on the History and Status of Peace Research)

http://www.webster.edu/peacepsychology/ (American Psychology Association, Division of Peace Psychology)

Peace Zones

PUSHPA IYER

Peace Zones (PZs) – alternatively known as Zones of Peace (ZoPs) – are zones that are meant to provide safety from the chaos of conflict. In the context of violent conflict, PZs can be geographical, personal, temporal, or goal specific. Territorially defined zones are generally safe havens for communities wanting to escape from fear and violence. Individuals or groups who are threatened, endangered, or have some special status can be declared as ZoPs when warring parties agree to specifically not target them during conflict. Temporal ZoPs are ones that are declared for specific periods of time, for clearly defined purposes, and during which time warring parties agree to halt violence. Goal-specific PZs are ones that are created for certain purposes; when these purposes are served, the PZs are usually dissolved or take on newer goals. PZs may be created in the period before violence breaks out or in the midst of war. They may also emerge in the period after a negotiated settlement to war and/or a ceasefire agreement is in place, that is, in times of relative calm.

An important aspect of any PZ is to identify the primary actors behind the creation of the zone. Most often, PZs are created through the presence and efforts of a third party; that is, an institution or an individual who comes from outside the immediate communities caught in the midst of conflict. However, there are many examples around the world of peace zones that are created by those who are affected by the violence, i.e., civil society.

Conflict resolvers are well aware that developing mechanisms for mitigating a violent conflict is often a more humble goal than resolving a conflict. PZs are a classic example of how violent conflicts can be managed through the institutionalizing of conflict. Institutionalizing conflict is the encouragement of conflict through rules. PZs are the zones where – by some form of consensus – certain acts are allowed and encouraged and others disallowed. Understanding the creation, maintenance, and termination or collapse of PZs provides useful insight on the chances of sustainability of PZs (Hancock & Iyer, 2007). PZs evaluated against the specific goals for which they were set up is one aspect of the measurement of the success of the zone; however, understanding the conflict context in which they function is crucial in the assessment of the impact of a PZ.

HISTORY OF PEACE ZONES

PZs are not a new phenomenon associated with wars and violence. Rules in war, fostering good relations among warring communities and factions and promoting conditions to stem violence, are all age-old concepts present in every society. *Mahabharata*, the epic war described in Hindu mythology, details the rules for combat. Noncombatants and unarmed people could not be targeted – an example of personal ZoPs. Similarly, at dusk, arms would be laid down and combatants were free to roam without fear of being attacked – an example of temporal ZoPs. Examples abound of historical monuments and religious sites that have been accepted by many warring parties as PZs. Mitchell (2007) provides an overview of the kinds of ZoPs that existed in pre-modern times in Moroccan, Greek, and other Middle Eastern societies. In modern society, often diplomats are offered immunity and enjoy some kind of relatively peaceful overtures even from hostile actors. Religious leaders and certain individuals in some cultures are other examples of personal zones of peace. Organizations like Médecins Sans Frontières (Doctors without Borders) and Peace Brigades International (PBI) enjoy immunity in

violent conflict and are subsequently able to extend and provide safety to those among whom they work.

Recently, the United Nations has declared many land and maritime territories as PZs to facilitate peace, security, and trade. Environmental ZoPs are also increasingly seen; known as Peace Parks, the primary goal of the park is the protection of the environment through collaboration of warring communities for whom the environment is equally important. These zones are particularly important in today's context where many wars are fought over resources.

PZs that emerge from initiatives of civil society or local nongovernmental organizations (NGOs), including religious organizations, during periods of intense conflict are becoming an important strategy of grassroots resistance to violence.

The following section provides a few examples from around the world of peace zones created during periods of violent conflict or during periods of peace. Lessons learnt from these experiences are also highlighted.

PEACE ZONES IN CONFLICT AND PEACE ZONES DURING PEACE

Some of the earliest examples of PZs initiated by communities suffering from violent conflict come from the Philippines. The country has seen waves (generations) of peace zones. The initial ZoPs – territorially defined – were created owing to a need for safety and security where residents declared themselves "off limits to war and other forms of armed hostility" (Garcia, 1997). Over years, PZs sprung up all over the country, providing a space for dialogue among the many divided communities that lived in close proximity. The ability of these PZs to survive through simple agreements with local military commanders and local leaders of armed groups drew attention to

"People Power." (See PEOPLE POWER.) This led to the second wave of PZs when the national government – wanting to invest in these successful grassroots initiatives – set up the Special Zone of Peace and Development Social Fund (SZOPAD) as part of the national-level peace agreement. The result was an inflow of huge amounts of money for the creation of peace zones to support development, infrastructure building, and reintegration of ex-combatants. This led to the general disintegration of the PZ in itself with greater emphasis being put on "development." The second wave led also to the creation of peace zones that were initiated by church institutions and NGOs. Many of these also focused on the economic development of communities, together with the goal of dialogue, violence prevention, and reconciliation. It was very evident that without the economic aspect, the survival or sustainability of the PZ would be negatively impacted (Iyer, 2004). Two key lessons emerge from the Philippine experience: the greater the involvement of the local communities in the creation and maintenance of the PZ and the more the zone catered to a variety of basic needs of the people, the more its chances of survival.

In Sri Lanka, the Butterfly Garden in Batticaloa, a city in the eastern part of the country, is an example of both a personal and a territorial ZoP. In what was one of the most tense and violent conflict areas, the camp quarters of Butterfly Garden were a totally safe haven for children from Sinhala, Tamil, and Muslim communities to come and spend time engaging in theater, arts, and crafts. The Butterfly Garden – created through the initiatives of academics at the University of Manitoba, Canada – had goals that extended from providing safety and security to the children who lived amid violence, to trauma healing through a variety of means. Another example of PZs that were specifically focused on children are the "days of tranquility" negotiated by UNICEF in El Salvador, Afghanistan, and Uganda, among others. In these cases, through an agreement with various armed factions, UNICEF secured a temporal ZoP, usually three days, when all fighting came to a halt with the single purpose of immunizing children.

The key lesson from child-focused PZs is that it is hard for parties in a conflict to refuse to support the idea of keeping children safe from violence. Although individual armed groups and militaries might recruit children and even target schools, they could rarely refuse the protection of children when the appeal came from civil society or NGOs.

Another example of a territorial ZoP comes from northwestern Sri Lanka, where a Catholic church in Madhu provided a safe haven to people of all religions whenever fighting broke out. Through some kind of unwritten agreement, no armed faction would ever target the church. However, during one intense period of conflict, a stray bullet hit the church and that led to the subsequent disintegration of the sanctuary. A key aspect of the experience is that PZs are not always created through formal agreements but often through custom, tradition, and culture.

The PZs that were declared in certain geographical areas of Aceh, as part of the implementation of peace agreements, were primarily zones for demilitarization and demobilization. Emphasis was placed on providing a safe environment for armed combatants to surrender weapons and to stock these with neutral authorities. The PZs also had rules about the kinds of criminal and violent acts that were prohibited within them. An incentive was also given to the PZs through the commitment of the international community to invest first within these PZs before meeting the needs of the rest of the country. A key feature of the PZs in Aceh was the list of sanctions noted for any kind of violence that took place in the PZs. In spite of all this, the PZs in Aceh never took off because the imposition of the idea of a ZoP from outsiders meant the community never felt involved or committed to the idea (Iyer & Mitchell, 2007).

The Assembly Points of Rhodesia provide another example of a DDR zone; that is, a zone for Disarmament, Demobilization, and Reintegration. Supervised by the commonwealth, these zones were camps where ex-combatants were encouraged to visit with their arms, surrender, and then be slowly reintegrated into society.

The Local Zone of Peace in El Salvador is an example of a ZoP created to build a culture of peace through restoration of human rights, promotion of indigenous methods of conflict resolution, and fostering peace and democracy (Chupp, 2003). Created by NGOs after the end of war and the initiation of a peace agreement, this PZ is less territorially bound and much broader in scope. The ambiguity comes from the fact that if the primary purpose of the PZ is not that of providing peace and security, do they need to be identified as such or could they just be another peacebuilding activity?

IMPORTANCE OF PEACE ZONES IN RESOLVING CONFLICTS

Conflict resolution theories explain the ability of human beings to engage in violent actions when basic needs of survival, identity, and security are not met. Conflicts over deep-rooted issues that emerge when basic needs of humans are not satisfied are the ones that are most difficult to resolve. They often require structural changes in society in order to ensure that the root cause of the conflict is addressed. While such long-term measures need to be taken to "resolve" the conflict, the pressing need to immediately end violence becomes the primary task of conflict resolvers.

PZs as tools of conflict mitigation can be useful not just to bring an end to violence in some limited sense but to ensure that conflict is carried out with some rules. While the need for sanctuaries is most appreciated by those caught in the midst of war, the survival of the zones as a safe haven is often at the mercy of those who are outside the zone, that is, the armed actors. Therefore, the conflict resolver's task becomes one of institutionalizing conflict within the zones through an agreement reached with warring parties. In short, grassroots-level peace agreements are the key. However, when these grassroots-level PZ initiatives are not linked to a broader and high-level peace process, they remain just "safe havens," making them susceptible to failure when peace processes at the high level collapse. The survival of high-level peace processes can help ensure the successful achievement of the limited goals of a PZ such as demobilization, or providing a safe haven, or immunizing children. Ideally, if the PZ survives, then its goals should be extended to the larger task of building peace and rebuilding society. In short, findings from around the world demonstrate that "humble" and realistic goals for a PZ, together with emphasis on sustainability and creativity, may contribute significantly to peace.

SEE ALSO: People Power.

REFERENCES

Chupp, M. (2003). Creating a culture of peace in postwar El Salvador. In C. Sampson, M. Abu-Nimer, & C. Liebler (Eds.), *Positive approaches in peacebuilding: A resource for innovators*. Washington, DC: Pact Publications.
Garcia, E. (1997). Filipino zones of peace. *Peace Review, 9*(2), 221–224.
Hancock, L. E., & Iyer, P. (2007). The nature, structure and variety of peace zones. In

L. E. Hancock & C. Mitchell (Eds.), *Zones of peace*. Bloomfield, CT: Kumarian Press.

Iyer, P. (2004). *Peace zones of Mindanao, Philippines: Civil society efforts to end violence*. Cambridge, MA: CDA-Collaborative Learning Projects.

Iyer, P., & Mitchell, C. (2007). The collapse of peace zones in Aceh. In L. E. Hancock & C. Mitchell (Eds.), *Zones of peace*. Bloomfield, CT: Kumarian Press.

Mitchell, C. (2007). The theory and practice of sanctuary. In L. E. Hancock & C. Mitchell (Eds.), *Zones of peace*. Bloomfield, CT: Kumarian Press

Peaceful Personality

LINDEN L. NELSON

Although psychologists have often recognized and measured individual differences in social dispositions ranging from aggressiveness to helpfulness, there have been relatively few efforts to define and measure a more general tendency for peacefulness. One approach with a rather specific focus involves conflict resolution styles. (See CONFLICT MANAGEMENT STYLES.) For example, Sternberg and colleagues (Sternberg & Dobson, 1987) developed methods for measuring conflict resolution styles. In their studies the participants either evaluated the desirability of various conflict resolution tactics in specific situations or indicated how they would deal with examples of conflict. Although most of the examples involved interpersonal conflict, some involved conflict between groups and nations. They conducted factor analyses in several studies that suggested the various styles could be usefully classified as active/mitigating, passive/mitigating, active/intensifying, or passive/intensifying. For example, the passive/mitigating style includes actions such as giving in and waiting, and the active/mitigating style includes behaviors like bargaining and mutual

discussion. The conflict mitigating styles could be seen as peaceful dispositions.

Nelson and Christie (1995) offered a conceptualization of "peaceful people" in the context of a discussion about the objectives of peace education. In order to facilitate development of peaceful people, peace educators would need to teach the values, competencies, and efficacy expectancies that enable and motivate peaceful behavior. Therefore, peaceful people are characterized as holding a particular set of values (e.g., social justice, nonviolence), possessing certain competencies (e.g., communication and conflict resolution skills), and believing that their peaceful actions will have positive results.

Ziller, Moriarty, and Phillips (1999) defined the "peace personality" as the disposition to attend to similarities rather than differences in other people. They theorized that selective attention to similarities between the self and others would lead to the concept of oneness or universal orientation. Universal orientation, in turn, would lead to empathy with others and reduced hostility during conflict. They used the Universal Orientation Scale developed by Ziller to measure the peace personality, and their research demonstrated that people scoring high on Universal Orientation were more empathic in response to images of war depicting the suffering of "the enemy."

Another approach for assessing peaceful dispositions is based on the Gandhian philosophy of nonviolence. (See NONVIOLENT DISPOSITIONS.) Mayton et al. (2007) operationally defined a "peaceful person" as someone scoring above the median on four of five scales on the Teenage Nonviolence Test (TNT). Those scales are labeled as physical nonviolence, psychological nonviolence, helping/empathy, *satyagraha* (seeking truth), and *tapasya* (willingness to endure suffering). Mayton and colleagues compared undergraduates who qualified as peaceful persons with nonpeaceful students (i.e., those scoring below the median on four of five TNT subscales). The peaceful students were found to be more benevolent, spiritual, and empathic, and had a higher need for cognition. They placed lower priorities on power and hedonistic values, and were less materialistic and less prone to anger.

If peacefulness can be considered a personality trait, the Big Five personality trait of Agreeableness may be useful for characterizing a general disposition for peaceful behavior. High scores on Agreeableness suggest tendencies toward cooperating vs. competing, relate to lower levels of anger and aggressiveness, and are associated with less interpersonal conflict and less use of threats in situations of conflict. In one study, priming aggression cues increased aggressive behavior only for people low in Agreeableness. In other studies, Agreeableness correlated negatively with tendencies to justify war and with militaristic attitude.

PEACEFULNESS AS A PERSONALITY TRAIT

The suggestion that peacefulness might be conceptualized as a "common" personality trait assumes that people tend to be consistent on the dimension of peacefulness across relevant situations and over time. That is, the assumption is that some people are consistently very peaceful, some are consistently moderate in peacefulness, and some are consistently low in peacefulness. It is also possible that peacefulness might be better conceptualized as an "idiosyncratic" trait, in which case the assumption would be that people show unique patterns of consistency in their peaceful behaviors. This would include the possibility that some people may be consistently peaceful even if most people were inconsistent in peacefulness. Personality research is generally based on the assumptions of the common trait

approach and personality tests are more easily constructed on that basis, so it seems desirable to explore the possibility that most people exhibit consistency in level of peacefulness. However, before investigating whether people are consistent in peaceful behavior, it is necessary to identify the range of situations for which peacefulness is a meaningful concept.

The numerous situations for which peacefulness is a relevant concept may be grouped into a shorter list of general contextual domains. For example, Anderson (2004) listed seven domains where peace may exist, from micro to macro contexts: personal (within the individual), interpersonal (among individuals / within the group), social (among social groups), civil (within the community), national (within the nation), international (among nations), and ecological (with the natural world). Whereas Anderson focused on peace as a nonviolent and harmonious condition, the focus here as it relates to peaceful personality is on individual behavior, attitude, and emotion. Thus, the personal domain is concerned with how individuals behave toward self, their attitudes about self, and their emotional state (e.g., calm vs. agitated). The interpersonal, civil, and national domains concern how individuals behave toward other ingroup individuals. The social domain is concerned with individuals' behaviors and attitudes toward outgroups. The international domain concerns attitudes regarding relations with other nations, and the ecological domain concerns behaviors and attitudes toward the natural environment. Perhaps another important domain to add to Anderson's list is the existential (i.e., attitude toward ultimate reality or to God). All of these domains pertain to the person's relationships, and all these relationships have a potential for conflict or peace.

Peacefulness as a trait could be defined as involving consistent behavior, attitudes, or emotional states across situations within one of these domains, or it could be defined as consistent behavior and attitudes across two, several, or all these domains. Scholars and researchers should be careful to specify the relevant contextual domains for their conceptualizations of peaceful personality. The question of whether peacefulness is a widely generalized disposition involving consistency across several domains, for some or most people, is an important issue for investigation.

There are at least two reasons for expecting that peacefulness may be a widely generalized disposition. First, conflict is a common stimulus in each domain and whatever responses to conflict a person has learned in one domain seems likely to have generalized to other domains. Second, the values and other dispositions that promote peacefulness in one domain are likely to be active in other domains as well. There is an additional reason to expect that personal (or inner) peacefulness may relate to interpersonal peacefulness. A person who is consistently peaceful interpersonally is likely to experience less conflictual and more harmonious and friendly relationships with others and therefore is likely to consistently experience peaceful feelings.

Conceptualized as a personality trait, peaceful personality may be operationally defined as consistent behavior, attitudes, and emotional states across time and situations on the dimension of peacefulness. Following Anderson's (2004) definition of peace as a nonviolent and harmonious condition, peaceful *behavior* may be defined as *behavior* that creates and maintains nonviolent and harmonious conditions. Cooperative behavior would be a good example of peaceful behavior. Peaceful *attitudes* may be defined as *attitudes* that facilitate the creation and maintenance of nonviolent and harmonious conditions, and peaceful emotional *states* include calmness, serenity, and other subjective/physiological states

associated with experiencing harmony and nonviolence.

INVESTIGATIONS OF CONSISTENCY IN PEACEFULNESS ACROSS SITUATIONS AND DOMAINS

Only a small number of studies have investigated individual consistency in peacefulness either between situations within the domains described above or between domains. Sternberg and Dobson (1987) reported studies where undergraduates rated the extent to which various interpersonal conflict resolution styles characterized their actual and ideal behavior in recent conflicts they had experienced with roommates, teachers, parents, and romantic partners. They found strong consistencies in the styles used by individuals across interpersonal situations, and they concluded that individual consistencies extend across actual and hypothetical situations, real and ideal styles, and various interpersonal relationships. They also reported an earlier study by Sternberg and colleagues where college students responded to nine stories involving conflict in three different domains: interpersonal, interorganizational, and international. There were three stories for each domain. Participants evaluated the quality of seven possible conflict tactics for each story. They found that individuals were "quite consistent" both within and across conflict domains.

Several researchers have reported small or moderate correlations within and between measures of individual aggressiveness and militaristic attitudes. Studies on people's values have revealed associations between tendencies to value peacefulness in the personal, interpersonal, international, and ecological domains.

Nelson (2007) reported two studies designed to investigate correlations between peaceful emotions, interpersonal peacefulness, and global peacefulness. In the first study, four measures of interpersonal behavior and attitudes were correlated with six measures of global attitudes (including opinions about social issues and international conflict issues). For men, 22 of the 24 correlations were statistically significant in the expected direction, and 15 of the 24 correlations were significant for women. The second study investigated correlations between a measure of peaceful emotions, three measures of interpersonal peacefulness (Peaceful Traits, Personal Revenge, Nonviolence), and two measures of global attitudes (Militaristic Attitude, National Revenge). All six of the correlations between interpersonal peacefulness and global attitudes were significant in the expected direction for men, and three of those correlations were significant for women. Regarding the three possible correlations between peaceful emotions and interpersonal peacefulness, two were significant for men and one for women. Neither of the two possible correlations between peaceful emotions and global attitudes was significant for men or women.

Overall, the research suggests that people tend to be somewhat consistent across situations within the interpersonal and international domains and that interpersonal peacefulness is related to attitudes about international relations. For these domains, the amount of consistency in peaceful behavior and attitudes that has been demonstrated by researchers is similar to what has been shown for other personality traits. Although there is also some evidence of relationships between the other domains, the research is limited and inconclusive Therefore, the evidence appears to support conceptualization of a peaceful personality trait relevant to interpersonal behavior and attitudes about international relations. Further research is necessary to investigate the validity of conceptualizing peacefulness as an even more general disposition that might also apply to personal, ingroup, outgroup, ecological, and existential domains.

CHARACTERISTICS OF THE PEACEFUL PERSON

Based on the evidence described above regarding consistency in peacefulness between the interpersonal and international domains, Nelson (2008) operationally defined a peaceful person as an individual with scores above the median on interpersonal peacefulness and below the median on militaristic attitude. (See MILITARISTIC ATTITUDE.) In one of his studies, interpersonal peacefulness was measured by a self-report instrument assessing interpersonal cooperativeness, and in a second study interpersonal peacefulness was measured by self-report ratings on peaceful interpersonal traits. Note that a low score on militaristic attitude indicated peaceful attitudes regarding international relations. Peaceful people were compared to people who scored below the median on interpersonal peacefulness and above the median on militaristic attitude. The results indicated that peaceful people scored higher on Universal Orientation, Fantasy Empathy, Perspective Taking, Empathic Concern, Ethnocultural Empathy, Peaceful Emotions, Benevolent Values, Hedonistic Values, Universal Values, and Humanistic Goals. (See VALUES, NONVIOLENCE, AND PEACE PSYCHOLOGY.) Peaceful people had lower scores on Social Dominance Orientation, Power Values, Religious/Moral Imposition, National Strength Goals, Closed Mindedness, and Endorsement of Negative Reciprocity Norms.

CONCLUSIONS AND SUGGESTIONS FOR FUTURE STUDIES

The study of peaceful personality is at an early stage. Basic issues concerning measurement of peaceful traits, identification of relevant contextual domains, and investigation of individual consistency in peacefulness within and across domains have not been adequately addressed. Nevertheless, the initial studies suggest that peaceful personality can be meaningfully conceptualized as a personality trait. Further investigations of peaceful personality traits and of the characteristics of peaceful people would probably be useful for identifying specific outcome objectives for parents and educators concerned with development of peaceful people.

Some additional important issues for future study include the following questions: What are the implications of the apparent gender differences in consistency across contextual domains? When peacefulness is conceptualized and measured as a personality dimension, should low scores be defined as violent and uncooperative or only as not peaceful? Would it be more meaningful and useful to conduct idiosyncratic studies of exceptionally peaceful individuals, much as Maslow studied self-actualizing people, than to study peacefulness in the general public? It would also be desirable to investigate the stability of peacefulness (i.e., consistency across the life span) and to study peaceful personality in various age and cultural groups.

SEE ALSO: Conflict Management Styles; Militaristic Attitude; Nonviolent Dispositions; Values, Nonviolence, and Peace Psychology.

REFERENCES

Anderson, R. (2004). A definition of peace. *Peace and Conflict: Journal of Peace Psychology*, 10, 101–116.

Mayton, D. M., Solom, R. C., Wilder, A. M., Sawa, M., Stephens, A. M., Smith, H. L., & Garrison, M. T. (2007, August). *An empirical view of a "peaceful person."* Paper presented at the Annual Meeting of the American Psychological Association, San Francisco, CA.

Nelson, L. L. (2007, August). *Correlations between inner peace, interpersonal behavior, and global attitudes.* Paper presented at the Annual Meeting of the American Psychological Association, San Francisco, CA.

Nelson, L. L. (2008, August). *Cognitive and motivational predictors of interpersonal peacefulness and militaristic attitude.* Paper presented at the Annual Meeting of the American Psychological Association, Boston, MA.

Nelson, L. L., & Christie, D. J. (1995). Peace in the psychology curriculum: Moving from assimilation to accommodation. *Peace and Conflict: Journal of Peace Psychology*, 1, 161–178.

Sternberg, R. J., & Dobson, D. M. (1987). Resolving interpersonal conflicts: An analysis of stylistic consistency. *Journal of Personality and Social Psychology*, 52, 794–812.

Ziller, R. C., Moriarty, D. S., & Phillips, S. T. (1999). The peace personality. In A. Raviv, L. Oppenheimer, & D. Bar-Tal (Eds.), *How children understand war and peace: A call for international peace education* (pp. 78–90). San Francisco, CA: Jossey-Bass.

ADDITIONAL RESOURCES

Mayton, D. M. (2009). *Nonviolence and peace psychology: Intrapersonal, interpersonal, societal, and world peace.* New York, NY: Springer Science and Business Media.

Peacekeeping, Psychology of

HARVEY J. LANGHOLTZ

The psychology of peacekeeping is a complex and multi-level topic that can be viewed from several different perspectives and taken to mean different things. One perspective is that of the psychology of peacekeeper on the ground – the soldier serving on a peacekeeping mission. Other perspectives include the psychological issues faced by international civilian police serving on peacekeeping missions, civilian humanitarian relief workers, ex-combatants, and the indigenous population living in the area of conflict. Separate from this are the psychological aspects of conflict resolution and diplomacy. And perhaps most important – and most broadly – are widely accepted assumptions about the psychology of relations between nations and peoples. Each of these topics certainly deserves a book-length examination, but they will all be briefly addressed here (Langholtz, 1997).

ETHOS: THE HEART OF A SOLDIER

"You don't have to be a soldier to serve as peacekeeper, but only soldiers can do it," said Dag Hammarskjöld, Secretary-General of the United Nations from 1953 to 1961. He certainly captures the point. Peacekeeping by definition takes place in an environment that is either violent or potentially violent. So-called "traditional peacekeeping" involves the interpositioning, following a ceasefire, of unarmed or lightly armed military peacekeepers between previously warring armies. In this case it is the job of the peacekeepers to monitor the actions of both sides and support the terms of a truce or peace agreement. In contrast, peace enforcement and other forms of peace support operations occur while fighting is still ongoing, when armed factions still exist, and in the absence of any ceasefire or truce. In these cases there is no peace to keep. But whether the mission is traditional peacekeeping or peace enforcement, the peacekeeper must still be a soldier who knows how to survive in a battlefield environment, and who is skilled at observing, recognizing, and monitoring military activities.

The ethos of the soldier–peacekeeper is by its nature the antithesis of the ethos of the soldier–warrior. Soldiers are trained first to be war-fighters. The war-fighter's ethos is to find and engage a clearly defined foe and to use escalating levels of aggression and force to intimidate, overwhelm, and destroy the enemy. The soldier's job is to be victorious in the battlefield through the use of stealth and the application of force. But the ethos of the soldier–peacekeeper is significantly different from this. The peacekeeper is not a participant in the conflict, but rather is a third party to someone else's conflict. It is the job of the peacekeeper to de-escalate or contain the use of violence through mediation, negotiation, and compromise and to instill a sense of trust and confidence in all parties by being open and transparent. The peacekeeper–soldier must deal with some of the psychological ambiguities of peacekeeping. There are some who argue that serving as a peacekeeper can undermine and weaken a war-fighter's ethos, or at least require a period of readjustment before the soldier is ready to return to the battlefield as a war-fighter.

While it is not easy to switch back and forth between being a peacekeeper and a war-fighter, it is important to point out the psychological impossibilities of making such switches in the field. A peacekeeper must develop the trust of both sides in a conflict and to be effective must be seen by both sides as an impartial arbiter. Any use of force against one side will seriously jeopardize this perception of neutrality. While it may be possible to make the switch one time from peacekeeper to war-fighter, there is no way back, as the essential trust will be lost. Neither is it possible to have peacekeeping and peace enforcement going on in the same area at the same time. This was tried and failed in Yugoslavia, with the psychological environment necessary for the success of peacekeeping on the ground being undermined by enforcement of a no-fly zone in the air.

CIVILIAN POLICE: RESTORING ORDER FOLLOWING HOSTILITIES

Since the 1990s, international police have played a wider role in peacekeeping missions. Peace and civil order do not immediately resume with the signing of a ceasefire, but the lawlessness and anarchy of war will continue until there is some civic order, and this requires the establishment of a police force (along with courts and prisons). It is worth reflecting on the psychological differences between international civilian police and military peacekeepers. Military peacekeepers are by definition foreigners. They come in formed units, wear helmets, boots, and camouflaged uniforms of war, live in barracks, and patrol in military vehicles and carry heavy weapons. Police typically patrol as individuals or in pairs. They wear uniforms consisting of caps, shoes, and badges that identify them. If they are armed, it is with nightsticks or pistols. They are seen as part of the community and enforce indigenous laws that stem from indigenous culture. It is the ultimate goal of international police serving on peacekeeping missions to restore a psychological sense of civil order where lawlessness is not accepted, train an indigenous police force, and withdraw to permit full self-governance.

HUMANITARIAN RELIEF WORKERS

Civilian humanitarian workers serving in an area where a peacekeeping mission is in place will face their own unique set of psychological issues. These civilians may be UN employees (known as International Staff) or United Nations Volunteers (see www.unv.org), or they may be serving with an organization other than the UN – e.g., the Red Cross, Doctors Without Borders, or other non-governmental organizations (NGOs). These civilians will be unarmed in an environment that can be violent. They want to be careful that they are not perceived by the indigenous population as being associated with the military, as this will only instill a sense of distrust and rejection. It can be interesting to observe the

two side by side in the mission area – the soldier (usually a man) armed and in full military gear, the civilian humanitarian worker (often a woman) in sandals and shorts.

Civilian humanitarian relief workers can face difficulties readjusting to "normal" life when they return to their countries of origin. While soldiers are expected to be trained before deployment and steeled for the suffering they may witness, this is not always the case with civilian humanitarian relief workers. These may be motivated by a sense of idealism and service, but they may not be fully ready for what they will encounter. Additionally, they may be functioning in very small groups and can be more dependent on the local economy than soldiers or police will be, leading to a sense of exposure and vulnerability. These factors can combine to produce high levels of stress for civilian humanitarian workers while they are on a mission, and feelings of guilt when they conclude their mission and return home. (See HUMANITARIAN WORKERS, MANAGING STRESS IN.)

EX-COMBATANTS

Traditional peacekeeping typically took place in cases where nations had been at war. With the conclusion of the conflict the soldiers of these nations would return to their peacetime posture within the military, or leave the military and return to civilian life. But since the 1990s and the end of the Cold War, the more common peacekeeping environment has been one of civil war, with Cambodia, Sierra Leone, Liberia, Sudan, Ivory Coast, and the Congo all serving as examples. One of the psychological challenges that emerges in these situations is the reinsertion of ex-combatants into civil society. In some cases this can include child soldiers, who have been taken from their villages, armed and trained, and who have spent their late childhood and adolescent years forced to be killers. The psychological difficulties lie in de-programming the child ex-combatant from a life of constant violence and killing, and preparing him (and in some cases her) to serve as a constructive member of society. Often, the families from which they were taken do not want them back. A 15-year-old who has spent the past five years as a child soldier cannot simply be mainstreamed with non-combatants in a school to learn literacy and a trade. (See CHILD SOLDIERS.)

The whole psychological process of de-escalation following a war is known as Disarmament, Demobilization, and Reintegration (DDR). This starts with programs for ex-combatants to turn in their arms, and often involves payment or some other incentive for this voluntary surrender. Demobilization is the closing of military units, and often first requires restricting units to "cantonment" areas. Reintegration includes programs to teach ex-combatants a productive trade, and in some cases wider economic or social programs of economic development. It is only through successful DDR programs that include psychological adjustment – either explicit or implicit – that a conflict can truly end, as ex-combatants from all sides resume constructive roles in civil life.

THE INDIGENOUS POPULATION

One group that can be easily overlooked is the indigenous population. It is this population that has of course endured war, seen its members in combat, had its infrastructure destroyed, and lived with violence for years. While the military peacekeepers, civilian police, and humanitarian workers will return to their home countries following their deployment, the indigenous population will remain. They will return to their farms and homes to find them destroyed – or perhaps

occupied by spoilers. Where the conflict was ethnically based, there will be lingering hatreds. Kosovo is a perfect example of where the actual fighting has stopped, but where the formerly fighting factions live an uneasy existence in ethnically separate villages and neighborhoods.

CONFLICTS, DIPLOMACY, AND THE PSYCHOLOGY OF RELATIONS BETWEEN NATIONS

Although there are no scholarly articles explicitly addressing the topic, informal discussions will indicate the academic community of psychologists is divided on whether psychological theories – developed to explain and understand the behavior of individuals – can be useful in explaining and understanding the behavior of nations. Diplomats and those who study international relations are probably less divided, seeing psychological theory as applicable only to the behavior of individuals.

While this topic of psychological theory as applied to the study of international relations can certainly lead to some lively cross-discipline debates, there is one aspect that all will agree on, and that is the long-term shift of some of the psychological assumptions of the relationship between nations and their obligations to each other. This shift can perhaps best be seen by starting with the relationship between nations as defined by Prussian General Carl von Clausewitz in his 1832 classic On War. Clausewitz captured and clarified the psychological assumptions of the day that undergirded the relations between nations. According to Clausewitz, war was simply one phase of the normal relations between nations. Nations might be at war or they might be at peace, but neither state was necessarily desirable over the other. Clausewitz also recorded that the concerns of the sovereign should be only for the welfare of his own nation and population. If suffering occurred outside his own borders, it was simply not something to be concerned about. Clausewitz also asserted that war was an extension of domestic politics (Clausewitz, 1832/1968).

It is interesting to compare this view to that of American psychologist William James, who 80 years after Clausewitz, in his 1910 *The Moral Equivalent of War*, objected to the tolerance the world had for war and called for a future where "acts of war shall be formally outlawed as between civilized peoples" (James, 1910/1995, p. 23).

It is instructive to compare this to the 1932 exchange of letters between Einstein and Freud. In his letter of July 30, 1932, Einstein wrote to Freud, asking:

Is there any way of delivering mankind from the menace of war? . . . I can do little more than enable you to bring the light of your far-reaching knowledge of man's instinctive life to bear upon the problem. There are certain psychological obstacles whose existence a layman in the mental sciences . . . is incompetent to fathom: You, I am convinced, will be able to suggest educative methods, lying more or less outside the scope of politics, which will eliminate these obstacles. . . . The ill-success . . . of all the efforts made during the last decade to reach this goal leaves us no room to doubt that strong psychological factors are at work, which paralyze these efforts. (Einstein & Freud, 1933, pp. 3–4)

Freud responded to Einstein's questions in his letter of September 1932:

Conflicts . . . are resolved, in principle, by recourse to violence. . . . There is but one sure way of ending war and that is the establishment, by common consent, of a certain control which shall have the last word in every conflict. . . . The League of Nations . . . has no force at its disposal and can only get it if the members of the new body, its constituent nations, furnish it. (Einstein & Freud, 1933, pp. 10–14)

It was perhaps a growing awareness among world leaders in the closing days of World War II of the validity of Freud's assertion that there needed to be some international organization, a United Nations, established by common consent, to address these issues of conflict between nations. The United Nations and United Nations peacekeeping certainly represent a contrast to the assumptions of Clausewitz's time. But it is this evolving psychological view of international relations and human relations that motivates nations to contribute their troops to serve as peacekeepers, with all the psychological implications that come with such cooperation.

SEE ALSO: Child Soldiers; Humanitarian Workers, Managing Stress in.

REFERENCES

Clausewitz, A. (1832/1968). *On War*. New York, NY: Penguin.
Einstein, A., & Freud, S. (1933). *Why War?* Paris, France: Institute of Intellectual Cooperation, League of Nations.
James, W. (1910/1995). The moral equivalent of war. *Peace and Conflict: Journal of Peace Psychology*, 1(1), 17–26.
Langholtz, H. (Ed.). (1997). *The psychology of peacekeeping*. Westport, CT: Praeger.

ADDITIONAL RESOURCES

http://humanitarian-psy.org (Geneva Centre on Humanitarian Psychology)
http://www.brill.nl/joup (Journal of International Peacekeeping)
http://www.peaceopstraining.org (Peace Operations Training Institute)
http://www.stimson.org (The Stimson Center)
http://www.un.org (United Nations)

People Power

CRISTINA JAYME MONTIEL AND
CARLO MIGUEL BERBA

In an unexpected press conference in Camp Aguinaldo at around 6:30 p.m. on February 22, 1986, Philippine Vice Chief of Staff General Ramos and Defense Minister Enrile announced their withdrawal of support for strongman Ferdinand Marcos in the midst of political instabilities following nearly 14 years of dictatorship, countless political killings and human rights violations, the assassination of leading opposition senator Ninoy Aquino, and a recent election marred by massive fraud and violence. By 9:00 p.m., Jaime Cardinal Sin, Archbishop of Manila, went on radio, asking the Filipino people to support "our two good friends." The popular archbishop made subsequent calls on radio, summoning people to fill the streets precisely to avoid bloodshed. By 10:20 p.m., Butz Aquino, leading social activist, called on all concerned citizens and political groups to gather in front of Camp Aguinaldo, along Epifanio de los Santos Avenue (EDSA). Through the first night, the number of people on the street had quickly risen to 30,000. This was the start of the Philippine People Power revolution, or what is now locally referred to as the EDSA revolution.

Over the next three days the people's gathering on EDSA bourgeoned to hundreds of thousands. It was a massive nonviolent demonstration in which Marcos's tanks and weapons were confronted by huge numbers of protesters bearing flowers, rosaries, and prayers. The throng of nonviolent protesters sat, ate, sang, prayed, and slept on the main highway in front of the military camp, despite the constant danger of violence and possible death.

By 9:05 p.m. on February 25, Marcos had fled the presidential palace on a US-provided military helicopter. His oppressive regime ended and democracy was restored in the Philippines without much bloodshed, through a globally unprecedented demonstration of forceful peace during power shifts in a developing society.

People Power is a mass-based political phenomenon wherein large collectivities of individuals and social movements band together into a united front to transform an oppressive political situation. It was first seen in history as a form of nonviolent democratic transition in the post-Cold War years, where its main goal was to overturn strong authoritarian regimes. Examples of these are found in the histories of the Philippines (1986), Taiwan (1987), South Korea (1987), Indonesia (1998), and East Timor (2002), among others. However, in more recent years, as new democracies matured, People Power has also become a state-building tool. For instance, in Bangkok (2008) a mass sit-in at the city's main airport helped unseat an unpopular prime minister, and in Ukraine (2004) fraudulent polls were annulled after mass protests.

People Power may be understood as a means of structural peacebuilding, as a process of transforming structurally violent social or state elements into new configurations where all groups have more equitable control over politico-economic resources needed to satisfy basic needs. In the first part of this essay, we describe the social psychological nature of People Power (Montiel, 2001). Then we discuss specific social psychological elements that are associated with, or increase the probability of, successful People Power.

People Power is political, highly informed, organized, and purposeful. It is political because its tackles matters related to the state. People Power is an example of human agency on a collective rather than an individual level, as large groups of people band together to change their oppressive political conditions. It does not refer to mob rule. Like other agentic interventions, People Power is highly informed and purposeful.

Group conscientizing shapes political consciousness and collective intent.

CONSCIENTIZING

Before challenging the status quo, there must first be a critical mass within society that is aware of the social and structural issues being protested against, as well as possible avenues for action. In light of this, political education becomes crucial in any People Power movement. It is through collective political formation that huge numbers of people develop a shared collective action frame, in order to move as one massive group. A collective action frame refers to a common frame of reference which guides group political action.

Paolo Freire (1970) popularized the process of conscientization as a liberating process for oppressed groups. He emphasized that the pedagogical style of liberating political education must promote equality and evoke knowledge already embedded among the oppressed. The political-education content of People Power has evolved over the last 40 years from being heavily ideological (conscientization) to being more issues based (collective action frames). Examples of modules in a political seminar include: Social and Structural Analysis, Basic Principles of the Movement, Process of Change (including active nonviolence), and Commitment or Oath Taking. (See CONSCIENTIZATION.)

NETWORKING AND MOBILIZATION

People Power likewise requires the production of unified and collective action among diverse groups, where large numbers provide safety as well as intensify political potency. Networking and mobilization make unified collective action possible.

Networking creates the political infrastructure, which is then activated during mobilizations. Networking is done outside the political status quo, by forming bonds or connections among groups and organizations that share the same anti-regime sentiments. It is this network that becomes the social capital for counterstructural moves that contest the status quo.

Mobilization involves activating the network of resources and people in order to collectively generate a massive amount of social pressure in a deliberate and coordinated manner. For example, after the fraudulent Philippine elections in early February 1986, Corazon Aquino mobilized her network of electoral supporters and asked them to boycott the products of government cronies' companies as part of a civil disobedience campaign aimed at overthrowing Marcos. Over the next few days, seven Marcos-affiliated banks experienced runs, restaurants throughout the nation refused to serve Coca-Cola (which was bottled by a Marcos-affiliated company), Marcos companies made minimal sales, and several popular department stores were absolutely empty.

GENERATING SOCIAL PRESSURE

The goal of conscientizing, networking, and mobilizing is the production of social pressure. Paradoxically, if violent structures are to be transformed into more structurally peaceful ones, as is in the case of People Power, social strain must be increased, not reduced. This is because structural shifts usually arise from strains internal to the system.

This strain is generated by producing relationships between groups (i.e., state elements and people) that are incompatible with the dominant structure. Conscientization generates this by developing a subjective structure within the individual incompatible with dominant state-controlled narratives, while networking and mobilization work toward making that incompatibility publicly visible in large numbers, thus addressing the objective structure.

Conscientization, networking, and mobilizing do not unfold in a linear fashion, where the subjective mind-change precedes the objective actions, or vice versa. Rather, the relation between subjective and objective transformation is cyclic and two-way, where mass actions feed into group reflections, and conscientization produces a subjective frame that synchronizes mass actions.

NONVIOLENCE

One of the most poignant and powerful elements of People Power is that these are collective actions that insist on being nonviolent despite facing military and political power. An example of nonviolence during People Power was to stay firmly in position while facing the military's armored vehicles, rather than hiding in fear, or moving against the tanks.

Collective nonviolence requires a high level of internal discipline and psychological tolerance for the enemy, often even a genuine intent to win over their good will. Active nonviolence while facing a militarized enemy requires knowledge of and insistence on one's human rights, the buddy or partner system, unquestioned obedience to the group's security marshals, and protective, not offensive, collective behaviors in response to acts of direct violence. Information about nonviolent tactics may be given to the rallyists prior to any public demonstration through leaflets and text messages.

During rallies, one is required to identify a buddy or partner, and when tear gas is sprayed on the group, the buddy-pair should not separate from each other while they find a place with better air; individuals who separate from the group become easy prey for snatching by intelligence agents. The group security marshals direct where to march and

when to walk, run, or sit. Complete obedience to marshals' instructions is required so that massive groups can act in a disciplined manner, rather than in a chaotic or hysterical way. Marshals' instructions are especially important when government troops begin to push forward and try to scatter the protesters.

SHARED SPIRITUALITY

Remaining faithful to a credo of nonviolence entails a firm willingness to sacrifice one's self for the collective purpose of political change. A shared sense of spirituality is important. Such spirituality is not necessarily religious or dogmatic, but about the Good that is in people and society, and can be derived from Christian, Buddhist, Islamic, Hindu, Taoist, and other traditions. Spirituality operates both on a personal level and a collective level. On a personal level, spirituality augments the conviction of the individual to be ready to give up their life, without harming anyone else. On a collective level, spirituality provides people a space to collectively identify themselves as one body.

LEADERSHIP

The leaders of People Power movements often command immense social influence. However, their social authority emanates not from their ability to wield brute force, but from a capacity for self-sacrifice and kind acts effectively coupled with pragmatic political tactics. In several People Power movements, like in the Philippines (1986), East Timor (2002), and Cambodia (1992), it was the spiritual leaders of the communities who first rallied people together for their cause.

The leadership structure of People Power is often decentralized for very practical reasons. If someone is killed or detained, a decentralized organization can compartmentalize the strain the loss causes. Furthermore, the call for self-sacrifice cannot be imposed by a centralized leadership and must be voluntary. Self-sacrifice is a daily personal decision that is carried out in the context of a small group.

OPPORTUNITY WITHIN
THE POLITICAL CONTEXT

People Power movements do not always succeed, especially when social strain is prematurely silenced by overwhelming state violence. China's Tiananmen Square (1989) and Malaysia's *Reformasi* (1998) stand as examples where the collective actions of prodemocracy movements did not result in positive social change. There is an optimal political context that provides the opportunity for successful People Power. This is the dual condition of a weakened and fractured authoritarian regime and an active nonviolent movement with a strong domestic and international base. (See NONVIOLENT DEMOCRATIC TRANSITIONS.)

CAVEAT: NON-ABSOLUTE PEACE

As a final note, although one salient principle of People Power is nonviolence, such a condition does not always hold true in most developing countries. What may appear to be peaceful People Power is usually brought about by a mix of peaceful and violent forms of political opposition, but international media may tend to feature the peaceful aspects of People Power. In the Philippines, for example, behind the anti-Marcos united front were different types of political movements, with varying political orientations toward using violence. Armed groups from the left dominated the anti-dictatorship struggle in the 1970s. And even as nonviolent opposition groups took the political

lead in the years before the 1986 People Power, there was also an expansion of anti-Marcos underground activities among junior officers in the Armed Forces of the Philippines (AFP). When People Power erupted on EDSA on February 22, 1986, junior AFP officers with high-powered weapons surrounded Defense Minister Enrile in Camp Aguinaldo, as he declared his rebellion against President Marcos. A similar combination of armed and peaceful forces can be observed in other People Powers as well, such as in East Timor in 2002 and Nepal in 2006.

Peace psychologists may need to acknowledge and appreciate the existence of nonabsolute peace in People Power's *realpolitik*. Such is the case among huge numbers of individuals and social movements in developing societies, who face variations of peace and violence in their everyday political lives, as they struggle for structural change amid political oppression.

SEE ALSO: Conscientization; Nonviolent Democratic Transitions.

REFERENCES

Freire, P. (1970). *Pedagogy of the oppressed* (M. B. Ramos, Trans.). New York, NY: Herder and Herder.
Montiel, C. J. (2001). Toward a psychology of structural peacebuilding. In D. J. Christie, R. V. Wagner, & D. D. Winter (Eds.), *Peace, conflict, and violence: Peace psychology for the 21st century* (pp. 282–295). Englewood Cliffs, NJ: Prentice-Hall.

ADDITIONAL RESOURCES

Galtung, J. (1996). *Peace by peaceful means*. London, UK: Sage.
Macapagal, M. E., & Nario-Galace, J. (2003). Social psychology of People Power II in the Philippines. *Peace and Conflict: Journal of Peace Psychology, 9*, 219–233.

Magno, F. (1986). The political dynamics of People Power. *Kasarinlan (Sovereignty): Philippine Quarterly of Third World Studies, 3,* 13–18.

Personality Processes in Interpersonal Conflict, Assessing

KATHERINE E. SULLIVAN,
PRIYA A. IYER, ERIKA VENZOR,
AND LAURI A. JENSEN-CAMPBELL

Interpersonal conflict is an inevitable part of life and has been linked to important developmental outcomes. The sequelae associated with interpersonal conflicts are not exclusively negative; conflicts can have both positive and negative consequences for individuals. In order to understand why some conflicts are harmful while others may actually lead to personal and social growth, one must consider that interpersonal conflict involves mutual opposition between two or more persons. Research has consistently found that personality is an important influence on how individuals deal with conflict, which in turn, influences the potential deleterious effects of these conflicts (Jensen-Campbell & Graziano, 2001). (See PEACEFUL PERSONALITY.) This paper will examine different methodological and statistical assessments that may be employed in determining how personality influences conflict in conjunction with situational influences. We will begin by examining important ways to assess personality followed by how to incorporate these personality assessments into conflict research.

COLLECTING PERSONALITY DATA

One of the easiest ways to obtain individual difference data is through self-reports. Surveys such as the Big Five Inventory can be used to measure different personality traits easily with a single assessment. If researchers want corroboration for these assessments, they can get reports from others (e.g., peers, spouses, parents, coworkers). Finally, individual differences can also be assessed through analysis of genetic polymorphisms. Genetic variations can be associated with personality differences which can ultimately lead to differences in conflict behavior. For example, Caspi et al. (2002) found that maltreated children with a certain MAO-A (monoamine oxidase A) genetic polymorphism have a greater likelihood of developing antisocial problems, which is directly relevant to conflict research.

SELF-REPORT METHODOLOGIES

One of the most common methodologies utilized by researchers to assess conflict is that of self-report questionnaires which ask participants to respond to items relating to their conflicts in a given situation at a specific point in time. These surveys are very easy to use; however, issues of causality, extraneous third variables, social desirability, common method variance, and retrospective reporting threaten their validity (Jensen-Campbell & Graziano, 2005).

When personality and conflict behavior are collected simultaneously, questions of causality arise. Researchers need to assess personality and conflict behavior at multiple time points (e.g., longitudinal studies) in order to assess the directionality of effects. For example, not only can personality influence conflict behavior over time, but conflict behavior can also influence the development of personality. Similarly, extraneous third variables may be responsible for the personality–conflict relationship. For example, agreeable people may report more positive conflict behavior because they want to portray themselves as "nice" people. To rule out such an explanation, the investigators must measure and determine that the relationship between personality and conflict exists after measuring and controlling for the effects of participants providing socially desirable responses.

Shared method variance often occurs when data points are collected from the same source, which can inflate the reported association between two variables. As such, it is necessary to assess these two constructs using multiple raters such as parents, co-workers, teachers, and peers (Jensen-Campbell & Graziano, 2005). With multiple convergent sources of information, one is able to report the link between personality and conflict behavior more confidently.

A final problem with self-report methodologies is retrospective reporting. Participants may be asked to recall conflicts occurring days, weeks, or several months ago. This is problematic due to the participant's need to select, recall, and aggregate the memory (Reis & Wheeler, 1991). Furthermore, if they have not been given proper instructions, participants may use their own criteria to select events. Worse still, personality may influence the saliency and mood of the individual, which in turn may affect the reported conflict behaviors. In other words, the personality of the participant may color what events are recalled, leading to spurious findings (e.g., Ebner-Priemer, Kubiak, & Pawlik, 2009). One possible solution is to utilize event-by-event recordings (see below).

HYPOTHETICAL SITUATIONS/ ROLE PLAY

Hypothetical situations/role-playing is another classic technique that has been employed to assess conflict behavior (Jensen-Campbell & Graziano, 2005). In this paradigm, participants are usually assessed on some personality measure (concurrently or during an earlier session) and are then asked

to answer how they would behave in a given situation. For example, Jensen-Campbell and Graziano (2001) presented participants who were previously assessed on agreeableness with vignettes of different conflict scenarios. The participant's task was to determine the effectiveness of the conflict resolution strategy described. Some researchers provide participants with vignettes from different conflict partners to examine potential differences in conflict interactions. For example, Borbely, Graber, Nichols, Brooks-Gunn, and Botvin (2005) asked adolescents to interact with the role player who was a teacher, peer, or parent. They determined that participants were better at conflict resolution when they were role-playing as friends than when they were interacting as a child with a parent.

This method continues to be used because many researchers argue that role-playing is similar to natural observations and has more of a "real life" component than self-report measures. (See ROLE PLAYING AS A TRAINING AND ASSESSMENT TOOL.) Another benefit of vignettes is that researchers are able to control the conflict situation and to bring a focus to the characteristics and variables of conflict and personality. However, this method has many potential flaws that include problems with social desirability (Tobin, Graziano, Vanman, & Tassinary, 2000). An additional problem with this methodology is the generalizability of the findings. Researchers cannot conclude that individuals have a set of skills that they use in all situations based on vignette responses. Perhaps more problematic is that the hypothetical vignette method relies heavily on simplistic, singular, deterministic views of personality. In other words, these designs typically involve "main effects" models where personality predicts conflict behavior while ignoring equally important contextual factors (e.g., conflict partner's contributions) that may influence the conflict behavior in important ways.

EVENT-BY-EVENT RECORDINGS

A method that focuses on examining daily interpersonal conflicts is event-by-event recordings. Jensen-Campbell and Graziano (2005) describe three types of event-by-event recordings that meet this goal: interval-contingent recording, signal-contingent recording, and event-contingent recording. With interval-contingent recording, participants are requested to list activities given at certain, generally theoretically or logically driven, time intervals. For example, participants may be asked to indicate interactions that occurred during the hour, day, or week. One issue that may arise is that of recall. It may be difficult to remember a specific instance that occurred earlier in the day if it did not seem important at the time. Furthermore, in investigating conflict or conflict resolution, participants may inflate or leave out details that are not socially desirable.

In signal-contingent recording, the participant records their activities at the given moment of a certain signal provided by the researcher. They may indicate their feelings at that time, what types of conflict they are experiencing, and how they handle it. The researcher may call the participant, or prompt them with the use of a cell phone (Jensen-Campbell & Graziano, 2005). The problem with this method is that generally researchers are interested in a certain event and the probability of that event and the signal occurring in a similar time period is low; however, the aspect of recall has been eliminated. Participants are able to record what is happening at that particular moment without having to select, recall, and recognize important events (Reis & Wheeler, 1991).

Finally, in event-contingent recording, participants must record events that meet a definition predetermined by the researcher (Jensen-Campbell & Graziano, 2005). For example, Jensen-Campbell and Graziano (2001) defined conflict as when "what you are doing or saying is opposed, blocked, or objected to by another person and you object back. In other words, someone does or says something against you, and you do or say something against them back" (p. 334). It is necessary to provide a clear definition so that participants all have the same idea of what type of event to record. Jensen-Campbell and Graziano (2005) describe several benefits to the use of this methodology. It is, like signal-contingent recording, not susceptible to reappraisal. In addition, they observe that event-contingent recordings are best used with discrete events, and it is best to sample a large number of events to investigate the variation within an event. The same authors utilized interval-contingent recordings in 2001. After being provided with a definition of conflict, participants filled out forms daily describing interactions that lasted longer than 10 minutes. Following this, they indicated how they felt about these interactions as well as what occurred in them. For example, they were asked how angry they were, whether force was used, and whether or not their feelings were hurt.

BEHAVIORAL OBSERVATIONS

To further eliminate the errors associated with participant self-reporting, behavioral observations may be used. Jensen-Campbell and Graziano (2005) argue that this method provides a very rich source of data. However, with this assessment, the situation is often fixed, and the environment is generally a laboratory. For example, Downey, Freitas, Michaelis, and Khouri (1998) conducted a two-part study where romantic couples first used a diary recording of daily interactions with their partner (Study 1) and then came into a laboratory setting for observation (Study 2), to determine the relationship between rejection sensitivity and conflict.

These couples were brought into the laboratory and given a list of common issues of conflict in relationships. Each couple was asked to pick several problems that they were personally experiencing in their relationship and to indicate what they believed to be the most salient one. They then discussed the issue with each other for about 20 minutes, and their behaviors were recorded. Behaviors such as mocking, denying responsibility, and voice tone were scored by trained researchers. One benefit of this particular experiment is the reality of the situation. The conflict was something that the couple was currently experiencing, and not just one that the researcher had picked out.

With new technology, we can begin to assess the influence of personality on conflict behavior in more naturalistic settings using ecological momentary assessments (EMA) (Ebner-Primer et al., 2009), also known as ambulatory assessments. That is, normal daily activities that involve conflict can now be assessed with computer-assisted technologies such as digital audio or video recordings, electronic communication, and physiological measurement. For example, texting via cell phones can be used to track individuals' conflict behavior within this medium. Indeed, recent studies have used these new social media to assess personality's influence on interpersonal activity on networking sites. Content analysis of chatroom conversations can also be used to further examine the effect of personality on conflict behavior. In summary, a wide range of new technologies have opened up a new social space for communication and conflict, making it possible to further examine personality's influence via observation.

STATISTICAL METHODOLOGIES

While all these methods contribute to our understanding of personality's influence on conflict behaviors, we need to move past simple "main effects" models that focus on one person's personality influencing conflict outcomes. As such, we will briefly describe some of the statistical methodologies that move beyond simple main effects models. (For a more comprehensive review, see Jensen-Campbell & Graziano, 2005.) A few of the statistical methods described by Jensen-Campbell and Graziano (2005) include moderated multiple regression, multi-level modeling, mediation analysis, social relations model analysis, and dyadic analysis.

The social relations model is especially useful in conflict research in that it employs a round robin design, allowing the researcher to decompose self, partner, and relationship effects associated with the interpersonal conflict. For this design, groups of individuals can be placed in some conflict-inducing task. All participants interact with each other and rate each other so that the personality effects of the individual can be partitioned out from partner and relationship effects.

Similarly, the actor–partner interdependence model examines the influence of personality while also accounting for the interdependence between conflict partners. In other words, the researcher can treat the conflict dyad as the major unit of analysis while partitioning the variance for personality into effects due to the actor, the partner, and the actor × partner interaction.

SUMMARY

Given that conflict is defined in terms of mutual opposition, it is critical to examine both the personality of individuals and the *interpersonal* aspects of conflict when considering potential methodologies and statistical analyses. Future research must also utilize multiple, converging methods. Finally, transactional models that look past simple main effects will lead to a better understanding of the causes, processes, and outcomes associated with interpersonal conflict.

SEE ALSO: Peaceful Personality; Role Playing as a Training and Assessment Tool.

REFERENCES

Borbely, C. J., Graber, J. A., Nichols, T., Brooks-Gunn, J., & Botvin, G. J. (2005). Sixth graders' conflict resolution in role plays with a peer, parent, and teacher. *Journal of Youth and Adolescence, 34*, 279–291.

Caspi, A., McClay, J., Moffitt, T. E., Mill, J., Martin, J., Craig, I. W., Taylor, A., & Poulton, R. (2002). Role of genotype in the cycle of violence in maltreated children. *Science, 297*, 851–854.

Downey, G., Freitas, A., Michaelis, B., & Khouri, H. (1998). The self-fulfilling prophecy in close relationships: Rejection sensitivity and rejection by romantic partners. *Journal of Personality and Social Psychology, 75*, 545–560.

Ebner-Priemer, U. W., Kubiak, T., & Pawlik, K. (2009) Ambulatory assessment. *European Psychologist, 14*, 95–97.

Jensen-Campbell, L. A., & Graziano, W. G. (2001). Agreeableness as a moderator of interpersonal conflict. *Journal of Personality, 69*, 323–362.

Jensen-Campbell, L. A., & Graziano, W. G. (2005). Methodologies for studying personality processes in interpersonal conflict. *International Negotiation, 10*, 165–182.

Reis, H. T., & Wheeler, L. (1991). Studying social interaction with the Rochester Interaction Record. In M. P. Zanna (Ed.), *Advances in experimental social psychology* (Vol. 24, pp. 269–318). New York, NY: Academic Press.

Tobin, R. M., Graziano, W. G., Vanman, E., & Tassinary, L. G. (2000). Personality, emotional experience, and efforts to control emotions. *Journal of Personality and Social Psychology, 79*, 656–669.

ADDITIONAL RESOURCES

Division 48 of the American Psychological Association: Society for the Study of Peace, Conflict, and Violence: Peace Psychology: http://www.apa.org/about/division/div48.html
Social Psychology Network: at http://www.socialpsychology.org/

Police–Community Relations

EDUARDO I. DIAZ

The nature of policing has changed considerably in the United States, and in many other countries, since the advent of the Civil Rights movement in the 1950s and '60s. It is important to note that, historically, police officers have been the enforcers of racist laws and unjust political administrations (Gabbidon & Greene, 2009). Modern policing varies greatly in policy and practice, depending on the agency's adherence to democratic principles and human rights. Unfortunately, in too many places police may still be involved in oppression; consciously, by the unquestioning following of orders, or subconsciously as a consequence of ethnocultural bias. This article aims to introduce the reader to mechanisms that have been set up worldwide to address both direct and structural violence associated with policing (Diaz, 2009).

Police misconduct is found everywhere, but to varying degrees because police accountability mechanisms vary greatly. This is in part due to differences in values and commitments to human rights. It is generally understood that a noncorrupt and fair police force depends on adequate civilian control of the police department. However, most police misconduct does not rise to the level of criminal activity; the majority involves misuse of power and discretion.

This kind of misconduct is observable in the broader population but the difference in quality is due to the police's extraordinary power to question, detain, and arrest.

Independent civilian oversight of law enforcement is a growing worldwide movement that aims to encourage policing that maintains order in a manner respectful of human rights. Independent oversight agencies should address citizen complaints in a respectful manner that avoids the "us versus them" trap that fuels poor police community relations.

Peer accountability via internal affairs investigations is the most common type of police accountability mechanism. Yet, critics point to a "police culture," that is sometimes described as being "like family," as problematic. Similar dynamics found in family violence, like masking the secrets of incest, intimate partner violence, or intrafamilial child abuse, are found in police departments. It is difficult for officers to observe wrongdoing by fellow members of their "family" and report the wrongdoer.

External oversight provides the community with a "check and balance" addition to the peer accountability system. External oversight, that is independent of the self-watched police department, also looks for internal investigations that have been subject to political interference. Investigation objectivity can be compromised when a politically connected colleague or a friend is being investigated.

The power of police to deprive someone of liberty is deemed essential in maintaining order. Institutional safeguards must exist to prevent misuse of this power; to minimize structural violence primarily experienced by those most likely to be subject to police action – namely, minorities and the less affluent. The degree to which police leadership is progressive and concerned about human rights in large part determines policy and practice. Unfortunately, many countries are in real need of more progressive policing.

Criminologists have documented that, internationally, regardless of world region, minorities and the less powerful are frequently overrepresented in the criminal justice systems of their respective country. (See SOCIAL DOMINANCE THEORY.) Gabbidon (2010) has recently published an analysis of race and crime comparing ethnic and racial injustice as manifested in the United States, Canada, Great Britain, South Africa, and Australia. He clearly identifies a key factor that contributes to the institutional racism as evidenced by the overrepresentation of Blacks in prisons. That factor is the systematically enhanced police vigilance of poor people of color.

There is a big problem in the front end of the criminal justice system because of the disproportionate attention given by police to the poor and less powerful. They are relatively easy to arrest during "get tough on crime" campaigns often championed by politicians who devalue the fact of social class privilege inequities. Unconscious social exclusion and a failure to assess the potentiality of racist outcomes from enhanced enforcement activities are issues to which all decision-makers must be sensitized to fully explore peace with justice. (See MORAL EXCLUSION; MORAL DISENGAGEMENT.) It is time for peace psychologists to investigate this international phenomenon so as to develop structural violence intervention designs that may be implemented by progressive governments and world bodies committed to human rights. (See PEACE PSYCHOLOGY: DEFINITIONS, SCOPE, AND IMPACT.)

There are many different models of police oversight and thorough reviews are provided by Goldsmith and Lewis (2000), Walker (2001), and Cintrón Perino (2006). Generic models, in the US, include citizen review boards, police auditor/monitor, police ombudsman, inspector general, and investigative panel models. Generally the preferred models are clearly independent agencies with investigatory authority; but no model is suitable for communities everywhere given vast differences in laws between municipalities, provinces, states, and nations.

States like California severely restrict what can be made public about police investigations. Florida, on the other hand, is known for its Government in the Sunshine Act. This allows public review of investigatory statements and discipline. This law gives external oversight agencies access to any completed internal affairs report. The level of transparency is determined by what the law allows in each jurisdiction. There is no single "best practices" model, no one-size-fits-all solution.

The structure of independent oversight of policing is very different depending on where in the world you live. In some countries, like the US, external oversight agencies are organized at the municipal or county government level. In countries like Canada and Australia the external oversight agencies are organized at the province or state level. In Europe and New Zealand the external oversight is organized at the national level. For more information, see European Partners Against Corruption (EPAC) (www.epac.at) and for New Zealand, the Police Complaints Authority (www.pca.govt.nz). Australia has the Commonwealth Ombudsman (www.ombudsman.gov.au), the Queensland Criminal and Misconduct Commission (www.cmc.qld.gov.au), the Police Integrity Commission (www.pic.nsw.gov.au), and the New South Wales Ombudsman's Office (www.nswombudsman.nsw.gov.au) as notable sample agencies.

The strongest form of civilian oversight of law enforcement is found in Northern Ireland, given that there is a very strong legislative mandate to initiate investigations and compel the production of records from the police department and witness testimony. The Police Ombudsman of Northern Ireland (www.policeombudsman.org) exercises considerable authority to conduct independent investigations followed by the Independent Police Complaints Commission (IPCC) of England and Wales (www.ipcc.gov.uk) as the closest in legislated authority.

How to help police reform movements in developing countries is a big challenge. Bayley (2001) has developed a useful guide. He posits that democratic policing shares certain qualities: "Police must give top operational priority to servicing the needs of individual citizens and private groups . . . Police must be accountable to the law rather than to the government . . . Police must protect human rights, especially those that are required for the sort of unfettered political activity that is the hallmark of democracy . . . Police should be transparent in their activities" (pp. 13–14). These admirable traits are not found in all developed countries and should be considered everywhere as desirable guidelines.

The United Nations Crime and Justice Information Network has relevant standards and information available to assist in the development of progressive policing. At www.uncjin.org/Standards/standards.html, the *Code of Conduct for Law Enforcement Officials*, the *Basic Principles on the Use of Force and Firearms by Law Enforcement Officials*, and the *Compendium of United Nations Standards and Norms in Crime Prevention and Criminal Justice* are readily available. Articles 6 and 7 of the International Covenant on Civil and Political Rights specifically call for "investigation independent of the alleged perpetrators" for harm caused by "the hand of the state."

Overall, with one notable exception, which is South Africa's Independent Complaints Directorate (www.icd.gov.za), African, South American, and Asian countries trail in the development of independent oversight of policing. However, each of these world regions is still recovering from the aftereffects of colonialism and it is important to consider that imposition of models that may work in more developed countries could be highly inappropriate. Each country must take into consideration what the law allows in a particular jurisdiction and whether political structures exist that would permit the development of local political will to sustain an effective police accountability system.

Civilian oversight of law enforcement is truly a world movement with new seeds sown wherever community leaders strive for improved police/community relations. Transparency, the idea that no cover-up of wrongdoing will be tolerated, is an essential value at the core of the movement. Police departments should be encouraged to send the community a message – that the police have nothing to hide. The desired outcome of any oversight agency is constructive change in police department policy and practice.

There is a new and very promising development in the field of police accountability that merits special attention. It is called the Consortium for Police Leadership in Equity (CPLE) (http://cple.psych.ucla.edu) and is a prime example of police and research community collaboration to help improve police/community relations. Created by Denver Police Division Chief, Dr. Tracie L. Keesee, and UCLA social psychologist, Dr. Phillip Atiba Goff, this consortium facilitates research collaborations between social scientists and law enforcement agencies aimed at improving police accountability and transparency.

The leadership of the National Association for Civilian Oversight of Law Enforcement (NACOLE) expects that the US Department of Justice will become increasingly vigilant of patterns and practice of misconduct by police agencies, an area where federal law allows the intervention of the federal judiciary in the affairs of local governments. In addition, it is expected that the United Nations will be prodded by human rights-oriented nongovernment organizations to enhance international efforts towards the professionalization of police around the world. This is an exciting field for those who are committed to social justice and who are prepared to deal with resistance from those with the power to control the police for their own political agenda.

SEE ALSO: Moral Disengagement; Moral Exclusion; Peace Psychology: Definitions, Scope, and Impact; Social Dominance Theory.

REFERENCES

Bayley, D. H. (2001). *Democratizing the police abroad: What to do and how to do it* (NCJ 188742). Washington, DC: National Institute of Justice.

Cintrón Perino, J. (Ed.). (2006). *Citizen oversight of law enforcement.* Chicago, IL: American Bar Association.

Díaz, E. I. (2009). Police oversight. In J. de Rivera,(Ed.), *Handbook on building cultures of peace* (pp. 287–301). New York, NY: Springer.

Gabbidon, S. L. (2010). *Race, ethnicity, crime, and justice: An international dilemma.* Thousand Oaks, CA: Sage.

Gabbidon, S. L., & Greene, H. T. (2009). *Race and crime* (2nd ed.). Thousand Oaks, CA: Sage.

Goldsmith, A., & Lewis, C. (Eds.). (2000). *Civilian oversight of policing: Governance, democracy, and human rights.* New York, NY: Hart Publishing.

Walker, S. E. (2001). *Police accountability: The role of citizen oversight.* Belmont, CA: Wadsworth.

ADDITIONAL RESOURCES

National Association for Civilian Oversight of Law Enforcement (NACOLE): www.nacole.org

Canadian Association for Civilian Oversight of Law Enforcement (CACOLE): www.cacole.ca

International Network for the Independent Oversight of Policing (INIOP): www.iniop.org